Sofija Rašić Jung

GDPR Transplantation in Third Countries

Global and Comparative Data Law

Edited by

Moritz Hennemann
Lea Katharina Kumkar
Linda Kuschel
Björn Steinrötter

Volume 7

Sofija Rašić Jung

GDPR Transplantation in Third Countries

A Comparative Study on the Western Balkans

DE GRUYTER

ISBN 978-3-11-914294-6
e-ISBN (PDF) 978-3-11-222101-3
e-ISBN (EPUB) 978-3-11-222128-0
ISSN 2751-0174

Library of Congress Control Number: 2025946805

Bibliographic information published by the Deutsche Nationalbibliothek
The Deutsche Nationalbibliothek lists this publication in the Deutsche Nationalbibliografie; detailed bibliographic data are available on the internet at http://dnb.dnb.de.

Cover image: peshkov / iStock / Getty Images
Printing and binding: CPI books GmbH, Leck

www.degruyterbrill.com
Questions about General Product Safety Regulation:
productsafety@degruyterbrill.com

Foreword and Acknowledgements

This study was accepted as a doctoral dissertation by the Faculty of Law at the University of Passau during the summer semester of 2024. It was completed in February 2024, with relevant developments considered up to March 2025.

First and foremost, I extend my sincere gratitude to my doctoral supervisor, Professor Dr. Moritz Hennemann, M.Jur. (Oxford) for his exceptional supervision. His insightful feedback and commitment were instrumental to the success of this work. I also wish to thank Professor Dr. Kai von Lewinski for his prompt and constructive second review.

My deepest thanks go to my husband, Alexander Jung. This achievement would not have been possible without his constant encouragement, patience, and belief in me. I am equally grateful to my family and closest friends for their unwavering support and continuous motivation throughout the course of my doctoral studies.

In particular, I would like to thank my team lead at Vinted, Ona Valainienė, for recognising the practical relevance of my academic work. I am also sincerely grateful to Vinted for its financial support in the publication of this dissertation. Finally, I am especially thankful to my colleagues from the Western Balkans, whose collaboration significantly enriched this research.

Berlin, July 2025 Sofija Rašić Jung

https://doi.org/10.1515/9783112221013-001

Overview

List of Abbreviations —— XXI

List of Tables —— XXIV

Chapter 1 – Introduction —— 1

Chapter 2 – Fundamentals of Data Protection Law and Privacy —— 9

Chapter 3 – The GDPR Impact on non-EU Countries —— 24

Chapter 4 – The GDPR Transplantation in the WB6 —— 41

Chapter 5 – Government Access to Personal Data in the WB6 —— 238

Chapter 6 – Privacy-Infringing Technologies in the WB6 —— 300

Chapter 7 – Towards Adequacy Decision(s): Prospects for the WB6 —— 316

Chapter 8 – Conclusion —— 367

Tables —— 371

Bibliography —— 382

Contents

List of Abbreviations —— XXI

List of Tables —— XXIV

Chapter 1 – Introduction —— 1

A Research Subject —— **2**
B Course of Study —— **3**
C State of Research —— **4**
D Research Aim —— **8**

Chapter 2 – Fundamentals of Data Protection Law and Privacy —— 9

A Evolution of European Data Protection Laws —— **10**
 I First Data Protection Laws —— **10**
 II OECD —— **11**
 III Convention 108 —— **11**
 IV ECHR —— **12**
 V CFR —— **13**
 VI TFEU and TEU —— **14**
 VII DPD —— **15**
 VIII GDPR —— **16**
 IX Conclusion to A —— **16**
B Evolution of Privacy and Data Protection Rights in the WB6 —— **17**
 I FRY Constitution —— **17**
 II Albania —— **18**
 III EU Acquis Alignment —— **19**
 IV Data Protection Laws in the WB6 2008 – 2025 —— **20**
 V Conclusion to B —— **22**
C Conclusion to Chapter 2 —— **22**

Chapter 3 – The GDPR Impact on non-EU Countries —— 24

A Territorial Scope of the GDPR —— **25**
 I Art. 3(1) GDPR —— **26**
 II Art. 3(2) GDPR —— **27**
  1 Offering of Goods or Services —— **28**
  2 Monitoring —— **28**
 III Conclusion to A —— **29**

B Data Transfers — 29
I Adequacy Decision — 30
1 Criteria Under Art. 45 GDPR — 32
a) Art. 45(2)(a) GDPR — 33
b) Art. 45(2)(b) GDPR — 34
c) Art. 45(2)(c) GDPR — 35
2 Art. 29 Working Party and EDPB — 35
3 CJEU and Schrems Decisions — 36
4 Procedure of Adoption — 36
5 Adequacy Paradox — 37
II Alternatives to Adequacy Decisions for the WB6 — 38
III Conclusion to B — 39
C Conclusion to Chapter 3 — 40

Chapter 4 – The GDPR Transplantation in the WB6 — 41
A Albania — 42
I Constitutional Parameters and International Commitments — 43
1 Conclusion to I — 44
II Data Protection Legislation — 44
1 Status Quo of GDPR Alignment — 45
2 Overview of the ADPL 2024 — 46
3 Scope of the ADPL 2024 — 46
4 Data Protection Principles — 47
5 Lawfulness of Data Processing — 47
a) Consent — 47
6 Special Categories of Personal Data — 48
7 Rights of Data Subjects — 48
8 Redress Mechanism — 49
9 Personal Scope — 49
a) DPO — 50
b) Security — 51
10 Transfer of Personal Data — 52
a) Adequacy Decisions — 53
11 Penalties — 53
12 Specific Processing Situations — 54
13 Conclusion to II — 55
III Supervisory Authority — 56
1 General Functions — 56
2 Independence — 57
3 Powers — 58

4 Challenges — 58
5 Conclusion to III — 59
IV Case Law and Enforcement — 59
1 Complaints and Investigations Before the Supervisory Authority — 60
2 Data Leaks Scandals — 61
a) Patronage System — 61
b) WhatsApp Data Leak(s) — 62
3 Conclusion to IV — 63
V Conclusion to A — 63
B Bosnia and Herzegovina (BiH) — 64
I Constitutional Parameters and International Commitments — 65
1 Conclusion to I — 66
II Data Protection Legislation — 67
1 Status Quo of GDPR Alignment — 67
2 Overview of the BDPL 2006 — 68
3 Scope of the BDPL 2006 — 69
4 Data Protection Principles — 70
5 Lawfulness of Processing — 70
a) Consent — 71
6 Special Categories of Personal Data — 72
7 Rights of Data Subject — 73
a) Nature and Manner of Implementation of Data Subjects' Rights — 74
b) Restrictions — 74
8 Redress Mechanism — 75
9 Personal Scope — 76
a) Obligations of Controller and Processor — 77
b) Third Party — 78
c) Representative — 79
10 Transfer of Personal Data — 79
11 Penalties — 81
12 Specific Processing Situations — 81
13 Conclusion to II — 81
III Supervisory Authority — 82
1 General Functions — 82
2 Independence — 83
3 Powers — 84
a) Supervisory Powers — 84
b) Authorisation and Advisory Powers — 85

c) Complaint Related Powers — 85
4 Challenges — 85
5 Conclusion to III — 87
IV Draft Law — 87
1 Overview of the Draft Law — 88
2 Conclusion to IV — 90
V Case Law and Enforcement — 90
1 Activities of the Supervisory Authority — 90
2 Complaints and Investigations Before the Supervisory Authority — 92
3 Court Cases — 93
4 Conclusion to V — 94
VI Conclusion to B — 94
C Kosovo — 95
I Constitutional Parameters and International Commitments — 95
1 Conclusion to I — 96
II Data Protection Legislation — 96
1 Status Quo of GDPR Alignment — 97
2 Overview of the KDPL 2019 — 97
3 Scope of the KDPL 2019 — 98
4 Definitions — 99
5 Data Protection Principles — 99
6 Lawfulness — 100
a) Consent — 100
7 Special Categories of Personal Data — 100
8 Rights of Data Subject — 100
9 Redress Mechanism — 101
10 Personal Scope — 101
a) Security of Personal Data — 102
b) DPO — 104
c) Codes of Conduct and Certification — 105
11 Transfer of Personal Data — 105
a) Adequacy Decisions — 105
b) Transfer Approval — 107
12 Penalties — 108
13 Specific Processing Situations — 109
a) Direct Marketing — 109
b) Biometric Data — 110
c) Video Surveillance — 111
14 Conclusion to II — 111

III Supervisory Authority — 112
1 General Functions — 113
2 Independence — 113
3 Powers — 114
4 Challenges — 114
5 Conclusion to III — 116
IV Case Law and Enforcement — 116
1 Activities of the Supervisory Authority — 117
2 Court Case Law — 118
3 Conclusion to IV — 119
V Conclusion to C — 119
D Montenegro — 120
I Constitutional Parameters and International Commitments — 121
1 Conclusion to I — 121
II Data Protection Legislation — 122
1 Status Quo of GDPR Alignment — 122
2 Overview of the MDPL 2008 — 123
3 Scope of the MDPL 2008 — 124
4 Definition of Personal Data — 124
5 Data Protection Principles — 125
6 Lawfulness of Processing — 125
a) Consent — 126
b) Consent of Deceased Persons — 126
7 Special Categories of Personal Data — 127
8 Rights of Data Subject — 127
9 Redress Mechanism — 129
10 Personal Scope — 130
a) Security Measures — 130
b) Data Breach Notification — 131
c) Records of Processing Activities and Notifying the Supervisory Authority — 132
d) DPO — 132
e) Representative — 133
11 Transfer of Personal Data — 133
12 Penalties — 134
13 Specific Processing Situations — 135
a) Biometric Measures — 135
b) Records on Entry and Exit from Business or Official Premises — 135

c) Video Surveillance — 135
14 Conclusion to II — 136
III Supervisory Authority — 137
1 General Functions — 137
2 Independence — 137
3 Powers — 138
4 Challenges — 139
a) Lack of Enforcement Powers — 139
b) Understaffing — 139
c) Political Influence — 140
5 Conclusion to III — 141
IV Draft Law — 142
1 Overview of the Draft Law — 142
2 Particularities — 143
a) Scope — 143
b) Rights of Data Subject — 144
c) Lawfulness of Processing — 144
d) Consent — 145
e) Redress Rights — 146
f) Personal Scope — 146
g) Data Transfers — 147
h) Supervisory Authority – Agency — 148
3 Conclusion to IV — 148
V Case Law and Enforcement — 149
1 Activities of the Supervisory Authority — 149
2 Complaints and Investigations Before the Supervisory Authority — 150
3 Court Cases — 150
4 Conclusion to V — 152
VI Conclusion to D — 152
E North Macedonia — 153
I Constitutional Parameters and International Commitments — 154
1 Conclusion to I — 155
II Data Protection Legislation — 155
1 Status Quo of GDPR Alignment — 156
2 Overview of the MDPL 2020 — 157
3 Scope of the MDPL 2020 — 157
4 Data Protection Principles — 158
5 Lawfulness of Processing — 159
6 Special Categories of Personal Data — 160

7 Rights of Data Subject — 160
8 Redress Mechanism — 161
9 Personal Scope — 161
a) Specific Security Obligations — 162
b) High-risk Filing Systems — 162
c) DPIA — 164
d) DPO — 165
e) Representatives — 166
f) Codes of Conduct — 166
g) Certifications — 166
10 Transfer of Personal Data — 167
a) Adequacy Decisions — 168
b) Transfers Based on Safeguards — 170
c) Derogations — 170
d) Data Transfers in Practice — 171
11 Penalties — 171
12 Specific Processing Situations — 172
a) Processing and Freedom of Expression and Information (Art. 81) — 173
b) Processing of Citizens' National Identification Number (Art. 83) — 173
c) Prior Approval(s) — 174
d) Deceased Persons — 174
e) Direct Marketing — 175
f) Video Surveillance — 175
g) Recipients — 177
13 Conclusion to II — 178
III Supervisory Authority — 179
1 General Functions — 179
2 Independence — 179
3 Powers — 180
a) Cooperation with State Administration Bodies — 181
4 Challenges — 181
5 Conclusion to III — 183
IV Case Law and Enforcement — 184
1 Activities of the Supervisory Authority — 184
2 Data Subjects' Complaints Before the PDPA — 186
3 Data Breach 'Scandals' — 186
a) Wiretapping — 187
b) State Election Commission — 187

c) Stop Corona App — 188
4 Court Cases — 188
5 Conclusion to IV — 190
V Conclusion to E — 190
F Serbia — 191
I Constitutional Parameters and International Commitments — 192
1 Conclusion to I — 193
II Data Protection Legislation — 193
1 Status Quo of GDPR Alignment — 194
a) The EU Commission Assessment — 197
2 Overview of the SDPL 2019 — 198
3 Scope of the SDPL 2019 — 198
4 Data Protection Principles — 199
5 Lawfulness of Processing — 199
6 Special Categories of Personal Data — 201
7 Rights of Data Subject — 202
a) Art. 21 – Transparent Information — 202
b) Art. 30 – Right to be Forgotten — 202
c) Art. 38 – Automated Individual Decision-Making, Including Profiling — 203
d) Art. 40 – Restrictions and Controversy — 204
8 Redress Mechanism — 205
9 Personal Scope — 205
a) Security of Personal Data — 206
b) DPO — 207
c) Representatives of Foreign Entities — 208
d) Codes of Conduct and Certification — 210
10 Transfers of Personal Data — 211
a) Art. 64 – Adequacy Decisions — 211
b) Adequate Safeguards — 214
c) DPC's Approval — 215
d) Special Cases — 216
11 Penalties — 216
12 Specific Processing Situations — 217
a) Processing in the Field of Labour and Employment — 217
b) Processing for Humanitarian Purposes by the Public Authorities — 218
13 Conclusion to II — 219
III Supervisory Authority — 219
1 General Functions — 220

2 Independence — 220
3 Powers — 221
4 Challenges — 221
a) Election of DPC's Head and Controversy — 222
b) President's Son's Wine Shop Case — 223
5 Conclusion to III — 224
IV Case Law and Enforcement — 225
1 Activities of the Supervisory Authority — 225
2 Cases Before the Supervisory Authority — 227
a) The President's Letters — 228
b) Senior Cards — 229
3 Court Cases — 230
a) SDPL 2008 — 231
b) Criminal Complaints (Art. 146 Criminal Code) — 231
c) SDPL 2019 — 232
4 SHARE as Data Privacy Watchdog in the WB6 — 232
5 Conclusion to IV — 234
V Conclusion to F — 235
G Conclusion to Chapter 4 — 236

Chapter 5 - Government Access to Personal Data in the WB6 — 238
A Criteria — 238
B Challenges in Aligning Government Access Legislation — 241
C Albania — 242
I Criminal Law Enforcement Purposes — 242
1 Rules for Authorising and Limiting Interception Measures — 243
2 Redress — 243
3 Oversight — 244
II National Security Purposes — 245
1 Rules for Authorising Interception Measures — 246
2 Limits and Safeguards — 247
3 Redress — 248
4 Oversight — 248
III Conclusion to C — 249
D Bosnia and Herzegovina — 250
I Criminal Law Enforcement Purposes — 251
1 Rules for Authorising and Limiting Interception Measures — 251
2 Redress — 253
3 Oversight — 253

II National Security Purposes — 254
1 Rules for Authorising Interception Measures — 255
2 Limits and Safeguards — 257
3 Redress — 259
4 Oversight — 260
III Conclusion to D — 261
E Kosovo — 261
I Criminal Law Enforcement Purposes — 262
1 Rules for Authorising and Limiting Interception Measures — 263
2 Redress — 264
3 Oversight — 264
II National Security Purposes — 265
1 Rules for Authorising Interception Measures — 266
2 Limits and Safeguards — 266
3 Redress — 268
4 Oversight — 268
III Conclusion to E — 269
F Montenegro — 270
I Criminal Law Enforcement Purposes — 270
1 Rules for Authorising and Limiting Interception Measures — 271
2 Redress — 271
3 Oversight — 272
II National Security Purposes — 273
1 Rules for Authorising Interception Measures — 273
2 Limits and Safeguards — 274
3 Redress — 276
4 Oversight — 276
III Conclusion to F — 277
G North Macedonia — 278
I Criminal Law Enforcement Purposes — 279
1 Rules for Authorising and Limiting Interception Measures — 279
2 Redress — 281
3 Oversight — 281
II National Security Purposes — 282
1 Rules for Authorising Interception Measures — 283
2 Limits and Safeguards — 284
3 Redress — 285
4 Oversight — 286
III Conclusion to G — 286

H Serbia — 287
I Criminal Law Enforcement Purposes — 288
1 Rules for Authorising and Limiting Interception Measures — 289
2 Redress — 290
3 Oversight — 291
II National Security Purposes — 292
1 Rules for Authorising Interception Measures — 293
2 Limits and Safeguards — 294
a) Challenges — 295
4 Redress — 296
5 Oversight — 297
III Conclusion to H — 298
IV Conclusion to Chapter 5 — 298

Chapter 6 – Privacy-Infringing Technologies in the WB6 — 300
A The Beijing Effect — 301
I Beijing Technologies in the WB6 — 303
1 Safe City Projects — 306
a) Safe Society Project in Serbia — 307
b) Huawei in BiH — 309
II Developments in the EU — 310
III Conclusion to A — 311
B Challenges for the Adoption of Adequacy Decisions — 312
I Conclusion to B — 314
II Conclusion to Chapter 6 — 314

Chapter 7 – Towards Adequacy Decision(s): Prospects for the WB6 — 316
A Current Developments in the WB6 — 317
I Countries with Adopted GDPR-like Laws — 317
II Countries without Adopted GDPR-like Laws — 321
III Regional Initiatives and State of Play of Mutual Recognition of Adequacy — 323
IV Conclusion to A — 325
B Current State of Play: Fulfilment of Art. 45(2) GDPR? — 326
I Rule of Law — 326
II Legislation — 327
1 Constitutional Provisions — 327
2 Data Protection Laws — 329
3 Essential Guarantees National Security and Criminal Laws — 331
4 Implementation of Legislation — 332

III Case Law — 333
IV Effective Redress — 333
V International Instruments — 334
VI Supervisory Authorities — 335
VII Conclusion to B — 337
C Beyond EU Accession: Possible Adequacy Decision(s) for the WB6? — 338
I Challenges — 341
II Transplantation Approach and Dilemmas — 342
III Evaluating Alternatives to GDPR Transplantation: Lessons and Models — 344
1 Other Adequacy Decisions — 346
a) Israel's Adequacy Decision — 346
b) Japan's Adequacy Decision — 348
c) South Korea's Adequacy Decision — 350
d) Hungary — 351
2 A Unique Solution for the WB6? — 352
a) Specifics of the WB6's Legal Systems — 353
b) Shift from a 'One Size Fits All' to a 'Risk Based' Approach? — 356
c) Strengthening Enforcement — 358
d) Amending the Legal Framework to Strengthen Data Protection Compliance — 358
e) Enhancing Regional Cooperation to Obtain Adequacy Decision(s) — 360
f) Regional Approach Versus the 'Regatta Principle' — 361
IV Conclusion to C — 364
D Conclusion to Chapter 7 — 365

Chapter 8 – Conclusion — 367

Tables — 371
Table of Cases — 371
Table of Legislation — 372
Table of Interview, Panel, and Accessed Public Information — 378
Table of Activity Reports on Data Protection in the WB6 — 379
Table of WB6 Supervisory Authorities' Decisions — 380

Bibliography — 382

List of Abbreviations

ACPP	Albanian Code of the Penal Procedure
ADPL 2008	Former Albanian Data Protection Law
ADPL 2024	Albanian Data Protection Law in Force
AIEC	Albanian Law on the Interception of Electronic Communications
APC	Albanian Penal Code
Art.	Article
Artt.	Articles
BA	Bosnian Personal Data Protection Agency
BCPL	Bosnian Criminal Procedure Law
BDPL 2008	Bosnian Data Protection Law 2008
BDSG	German Federal Data Protection Act
BIA	Serbian Security Information Agency known as "BIA"
BLC	Bosnian Law on Communication
BRI	Chinese Belt and Road Initiative
CFU	Chapter of Fundamental Rights of the European Union
CJEU	Court of Justice of the EU
CoE	Council of Europe
COIC	Kosovo Commissioner for Oversight of Interception of Communication
Convention 108	The Convention for the Protection of Individuals with regard to Automatic Processing of Personal Data (CETS No. 108)
Convention 108+	Modernised Convention for the Protection of Individuals with Regard to the Processing of Personal Data
DPC	Serbian Commissioner for Public Information and Data Protection
DPD	Directive 95/46/EC of the European Parliament and of the Council of 24 October 1995 on the protection of individuals with regard to the processing of personal data and on the free movement of such data
DPIA	Data Protection Impact Assessment
DPO	Data Protection Officer
ECHR	European Convention on Human Rights
ECPSA	Electronic Communications and Postal Agency of Montenegro
ECtHR	European Court on Human Rights
EDPB	European Data Protection Board
EU	European Union
EU Commission	European Commission
EU Data Retention Directive	Directive 2006/24/EC of the European Parliament and of the Council on the retention of data generated or processed in connection with the provision of publicly available electronic communications services or of public communications networks and amending Directive 2002/58/EC (2006)
EUPM	EU Police Mission in Bosnia and Herzegovina
GDPR	Regulation (EU) 2016/679 of the European Parliament and of the Council of 27 April 2016 on the protection of natural persons with regard to

https://doi.org/10.1515/9783112221013-002

	the processing of personal data and on the free movement of such data, and repealing Directive 95/46/EC
IPTF	International Police Task Force in Bosnia and Herzegovina
ISA	Intelligence-Security Agency of Bosnia and Herzegovina
JMBG	Jedinstveni Matični Broj Građana (Unique Citizen Identification Number)
KDPL 2010	Kosovo Data Protection Law 2010
KDPL 2019	Kosovo Data Protection Law 2019
KIA	Kosovo Intelligence Agency
KIEC	Kosovo Law on Interception of Electronic Communications
LED	Directive on the protection of natural persons with regard to the processing of personal data by competent authorities for the purposes of the prevention, investigation, detection or prosecution of criminal offences or the execution of criminal penalties, and on the free movement of such data
LKISA	Law on Kosovo Intelligence Agency
LMSIA	Law on Military Security Agency and Military Intelligence Agency of Serbia
LNSA	Law on the Agency for National Security of North Macedonia
LSIA	Military Intelligence Agency of Serbia
MCC	Criminal code of Montenegro
MCPC	Criminal Procedure Code of Montenegro
MDPL 2008	Montenegrin Data Protection Law 2008
MDPL 2020	Macedonian Data Protection Law 2020
MoJ	Ministry of Justice Serbia
MSA	Military Security Agency of Serbia
NCT	The National Coordination Council of Montenegro
NGO	Non-governmental Organisation
NMCPL	Criminal Procedure Law of North Macedonia
NMLEC	Law on Electronic Communications of North Macedonia
NMLIC	Law on Interception of Communications of North Macedonia
NSA	Agency for National Security of North Macedonia
OECD	Organisation for Economic Cooperation and Development
OECD Recommendations	Recommendations of the Council Concerning Guidelines Governing the Protection of Privacy and Transborder Flow of Personal Data
OHR	Office of the High Representative in Bosnia and Herzegovina
Para.	Paragraph
Paras.	Paragraphs
PDPA	Personal Data Protection Agency of North Macedonia
PIPL	China Personal Information Protection Law
RCC	Regional Cooperation Council
SCCs	Standard Contractual Clauses
SCPC	Serbian Criminal Procedure Code
SEC	State Election Commission of North Macedonia
SIS	Albanian State Intelligence Service
SLEC	Serbian Law on Electronic Communications
SDPL 2019	Serbian Data Protection Law 2019
SDPL 2008	Serbian Data Protection Law 2008

TEU	Treaty on European Union
TOMs	Technical and Organisational Measures
UDHR	UN's Universal Declaration of Human Rights of 1948
WB6	6 Western Balkan Countries (Albania, Bosnia and Herzegovina, Kosovo, Montenegro, North Macedonia and Serbia)
WP29	Article 29 Working Party

List of Tables

Table 1: Overview of Data Protection Laws in the WB6 (2008 – 2003) p. 21
Table 2: Overview of Constitutional Parameters on Privacy and Data Protection in the WB6 p. 328
Table 3: Overview of the Data Protection Laws and Their Status in the WB6 p. 329
Table 4: Overview of International Instruments in the WB6 p. 335
Table 5: Overview of Supervisory Authorities in the WB6 p. 336

Chapter 1 – Introduction

The adoption and implementation of the General Data Protection Regulation (hereinafter: "GDPR") have had essentially global consequences with regard to the determination of its territorial jurisdiction and the instrument of adequacy decisions.[1] The GDPR has set a global standard for data protection and, as it is available in many languages, has made it more accessible to third countries.[2] From the point of view of the European Union (hereinafter: "EU"), the transfer of personal data to places outside of the EU ('third countries') may result in the loss of the protection afforded within the EU.[3] It is therefore necessary that appropriate safeguards are put in place to ensure a comparable level of data protection.[4]

This impact of the GDPR had required many non-EU countries to quickly choose their approach to continue cooperating with the EU. Many of these countries are striving to harmonise their legislation to get on the EU Commission's list of countries providing adequate data protection in accordance with Art. 45 GDPR or to retain their current position on the list. However, the GDPR is a highly complex law, enacted as a general regulation directly applicable in EU Member States, but giving EU Member States the right to further specify the application of its provisions in accordance with their domestic legal system ('opening clauses').[5]

Thus, many third countries, which may not possess a culture of data protection and privacy awareness that matches EU Member States, are now in a challenging position. For the Western Balkans six countries (hereinafter: "WB6") – all of them in the EU accession process – this situation is particularly pressing, as their legal systems are required to adapt to the EU's acquis communautaire and their businesses are already heavily intertwined with the EU market. None of the WB6 countries has been included in the EU Commission's adequacy list, despite their longstanding EU accession process, which aims at overall harmonisation with the EU acquis.

All WB6 countries have initiated the process of harmonising their national legislation with the GDPR. However, they face various obstacles, ranging from challenges during the legislative process to a lack of understanding of the GDPR

---

1 Artt. 3, 45 GDPR.

2 Moritz Hennemann, "Wettbewerb der Datenschutzrechtsordnungen? – Zur Rezeption der Datenschutz-Grundverordnung", RabelsZ, vol. 84, pp. 864–895 (2020), p. 890.

3 Christopher Kuner, "Protecting EU data outside EU borders under the GDPR", Common Market Law Review, Volume 60, Issue 1 (2023), pp. 77–106.

4 *Ibid.*

5 Julian Wagner and Alexander Benecke, "National Legislation within the Framework of the GDPR," 2 Eur. Data Prot. L. Rev. 353 (2016).

https://doi.org/10.1515/9783112221013-003

principles that need to be incorporated into their national legislation. Opting for a simple replication of the GDPR instead of a critical assessment of its compatibility with the respective legal systems has resulted in laws that are inherently difficult to interpret and apply. In addition, limited resources are an obstacle to the effective implementation of the harmonisation process and the enforcement of the newly adopted GDPR-like rules.

Lastly, the EU is not the sole influential force in the WB6 region. The influence of Chinese companies investing in extensive projects and introducing innovative technologies also contributes to the shaping of data protection standards in this region.

A Research Subject

Against this background this dissertation seeks to analyse the approach taken by the WB6 in dealing with the challenges posed by the GDPR, taking into account their special position as countries seeking EU membership. The study will provide a comprehensive overview of the data protection compliance profile of each of the WB6: Albania, Bosnia and Herzegovina, Kosovo, Montenegro, North Macedonia and Serbia. Specifically, it will look at data protection laws and laws governing law enforcement access rights to identify areas where improvements are needed that would ultimately facilitate obtaining an adequacy decision from the EU Commission.

Given the interdependence of the economies of the WB6 with the EU market, the free flow of personal data between these countries is of great importance to the WB6 countries. The study therefore addresses the issue of data transfers between the EU and the WB6 countries and the criteria required for an adequacy decision for the WB6 countries. In assessing the criteria essential for adequacy decisions, the dissertation will take a multi-layered approach, including an analysis of data protection laws, the effectiveness of data protection authorities, the role of non-governmental organisations (hereinafter: "NGO") and relevant case law with the aim to provide a complete picture of data protection standards in the WB6 countries.

As the EU is not the only influencer in the WB6 countries, the study will also analyse the influence of Chinese companies in the region and how such influence may shape data protection standards and thus affect the prospects of an adequacy decision. Given the increasing prevalence of privacy-infringing technologies, maintaining an adequate level of data protection is of paramount importance. Therefore, the study examines the adoption of modern technologies by WB6 governments and their potential impact on the adequacy decision, particularly with regard to the EU's scrutiny of Chinese privacy standards.

The study will delve deeper into the inherent challenges and limitations associated with the transposition of the GDPR text by the WB6 countries. While the GDPR serves as a robust framework for data protection regulation within the EU context, its 'applicability' to the WB6 countries necessitates careful consideration of the unique legal, cultural, and economic factors at play in these countries

B Course of Study

This dissertation begins by providing pertinent information to understand the fundamentals of data protection, including the principles and the legal framework established by the GDPR. This is important to assess the EU standards for protection of personal data and compare them with those of the WB6 (Chapter 2). Chapter 3 will focus on the impact of the GDPR on non-EU countries, including the possibilities for direct application of the GDPR in third countries. Furthermore, the possible venues for data transfers from the EU to third countries will be analysed, with a particular emphasis on adequacy decision as the easiest basis for transfers of data outside of the EU. The most important criteria considered by the EU Commission in making adequacy decisions will be elaborated in detail. Chapter 4 will provide a comprehensive overview of the data protection framework in each of the WB6 countries, in order to assess the level of data protection and identify the main issues in each country that are relevant for the adoption of an adequacy decision. A solid data protection framework alone may not be enough for the adoption of an adequacy decision, but the handling of and access to sensitive data by state authorities also needs to be taken into account. Therefore, the Chapter 5 will examine the legislation in each WB6 country relevant to the essential access to personal data transferred from the EU to the WB6 by public authorities for criminal enforcement and national security purposes. In this part, the jurisprudence of the Court of Justice of the European Union (hereinafter: "CJEU") and European Court of Human Rights (hereinafter: "ECHR") will also be analysed in more detail. Chapter 6 will focus on the potential impact of non-EU influences, such as Chinese influence (the so-called "Beijing effect") and technological innovations in the region, on data protection standards in the WB6 countries. Possible negative impacts of these influences for the adoption of an adequacy decision will also be assessed. Finally, Chapter 7 examines the extent to which the WB6 fulfil the criteria necessary for the adoption of an adequacy decision and provides a preview to expected future developments in the field of data protection in the WB6 countries. It will question the suitability of merely transposing the GDPR text to WB6's data protection laws and its potential impact on possible future EU Commission adequacy decisions. Moreover, it also provides recommendations for the WB6 countries to contemplate while aligning their domestic data protection laws with the EU framework, and for the EU Commission to consider when entering into potential adequacy negotiations with the WB6 countries.

C State of Research

The GDPR was adopted in April 2016 and since then has been the subject of numerous discussions as it brings many novelties in the field of data protection and leaves space for plenty of interpretations. The extraterritorial dimension of GDPR applicability has been regularly discussed, especially after the publication of the initial GDPR proposal.[6] Jules Polonetsky and Christopher Wolf highlighted that the extension of the extraterritorial GDPR application constitutes a dramatic shift from a country of origin to a country of destination approach and threatens to create uncertainty about when EU law will be deemed to apply and cause conflicts with other privacy regimes at a time when interoperability is key.[7] Criticisms of the effectiveness of the GDPR's extraterritorial jurisdiction are mostly based on the fact that non-EU data protection regulators have a certain margin of manoeuvre to refuse cooperation with EU supervisory authorities.[8] As a former vice president Omer Tene at the International Association of Privacy Professionals stated, even if the EU persuades other countries to adopt its policies, it will be hard to ensure the laws work: "It's one thing to have rules on the books, but it's quite an-

---

6 Paul De Hert and Michal Czerniawski, "Expanding the European Data Protection Scope Beyond Territory: Article 3 of the General Data Protection Regulation in its Wider Context" International Data Privacy Law, Volume 6, Issue 3, (August 2016), pp. 230–243; Peter Gola and Dirk Heckmann, Art. 3 "Räumlicher Anwendungsbereich, Datenschutz-Grundverordnung – Bundesdatenschutzgesetz", (3th edn. C.H. Beck. 2022); Philip Laue und Sascha Kremer, Das neue Datenschutzrecht in der betrieblichen Praxis, (2nd edn, C.H. Beck 2019); Boris P. Paal und Daniel A. Pauly, "Art. 3 Räumlicher Anwendungsbereich, Datenschutz-Grundverordnung Bundesdatenschutzgesetz", DS-GVO BDSG Kommentar (3rd edn. C.H. Beck 2021); Alexander Golland, "Der räumliche Anwendungsbereich der DS-GVO", Datenschutz Datensich 42, 351–357 (2018), Omer Tene and Christopher Wolf, White Paper "Overextended: Jurisdiction and Applicable Law under the EU General Data Protection Regulation", The Future of Privacy Forum White Paper (January 2013); Dan Jerker B Svantesson, "Extraterritoriality and targeting in EU data privacy law: the weak spot undermining the regulation," International Data Privacy Law, Volume 5, Issue 4, November 2015, pp. 226–234.

7 Omer Tene and Christopher Wolf (n. 6).

8 See more broadly a criticism of the GDPR exterritorial application: Cedric Ryngaert and Mark Zoetekouw, "The End of Territory? The Re-Emergence of Community as a Principle of Jurisdictional Order in the Internet Era" (October 2014).

other thing to implement these rules on the ground."[9] The venues for data transfers to third countries and criteria for the adoption of adequacy decisions have been also a subject of academic research.[10] In particular, the instrument of adequacy decisions received plentiful attention (which will be discussed further in Chapter 3).[11] In addition, the 'one-size-fits-all' approach of the GDPR was subject of criticism[12], as it is particularly challenging for third countries, placing a heavy burden on their businesses, especially small and medium-sized enterprises.

In examining the existing academic discourse on data protection legislation in the countries of the WB6 there are several researchers who focus on data protection developments in each country. Their contributions include the provision of comprehensive overviews of the GDPR and the relevant national legislations.[13]

---

9 The New York Times' article "G.D.P.R., a New Privacy Law, Makes Europe World's Leading Tech Watchdog", published in May 2018 <https://www.nytimes.com/2018/05/24/technology/europe-gdpr-privacy.html> (accessed on 15.10.2021).

10 See also: Julian Wagner, "The transfer of personal data to third countries under the GDPR: when does a recipient country provide an adequate level of protection?", *International Data Privacy Law*, Volume 8, Issue 4, (November 2018), pp. 318–337; Laura Drechsler "What Is Equivalent? A Probe into GDPR Adequacy Based on EU Fundamental Rights" Jusletter IT (February 21, 2019).

11 Oskar Josef Gstrein and Andrej Zwitter, "Extraterritorial Application of the GDPR: Promoting European Values or Power?" Internet Policy Review 2021, Volume 10 Issue 3 (September 30, 2021); W. Gregory Voss, "Cross-Border Data Flows, the GDPR, and Data Governance," 29 Wash Int'l L.J. 485 (2020); Ira Rubinstein and Bilyana Petkova, "The International Impact of the General Data Protection Regulation" Commentary on the General Data Protection Regulation, Marc Cole and Franziska Boehm, Edward Elgar 2018 (April 23, 2018).

12 Winfried Viel, "The GDPR: The Emperor's New Clothes – On the Structural Shortcomings of Both the Old and the New Data Protection Law", Neue Zeitschrift für Verwaltungsrecht 10/2018, pp. 686–696 (December 21, 2018).

13 Andrej Diligenski, Dragan Prlja and Dražen Cerović, Data Protection Law, GDPR, , Institute of Comparative Law, Belgrade (2020) <https://iup.rs/wp-content/uploads/2021/05/2018-Pravo-za%c5%a1tite-podataka-Diligenski-Prlja.pdf>; Dragan Milić, "Legitimni interes kao osnov obrade podataka o ličnosti" (Eng. Legitimate Interest as a Basis for Processing Personal Dat), The Personal Data Protection Rights in Serbia (2020), Serbian Institute of Comparative Law, pp. 50–59; Karanovic & Partners "North Macedonia: Informal Requirement for Transfer Impact Assessments in the New Yea", Lexology (15.12.2021) <https://www.lexology.com/library/detail.aspx?g=a36a570d-5777-45a8-89a3-e19e4356b7ef> accessed on 28.05.2023; Arben Murtezić, "Opšta Uredba o Zaštiti podataka: Odnos Prava na Privatnost i Zaštite Ličnih Podataka s osvrtom na Bosnu i Hercegovinu", Anali Pravnog fakulteta Univerziteta u Zenici, ISSN 1986–5791, pp. 35–51 (2019); Nora Osmani, "Privacy and data protection: Legal aspects in the Republic of Macedonia", Information Technology Law,Ss. Cyril and Methodius University, Skopje, Republic of Macedonia (2016); Gliqiri Riza, "GDPR and personal data protection in non-EU countries: Albanian case of data protection legislation," University of Tirana, Faculty of Economics, Tirana, Albania, RTA-CSIT (May 2021); Sara Zotaj, "Protection of the Personal Data in Albania in Compliance with the General Data Protection

Some scholars go even deeper in their analysis and focus on the significant impact of the GDPR on these national legal frameworks.[14] However, when it comes to the impact of the GDPR in the WB6 countries as a whole region, there is little up-to-date scientific research available that specifically tackles developments in the WB6 region in the area of data protection and new technologies.[15] In the work "Privacy Concern in Western Balkan Countries: Developing a Typology of Citizens"[16] authors examined which segments of the populations with similar attitudes towards data protection and privacy exist in the WB6. Nevertheless, the work was published before the adoption of the GDPR and it did not analyse data protection legislation in the WB6 countries. More recently, a notable academic contribution is the research "Nationalising the General Data Protection Regulation in Western Balkan" by Nevena Ružić.[17] This article provides a concise overview of the ongoing harmonisation process in the WB6 with the GDPR until 2021. Nonetheless, this dissertation aims to extend upon this work by providing more comprehensive profiles of each country within the WB6, focusing specifically on

Regulation", Central European University Private University (2021); Anisa Tomić, "Bosnia & Herzegovina – Data Protection Overview", OneTrust Data Guidance (August 2022) available at the following link <https://www.dataguidance.com/notes/bosnia-herzegovina-data-protection-overview> (accessed on 22.04.2023).

14 Merisa Çeloaliaj, "General Regulation on Personal Data Potection: Certain Aspects of the GDPR's Impact on Legal Entities in the Republic of Albania", International Journal, Vol.34.5 (September 2019); Bledar Abdurrahmani, "Data Protection in Albania: A Challenge Towards Improving Legislation on the Way to EU Integration", Aleksandër Moisiu University, Durrës (2022); Petrit Hajdari, Petrit Nimani, Deshnim Hebibi, and Artan Maloku, "Implementation of the right to privacy in the Republic of Kosovo, International Journal of Health Sciences", (2022), pp. 5036–5044; Njomëza Zejnullahu, "Personal Data Protection in Kosovo, Three Years of Failure", European Data Protection Law Review, Volume 6 (2020), Issue 2, p. 309.

15 Stefan Andonović and Dragan Prlja, "The Basics of Personal Data Protection Rights", Institute of Comparative Law, Belgrade (2020) <https://iup.rs/wp-content/uploads/2020/09/2020-Andonovic-Prlja-Osnovi-prava-zastite-podataka-o-licnosti.pdf> (accessed on 23.04.2021); Bashkim Nuredini, Jorida Xhafaj, Vesna Paukovska Dodevska, "A Comparative Overview of Data Protection in e-Commerce in the European Union, the United States of America, the Republic of North Macedonia, and Albania: Models and Specifics", Studia Iuridica Lubliensia, Vo 31, No 3 (2022); Milos B. Stanic, "Election of Members of the Supervisory Body for Personal Data Protection as a Guarantee of Their Independence – Examples of Albania, Bosnia and Herzegovina, Montenegro and North Macedonia", Foreign Legal Life (2020).

16 Elena Budak and Edo Rajh and Ivan-Damir Anic, "Privacy Concern in Western Balkan Countries: Developing a Typology of Citizens", Working Papers 1402, The Institute of Economics, Zagreb (2014).

17 Nevena Ružić, "Nationalising the General Data Protection Regulation in Western Balkan", Regional L. Rev. 313 (2021).

the criteria pertinent to an adequacy decision and the challenges of the copy-paste approach of the GDPR into the national laws of the WB6 countries.

In addition to the academic debate on the impact of the GDPR on the national WB6 legislation, it is essential to acknowledge the significant contributions of various stakeholders to the ongoing dialogue on the development of data protection in the WB6 countries after the adoption of the GDPR. The initiative by the Regional Cooperation Council (hereinafter: "RCC") on assessing the state of play in each WB6 country in aligning national legislation with the EU acquis in the area of data protection and the GDPR is one of them.[18] While this report is not a scientific work, it represents a programme of the RCC involving different experts from each WB6 country where they analysed the developments of the harmonisation processes in the WB6 until 2020.

Furthermore, the commendable efforts of the SHARE Foundation, an NGO (hereinafter: "SHARE") with a strong commitment to data protection in the WB6, deserve due recognition. SHARE has made substantial contributions to the discourse on data protection legislation, disseminating a number of educational materials aimed at promoting an understanding of the GDPR and emerging data protection laws.[19] This organisation also prepared a comparative analysis of data protection laws in the WB6.[20] In addition, SHARE has been actively involved in the investigation of data breaches, particularly within Serbia and, to some extent, other WB6 countries.[21] The lessons learned from these efforts, particularly those conducted within Serbia and other WB6 jurisdictions, will be subject to analysis in the dissertation.

Finally, it is imperative to underline the importance of the opinions and recommendations offered by the data protection authorities operating in the WB6 countries. Their work will be an important focus of discussion in this dissertation.[22]

---

18 Regional Cooperation Council, "Compliance of Legal Framework in the Western Balkans Economies with the General Data Protection Regulation (GDPR) Requirements", (December 2020), <https://www.rcc.int/pubs/113/compliance-of-legal-framework-in-the-western-balkans-economies-with-the-general-data-protection-regulation-gdpr-requirements> (accessed on 03.09.2021)

19 SHARE, "Vodič kroz zakon o zaštiti podataka o ličnosti i GDPR: Tumačenje novog pravnog okvira" (Eng. Guide on the Law on Data Protection and GDPR – Interpretation of the New Legal Framework). Other material of SHARE will be particularly analysed in Chapters 4, 5 and 6.

20 SHARE, "Regulatory Framework in the field of Digital Rights, Comparative Analysis: Albania, Bosnia and Herzegovina, Kosovo, Montenegro, North Macedonia, Serbia" (December 2021).

21 The work of SHARE will be particularly analysed in Chapters 4, 5 and 6.

22 The opinions and recommendations of the data protection authorities are analysed separately in the individual country profiles in Chapter 4.

D Research Aim

This study pursues to comprehensively examine the data protection frameworks in the WB6 countries that are aspiring to EU membership and to compare them with EU standards. The absence of such a thorough overview in the English language literature underlines the importance of this study. Through an in-depth analysis of the data protection regulatory landscape in the WB6 and considering the EU Commission's approach to data protection adequacy assessment, the main analytical part of this study aims to identify the shortcomings that prevent the WB6 countries from meeting the criteria for an EU Commission's adequacy decision. To provide a comprehensive understanding of the data protection standards in the region, the study will also explore the influences of non-EU political actors, particularly countries like China, which are introducing advanced technologies in the region. It will evaluate their impact on data protection standards and possible negative effects on future negotiations with the EU Commission regarding obtaining adequacy decisions. Having elaborated this analytical basis in the final part this study will challenge the predominant approach which consists in the WB6 merely copying the GDPR text as part of their endeavour to align with the EU acquis and obtain adequacy decisions by the EU Commission. Thus, another aim of this study is to test the hypothesis whether by considering alternative approaches beyond mere GDPR replication in each country individually, policymakers could embark on a better path towards sustainable and effective data protection governance that balances regulatory compliance with the region's unique needs and political aspirations. Ultimately, the study seeks to offer pragmatic and context-sensitive recommendations for the WB6 countries as they navigate the complexities of the GDPR alignment in the context of EU accession of the region.

Chapter 2 – Fundamentals of Data Protection Law and Privacy

Different interpretations and definitions of the right to privacy exist. Often said to be the founders of the definition of the right to privacy, Samuel Warren and Louis Brandeis, who at the end of the 19th century, defined privacy as "the right to be left alone" and pointed out that political, social and economic changes conditioned the adoption of new laws and the improvement of the concept of privacy.[23] Moreover, they laid down the foundations for the whole modern corpus of privacy protection, private communication, and even personal data. At the same time, they introduced some limitations to these rights, such as the public interest or consent to the publication of private communications, and recognised the right to compensation in the event of data breaches, which all remain applicable today.[24] In the days of Warren and Brandeis, the greatest threat to privacy were cameras and the printed means of public information with gossip columns and slander to increase their circulation.[25] Already at that time, lawyers took the view that the law must respond to the evolution of technology, understanding that this evolution would not halt at cameras.[26] Nowadays, the development of technology has accelerated dramatically, and modern societies use various technological means to achieve individual, economic, social and political goals including by monitoring citizens' behaviour. Therefore, legislators have the difficult task of keeping up with technological trends. They often face a trade-off between the aim to protect privacy and economic interests of large corporations. EU legislators have led the way in finding compromise solutions to this dilemma, and the legal formulae they have developed have in many cases influenced regulation in other parts of the world.[27]

The following Chapter focuses on the development of data protection legislation in Europe, with a particular focus on the EU as the forerunners of data protection regulation, also taking into account the legal instruments of the Council of

---

23 Samuel D. Warren and Louis D. Brandeis, "The Right to Privacy", Harvard Law Review, Vol. 4, No. 5. (1890), pp. 193–220; Rodotà, Stefano, "Data Protection as a Fundamental Right," in: Gutwirth, S., Poullet, Y., De Hert, P., de Terwangne, C., Nouwt, S. (eds) Reinventing Data Protection? Springer, Dordrecht (2009); Orla Lynskey, "Deconstructing Data Protection: The 'Added-Value' Of A Right to Data Protection in the EU Legal Order", International and Comparative Law Quarterly, 63(3), pp. 569–597, (2014).

24 Samuel D. Warren and Louis D. Brandeis (n. 23), pp. 218–219.

25 *Ibid*, pp. 195–196.

26 *Ibid.*

27 Anu Bradford, "The Brussels Effect", Northwestern University Law Review, Vol. 107, No. 1, 2012, Columbia Law and Economics Working Paper No. 533 (2012).

https://doi.org/10.1515/9783112221013-004

Europe (hereinafter: "CoE"). In addition, this Chapter will shed light on the evolution of data protection legislation in the WB6 countries, which have consistently adopted and drawn inspiration from EU legislation. In order to understand the historical development of data protection legislation in the WB6 countries, it is essential to look at the data protection framework established in the EU, given the WB6's tendency to emulate EU rules, motivated by their prolonged involvement in the EU accession process over almost two decades.

A Evolution of European Data Protection Laws

Data protection is a relatively new right, compared to other human rights, as it first emerged in the 1970s in response to concerns about the increasingly centralised processing of personal data and the creation of vast databases.[28]

I First Data Protection Laws

In 1968, the Parliamentary Assembly of the CoE addressed Recommendation 509 to the Committee of Ministers, calling on it to consider whether the European Court of Human Rights (hereinafter: "ECtHR") and the domestic law of the Member States provide adequate protection of the right to privacy with respect to modern science and technology.[29] A study conducted on behalf of the Committee of Ministers found that current national laws do not adequately protect privacy and other individual rights and interests with respect to automated databases.[30] Based on these findings, the Committee of Ministers adopted two resolutions on data protection in 1973 and 1974. The first, Resolution (73) 22, established principles of data protection for the private sector and the second, Resolution (74) 29, did the same for the public sector.[31]

Shortly after the adoption of these two resolutions, the first piece of data protection legislation was enacted in 1970 by the German state of Hesse.[32] The law

28 Lee A. Bygrave, "Data Protection Law, Approaching its Rationale, Logic and Limits", Kluwer Law International (2002), p. 93.

29 European Treaty Series – No. 108, Explanatory Report to the Convention for the Protection of Individuals with regard to Automatic Processing of Personal Data, Strasbourg, 28.01.1981.

30 *Ibid.*

31 *Ibid.*

32 Bundesdatenschutzgesetz. BGBl, I 1977 <https://offenegesetze.de/veroeffentlichung/bgbl1/1977/7#page=1> (accessed on 21.03.2022).

had 17 articles and applied only to state authorities.[33] The law also introduced the data protection authority (ger. *Datenschutzaufsichtsbehörde*).[34] The Hessian Data Protection Act was followed by the Swedish Data Protection Act in 1973 – which was also the world's first national data protection legislation – and subsequently, by other European countries, such as Germany, Austria, Denmark, France, and Luxembourg.[35]

II OECD

Developments in data protection were not confined only to Europe. In 1980 the Council of the Organisation for Economic Cooperation and Development (hereinafter: "OECD") adopted Guidelines Governing the Protection of Privacy and Transborder Flow of Personal Data, (hereinafter: "OECD Recommendations").[36] The OECD Recommendations, contained seven principles: (1) Collection Limitation Principle (2) Data Quality Principle – data collection should be relevant and up-to-date (3) Purpose Specification Principle (4) Use Limitation Principle, (5) Security Safeguards Principle, (6) Openness Principle – data subjects should have the right to have information on what data are collected about them and (7) Accountability Principle – controllers of personal data should be accountable for complying with the law.[37] The OECD Recommendations not only introduced the principles, but also defined the terms that were to become familiar in data protection law, such as 'controller' and 'personal data'.[38]

III Convention 108

The CoE Convention for the Protection of Individuals with regard to Automatic Processing of Personal Data, European Treaty Series – no. 108, adopted by the CoE Committee of Ministers on (hereinafter: "Convention 108") was adopted in

33 Art. 1 Hessian Data Protection Act, GVBI. II 300–20, October 1970.
34 Art. 7, Hessian Data Protection Act, GVBI. II 300–20, October 1970.
35 Gloria González Fuster, "The Emergence of Personal Data Protection as a Fundamental Right of the EU", Law, Governance and Technology Series 16. Springer (2014), p. 21.
36 OECD, "Guidelines on the Protection of Privacy and Transborder Flows of Personal Data," (2013), <https://www.oecd.org/digital/privacy/> (accessed 06.03.2022).
37 *Ibid.*
38 Philip Coppel KC, "Information Rights: A Practitioner's Guide to Data Protection, Freedom of Information and other Information Rights," Bloomsbury Publishing (2020), p. 132.

January 1981. Convention no. 108 is an international treaty dealing specifically with data protection. Convention 108 is open to non-European states and consists now of 55 parties – the latest to join being Marocco.[39] Convention 108 was also a model for many third countries in adopting their national legislation, as well as for the WB6 countries, since they had all incorporated the principles provided in Convention 108. Convention 108 was further modernised by an additional Amending Protocol in 2018 (hereinafter: "Convention 108+"). In 2023, Argentina was the 23rd party to ratify Convention 108+.[40] Almost all WB6 countries have signed Convention 108+, with the exception of Kosovo, while Montenegro has not yet signed Convention 108+.[41]

IV ECHR

Respect for privacy is defined in Art. 8 by the 1950 Convention for the Protection of Human Rights and Fundamental Freedoms (hereinafter: "ECHR"). Although the right to the protection of personal data is not an autonomous right among the various ECHR rights and freedoms, the ECtHR has nevertheless acknowledged that the protection of personal data is of fundamental importance to a person's enjoyment of their right as guaranteed by Art. 8 ECHR.[42] This article is the main vector through which personal data is protected in the ECHR system, even though considerations related to this protection may also come into play under other provisions of the ECHR and its protocols.[43] One of the important aspects discussed in the ECtHR case law is also the technological progress that has led to a quantum leap in surveillance, interception of communications and data retention, in turn leading to major challenges for personal data protection.[44] Since the Leander v. Sweden judgment of 1987, in which the 'old' ECtHR analysed, for the first time,

39 Chart of signatures and ratifications of Treaty 108, Convention for the Protection of Individuals with regard to Automatic Processing of Personal Data (ETS no. 108), status as of 19.05.2023.

40 CoE, "Argentina becomes the 23rd state to ratify Convention 108+ on data protection" (published 17.04.2023) <https://www.coe.int/en/web/human-rights-rule-of-law/-/argentina-ratifies-convention-108-during-the-privacy-symposium> (accessed on 19.05.2023).

41 A complete overview of the international instruments applicable in WB6 can be found in Chapter 7, A.III.

42 Case of Satakunnan Markkinapörssi Oy and Satamedia Oy v. Finland [GC], 2017, § 137; Z v. Finland, 1997, § 95.

43 Guide to the Case-Law of the of the European Court of Human Rights Data protection, (31.08.2022), <https://www.echr.coe.int/Documents/Guide_Data_protection_ENG.pdf> (accessed on 05.05.2023).

44 *Ibid.*

the question of the storage by a public authority of an individual's personal data, the case-law of the ECHR in this field has seen a significant development.[45]

V CFR

Different rules and legal instruments govern the protection of personal data in the EU.[46] The Charter of Fundamental Rights (hereinafter: "CFR"), stemming from the case law of the Court of Justice of the EU (hereinafter: "CJEU") and the ECHR, further consolidate fundamental rights in the EU.[47] The CFR incorporates the general principles laid down in the ECHR, but refers specifically to privacy in Art. 7 and data protection in Art. 8.[48] Unlike the ECHR, the CFR draws a distinction between the conventional right to privacy (Art. 7 CFR), modelled after Art. 8 ECHR, and the right to data protection (Art. 8 CFR), which becomes thereby a new, autonomous fundamental right.[49]

According to Art. 7 CFR, everyone has the right to respect for his or her private and family life, home and communications. As indicated in the explanatory note to Art. 8 CFR, the roots of the right to data protection lie in the right to privacy.[50] Some authors argue that in the EU constitutional context, data protection contributes an additional dimension to privacy.[51] The CJEU refers to them as "fused species"[52] and emphasizes that both rights are "closely connected" with each other.[53]

---

45 *Ibid.*

46 Maria Tzanou, "Data protection as a fundamental right next to privacy? 'Reconstructing' a not so new right" International Data Privacy Law, Volume 3, Issue 2, (May 2013), pp. 88–99; P. Peter Hustinx, "EU Data Protection Law: The Review of Directive 95/46/EC and the Proposed General Data Protection Regulation", (September 2014); J. Kokott and C. Sobotta, "The distinction between privacy and data protection in the jurisprudence of the CJEU and the ECtHR", International Data Privacy Law 3(4) (2013) pp. 222–228.

47 European Data Protection: Law and Practice, Second Edition, International Association of Privacy Professionals (January 1, 2018) IAPP (2018), pp. 26–27.; Gloria González Fuster and Raphaël Gellert, "The fundamental right of data protection in the European Union: in search of an uncharted right", International Review of Law, Computers & Technology (2012), pp. 73–81.

48 González Fuster, G. (2014), pp. 261–262 (n. 35).

49 Stefano Rodotà, "Data Protection as a Fundamental Right", in Gutwirth, S., Poullet, Y., De Hert, P., de Terwangne, C., Nouwt, S. (eds) Reinventing Data Protection?. Springer, Dordrecht (2009).

50 The EU Charter of Fundamental Rights, A Commentary Published by Prof. Steve Peers, Prof. Tamara Hervey, Prof. Jeff Kenner, Prof. Angela Ward, Nomos, Second Edition (2022), p. 251.

51 Maria Tzanou, (2013), p 89 (n. 46).

52 Orla Lynskey, "The Foundations of EU Data Protection Law", Oxford University Press, (2015), p. 15.

According to Art. 8 CFR, everyone has the right to the protection of their personal data and the processing of personal data must be based on a lawful basis. Moreover, compliance with Art. 8 must be subject to control by an independent authority.[54] Any limitation to Art. 8 CFR must be in accordance with Art. 52 CFR, which reflects the limitations based on necessity and proportionality contained in the ECHR.[55] The right to data protection and the limitations of Art. 8 CFR have been further discussed in case law of the CJEU.[56]

The rights enshrined in Artt. 7 and 8 CFR play a crucial role, as the CJEU has developed an extensive body of case law on the right to privacy through its interpretation of these fundamental rights. Notably, in the cases *Digital Rights Ireland* and *Schrems*, the CJEU, for the first time, defined the modalities of breaches concerning the essence of fundamental rights to privacy and data protection, thereby laying the constitutional foundations for interpreting these concepts.[57]

VI TFEU and TEU

Two Treaties, the Treaty on European Union (hereinafter: "TEU") and the Treaty on the Functioning of the European Union (hereinafter: "TFEU") form the foundation of the EU since the Treaty of Lisbon entered into force in 2009.[58] Art. 16 TFEU mirrors Art. 8 CFR and provides that everyone has the right to protection of their personal data. In particular, Art. 16(2) of the TFEU introduced a specific legal basis for the adoption of data protection legislation, with the aim of ensuring a consistent application of data protection rules in all areas of the EU.[59] Art. 2 TEU de-

53 Paul de Hert and Serge Gutwirth, "Privacy, Data Protection and Law Enforcement. Opacity of the individual and transparency of power", in Erik Claes and others (eds), Privacy and the Criminal Law (2006).

54 Art. 8(3) CFR.

55 Eleni Kosta, "A divided European data protection framework: A critical reflection on the choices of the European legislator post-Lisbon", in E. Kosta, R. Leenes, and I. Kamara (Eds.), Research handbook on EU data protection law (2022) (1st ed., pp. 68–90).

56 See for more: CJEU Fact sheet on Protection of personal data, (March 2021), <https://curia.europa.eu/jcms/upload/docs/application/pdf/2018-10/fiche_thematique_-_donnees_personnelles_-_en.pdf> (accessed on 05.02.2022).

57 Maja Brkan, "The Essence of the Fundamental Rights to Privacy and Data Protection: Finding the Way Through the Maze of the CJEU's Constitutional Reasoning"; Cambridge University Press, (2019); Federico Fabbrini, Five Years of Legally Binding Charter of Fundamental Rights (Oxford, Hart Publishing, 2015).

58 Eleni Kosta, pp. 71–73, (n. 55).

59 *Ibid.*

clares that the EU is founded on the principles of respect for human rights and Art. 6 TEU affirms that the fundamental rights enshrined in the ECHR serve as general principles of EU law.

VII DPD

Directive 95/46/EC of the European Parliament and of the Council of Europe on the protection of individuals with regard to the processing of personal data and on the free movement of such data (hereinafter: "DPD") was adopted by the European Parliament and the CoE in 1995 and came into force in 1998.[60]

The DPD was built on the seven general principles contained in the OECD Recommendations. The DPD was incorporated into the 1992 Agreement on the European Economic Area, and therefore the states which are not part of the EU could be legally bound to bring their legislation into conformity with the DPD.[61] Similarly to the GDPR, the DPD has had an impact on other countries outside the EU as it prohibited the transfer of personal data to countries which do not provide an 'adequate level of data protection'.[62]

Nevertheless, the DPD overcame to some extent the problem, recognised at the EU level, that even between countries that have a very similar system of data protection laws, problems arise in the practical application of the law and state jurisdiction.[63] As an EU directive, the DPD had to be transposed into the national law of the EU Member States, due to which reason a full uniformity of data protection standards has not been achieved.[64] EU Member States were allowed a margin for manoeuvre in implementing the DPD, due to its status as a 'directive' as opposed to a 'regulation' – directly applicable in their entirety on all EU countries.[65]

---

60 See for a detailed overview of the DPD: Neil Robinson, Hans Graux, Maarten Botterman, Lorenzo Valeri, "Review of the European Data Protection Directive", Information Commissioner's Office (ICO) (May 2009); Michael D. Birnhack, "The EU Data Protection Directive: An engine of a global regime", Computer Law & Security Review, Volume 24, Issue 6 (2008) pp. 508–520.

61 Lee A. Bygrave (2002), (n. 28).

62 *Ibid.*

63 Orla Lynskey, "The Foundations of EU Data Protection Law", Oxford University Press (November 2015); Rebecca Wong, "The Data Protection Directive 95/46/EC: Idealisms and realisms", International Review of Law, Computers & Technology, (2012).

64 Mariusz Krzysztofek and Wolters Kluwer, "General Data Protection Regulation (EU) 2016/679: Post-reform Personal Data Protection in the European Union," Band 107 von European monographs, (2019), pp. 7–8; P. Hustinx (September 2014), (n. 46).

65 Lee A. Bygrave (2002), (n. 28).

VIII GDPR

Given the flaws in the DPD and the changes that have occurred as a result of increasing globalisation, the EU took the view that new legislation should be enacted to address any shortcomings, ensure legal certainty in the EU, and expand the scope of data protection powers to ensure that EU rules are respected beyond its borders.[66] The preamble of the GDPR acknowledges "the objectives and principles of Directive 95/46/EC remain sound, but it has not prevented fragmentation in the implementation of data protection across the Union, legal uncertainty or a widespread public perception that there are significant risks to the protection of natural persons, in particular with regard to online activity."[67] The result was the reform of data protection legislation which led to the adoption of the GDPR in April 2016. The GDPR entered into force on 25 May 2018.[68] The GDPR, as a regulation, is directly applicable, meaning that national implementation is not required, which brings more legal certainty on the EU level. The GDPR also established an independent body at the EU level – the European Data Protection Board (hereinafter: "EDPB") – a body designed to ensure the consistent application of data protection rules across the EU.[69]

IX Conclusion to A

The evolution of data protection legislation in Europe has witnessed significant advancements and transformations over the years. Europe's data protection journey began with the recognition of privacy as a fundamental right enshrined in various international and regional human rights instruments. This recognition laid the foundation for the development of comprehensive data protection legislation. In the 1970s, the first data protection laws were enacted in Europe, such as in Sweden and Germany. The introduction of the DPD in 1995 marked a pivotal moment, harmonising data protection laws across EU Member States and setting the stage for greater cooperation in this domain. The evolution of data protection legislation gained momentum with the enactment of the GDPR in 2016. The GDPR represented a significant shift, introducing stricter obligations and enhanced rights for individuals. It not only consolidated data protection principles but

66 Recitals 6–7 GDPR.
67 Recital 9 GDPR.
68 Art. 90 GDPR.
69 Art. 94 GDPR.

also extended the extraterritorial reach of European data protection laws, impacting organisations worldwide.

B Evolution of Privacy and Data Protection Rights in the WB6

The evolution of privacy and data protection rights in the WB6 countries has been a relatively recent development, lagging behind the EU. In contrast to the EU, where data protection and privacy rights have been a longstanding concern, the WB6 countries were relatively slower in recognising the significance of these rights. This can be attributed to various factors, including differences in political systems, historical circumstances, and legal frameworks. As part of their EU integration process, the WB6 countries recognised the importance of harmonising their legislation with EU norms and standards. This involved introducing EU-like rules and laws related to data protection and privacy. The Stabilisation and Association Agreements (hereinafter: "SAAs") signed between the EU and individual WB6 countries provided a framework for enhancing data protection and privacy within the region.

I FRY Constitution

The first legal document which mentions the right to data protection was the Constitution of the Federal Republic of Yugoslavia from 1992 (hereinafter: "FRY Constitution"), the first constitution adopted after the collapse of the socialist political system. The right to data protection was envisaged in Art. 33: "The protection of personal data is guaranteed. The use of personal data outside the purpose for which they were collected is prohibited. Everyone has the right to be informed of the collected personal data relating to him, as well as the right to judicial protection in the event of their misuse. The collection, processing, use and protection of personal data are regulated by federal law."[70]

The FRY Constitution was also the basis for the enactment of the first data protection law in 1998 with only 27 Articles (hereinafter: "FRY DPL").[71] The FRY DPL was adopted, still under the auspices of the Federal Republic of Yugoslavia, in order to harmonise legislation with Convention 108. Prior to the adoption of

70 Art. 33 Constitution of the Federal Republic of Yugoslavia (1992).

71 Law on Personal Data Protection (Official Gazette of the FRY, no. 24/98 and 26/98).

the FRY DPL, in 1992, the Law on Ratification of the Convention on Automatic Processing of Personal Data was adopted,[72] which made Convention 108 an integral part of the domestic legal order.

In terms of basic principles, the FRY DPL was close to the EU standards in force at the time (it included, for example, a 'right to erasure'), but it remained without real impact in its application. The FRY DPL has never been applied, nor has anyone sought protection of the rights prescribed by the law.[73] As an explanation for this phenomenon, there were two equally plausible reasons.

The first was the very low level of citizens' awareness of their own rights and the degree of their endangerment, as well as the lack of readiness to protect effectively those rights.[74]

The second reason is that during the turbulent years when the Federal Republic of Yugoslavia was first dissolved, there was a failure to designate a supervisory authority responsible for monitoring the implementation of the FRY DPL.[75] The FRY DPL stated that a "competent federal authority" will supervise the implementation of the law. This provision was in contradiction to the DPD, which stipulated that such competence must be entrusted to an independent body and not to a part of the executive authorities.[76] The FRY DPL was valid until January 2009 and was thus applicable also in the State Union of Serbia and Montenegro.

II Albania

In Albania, which was not part of the former Federal Republic of Yugoslavia, the first data protection law emerged in 1999.[77] This law did not provide a comprehensive data protection regime, but it introduced essential instruments such as the

---

72 Law on Ratification of the Convention on Automatic Processing of Personal Data (Official Gazette of the FRY – International Agreements, no. 1/92).

73 Nataša Pirc Musar, "Vodič kroz Zakon o Zaštiti Podataka o Ličnosti" (Eng: Guide to the Law on Personal Data Protection), Commissioner for Information of Public Importance and Personal Data Protection, Belgrade, (May 2009), p. 11.

74 *Ibid.*

75 Center for Democracy and Human Rights (CEDEM) and AIRE CENTER, "The right to privacy in Montenegrin legislation and European practice", (March 2012), p.3, available at the following link <http://www.cedem.me/publikacije/studije-i-javne-politike/send/69-studije-i-javne-politike/678-policy-paperpravo-na-privatnost> (accessed on 23.04.2022).

76 *Ibid.*

77 Albania: Law no. 8517 of 1999 on the Right to Information and Protection of Personal Data, 1 June 1999, available at the following link: <https://www.refworld.org/docid/3ae6b5fa0.html> (accessed on 10.04.2023).

establishment of a supervisory authority (Chapter 4), rules on consent (Article 16), data transfers (Article 20) and the right of redress for data subjects (Chapter 5).

III EU Acquis Alignment

The EU has developed its accession procedures and criteria to ensure that aspiring member states not only express their willingness but also demonstrate their capacity and commitment to adhere to the EU's political, economic, and legal standards. Under Art. 49 TEU any European state that upholds and actively promotes the values enshrined in Art. 2 TEU is eligible to apply for EU membership. The requirement to uphold the values expressed in Art. 2 TEU codifies earlier practice and was first formally articulated in 1993 when the European Council introduced the so-called Copenhagen criteria for enlargement.[78]

For a European state to attain EU membership, it must satisfy conditions outlined in the Copenhagen criteria.[79] These criteria serve as the fundamental prerequisites for EU accession. They assess a country's readiness based on three primary dimensions: institutional stability guaranteeing democracy and the rule of law, a functioning market economy, and the ability to assume and effectively implement the obligations of EU membership.[80] This includes the ability to incorporate and enforce the rules, standards, and policies that constitute the body of EU law, known as the acquis communautaire or "EU acquis".[81] As a matter of principle it is the responsibility of the candidate country to adapt its legal framework to align with that of the EU, a process commonly referred to as "legal approximation".[82]

---

78 Friedrich Erlbacher, "Article 49 TEU", in Manuel Kellerbauer, Marcus Klamert, and Jonathan Tomkin (eds), The EU Treaties and the Charter of Fundamental Rights: A Commentary, online edn, Oxford Academic, (2019), pp. 313–315; Christophe Hillion, "The Copenhagen Criteria and Their Progeny" (2014), in C. Hillion (ed), EU enlargement, Oxford, Hart Publishing (2004).

79 See Accession criteria (Copenhagen criteria), EUR-Lex, Access to European Union law, available at <https://neighbourhood-enlargement.ec.europa.eu/enlargement-policy/glossary/accession-criteria_en> (accessed on 25.01.2025).

80 Friedrich Erlbacher, (2019), (n. 78), pp. 315–316.

81 *Ibid.*, Dimitry Kochenov, "The Acquis and Its Principles: The Enforcement of the 'Law' versus the Enforcement of 'Values' in the European Union", A. Jakab and D. Kochenov (eds.), The Enforcement of EU Law and Values University of Groningen Faculty of Law Research Paper, (2018), pp. 9–27.

82 Christophe Hillion, (2004), (n. 78), p. 9; This term is also being used in the SAA agreements, e.g. SAA with Serbia, Art. 1(d).

Consequently, the WB6 countries, aspiring EU membership, must meet the Copenhagen criteria. To facilitate this process, the EU has entered into a SAA with each WB6 country as part of the Stabilization and Association Process.[83] Under the SAAs, these countries are explicitly required to harmonise their national data protection laws with the EU acquis.[84] As the EU legal order is constantly reviewed and enriched through the legislative activities of the institutions, the 'acquis' criterion has naturally become more demanding for the latest candidates.[85]

Thus, the WB6 countries, all of which aim to join the EU, are obligated to respect and uphold the right to personal data protection as articulated in the EU's founding documents. Moreover, they are continuously obliged to align their national data protection frameworks with evolving EU legislation. This obligation has prompted the adoption of national legislation modelled upon the EU standards, including data protection frameworks modeled on EU norms, even prior to the implementation of the GDPR.

IV Data Protection Laws in the WB6 2008 – 2025

After the complete dissolution of the Federal Republic of Yugoslavia and the full separation of Serbia and Montenegro, new laws were adopted correspondingly in all newly established countries which were modelled on the DPD provisions, except Albania, where the first law was adopted in 1999. In Kosovo, the first data protection law was enacted in 2010, following its declaration of independence from Serbia in 2008. The initial data protection frameworks in the WB6 were largely based on the DPD, reflecting the obligation of these countries to align their legal systems with the EU acquis.

---

83 This process was initiated to stabilise the region following the conflicts of the 1990s. Some authors note that, in addition to the general Copenhagen criteria, the EU introduced an additional criterion requiring the countries concerned to engage in the so-called Stabilisation and Association Process as a preliminary step, thereby addressing bilateral issues in a structured way and fostering good neighbourly relations between them, see: Friedrich Erlbacher, (2019), (n. 78), pp. 315 – 316.

84 E. g. Art. 84 Stabilisation and Association Agreement between the European Union and Kosovo, 10728/1/15 REV 1 available at the following link <https://data.consilium.europa.eu/doc/document/ST-10728-2015-REV-1/en/pdf> (accessed on 29.04.2023) or Art. 68 Stabilisation and Association Agreement between the European Communities and their Member States, of the one part, and the Republic of North Macedonia, of the other part, OJ L 84, (20.3.2004) p. 13, available at the following link <https://eur-lex.europa.eu/legal-content/EN/TXT/PDF/?uri=CELEX:02004A0320(03)-20210909&from=EN> (accessed on 16.04.2023).

85 Christophe Hillion, (2004), (n. 78), pp. 10 – 11.

The following table provides a brief overview of data protection laws in the WB6, from the first law enacted to the current law in force. Chapter 4 will provide a detailed profile of the data protection framework for each country separately.

Table 1: Overview of Data Protection Laws in the WB6 (2008 – 2025)

Country	First Enacted Law	Currently Applicable Law	GDPR-aligned[86]	New GDPR-like law announced
Albania	Law n. 8517 of 1999 on the Right to Information and Protection of Personal Data	Law on personal data protection no. 124/2024 dated 19.12.2024.	Yes	–
BiH	Law on Personal Data Protection 2001[87] (amended in 2006[88] and 2011[89])	First law still in force	No	Yes
Kosovo	Law No.03/L – 172 on the Protection of Personal Data 2010	Law 06/L-082 on Personal Data Protection 14.02. 2019	Yes	–
Montenegro	Law on Personal Data Protection 2008[90] (last time amended in 2017)[91]	First law still in force	No	Yes
North Macedonia	Law on Personal Data Protection 2005[92] (last time amended in 2018)[93]	Law on Protection of Personal Data no. 42/20[94] 16.02.2020 and amended in 2021	Yes	–

86 For the purposes of this dissertation, *GDPR-aligned* refers to data protection laws adopted with the aim of harmonising national frameworks with the terminology, principles, and standards of the GDPR. However, this term does not imply full compliance, as these national laws may still diverge in certain aspects, either due to legislative gaps, differences in implementation, or contextual adaptations within the respective legal systems.

87 Law on Personal Data Protection (Official Gazette of BiH, no. 32/01).

88 Amendments on Law on Personal Data Protection (Official Gazette of BiH, no. 49/06).

89 Amendments on Law on Personal Data Protection (Official Gazette of BiH, no. 76/2011 and 89/2011 – corrected).

90 Law on Personal Data Protection (Official Gazette of Montenegro, no. 079/08 dated 23.12.2008, 070/09 dated 21.10.2009, 044/12 dated 09.08.2012, 022/17 dated 03.04.2017).

91 Amendments on Law on Personal Data Protection (Official Gazette of Montenegro, no. 22/2017).

92 Law on Personal Data Protection (Official Gazette of the Republic of Macedonia, no. 7/2005).

93 Law on Personal Data Protection (Official Gazette of the Republic of Macedonia no. 7/2005, 103/2008, 124/10, 135/11, 43/14, 153/15, 99/16 and 64/18).

94 Law on Personal Data Protection (Official Gazette of the Republic of North Macedonia, no. 42/20 and 294/21).

Table 1 *(Continued)*

Country	First Enacted Law	Currently Applicable Law	GDPR-aligned[86]	New GDPR-like law announced
Serbia	Law on Personal Data Protection 2008[95] (last time amended in 2012)[96]	Law on Personal Data Protection[97] 13.11.2018	Yes	–

V Conclusion to B

In the WB6 countries, although data protection laws emerged in the 1990s, their practical enforceability was limited. The significance of data protection standards in the WB6 countries gained prominence due to their EU accession process, which necessitated the alignment of their national data protection legislation with the EU acquis as outlined in the signed SAAs. Hence, the incorporation of the GDPR into the WB6 countries' national data protection laws is not the first instance of EU legal instruments being transposed in these jurisdictions. It is important to note that when the first data protection laws were adopted in the WB6 (as separate countries), as indicated in the table providing an overview of data protection legislation, the WB6 countries were already identified as potential candidates for EU membership. As a consequence, these countries have been continuously aligning their standards with the EU in various aspects, including data protection.

C Conclusion to Chapter 2

Compared to other human rights, the right to data protection is a genuinely new right that has emerged in response to the digital transformation of recent decades. However, although it has been in existence for many years, it has not had the same prominence around the world as it has in the EU. The EU has been at the forefront of developing new data protection legislation and has had a significant impact on the rest of the world. The right to protect personal data in the EU is guaranteed

95 Law on Personal Data Protection (Official Gazette of RS, no. 97/2008).
96 Law on Personal Data Protection (Official Gazette of RS, no. 97/2008, 104/2009 – other law, 68/2012 – decision of CC and 107/2012).
97 Law on Personal Data Protection (Official Gazette of RS, no. 87/2018).

and upheld by several instruments, including Artt. 7 and 8 CFR, Art. 8 ECHR and the GDPR.

In contrast, the WB6 countries have generally followed the lead of the EU in developing their national data protection laws due to their geographic and political situation, rather than developing their own rights-driven approach. Their national data protection laws were aligned with the Convention 108 and in particular with the DPD but often lacked enforcement. Following the adoption of the GDPR, these countries faced a new legal framework in the field of data protection on the EU side and needed to align their national legislation again. Compounding these challenges is the fact that the WB6 countries are EU candidates or potential candidates, which means that they are required to bring their national laws into line with the EU Acquis. This creates an additional burden on these countries as they work to develop effective data protection frameworks that meet EU standards, as not all of them transpose GDPR provisions at the same pace. In addition, they are likely to struggle with the enforcement of new GDPR-like laws, as they must strike the right balance between the incorporation of GDPR articles and the effectiveness of such laws tailored to their systems. Ultimately, these challenges demonstrate the importance of ongoing analysis and evaluation of data protection frameworks in the WB6 countries, as well as the need for continued dialogue and collaboration between these countries and the EU to ensure effective enforcement.

Chapter 3 – The GDPR Impact on non-EU Countries

One of the most significant novelties in data protection law worldwide is the extent of the territorial application of the GDPR. The EU Commission stated in its evaluation of the GDPR: "The GDPR has already emerged as a key reference point at the international level and acted as a catalyst for many countries around the world to consider introducing modern privacy rules. This trend towards global convergence is a very positive development that brings new opportunities to better protect individuals in the EU when their data is transferred abroad while, at the same time, facilitating dataflows."[98]

The exterritorial influence of EU legislation is also known as a 'Brussels effect',[99] under which relatively strict EU rules have shaped policy development in areas outside the EU, leading to a 'Europeanisation' of numerous norms across the globe.[100] This effect is measured not just in terms of legislative change, but also in terms of what corporate boardrooms around the world view as the 'gold standard' to guide or otherwise shape their behaviour.[101] The area of data protection is commonly seen as the quintessential example of this effect, with both the DPD and the GDPR playing leading roles.[102]

However, while many countries across the world have responded to the GDPR by developing new data protection laws, not all of them may have the same resources as the EU. Enacting a legal framework for data protection based on EU standards can be a significant burden, considering that the GDPR is more complex and lengthier than its predecessor, the DPD. Furthermore, adopting data protection legislation that is essentially equivalent to the GDPR, or revising existing legislation to meet this standard, requires third countries to invest in a large-scale legislative project that could take many years.[103]

---

98 European Commission, "Data protection as a pillar of citizens' empowerment and the EU's approach to the digital transition – two years of application of the General Data Protection Regulation", no. 264, 2020, p. 12.

99 Anu Bradford, The Brussels Effect, pp. 1–67, (n. 27).

100 Lee A. Bygrave, "The 'Strasbourg Effect' on data protection in light of the 'Brussels Effect': Logic, mechanics and prospects, 2021", p. 2.

101 *Ibid.*

102 *Ibid.*

103 Christopher Kuner, Dan Jerker, B. Svantesson, Fred H. Cate, Orla Lynskey, Christopher Millard, Nora Ni Loideain Author Notes, "The GDPR as a chance to break down borders", International Data Privacy Law, Volume 7, Issue 4, (November 2017), pp. 231–232.

https://doi.org/10.1515/9783112221013-005

This Chapter will focus on the territorial scope of the GDPR and possible venues for data transfers between the EU and the WB6 countries. It will focus mostly on adequacy decisions, as this venue for data transfers is most relevant for WB6 countries pursuing the EU accession path. Prior to the introduction of the GDPR, evaluating the adequacy level of data protection in a third country was not a straightforward process, due to DPD ambiguity and lack of adequacy standards.[104] Also, Art. 26(2) DPD allowed Member States to make ad hoc decisions, notably of a contractual nature, and allow data transfers to third countries in cases of absence of an adequacy decisions within the meaning of Art. 25(2) DPD, with the obligation to inform EU Commission.[105] The GDPR replaced this approach with a centralised system, in which the EU Commission is solely responsible for determining whether a third country provides an adequate level of protection and Member States might not make any ad hoc decisions.[106] This Chapter will focus on general remarks regarding adequacy decisions, the procedure for their adoption and their possible effects on the WB6 countries.

A Territorial Scope of the GDPR

The territorial scope of the GDPR is regulated by Art. 3 GDPR. Firstly, under Art. 3(1) the scope of the GDPR is extended to processing of personal data in the context of the activities of an establishment of a controller or a processor in the EU, regardless of whether the processing takes place within the EU or not.[107] In addition, under Art. 3(2) a non-EU company acting as a controller or processor is obliged to apply the GDPR if its activities are related to 1) offering goods or services to EU residents, and 2) monitoring the behaviour of data subjects, provided that their behaviour takes place within the EU.[108]

The extraterritorial reach has also been provided for in the DPD, by virtue of Art. 4(1). The most important grounds for such exterritorial reach under the DPD

---

104 Patrick J. Murray, "The Adequacy Standard under Directive 95/46/EC: Does U.S. Data Protection Meet This Standard", 21 FORDHAM INT'l L.J. 932 (1998).

105 Working Party on the Protection of Individuals with Regard to the Processing of Personal Data, First Orientations on Transfers of Personal Data to Third Countries – Possible Ways Forward in Assessing Adequacy, XV D/5020/97-EN Final, (26.06.1997).

106 Recital 103 and Art. 45 GDPR. See also Christopher Kuner, "Article 45 Transfers on the basis of an adequacy decision", The EU General Data Protection Regulation (GDPR): A Commentary, Oxford University Press (2020) for an overview of the differences between Art. 25 DPD and Art. 45 GDPR, p. 775–776.

107 Art. 3(1) GDPR.

108 Art. 3(2) GDPR.

were (1) the location of an establishment of the controller – where the controller must be involved in activities implying the processing of personal data in question,[109] and (2) the location of equipment being used.[110] The application of Art. 4 DPD has been further elaborated by the CJEU in the case Google Spain.[111] In this context, the CJEU held that an online search engine operator qualifies as a controller within the meaning of Art. 2(d) DPD[112] and concluded that the processing relating to the search engine service should be viewed as taking place "in the context of the activities of an establishment" located on EU territory, consistent with Art. 4(1)(a) DPD.[113]

I Art. 3(1) GDPR

Under Art. 3(1) the GDPR applies to any processing of personal data "in the context of the activities of an establishment in the EU", regardless of whether the processing itself takes place inside or outside the EU. Yet, Art. 3(1) does not define the term 'establishment', but Recital 22 GDPR gives some orientation.[114] This solution repeats the jurisdiction nexus from Art. 4(1)a DPD.[115] The case law of the CJEU[116] concerning DPD clearly favours a broad interpretation of the notions of 'establishment' and 'in the context of the activities'.[117] With the adoption of Art. 3(1) GDPR, the EU legislator has chosen to confirm the CJEU's broad interpretation of these

109 Art. 4(1)(a) DPD.

110 Art. 4(1)(c) DPD.

111 C-131/12 Google Spain SL and Google Inc. v Agencia Española de Protección de Datos (AEPD) and Mario Costeja González, (13 May 2014).

112 CJEU, Case C-131/12, para 41.

113 CJEU, Case C-131/12, para 56.

114 According to Recital 22 GDPR "establishment implies the effective and real exercise of activity through stable arrangements. The legal form of such arrangements, whether through a branch or a subsidiary with a legal personality, is not the determining factor in that respect".

115 Art. 4(1)(a) DPD "the processing is carried out in the context of the activities of an establishment of the controller on the territory of the Member State; when the same controller is established on the territory of several Member States, he must take the necessary measures to ensure that each of these establishments complies with the obligations laid down by the national law applicable".

116 E. g. Case C-131/12 Google Spain SL and Google Inc v Agencia Espa~nola de Proteccion de Datos (AEPD) and Mario Costeja Gonzalez and Case C230/14 *Weltimmo s. r. o.* v. *Nemzeti* Adatvédelmi és Információszabadság Hatóság.

117 See also Brendan Van Alsenoy and Marieke Koekkoek, "Internet and jurisdiction after Google Spain: the extraterritorial reach of the 'right to be delisted'', International Data Privacy Law, Volume 5, Issue 2, (May 2015), pp. 105–120.

concepts and reaffirms its exterritorial reach.[118] Referring to the Weltimmo case, the EDPB guidelines[119] summarised the CJEU's ruling "that the notion of establishment extends to any real and effective activity – even a minimal one – exercised through stable arrangements" where the threshold for 'stable arrangements' is quite low.[120]

Furthermore, the EDPB stressed in its interpretation of Art. 3(1) GDPR that if a controller subject to GDPR chooses to use a processor located outside the EU for a given processing activity, it will still be necessary for the controller to ensure by contract or other legal act that the processor processes the data in accordance with the GDPR.[121] The processor located outside the EU will therefore become indirectly subject to some obligation imposed by controllers subject to the GDPR by virtue of contractual arrangements under Art. 28 GDPR.[122]

II Art. 3(2) GDPR

Even more remarkable is Art. 3(2) GDPR under which the GDPR applies to certain companies, even if they do not have an establishment in the EU.

Art. 3(2) GDPR applies to the processing of personal data of data subjects who are in the EU by a controller or processor not established in the EU, where the processing activities are related to 1) the offering of goods or services, irrespective of whether a payment of the data subject is required, to such data subjects in the EU; or 2) the monitoring of their behaviour as far as their behaviour takes place within the EU. Both extensions of scope are clarified further in the Recitals – Recital 23 for Art. 3(2)(a) GDPR, and Recital 24 for Art. 3(2)(b) GDPR. This article has been much debated as GDPR's exterritorial innovation.[123] Art. 3(2) is intended to ensure that individuals in the EU should not be deprived of GDPR protection, even if the data processing takes place outside of the EU.[124]

---

118 See also Paul de Hert, Michal Czerniawski (2016) (n. 6); Mistale Taylor, "Permissions and prohibitions in data protection jurisprudence" Vol. 2, Brussels Privacy Hub Working Paper, (May 2016); Merlin Gömann, "The new territorial scope of EU data protection law: Deconstructing a revolutionary achievement", 54, Common Market Law Review, Issue 2, (2017), pp. 567–590.

119 EDPB, Guidelines 3/2018 on the Territorial Scope of the GDPR (Article 3) (2019).

120 *Ibid.* See also Paul de Hert, Michal Czerniawski (2016) (n. 6).

121 EDPB, Guidelines 3/2018 (Article 3), p. 11. (n. 119).

122 *Ibid.*

123 Paul de Hert, Michal Czerniawski, (2016) (n. 6); Gstrein and Zwitter (2021) (n. 11); Benjamin Greze, "The extra-territorial enforcement of the GDPR: a genuine issue and the quest for alternatives," *International Data Privacy Law*, Volume 9, Issue 2, (May 2019), pp. 109–128.

124 Paal/Pauly/Ernst, DS-GVO Art. 3, para. 13–20, (n. 6).

1 Offering of Goods or Services

A non-EU company is required to respect the GDPR rules if it offers goods or services to data subjects in the EU. It is also important to understand the definition of "data subjects who are in the EU".[125] Recital 14 GDPR states that the protection afforded by the GDPR should apply to natural persons regardless of their nationality or residence with respect to the processing of their personal data. This provision of the GDPR mirrors EU primary law, which establishes a broad scope for the protection of personal data that is not limited to EU citizens, with Art. 8 CFR providing that the right to the protection of personal data is not limited but applies to 'everyone'[126] Similarly, it is important to define what constitutes an 'offer of goods and services'. This concept has already been addressed in EU legislation and case law.[127] In order to determine whether a data controller or data processor is offering goods or services to individuals in the EU, the decisive factor is whether the data controller or data processor manifestly intends to offer services to data subjects in one or more Member States.[128] In this context, conduct on the part of the controller or processor which demonstrates their intention to offer goods or services to data subjects located in the EU is required.[129] The mere accessibility of a website is considered insufficient to ascertain such an intention, however, "the use of a language or a currency generally used in one or more Member States with the possibility of ordering goods and services in that other language, or the mentioning of customers or users who are in the Union, may make it apparent that the controller envisages offering goods or services to data subjects in the Union".[130]

2 Monitoring

For the application of Art. 3(2)(b) GDPR, it is necessary that the behaviour of data subjects takes place within the territory of the EU. According to Recital 24 GDPR monitoring of data subjects' behaviour takes place when "natural persons are tracked on the internet including potential subsequent use of personal data processing techniques which consist of profiling a natural person, particularly in order to take decisions concerning her or him or for analysing or predicting

---

125 Art. 3 (2)(a) GDPR.

126 Charter of Fundamental Right of the European Union, Article 8(1), "Everyone has the right to the protection of personal data concerning him or her".

127 EDPB, Guidelines 3/2018 (Article 3), p. 16 (n. 119).

128 *Ibid.* p. 17.

129 *Ibid.* p. 18.

130 *Ibid.*

her or his personal preferences, behaviours and attitudes".[131] Thus, this includes techniques for gathering information on individuals via their internet activities, such as tracking/profiling and targeting in advertising.[132] This exterritorial approach has been criticised, on the one hand, for creating a de facto global application of the GDPR via overstepping of its jurisdictional boundaries,[133] and on the other hand, not distinguishing between large companies such as Meta and Google and other small and medium-sized enterprises.[134]

III Conclusion to A

The GDPR has established a global scope, characterised by two main elements: 'the establishment criterion' under Art. 3(1) GDPR and the 'targeting criterion' under Art. 3(2) GDPR. This territorial scope extends the protection of data subjects' rights beyond the borders of the EU and may apply to foreign companies. The extraterritorial effect has strong impacts on the WB6 countries, given their geographical proximity to the EU and the close interdependence of their economies with the EU. This factor underlines the importance for the WB6 countries to align their national legislation with the GDPR and obtain an adequacy decision. This will enable WB6 companies to more easily comply with their obligations where Art. 3 GDPR is applicable to them, and the free flow of personal data will be facilitated.

B Data Transfers

The exterritorial effect of the GDPR is not the only influential aspect of the GDPR. Under Art. 44 GDPR data transfers outside of the EU are allowed only under special conditions, which require that the recipient country provides an equivalent

131 Recital 24 GDPR.

132 Paal/Pauly, DS-GVO Art. 3, (n. 6).

133 Omer Tene and Christopher Wolf 2013 (n. 7); Alexander Kloth, "One law to rule them all – On the extraterritorial applicability of the new EU General Data Protection Regulation", Völkerrechtsblog, (05.02.2018).

134 See M. Scott, L. Cerulus and L. Kayali "Six months in, Europe's privacy revolution favors Google, Facebook", Politico.eu (23.11.2018) <https://www.politico.eu/article/gdpr-facebook-google-privacy-data-6-months-in-europes-privacy-revolution-favors-google-facebook/>, or M. Scott, L. Cerulus and S. Overly, "How Silicon Valley gamed Europe's privacy rules", Politico.eu, (22.05.2019) <https://www.politico.eu/article/europe-data-protection-gdpr-general-data-protection-regulation-facebook-google/> (both accessed on 05.03.2022).

level of protection as that provided by the EU rules. Thus, the central regulatory purpose of Art. 44 GDPR is to perpetuate the level of protection under EU law if the data importer is not already covered by the territorial scope of Art. 3 GDPR.[135] The GDPR offers three main venues for transfers: adequacy decisions (Art. 45), appropriate safeguards (Artt. 46–47)[136] and derogations (Art. 49).[137] Given the WB6 countries' high level of commercial connection with the EU internal market and their obligation to fully align their legislation with the EU acquis communautaire, their most effective solution would be adequacy decisions, instead of case-by-case arrangements.[138] This study will therefore concentrate on this venue, with the aim to also assess the adequacy criteria needed for obtaining an adequacy decision.

I Adequacy Decision

Transfers of data from the EU or other countries to a third country have been restricted already for decades and the concept of 'adequate level of protection' is not new. In 1973, Sweden was the first country to regulate data exports to third countries by making such exports subject to approval by the competent Swedish authority.[139] Austria followed suit in 1978 by making the export of personal data to other countries subject to the condition that they guarantee a level of data pro-

135 Jürgen Taeger and Detlev Gabel, "DS-GVO Art. 44 Allgemeine Grundsätze der Datenübermittlung", paras. 1–4, Kommentar DSGVO – BDSG – TTDSG (4th edn. C.H. Beck. 2022).

136 According to Art. 46 GDPR "in the absence of a decision pursuant to Art. 45(3) GDPR, a controller or processor may transfer personal data to a third country or an international organisation only if the controller or processor has provided appropriate safeguards, and on condition that enforceable data subject rights and effective legal remedies for data subjects available." Appropriate safeguards are listed within Art. 46(2) and include instruments such as, standard contractual clauses, binding corporate rules, approved code of conducts and approved certifications.

137 According to the Art. 49 GDPR "in the absence of an adequacy decision pursuant to Article 45 (3), or of appropriate safeguards pursuant to Article 46, including binding corporate rules, a transfer or a set of transfers of personal data to a third country or an international organisation shall take place only on one of the following conditions". These conditions include concepts such as explicit data subject's consent, performance of contract between the data subject and the controller and public interest.

138 Only an adequacy decision allows the transfer of personal data in all cases where the additional requirements are not necessary. For example, companies do not need to sign standard contractual clauses for data transfers every time they transfer personal data to a WB6 company.

139 Para 11 of the Datalag of 11 May 1973, SFS 1973:289. See also Dan Svantesson, "The Regulation of Cross-Border Data Flows" 1(3) International Data Privacy Law (2011).

tection equivalent to that in Austria.[140] The OECD also established a minimum standard for privacy protection to facilitate cross-border data flows and eliminate differences in data protection levels among countries.[141] The DPD introduced in 1995 restrictions on the transfer of personal data to third countries which did not guarantee an equivalent standard of protection.[142] This concept has been further developed by the CJEU in several cases as explained later.[143]

The purpose of adequacy decisions by the EU Commission, introduced by the DPD, was to formally confirm with binding effects on Member States that the level of data protection in a third country or an international organisation is essentially equivalent to the level of data protection within the EU.[144] Therefore, one of the main objectives of the EU data protection approach was to introduce laws that prohibit the circumvention of the high EU personal data protection level by exporting the data to third countries with a lower data protection level.[145] This concept is also substantiated by the GDPR.

The extraterritorial effect of the GDPR and the concept of adequacy have triggered third countries outside the EU to adopt and incorporate EU data protection principles and concepts. The aim is to align their data protection legislation more closely with the EU acquis communautaire and to ensure an adequate level of protection from the EU's point of view, which would facilitate the exchange of data.[146] Even countries which already obtained their adequacy decisions, before the adoption of the GDPR, are now being very careful in order not to have major divergences from the EU acquis, fearing not to lose their 'prestige status'.[147] When com-

---

140 Christopher Kuner, "International Regulation of Transborder Data Flows", *Transborder Data Flows and Data Privacy Law* (Oxford, 2013; online edn, Oxford Academic, 26 Sept. 2013); Para 32 of the Bundesgesetz über den Schutz personenbezogener Daten (Datenschutzgesetz) of 18 October 1978, BGBl Nr 565/1978.

141 OECD, 'Original Explanatory Memorandum to the OECD Privacy Guidelines (OECD, Paris 1980)' in OECD (ed), The OECD Privacy Framework (2013) 39 ff.

142 Recitals 56–57, Art. 25 DPD. Also discussed in Chapter 2.

143 Data Protection Commissioner v Facebook Ireland Limited and Maximillian Schrems, case C-311/18 (16.07.2020) (Schrems II) and Maximillian Schrems v Data Protection Commissioner, case C-362/14 (06.10.2015) (Schrems I).

144 Case C-362/14, Maximillian Schrems v Data Protection Commissioner, 6 October 2015 (§§ 52).

145 Julian Wagner 2018 (n. 10).

146 Graham Greenleaf, "The influence of European data privacy standards outside Europe: implications for globalization of Convention 108," International Data Privacy Law, Volume 2, Issue 2 (2012), pp. 68–92.

147 E.G. In September 2020 Swiss Federal Data Protection Authority removed the US from its List of adequate countries. See Policy paper on the transfer of personal data to the USA and other countries lacking an adequate level of data protection within the meaning of Art. 6 Para. 1 Swiss

paring the different options for exporting data, it becomes clear that data transfer on the basis of an adequacy decision is the most straightforward route. In that case, no additional safety measures have to be applied by the exporter, and in practice, the data transfer can be carried out just like the transfer of personal data to a recipient within the EU.[148]

1 Criteria Under Art. 45 GDPR

The GDPR has to some extent clarified the adequacy rules, as the DPD it replaced did not provide an explanation of adequacy or specify its criteria.[149] Requirements for data adequacy are formulated in Art. 45(2) GDPR. The assessment of adequacy is made by the EU Commission in a formal procedure, which was already the case with the DPD. According to Art. 45(2) the EU Commission shall take into account in particular:

a) Respect for fundamental general and data protection rights: "the rule of law, respect for human rights and fundamental freedoms, relevant legislation, both general and sectoral, including concerning public security, defence, national security and criminal law [...], as well as the implementation of such legislation, data protection rules, [...], including rules for the onward transfer of personal data to another third country[...] which are complied with in that country [...], case-law, as well as effective and enforceable data subject rights and effective administrative and judicial redress for the data subjects whose personal data are being transferred";
b) An independent supervisory authority: "the existence and effective functioning of one or more independent supervisory authorities in the third country [...], with responsibility for ensuring and enforcing compliance with the data protection rules, including adequate enforcement powers, for assisting and advising the data subjects in exercising their rights and for cooperation with the supervisory authorities of the Member States"; and
c) International conventions being defined as "the international commitments [...] or other obligations arising from legally binding conventions or instruments as well as from its participation in multilateral or regional systems [...]".

Federal Act on Data Protection <https://www.newsd.admin.ch/newsd/message/attachments/64261.pdf> (accessed on 14.05.2022).

148 Julian Wagner 2018 (n. 10).

149 Patrick J. Murray, "The Adequacy Standard under Directive 95/46/EC: Does U.S. Data Protection Meet This Standard", McGill Guide 9th ed. (1998).

Art. 45(2) GDPR, therefore, gives an extensive, though non-exhaustive, list of elements to be taken into account in the assessment of the adequacy of the level of protection provided by a third country. Further, important criteria are also the existence of effective and enforceable data subjects' rights and effective administrative and judicial redress for the data subjects whose personal data are being transferred. This implies, that the third country needs to provide such rights to EU citizens as well.

a) Art. 45(2)(a) GDPR

The wording of Art. 45(2)(a) GDPR makes it clear that the requirements listed therein are subdivided into general criteria, such as the rule of law, the respect for human rights and fundamental freedoms, relevant legislation both general and sectoral, on the one hand, and specific data protection requirements on the other hand. Insofar as Art. 45(2)(a) GDPR refers to the rule of law and to the respect for human rights and fundamental freedoms, these requirements are founded on Artt. 2, 6, and 21 TEU which use the same terms to define the fundament of the EU.[150] Further, the term 'legislation' goes beyond specific data protection laws and explicitly covers the legislation concerning public security, defence, national security, and criminal law.[151] This has already been confirmed by case law and the adequacy decisions adopted by the EU Commission. Even more relevant, the 'Copenhagen criteria' include, inter alia, "the rule of law and human rights" and therefore require third countries striving to become members of the EU to guarantee them.[152] Art. 49 TEU demands accession countries to respect the values referred to in Art. 2 TEU.[153] The Copenhagen criteria are particularly relevant for the WB6 countries, having signed SAAs with the EU, as part of their EU accession process.

Lastly, under Art. 45(2)(a) GDPR case law, effective and enforceable data subjects' rights as well as effective administrative and judicial redress are crucial criteria. While the majority of accession countries have made substantial progress with regard to the adoption of the EU acquis, its implementation and enforcement

---

150 Julian Wagner 2018, p. 322 (n. 10).

151 Leonie Wittershagen, The Transfer of Personal Data from the European Union to the United Kingdom post-Brexit, Volume 1 in the series Global and Comparative Data Law, (2023), p. 58.

152 Christophe Hillion, "The Copenhagen Criteria and Their Progeny", C. Hillion (ed), EU enlargement (Oxford, Hart Publishing, 2004); Julian Wagner (2018), p. 322 (n. 10).

153 Laurent Pech, "A Union Founded on the Rule of Law": Meaning and Reality of the Rule of Law as a Constitutional Principle of EU Law' (2010) 6(3) European Constitutional Law Review Vol. 6, pp. 359–396, (January 201); Tanja Marktler, "The Power of the Copenhagen Criteria" 2 Croatian Yearbook of European Law and Policy (2006) pp. 343–348.

are still highly insufficient and problematic.[154] This is the case with the WB6 countries who struggle with the implementation of the new legislation aligned with the EU acquis.

The WP29 also emphasised that efficient enforcement mechanisms are of "paramount importance" when assessing the adequate level of personal data protection.[155] Thus, this last criterion will be of significant importance for the WB6 countries.

b) Art. 45(2)(b) GDPR

Art. 45(2)(b) GDPR requires third countries to have established one or more functional and independent supervisory authorities. The supervisory authority must have the necessary powers to enforce data protection law in the third country.[156] This includes having sufficient investigative and sanctioning powers, which the supervisory authority must actually use.[157] Whereas it is not necessary that the authority entrusted with data protection supervision is only competent for this task, the independence factor is decisive, meaning that it can fulfil its task without being influenced by politics or third parties.[158] Furthermore, the CJEU has defined in its case law that supervisory authorities must also be provided with "the human, technical and financial resources, premises and infrastructure necessary for the effective performance of its tasks and the exercise of its powers [...]."[159]

It is important to note that the WB6 countries have already committed themselves to the establishment of supervisory authorities in line with the EU acquis in the framework of the signed SAAs. The fulfilment of the criteria for an independent supervisory authority free from political influence and the criteria for adequate supervision are of particular importance for the WB6 countries and will be the subject of Chapters 4 and 7.

---

154 Tanja Marktler, (2006), (n. 153).

155 WP29, Working Document on Adequacy Referential 18/EN, WP 254rev.01, February 2018, p. 3.

156 Art. 52(4) GDPR.

157 WP29 Adequacy Referential, p. 7 (n. 155).

158 Boris P. Paal und Daniel A. Pauly, "DS-GVO Art. 45 Datenübermittlung auf der Grundlage eines Angemessenheitsbeschlusses", "Datenschutz-Grundverordnung Bundesdatenschutzgesetz: DS-GVO BDSG", paras 13–20, (3d edn. C.H. Beck. 2021).

159 Felix Bieker, "Enforcing Data Protection Law – The Role of the Supervisory Authorities in Theory and Practice", In: Lehmann, A., Whitehouse, D., Fischer-Hübner, S., Fritsch, L., Raab, C. (eds) Privacy and Identity Management. Facing up to Next Steps. Privacy and Identity 2016. IFIP Advances in Information and Communication Technology(), vol 498. Springer, Cham. (2017).

c) Art. 45(2)(c) GDPR

As also emphasised by Recital 105 GDPR, international instruments and participation in multilateral or regional systems, in particular in relation to the protection of personal data, constitute an indication of the commitment to the protection of personal data. The relevant international instruments are, inter alia, the ECHR, Convention 108 and Convention 108+. However, the existence of ratified international instruments is neither necessary nor sufficient for the adoption of an adequacy decision by the Commission.[160] The international instruments ratified by the WB6 countries will be analysed in Chapters 4 and 7.

2 Art. 29 Working Party and EDPB

Considering that the criteria for adequacy decisions established by the DPD were still too broad, the WP29 published a Working Document on transfers of personal data to third countries in 1998.[161] With the replacement of the DPD, WP29 revised this document, with the aim to update it in the context of the new legislation and recent case law of the CJEU.[162] The EDPB endorsed these guidelines, which are also used as guidance to assess third countries' data protection levels when the EDPB is asked to adopt an opinion for the EU Commission's decision.

The WP29 explicitly cites the *Schrems case* as its starting point emphasising that third country legislation does not have to mirror the EU data protection regime point by point, but instead has to guarantee the core requirements of the EU legislation. However, the standards required for the WB6 countries might be considerably higher as they have committed to fully align with the EU acquis.

The WP29 compiled a list of general content principles which have to be contained in the third country's data protection system.[163] They present the core general data protection principles[164] and basic data protection concepts of the GDPR[165] to ensure that the level of data protection in a third country or interna-

---

160 Zuzanna Gulczyńska, "A certain standard of protection for international transfers of personal data under the GDPR, International Data Privacy Law", Volume 11, Issue 4, November 2021, pp. 360–374.

161 WP29, Working Document: Transfers of personal data to third countries: Applying Art. 25 and 26 of the EU data protection directive (24 July 1998).

162 WP29 Adequacy Referential (n. 155).

163 *Ibid.*

164 WP29 lists principles like the limitation principle, the data quality and proportionality principle, the security principle, the, transparency principle, the rights of access, rectification and objection, and the principle of restricting onward transfers.

165 Concepts like: 'personal data', 'processing of personal data', 'data controller', 'data processor', 'recipient' and 'sensitive data'.

tional organisation is essentially equivalent to the one established by the EU legislation. WP29 has provided further guidance on the essential guarantees that third countries must have in place to limit interferences with fundamental rights in cases of law enforcement and national security access, which will be examined in more detail in Chapter 5.

Thus, it is not sufficient for third countries to simply translate the provisions of the GDPR, but they must also have essential guarantees in place for limiting government access to personal data. This may pose a particular challenge for the WB6 countries, as they are currently focusing only on adopting the GDPR into their national legislation without necessarily considering these essential guarantees, as also explained in Chapter 5.

3 CJEU and Schrems Decisions

The CJEU has addressed the tangle of different concepts related to the required standards of protection for international data transfers in three cases: *Schrems I*, *Schrems II*, and *Opinion 1/15*. In the most recent judgment, *Schrems II*, the CJEU assessed the criteria of 'essentially equivalent'.[166] The motive for the decision was assessing the level of safeguards regarding the interferences arising from US surveillance programs, where the CJEU found that the level of protection provided by the EU-US Privacy Shield is invalid.[167] It also assessed the criteria for an independent supervisory authority[168] and effective and enforceable data subjects' rights.[169] The Schrems judgments have been widely discussed in academia, and will therefore not be the subject of further discussion here.

4 Procedure of Adoption

The EU Commission carries out a comprehensive analysis of the third country's legal order, covering both the specific data protection laws and the limitations and safeguards on access to personal data by public authorities. However, the EU Commission does not play an entirely independent role in the adequacy assessment. The EU Commission submits its adequacy proposal to the EDPB with the aim of enabling the EDPB to make its own assessment of the level of data protection in the third country.[170] The EDPB then issues a non-binding opinion on the EU Com-

166 Schrems II, (n. 143).
167 Schrems II, para 201 (n. 143).
168 Schrems II, paras 48, 116, 120, 150, 151, 193–197 (n. 143).
169 Schrems II, paras 91, 131, 177 (n. 143).
170 WP29 Adequacy Referential (n. 155).

mission's findings and identifies any shortcomings in the adequacy framework.[171] The EDPB may also seek to propose changes or additions to address any shortcomings.[172] Lastly, the EU Commission then seeks approval from a committee of Member State representatives.[173] In addition, the European Parliament has a right of scrutiny over adequacy decisions.[174] Once this process is complete, the EU Commission can adopt the final adequacy decision. The adequacy decision also provides for a periodic review mechanism, taking into account all relevant developments in the third country at least every four years.[175]

5 Adequacy Paradox

The instrument of adequacy decisions, together with the so-called Brussels effect, has been much criticised. Not only because the EU has the power to decide on data protection levels in third countries, but also because the Member States themselves may not pass the adequacy test. This paradox was pointed out by Christakis[176] and Zuzanna Gulczyńska[177], who noted that the ECtHR found the surveillance measures deployed by several Member States, most recently Hungary[178] and the UK[179] (while it still was an EU Member State) as violating the ECHR. Similarly, the CJEU considered that the laws of France, Belgium, and the UK (former EU country)[180] do not meet the EU standards either.[181] Yet, due to the principle of equivalent protection, intra-EU transfers cannot be restricted.[182] The level of pro-

171 *Ibid.*

172 *Ibid.*

173 European Commission – Press release, Commission starts process to adopt adequacy decision for safe data flows with the US (13.12.2022).

174 *Ibid.*

175 Article 45(3) GDPR.

176 Theodore Christakis, '"Schrems III"? First Thoughts on the EDPB post-Schrems II Recommendations on International Data Transfers (Part 1)' European Law Blog, (13 November 2020) <https://europeanlawblog.eu/2020/11/13/schrems-iii-first-thoughts-on-the-edpb-post-schrems-ii-recommendations-on-international-data-transfers-part-1/> (accessed on 22.01.2023).

177 Zuzanna Gulczyńska (2021) (n. 160).

178 Szabo´and Vissy v Hungary, application no. 37138/14 (ECtHR 12.12.2016).

179 Big Brother Watch, applications nos. 58170/13, 62322/14, and 24960/15 (ECtHR 13 September 2018). The violation has been confirmed recently by the Grand Chamber (ECtHR, 25.05.2021).

180 Joined Cases C-511/18, C-512/18, C-520/18 La Quadrature du Net (n82); Case C-623/17 Privacy International.

181 Theodore Christakis (2020), (n. 176).

182 *Ibid.*

tection of personal data required from third countries is therefore, at least in some instances, higher than the one followed by Member States.[183]

It can also be noted that adequacy assessments are to a certain extent influenced by political and economic considerations to the effect that criteria whether and how to engage in an adequacy process with a third country might not be the same for every country depending on the economic benefits at stake for the EU.[184] The approach taken by the EU Commission to develop adequacy decisions is to actively engage with key trading partners and establish dialogue and close cooperation with the concerned third country.[185] Before starting a dialogue with a third country, the EU Commission also takes into account the EU's commercial relations with the third country, the extent of personal data flows, a potential pioneering role that country plays in the field of privacy and data protection and also the overall political relationship with that country.[186] Evidence for this connection is given by the number of attempts the EU Commission has made to come to at least partial adequacy decisions based on agreements and safeguards with the US, whose data protection laws and essential safeguards for government access to personal data raise ample doubts to be considered 'adequate'.[187] The strong interest of both sides to reach a legal framework that allows the free flow of data has been confirmed with the conclusion of an EU-U.S. Data Privacy Framework.[188]

II Alternatives to Adequacy Decisions for the WB6

It should be mentioned that also under the GDPR, other than through adequacy decisions, the transfer of personal data may be legalised by an international

183 *Ibid.*
184 Gstrein and Zwitter also noted that both adequacy assessments with South Korea were part of a larger political package; Gstrein and Zwitter, p. 12 (2021) (n. 11).
185 *Ibid.*
186 Communication from The Commission to The European Parliament and The Council Exchanging and Protecting Personal Data in a Globalised World COM (2017) 7 final (2017 Communication), 9 and footnote 42. An adequacy finding is a unilateral implementing decision by the Commission in accordance with EU data protection law, based on the criteria therein. The EU data protection rules cannot be the subject of negotiations in a free trade agreement.
187 These doubts are detailed in the draft motion of the European Parliament's Committee on Civil Liberties, Justice and Home Affairs in a draft motion for a resolution in March 2023 <https://www.europarl.europa.eu/doceo/document/LIBE-RD-740749_EN.pdf> (accessed on 12.05.2023).
188 EU-U.S. Data Privacy Framework, available at the following link <https://ec.europa.eu/commission/presscorner/detail/en/qanda_22_6045> (accessed on 14.02.2023).

agreement.[189] Yet, the GDPR articles do not define this explicitly as it is not a preferred option under the new regulation. Art. 96 GDPR confirms that international agreements which were concluded before the adoption of the GDPR remain in force. Recital 102 GDPR addresses this data transfer venue as well, by stating that "this Regulation is without prejudice to international agreements concluded between the Union and third countries regulating the transfer of personal data [...]." Further, Recital 102 GDPR opens the possibility for Member States to conclude international agreements which involve the transfer of personal data to third countries.[190] These agreements must also ensure an adequate level of protection for personal data transferred under such an instrument.[191] However, the scrutiny of data protection standards when negotiating an international agreement may not be as thorough as the one for adequacy findings.[192] Therefore, the EU Commission prefers to legalise data transfers outside the EU through adequacy decisions in order to keep trade agreements politically uncontroversial.[193] For the WB6 countries, given the fact that they already have SAAs in place obliging them to fully align their legislation with the EU acquis communautaire there is no indication that the EU Commission would explore ways to come to an international agreement on adequacy. Hence the only way, short of becoming a member of the EU, is striving for an adequacy decision.

III Conclusion to B

An adequacy decision is the preferred venue to transfer data from the EU to a third country, as it does not necessitate any additional requirements. Thus, the transfer via an adequacy decision has the same status as intra-EU data transfers. However, the criteria for adopting an adequacy decision are complex and not always clear. Furthermore, the economic relationship between a third country and the EU has a significant impact on the EU Commission's decision-making process. Currently, the WB6 countries are not on the EU Commission's adequacy list, nor are there any adequacy talks between the EU and the WB6 countries. This situa-

189 Leonie Wittershagen (2023), p. 58 (n. 151).

190 Recital 102 GDPR: "Member States may conclude international agreements which involve the transfer of personal data to third countries or international organisations, as far as such agreements do not affect this Regulation or any other provisions of Union law and include an appropriate level of protection for the fundamental rights of data subjects."

191 *Ibid.*

192 Leonie Wittershagen, p. 58 (n. 151).

193 *Ibid.*

tion presents challenges for the free flow of data, particularly given the WB6's geographic location, surrounded by EU Member States.

C Conclusion to Chapter 3

The extraterritorial application of the GDPR has significant data protection implications for third countries. In the context of the EU accession process, the WB6 countries are particularly affected by the GDPR. Not only can the GDPR be directly applied in certain situations within the WB6 countries, but these countries are also legally obliged to harmonise their national legislation with the GDPR under the SAAs they have individually concluded with the EU.

In addition, the EU Commission plays a role in assessing the data protection frameworks of the WB6 countries through annual reports as part of the evaluation process within the EU accession process. Despite these ongoing efforts, no adequacy decisions or discussions have been initiated specifically for the WB6 countries. Consequently, this situation raises questions about the underlying rationale and factors that may influence the possible adoption of adequacy decisions for these countries.

Chapter 4 and Chapter 5 will delve into the comprehensive profiles of each of the WB6 data protection frameworks, providing a deeper understanding of the challenges that may influence the adoption of adequacy decisions for these countries.

Chapter 4 – The GDPR Transplantation in the WB6

The right to the protection of personal data and the adequacy of the protection afforded to that right are of paramount importance in the process of WB6 countries joining the EU. This is also indicated in the SAAs, which all WB6 countries have signed with the EU. WB6 countries are closely tied with EU Member States, having a high number of EU investors operating and opening their companies in the region.[194] For them it is therefore also important to have strong data protection and privacy laws, in order to be even more attractive for EU investors. However, the protection of personal data in WB6 countries is not at the same level as in the EU countries, which is why the EU Commission has decided not to put the WB6 countries on the list of countries providing adequate protection. One of their critical issues, is that most of them do not have efficient institutional mechanisms – operational or legislative – to address emerging developments in the field of data protection.[195] This comes primarily as a result of the lack of political awareness of the problem and institutional capacities to recognise the risk and act upon it in a cooperative manner on the regional level.[196]

Despite the fact that the EU supports the alignment of WB6 countries with the EU acquis through various financial and technical instruments, such as twinning projects,[197] including these countries in an adequacy decision seems to be a lower

194 The EU is the leading trade partner for all WB6 countries, with almost 70 % of the region's total trade. In 2018, EU companies accounted for over 65 % of foreign direct investment in the region. See for more information at the following link <https://www.eeas.europa.eu/eeas/eu-and-western-balkans-towards-common-future_en> (accessed on 21.12.2020).

195 See also DiploFoundation, Cybersecurity in the Western Balkans: Policy gaps and cooperation opportunities Research report under the project "Cybersecurity Capacity Building and Research Programme for South-Eastern Europe" implemented with the support of the Federal Department of Foreign Affairs of Switzerland, (September 2016), available at the following link <https://www.diplomacy.edu/resource/cybersecurity-in-the-western-balkans-policy-gaps-and-cooperation-opportunities/> (accessed on 10.12.2020).

196 *Ibid.*

197 Twinning is a European Union instrument for institutional cooperation between Public Administrations of EU Member States and of beneficiary or partner countries. Twinning in the Western Balkans aims to provide support for the transposition, implementation and enforcement of the EU legislation (the Union acquis). See for more information at the following link <https://neighbourhood-enlargement.ec.europa.eu/funding-and-technical-assistance/twinning_en.> (accessed on 09.04.2023).

https://doi.org/10.1515/9783112221013-006

priority for the EU, compared to some other countries.[198] This Chapter examines how the WB6 countries have implemented the GDPR or are in the processes of the implementation in their national laws and the challenges they face in ensuring compliance with the GDPR. The Chapter will also explore how the GDPR's implementation affects data protection framework in the WB6 countries and the free flow of data in the region.

A Albania

Albania was identified as a potential candidate for EU membership during the Thessaloniki summit in June 2003.[199] In October 2012, the EU Commission recommended that Albania should be granted EU candidate status after completing key measures in the areas of judicial and public administration reform.[200] Finally, in June 2014, the EU granted Albania candidate status. However, due to the need for Albania to improve its rule of law, Albania was not able to start accession talks with the EU immediately.[201] Only in March 2020 the European Council endorsed the General Affairs Council's decision to open accession negotiations with Albania and in July 2020 the draft negotiating framework was presented to the Member States.[202] In July 2022, the EU and Albania held the first Intergovernmental Conference opening negotiations for the country's EU accession.[203]

Albania has recently aligned its national data protection legislation with the GDPR. This Section will examine the newly adopted data protection law currently in force while also briefly reviewing the previous legal framework to highlight the

198 The Commission has identified East and South-East Asia as a first target group, and already adopted adequacy decisions with Japan and Korea. As to other strategic partners, they include India as well as countries in Latin America, in particular the Mercosur trading bloc. See also EU Commission, Exchanging and Protecting Personal Data in a Globalised World (n. 186) and UNCTAD, "Data protection regulations and international data flows: Implications for trade and development", (2016), available at the following link <http://unctad.org/en/PublicationsLibrary/dtlstict2016d1_en.pdf> (accessed on 09.04.2023). Chapter 7 analyses this aspect in more detail.

199 European Neighbourhood Policy and Enlargement Negotiations, Negotiation Status of Albania, available at the official website of the EU Commission at the following link <https://ec.europa.eu/neighbourhood-enlargement/enlargement-policy/negotiations-status/albania_en> (accessed on 17.06.2022).

200 *Ibid.*

201 *Ibid.*

202 *Ibid.*

203 Achieving progress on Albania's pathway to EU accession, GIZ, (February 2023), available at the following link <https://www.giz.de/en/worldwide/120333.html> (accessed on 09.04.2023).

key changes introduced. Analysing both the current and former legislation is essential for understanding the evolution of Albania's data protection framework, assessing the extent of alignment with the GDPR, and identifying persisting gaps or challenges.

I Constitutional Parameters and International Commitments

The right to data protection is guaranteed at the constitutional level in Albania. Art. 35 guarantees the right to data protection by stating that "no one may be obliged, except when the law requires it, to make public data connected with his person. The collection, use and making public of data about a person is done with his consent, except for the cases provided by law. Everyone has the right to become acquainted with data collected about him, except for the cases provided by law. Everyone has the right to request the correction or expunging of untrue or incomplete data or data collected in violation of law".

Hence, the Albanian Constitution enshrines several rights that are also foreseen in the GDPR: the principle of lawfulness of data processing (Art. 6 GDPR), the right of access of data subjects (Art. 15 GDPR) and the right of rectification (Art. 16 GDPR). The Albanian Constitution also recognises the right to privacy, including the freedom and secrecy of correspondence and communication,[204] inviolability of the home,[205] and the right to family life.[206]

Relevant international instruments and international law are also an integral part of the Constitution. The Albanian Constitution referrers to international law and instruments at several places. Firstly, under Art. 5 "the Republic of Albania applies international law that is binding upon it". Secondly, in Part II of the Constitution, which regulates the fundamental human rights and freedoms, the Constitution makes a fundamental reference to the norms of international law when it stipulates that "the limitations of the fundamental human rights and freedoms cannot supersede the limitations set by the ECHR".[207] Thirdly, part VII of the Constitution refers specifically to international agreements and their place in the hi-

---

204 Art. 36 Albanian Constitution.
205 Art. 37 Albanian Constitution.
206 Art. 53 Albanian Constitution.
207 Armand Skapi, "The law of treaties and its implementation in Albania, Pillar 1 Albanian Legislation", Law Journal ISSN 2523–1766, November 2017, available at the following link <https://www.lawjournal.al/sites/default/files/Pillar%20I%2C%20ALJ%20No.%204%20-%20ENGL.pdf> (accessed on 18.05.2022).

erarchy of the norms of Albania.[208] Ratified agreements are listed immediately after the Constitution in the hierarchy of norms.[209] As a result, all laws and sub-legislative acts must be in conformity not only with the Constitution, but also with the international agreements ratified by the parliament of Albania.[210]

As a member of both CoE and the United Nations (hereinafter: "UN"), Albania is committed to respecting human rights both regionally and globally. In June 2005, the country acceded to Convention 108 and in 2022, it signed the Protocol (CETS No. 223) to Convention 108.[211]

1 Conclusion to I

The right to data protection and privacy is enshrined at the constitutional level in Albania. The definition of the right to data protection is comprehensive and includes several rights that are also foreseen in the GDPR, such as the principle of lawfulness of data processing, the right of access of data subjects, and the right of rectification. Additionally, Albania's Constitution refers to international law and instruments at multiple points, highlighting the country's commitment to upholding human rights both regionally and globally. As a member of the CoE and the UN, Albania is obligated to adhere to international human rights standards, further underscoring its commitment to protecting the right to data protection and privacy.

II Data Protection Legislation

In December 2024, Albania passed a law on the protection of personal data (hereinafter: "ADPL 2024"),[212] which replaced the previous legislation – Albanian data protection law from 2008 ("ADPL 2008").[213] The ADPL 2024 is a third-generation

---

208 Art. 116 Albanian Constitution.
209 *Ibid.*
210 Armand Skapi, "The law of treaties and its implementation in Albania", Law Journal Albania, (30.11.2.17), the article available at the following link <https://www.lawjournal.al/?q=article/law-treaties-and-its-implementation-albania> (accessed on 02.09.2022).
211 CoE, "With Albania Convention 108+ reaches half the needed ratifications", (22.07.2022), available at the following link <https://www.coe.int/en/web/data-protection/-/with-albania-convention-108-reaches-half-the-needed-ratifications> (accessed on 02.09.2022).
212 Law on personal data protection no. 124/2024 dated 19.12.2024.
213 Law on the protection of personal data no. 9887/2008 dated 10.03.2008 (with amendments). English version of ADPL 2008 available at the following link <https://www.idp.al/wp-content/uploads/2016/11/law_data_protection_new-2.pdf> (accessed on 02.09.2022).

data protection law and an umbrella legislation that comprehensively regulates the protection of personal data. Its adoption came as a response to Albania's efforts to align with GDPR and its adoption took several years.

1 Status Quo of GDPR Alignment

The adoption of the ADPL 2024 was a lengthy and complex process for Albania, requiring significant legislative effort. The Albanian Information and Data Protection Commissioner (hereinafter: "AC") has been recognising the impact of the GDPR on Albania and the importance of brining the national legislation in line with the EU standards, by stating "GDPR is a regulation that extends to non-EU countries, we note from the perspective of Albanian reality that the impact of this regulation on Albanian territory will be inevitable as long as personal data of European citizens are generated, collected and processed. The expansion of Albanian trade and cooperation with EU countries, globalisation and the spread of online platforms make the impact of the GDPR in Albania inevitable."[214] At the end of 2021, the AC published a notice for public consultation on the proposed amendments to the ADPL 2008.[215] The proposed law was consolidated with the support of the EU in the framework of a twinning project.[216] The National Plan for European Integration envisaged that the new draft law on personal data protection would be approved in the fourth quarter of 2021.[217] Moreover, the AC's strategy for 2020–2025 envisaged as its first objective the adoption of the draft law on personal data protection "approximated with the EU acquis in this field and relevant secondary legislation for its implementation".[218] While the deadline was missed, the ADPL 2024 was finally adopted on 19 December 2024 and published in January 2025.[219]

---

214 Merisa Çeloaliaj, "General Regulation on Personal Data Potection: Certain Aspects of the GDPR's Impact on Legal Entities in the Republic of Albania", International Journal, Vol.34.5 (September 2019).

215 Proposed new data protection law published on the Commissioner's website, available at the following link <https://www.idp.al/projekt-akte-te-zyres-se-komisionerit/> (accessed on 01.07.2022).

216 Twinning Project, Albania – Italy – Austria, "Institution-building for Alignment with the European Union Acquis on the Protection of Personal Data" (2020–2021).

217 The AC's Annual Report 2021, available at the following link <https://www.idp.al/wp-content/uploads/2016/11/Annual-report-2021.pdf> (accessed on 23.09.2022) pp. 28–29.

218 Art. 4(2) AC's Institutional Strategy 2022–2025, available at the following link <https://www.idp.al/wp-content/uploads/2016/11/ENGLISH_Strategjia-Institucionale-2022-2025_revised.pdf> (accessed on 20.05.2023).

219 Official Journal of the Republic of Albania, no 9, 2025, available at the following link < https://qbz.gov.al/eli/fz/2025/9/b9ea0ec9-b6ad-4464-9fe7-ca419a989852;q=P%C3%ABr%20mbrojtjen%20e%20t%C3%AB%20dh%C3%ABnave%20personale> (accessed on 01.02.2025).

The ADPL 2024 largely mirrors the GDPR provisions, although it lacks the Recitals that provide valuable context for understanding such a complex piece of legislation. Moreover, it incorporates provisions from the Law Enforcement Directive (hereinafter: "LED") into part three.

The ADPL 2024 expands the scope by introducing a set of detailed rules to ensure stronger enforcement and new concepts such as: profiling, pseudonymisation, anonymisation, genetic and biometric data. The key novelties also include easier access to personal data and right to portability, right to be forgotten, data protection by design and by default, mandatory breach notifications, DPIA, certification and new enforcement rules and provisions on the fines. It also transposes the definition of personal data under the GDPR, including location and online identifiers, which was lacking in the previous legislation.[220] Few differentiations however, do exist, and will be presented in this Section.

2 Overview of the ADPL 2024

The ADPL 2024 is structured into six distinct parts. Part 1 outlines the objectives and general principles, including definitions and the scope of the ADPL 2024 (general provisions). Part 2 stipulates the principles of data processing, lawfulness of processing and defines conditions for valid consent (first chapter). It further elaborates on the data subject rights (second chapter), defines the obligations of controllers and processors (third chapter) and sets forth provisions related to international data transfer (fourth chapter). Additionally, it provides provisions relating to specific processing situations (fifth chapter). Part 3 provides dedicated provisions related to data processing by competent authorities for the purposes of the national security and public authorities for prevention and prosecution of criminal offences. This part of the legislation comprises five autonomous chapters exclusively dedicated to such authorities. Part 4 defines the role, competencies, and responsibilities of the AC. Part 5 consolidates the enforcement of the data protection legislation, including penalties and legal remedies. Lastly, Part 6 stipulates the transitional and final provisions of the ADPL 2024.

3 Scope of the ADPL 2024

The ADPL 2024 defines both the material and territorial scope. In particular, Art. 4 ADPL 2024 adopts the extraterritorial effect of GDPR. It is noteworthy, however, that Art. 4(1) ADPL 2024 differs from Art. 3(2) GDPR in a significant way, by stating that "the law shall also apply to the processing of data by controllers not estab-

220 Art. 3(1)(1) ADPL 2008.

lished in Albania, if the processing operations are related to: i) the provision of goods or services, regardless of whether a payment by the data subject to such persons in Albania is required, or ii) the monitoring of the behaviour of persons located in the territory of Albania".[221] While it omits any mention of processors in this context, it specifies that when a controller not established in Albania, contracts a processor who is not established in the Albania, Chapter IV, "International data transfers" shall apply in such a case. Thus, Art. 4(1) ADPL 2024, has a different exterritorial scope compared to the GDPR, as it applies as a whole only to data controllers not established in Albania, whereas for data processors, international data transfer rules apply.[222]

4 Data Protection Principles

Data protection principles envisaged by ADPL 2024 include the same seven principles relating to processing of personal data, including the principles of transparency, accountability and integrity and confidentiality, which were not explicitly defined in the previous ADPL 2008.

5 Lawfulness of Data Processing

As per the principle of lawfulness, data processing is only allowed if there is a valid legal ground for data processing. The ADPL 2024 provides for the same grounds for lawfulness of processing as in Art. 6 GDPR.

a) Consent

Art. 8 ADPL 2024 incorporates Art. 7 GDPR, and on a positive note, compared to the old legislation,[223] lays down specific rules on validity of consent and provides specific examples where consent is not deemed to be freely given.[224] The examples include elements of coercion, pressure or inability to exercise free will. This might be the case in situations of imbalance between the controller and the data subject, as may be the case, inter alia, where a public authority requires the consent of a citizen or an employer requires that of an employee.[225] These examples are not mentioned in Art. 7 GDPR, but are listed in Recital 43 GDPR. Although the Recitals of GDPR are not reproduced in the ADPL 2024, it seems that

221 Art. 4(1) ADPL 2024.
222 Art. 4(2) ADPL 2024.
223 Art. 6 ADPL 2008.
224 Art. 8 ADPL 2024.
225 *Ibid.*

the Albanian legislator intends to give legal effect to them. Moreover, it pays close attention to the assurance that the consent declaration needs to be presented in a manner which is clearly distinguishable from other matters (when the consent is only a part of another document), in an intelligible and easily accessible form, using clear and plain language.[226]

6 Special Categories of Personal Data

The ADPL 2024 adopts a definition of 'sensitive data'[227] instead of the 'special categories of personal data' as defined in the GDPR. However, despite the difference in the terms, the ADPL 2024 provides the same protection to sensitive data by stipulating a general prohibition of processing sensitive data.[228] These data include personal data revealing racial or ethnic origin, political opinions, religious beliefs or philosophical views, trade unions membership, genetic data, biometric data, data concerning health, life or sexual orientation of a person.[229] This definition provides a modernised solution, considering that the ADPL 2008 did not recognise biometric data as special categories of personal data.[230] Regarding the exemptions from the general prohibition for processing sensitive data, they seem to align with the exemptions envisaged by the Art. 9(2) GDPR.

7 Rights of Data Subjects

Chapter 3 (part 2) ADPL 2024 incorporates all the data subject's rights enumerated in the GDPR. In comparison to the restrictions defined by Art. 23 GDPR, which include also inter alia, economic or financial interests of the EU or Member States or the enforcement of civil law claims, Art. 21 ADPL 2024 stipulates that the data subject's rights may be limited by law, whereas the limitation must respect the essence of the fundamental rights and freedoms and be necessary and proportionate to a democratic society to ensure national security, public safety or the economic interests of the country, for the prevention of disorder or criminal offences, or for the protection of the rights and freedoms of others. Thus, the list of situations in which it would be possible to restrict the rights is narrower compared to the GDPR. Art. 21(2) ADPL 2024 also specifies which specific provisions any legislative measures should contain to safeguard the core fundamental rights

226 Art. 8(2) ADPL 2024.
227 Art. 9 ADPL 2024.
228 Art. 7(1) GDPR.
229 Art. 5(28) ADPL 2024.
230 Art. 3(2) ADPL 2008.

and freedoms of data subjects, listing the same provisions as those defined by Art. 23(2) GDPR.

8 Redress Mechanism

The ADPL 2024 provides a dedicated part (part 5) which regulates legal remedies. This part follows in most part the Chapter 8 GDPR. Data subjects have the right to file a complaint with the AC (Art. 86) and the right to appeal against the AC's decision before the competent administrative court (Art. 87). Moreover, data subjects who have suffered financial or other damage as a result of data misuse have the right seek compensation from responsible controllers or processors before the competent civil courts (Art. 88). In contrast to the Art. 79, the ADPL 2024 does not specifically mentions the right to an effective judicial remedy against a controller or processor. Additionally, Art. 91 ADPL 2024 stipulates that during the appeal procedure initiated by submitting a complaint by the AC, a complainant may request the AC to issue a preliminary restriction order in relation to specific processing operations by the other party, due to the serious and irreparable risk that threatens the rights of the complainant under this law.[231] This specific possibility is not envisaged by the GDPR.

9 Personal Scope

The ADPL 2024 recognises the two main terms 'controller' and 'processor'. The law introduced the term join controllers[232], which did not exist under previous legislation. It mostly imposes the same obligations on controllers and processors as the GDPR. Just as provided by Art. 28 GDPR, Art. 26(3) ADPL 2024 provides that the relationship between the controller and the processor must be governed by a written agreement, and it includes necessary elements which each such a written agreement should entail. The controller can only entrust processors that ensure the lawful and secure use of data and data subjects' rights, imposing numerous obligations on the processor.[233] These obligations, inter alia, require the processor to process data solely based on the instructions of the controller, to maintain confidentially of data, not to engage another processor without the prior specific or general written authorisation of the controller and to make available to the controller all information necessary to control the compliance with the obligations provided by the law.[234]

---

231 Art. 91 ADPL 2024.
232 Art. 24 ADPL 2024.
233 Art. 26 ADPL 2024.
234 *Ibid.*

a) DPO

The ADPL 2024 law incorporates provisions regarding the appointment of a Data Protection Officer (hereinafter: "DPO") influenced by the GDPR (Art. 42). The previous legislation did not impose a mandatory requirement to appoint a DPO, thus, this presents a novelty introduced by the recent law. Nevertheless, even though the previous legislation did not define the institute of a DPO, the AC's Instruction no. 47 dated 14.09.2018 on determining rules for safeguarding personal data processed by large controllers (hereinafter "Instruction no. 47"), provided that large data processing entities in Albania are required to appoint a person which shall be responsible for the internal compliance with the data protection law and acting as the primary point of contact with the AC.[235] The designated person must fulfil specific legal requirements, including holding a university degree in law or computer science, demonstrating integrity, possessing recognised professional skills and ethical and moral integrity, accumulating at least five years of work experience as a lawyer or IT expert or a minimum of three years of work experience in the AC's office as a lawyer or IT expert, and no criminal record.[236] According to ADPL 2024, the DPO is entrusted with the same responsibilities as outlined in the GDPR.[237] The ADPL 2024 mandates that DPOs must possess appropriate qualifications to fulfil their duties, although it is less specific in this regard than the Instruction no. 47.[238] However, as the ADPL 2024 provides that the current bylaws remain applicable until the new ones are published, the Instruction no. 47 remains in force.[239] Additionally, controllers or processors are obligated to publish the contact details of the DPO and to communicate them to the supervisory authority.[240]

Moreover, the ADPL 2024 gives DPOs a unique opportunity to organise themselves under the national chamber of data protection officers,[241] potentially giving them a stronger voice in their roles. This provision goes beyond the scope of the GDPR, and underlines the importance of fostering cooperation and mutual support among data protection professionals. By providing a platform for DPOs to co-

---

235 According to Instruction no. 47 dated 14.09.2018 on determining rules for safeguarding personal data processed by large controllers, large controllers include controllers and processors that process personal data manually or electronically, by employing 6 or more persons for the processing, either directly or by virtue of processors.

236 Instruction no. 47 (n. 235).

237 Art. 33 ADPL 2024.

238 Art. 34(2) ADPL 2024.

239 Art. 99(2) ADPL 2024.

240 Art. 34(2) ADPL 2024.

241 Art. 33(6) ADPL 2024.

ordinate and advocate for data protection, the ADPL 2024 may facilitate more effective implementation of data protection practices in Albania.

b) Security

The ADPL 2024 introduces data protection by design and default, which require controllers to integrate data protection measures into every stage of their operations and implement technical and organisational measures (hereinafter: "TOMs").[242]

Moreover, the law introduced several obligations and security related provisions that were absent in the previous legislation, and are modelled upon the GDPR. First, it defines the obligation to notify data breaches to the supervisory authority or data subjects.[243] Second, the ADPL 2024 requires data controllers to conduct data protection impact assessment (hereinafter: "DPIA") for processing which is likely to result in a high risk to the rights and freedoms of natural persons.[244] Thirdly, the ADPL 2024 provides for the possibility for controllers and processors to prepare codes of conduct, or obtain certifications for the purpose of demonstrating compliance with the ADPL 2024.[245]

In addition, Instruction no. 47, which is still in force, states that all large controllers and processors are required to establish and maintain an information security management system (hereinafter: "ISMS") for the protection of personal data.[246]

Finally, the AC's Decision no. 6 "On establishment of detailed rules for personal data security" (hereinafter: "Decision no. 6") sets out additional rules for controllers to ensure an adequate level of data security and for processing activities.[247]

---

242 Art. 23 ADPL 2024.

243 Art. 29 ADPL 2024.

244 Artt. 31–32 ADPL 2024.

245 Artt. 35–38 ADPL 2024. Codes of conduct are governed by Artt. 40–41 GDPR and certifications by Artt. 42–43 GDPR.

246 *Ibid.*

247 The following are the obligations of the data controller according to the Decision no. 6: (1) determine the categories of personal and sensitive data to be processed; (2) determine the levels of access to data, in accordance with their job profile, in function of the processing and protection of data; (3) draft and approve a regulation "On the protection, processing, storage and security of personal data" based on the template draft/regulation provided by the Commissioner; (4) take the necessary measures and ensure that staff are aware of and trained in the need for data security; (5) draw up and implement a privacy policy and rules on access security in the premises where data processing is carried out; (6) ensure that each employee involved in data processing has agreed to a 'agreement' in accordance with the model annexed to the Decision; (7) draw up and

10 Transfer of Personal Data

In the course of evaluating adequacy decisions, the EU Commission duly factors in the 'onward transfers', which from the perspective of the third country's controller or processor constitute international transfers.[248] Such onward transfers "should be permitted only where the further recipient outside the third country is itself subject to rules ensuring a similar level of protection to that guaranteed within the third country's legal order."[249] Therefore, national rules governing data transfers play a key role in determining adequacy decisions.

The ADPL 2024 largely aligns with the GDPR in regulating data transfers, distinguishing between transfers based on adequacy decisions[250] and those occurring in the absence of such decisions.[251] It also includes provisions for onward transfers,[252] albeit with certain deviations from the GDPR framework. Notably, the ADPL 2024 incorporates provisions for data transfers to countries that maintain an adequate level of data protection. The adequacy of a country, territory, sector, or international organisation is determined by a decision of the AC. However, unlike the GDPR, the law does not establish a mandatory mechanism for periodic adequacy reviews, which, under the GDPR, must occur at least every four years. Instead, the ADPL 2024 imposes a general obligation to monitor developments in third countries, without specifying a strict review timeline.[253] Furthermore, the ADPL 2024 explicitly stipulates that foreign court rulings and administrative decisions requiring a data controller or processor to transfer or disclose personal data may be recognised or enforced if they are based on an international agreement.[254] This includes treaties on mutual legal assistance in force between the requesting foreign state and Albania.[255]

Finally, it is important to note that, unlike the data protection law of North Macedonia, which was adopted to align with the GDPR, the ADPL 2024 does not

---

implement procedures for keeping records of possible changes, destruction and transfers of data during their processing.

248 EU Commission implementing decision of 28.06.2021 pursuant to Regulation (EU) 2016/679 of the European Parliament and of the Council on the adequate protection of personal data by the United Kingdom C(2021) 4800 final (28.06.2021), para. 120.

249 WP29 Adequacy Referential, p. 6 (n. 155).

250 Art. 40 ADPL 2024.

251 Art. 41 ADPL 2024. These include equivalent safeguards provided by Art. 46 GDPR and derogations for specific situations provided by Art. 49 GDPR.

252 Art. 39 ADPL 2024.

253 Art. 40(4) ADPL 2024.

254 Art. 39(2) ADPL 2024.

255 *Ibid.*

explicitly recognise EU member states as providing an adequate level of data protection by default under the law.

a) Adequacy Decisions

Considering that the bylaws are still in force, adopted under the previous ADPL 2008, the AC' decision from 2016 which provides the list of countries that ensure adequate protection of personal data ("Albanian Adequacy Decision") is still in force. This decision includes, in principle, the members of the EU and the EEA, as well as countries that have ratified Convention 108+.[256] However, the Albanian Adequacy Decision does not include all the countries that have signed the Convention 108 + per se, but sets additional criteria: 1) the country has adopted a specific data protection law, 2) the country has established a supervisory authority that performs its functions with complete independence and 3) the country provides for adequate legal remedies, including the handling of complaints, and ensuring transparency in the processing of personal data.[257] Accordingly, the following countries are assessed as countries providing an adequate level of protection: Georgia, Bosnia and Herzegovina, Montenegro, Moldavia, Principality of Monaco, North Macedonia and Serbia.[258] Further, the Albanian Adequacy Decision recognises the EU Commission's adequacy decision and includes these countries as well.[259] However, it is not updated to the latest status quo list because it includes the US under the previous Privacy Shield regime.[260] The question remains if the list will be updated as well, to exclude the countries which are not recognised by the EU Commission, as the law aims to be aligned with the GDPR.

11 Penalties

The ADPL 2024 introduces stringent financial penalties for significant data breaches, with fines for non-compliance reaching up to 1 billion ALL (approximately EUR 10.2 million) or, in the case of corporate entities, up to 2% of their global annual turnover. For particularly serious violations, such as unauthorised international data transfers or breaches of fundamental data processing principles, these penal-

256 Decision no. 8 dated 31/ 10/ 2016 "on Determining States that ensure an Adequate Level of Personal Data Protection", p. 1, available at following link <https://www.idp.al/wp-content/uploads/2020/10/Decision_no_8.pdf> (accessed on 10.04.2023).
257 *Ibid*, p. 3.
258 *Ibid*, p. 3.
259 *Ibid*.
260 *Ibid*, p. 4.

ties are even more severe, doubling to 2 billion ALL (approximately EUR 20.4 million) or up to 4% of global annual turnover, whichever is higher.[261]

To put these penalties into perspective, under the previous legislation, the maximum fine was significantly lower, capped at just 2 million ALL (approximately EUR 20,000),[262] a fraction of the new upper limits established by the ADPL 2024.

The fines are imposed by the AC[263], and an appeal against administrative sanction with fine is addressed at the court in the terms and under the procedures governing administrative proceedings.[264]

12 Specific Processing Situations

The aim of the GDPR, according to the will of the European legislator, is to create "a strong and more coherent data protection framework in the Union", and in particular to promote "digital economy across the internal market" (Recital 7). An equivalent level of protection for processing in all Member States of the EU is intended to "ensure a consistent and high level of protection of natural persons and to remove the obstacles to flows of personal data within the Union [...]" (Recital 10). However, the GDPR contains, in various contexts clauses for both the EU and the national legislator – the so-called 'opening clauses'.[265] These allow – depending on the specific regulatory context – to replace the provisions of the GDPR with other legal provisions, to supplement them or to specify them in more detail.[266] This affects both various rights and obligations in different individual regulations as well as possible requirements in special processing situations, which are listed in Chapter IX of the GDPR.[267] However, this may be a challenge for non-EU countries seeking an adequacy decision, as there is no specific guidance for third countries in this regard, except that WP29 has noted that "general provisions regarding data protection and privacy in the third country are not sufficient [...] specific provisions addressing concrete needs for practically relevant aspects of the right to data protection must be included in the third country's [...] legal framework."[268] Furthermore, the EU Commission stressed that the "national legislator can neither copy the text of the GDPR when it is not necessary in the light of the criteria provided by the case law, nor interpret it or add additional

261 Art. 94 ADPL 2024.
262 Art. 39 ADPL 2024.
263 Art. 93 ADPL 2024.
264 Art. 95 ADPL 2024.
265 Philip Laue und Sascha Kremer, para. 114 (n. 6).
266 *Ibid.*
267 *Ibid.*
268 WP29 Adequacy Referential, pp. 4–5 (n. 155).

conditions to the rules directly applicable under the GDPR. If they did, operators throughout the Union would again be faced with fragmentation and would not know which rules they have to obey."[269] This may open up more room for manoeuvre, as third countries will not have to ensure uniform application of the rules that exist at EU level, but of course such rules will have to be in line with the principles of the GDPR. For Albania and other WB6 countries, it may be advisable to look at the standards of the EU acquis due to their specific situation as countries aspiring to EU membership.

Looking at Albanian national legislation, the ADPL 2024 recognises similar specific situations for data processing: Processing of personal data and freedom of expression,[270] processing of personal data and access to information in the public sector,[271] processing of personal data for archiving purposes in the public interest[272] and for direct marketing purposes.[273] Art. 46 ADPL 2024, regulating direct marketing, explicitly states that personal data processing for direct marketing purposes may be based on legitimate interest, provided that the rights and interests of data subjects are not overridden. Notably, the law specifies that legitimate interest may be particularly relevant when data is obtained from publicly available sources for direct marketing purposes. Furthermore, the article clarifies that explicit consent from the data subject is required only for the processing of sensitive data in the context of direct marketing. Compared to the GDPR, this represents a more permissive approach, as the GDPR does not explicitly affirm the use of legitimate interest as a legal basis for direct marketing in its main provisions.[274]

Additionally, compared to the GDPR, the ADPL 2024 does not include specific provisions related to national identification documents or in the context of employment. This narrower regulatory scope may fall short of ensuring comprehensive data protection, as the GDPR encourages member states to provide more detailed regulations in these areas.

13 Conclusion to II

The data protection framework in Albania follows the structure and principles of the GDPR. While the ADPL 2024 largely mirrors GDPR provisions, it notably omits

269 Karen Mc Cullagh, Olivia Tambou and Sam Bourton, "National Adaptations of the GDPR, Collection Open Access Book, Blogdroiteuropeen, Luxembourg" (February 2019), p. 26.
270 Art. 43 ADPL 2024.
271 Art. 44 ADPL 2024.
272 Art. 45 ADPL 2024.
273 Art. 46 ADPL 2024.
274 GDPR only provides in its Recital 47 that the processing of personal data for direct marketing purposes may be regarded as carried out for a legitimate interest.

the Recitals, which serve as essential interpretative guidance for controllers and processors. The absence of Recitals may create challenges in understanding and applying certain provisions, potentially requiring stakeholders to refer directly to the GDPR for clarification. However, in some instances, Recitals have been incorporated into the legal text, such as the conditions for obtaining valid consent, thereby granting them legal force.

Despite its overall alignment with the GDPR, the ADPL 2024 contains certain divergences. Notably, its extraterritorial scope does not extend to processors, which differs from the GDPR's broader application. Additionally, the law's adequacy framework includes countries that have not been recognised as adequate by the EU Commission, raising potential concerns regarding data (onward) transfer standards. Furthermore, while the ADPL 2024 recognizes legitimate interest as a basis for direct marketing, it does not provide further clarification on other specific processing scenarios. The EU Commission will likely scrutinise these differences to evaluate the ADPL 2024 alignment with GDPR.

III Supervisory Authority

When assessing adequacy, the EU Commission must also consider "the existence and effective functioning" of an independent supervisory authority.[275] An independent supervisory authority tasked with monitoring, ensuring and enforcing compliance with the data protection rules should be in place to ensure an adequate level of data protection is guaranteed in practice.[276] The data protection system must provide support and help to the individual data subjects to exercise their rights and appropriate redress mechanisms.[277]

1 General Functions

The AC carries numerous functions and is granted various powers. The AC's role is to promote compliance with the ADPL 2024 and monitor and supervise its implementation.[278] The AC's powers also include addressing complaints from data subjects related to the protection of their rights and freedoms regarding the processing of personal data.[279] The AC shall also cooperate with supervisory authorities in

275 Art 45(2)(b) GDPR.
276 WP29 Adequacy Referential, p. 7 (n. 155).
277 *Ibid.*, p. 8.
278 Art. 81 ADPL 2024.
279 Art. 82 ADPL 2024.

foreign states concerning the protection of individuals who reside in those states.[280]

2 Independence

In Albania, the public authority responsible for overseeing data protection is the AC ("Komisionieri per te Drejten e Informimit dhe Mbrojtjen e te Dhenave Personale" in Albanian). As outlined in the ADPL 2024, the AC is an independent public legal entity tasked with supervising and monitoring the protection of personal data with the aim of protecting the rights and fundamental freedoms of natural persons with regard to the processing of personal data.[281]

The AC reports to the Albanian Parliament and is dismissed by Parliament.[282] The AC submits an annual report to Parliament and reports in front of Parliament when asked to do so.[283]

The role of the Commissioner as a head of AC office is incompatible with any other state function, political party affiliation and participation in their activities, or any other profitable activity.[284] The ADPL 2024 stipulates that a Commissioner shall act in complete independence when performing their duties and exercising their powers in accordance with this law, and shall not be influenced, either directly or indirectly, and shall not seek or receive instructions.[285]

The ADPL 2024 outlines the criteria for appointing an Albanian citizen as the head of the AC's office: Eligible candidates must hold a university degree in law, possess extensive knowledge and experience in the field of human rights and fundamental freedoms, in particular, in the field of personal data protection and the right to information, possess a minimum of fifteen years of experience as a legal professional, have no criminal convictions and not have held the office of member of the Council of Ministers or deputy during the last 4 (four) years.[286] In comparison to the old legislation, this is the first time that there is a provision related to the knowledge of data protection law and experience in this field. This requirement is in line with the provisions of the GDPR, which mandate that each member of supervisory authority needs to have the necessary qualifications, experience,

280 *Ibid.*
281 Art. 75 ADPL 2024.
282 Artt. 76, 78 and 80 ADPL 2024.
283 Art. 82(2) ADPL 2024.
284 Art. 76(2) ADPL 2024.
285 Art. 76(1) ADPL 2024.
286 Art. 79 ADPL 2024.

and skills, particularly in the area of personal data protection, to carry out their duties and exercise their powers.[287]

3 Powers

The AC is entrusted with several responsibilities that can be categorised as follows: supervisory powers, correction powers, advisory and authorisation powers.

Firstly, the supervisory and correction powers include conducting investigations of the compliance with ADPL 2024, issuing fines, and overseeing the execution of fines.[288] In line with this, private and public institutions are obliged to collaborate and provide all the necessary information.[289] Secondly, under the advisory powers, the AC is authorised to provide opinions to the Parliament, the Council of Ministers and other central institutions for legislative and administrative measures regarding the processing of personal data.[290] The AC also issues recommendations, guidelines, advises data controllers organises publications and training programs/modules with special attention to activities that focus on minors and data protection officers.[291] Furthermore, it releases guidelines that govern the retention period of personal data and provides guidelines on security measures in specific sectors.[292] Finally, the authorisation powers include authorisation for data transfers in case of absence of an adequacy decision or appropriate safeguards, the approval and publication of standard contractual clauses for contracts between controllers and processors, and binding company rules.[293]

4 Challenges

The AC has many powers comparable to Chapter 6 GDPR, such as the power to conduct investigations, impose fines and handle complaints from data subjects. Nevertheless, several challenges are present. Notably, the AC's institutional capacity is understaffed, which is particularly challenging as it is responsible for enforcing both data protection and public information rights legislation.[294] This issue has been repeatedly highlighted in the EU Commission's annual reports for Alba-

287 Art. 58(2) GDPR.
288 *Ibid.*
289 Art. 84 ADPL 2024.
290 Art. 82 ADPL 2024.
291 *Ibid.*
292 *Ibid.*
293 *Ibid.*
294 RCC Report 2020, p. 27 (n. 18).

nia.[295] The WP25 Guidelines note that "consideration should also be given to the staff and budget of the supervisory authority" when considering the procedural and enforcement mechanism of the supervisory authority.[296] Given the lack of resources and personnel, the AC will likely face significant challenges in preparing private and public sector for the changes that were introduced by the ADPL 2024.

It's worth to note that the ADPL 2024 introduces some changes that pertain to the role of the AC and aim to improve its role. Specifically, it included that the Commissioner needs to have knowledge in the field of data protection. Furthermore, the ADPL 2024 endows the AC with stronger and more comprehensive powers that are derived from GDPR provisions, compared to the powers this institution had under the previous legislation. The ADPL 2024 adds a provision under which the AC's office must be equipped with the requisite human, technical, and financial resources, as well as the necessary infrastructure and environment, for effective duty performance and exercise of powers.[297] This provision is optimistic, as resource allocation has remained a significant challenge for the AC. Given that the AC is now set to receive stronger inspection and corrective powers, it is of paramount importance that the AC has the appropriate resources to effectively fulfil its duties.

5 Conclusion to III

When assessing the adequacy of the data protection framework in a non-EU country, the EU Commission has to take into account the existence and effectiveness of an autonomous supervisory authority with the task of monitoring and enforcing compliance with data protection rules. The AC is responsible for this function in Albania, operating independently in accordance with the ADPL 2024. However, the AC faces challenges that may impede its autonomy as a regulatory watchdog. In particular, the AC's institutional capacity and resources are limited, hampering its ability to effectively enforce data protection legislation.

IV Case Law and Enforcement

Despite ongoing efforts to align personal data protection legislation with EU standards, which brought also the adoption of the ADPL 2024, mass data breaches re-

295 RCC Report 2020, p. 27, (n. 18). See also EU Commission Report for Albania 2022, SWD(2022) 332 final (12.10.2022), p. 26.
296 WP29 Adequacy Referential, p. 7 (n. 155).
297 Art. 77 ADPL 2024.

main prevalent in Albania.[298] This was highlighted also by the EU Commission in its 2023 Report on Albania. The AC's Report for 2021 notes that unlawful personal data leaks constitute over 25 % of all complaints from data subjects.[299] Neverthe-less, the number of data subject complaints appears to be increasing, indicating a potential rise in awareness among data subjects. The present part will only consider cases before the AC,[300] including those that have raised public concerns.

1 Complaints and Investigations Before the Supervisory Authority

The AC publishes on annual base the reports on its activities in the field of data protection.[301] In the latest available report, the AC's office noted an increase in the number of data subjects' complaints.[302] The majority of complaints (nearly 60 %) relate to non-compliance with the right of access, over 25 % of complaints pertaining to unlawful personal data leaks, and the remainder relating to direct marketing.[303]

Furthermore, the AC conducted 46 administrative inquiries in 2021, a decrease compared to the highest number of investigations performed in 2019 (190).[304] It appears that the AC was less active after 2020, despite the increasing number of complaints. This could be due to a lack of staff and other resources.

During the administrative inquiry process in the course of 2021, the AC noted several issues, including an inadequate level of knowledge of data protection standards of data controllers and processors with a lack of willingness to fulfil and comply with the provisions of ADPL, lack of attention to taking technical and organisational measures, lack of data processing agreements with processors, and systematic non-compliance with legislation by all controllers regarding their responsibility to seek feedback and opinions from the AC's office on draft acts, laws, and bylaws pertaining to personal data.[305]

---

298 EU Commission Report for Albania 2023, SWD(2023) 690 final (8.11.2023), p. 28.
299 The AC's Annual Report 2021, p. 20 (n. 217).
300 Cases before national courts were not taken into account due to the language barrier.
301 Art. 30(1)(h) ADPL 2008. All AC's activity reports are available in English at the following link <https://www.idp.al/annual-reports/?lang=en> (accessed on 29.03.2023).
302 The AC' Annual Report 2021, p. 20 (n. 217).
303 *Ibid.*
304 The AC's Annual Report 2018, p. 21 available at the following link <https://www.idp.al/wp content/uploads/2019/03/ENGLISH_Annual_Report_2018_KDIMDP.pdf> (accessed on 20.03.2023).
305 AC's Annual Report 2021, p. 22 (n. 217). Similar issues were identified in previous years based on the Annual AC's annual reports (n. 217).

2 Data Leaks Scandals

Notably, in 2021, there were three high-profile data breaches cases of mass personal and sensitive data leaks, which will be discussed in this Section. Information regarding these cases was primarily obtained through an interview with Erida Skendaj, Executive Director of the Albanian Helsinki Committee in December 2021 (hereinafter: "Interview with Director of Albanian Helsinki").

a) Patronage System

In the first case, the Socialist Party in Albania published a database of personal and sensitive data of almost 900,000 Albanian voters during the pre-election period.[306] The database contained detailed personal information, such as ethnicity, religion, gender, Facebook profiles, place of work, voting records, health information, and employment status, including the employment status of their family members.[307] The data was collected through various means, including the 'patronage system' that allowed for the collection of data without the consent of relevant data subjects.[308] Concretely, this patronage system allowed to collect data of third persons without their consent, via the column 'recommend your friend'.[309] Following this data leak, the AC performed an ex officio investigation, which resulted in several recommendations issued to the Socialist Party, including the recommendation to assure that the prior consent is collected when using the column 'recommend your friend' and to improve the security of personal data.[310] The Special Prosecution against Corruption and Organised Crime (hereinafter: "SPAK") launched also an investigation into the media portal that first published informa-

---

306 Interview with the Director of the Albanian Helsinki Committee conducted in December 2021. See also Gjergj Erebara, "Albania Prosecutors Investigate Socialists' Big-Brother-Style Database", *Balkan Insight* (16.04.2021), article available at the following link <https://balkaninsight.com/2021/04/16/albania-prosecutors-investigate-over-socialist-party-big-brother/> (accessed on 02.09.2022).

307 Article "Soldiers among Albanian Ruling Party's Voter Tracking 'Army'" Eurasia, article available at the following link <https://eurasia.ro/2021/04/23/police-soldiers-among-albanian-ruling-partys-voter-tracking-army/>; Analysis "Police, Soldiers among Albanian Ruling Party's Voter Tracking 'Army'", Balkaninsight, available at the following link <https://balkaninsight.com/2021/04/21/police-soldiers-among-albanian-ruling-partys-voter-tracking-army/> 21.04.2021 (both accessed on 28.08.2022).

308 According to the Director of the Albanian Helsinki Committee "the Patronage system is one whereby every person in the country has a 'patronazhist'. This is a low-ranking party official or even just a party member who is assigned several members of the public to 'watch over'."

309 Interview with the Director of the Albanian Helsinki Committee (n. 306).

310 AC's Recommendation no 44 to Socialist Party of Albania, (19.08.2021), available only in Albanian at the following link <https://www.idp.al/rekomandime-2021/> (accessed on 02.09.2022).

tion about the database, but no similar investigations were conducted on the other government institutions or political party.[311] The EU Commission's 2021 Report on Albania also urged the authorities responsible for implementing its decision making.[312] The Albanian Helsinki Committee expressed also concerns over the reaction of the AC, and stated that it is not clear if the administrative investigation was comprehensive enough in the sense that it scrutinized the whole computer system of the 'patronage system'. They also criticised that the recommendations addressed to the Socialist Party do not contain a clear deadline but are referred to be addressed in continuity.[313]

b) WhatsApp Data Leak(s)

In the second and third cases, sensitive information was published and distributed through WhatsApp. The second case affected around 600,000 public and private sector employees, whose names, ID numbers, employer names, job positions and salaries of January and April 2021 were published.[314] The third data leak which happened in December 2021 contained information of vehicle license plates/ model/ colour and other data of over 500,000 Albanian private citizens and businesses.[315] The AC launched an administrative investigation and was interacting with the parent company of WhatsApp, Meta, to take measures for minimising the risks of further violations.[316]

311 Article "ECHR Ruling in Privacy Case Shows Similarities to Albania's Massive Data Leak" published on the Exit news portal, available at the following link <https://exit.al/en/echr-ruling-in-privacy-case-shows-similarities-to-albanias-massive-data-leak/> (accessed on 02.09.2022).

312 EU Commission Report Albania 2021, pp. 27–28, available at the following link <https://ec.europa.eu/neighbourhood-enlargement/albania-report-2021_en> (accessed on 23.03.2023).

313 The concern was expressed in the Interview with the Director of the Albanian Helsinki Committee (n. 306).

314 The AC's Annual Report 2021, p, 25 (n. 217); See also Catalin Cimpanu, "Personal and salary data for 637,138 Albanian citizens leaks online", published on The Record, (23.12.2021), available at the following link <https://therecord.media/personal-and-salary-data-for-637138-albanian-citizens-leaks-online> (accessed on 02.09.2022).

315 The AC's Annual Report 2021, p. 25 (n. 217); See also Eduart Halili, "Commissioner Asked to Close Probe on Salaries, Plates Data Leak Scandal", (02.05.2022), available at the following link <https://albaniandailynews.com/news/commissioner-asked-to-close-probe-on-salaries-plates-data-leak-scandal> (accessed on 02.09.2022).

316 The AC's Annual Report 2021, p. 25 (n. 217).

3 Conclusion to IV

While it seems that the AC is active in working to address complaints and investigate cases of non-compliance with data protection laws, the cases of mass data breaches in Albania have highlighted that the system does not necessarily ensure a good level of compliance with the data protection legislation. The above-mentioned cases demonstrate the need for stronger measures to protect personal data in Albania, and the importance of active enforcement and investigations by the AC. The EU Commission's 2021 and 2023 Report on Albania urged the authorities to take steps to implement decision-making in this regard. The Albanian Helsinki Committee also expressed concerns over the AC's investigation and the need for a comprehensive examination of the patronage system. It is essential that measures are taken to ensure the protection of personal data and that any violations are appropriately addressed to prevent further breaches and ensure better compliance.

V Conclusion to A

Albania has recently adopted the new legislation with the aim to align it with the GDPR. The ADPL 2024 mirrors the provisions of the GDPR. Nevertheless, ensuring a good level of compliance remains a significant challenge, which is a crucial element for the adoption of adequacy decisions.

This has been demonstrated with the level of implementation of the former data protection legislation – ADPL 2008. One of the biggest challenges in the implementation of ADPL 2008 was the lack of knowledge and understanding among controllers and processors of their obligations. While multinational and domestic technology companies in Albania are generally more familiar with the requirements of data protection legislation and the GDPR, many small and medium-sized private companies and public institutions are unaware of their obligations arising from their data processing activities, despite awareness campaigns organised by the AC.[317] The lack of awareness among public institutions is even more worrying, given the data leak scandals discussed previously. This can be partly attributed to the mild penal policy provided in the ADPL 2008, as well as to the practice of the AC, which tended to issue mere recommendations to infringing entities prior to imposing fines under the ADPL 2008.[318] With the adoption of the new GDPR-like data protection law, private and public entities may face new

---

317 RCC Report 2020, p. 30 (n. 18).
318 *Ibid.*

challenges implementing new principles and standards, such as accountability principle. An additional challenge to this is that the new GDPR-like law is without Recitals, which are an important guidance for understanding the GDPR provisions.

Data subjects also exhibit a low level of understanding regarding their data protection and privacy rights, which compounds the challenges of enforcing data protection laws in Albania.[319] Nonetheless, the AC's annual reports show an increase in the number of complaints from data subjects, which indicates that citizens are aware of and recognise the rights guaranteed by the law on the protection of personal data. Finally, a better level of compliance may be ensured, as the adoption of the new GDPR-like law gives the AC greater powers, including the right to impose higher fines, which may motivate data controllers and processors to start implementing data protection standards.

B Bosnia and Herzegovina (BiH)

BiH is an EU candidate country. The SAA was signed between the EU and BiH in 2008 and came into effect in 2015.[320] Subsequently, in February 2016, BiH submitted an application for EU membership.[321] The EU Commission formulated its opinion (known as "Avis") on the country's EU membership application in May 2019, outlining 14 critical priorities that BiH must satisfy to start EU accession negotiations.[322] This opinion provided a comprehensive roadmap for significant reforms in areas such as democracy, the rule of law, fundamental rights, and public ad-

319 Indicated in the RCC Report 2020 (n. 18) and by the Albanian Helsinki Committee (n. 306). See also Gliqiri Riza, "GDPR and personal data protection in non- EU countries: Albanian case of data protection legislation," University of Tirana, Faculty of Economics, Tirana, Albania, RTA-CSIT (May 2021).

320 Council Decision (EU) 2015/997 of 16 June 2008 on the signing on behalf of the European Community of the Stabilisation and Association Agreement between the European Communities and their Member States, of the one part, and Bosnia and Herzegovina, of the other part, 2015, O.J. (L164), available at the following link <https://eur-lex.europa.eu/legal-content/EN/TXT/?uri=CELEX%3A32015D0997> (accessed on 01.09.2021).

321 See for a complete timeline of BiH accession: European Neighbourhood Policy and Enlargement Negotiations available at the following link <https://neighbourhood-enlargement.ec.europa.eu/enlargement-policy/bosnia-and-herzegovina_en> (accessed on 22.04.2023).

322 Commission Opinion on Bosnia and Herzegovina's application for membership of the European Union, 29.5.2019 {SWD(2019) 222 final}, available at the following link <https://neighbourhood-enlargement.ec.europa.eu/system/files/2019-05/20190529-bosnia-and-herzegovina-opinion.pdf> (accessed on 21.09.2021).

ministration reform. Finally, in late 2022 BiH was recognised by the EU as a 'candidate country' for accession, signifying that the country has taken important steps towards meeting the criteria for EU membership, but still expressed its concerns over limited progress in reforms of rule of law.[323] BiH is under Art. 79 SAA obliged to harmonise its national data protection legislation with the EU acquis, which includes the establishment of an independent supervisory authority.

I Constitutional Parameters and International Commitments

The General Framework Agreement for Peace in Bosnia and Herzegovina, signed on 14 December 1995 (hereinafter: "Dayton Agreement"), established the basic principles of the state and political organisation of BiH.[324] An integral component of the Dayton Agreement is the Constitution of BiH, set out in Annex 4 (hereinafter: "Constitution of BiH").[325] The Constitution of BiH guarantees the right to private and family life, home and correspondence.[326] In contrast to other WB6' constitutions, data protection is not guaranteed by the Constitution of BiH. However, the Constitution of BiH stipulates that the rights and freedoms enshrined in the ECHR are directly applicable and take precedence over all other laws.[327] Therefore, although not explicitly mentioned, data protection is considered a basic right on the constitutional level through the application of the ECHR in BiH.

It is also worth noting that the two entities of BiH have separate constitutions, namely the Constitution of the Federation of Bosnia and Herzegovina[328] (herei-

---

323 Council of the European Union Enlargement and Stabilisation and Association Process, 15935/22, 13 December 2022, paras. 82–86, available at the following link <https://www.consilium.europa.eu/media/60797/st15935-en22.pdf> (accessed on 22.04.2023).

324 Dayton Agreement. Annex 11: Agreement on International Police Force, available at the following link <https://peacemaker.un.org/sites/peacemaker.un.org/files/BA_951121_DaytonAgreement.pdf>, (accessed on 22.04.2023). The Dayton Agreement divides the country into two federal entities: the Federation of Bosnia and Herzegovina (FBiH) and the Republika Srpska and one condominium named the Brčko District.

325 Constitution of BiH no. 327/09, 26 March 2009.

326 Article II (3)(f) Constitution of BiH.

327 Article II (2) Constitution of BiH.

328 Constitution of the Federation of Bosnia and Herzegovina (Official Gazette of FBiH, no. 1/1994, 1/1994 - Amendment I, 13/1997 - Amendments II–XXIV, 13/1997 - Amendments XXV and XXVI, 16/2002 - Amendments XXVII -LIV, 22/2002 - Amendments LVI–LXIII, 52/2002 - Amendments LXIV–LXXXVII, 60/2002 - Amendment LXXXI, 18/2003 - Amendment LXXXVIII, 63/2003 - Amendments LXXXIX–XCIV, 9/2004 - Amendments XCV–CII, 32/2007 - corr., 20/2004 - Amendments CIII and CIV, 33/2004 - Amendment CV, 71/2005 - Amendments CVI–CVIII, 72/2005 - Amendment CVI, 88/2008 -

nafter: “Federation Constitution”) and the Constitution of the Republika Srpska[329] (hereinafter: “RS Constitution”). The Federation Constitution only recognises the right to privacy in Art. 2(1)(g), whereas the RS Constitution recognises both the right to privacy (Art. 13) and the right to data protection (Art. 23). The latter article is relatively extensive, stipulating “Protection of secrecy of personal data shall be guaranteed. Collection, processing and the purpose of the use of personal data shall be regulated by law. The use of personal data contrary to the determined purpose of their collection shall be prohibited. Citizens shall be entitled to demand and receive all data on them contained in acts of State bodies and other official registers.”

Last but not least, looking at the other international instruments relevant for data protection, BiH has ratified the Convention 108. In July 2020, BiH signed the Protocol (CETS no. 223) and in July 2023 has ratified it.[330]

1 Conclusion to I

Data protection in BiH is governed by a complex legal framework that includes international treaties, national laws, and constitutions both on the level of the state and its two entities. Despite the absence of explicit constitutional recognition of data protection in the Constitution of BiH, data protection is implicitly recognised as a fundamental right via direct application of the ECHR standards and jurisprudence, which also take precedence over all other laws. Furthermore, one of the entities, Republika Srpska, also recognises data protection on a constitutional level. As BiH moves towards EU accession, it must ensure that its data protection legislation is aligned with EU standards and continue to prioritise the protection of personal data as a fundamental right.

Amendment CIX , 79/2022 - Amendments CX – CXXX, 80/2022 - correction and 31/2023 - Amendment CXXXI).

329 Constitution of Republika Srpska (Official Gazette of the Republic of Srpska, no. 21/92 – revised text, 28/94, 8/96, 13/96, 15/96, 16/96, 21/96, 21/02, 26/02, 30/02, 31/02, 69/02, 31/03, 98/03, 115/05, 117/05).

330 Council of Europe, Bosnia and Herzegovina and Malta, two new signatures for Convention 108+, available at the following link <https://www.coe.int/en/web/data-protection/-/bosnia-and-herzegovina-and-malta-two-new-signatures-for-convention-108-> (accessed on 22.04.2023); A comprehensive overview of all parties to the Convention 108+ is available at the website of Council of Europe <https://www.coe.int/en/web/conventions/full-list?module=signatures-by-treaty&treatynum=223> (accessed on 04.02.2023).

II Data Protection Legislation

Pursuant to the Constitution of BiH and the Convention 108, BiH has enacted the Personal Data Protection Law (hereinafter: "BDPL 2006") in 2006.[331] This is the second-generation data protection legislation in BiH. The first data protection law of 2001[332] already established a number of key data protection concepts, including controllers and processors, special categories of personal data, principles of data protection and provided some limited penalty provisions. The current data protection law, BDPL 2006, was modelled on the DPD and is not aligned with the GDPR.

1 Status Quo of GDPR Alignment

BiH has not yet harmonised its legislation in the area of personal data protection with the GDPR, although efforts towards legislative harmonisation have been initiated. The supervisory authority has prepared a new draft law on data protection and published it for public consultations in 2018.[333] The Ministry of Justice subsequently submitted numerous objections and suggestions, that ultimately led to a failure to reach an agreement, resulting in the proposed law not being sent to the further legislative process.[334] In view of this, the Ministry of Justice and the supervisory authority jointly concluded that the EU Delegation to BiH should be involved in the process of drafting the new law.[335]

Despite attempts to harmonise the current legislation, there appears to be limited support for its adoption. The supervisory authority has repeatedly expressed concerns over the lack of progress in the legislative process and called on the Council of Ministers of BiH and the Parliamentary Assembly to adopt a new legal framework on data protection so that "Bosnia and Herzegovina like other neighbouring countries can reach the required level of personal data protec-

331 Personal Data Protection Law (Official Gazette of Bosnia and Herzegovina, no. 49/2006, 76/2011 and 89/2011 – correction).

332 Personal Data Protection Law (Official Gazette of Bosnia and Herzegovina, no. 32/01).

333 See for more information and the available text of the draft law: Anisa Tomić, "Bosnia & Herzegovina – Data Protection Overview", OneTrust Data Guidance (August 2022) available at the following link <https://www.dataguidance.com/notes/bosnia-herzegovina-data-protection-overview> (accessed on 22.04.2023).

334 This information was provided by the Civil Ministry, via an email on 26.11.2021. Since then, no other information is publicly available.

335 *Ibid.*

tion".[336] In an interview given to the BBC in 2019, one of the employees of the supervisory authority stated: "Law enforcement is difficult when there is no support, in 2017, this agency informed the Council of Ministers of Bosnia and Herzegovina that it is urgent to adjust the law from 2006 to the new legislation of the European Union. At that moment, there was no adequate reaction."[337] In early 2023, the director of the supervisory authority stated, "Regarding legal protection, I can freely say that the level of legal protection that the citizens of BiH have is inferior to that of citizens of neighbouring countries."[338] He further noted that a new law had been drafted but had yet to be adopted.[339]

As a result, BiH now faces the challenge of both enforcing the current data protection framework and harmonising it with the EU acquis. This Section will not only focus on the provisions of the BDPL 2006 but will also provide an overview of the currently proposed draft law in part IV.

2 Overview of the BDPL 2006

BDPL 2006 consists of six parts. Part 1 covers the general provisions and includes the scope of the law and definitions (first chapter). Part 2 contains diverse provisions, including the principles governing data processing, rules governing consent, special categories of personal data, security of personal data, obligations of controllers and processors, rules governing data transfers, and rules for special processing situations, all of which are contained in its second chapter. Part 3 defines rights of data subject (third chapter). Part 4 clarifies the role of the supervisory authority and its functions and powers (fourth chapter). Part 5 includes misdemeanours provisions (fifth chapter). Lastly, part 6 contains transitional and final provisions, including rules for the adoption of bylaws, and constitutes the sixth and final chapter.

---

336 Annual Report on Data Protection in BiH for 2020, no. 01–02–4–661–1/21, (04.06.2021) p. 59 and the Annual Report on Data Protection in BiH for 2021, no. 01–02–4–489–1/22 (22.06.2022).
337 Petra Živić, "Problemi sa ličnim podacima na Balkanu: Od ličnih karata do video nadzora" (Eng: Problems with personal data in the Balkans: From ID cards to video surveillance), BBC News (08.10.2019), available at the following link <https://www.bbc.com/serbian/lat/balkan-49919849> (accessed on 24.05.2022).
338 Dragoljub Reljić, "Potrebno usvajanje novog zakona o zaštiti ličnih podataka" (Eng: The adoption of a new law on the protection of personal data is necessary) TRT Balkan, (27.02.2023), available at the following link <https://bhsc.trtbalkan.com/region/bih-potrebno-usvajanje-novog-zakona-o-zastiti-licnih-podataka-11841199> (accessed on 22.04.2023).
339 *Ibid.*

3 Scope of the BDPL 2006

The material scope of the application of the BDPL 2006 is explicitly defined in Art. 2. It applies to personal data processed by all public bodies, natural and legal persons, but excludes personal data processed by natural persons exclusively for personal or household activities.[340] The BDPL 2006, as opposed to the GDPR, also applies to deceased persons. As outlined in Art. 3, the declared legal successors of the deceased inherit the ownership of their personal data. This provision has been found to be important in practice, particularly in the area of inheritance law. For instance, in a case where a bank refused to disclose information to the heirs of a deceased individual citing privacy concerns, the supervisory authority held that the deceased was no longer a legal subject and their personal and property rights had been transferred to the beneficiaries at the time of their death.[341] In another case, directed against the Sarajevo Canton Memorial Fund, the supervisory authority imposed administrative measures for processing copies of ID cards not only of applicants for the burial of a deceased individual but also of copies of ID cards pertaining to deceased persons.[342]

The MDPL 2006 does not explicitly specify its territorial scope. Nevertheless, the objective of this law, as stated in Art. 1, is to safeguard human rights and fundamental freedoms, including the right to privacy and data protection in relation to the processing of personal data "for all individuals present within the territory of Bosnia and Herzegovina, regardless of their nationality or residency". As such, the aim of the law implies a territorial scope covering all individuals residing within BiH's borders.

Furthermore, exterritorial elements of the BDPL 2006 can be found in Art. 12(a). This provision stipulates that controllers who are not established within the territory of BiH but use automated or other equipment in BiH for personal data processing must designate a representative for such processing, unless they solely use such equipment to transfer data through BiH. This provision originates from the DPD and was incorporated into BiH's applicable law through legislative amendments in 2011.[343] This kind of extraterritorial scope is not in line with Art. 3 GDPR.[344]

340 Art. 2 BDPL 2006.

341 Annual Report 2021, p. 36 (n. 336).

342 *Ibid*, p. 29.

343 The Law on Amendments to the Law on the Protection of Personal Data, no: 01,02–02–1–2/11 September 14, 2011.

344 Exterritorial effect under the DPD was also explained in Chapter 4, A.II.3.

4 Data Protection Principles

In accordance with the BDPL 2006, all personal data, regardless of their type, categories of data subjects, and the scope of a particular processing, must be processed in compliance with explicit processing principles laid out by this law. These principles are as follows: (1) processing of personal data must be conducted lawfully and fairly, (2) personal data must be processed for specified, explicit, and legitimate purposes, (3) processing must be limited to personal data necessary for the realisation of the processing's purpose(s), (4) personal data must be accurate and, where necessary, kept up to date, and incorrect and incomplete data must be deleted or corrected, (5) personal data must not be retained longer than necessary for the purpose(s) for which they are processed, and (6) personal data obtained for various purposes may not be combined or merged.[345]

While the above data processing requirements are generally consistent with the relevant principles of the GDPR, there are specific dissimilarities. For instance, the BDPL 2006 does not explicitly provide for the principles of integrity[346] and accountability.[347] Furthermore, there is no specific requirement for transparency[348] defined as a principle.

5 Lawfulness of Processing

Pursuant to the principle of lawfulness as provided for in Art. 4(1)(b), several legal grounds are foreseen by MDPL 2006, including a data subject's consent, compliance with a legal obligation to which the data controller is subject, performance of a contract to which a data subject is party, the protection of the vital interests of the data subject (in which case the consent must be obtained without delay or the processing has to be terminated and collected data destroyed), the performance of a task carried out in the public interest, realisation of the legitimate interests pursued by the controller or by a third party (except where such interests are overridden by the interests or fundamental rights and freedoms of the data subject), and legitimate activities of political parties, movements, civic associations, trade union organisations, religious communities (except where such interests are overridden by the interests or fundamental rights and freedoms of the data subject which require protection of personal data).[349]

---

345 Art. 4 BDPL 2006.

346 Art. 5(1)(f) GDPR.

347 Art. 5(2) GDPR.

348 Art. 5(1)(a) and Recital 39 GDPR.

349 Artt. 5–6 BDPL 2006.

The legal bases foreseen in the BDPL 2006 do not fully correspond to the legal bases for data processing laid down in the GDPR. Particularly of concern is the legal ground provided for in Art. 6(1)(f) – the legitimate interest of political parties, movements, civic associations, trade union organisations and religious communities. This legal ground is not recognised by the GDPR as a legal basis for general data processing, nor was recognised by the DPD upon which the BDPL 2006 is modelled. This clause creates opportunities for misusing personal data by political parties, which often have great interest in using citizens' personal data. On a positive note, as explained further in part IV, an effect of future alignment with the GDPR will be that this 'legitimate interest' of political parties etc. as a legal ground is excluded from the proposed new law on data protection.

a) Consent

Under the GDPR, consent plays a central role as an element of permissibility for lawful data processing.[350] The GDPR has, compared to the DPD, strengthened the rules on obtaining consent by clarifying elements for consent, such as criteria for unambiguous and specific consent.[351] Recital 32 GDPR states that "consent should be given by a clear affirmative act establishing a freely given, specific, informed and unambiguous indication of the data subject's agreement [...] such as by a written statement, including by electronic means, or an oral statement. This could include ticking a box when visiting an internet website, choosing technical settings for information society services [...]." Thus, the GDPR sets out also the rules on obtaining consent electronically.

In contrast, the BDPL 2006 provides limited rules on consent, only requiring the controller to prove, upon request by the supervisory authority, that consent was really obtained for the period of personal data processing[352] and that the consent may be withdrawn at any time.[353] The BDPL 2006 sets out special provisions on consent for special categories of personal data. It requires that consent for the processing of a special category of personal data must be given in writing and signed by the data subject.[354] This means that a data controller must obtain a physical signature from the data subject indicating their agreement to the process-

350 Bürgen Kühling and Benedikt Buchner, "Art. 7 DS-GVO Bedingungen für die Einwilligung" in Jürgen Kühling and Benedikt Buchner, Datenschutz-Grundverordnung, Bundesdatenschutzgesetz: DS-GVO/BDSG (3rd edn, C.H. Beck 2020) para 9.

351 See also WP29, Guidelines on Consent under Regulation 2016/679 (wp259rev.01).

352 Art. 5(3) BDPL 2006.

353 Art. 5(4) BDPL 2006.

354 Art. 5(2) BDPL 2006.

ing of their sensitive data. This requirement may present practical difficulties in the context of electronic processing of personal data. With most companies processing personal data electronically, obtaining a physical signature from data subjects for sensitive data processing may be inconvenient, time-consuming, and potentially costly. The GDPR does not require written consent for the processing of special categories of personal data. Instead, the GDPR requires that consent for sensitive data processing be 'explicit', meaning that it must be given through a clear affirmative action by the data subject.[355]

6 Special Categories of Personal Data

The same as under the GDPR, the BDPL 2006 envisages for a general prohibition of special categories of personal data.[356] According to the BDPL 2006 special categories of data include all personal data that reveal: a) racial origin, national or ethnic origin, political opinion or party affiliation, or trade union membership, religious, philosophical or other beliefs, health status, genetic code and sexual life; b) criminal convictions; c) biometric data.[357] This definition of special categories of personal data does not contradict Art. 9 GDPR, however, it is not entirely aligned either. In particular, data relating to a natural person's sexual orientation is not included in the BDPL 2006, while some other data not considered as special categories of personal data by the GDPR are provided for in the BDPL 2006 (such as data relating to criminal convictions).

Furthermore, as already mentioned, obtaining consent for processing special categories of personal data under the BDPL 2006 does not conform to the GDPR's provisions. Specifically, the BDPL 2006 does not allow for online consent forms, which is not in line with day-to-day business practices of companies. Other exceptions under which processing of special categories of personal data may be allowed are in general in line with the Art. 9(2) GDPR.[358]

---

355 Art. 9(2)(a) GDPR.

356 Art. 9(1) BDPL 2006.

357 Art 3(1) BDPL 2006.

358 Art. 9(2) BDPL 2006 includes the same exceptions as Art. 9 (2) GDPR, such as consent, vital interests, data made public by the data subject, etc. However, Art. 9 (2) (b) specifies, besides the protection of vital interests, also "the protection of the life, health, property and other vital interests of the data subject or of another person from whom consent cannot be obtained, in particular if the person is physically, mentally or legally incapacitated, or if the person is considered to be missing, or for other similar reasons".

7 Rights of Data Subject

In chapter three, the BDPL 2006 outlines various rights that are afforded to data subjects, including the right to request information on a particular processing (which corresponds to Art. 13 and 14 GDPR),[359] right to access,[360] and right to obtain a copy.[361] Additionally, data subjects have the right to rectification (e.g., if the processed data's accuracy is contested by the data subject), deletion and processing's cessation,[362] and the right to object to the data processing (e.g., if the processing is based on a legitimate interest or performed for direct marketing purposes).[363] They also have the right not to be subject to a decision based solely on automated processing, which produces legal effects concerning the data subject or significantly affects them.[364]

These rights tend to be consistent with the GDPR but differ in a few respects. First of all, the BDPL 2006 does not recognise the right to data portability, an innovation in data protection law introduced by the GDPR. The aim of the GDPR was to give data subjects back control over their personal data, also via giving them the possibility of at least transferring their personal data to the processing system of another controller and possibly even having it transferred directly between controllers.[365] Given that the BDPL 2006 predates the GDPR, this is not reflected in the text of the law. Secondly, the right to obtain a copy of the personal data is regulated differently compared to Art. 15(3) GDPR. The BDPL 2006 does not use term 'copy' but rather "providing information on data processing in writing". Also, this right is limited financially. The data subject can only receive a free copy once a year, and for each additional copy the data subject must pay a reasonable fee.[366]

Lastly, there is also a different regime for the right not to be subject to a decision based solely on automated processing. The BDPL 2006 does not use term 'profiling'[367] but "accessing certain personal characteristics of data subject" and

359 Artt. 22–23 BDPL 2006.
360 Art. 24 BDPL 2006.
361 Art. 25 BDPL 2006.
362 Art. 27 BDPL 2006.
363 Art. 26 BDPL 2006.
364 Art. 29 BDPL 2006.
365 Carlo Piltz, "DS-GVO Art. 20 Recht auf Datenübertragbarkeit", in Gola/Heckmann, Datenschutz-Grundverordnung, Bundesdatenschutzgesetz (3d edn, C.H. Beck 2022), paras. 1–4.
366 Art. 25(3) BDPL 2006.
367 Art. 22 GDPR recognises automated decisions which can be made with or without profiling. Profiling is defined under Art. 4 4) GDPR as any form of automated processing of personal data consisting of the use of personal data to evaluate certain personal aspects relating to a natural person, in particular to analyse or predict aspects concerning that natural person's performance

only provides for two exceptions in which automated decision making may be allowed, namely the performance of a contract and the legal obligation of the controller. On the other hand, Art. 22(2)(c) GDPR also provides for consent of the data subject as a third exception.

a) Nature and Manner of Implementation of Data Subjects' Rights

As opposed to the GDPR, the BDPL 2006 does not explicitly prescribe the procedure within which the controllers are obliged to ensure realisation of the relevant rights. The GDPR here pays greater attention, by imposing the obligation on the controller to take appropriate measures to provide the data subject with the information pursuant to Art. 13 in a precise, transparent, intelligible and easily accessible form in plain and simple language.[368] Further, the controller must actively provide information e.g. by providing or purposefully leading to the information.[369] In this aspect, WP29 has provided even more detailed guidance in relation to multiple layers in the digital context and 'push' and 'pull notices' such as privacy dashboards or just in time notices.[370]

Moreover, there are no deadlines for data controllers and processor under which they shall ensure the realisation of the data subject's rights, the exception being the right to access and to obtain the copy of data which must be realised within a 30 day-term.[371]

b) Restrictions

The restrictions on data subjects' rights are provided in Art. 28 BDPL 2006. Under this article, the "data controller shall not be obliged to provide information on processing of personal data or to enable access to personal data if that action could cause significant damage to legitimate interests" of certain categories in BiH. These categories include state security, defence, public security, prevention, investigation, detection of crimes and prosecution of perpetrators as well as violations of ethical regulations of the profession, economic and financial interests,

---

at work, economic situation, health, personal preferences, interests, reliability, behaviour, location or movements. See also WP29, Guidelines on Automated individual decision-making and Profiling for the purposes of Regulation 2016/679 (wp251rev.01), (22.08.2018).

368 See also Boris P. Paal und Moritz Hennemann, "DS-GVO Art. 14 Informationspflicht, wenn die personenbezogenen Daten nicht bei der betroffenen Person erhoben wurden", DS-GVO BDSG, Paal/Pauly, (3d edn. C.H. Beck. 2021), paras. 5–6a.

369 *Ibid.*

370 Guidelines on Consent under Regulation 2016/679, pp. 18–22 (n. 351).

371 Art. 25(3) BDPL 2006.

including monetary, budgetary and tax issues, inspection and duties related to control, protection of data subjects or rights and freedoms of other people.[372]

While these restrictions align with those specified by Art. 23 GDPR, the BDPL 2006 does not explicitly state that these restrictions should only be imposed by legislative measures, nor does it specify the provisions that such measures should include to safeguard the rights of data subject. The BDPL 2006 stipulates only that "the restrictions may be allowed only to the extent required in a democratic society".[373] Yet, as an additional safeguard measure the data controller is obliged to submit to the supervisory authority an annual report on the rejected requests of the data subject.[374]

8 Redress Mechanism

The BDPL 2006 does not provide for a separate chapter on redress mechanism and liability of controllers and processors, such as the GDPR does (chapter eight). Instead, the rights to redress are established within the chapter which governs data subjects' rights (chapter three). Data subjects have the right to file a complaint with the supervisory authority if they believe that their rights have been breached or if there is a risk of such a breach.[375] Through a complaint, they may request that the controller or processor desist from any such activities and remedy any factual situations caused by such activities.[376] Additionally, data subjects may request that the controller or processor correct or amend personal data to ensure accuracy, or to block or destroy them[377] While no appeal is permitted against the supervisory authority's decision, it is possible to initiate an administrative dispute before the competent courts.[378]

Beside the right to file a complaint to the supervisory authority, data subjects also have the right to compensation for material and nonmaterial damage resulting from a breach of their right to privacy.[379] The BDPL 2006 uses the term "violation of privacy" instead of "violation of personal data," raising questions if and in which cases processing in violation of the BDPL 2006 would also constitute a breach of the right to privacy. The competent court with jurisdiction over the data subject's permanent or temporary residence, or the competent court with ju-

372 Art. 28(1) BDPL 2006.
373 Art. 28(2) BDPL 2006.
374 Art. 28(4) BDPL 2006.
375 Art. 30 BDPL 2006.
376 Art. 30(1)(a) BDPL 2006.
377 Art. 30(1)(b)(c) BDPL 2006.
378 Art. 30(3) BDPL 2006.
379 Art. 32(1) BDPL 2006.

risdiction over the controller's seat, is responsible for deciding on such complaints.[380] Furthermore, the BDPL 2006 distinguishes between a 'material' and 'non-material' damage, similar like the GDPR does. However, while the competent court determines the compensation for material damage (unless the parties reach an amicable settlement), non-material damage may be compensated via public apology and payment of a just compensation.[381] Finally, if the data processor is responsible for any damage caused, the data controller is held liable.[382]

Having in mind the above, the rules on remedies and liability are not completely in line with Chapter 8 GDPR. There is no provision for an effective judicial remedy against a controller or processor, the rules on the right to compensation are regulated differently by conditioning compensation on the violation of privacy rather than personal data protection violations and the right to complaint to the supervisory authority is restricted to specific requests such as deletion, blocking, or correction.

9 Personal Scope

The BDPL 2006 recognises the roles of data controllers and data processors. However, the law places greater responsibility on the controllers. The principles enshrined in the law apply explicitly only to the controller, as per Art. 4, which states, "the controller shall be required to [...]" and lists the principles without reference to the processor. In addition, the law imposes fines solely on controllers pursuant to Artt. 49–50, while the sanctions for non-compliance with the provisions of the BDPL 2006 are to be borne by the controller in certain circumstances, e.g., if the processor fails to provide the information requested by the supervisory authority.[383]

The BDPL 2006 stipulates that in case a controller engages another entity (processor) for processing personal data on behalf of a controller, the controller must conclude a written contract with a processor. Art. 12(2) governs the details which a data processing agreement shall include, such as the scope, purpose, and duration, as well as the processor's adequate guarantees regarding implemented TOMs and that they will act only on the basis of the controller's instructions. Moreover, the processor is responsible for processing personal data based on the controller's instructions and may not delegate this responsibility to other processors (sub-pro-

380 Art. 32(2) BDPL 2006.
381 Art. 32(4) BDPL 2006.
382 Art. 32(5) BDPL 2006.
383 Art. 49(1)(lj) BDPL 2006.

cessors), except with the explicit instruction of the data controller.[384] This mostly aligns with the logic of Art. 28 GDPR.

a) Obligations of Controller and Processor

The BDPL 2006 sets out several obligations on both data controllers and processors, aimed at safeguarding personal data and protecting the rights of data subject. These provisions are largely based on DPD and similar to the legal framework of other WB6 countries that are not yet aligned with the GDPR.

aa) Obligation to Notify

One of the obligations which stems from the DPD is the obligation to notify the supervisory authority on each data processing. The provisions on record keeping under the GDPR deviate from the strategy of notification obligations under the DPD. The DPD envisaged an authorisation-like approach, allowing data protection authorities to keep a register of data processing activities and to assess planned initiatives in advance or to intervene at an early stage. Obviously, this was not feasible and the GDPR has abolished this ex ante approach. Under the BDPL 2006, data controllers are obliged to keep records (either manually or by means of automatic data processing tools) for each database containing personal data that they have set up.[385] They are also obliged to register their records with the supervisory authority, which consolidates the data provided in the so-called 'Central Register' – open to public.[386] The processing may not commence until the supervisory authority has authorised the processing or until two months have elapsed from the date on which the supervisory authority received the request and failed to respond.[387]

bb) Specific Security Obligations

The BDPL 2006 provides for some security obligations which are also modelled upon the DPD. Under Art. 11, both data controllers and processors (within the scope of its competences) are required to take care of data security and implement TOMs necessary for the enforcement of the BDPL 2006 and other regulations concerning data protection.[388] Controllers and processors are also required to imple-

---

384 Art. 12(3)(4) BDPL 2006.
385 Art. 13 BDPL 2006 stipulates the details which such records on data processing shall include.
386 Art. 14(1)(7) BDPL 2006.
387 Art. 14(3) BDPL 2006.
388 Art. 11(1) BDPL 2006.

ment measures against unauthorised or accidental access to personal data, their alteration, destruction or loss, unauthorised transfer, other forms of illegal data processing, as well as measures against misuse of personal data.[389] Additionally, Art. 16 sets out confidentiality requirements for personal data processed by controllers or processors, which shall be considered an official secret for employees. This includes a requirement that employees engaged in the processing of personal data may process such data only under the conditions and in the scope specified by the controller or the processor.[390]

It is important to note that the BDPL 2006 fails to regulate the specific rules envisaged by the GDPR, such as the rules on data breach notifications and conducting a DPIA. Moreover, the BDPL 2006 makes no reference to security measures and concepts such as privacy by design and default, pseudonymisation or encryption of personal data, etc.

b) Third Party

The BDPL 2006 provides more detailed provisions on third parties compared to the GDPR. Third party is defined under Art. 3(c) as any natural or legal person, public authority, agency or any other body other than the data subject, controller, processor and persons under the direct jurisdiction of the controller or processor authorised to process the data.[391] This definition corresponds to the concept of third party under Art. 4(10) GDPR. The BDPL 2006 mandates that prior consent of the data subject is required for disclosing personal data to any third party, unless such disclosure is in the public interest.[392] Moreover, the controller may disclose personal data to a third party on the basis of a written request[393] provided that such disclosure is necessary for carrying out tasks within the competence specified by law or for the lawful interests of the user.[394] Additionally, controllers are obliged to keep specific records of personal data disclosed to a third party.[395] Conversely, no such detailed provisions are made for recipients.[396]

---

389 Art. 11(2) BDPL 2006.

390 Art. 16(2) BDPL 2006.

391 Art 3(c) BDPL 2006.

392 Art. 17(1) BDPL 2006.

393 Under Art. 17(3) BDPL 2006 the written request must specify the purpose and legal grounds for the personal data use, and the type of personal data requested.

394 Art. 17(2) BDPL 2006.

395 Art. 17(5) BDPL 2006.

396 Art. 3(1) only has a definition of recipients and there is no further reference to recipients in the text of the law.

c) Representative

Controllers who are not established on the territory of BIH and who use automatic or other equipment located on the territory of BIH when processing personal data must appoint a representative for such processing, unless they use that equipment only for data transit through BiH.[397] This exterritorial element for appointment of a representative is taken from the DPD as mentioned above.[398] It should also be noted that, differently in comparison to the GDPR, the respective obligation to appoint a representative is prescribed solely for foreign data controllers (i. e. foreign data processors remain out of its scope).

Nevertheless, the supervisory authority's interpretation of the representative's role appears to be rigid. This was evidenced in an opinion issued on April 7th, 2022, in response to a query from Marbo Product doo Belgrade (Marbo), a company based in Serbia that sought clarification on whether it was obliged to appoint a representative under Art. 12 BDPL 2006.[399] Marbo was planning to engage a data processor in BiH to conduct a time-limited consumer preferences survey. The supervisory authority concluded that Marbo, as a data controller, was required to appoint a representative for the processing of personal data of participants in the survey in BiH.[400] This query was particularly intriguing as the processing was only temporary and intended for conducting the survey. In contrast, under the GDPR, controllers established outside the EU are not obliged to appoint representatives for processing which is "occasional, does not include, on a large scale, processing of special categories [...] and is unlikely to result in a risk to the rights and freedoms of natural persons, taking into account the nature, context, scope and purposes of the processing".[401]

10 Transfer of Personal Data

The regulation of data transfers under the BDPL 2006 is not as comprehensive as that under the GDPR. Art. 18 BDPL 2006 permits the transfer of personal data to countries or international organisations that "implement adequate safeguards for

397 Art. 12 BDPL 2006.

398 Article 4(1)(c) DPD reads as follows: "the controller is not established on Community territory and, for purposes of processing personal data makes use of equipment, automated or otherwise, situated on the territory of the said Member State."

399 Opinion of the supervisory authority "Application of the Personal Data Protection Law to a controller not based in Bosnia and Herzegovina" (from 07.04.2021), available in Bosnian at the website of supervisory authority at the following link <http://www.azlp.ba/misljenja/Archive.aspx?langTag=bs-BA&template_id=149&pageIndex=1> (accessed on 22.04.2023).

400 *Ibid.*

401 Art. 27(2) GDPR.

personal data."[402] This concept seems to be similar to the concept of adequacy decision under Art. 45 GDPR. The adequacy of safeguards is assessed based on the specific characteristics of each transfer, such as the type of personal data, the purpose and duration of processing, the destination country, relevant legal rules in the respective jurisdiction, and other relevant circumstances.[403]

Furthermore, Art. 18(3) BDPL 2006 permits data transfers to countries that do not provide adequate safeguards, but only in special cases similar to those provided under Art. 49 GDPR.[404] Moreover, in exceptional circumstances, even if none of the special cases under Art. 18(4) apply, data can be legitimately transferred out of BiH if the supervisory authority approves the transfer and a data controller in the recipient country provides sufficient safeguards for the protection of privacy and fundamental rights and freedoms of individuals or if similar rights are guaranteed under a special agreement.[405] As such, the provisions on data transfers under the BDPL 2006 are not defined extensively enough. The use of special cases for derogations seems to be rather unrestricted. Also, Art. 18(4) under which the supervisory authority may authorise data transfers, does not impose any additional restrictions, such as that the transfer is not repetitive and concerns only a limited number of data subjects.[406]

Moreover, the BDPL 2006 does not cover transfers subject to appropriate safeguards, as provided for under Art. 46 GDPR, which leaves fewer options for transfer mechanisms for data controllers and processors. Consequently, the current solution is inadequate to restrict onward transfers, a key criterion for the adoption of an adequacy decision by the EU Commission. However, the proposed new law aims to enhance the rules on data transfers, which will be elaborated in Part IV.

---

402 Art. 18(1) BDPL 2006.

403 Art. 18(2) BDPL 2006.

404 The exceptions include: the disclosure of personal data is provided for by a special law; the prior consent of the data subject whose data are transferred has been obtained and the data subject has been informed of the possible consequences of the data transfer; the disclosure of personal data is necessary for the performance of the contract between the data subject and the controller or the fulfilment of pre-contractual obligations undertaken at the request of the person whose data are processed; the transfer of personal data is necessary to save the life or vital interests of the data subject; the personal data are transferred from files or records which are accessible to the public in accordance with law or other regulations; the transfer of personal data is necessary for reasons of the public interest; the transfer of personal data is necessary for the conclusion or performance of a contract between the controller and a third party when the contract is in the interest of the data subject.

405 Art. 18(4) BDPL 2006.

406 Such limitations are listed in Art. 49(2) GDPR.

11 Penalties

Penal provisions are outlined in chapter five of the BDPL 2006, wherein the power to impose fines rests with the supervisory authority.[407] It is important to note that the fines specified in the BDPL 2006 are considerably lower compared to those of the GDPR. The BDPL 2006 provides for civil liability in case of non-compliance with its provisions, with the maximum fines being BAM 100,000 (equivalent to approximately €50,000) for a legal entity, and BAM 15,000 (equivalent to approximately €7,000) for a natural person or a representative of a legal entity per offence. These pecuniary penalties are not compatible with the GDPR, which stipulates more substantial fines.

12 Specific Processing Situations

The BDPL 2006 outlines several specific situations in which personal data processing is permissible. These situations are not addressed in a distinct chapter, but rather are covered in the chapter that establishes the fundamental principles governing lawful data processing (chapter 2). The specific situations include processing personal data in mass media (Art. 19), data processing for statistical, historical and scientific purposes (Art. 20), publication of personal data in research institutes (Art. 21), and processing personal data through video surveillance (Art. 21a).

It is worth noting that Art. 19(2) – regulating processing of personal data in mass media – explicitly excludes the application of the BDPL 2006 (except for provisions concerning security and confidentiality, as well as liability for damages). Also, the BDPL 2006 does not include all specific situations of personal data processing that are provided for under the GDPR, such as national identification numbers or employment.[408] Furthermore, there are no specific safeguards in place for the processing of personal data for statistical, historical, and scientific purposes under the BDPL 2006.[409]

13 Conclusion to II

The current data protection framework in BiH does not meet all the EU standards. The BDPL 2006 is largely derived from the DPD and still contains some outdated provisions, such as the requirement to notify the BA of data processing activities. Additionally, the BDPL 2006 envisages some concerning legal grounds for data

---

407 Art. 41(1)(k) BDPL 2006.
408 As provided by Artt. 87–88 GDPR.
409 As provided by Art. 89 GDPR.

processing, such as the legal interest of political parties. The provisions relating to consent are particularly problematic, as there is a lack of specificity with regards to the method by which consent should be obtained. Furthermore, consent for the processing of sensitive personal data can only be obtained in writing. The legislation also fails to provide clear guidelines on the means by which data subjects' rights should be exercised, such as providing transparent information on data processing in an intelligible and easily accessible form using plain and simple language. Also, the rules on data transfers are not aligned with the GDPR either and may not satisfy the criteria for restricting onward transfers. The BDPL 2006 further lacks some provisions related to specific processing of personal data, such as ID numbers or for employment purposes (which are among the most common causes of data breaches as discussed in part V). Finally, the fines stipulated in the BDPL 2006 are significantly lower than those outlined in the GDPR.

Hence, the current legal framework still does not meet the criteria required for the adoption of an adequacy decision. Nevertheless, the BA has acknowledged the issue and has drafted a proposal for a new data protection law, however, its adoption has been significantly delayed and has yet to happen.

III Supervisory Authority

The Personal Data Protection Agency (hereinafter: "BA") (in Bosnian, *Agencija za zaštitu ličnih podataka*) is the public authority entrusted with the competence to oversee data protection matters. As a sole authority, it holds jurisdiction over data protection matters throughout the territory of BiH.

1 General Functions

The BA's primary role is to supervise compliance with the BDPL 2006.[410] The BA is empowered to handle complaints from data subjects related to the protection of their rights and freedoms with respect to the processing of personal data.[411] Furthermore, the BA is authorised to propose new legislation or amendments to existing legislation governing the processing of personal data, as well as to ensure compliance with data protection criteria that are derived from international treaties binding for BiH.[412] The BA is also mandated to collaborate with similar authorities in other countries.[413]

---

410 Art. 40(1)(a) BDPL 2006.
411 Artt. 40(1)(b), 41(1)(c) BDPL 2006.
412 Art. 40(1)(d) BDPL 2006.

2 Independence

According to the BDPL 2006 the BA is "an independent administrative organisation established for the purpose of ensuring the protection of personal data".[414] The director of the BA leads the organisation.[415] The funds required for its operation are provided from the budget of the institutions of BiH and "international obligations of BiH".[416]

The director and deputy director of BA are appointed and dismissed by parliament.[417] Employees of the BA have the status of civil servants and employees.[418] Moreover, the BA is responsible before parliament, which may request carrying out the control of the BA's operation.[419] The BDPL 2006 sets out specific requirements for the appointment of the director and deputy director, including a law degree, five years of work experience in leadership positions in the administration, proven experience in the field of human rights, and recognised high moral status.[420] However, there are no specific requirements for knowledge or experience in data protection matters.

Regarding inspections of the public sector, the BDPL 2006 provides that all authorities must assist the BA in carrying out its duties upon request.[421] State and official secrets cannot hinder the BA from exercising its rights, but the confidentiality provisions remain binding for this authority.[422]

In comparison to the GDPR, the regulations governing the independence of the BA are deemed insufficient. Specifically, there are no provisions stipulating the obligation to avoid actions that are incompatible with the duties of BA's members, nor provisions addressing whether political party affiliations have an impact on their performance of duties. Additionally, there is no provision requiring the provision of human, technical, and financial resources, premises, and infrastructure necessary for the BA to effectively perform its functions and exercise its powers.

---

413 Art. 40(2)(h) BDPL 2006.
414 Art. 35 BDPL 2006.
415 Art. 42(1) BDPL 2006.
416 Art. 36 BDPL 2006.
417 Art. 43 BDPL 2006.
418 Art. 38(1) BDPL 2006.
419 Art. 47 BDPL 2006.
420 Art. 44 BDPL 2006.
421 Art. 41(5) BDPL 2006.
422 Art. 41(4) BDPL 2006.

3 Powers

In order to exercise its powers and perform the duties within its remit, the BA has three main types of authority stemming from Art. 40 BDPL 2006. Namely supervisory, advisory, and complaint-related powers. It should be noted that unlike the GDPR, the BDPL 2006 does not distinguish between these powers and lists them together (Art. 40).

a) Supervisory Powers

The supervisory powers of the BA derive from its role as the supervisory authority responsible for the enforcement of the BDPL 2006. The BA has the power to carry out inspections of compliance with the obligations for controllers and processors set out in the BDPL 2006.[423] Supervisory powers also comprise corrective powers, as the BA is entitled, inter alia, to issue decisions ordering controllers and processors to take certain corrective measures[424] (e.g., to order blocking and deletion of personal data, to order a ban on data processing, issue warnings, etc.) and to impose fines.[425] In the exercise of its functions, the BA has the power to require a controller or processor to provide the BA with information on any matter and to inspect all documents and records likely to contain personal data.[426] This also includes the right to enter any premises where data are processed.[427] Controllers and processors have the right to appeal against this decision to the director of the BA as a second instance.[428] Against the decision of the director, they are entitled to bring an administrative action before the competent courts.[429] Lastly, the BA has the power to submit a request for misdemeanour proceedings against data controllers and processors before the competent courts if it finds that the controller's or processor's actions constitute serious offences, such as commercial or criminal offences.[430]

423 Art. 40(2)(a) BDPL 2006.
424 Artt. 40(2)(c), 41(1) BDPL 2006.
425 Art. 40(2)(k).
426 Art. 41(2) BDPL 2006.
427 Art. 41(3) BDPL 2006.
428 Art. 20(1) the Rulebook on Supervision Inspection Regarding Personal Data Protection (Official Gazette of Bosnia and Herzegovina, no. 32/02).
429 Art. 20(3) Rulebook on Supervision Inspection (n. 428).
430 Art. 40(2)(f) BDPL 2006 and Art. 17(4) the Rulebook on Supervision Inspection (n. 428).

b) Authorisation and Advisory Powers

In addition to its supervisory powers, the BA possesses authorisation and advisory powers. The BA is authorised to give advice and opinions on matters concerning the protection of personal data[431] and adopt bylaws, guidelines, or other legal acts, in accordance with the BDPL 2006.[432] Furthermore, the BA maintains the Central Register of personal data filing systems of controllers in BiH.[433] In line with this, the BA also approves the establishment of personal data filing systems after verifying the compliance of data processing operations with the law.[434] In certain cases, the BA may carry out preliminary control upon receiving requests from controllers for the establishment of personal data filing systems, particularly when data filing systems include processing of special categories of personal data or processing personal data intended to assess the identity of data subjects, including decision-making based on such processing.[435]

c) Complaint Related Powers

The BA, in its capacity as a supervisory authority, also has powers in relation to the handling of complaints from data subjects.[436] Depending on whether the BA considers a data subject's complaint to be well-founded, it may reject it or order the controller or processor to act upon a request within a specified period.[437] In any case, a decision of the BA may not be appealed, but an administrative dispute may be brought against such a decision before the competent court of BiH.[438]

4 Challenges

The failure of the BDPL 2006 to provide sufficient provisions to ensure the independence of the BA has led to various challenges that threaten the authority's independence. One significant topic related to the BA's work and organisation is the support it receives for the development of data protection guidelines and by-

---

431 Art. 41(2)(g) BDPL 2006.
432 Art. 41(2)(d) BDPL 2006.
433 Art. 40(2)(b) BDPL 2006.
434 Art. 14(3) BDPL 2006.
435 Art. 14(4) BDPL 2006.
436 Art. 40(1)(b) BDPL 2006.
437 Art. 30(2) BDPL 2006. Also, Rulebook on the Procedure for Complaints by Data Subjects before the Personal Protection Agency in Bosnia and Herzegovina (Official Gazette of Bosnia and Herzegovina, no. 32/02) regulates handling data subjects' complaints in detail.
438 Art. 30(3) BDPL 2006.

laws.[439] Per the annual reports published by the BA, it appears that the authority abstained from contributing to a substantial number of initiatives owing to their non-inclusion in the budgetary allocation.[440]

The lack of personnel, particularly in the department handling data subjects' complaints, poses another significant challenge.[441] The current solution under which employees have the status of civil servants seems to be problematic, as under the Law on Civil Service in the Institutions of BiH,[442] the Civil Service Agency is the main institution in the process of hiring civil servants and accordingly needs to approve the hiring of new BA's members.[443] The BA has already noted that this negatively affects its independence, especially as the BA also has the power to supervise the work of the Civil Service Agency under the BDPL 2006.[444] In its 2022 report, the EU Commission recognised this problem and noted that no steps were taken to make the BA more independent or to increase its human and financial resources necessary for effective performance and exercising of its powers.[445] Moreover, the BA also lacks the premises and infrastructure necessary for the effective performance of its tasks and exercise of its powers.[446]

Furthermore, it appears that the influence of the BA on the government is not significant. Despite being granted the power to monitor the conditions for the protection of personal data and propose the adoption or amendment of laws related to the processing of personal data under Art. 40(1)(b) of the BDPL 2006, this power of the BA appears to be more hypothetical than feasible in practice, which is evidenced by the delay in adopting the new law aligned with the GDPR. The BA's Annual Report 2021 also condemns the delay in passing the law and emphasizes the importance of involving this authority in finalising the proposed data protection legislation.[447]

439 RCC Report 2020, p. 52 (n. 18).

440 *Ibid.*

441 Annual Report 2021, p. 15 (n. 336).

442 Under Art. 4 Law on Civil Service in the Institutions (Official Gazette of BiH, no. 12/2002, 19/2002, 8/2003, 35/2003, 4/2004, 17/2004, 26/2004, 37/2004, 48/2005, 2/2006, 50/2008 – other laws, 43/2009, 8/2010, 40/2012 and 93/2017) employees of the Central Bank of BiH and the Office of the Ombudsman for Human Rights from its application are exempted.

443 Annual Report 2021, p. 15 (n. 336).

444 *Ibid.*

445 EU Commission Report for Bosnia and Herzegovina 2022, SWD(2022) 336 final, (12.10.2022), p. 30.

446 Annual Report on Data Protection in BiH for 2019, no. 01–02–4–568–1/20, (27.07.2020), p. 11.

447 Annual Report 2021, p. 63 (n. 336).

Lastly, as already noted, the BA can either impose a fine directly or submit a misdemeanour request to the competent court. However, the authority has confirmed that if it imposes fines directly, it can only impose minimal penalties, while the competent court may impose a fine of up to its maximum prescribed amount.[448] So far, the BA has opted for imposing lower fines directly,[449] for two reasons. Firstly, misdemeanour proceedings before courts are lengthy, and secondly, if data controllers initiate administrative proceedings challenging orders of the BA, the courts usually pass decisions by which the penalties are suspended or impose even lower penalties than those imposed by the BA, raising concerns over the effectiveness of the protection.[450]

5 Conclusion to III

BiH has an established supervisory authority, the BA, responsible for enforcement of data protection legislation. The BA is vested with several powers that enable it to perform its mandated duties, including conducting investigations of controllers and processors, imposing fines and corrective measures, redressing complaints from data subjects, issuing opinions and granting authorisations for data processing. Nevertheless, the BA may not meet the criteria of an independent supervisory authority since it lacks sufficient resources to carry out its tasks, including but not limited to, human, technical and financial resources. Moreover, the BA is reliant on the Civil Agency for employment, resulting in limited authority to freely choose its staff. Additionally, the fines imposed by the BA are comparably low, and the BA is inclined to impose corrective measures instead of fines. Overall, this does not guarantee data subjects in BiH adequate protection of their rights and freedoms.

IV Draft Law

As previously noted in part II, the BA has formulated a draft proposal for new law on data protection. This proposal was first presented in 2020 and was subsequently accepted by the Interdepartmental Working Group, in which a representative of the BA participated.[451] As the BA lacks the authority to propose new legislation,

---

448 RCC Report 2020, p. 56 (n. 18).

449 The fines issued by the BA ranged between EUR 150 to EUR 5,000 (while the fines stipulated by the BDPL 2006 may amount up to EUR 50,000). RCC Report 2020, p. 62 (n. 18).

450 *Ibid.*

451 The Decision on the Formation of the Interdepartmental Working Group for Drafting the Draft Law on the Protection of Personal Data (Official Gazette of Bosnia and Herzegovina, number

the proposal was submitted to the Ministry of Civil Affairs as the official proponent for further legislative procedure. At the 12th session of the House of Representatives of Parliament on September 15, 2020, the Council of Ministers was instructed to submit the official draft law to the parliamentary procedure by the end of 2020 (hereinafter: "Draft Law").[452] However, it appears that the Ministry of Justice did not endorse the proposal, resulting in a pause in the legislative procedure and a failure to submit the Draft Law to Parliament. It is up to date unclear whether an alternative proposal or draft legislation has been put forward.

1 Overview of the Draft Law

The Draft Law consists of 10 parts and is structured in a manner similar to the GDPR. It presents mostly a replica of the GDPR, copying provisions such as definitions, legal grounds, principles, special categories of personal data, data subject rights, rules on controllers and processors, rules on data transfers etc., while omitting the Recitals contained in the GDPR. Consequently, the Draft Law introduces concepts that were previously absent in the BDPL 2006, such as the right to data portability,[453] DPIA,[454] data breach notification,[455] data protection by design and default,[456] and transparency.[457] Although the Draft Law largely aligns with the GDPR, it differs in some respects.

Firstly, the scope of the Draft Law differs from that of the GDPR. It sets out general regulations for the protection of natural persons concerning the processing of personal data, which is consistent with the GDPR material scope, as well as regulations for the protection of natural persons concerning the processing of personal data by competent authorities, as laid down in the LED.[458] The Draft Law includes provisions on LED in a separate chapter (chapter seven), which makes it more readable than other data protection laws that have been aligned with the GDPR, such as the SDPL 2019 (Serbian data protection law). Thus, the Draft Law aims to cover the entire package of reforms with the EU acquis in the field of data protection. Additionally, the Draft Law distinguishes between the material scope of application (Art. 2) and the territorial scope of application (Art. 3), which

49/18), available in Bosnian at the following link <http://www.sluzbenilist.ba/page/akt/zAxqEkGJ7Uc=>, (accessed on 23.04.2023).

452 Official Answer of the BA, no. 04–02–1–1042–3/21, (24.11.2021).

453 Art. 20 Draft Law.

454 Artt. 35–36 Draft Law.

455 Artt. 33–34 Draft Law.

456 Art. 25 Draft Law.

457 Art. 12 Draft Law.

458 Art. 1(4) Draft Law.

is replicated from the GDPR, thereby conferring an extraterritorial effect based on the rationale of Art. 3 GDPR.

Secondly, the chapter regulating special processing situations contains several provisions that are absent in the GDPR. For instance, video surveillance (Art. 55) and confidentiality obligations (Art. 57) are included. Under the latter provision, state and official secrets do not constitute an impediment to the supervisory authority in performing its supervisory duties if such action is necessary and proportionate to align the right to the protection of personal data with the obligation of secrecy. Additionally, unlike the BDPL 2006, the Draft Law proposes the processing of national ID numbers.[459] These provisions are aimed at enhancing the implementation of data protection regulations, particularly since use of video surveillance and ID numbers are frequently associated with data breaches.

Furthermore, one of the most significant enhancements of the Draft Law pertains to the provisions governing the supervisory authority, particularly those relating to the independence of the BA. As previously stated, the Law on Civil Service in the Institutions of BiH mandates that the Civil Service Agency must authorise the appointment of new members to the BA. However, the Draft Law offers a solution that excludes the employees of the BA's Institution from this requirement of the Law on Civil Service in the Institutions of BiH.[460] Moreover, the BA shall change its name to the "Institution of the Commissioner for the Protection of Personal Data in Bosnia and Herzegovina".[461] As the legal successor of the BA, the new institution shall take over its affairs, archives and other documentation, work resources, financial resources, rights and obligations, as well as its employees.[462]

Finally, the Draft Law proposes the imposition of ambitious fines, which could amount to up to 2% and 4% of the total worldwide annual turnover of the previous fiscal year for non-compliance by legal entities acting as controllers and processors.[463] This provision stands out as the fines are based on the company's annual worldwide turnover and could be substantial for major companies such as Facebook and Google. The substantial fines proposed may be due to the fact that the BA drafted the law, and this article is likely to be altered in the future.

459 Art. 52 Draft Law.
460 Art. 95(6) Draft Law.
461 Art. 94(1) Draft Law.
462 Art. 94(2) Draft Law.
463 Art. 10 (4)(5) Draft Law.

2 Conclusion to IV

The proposed Draft Law represents a significant step towards aligning the BiH national legislation with contemporary data protection standards. By introducing several key concepts, such as data breach notification, the right to data portability, DPIA, and data protection officer, the Draft Law brings BiH's national legislation in line with the GDPR. Beyond this, the provision of the Draft Law introduced, would not only align with the GDPR, and potentially bring the country closer to negotiating the adoption of an adequacy decision with the EU Commission, but would also enhance the existing data protection framework and enforcement. In particular, as the supervisory authority would be given a more independent position (as one of the key criteria for the adoption of an adequacy decision) and as the Draft Law would introduce some specific provisions which were lacking in the previous legislation, such as processing of national ID numbers. However, given that the Draft Law was prepared by the BA, the question remains whether it will be accepted as such.

V Case Law and Enforcement

Case law and the level of enforcement of data protection law is one of the key aspects that the EU Commission takes into account when assessing the level of data protection in a third country. The WP29 also stressed that any meaningful analysis of adequate protection must include the two basic elements of "the content of the applicable rules" and "the means to ensure their effective application".[464] This means that the EU Commission must verify that the rules in force are also effective in practice.[465] Therefore, this Section will analyse the enforcement of data protection in BiH, including the activities of the BA in raising the awareness of data subjects. It will also provide an overview of cases before the BA and the competent courts.

1 Activities of the Supervisory Authority

The BA's activities as a supervisory authority are crucial to enforcing data protection standards. The BA plays an important role in monitoring compliance with data protection rules and in educating the relevant stakeholders on important data privacy and security issues.

464 WP29 Adequacy Referential, p. 3 (n. 155).
465 *Ibid.*

Notwithstanding the various challenges confronting the BA, the authority has demonstrated significant activity, by organising seminars and lectures, especially in the public sector, for civil servants, local government employees, police officers, judicial officers, law students, as well as trainings in the business sector.[466] Furthermore, the BA is proactive in its dissemination of useful information on its website for both data subjects and data controllers/processors. Notably, the BA has dedicated a section of its website exclusively to GDPR matters, featuring translated Guidelines of the EPDB into Croatian, which is a language readily comprehensible to the people of BiH. The primary objective of this section on the BA' website is to facilitate companies' understanding of the GDPR provisions and provide access to other relevant literature on data protection in the EU.[467] Furthermore, the BA's website highlights the importance of the role of the DPO. The authority strongly recommends that all companies appoint a DPO, even though this is not yet a legal requirement under the current Bosnian data protection framework.[468] The BA also publishes the decisions of EU regulators, including significant fines imposed by supervisory authorities.[469] This approach is an excellent strategy to prepare companies in advance for the forthcoming changes once the new data protection legislation takes effect.

In 2022, the BA made public its Medium-Term Plan for the 2023–2025 period, outlining the objectives and actions to be taken by the institution. Given the absence of a national data protection strategy, this plan assumes particular significance. A key aim identified in the plan is the enactment of a new law that conforms fully to the GDPR.[470] In addition, crucial tasks set forth in the plan include monitoring the implementation of data protection legislation, fostering public awareness of personal data protection, and collaborating with European authorities and organisations to adopt best practices and norms.[471] The plan recognises that the BA will need additional personnel and budgetary resources

466 RCC Report 2020, p. 62 (n. 18).
467 Information available on the BA's website at the following link <http://www.azlp.ba/GDPR_Menu/Sta_je_GDPR/default.aspx?id=2373&langTag=bsBA&template_id=149&pageIndex=1> (accessed on 24.04.2023).
468 Information available on the BA's website, section "Data Protection Officer" at the following link <http://www.azlp.ba/Sluzbenik_za_zastitu_podataka/Default.aspx?id=3463&pageIndex=1&langTag=en-US> (accessed on 24.04.2023).
469 The section "news" contains decisions by the EU Regulators, available at the following link <http://azlp.ba/aktuelnosti/Default.aspx?id=289&pageIndex=1&langTag=en-US> (accessed on 28.04.2023).
470 Medium-Term Plan work for the period 2023–2025, published in September 2022, p. 4.
471 *Ibid*, p. 5.

to achieve its objectives and goals, particularly since the new law will entail new responsibilities for the BA that demand greater capacities.[472]

2 Complaints and Investigations Before the Supervisory Authority

The BA has the authority to perform both regular and irregular inspections.[473] However, there has been a decrease in the number of inspections carried out by the BA, which may be attributed to a shortage of personnel.[474] Conversely, the number of complaints lodged by data subjects has been steadily increasing over the years, with 183 complaints registered in 2021 compared to only 35 in 2011.[475] This trend is indicative of a heightened awareness among data subjects of their rights.[476] However, the BA's record of imposing fines is very low. For example, the BA issued just nine fines during 2021, and the peak number for the past ten years was 2015, when the BA issued 25 fines.[477]

Case law before the BA reveals a variety of issues, such as video surveillance, non-compliance with the principle of data minimisation in ID card processing, data breaches in employment law during the hiring process and the retention of application documentation for non-selected candidates, failure to implement adequate personal data security measures, and others.[478] The BA's annual reports indicate that many public institutions have failed to comply with basic data protection principles when handling personal identification documents.[479] Furthermore, the case law demonstrates a widespread lack of awareness regarding the principles of minimisation and privacy by design and default, with many data controllers requesting irrelevant personal data, such as the sensitive personal identification number 'JMBG'.[480] Data breaches related to video surveillance are also very present, including public authorities.[481] For example, the BA issued corrective measures to the Ministry of Interior of the Republika Srpska for processing

---

472 *Ibid.* pp. 8–9.
473 Art. 13 Rulebook on Supervision Inspection (n. 428).
474 Information from the Annual Report 2021, p. 19 (n. 336). For example, 101 inspections were carried out in 2013, but only 19 in 2019. In 2020 the figure was 36 and in 2021 the figure increased to 78.
475 Annual Report 2021, p. 23 (n. 336).
476 The BA also noted this in its Annual Report 2020, p. 57 (n. 336).
477 Annual Report 2021, p. 35 (n. 336).
478 Information from the BA's annual reports (n. 336). See also Arben Murtezić, pp. 35–51 (n. 13).
479 Annual Report 2021, pp. 15–17 (n. 336).
480 In 2021, of the nine fines issued by the BA, three were for unlawful processing of the ID. Annual Report 2021, p. 34 (n. 336).
481 In 2020, most complaints concerned video surveillance. Annual Report 2020, p. 57 (n. 336).

personal data through video surveillance for facial recognition in public areas in Republika Srpska, and to the Office for Audit of BiH for processing personal data through video surveillance in official premises.[482]

3 Court Cases

With regard to the current case law, as already highlighted in part III.5., the BA has so far preferred to issue decisions directly instead of initiating misdemeanour proceedings before the courts. Moreover, data subjects do not have the right to seek direct judicial protection against data controllers and processors. As a result, the majority of court cases pertain to the challenge of BA decisions before the administrative court. It is noteworthy that the number of court cases challenging the BA's decisions is relatively high, particularly in comparison to other countries such as Serbia or Kosovo. Nevertheless, in the majority of instances, the courts have dismissed complaints against the BA's decisions. The BA has made court decisions available to the public on its official website. There are approximately 90 cases dating from 2014 to 2013, with the majority of these cases relating to employment purposes, video surveillance, identification numbers or documents, and health data.[483]

A recent data breach involving the unlawful processing of personal data by the Central Election Commission of Bosnia and Herzegovina (hereinafter: "CEC") serves as an illustration of the lack of data protection awareness and accountability on the part of public institutions as data controllers in Bosnia and Herzegovina. In October 2020, the CEC published on its official website (www.izbori.ba) a list containing personal data of 101,771 registered voters with the right to vote from abroad, including names, surnames, municipality of residence, year of birth, and foreign country of residence of registered voters. The BA determined that the CEC lacked the legal basis to publish such personal data and imposed the deletion of published personal data and a ban on further publishing personal data on the website. The CEC challenged the BA's decision in court, but the court dismissed the appeal in early 2023, finding that the BA's decision was adopted through the proper application of the BDPL 2006.

---

482 Annual Report 2021, p. 26 (n. 336).

483 Information on the court proceedings published on the respective page on the BA's website at the following link <http://azlp.ba/upravni_sporovi/Default.aspx?id=257&pageIndex=1&langTag=bs-BA> (accessed on 07.06.2034).

4 Conclusion to V

Data subjects in BiH do not enjoy the same level of redress as those in the EU. The only options available to data subjects are to file a complaint with the supervisory authority or to seek compensation through the courts. Nevertheless, the number of complaints filed with the supervisory authority has increased in recent years, which may indicate a positive impact of the GDPR and improved public awareness of data protection. Despite this, the supervisory authority lacks the necessary resources to effectively address data subjects' complaints and exercise its powers, such as investigations. The EU Commission has also noted in its report for 2022 that the BA needs to better balance the protection of privacy with objectives of general public interest, notably media freedom and electoral integrity.[484] This lack of real enforcement powers of the BA could pose a major obstacle for enforcing the BDPL 2006 and the new legislation, unless the new proposed law sets higher standards for ensuring the independence of the supervisory authority.

VI Conclusion to B

Given that BiH has not yet harmonised its legislation with the EU acquis, the existing laws fall short of incorporating several concepts outlined in the GDPR, such as the right to data portability, data breach notification, the appointment of DPO, conducting a DPIA, and the limitation of further (onward) data transfers. Moreover, the redress rights are not in line with the GDPR, as data subjects do not have the right to seek a judicial remedy against data controllers and processors. Consequently, the supervisory authority prepared the Draft Law, however, its adoption has been significantly delayed. If adopted, the Draft Law would enhance the data protection framework in line with the GDPR.

The supervisory authority faces numerous challenges, including a limited budget and inadequate resources to fulfil its powers and duties. The current BDPL 2006 also fails to stipulate the provisions which shall ensure the existence of an independent supervisory authority.

There is no national data protection strategy in place with the primary objective of obtaining an adequacy decision from the European Commission. However, the medium-term plan for 2023–2025 adopted by the supervisory authority clearly states that its main objective is to align the data protection law with the GDPR. To fortify its position in negotiating an adequacy decision, BiH shall adopt the new data protection law aligned with the GDPR and approve the changes related to the

484 EU Commission Report Bosnia and Herzegovina 2022, p. 30 (n. 445).

independence of the supervisory authority, as outlined in the Draft Law prepared by the supervisory authority.

C Kosovo

Kosovo has the status of a potential EU candidate country. A SAA between the EU and Kosovo was signed in 2015 and entered into force in 2016. The SAA also covers the issue of protection of personal data stating "the Parties shall cooperate on personal data protection legislation with a view to achieving a level of protection of personal data by Kosovo corresponding to that of the EU acquis. Kosovo shall ensure sufficient financial and human resources for one or more independent supervisory bodies in order to efficiently monitor and guarantee the enforcement of its personal data protection legislation."[485] Therefore, Kosovo is obliged not only to ensure that its data protection framework is aligned with the GDPR, but also to have an independent authority with enough resources to execute its powers.

I Constitutional Parameters and International Commitments

Data protection and right to privacy are afforded on constitutional level in Kosovo. Art. 36 of the Constitution of Kosovo guarantees the fundamental right to privacy, stipulating that privacy and family life, as well as the confidentiality of correspondence and other communications, are protected for all individuals.[486] The right to personal data protection is also enshrined in this article, which recognises that everyone has the right to the protection of their personal data and that the collection, storage, access, correction, and use of such data must be regulated by law.[487]

The Constitution of Kosovo elevates a number of international legal instruments in Art. 22 to constitutional rank. The Constitution specifies that "human rights and fundamental freedoms guaranteed by the following international agreements and instruments are guaranteed by this Constitution [...]".[488] These instruments include some of the key international and European conventions, such

485 Article 84 Stabilisation and Association Agreement between the European Union and Kosovo, 10728/1/15 REV 1 available at the following link <https://data.consilium.europa.eu/doc/document/ST-10728-2015-REV-1/en/pdf> (accessed on 29.04.2023).

486 Art. 36(1) Constitution of Kosovo 2008.

487 Art. 36(4) Constitution of Kosovo 2008.

488 Art. 22 Constitution of Kosovo 2008.

as the Universal Declaration of Human Rights (hereinafter: "UDHR") and the ECHR which both guarantee the right to respect for private and family life.[489] Thus, these instruments appear to have constitutional authority, to be part of the domestic constitutional system, and to be both source and binding documents on human rights issues within Kosovo's jurisdiction.[490] However, as Kosovo's statehood is not yet universally recognised, Kosovo is not still in the capacity to be a signatory to international instruments of consensual character (including the ECHR) and the 'constitutionalising' of these conventions has no significance for external relations unless Kosovo becomes a signatory to them.[491] As a consequence, the mentioned conventions are applied unilaterally.

1 Conclusion to I

The protection of data and privacy is enshrined as a fundamental right in Kosovo's constitution. However, as Kosovo is not yet a member of the CoE, it cannot be signatory of human rights conventions such as the ECHR or Convention 108(+). Nevertheless, the Constitution of Kosovo provides constitutional recognition to the international agreements and instruments listed in Art. 22.[492]

II Data Protection Legislation

The first-generation legislation regulating personal data protection, Law no. 03/L – 172 on the Protection of Personal Data was adopted in 2010 (hereinafter: "KDPL 2010") and was influenced by the DPD. The KDPL 2010 established fundamental data protection principles and rules for data processing. Nonetheless, it had sev-

---

489 According to Art. 22(1)-(8) Constitution of Kosovo 2008 the international human rights instruments which have been constitutionalised include the Universal Declaration of Human Rights, the ECHR and its Protocols, the International Covenant on Civil and Political Rights and its Protocols, the Council of Europe Framework Convention for the Protection of National Minorities, the Convention on the Elimination of All Forms of Racial Discrimination, the Convention on the Elimination of All Forms of Discrimination Against Women, the Convention on the Rights of the Child, and the Convention against Torture and Other Cruel, Inhumane or Degrading Treatment or Punishment. See also Comprehensive Proposal for the Kosovo Status Settlement, UN Doc. S/2007/168/Add. 1, Annex 1, Art. 2, para. 1.

490 Paul De Hert and Fisnik Korenica, "The New Kosovo Constitution and Its Relationship with the European Convention on Human Rights: Constitutionalization "Without" Ratification in Post-Conflict Societies", Max-Planck-Institut für ausländisches öffentliches Recht und Völkerrecht, p. 145 (2016).

491 *Ibid.*

492 Art. 22 Constitution of Kosovo 2008.

eral shortcomings, resulting in inadequate personal data protection for data subjects in Kosovo. One of the primary deficiencies was the limited authority of the supervisory authority to impose sanctions for data breaches, rendering data subjects vulnerable to potential violations of their rights.[493] The second-generation legislation, which aims to align the KDPL 2010 with the GDPR, was adopted in 2019.

1 Status Quo of GDPR Alignment

The process of harmonising Kosovo's data protection legislation with the GDPR began immediately after the adoption of the GDPR in 2016, with the assistance of an EU-funded project.[494] As a result, the new data protection law – Law 06/L-082 on personal data protection (hereinafter: "KDPL 2019") – came into force in early 2019. With the adoption of the KDPL 2019, a new data protection authority was established, the Information and Privacy Agency, replacing the previous supervisory authority, the National Agency for Personal Data Protection (hereinafter: "NAPDP").[495]

The KDPL 2019 represents for the most part a replication of the GDPR. This is a common phenomenon in the WB6 countries, as countries tend to copy EU law without necessarily adapting them to their specific legal orders.[496] The KDPL 2019 states in its Art. 1 that it "is in compliance with the Regulation (EU) 2016/679". Although some differences exist, the most significant variation relates to the stricter data transfer regulations in the GDPR and a milder penal policy in the KDPL 2019. Moreover, the KDPL 2019 does not include any of the Recitals introduced by the GDPR, as it is the case with the other two data protection laws adopted after the GDPR in the two countries of the Western Balkans (Serbia and North Macedonia). This Section will provide the differences between the KDPL 2019 and the GDPR.

2 Overview of the KDPL 2019

The KDPL 2019 consists of eight parts. Part 1 contains general provisions, including the scope of the law, definitions and principles (chapters 1 and 2). Part 2 sets out

493 Art 29(2) KDPL 2010.

494 EU Project "Support to Kosovo institutions in the field of Protection of Personal Data" EuropeAid/133806/C/SER/XK, (31.01.2016); Njomëza Zejnullahu, p. 309 (n. 14).

495 Art. 108 KDPL 2019.

496 Merita Kostanica, "Data Protection Regulation in the Republic of Kosovo and Compliance by the Companies: A Proposed Model for Kosovo", International In-House Counsel Journal, Vol. 2, Issue 8 (Summer 2009), pp. 1227–1238.

the rights of the persons concerned (chapters 2 to 6). Part 3 regulates controllers and processors, including their obligations in relation to the security of data processing (chapters 7 to 10). Part 5 lays down rules on international data transfers (chapter 11). Part 6 defines redress mechanisms (chapter 12). Part 7 sets out the role of the supervisory authority and its functions and powers (chapters 13 and 14). Part 8 lays down the provisions relating to specific situations of processing (chapters 15 to 20). Part 9 provides for sanctions for non-compliance with the provisions of the KDPL 2019 (chapter 21). Finally, Part 8 contains transitional and final provisions (chapter 22).

3 Scope of the KDPL 2019

The KDPL 2019 defines both the material and territorial scope. The material scope differs from the GDPR in the sense that Art. 2 of the KDPL 2019 stipulates that, with the exception of processing for purely personal purposes, it applies to the processing of personal data by both public and private entities.[497] In contrast to the Art. (2)(d) GDPR, the KDPL 2019 does not exclude public authorities from the scope of the LED. Furthermore, the KDPL 2019 does not explicitly specify the nature of data processing to which it applies (e.g., wholly and partially automated processing), in contrast to Art. 2(1) GDPR.

With regards to its territorial effect, the KDPL 2019 replicates the territorial scope of the DPD, as opposed to the GDPR. Specifically, it applies to data controllers who are not established in Kosovo but "which for the purposes of processing personal data make use of automatic or other equipment in Kosovo, unless such equipment is used only for purposes of transit through the territory of Kosovo".[498] In these circumstances the controller must designate a representative established in Kosovo as well.[499] It is worth noting that the concept of exterritorial scope and a representative are not new terms in Kosovo data protection legislation, as the KDPL 2010 provided for the same approach.[500] While the KDPL 2019 has adopted provisions from the GDPR and asserts compliance with the GDPR in its Art. 1, it has chosen an outdated approach that has proven inadequate in practice.[501] This raises questions as to the rationale behind the law's adoption of such an approach.

---

497 Art. 2(1) KDPL 2019.
498 Art. 2(3) KDPL 2019.
499 *Ibid.*
500 Art. 4(3) KDPL 2010.
501 The extraterritorial scope of the DPD and related issues have been the subject of discussion in section A, II.3 of this Chapter.

The KDPL 2019 has, however, broadened the territorial scope of data protection legislation. The KDPL 2010 excluded certain controllers from several security obligations, such as media processing personal data for the purpose of informing the public and artistic and literary expressions, as well as political parties, trade unions, associations, and religious communities in relation to their members.[502] The legislative reform has therefore already had a positive impact in this respect.

4 Definitions

The KDPL 2019 incorporates the same definitions as those set out in the GDPR, but there are some 'new' terms that are not present in the GDPR, like 'classification of personal data', 'privacy' and 'connecting code'.

Classification of personal data is defined as marking personal data in order to indicate their sensitive nature.[503] This serves as an additional safeguard measure for special categories of personal data, which is a leftover from the KDPL 2010. Similarly, the so-called connecting code has been carried over from the KDPL 2010,[504] and is defined as a "personal identification number or any other specific identification number defined by law relating to an individual that can be used to disclose or retrieve personal data from filing systems in which the connecting code is also processed."[505] Finally, while privacy is not explicitly defined by the GDPR, the KDPL 2019 defines it as "respect for private and family life, inviolability of the home and the secret of telephone and other communications correspondence, in compliance with the applicable law".[506]

5 Data Protection Principles

The KDPL 2019 incorporates the same seven data protection principles as outlined in the GDPR.[507] The majority of these principles had already existed under the KDPL 2010. However, the principle of accountability and the principles of integrity and confidentiality were not explicitly acknowledged as data protection principles by the KDPL 2010.

502 Art. 4(4)(5) KDPL 2010.
503 Art. 3(1)(1.1.) KDPL 2019.
504 Art. 2(1.3)(1.17) KDPL 2010.
505 Art. 3(1)(1.10.) KDPL 2019.
506 Art. 3(1)(1.23.) KDPL 2019.
507 Art. 4 KDPL 2019.

6 Lawfulness

The KDPL 2019 also recognises the same legal grounds in line with the principle of lawfulness of data processing, namely consent, performance of a contract, compliance with a legal obligation, legitimate interests, protection of vital interests, etc.[508]

a) Consent

The KDPL 2019 incorporates the conditions for consent as provided by Art. 7 GDPR.[509] It is worth noting that the KDPL 2019 introduced specific rules for obtaining children's consent[510] to data protection legislation, which were not present in the KDPL 2010.

7 Special Categories of Personal Data

The KDPL 2019 completely transposes Art. 9 GDPR in the regulation of special categories of personal data.[511] Moreover, the KDPL 2019 imposes identical rules and exceptions for processing special categories of personal data, while also introducing an additional obligation that is not present in the GDPR. Controllers have the obligation to classify special categories of personal data for the purpose of preventing unauthorised access and use.[512] As already mentioned, this is an additional safeguard and includes marking of personal data to indicate their sensitive nature.

8 Rights of Data Subject

The KDPL 2019 foresees a set of data subject's rights which completely correspond to the rights envisaged by the GDPR, as well as all rules and manners for the exercise of the data subject's rights and restrictions.[513] While most of the data subject's rights already existed under the KDPL 2010, certain rights are completely new or have been modified to be consistent with the GDPR. For instance, the KDPL 2010 did not recognise the obligation to provide information in a case when personal data have not been obtained from the data subjects (Art. 14

---

508 Art. 5 KDPL 2019.
509 Art. 6 KDPL 2019.
510 Art. 7 KDPL 2019.
511 Art. 8 KDPL 2019.
512 Art. 8(4) KDPL 2019.
513 Chapter III KDPL 2019.

GDPR). Moreover, the right to data portability[514] is a new concept introduced by the KDPL 2019.

9 Redress Mechanism

Data subjects are afforded various means to exercise their rights under the KDPL 2019. First of all, they have the right to file a complaint before the supervisory authority (Art. 52). Secondly, a right to an effective judicial remedy is envisaged against a legally binding decision of the supervisory authority or in cases of its silence (Art. 53). Furthermore, Art. 54 establishes the right of data subjects to seek an effective judicial remedy against a controller or processor. These rights are in complete correspondence with the provisions of Art. 77–79 GDPR.

An additional noteworthy aspect of the Kosovo legislation is the right of data subjects to designate a representative, an entity, organisation, or non-profit association with statutory objectives in the public interest, and activity in the field of the protection of data subjects' rights and freedoms regarding the protection of their personal data, to initiate a complaint on their behalf, exercise their rights on their behalf, and seek compensation on their behalf.[515] This right is also completely taken from Art. 80 GDPR. Moreover, the KDPL 2019 defines the right to compensation and liability as set out in the GDPR provisions.[516]

10 Personal Scope

The KDPL 2019 recognises data controllers (Art. 23), joint controllers (Art. 25) and data processors (Art. 27) as responsible actors for protection of personal data. The relationship between data controllers and data processors must be regulated by a written agreement.[517] The KDPL sets out the content of such agreements transposing Art. 28(3) GDPR.[518] Additionally, the KDPL 2019 gives greater control rights to data controllers over processors by explicitly granting them the right to supervise and carry out periodic visits to data processor premises.[519]

---

514 Art. 13 KDPL 2019.
515 Art. 55 KDPL 2019.
516 Art. 56 KDPL 2019.
517 Art. 27(3) KDPL 2019.
518 *Ibid.*
519 Art. 32(3) KDPL 2019.

a) Security of Personal Data

Similar to the GDPR, the KDPL 2019 does not prescribe an exhaustive list of the measures for protecting personal data, but envisages data protection by design and by default and solely provides some examples (such as pseudonymisation, minimisation and encryption).[520] The law also promotes the implementation of appropriate technical and organisational measures in order to ensure that "by default personal data are not made accessible without the individual's intervention to an indefinite number of natural persons"[521] as also set out in Art. 25(2) GDPR. It also promotes the creation of data privacy policies and certification mechanisms.[522] In addition, both the rules on notification of a personal data breach to the supervisory authority[523] and the rules on data protection impact assessment[524] are identical to the GDPR, and both are new in Kosovo's data protection legislation.

In contrast to the KDPL 2019, its predecessor KDPL 2010 contained a more comprehensive list of obligations of controllers and processors to ensure security of data processing. This included measures such as protection of premises, equipment and systems software.[525] Furthermore, it required the implementation of effective methods for deletion or anonymisation of personal data and enabling the subsequent determination of when personal data were entered into a filing system, accessed, modified, disclosed, destroyed, used, or otherwise processed, and by whom, for the entire storage period.[526] Lastly, in case personal data are processed via telecommunications networks data controllers had to implement additional security measures in order to ensure that processing takes place within the limits foreseen by law and that the hardware, the systems software and the software applications ensure an appropriate level of data protection.[527]

Considering that the KDPL 2019 does not provide an exhaustive list of security measures, the supervisory authority issued a Rulebook on security measures.[528] This rulebook outlines detailed provisions on security measures and distinguishes

---

520 Art. 24 KDPL 2019.
521 Art. 24(2) KDPL 2019.
522 Art. 23(2) KDPL 2019.
523 Artt. 33–34 KDPL 2019.
524 Artt. 35–36 KDPL 2019.
525 Art. 14 KDPL 2010.
526 *Ibid.*
527 *Ibid.*
528 Rulebook no. 05/2022 on Security Measures in the Course of Personal Data Processing (hereinafter "Rulebook on security measures"), 27.09.2022 < https://aip.rks-gov.net/download/rregullore-nr-05-2022-mbi-masat-e-sigurise-gjate-perpunimit-te-te-dhenave-personale/?wpdmdl=2557&refresh=6457478e379851683441550> (accessed on 07.05.2023).

between 'high risk controllers' and 'low risk controllers'. The term 'high risk controllers' refers to those data controllers who process personal data falling within the categories defined by the supervisory authority, including processing personal data relating to more than 200 data subjects, processing special categories of personal data, conducting profiling, processing personal data for the provision of health care, processing data for making decisions regarding specific individuals on a large scale, or conducting automated monitoring of publicly accessible areas on a large scale.[529] Moreover, the Rulebook on security measures imposes different security obligations on high and low risk controllers. High risk controllers are required, inter alia, to establish an information security management system (ISMS),[530] develop a disaster recovery plan,[531] conduct an analysis and assessment of filing system security,[532] perform a privacy impact analysis,[533] set up an information security policy,[534] apply additional safeguards for special categories of personal data,[535] respect specific provisions for cloud computing,[536] and conduct trainings in order to raise data security awareness among personnel.[537]

This represents a shift towards a more risk-based approach compared to the GDPR. The GDPR has been criticised that it does not differentiate between sectors or sizes of companies (one-size-fits-all approach).[538] It emphasizes risk-based measures that data controllers must implement to safeguard fundamental rights and freedoms, while at the same maintains a commitment to a more traditional legal approach described as 'rights-based'.[539] Specifically, it does not provide different obligations for the controllers based on their type, but it puts an obligation on data controllers to 'evaluate the risks inherent to the processing and implement

529 Art. 3(1.4) Rulebook on security measures (n. 528).
530 *Ibid.*, Art. 13.
531 *Ibid.*, Art. 14(2.6).
532 *Ibid.*, Art. 15.
533 *Ibid.*, Art. 16.
534 *Ibid.*, Art. 17.
535 *Ibid.*, Art. 20.
536 *Ibid.*, Art. 22.
537 *Ibid.*, Art. 23.
538 See for example, Winfried Veil (n. 12), Axel Voss, "Position Paper on Fixing the GDPR: Towards Version 2.0", (25.05.2021); Michael L. Rustad and Thomas H. Koenig. "Towards a Global Data Privacy Standard", Florida Law Review, vol. 71, no. 2 (March 2019) pp. 365–454.
539 Graça Canto Moniz, "The risk-based approach in the GDPR and the 'two-step test' within Article 44", *International Data Privacy Law*, Volume 14, Issue 2, (May 2024); Fred H Cate, Christopher Kuner, Christopher Millard, Dan Jerker B Svantesson and Orla Lynskey, "Risk Management in Data Protection", International Data Privacy Law (2015).

measures to mitigate those risks', without saying which measures should be implemented.

The Rulebook on security measures provides a nuanced approach to addressing the different levels of risk posed by different types of controllers. By distinguishing between 'high risk' and 'low risk' controllers, the Rulebook is able to tailor the security obligations imposed on controllers based on the specific risks they pose to the privacy and security of personal data. This approach is a departure from the one-size-fits-all approach of the GDPR and has the potential to enhance the protection of personal data in Kosovo.

b) DPO

Both controllers and processors are obliged to appoint a DPO pursuant to Art. 37 KDPL 2019. A similar role of the DPO has already been recognised by the KDPL 2010 prior to the entry into force of the GDPR, as was the case in many other EU countries.[540] However, under the KDPL 2010 only public institutions were obliged to appoint DPO.[541]

Additionally, Art. 40 KDPL 2019 obliges data controllers and processors to establish internal data protection policies, along with procedures and measures for ensuring the security of personal data. These policies must include the appointment of 'competent persons' responsible for implementing the rules under the KDPL 2019, among other things.[542] The use of the plural in this article suggests that there may be several individuals, in addition to the DPO, who are responsible for implementing the KDPL 2019. The Rulebook on security measures specifies this, and states that 'competent persons' include 1) administrators of information and communication technology systems 2), personal data operators (employees, contractors, etc.) which process personal data using information and communication technology means and 3) all other persons assigned by public and private entities to process personal data manually for the purpose of fulfilling their tasks.[543] The requirement to designate multiple individuals responsible for ensuring compliance with data protection standards is a commendable approach within the legal framework of Kosovo. This measure serves as an additional safeguard to uphold the role of a DPO, who, among many other responsibilities, must possess the

540 Germany, Belgium, Bulgaria, Estonia, Hungary, Luxembourg, Malta, Sweden etc, see more: Miguel Recio, "Data Protection Officer: The Key Figure to Ensure Data Protection and Accountability", ALWD 7th ed. 3 Eur. Data Prot. L. Rev. 114 (2017).
541 Art. 74(1) KDPL 2010.
542 Art. 40(2) KDPL 2019
543 Art. 3(1.8) Rulebook on security measures (n. 528).

capacity to effectively engage with data subjects and collaborate with relevant supervisory authorities.[544]

c) Codes of Conduct and Certification

Concepts of codes of conduct and data protection certification mechanisms is another novelty in Kosovar data protection legislation, transplanted from the GDPR. In terms of compliance monitoring for codes of conduct, the KDPL 2019 outlines more consistent rules compared to other WB6 laws, especially compared to the MDPL 2020 (Macedonian new GDPR-like data protection law). Under Art. 42 KDPL 2019, the responsible body for monitoring compliance with codes of conduct is accredited by the supervisory authority, with the conditions for accreditation taken from Art. 43(2) of the GDPR.[545]

Regarding the data protection certification mechanism, the KDPL 2019 designates the supervisory authority as a responsible body for the certification mechanism. Additionally, the KDPL 2019 explicitly stipulates that certificates issued by EU institutions or competent bodies are also valid in Kosovo.[546]

11 Transfer of Personal Data

The provisions governing transfer of personal data in the KDPL 2019 rely on the GDPR's approach, but with some distinctions. Firstly, the transfer of personal data may be carried out to a country that has an adequate level of data protection.[547] Secondly, if a country is not deemed by the supervisory authority to provide an adequate level of data protection, personal data may be transferred only if authorised by the supervisory authority.[548] Thirdly, the KDPL 2019 does not acknowledge other methods for data transfers to countries which do not provide an adequate level of data protection which would guarantee protection of personal data, such as appropriate safeguards (Art. 46 GDPR) or binding corporate rules (Art. 47 GDPR).

a) Adequacy Decisions

The supervisory authority is authorised to determine whether third countries offer a level of data protection that is comparable to that provided by the legal

---

544 See also WP29, Guidelines on Data Protection Officers ('DPOs') WP 243 rev.01, (05.04.2017).
545 Art. 41(1) KDPL 2019.
546 Art. 43(3) KDPL 2019.
547 Art. 44 KDPL 2019.
548 Art. 49 KDPL 2019.

system of Kosovo.[549] If so, the authority shall publish a list of such countries.[550] In making its determination, the supervisory authority may take into account decisions taken by competent EU authorities.[551]

In its assessment of whether a country offers an adequate level of data protection, the supervisory authority is guided by a range of criteria outlined in Art. 47 KDPL 2019. These criteria include those adopted from the GDPR, as well as some additional criteria not explicitly covered by the GDPR. The 'innovative' criteria stipulated by the KDPL 2019 include criteria such as the type of personal data to be processed, the purpose and duration of the proposed processing, the measures to secure personal data used in such countries, whether the foreign data controller or data processor performs adequate organisational and technical procedures and measures to protect personal data, the effectiveness of the technical and organisational measures implemented by foreign data controllers and processors to protect personal data etc.[552] These additional criteria seem to be very case specific, considering that it may be difficult to take into account factors such as the type of personal data or the purpose and duration of processing when determining whether a country provides an adequate level of data protection.

The supervisory authority has published a list of countries providing an adequate level of data protection in accordance with Art. 46 KDPL 2019.[553] Unlike in the Macedonian and Serbian GDPR-like data protection laws, EU Member States are not automatically per law recognised as countries providing adequate data protection, but they are on the supervisory authority's adequacy list.[554] However, none of the neighbouring countries are included on the adequacy list. This is questionable, considering that countries such as North Macedonia and Serbia have adopted new GDPR-like laws and could possibly be considered as providing an adequate level of data protection compared to Kosovo.[555]

Finally, the supervisory authority is required to periodically review the adequacy list at least every four years, taking into account any relevant developments

549 Art. 46(1) KDPL 2019.

550 *Ibid.*

551 Art. 46(2) KDPL 2019.

552 Art. 47 KDPL 2019.

553 Decision on the countries providing an adequate level of data protection, no. 11/2021 (13.09.2021), available at the following link <https://aip.rks-gov.net/download/decision-the-list-of-the-countries-and-international-organizations/> (accessed on 08.06.2023).

554 Moreover, the adequacy list (13.09.2021) also includes Argentina, Andorra, Canada, Guernsey, Isle of Man, Jersey, Faroe Islands, Israel, New Zealand, Uruguay, Japan and the United Kingdom as countries providing an adequate level of data protection (n. 553).

555 Chapter 7 discusses in more detail the possible reasons why other WB6 countries were not included in the supervisory authority's adequacy list.

in the third country or international organisation in question.[556] Meanwhile, it remains to be observed whether the supervisory authority decides to change its approach and not base its decisions exclusively on the EU Commission's decisions, finding instead new arrangements that are likely to be more beneficial for Kosovo.

b) Transfer Approval

The second option for transfer of personal data foresees the supervisory authority authorising transfers of personal data to countries or organisations which do not ensure an adequate level of data protection.[557] A 'transfer approval' can be granted if certain conditions outlined in Art. 49 KDPL 2019 are met. These conditions include cases set out in Art. 49(1) GDPR, as well as two additional criteria: 1) if this is provided by another law or binding international treaty and 2) if the controller provides adequate safeguards for the protection of personal data and the fundamental rights and freedoms of individuals. These safeguards can be in the form of contractual provisions or general terms of business activities which govern the transfer of personal data.[558] Furthermore, the KDPL 2019 stipulates that the supervisory authority is required to maintain a register of authorisations for data transfers, which enhances transparency and is published on the supervisory authority's website alongside the name of the data exporter.[559]

Despite not explicitly transposing the GDPR's provisions on appropriate safeguards (Art. 46) and binding corporate rules (Art. 47), one of the criteria for the transfer approval is that the data controller ensures adequate safeguards, which may result from "the provisions of the contract" or "the general terms of business activities governing the transfer of personal data". This implies that the KDPL 2019 does recognise some sort of additional safeguards, such as the SCCs under the GDPR. However, even in such cases companies would need to obtain an approval, which is a stringent approach compared to the GDPR. It is still unclear whether the supervisory authority will provide its own version of contract clauses for data transfers or adopt the EU Commission's SCCs.

According to the information available on the supervisory authority's website, only one data transfer to the USA has been authorised through this procedure. The

---

556 Art. 47(3) KDPL 2019.

557 Art. 49 KDPL 2019.

558 Art. 49(1.9) KDPL 2019.

559 In the Decision on the authorisation of personal data transfer on behalf of FINCA to the USA No. 03/2021 (19.11.2021) the name of both the data exporter (FINCA Kosovo) and the data importer (ACCION International) are publicly available at the following link <https://aip.rks-gov.net/bs/odluke/> (accessed on 17.12.2022).

supervisory authority based its decision on a data transfer agreement between the importer and the exporter, under which the importer is obliged to comply with the KDPL 2019.[560] In addition to the data transfer agreement, the supervisory authority also considered other circumstances, such as the fact that the data would be stored on a server provider, Amazon Web Service, which complies with international standards according to the supervisory authority, the purpose of the data transfer, and the six-month storage period of personal data.[561] However, it should be noted that a data transfer impact assessment (hereinafter: "TIA"), which is obligatory for data exporters under clause 14 of the new model of SCCs,[562] was not required.

12 Penalties

The KDPL 2019 stipulates the fines for non-compliance with the provisions of the KDPL 2019, differentiating between 'minor' and 'serious and great' violations. General conditions apply to minor violations which are specifically defined by the KDPL 2019[563] with a penalty of up to €40,000 for the breaching entity and up to €2,000 for its responsible person.[564] However, as an exception, the KDPL 2019 provides for penalties of up to 4 % of the general turnover of the previous fiscal year in line with the GDPR for situations in which the supervisory authority determines a 'serious and great' violation of personal data.[565] The terms 'serious' and 'great' have not been defined by the law, indicating that the supervisory authority has the freedom of interpretation to assess and determine when to impose such fines.

The KDPL 2019 also envisages a special responsibility of natural persons as responsible persons for both the private and public sectors, whereas the fine for responsible person in private sector is higher in comparison to the public sec-

560 Decision on the authorisation of personal data transfer on behalf of FINCA to the USA No. 03/2021 (n. 559).

561 *Ibid*, p 2.

562 Barbara Sandfuchs, "The Future of Data Transfers to Third Countries in Light of the CJEU's Judgment EUGH Aktenzeichen C-311/18 – Schrems II", GRUR Int. (2021), p. 245; EDPB, "Recommendations 01/2020 on measures that supplement transfer tools to ensure compliance with the EU level of protection of personal data (R01/2020)"; for a comprehensive summary and analysis, see also Caitlin Fennessy, "A breakdown of EDPB's recommendations for data transfers post-'Schrems II", IAPP (11.12.2020).

563 Offences are listed in the Artt. 92–104 KDPL 2019.

564 Art. 92 KDPL 2019.

565 Art. 105 KDPL 2019 states explicitly that these fines are in compliance with the GDPR.

tor.[566] In addition, the KDPL 2019 establishes a responsibility of individuals as controllers with a fine ranging from four hundred (€400) to one thousand (€1,000).[567]

The fines are generally lower with respect to the penalties introduced by the GDPR. However, in an analogous comparison, the KDPL 2010 provided for much lower penalties, up to €10,000 for the infringing company and up to €2,000 for the responsible person.[568] Hence, the new law represents a significant step of alignment with the penal provisions of the GDPR.

13 Specific Processing Situations

The KDPL 2019 stipulates several provisions relating to specifying processing situations, including direct marketing (Art. 73) together with the right to object to direct marketing (Art. 74), different situations of video surveillance (chapter 16), use of biometric features (chapter 17), records of entry and exit from premises (chapter 18), public books (chapter 19), and linking filing systems (chapter 20). This part contains certain provisions which are not envisaged by the GDPR or provisions that require attention due to potential difficulties in harmonisation with the GDPR.

a) Direct Marketing

The KDPL distinguishes two different types of consent for processing of personal data for direct marketing purposes – 'implicit consent' (soft opt-in) and 'explicit consent' (opt-in).[569] In the first case, data controllers may process personal data explicitly enumerated by the KDPL 2019 – personal name(s), permanent or temporary address, telephone number, e-mail address and fax number – for direct marketing purposes acquired from publicly accessible sources or within the framework of the lawful performance of activities for the purposes of offering goods, services, employment or temporary performance of work using postal services, telephone calls, electronic mail or other telecommunications means[570] in case they have obtained an implicit consent (soft opt-in).[571] Personal data beyond the

566 Each offence stipulates the fine for the responsible person separately.
567 E.g. Artt. 95(4), 98(4), 99(4), 102(4) KDPL 2019.
568 Art. 79 KDPL 2010.
569 Art. 73 KDPL 2019.
570 Art. 73(2) KDPL 2019.
571 IPA's Guidelines for the Processing of Personal Data for Direct Marketing Purposes MDHP Guidelines (24.05.2022) defines the soft-opt in as "implicit consent is a type of consent where the action of one party implies that consent has been given for the processing of personal data for a specific purpose. For example, this happens when the data subject discloses personal data in the

aforementioned types of personal may be processed with the 'explicit' consent (opt-in) of the data subject.[572] Transparency obligations and data protection principles need to be respected in both cases.[573]

This approach is comparatively more liberal than the GDPR. The GDPR does not provide detailed information on the possible legal basis for direct marketing. However, in general, the basis for assessing the permissibility of processing personal data for direct marketing purposes may be, in addition to the consent of the data subject, which must meet the criteria of Art. 7, a balancing of interests pursuant to Art. 6 (1)(f) GDPR (legitimate interest).[574] According to this, the processing must be necessary to protect the legitimate interests of the controller and the interests of the data subject must not be overridden.[575] Hence, companies who intend to rely on legitimate interest still must perform the balancing exercise prescribed by Art. 6 (1)(f) GDPR. In contrast, the KDPL 2019 does not reference to legitimate interest as a possible legal basis for direct marketing. Rather, Art. 73 KDPL 2019 explicitly allows for a 'soft-opt in' for the processing of personal data specifically enumerated in Art. 73(2). An 'explicit' consent is only required if the personal data in question is not included in the list provided by the KDPL 2019. It is worth noting that this is a similar approach as in the UK data protection law,[576] for which the EU Commission found that it ensures an adequate level of data protection.[577]

b) Biometric Data

The KDPL 2019 introduces specific regulations for the use of 'features' in both the public and private sectors. It stipulates that "determination and use of a data subject's biometric features and their comparison to allow his or her identification

context of obtaining a service, which implies that he/she agrees that his/her data may be processed for the purpose of providing the service in question".

572 Art. 73(3) KDPL 2019.

573 Art. 73(2) KDPL 2019.

574 See German Data Protection Conference ('DSK'), Orientierungshilfe der Aufsichtsbehörden zur Verarbeitung von personenbezogenen Daten für Zwecke der Direktwerbung unter Geltung der Datenschutz-Grundverordnung (DSGVO) available at the following link <https://www.datenschutzkonferenz-online.de/media/oh/OH-Werbung_Februar%202022_final.pdf> (accessed on 16.06.2023), p. 3.

575 *Ibid.*

576 See Information Commissioner Office's Guidance on direct marketing using electronic mail, available at the following link <https://ico.org.uk/for-organisations/guide-to-pecr/guidance-on-direct-marketing-using-electronic-mail/how-do-we-comply-with-the-rules-on-sending-marketing-by-electronic-mail/#howdoweusesoft> (accessed on 08.05.2023).

577 UK Adequacy Decision (n. 248).

shall be governed by the provisions of this law."[578] The private sector may only employ biometric features when necessary to perform tasks for the safety of individuals, securing property, or safeguarding confidential data or business secrets. However, prior approval of the supervisory authority is required before implementing the use of biometric features in the private sector.[579] In contrast, there is no obligation to obtain the supervisory authority's approval in the public sector.[580] As a result, the KDPL 2019 gives the public sector more room for manoeuvre in this area.

c) Video Surveillance

While the GDPR does not provide rules on video surveillance, the KDPL 2019 devotes significant attention to the subject. The KDPL 2019 establishes detailed provisions on video surveillance in both the public and private sectors,[581] introducing special rules for different types of video surveillance, including the monitoring of official and business premises (Art. 76), monitoring of apartment buildings (Art. 77), video surveillance in the employment sector (Art. 78), and video surveillance by drones (Art. 79). The KDPL 2019 sets forth additional measures aimed at protecting the privacy rights of data subject. To this end, data controllers are mandated to make a decision regarding the introduction of video surveillance, which includes determining where cameras may be placed, obligating the posting of visible and public notice concerning video surveillance, and informing data subjects in advance.[582] While the rules for the private sector seem to be more stringent and very detailed, the rules for the public sector are more general, leaving a lot of room for interpretation and regulation by other legislation.

14 Conclusion to II

Kosovo has adopted a new GDPR-like law, KDPL 2019, which replicates the GDPR provisions in most parts (definitions, data protection principles, personal scope, data transfers etc.). The KDPL 2019 sets out the core general data protection principles that the EU Commission shall take into account when assessing whether the third country ensures a level of data protection essentially equivalent to the one established by the EU legislation, but certain reservations exist. While the structural similarity between the KDPL 2019 and the GDPR is quite obvious, the

578 Art. 80 KDPL 2019.
579 Art. 83 KDPL 2019.
580 Art. 81 KDPL 2019.
581 Art. 75(2)(4) KDPL 2019.
582 *Ibid.*

KDPL 2019, like all other WB6 data protection laws, lacks the explanatory part found in the Recitals of the GDPR. Notwithstanding this absence, Kosovo's data protection framework demonstrates a careful approach to regulating certain GDPR-derived provisions, particularly regarding security obligations and specifying technical and organisational measures. The law also distinguishes between low-risk and high-risk data controllers, thereby imposing obligations in accordance with their respective processing activities and the nature of their business. This approach represents a shift from the 'one-size-fits-all' solution that has been criticised in the context of the GDPR. Furthermore, in addition to the appointment of a DPO, the legislation provides that companies must appoint other competent persons responsible for the implementation of the KDPL 2019, in particular with regard to security obligations.

Nevertheless, some provisions of the KDPL 2019 remain vague, especially those related to data transfers and the criteria for issuing an adequacy decision. Moreover, none of other WB6 countries are on the IPA's adequacy list, although some of these countries have aligned their legislation with the GDPR.[583] In this context, it appears that Kosovo's legal framework conforms to the EU Commission's decisions, possibly for fear of not being classified by the EU Commission as a country providing adequate level of data protection (onward data transfers). Lastly, the KDPL 2019 introduces additional specific processing situations, such as video surveillance or use of biometric features. Direct marketing, categorised as one of the specific processing situations is regulated in a relatively permissive manner, allowing for implicit consent for the processing of personal data for direct marketing purposes for certain types of personal data.

III Supervisory Authority

The public authority with the competence in the field of data protection in Kosovo is the IPA – Information and Private Agency (in Albanian, *Agjencia për Informim dhe Privatësi* and in Serbian: *Agencija za informacije i privatnost*). The IPA replaced the NAPDP as supervisory authority in the field of data protection. Prior to the establishment of the NAPDP in June 2011, Kosovo lacked any authority responsible for data protection, which left data subjects without effective protection.[584] This had numerous implications for the consolidation of its capacities,

583 Chapter 7 discusses in more detail the possible reasons why other WB6 countries were not included in the supervisory authority's adequacy list.

584 Merita Kostanica, pp. 1227–1238 (n. 496).

as the NAPDP had to react retroactively to data protection violations committed before its existence.[585] By adopting the KDPL 2019, the IPA took over all functions and rights as well as the staff of the NAPDP.[586]

1 General Functions

The organisational structure of the IPA is divided into two special professional scopes, one for access to public documents and another one for the protection of personal data.[587] The IPA's scope of personal data protection involves several key responsibilities, including the supervision of the implementation of the KDPL 2019, the promotion of the right to data protection and to raising public awareness of personal data protection.[588] The IPA has also competences to conduct investigations, impose fines, and handle data subjects' complaints.[589] Alongside these functions, the IPA's tasks include advising the parliament, the government, and other institutions and bodies on legislative and administrative measures concerning the processing of personal data.[590] In addition, the IPA has the task to publish regularly transparent information on its activities, including relevant material such as any court decisions concerning data protection, opinions, recommendations, public statements on inspections and professional literature.[591]

2 Independence

Pursuant to the KDPL 2019 the IPA is an autonomous public authority and acts free from any external influence, direct or indirect, in carrying out its duties and exercising its powers, and does not request or take instructions from anyone.[592] The IPA is led by the commissioner, who shall be elected by the parliament for a five years mandate with the right to be re-elected for another mandate.[593] The conditions for the appointment of the commission include, inter alia, experience and outstanding knowledge in the field of the protection of human rights, not having held any position in a political party during the last five years and not hav-

585 National Council for European Integration, Report, Thematic Roundtable on Justice, Freedom and Security 2020, pp. 104–106, available at the following link <https://president-ksgov.net/repository/docs/TRT_2_ENG.pdf> (accessed on 30.05.2023).
586 Art. 108 KDPL 2019.
587 Art. 57(1) KDPL 2019.
588 Art. 64(1) KDPL 2019.
589 Art. 64(1.5)(1.7) KDPL 2019.
590 Art. 64(1.6) KDPL 2019.
591 Art. 67 KDPL 2019.
592 Art. 57(1) KDPL 2019.
593 Art. 59 KDPL 2019.

ing been a member of Parliament or a member of the Government cabinet during the last term of office.[594]

The IPA is financed from the state budget and has its own budget line, which should guarantee its independence.[595] The IPA is obliged to submit an annual activity report on its work to the parliament and to publish it by 31 March each year for the previous calendar year.[596]

3 Powers

Rather than copying the GDPR in its entirety, the competences and authorities of the IPA have been further elaborated. The KDPL 2019 makes a distinction between tasks and competencies under Art. 64 and contains a separate chapter 14, specifically dedicated to inspections and audits. The inspections include regular inspections on the initiative of the IPA and irregular inspections following complaints from data subjects.[597] In case the IPA finds violations of data protection it may issue corrective powers, which include, inter alia, issuing warnings, imposing a temporary or definitive ban on the processing of personal data or transfer of personal data and ordering controllers or processors to comply with the requirements of data subjects to exercise their rights.[598] Thus, such corrective measures correspond to Art. 58(2) GDPR. Compared to its predecessor, the IPA now has greater powers and competencies under the KDPL 2019. For instance, the NAPDP was not entitled to impose fines under the KDPL 2010.[599]

4 Challenges

As set out in detail above, the IPA has a very wide scope of work and powers. However, one of the primary challenges in the work of the IPA is the need for additional capacity building and human resources to effectively cover this broad range of work and competences.[600]

---

594 *Ibid.*
595 Art. 62 KDPL 2019.
596 Art. 66 KDPL 2019.
597 Art. 68 KDPL 2019.
598 Art. 71 KDPL 2019.
599 Art. 49 KDPL 2010 regulating corrective powers did not include a power of the NDPA to impose fines. See more on critics of NDPA powers under the 2010 KDPL: Njomeza Zejnullahu, "Imposition of Monetary Sanctions as a Mechanism for Protection of Personal Data: Comparative Analysis of Kosovo and Slovenia", 2 Eur. Data Prot. L. Rev. 80 (2016).
600 RCC Report 2020, p. 88 (n. 18).

Despite this challenge, the IPA has already issued several guidelines to further clarify the implementation of the KDPL 2019, such as guidelines on security measures,[601] guidelines for the processing of personal data for direct marketing purposes,[602] guidelines for using the camera surveillance system for data controllers[603] and guidelines for political parties during the election campaign.[604] However, there remains a lack of guidance in other areas, in particular with regard to data transfer rules, as the KDPL 2019 does not provide adequate safeguards for data transfers to countries which do not ensure an adequate level of data protection and rules on deciding which countries provide an adequate level of data protection seem not to be completely clear.[605] Moreover, the IPA's guidelines are predominantly published exclusively in Albanian language, despite its obligation to publish documents in both Albanian and Serbian language.[606] The IPA's website is also primarily available only in Albanian, limiting accessibility for non-Albanian speakers in Kosovo. Furthermore, the annual work reports are not available on the IPA's website.[607]

Another issue that has been observed is the presence of political influence on the IPA. The election of the current commissioner was posed with difficulties as the IPA was unable to elect a commissioner for several months, considering that the recruitment process was cancelled due to allegations of several NGOs in Kosovo that the shortlisted candidates were close to certain political parties

601 Already explained in Chapter 4, C.II.9.

602 Guidelines for the Processing of Personal Data for Direct Marketing Purposes MDHP Guidelines (24.05.2022), available at the following link <https://aip.rks-gov.net/mbrojtja-e-te-dhenave-personale/mbrojtja-e-te-dhenave-personale/> (accessed on 30.05.2023).

603 Guidelines for Using the Camera Surveillance System for Data Controllers MDHP Guidelines (30.03.2022) available at the following link <https://aip.rks-gov.net/mbrojtja-e-te-dhenave-personale/mbrojtja-e-te-dhenave-personale/> (accessed on 30.05.2023).

604 Guidelines for political parties during the election campaign MDHP Guidelines (15.09.2021) available at the following link <https://aip.rks-gov.net/mbrojtja-e-te-dhenave-personale/mbrojtja-e-te-dhenave-personale/> (accessed on 30.05.2023).

605 Explained in Chapter 4, C.II.12.

606 Art. 1 (1.1.) Law No. 02/L-37 of 2006 on the Use of Languages 26 July 2006, available on the following link <https://www.refworld.org/docid/4ae96d832.html> (accessed 07.05.2023).

607 Despite Art. 66 KDPL 2019, which stipulates that the IPA shall submit an annual activity report on its work to the Assembly of Kosovo and publish it no later than 31 March of the following year, the IPA has published only information that it has submitted the annual report to the Assembly, while the report itself is not available. However, the IPA published a brief media report, currently available only for 2021: "Media report for 2021 (30.12.2021) " <https://aip.rks-gov.net/download/raporti-mediatik-per-vitin-2021-i-agjencise-per-informim-dhe-privatesi/> available at the following link (accessed on 03.04.2023).

and that there had been political influence in the procedure.[608] This overshadowed the independence of the newly established data protection authority, as it could not be functional without the elected commissioner. Finally, the commissioner was elected in June 2021.[609]

5 Conclusion to III

The IPA in Kosovo plays a crucial role in protecting personal data and supervising its processing. Its competencies and powers are now more comprehensive and include tasks such as monitoring compliance with the KDPL 2019, conducting investigations, handling data subjects' complaints and imposing fines. However, the IPA faces several challenges. As a newly-setup institution, taking over duties and rights from its predecessor, the NAPDP, and at the same time acquiring new competences and powers, achieving full functionality and independence is a challenging task. Nevertheless, the IPA has already issued important publications that help to clarify new concepts and obligations under the KDPL 2019, which are modelled on the GDPR. To address these challenges and strengthen the independence of the IPA, it is crucial that appropriate measures are taken to ensure that the IPA is not subject to political influence and is provided with sufficient resources and capacity-building initiatives to enable it to carry out its tasks effectively and independently.

IV Case Law and Enforcement

Case law in Kosovo does not appear to be extensive, not implying that there are no data protection violations, but rather that there is a lack of data protection awareness among citizens. Some authors argue that this lack is due to the fact that data protection rights are seen as a 'luxury' in the face of the ongoing problems of Kosovo society and the myriad of post-conflict issues that have hampered the in-

---

608 Egzon Dahsyla, "Political League: NGOs Demand Cancellation of selection of the Information and Privacy Commissioner", available at the following link <https://kallxo.com/shkurt/lidhja-politike-ojq-te-kerkojne-anulimin-e-perzgjedhjes-se-komisionerit-per-informim-dhe-privatesi/>; Xhorxhina Bami, Analysis "Kosovo Lawmakers Play Politics with Personal Data", published by BIRN, (21.09.2021), available at the following link <https://balkaninsight.com/2020/09/21/kosovo-lawmakers-play-politics-with-personal-data/> (both accessed on 07.05.2023).

609 Diellza Luzha, article "Krenare Sogojeva-Dërmaku zgjidhet komisionere e Agjencisë për Informim dhe Privatësi" (Enf. Krenare Sogojeva-Dërmaku is elected commissioner of the Agency for Information and Privacy) published by online Platform Kallxo.com, available at the following link <https://kallxo.com/lajm/krenare-sogojeva-dermaku-zgjidhet-komisionere-e-agjencise-per-informim-dhe-privatesi/> (accessed on 08.05.2023).

centives to develop a human rights approach.[610] Moreover, the fact that the NAPDP did not have the power to impose fines on data controllers and data processors limited the raising of awareness.[611] This authority could only in minor cases of violations warn or admonish the data controller or data processor or impose a temporary or definite ban on the processing of personal data.[612] This part will present both the activities of the supervisory authority and the case law before the national courts to provide a solid overview of the level of enforcement of data protection standards in Kosovo. However, considering that the IPA is a newly established institution, the activities of the supervisory authorities presented in this part are only related to the KDPL 2019.

1 Activities of the Supervisory Authority

The activities of the IPA in enforcing the KDPL 2019 have evolved over time since its establishment. According to the media report for 2021, in the field of data protection, the IPA has carried out the supervision of the implementation of the KDPL 2019 only through the review of complaints and requests addressed by citizens, public institutions and the private sector. There was none performed inspection due to limited capacities of the IPA.[613] The number of cases handled has been relatively low with twenty-two requests for legal advice, thirty-five complaints, and three requests for authorisation of international transfer of personal data.[614] These cases have mainly been related to personal data processing through camera surveillance systems, right to access, and direct marketing.[615] Nevertheless, recent data available on the IPA's website suggests that the IPA was significantly more active in 2022. It carried out 213 inspections and issued eight fines.[616] Moreover, the number of data subject complaints increased to 145, a significant increase compared to 2021.[617] Also, public authorities appear to be engaged in actions that

610 Thematic Roundtable on Justice, Freedom and Security 2020, p. 106 (n. 585).
611 Art. 29(2) KDPL 2010. See also Bluebook 21st ed. Njomeza Zejnullahu (n. 599).
612 Art. 49 KDPL 2010.
613 Media Report 2021 (n. 608).
614 *Ibid.*
615 *Ibid.*
616 General Overview of the Activities of the Information and Privacy Agency for 2022, available at the following link <https://aip.rks-gov.net/bs/opsti-prgled-aktivnosti-agencije-za-informacije-i-privatnost-za-2022-godinu/> (accessed on 08.05.2023).
617 *Ibid.*

fail to comply with data protection standards.[618] Nevertheless, data subjects do not seem to show a strong tendency to exercise their rights to challenge such infringements. This may be attributed to data subjects' insufficient understanding of their rights. The IPA's Commissioner confirmed this observation in November 2022, stating that the IPA has not received a single complaint from private individuals about data protection violations by public institutions since January 2022, which may be due to the fact that citizens are not aware of this possibility.[619]

It is also worth noting that, as mentioned above, the IPA has published several useful guidelines to controllers and processors, with a particular focus on security measures. The IPA has made great efforts to regulate detailed provisions and differentiate between high-risk and low-risk controllers, aimed at supporting smaller companies where the one-size-fits-all approach may not be appropriate. Moreover, the IPA is organising various workshops and lectures aimed at raising public awareness, which is of great importance given the low level of general awareness of data protection in Kosovo.[620] For instance, a survey of the former supervisory authority, NAPDP, in 2015 revealed that 56 % of respondents were unaware of the authority's existence, while 44 % were aware of its existence.[621]

2 Court Case Law

In Kosovo, there is limited judicial precedent regarding personal data protection. This can be partly attributed to the fact that under the old legislation, the supervisory authority did not have the power to impose fines on data controllers in cases of non-compliance, so there was no need for controllers or data subjects to challenge the supervisory authority's decisions imposing fines. On the other hand, the former supervisory authority failed to refer possible breaches of the data protection law to the competent courts for the purpose of requesting imposition of fines in accordance with the KDPL 2010.[622] Moreover, while data subjects did have the right to judicial remedy, they rarely exercised this right as court proceedings usually last very long and judges may lack the same expertise as employees of the supervisory authority.[623] As a consequence, only two cases have been

618 Article published in BIRN "In Kosovo and Albania, Personal Data Up for Grabs", (14.11.2022), available at the following link <https://balkaninsight.com/2022/11/14/in-kosovo-and-albania-personal-data-up-for-grabs/> (accessed on 04.03.2023).

619 *Ibid.*

620 Detailed information available on the IPA's website <https://aip.rks-gov.net/en/ipa-actions/> (accessed on 08.05.2023).

621 Hajdari, P., Nimani, P., Hebibi, D., and Maloku (2022), pp. 5036–5044, (n. 14).

622 Njomëza Zejnullahu, p. 311 (n. 14).

623 *Ibid.* p. 312.

ruled by the court regarding the right to protection of personal data until 2020.[624] The first court decision was in 2018, when the Basic Court of Pristina ruled on a case that had been brought on by the NAPDP in 2014 for the imposition of a fine amounting to €12,000 for unlawful processing of personal data through a video surveillance system.[625] In the second decision of the same year a fine of €9,000 was imposed on the Kosovo Electricity Supply Company (KESCO) for the failure to prevent unauthorised access to personal data of its customers.[626]

3 Conclusion to IV

The limited case law in Kosovo highlights the need for effective enforcement mechanisms to ensure compliance with personal data protection regulations. The introduction of the KDPL 2019, which grants the IPA the power to impose fines on data controllers and processors, represents a significant step forward in this regard. Moreover, while the IPA has made significant efforts to enforce the KDPL 2019, there remain challenges in raising awareness among data subjects and building the IPA's capacity to perform its duties effectively. However, recent developments indicate that the IPA is becoming more active and is taking important steps to raise public awareness about data protection and to regulate the implementation of the KDPL 2019 through various measures, such as the issuance of guidelines and the organisation of workshops. This positive development was also acknowledged by the EU Commission report for 2022.[627]

V Conclusion to C

Kosovo, a potential EU candidate country has largely aligned its national data protection framework with the GDPR. The KDPL 2019, which represents a replica of the GDPR, was adopted already in 2019 and has been in force for a considerable period. While the KDPL 2019 seems to be largely aligned with the GDPR, given its close resemblance to the GDPR provisions, certain obstacles remain regarding possible obtaining of an adequacy decision from the EU Commission.

---

624 No information in Serbian or English is publicly available after this period.

625 Njomëza Zejnullahu, p. 309 (n. 14).

626 *Ibid.*

627 EU Commission Report Kosovo 2022, SWD(2022) 334 final (12.10.2022), pp. 31–32, available at the following link <https://neighbourhood-enlargement.ec.europa.eu/system/files/2022-10/Kosovo%20Report%202022.pdf> (accessed on 23.05.2023).

The supervisory authority, IPA, possesses extensive tasks and powers, taken from the provisions of the GDPR regulating independent supervisory authority. However, it appears that the IPA lacks sufficient resources to execute effectively its responsibilities and educate adequately data controllers and processors. Additionally, there appears to be a general lack of awareness among the public in Kosovo regarding their data protection rights, as highlighted by the EU Commission. The limited number of case law, which cannot be solely attributed to companies and public authorities diligently adhering to the data protection framework, further underscores this observation. Furthermore, it seems that public authorities exhibit less caution when processing personal data. Nevertheless, with the IPA now empowered to impose fines for breaches of the KDPL 2019, there is potential for an increase in awareness among data controllers and processors, as well as overall enforcement of data protection legislation.

D Montenegro

Montenegro signed a SAA with the EU in October 2007 which entered into force in May 2010.[628] On 17 December 2010, Montenegro was granted EU candidate status.[629] So far, Montenegro is the most advanced country in its negotiation process, having opened all 33 screened chapters of the EU acquis, and has provisionally closed negotiations on three.[630] Harmonisation with EU legislation in the field of data protection, as well as the establishment of a data protection authority, are envisaged in Art. 81 SAA.

---

628 Stabilisation and Association Agreement between the European Communities and their Member States, of the one part, and Montenegro, of the other part (2010) O.J. (L 108), available at the following link <https://eur-lex.europa.eu/EN/legal-content/summary/stabilisation-and-association-agreement-with-montenegro.html> (accessed on 01.09.2022).

629 Information from EU Commission website “Candidate Countries and Potential Candidates”, available at the following link <https://ec.europa.eu/environment/enlarg/candidates.htm> (accessed on 20.9.2022).

630 Motion for a European Parliament Resolution on the 2019–2020 Commission Reports on Montenegro, 2019/2173(INI) (20.04.2021).

I Constitutional Parameters and International Commitments

The Constitution of Montenegro[631] envisages as one the basic human rights the right to privacy[632] and right to data protection.[633] The right to privacy is aligned with Art. 8 ECHR. The right to data protection encompasses several aspects of data protection, such as the prohibition of the use of personal data for purposes other than the ones for which they were collected, the right of individuals to be informed about the data collected about them, and the right to seek judicial protection.[634]

In terms of the hierarchy of international instruments in the legal system, the Constitution of Montenegro adopts the principle of the supremacy of international law.[635] Ratified international agreements and accepted rules of international law form an integral part of the domestic legal system.[636] They take precedence over domestic legislation and apply directly when domestic laws diverge from them.[637] In line with this principle, Montenegro ratified the Convention 108 under the auspices of the State Union of Serbia and Montenegro in 2005. However, Montenegro has yet to sign and ratify the Protocol (CETS no. 223) modifying the Convention.[638] As a member of the CoE, Montenegro must also respect the ECHR and individuals have the right to challenge decisions of national courts before the ECtHR.

1 Conclusion to I

In Montenegro, data protection is recognised as a fundamental human right at the constitutional level. The country also recognises international instruments as part of its legal order, including the ECHR and Convention 108. However, Montenegro

---

631 Constitution of Montenegro (Official Gazette of Montenegro, no. 1/2007 and 38/2013 – Amendments I-XVI) (hereinafter: Constitution of Montenegro).

632 Art. 49 Constitution of Montenegro.

633 Art. 43 Constitution of Montenegro.

634 *Ibid.*

635 Art. 9 Constitution of Montenegro.

636 *Ibid.*

637 *Ibid.*

638 CoE, Treaty list for a specific State or International Organisation: Montenegro, available at the following link <https://www.coe.int/en/web/conventions/by-non-member-states-of-the-coe-or-the-european-union?module=treaties-full-list-signature&CodePays=MOT> (accessed on 05.04.2025).

has not yet signed or ratified the Protocol (CETS no. 223), prompting criticism from the EU Commission.[639]

II Data Protection Legislation

The principal legal framework governing data protection in Montenegro is the Law on protection of personal data of 2008[640] (hereinafter: "MDPL 2008"). The MDPL 2008 was enacted in December 2008 and its last amendments were made in April 2017, which were endorsed by the EU Commission. However, the EU Commission also observed that "further efforts [were] needed to implement the national legislation in line with the EU acquis in this area," which was critical for cooperation with Eurojust.[641] Subsequently, the MDPL 2008 was further amended to include provisions relating to video surveillance, but the changes did not alter the substantial elements of the law that are relevant for complying with the EU acquis. With the entry into force of the GDPR, the need for harmonisation with the EU acquis has become even more pressing. Although the MDPL 2008 is not aligned with the GDPR, it is not entirely incompatible with it as it was based on the DPD.

1 Status Quo of GDPR Alignment

Montenegro has started with the drafting of a new data protection law which would be aligned with the GDPR (hereinafter: "Draft"). The Draft was published by the Montenegrin Ministry of Internal Affairs already in April 2019, but it still has not been adopted.[642] After its publication, a public hearing was held in July 2019, during which a number of objections to the Draft law were adopted.[643]

---

639 EU Commission Report for Montenegro 2022, SWD(2022) 335 final (12.10.2022) pp. 35–35, available at the following link <https://neighbourhood-enlargement.ec.europa.eu/system/files/2022-10/Montenegro%20Report%202022.pdf> (accessed on 29.04.2023) .

640 Personal Data Protection Law (Official Gazette of Montenegro, no. 079/08 dated 23.12.2008, 070/09 dated 21.10.2009, 044/12 dated 09.08.2012, 022/17 dated 03.04.2017).

641 EU Commission Report for Montenegro 2012, SWD(2012) 331 final, (10.10.2012), p. 50, available at the following link <https://ec.europa.eu/neighbourhood enlargement/sites/near/files/pdf/key_documents/2012/package/mn_rapport_2012_en.pdf> (accessed on 01.09.2022).

642 The Draft law (published on 10.04.2019) is publicly available on the Ministry of Interior's website at the following link <https://www.gov.me/dokumenta/2ca5b30b-16ef-4fcf-a043-c05e2afa8fe6> (accessed on 29.04.2023).

643 Report on the public discussion regarding the Draft Law on the Protection of Personal Data (published on 10.07.2019), available at the following link <https://www.gov.me/dokumenta/6c2470bc-aeee-4281-95de-3c40c591bb94> (accessed on 29.04.2023).

However, the consolidated text of the Draft after the public hearing is not publicly available. In its 2020 Report for Montenegro, the EU Commission also noted that a new law on protection of personal data was in preparation with the aim of aligning it with the GDPR.[644] This report mentioned that the Draft is expected to be finalised in autumn 2022.[645] However, this deadline was not observed. According to the latest publicly available information the Draft is expected to be adopted in the first half of 2023.[646]

This part will analyse the provisions of the MDPL 2008. The focus will be on the provisions which need to be further aligned with the EU acquis. However, considering that Montenegro is on the path to align its data protection legislation currently in force, an overview of the currently available Draft will be provided in the Section IV.

2 Overview of the MDPL 2008

The MDPL 2008 consists of eight parts. Part 1 contains the general provisions, which include the scope of the law, principles (which are not explicitly defined as principles and consolidated in one article, but found in several articles), definitions and rules for processing of personal data for statistical or scientific research purposes (Art. 2 (3)) (first chapter). Part 2 is the most comprehensive part and provides various concepts and outlines the lawfulness of data processing. Moreover, it governs data controllers and processors, including their obligations related to transparency and security of data processing (second chapter). Part 3 defines special categories of personal data and stipulates the provisions relating to specific processing situations (third chapter). Part 4 lays down rules on international data transfers (fourth chapter). Part 5 sets out the data subject's rights, including the redress rights (chapter five). Part 6 clarifies the role of the supervisory authority and its functions and powers (chapter six and seven). In part 7, the provisions on misdemeanours are defined (chapter eight). Finally, part 8 contains transitional and final provisions (chapter nine).

---

644 EU Commission Report for Montenegro 2020, SWD(2020) 353 final, (06.10.2020), available at the following link <https://www.ecoi.net/en/file/local/2040146/montenegro_report_2020.pdf> (accessed on 01.09.2022).

645 EU Commission Report Montenegro 2022 (n. 639).

646 One trust, Montenegro – Data Protection Overview, (December 2022), available at the following link <https://www.dataguidance.com/notes/montenegro-data-protection-overview> (accessed on 20.01.2023).

3 Scope of the MDPL 2008

The MDPL 2008 distinguishes between material scope and territorial scope. The material scope of the MDPL 2008 is consistent with Art. 3 DPD.[647] Consequently, this also means that the MDPL 2008 does not apply to the processing of personal data for defence, national, and public security purposes, except where otherwise stipulated by separate law.[648] However, a special provision is made for surveillance and interception measures for defence, national, and public security purposes, where the MDPL 2008 continues to apply.[649]

The territorial scope under the MDPL 2008 is also derived from Art. 4 DPD. Apart from applying to controllers and processors within Montenegro,[650] it extends to the personal data filing system of a controller with an establishment outside of Montenegro whose data processing equipment is located in Montenegro, unless such equipment is exclusively used for transit through the territory of Montenegro.[651] This provision is not aligned with the GDPR as the latter replaced the exterritorial scope model provided by the DPD.[652]

4 Definition of Personal Data

The definition of personal data in Montenegro is expounded in two distinct definitions, one defining personal data and the other defining the data subject. Under Art. 9(1) MDPL 2008 personal data include "any information relating to an identified or identifiable natural person", and under Art. 9 (9) a data subject is "a natural person whose identity has been established or can be established, directly or indirectly, and in particular by reference to a personal identification mark or one or more characteristics that are specific to the physical, physiological, mental, economic, cultural or social identity of that person." These definitions were taken from the DPD. They do not necessarily conflict with the definition envisaged by

647 Art. 7 MDPL 2008.

648 Art. 8(1) MDPL 2008; Pursuant to Art. 3 (2) DPD, processing operations concerning public security, defence, state security and the activities of the state in areas of criminal law were also excluded.

649 Art. 8(1) MDPL 2008. The provisions on government access to personal data and interception measures are covered separately in Chapter 5, E.

650 Art. 5(1) MDPL 2008

651 Art. 5(2) MDPL 2008.

652 The extraterritorial scope of the DPD is the subject of further discussion in this Chapter, A.II.3.

the GDPR,[653] but omit some of the newly introduced identifiers by the GDPR such as location data, genetic data, and online identifiers.[654]

5 Data Protection Principles

The MDPL 2008 foresees data protection standards that must be respected when processing personal data. This set of standards are not specifically defined as principles – the definition used by the GDPR – but as 'general provisions'.[655] They are, yet, comparable to principles provided by Art. 5 GDPR and include, inter alia, the principle of accuracy, the principle of lawfulness and fairness, purpose limitation. data minimisation, storage limitation, etc. The principles are largely consistent with Chapter II GDPR, even though the MDPL 2008 is not yet harmonised with the GDPR. However, the accountability principle, the principle of transparency are not explicitly enshrined in the MDPL 2008. Likewise, the concepts of data protection by design and by default (while not defined as principles by Art. 5 GDPR, but are closely connected to them) are neither envisaged by the MDPL 2008.

6 Lawfulness of Processing

The MDPL 2008 establishes six legal grounds for lawful processing of personal data in accordance with the principle of lawfulness. The MDPL 2008 places a strong emphasis on consent as one of the requirements for lawful processing.[656] Other remaining grounds explicitly prescribed by MDPL 2008 include performing the legally prescribed obligations of the controller, protection of life and other vital interests of a person who is not able to give consent in person, performance of a contract, performing activities of public interest or in the exercise of public authority, realisation of the law-based interest of the controller or a third party, i. e. data subjects, unless such interests need to be restricted in order to exercise and protect rights and freedoms.[657]

---

653 Benjamin Wong, "Delimiting the concept of personal data after the GDPR", Legal Studies, 39(3) (2019) pp. 517–532; Nadezhda Purtova, "The law of everything. Broad concept of personal data and future of EU data protection law", Law, Innovation and Technology, 10:1, pp. 40–81 (2018).

654 However, the WP29 stated in its Opinion on the concept of personal data (n. 286) that IP addresses are also personal data, and the question is whether the Montenegrin authority has taken the same approach.

655 Artt. 2–3, 4a MDPL 2008.

656 Art 10 (1) MDPL 2008 uses the formulation "The processing of personal data can be done with the previously obtained consent of the data subject, which can be revoked at any time. Personal data can be processed without the consent of the person if it is necessary to [...]."

657 Art. 10 MDPL 2008.

The above-mentioned legal bases are to a large degree already aligned with the GDPR. The main difference is the restricted legitimate interest as a legal ground for data processing, considering that the MDPL 2008 provides that the legitimate interest of the controller must be based on the law, in contrast to Art. 6(1) (f) GDPR.

a) Consent

Under the GDPR, consent is considered valid only when it possesses certain characteristics, including being freely given, informed, specific, and unambiguous (explicit).[658] The MDPL 2008 defines consent as “a free statement given in writing or orally on record by which an individual signifies his agreement to personal data relating to him being processed for a specific purpose”. As such, the consent under Art. 10(1) MDPL 2008 has several characteristics, including being freely given, in written or verbal form, informed, and specific. Art. 10(1) MDPL 2008 further specifies that consent can be revoked at any time. However, the MDPL 2008 does not provide further rules for obtaining consent, as outlined in Art. 7 GDPR.

Although the basic standard for valid consent is similar to that of the GDPR, the current rules on consent are not completely aligned with the GDPR. In addition to failing to provide rules for obtaining consent, such as using clear and plain language and making the consent intelligible and easily accessible, there are other shortcomings. Firstly, the MDPL 2008 does not recognise the possibility of obtaining consent online, as the precondition for consent is that it must be given in written or verbal form (on a record). This is not up-to-date with the reality of the modern digital world. Secondly, there are no specific rules for assessing whether the consent was given freely.

b) Consent of Deceased Persons

The GDPR does not apply to deceased persons, but it leaves it up to the Member States to regulate it.[659] Various solutions exist among the EU’s national data protection laws.[660] The MDPL 2008 also provides rules for processing data of deceased persons. Consent to the processing of personal data on behalf of a deceased person

658 Art. 7 GDPR.

659 Recital 27 GDPR.

660 E. g. German, Austrian and Belgian data protection laws do not lay down specific provisions on deceased persons, while some other countries, such as Slovakia, France, Denmark and Italy, do; See Bird & Bird “Personal data of deceased persons”, available at the following link <https://www.twobirds.com/en/capabilities/practices/privacy-and-data-protection/general-data-protection-regulation/gdpr-tracker/deceased-persons> (accessed on 30.12.2022).

is given by their legal successors, determined in accordance with the law of succession, unless the deceased person has prohibited the processing of personal data.[661] The Draft removes this provision following the GDPR, as explained in Section IV.

7 Special Categories of Personal Data

The MDPL 2008 recognises the special categories of personal data, admittedly following the definition from the DPD. Consequently, some categories of personal data recognised under the GDPR, such as biometric data, genetic data, and data concerning a person's sexual orientation, are not included in the definition. The DPD did not explicitly regulate biometric data and entrusted it to the Member States through the opening clause.[662] However, the MDPL 2008 governs biometric data as one of the so-called special cases of data processing.[663] In addition to biometric data processing, the remaining special cases of data processing include (1) video surveillance, and (2) records of access to business or official premises.[664]

Processing of special categories of personal data is prohibited unless in a few exceptional cases explicitly envisaged by the MDPL 2008.[665] Accordingly, no processing of special categories of personal data is allowed if it does not 'fit in' one of the exceptional cases. In this regard, the MDPL 2008 is aligned with the GDPR. However, the list of exceptional cases envisaged by the MDPL 2008 does not fully correspond to the list envisaged by the GDPR. For instance, one of the exceptional cases includes processing as part of the legitimate activities of a non-profit organisation or association with political, philosophical, religious, or trade union objectives.[666]

8 Rights of Data Subject

The MDPL 2008 provides for several rights of data subject in chapters II and V, including the right to be informed on a particular processing which involves their personal data,[667] the right to be informed where personal data have not been obtained directly from the data subject,[668] the right to rectification (if a

661 Art. 10(4) MDPL 2008.
662 Art. 8 DPD; WP 29 Working Document on Biometrics 2003 (WP80), p. 9.
663 Artt. 9(8), 31 MDPL 2008.
664 Specific processing situations are analysed later in this Chapter, D.II.10.
665 Art. 13(1) MDPL 2008.
666 Art. 13(1)(6) MDPL 2008.
667 Art. 20 MDPL 2008.
668 Art. 21 MDPL 2008.

data controller establishes that processed data are incomplete or incorrect, it is obliged to supplement or amend them, the same as if it receives the respective request from the data subject),[669] the right to erasure (if a particular data processing is not compliant with the law, a data controller is obliged to delete the processed data upon request of the data subject),[670] the right to restriction of the data processing (if the personal data's accuracy is contested by the data subject),[671] the right to object to the data processing (if the processing is to be performed for direct marketing purposes),[672] and the right not to be subject to a decision based solely on automated processing, including profiling.[673]

The above-mentioned rights are in correlation with the provisions of the GDPR, although not fully aligned. For instance, the right to erasure is not as comprehensive as 'right to be forgotten' envisaged by the GDPR.[674] The right to data portability (Art. 20 GDPR) is not covered by the MDPL 2008 at all. Moreover, same as in the BDPL 2006 (Bosnian Data Protection Law) the term 'profiling' is not explicitly used but rather "accessing certain personal characteristics and abilities of data subject" and there are only two exceptions in which automated decision making may be allowed, namely the performance of a contract and the legal obligation of the controller.[675]

The MDPL 2008 foresees the restriction of the rights of data subject. Rights may be restricted 1) for the purposes of defence, national security and public safety, 2) for the prevention of crime and the detection and prosecution of criminal offences, 3) for the protection of economic or financial interests, and 4) for the protection of persons or the rights and freedoms of others, to the extent necessary to achieve the purpose for which the restriction is established in accordance with a specific law.[676]

---

669 Art. 44 MDPL 2008.

670 Artt. 23, 44 MDPL 2008.

671 Art. 23 MDPL 2008.

672 Art. 15 MDPL 2008.

673 Art. 15a MDPL 2008.

674 According to Art. 17 GDPR the data subject has the right to obtain from the controller the erasure of personal data in several cases, such as if the data are no longer necessary, no legal basis exists, the data subject objects to the processing pursuant to Art. 21, the personal data have been collected in connection with the provision of information society services pursuant to Art. 8(1) GDPR, etc. The "right to erasure" pursuant to Art. 23 MDPL 2008 only provides for the general obligation of the controller to erase personal data "at the request of the data subject if processing is not in accordance with the law".

675 Art. 15a(2) MDPL 2008.

676 Art. 45 MDPL 2008.

Unlike the GDPR, which provides further guidance on the legislative measures by which rights may be restricted, the MDPL 2008 does not provide further specific rules, such as that such a restriction must respect the essence of fundamental rights and freedoms, or any specific provisions that must be included in the measure (scope of the restrictions, safeguards to prevent abuse or unlawful access or disclosure, retention periods, risks, etc.).[677]

9 Redress Mechanism

As already mentioned, the MDPL 2008 does not provide a separate chapter dedicated to remedies and liability, but instead includes few provisions in the chapter regulating the data subject's rights. Thus, redress mechanisms are not fully consistent with Chapter 8 GDPR. In particular, the MDPL 2008 does not define specifically a right to an effective judicial remedy, as provided for by the GDPR. The MDPL 2008 only provides for a "request for protection of rights" which shall be submitted to the supervisory authority.[678] This concept is similar to the right to lodge a complaint to the supervisory authority under Art. 77 GDPR. However, there is no right of appeal against the supervisory authority's decision, although an administrative dispute proceeding can be initiated before the competent court.[679] In addition, the MDPL 2008 provides for the right to "initiate the supervisory procedure", which grants everyone (including data subjects) the right to request that the supervisory authority conduct an investigation into the processing activities of controllers.[680] A decision concerning the supervisory procedure can be appealed to the supervisory authority.[681]

Apart from that, data subjects have the right to lodge a complaint with the controller if the controller fails to respond to the data subject's request to delete or supplement incomplete personal data, or to amend or delete inaccurate personal data.[682] Finally, the data subjects also have the right to compensation, under the special law regulating compensation.[683]

---

677 Art. 23 GDPR.
678 Art. 47 MDPL 2008.
679 *Ibid.*
680 This right is not provided for in the chapter dealing with the rights of data subject, but in chapter seven (Art. 65(2) MDPL 2008), which regulates the supervision exercised by the supervisory authority.
681 Art. 68(4) MDPL 2008.
682 Art. 44 MDPL 2008.
683 Art. 48 MDPL 2008.

10 Personal Scope

The concepts of controller, joint controllers and processor are essential for the proper application of the GDPR as they delineate the respective responsibilities for compliance with data protection standards and the ways in which data subjects can enforce their rights. In contrast, the MDPL 2008 only recognises the roles of data controller and data processor. The controller bears primary responsibility for data processing[684] and has a more extensive set of obligations.[685] The controller may engage a processor to carry out data processing activities on their behalf, subject to a written contract,[686] and only with a data processor which fulfils the conditions for implementing appropriate technical and organisational measures,[687] similar to the GDPR. Although the MDPL 2008 appears to align with the GDPR on this point, there are some significant differences. For instance, the MDPL 2008 does not mandate any specific content for a controller-processor agreement and there is no rule that a processor should not engage another processor (sub-processor) without prior written authorisation of the data controller. Indeed, the relationship between controller and processor and their responsibility stems from the DPD. Under the DPD, the controller shall be held liable for data protection compliance, meaning that there are no statutory obligations on processors.[688] Instead, processors can be subject to obligations that the controller imposes on them by contract to protect the controller against compliance risks.[689] This logic is transposed into the MDPL 2008.

a) Security Measures

Controllers and processors must implement appropriate technical, organisational and human resources measures, based on the nature of personal data and the state of the art, taking into account the cost of their implementation.[690] The MDPL 2008 stipulates non-exhaustive examples of these measures, such as protec-

---

684 Art. 48 MDPL 2008 stipulates that only the controller is responsible for the damage suffered by the data subject due to the violation of the rights prescribed in accordance with the general rules on compensation for damage.
685 According to Artt. 17–30 MDPL 2008 the controller shall bear all obligations in connection to the processing of the persona data.
686 Art. 16(1) MDPL 2008.
687 Art. 16(3) MDPL 2008.
688 DPD, see e.g., Art. 23.
689 Jenna Lindqvist, "New challenges to personal data processing agreements: is the GDPR fit to deal with contract, accountability and liability in a world of the Internet of Things?", International Journal of Law and Information Technology, Volume 26, Issue 1, pp. 45–63 (2018).
690 Art. 24(1) MDPL 2008.

tion of the personal data against loss, destruction, unauthorised access, modification, disclosure and misuse.[691] On top of that, the MDPL 2008 provides for some specific obligations[692] not explicitly set out in the GDPR, including 1) determining which types of processed data may be disclosed to third parties as data recipients (and under what conditions), 2) determining which types of personal data may be disclosed to third parties as data recipients (and under which conditions), 3) ensuring that, in case of electronic data processing, certain information about the respective processing is automatically recorded in their IT systems (e.g., data, type of data, time of login and logout, etc.) and 4) keeping records of the recipients of personal data, including the purpose and the legal basis for disclose of data to recipients. These records shall be kept for a period of 10 years, after which they shall be deleted.[693]

Although the above-mentioned security obligations are not strictly provided by the GDPR, they are in line with it. Keeping records of personal data recipients is particularly noteworthy, given recent CJEU case law recognising every person's right to know to whom their personal data has been disclosed and requiring controllers to provide the data subject, upon request, with the actual identity of those recipients.[694]

b) Data Breach Notification

The MDPL 2008 does not recognise concepts of data breach notifications. Nevertheless, the data breach notification concept is recognised by certain sectoral laws currently applicable in Montenegro, i.e., by the Law on Electronic Communications. The said law obliges operators to notify the Montenegrin Agency for Electronic Communications and Postal Services as well as the supervisory authority for data protection in the event of any breach of personal data or privacy of the data subjects, without undue delay.[695] In addition to notifying the relevant authorities, this law obliges the operator to notify the data subjects (i.e. users of the respective telecommunication services) as well, if a particular breach may influence detrimentally the users' personal data or privacy.[696]

691 Art. 24(2) MDPL 2008.
692 Art. 24(3)(4)(5) MDPL 2008.
693 Art. 19 MDPL 2008.
694 Rw v Österreichische Post, CJEU C-154/21, (12.01.2023).
695 Artt. 170–171 Law on Electronic Communications no. 40/2013.
696 Art. 170(3) Law on Electronic Communications no. 40/2013.

c) Records of Processing Activities and Notifying the Supervisory Authority

The MDPL 2008 imposes two distinct obligations to notify the supervisory authority prior to the commencement of personal data processing, as a remnant of the DPD,[697] which ceased to exist with the adoption of the GDPR.[698] The first one presents a general obligation to keep records of filing systems (similar to records of processing activities under the Art. 30 GDPR)[699] and to submit a notification to the supervisory body before the establishment of an automatic personal data collection.[700] The supervisory authority maintains the register of such records, which are available to the public.[701]

The second obligation applies to automatic processing of personal data that presents a special risk to individuals' rights and freedoms, requiring prior consent from the supervisory authority for each processing instance, especially for the processing of special categories of personal data, personality and behaviour assessments of data subjects, video surveillance, and biometric data.[702] The MDPL 2008 foresees some exceptions, such as consent, legal obligation or performance of a contract between the controller and the data subjects.[703] This concept seems to have some similarities with the concept of DPIA under Art. 35 GDPR.

d) DPO

Although the MDPL 2008 does not provide for the concept of a DPO, Art. 24(3) MDPL 2008 states that a controller employing more than 10 employees must designate a person responsible for the protection of personal data after establishing automatic personal data collection.[704] Thus, it seems similar to the concept of the DPO. Unlike the GDPR's rules on the appointment of a DPO, the number of employees is the sole criterion for determining the existence of this obligation, and neither the types of personal data nor the nature or purpose of the data processing activities are relevant.

---

697 Artt. 18–19 MDPL 2008.

698 Recital 89 GDPR states that DPD's general obligation to notify the processing of personal data to the supervisory authorities produced administrative and financial burdens, it did not in all cases contribute to improving the protection of personal data.

699 Art. 26(2) MDPL 2008.

700 Art. 27 MDPL 2008.

701 Artt. 29–30 MDPL 2008.

702 Art. 28 MDPL 2008.

703 *Ibid.*

704 Art. 27 MDPL 2008.

e) Representative

The MDPL 2008 also recognises the concept of a representative.[705] Given the territorial scope of the MDPL 2008[706] the obligation to appoint a foreign representative differs from the GDPR.[707] A foreign controller is obliged to appoint a representative in Montenegro only if it uses equipment located on Montenegrin territory for data processing, unless the equipment is used solely for transferring data over Montenegrin territory.

11 Transfer of Personal Data

Under the MDPL 2008, rules for data transfer are generally more stringent than under the GDPR. There are two main streams of the respective regime: 1) transfers subject to consent of the supervisory authority and 2) transfers without the consent of the supervisory authority. Under the first stream, personal data may be transferred out of Montenegro to another country or organisation if there are adequacy measures in place.[708] The term 'adequacy measures' should not be confused with adequacy decisions under Art. 45 GDPR, though not entirely different in approach. The data controller must obtain prior approval from the supervisory authority each time they plan to transfer personal data. Unlike the GDPR, there are no pre-approved countries which provide an adequate level of data protection. The supervisory authority will only grant an authorisation if it determines that adequate measures are in place to protect personal data (e.g., considering the nature of the data, the purpose of the transfer, the legal provisions in force in the country to which the data will be transferred).[709] The second stream of the data transfer regime includes the explicitly prescribed cases by the MDPL 2008 when a data transfer can be performed without any approval.[710] These cases include situations where the data subject has given prior consent, data transfer is required by law or international agreement, or is necessary for the fulfilment of a contract between the data subject and the data controller. Data transfer is also allowed when it is in the public interest, for the protection of the data subject's life or legal interests, or when the transfer is made from publicly available registries or records. In addition, under this second stream, personal data can be transferred to countries that are members of the EU and EEA or those included

---

705 Art. 5(2) MDPL 2008.
706 The territorial scope stems from the DPD.
707 Art. 3 GDPR.
708 Art. 41(1) MDPL 2008.
709 Art. 41(2) MDPL 2008.
710 Art. 42 MDPL 2008.

in the EU Commission's adequacy list, or when an agreement is made with a data processor from a non-EU country that includes adequate contractual obligations accepted by EU Member States.

The second stream of data transfers that do not require the prior consent of the supervisory authority is a combination of cases covered by Art. 46 and Art. 49 GDPR, with additional specific cases explicitly mentioned in the MDPL 2008. Such specific cases include EU/EEA countries and countries on the EU Commission's adequacy list. However, as other WB6 countries are not on the EU Commission's adequacy list, this also means that they are automatically excluded from the scope of the second stream of data transfers. This creates difficulties in practice, as the WB6 countries are very much economically interlinked.

12 Penalties

The penal policy prescribed by the MDPL 2008 is significantly, although not surprisingly, milder than the penal policy introduced by the GDPR. While the GDPR imposes strict penalties, the MDPL 2008 only provides for liability in case of breach of the law, with the highest fines amounting to EUR 20,000 for legal entities and EUR 2,000 for representatives or natural persons as controllers per offence.[711] Although offence liability under some other laws in force in Montenegro (for example, Consumer Protection Law, Law on Electronic Communications, Corruption Prevention Law, etc.) includes, besides fines, certain corrective measures (e.g., prohibition to perform certain business activities/duties within certain period of time),[712] such measures are not envisaged by the MDPL 2008.

Additionally, criminal liability is also prescribed by the relevant Montenegrin legislation. Specifically, the Montenegrin Criminal Code, introduces a criminal offence of unauthorised collection and use of personal data.[713] This criminal offence is envisaged as one of the criminal offences within the group of criminal offences jointly named "Criminal offences against freedoms and rights of people and citizens."[714] The prescribed sanction is fine (in the amount to be determined by the court) or imprisonment up to three years.[715] However, in general, considering the existing practice, criminal liability remains to be a theoretical possibility.[716]

---

711 Art. 74 MDPL 2008.

712 RCC Report 2020, p. 108 (n. 18).

713 Art. 176 Montenegrin Criminal Code (Official Gazette of the Republic of Montenegro, no. 70/2003, 13/2004 – corrected and 47/2006 and Official Gazette of the Republic of Montenegro, no. 40/2008, 25/2010, 32/2011, 64/2011 40/2013, 56/2013 – amended, 14/2015, 42/2015, 58/2015 – Law, 44/2017, 49/2018 and 3/2020).

714 Chapter XV Montenegrin Criminal Code.

715 Art. 176(4) Montenegrin Criminal Code.

13 Specific Processing Situations

The MDPL 2008 provides for some special types of personal data processing, including biometric measures, records on entry and exit from business or official premises and video surveillance.

a) Biometric Measures

The MDPL 2008 explicitly authorises the public sector to use biometric measures for verifying the identity of individuals entering business or official premises or for monitoring employees, if required by law.[717] Biometric measures are defined as the process of determining and comparing the physical characteristics of an individual.[718] The use of these measures is allowed only if they are necessary for the protection of individuals, property, or confidentiality, and if these aims cannot be achieved by other means or to comply with international obligations and establish the identity of individuals crossing the state borders.[719] These provisions have been carried over to the Draft, as explained in part IV.

b) Records on Entry and Exit from Business or Official Premises

The MDPL 2008 also defines the rules for processing personal data for the purpose of entering business or official premises. In order to protect the safety of persons and property within business or official areas, a legal entity has the right to require a person to state the reasons for entering the business or official areas, provide their personal data and present an identity document for inspection, if so required.[720] The data controller may keep records of entries into and exits from business or official areas, which shall be kept for no longer than one year from the date of collection.[721] These provisions continue to be included in the proposed Draft.

c) Video Surveillance

The MDPL 2008 sets out rules for video surveillance.[722]There are four situations explicitly prescribed by the law: (1) video-surveillance of access to official or busi-

---

716 RCC Report 2020, p. 108 (n. 18).
717 Art. 32(1) MDPL 2008.
718 Art. 31 MDPL 2008.
719 Art. 32(2) MDPL 2008.
720 Art. 33 MDPL 2008.
721 Art. 34 MDPL 2008.
722 Chapter III MDPL 2008.

ness premises,[723] (2) video-surveillance in official or business premises,[724] (3) video-surveillance of entrance to/exit from residential buildings and of joint premises,[725] and (4) video-surveillance of public surfaces.[726] In any case, MDPL 2008 envisages set of safeguards, such as visible notice of video-surveillance,[727] territorial restrictions on video-surveillance,[728] prohibition of transmission of video-surveillance data via electronic means of communication,[729] obligation to keep records of video-surveillance[730] (with personal data being kept for a maximum of six months from the date of creation), previous consent from the supervisory authority for introducing video surveillance of public surfaces[731] and some special safeguards for video-surveillance in employment.[732] The provisions on video surveillance are preserved without modification in the Draft.[733]

14 Conclusion to II

Although the data protection framework in Montenegro is not in line with the GDPR, there are already many similarities with the GDPR, as the MDPL 2008 was adopted on the basis of the provisions of the DPD. However, this underscores the need for updating the existing legislation, not only to accommodate the modifications introduced by the GDPR, but also to address present-day realities. For instance, the inadequacy of the current legal regime is highlighted by unsuitable consent requirements for online data processing, reliance on DPD's exterritorial effect provisions, and the absence of suitable redress mechanisms for data subjects beyond complaints to the supervisory authority. It is commendable that Montenegro has begun the alignment process with the GDPR and has proposed a Draft for a new data protection law in 2019. However, since then there is no further available information nor the publicly available version of the Draft, it is essential for Montenegro to expedite its efforts to ensure its data protection regime is compliant with the EU Acquis.

---

723 Art. 35 MDPL 2008.
724 Art. 36 MDPL 2008.
725 Art. 38 MDPL 2008.
726 Art. 40 MDPL 2008.
727 Art. 39(1) MDPL 2008.
728 Art. 35(3) MDPL 2008.
729 Art. 35(6) MDPL 2008.
730 Art. 37 MDPL 2008.
731 Art. 40a MDPL 2008.
732 Art. 36 MDPL 2008.
733 Chapter V Draft law.

III Supervisory Authority

The supervisory authority in Montenegro is the Agency for Personal Data Protection and Free Access to Information (hereinafter: "Agency"). The Agency is an autonomous public authority established by the MDPL 2008.

1 General Functions

The Agency is responsible for performing the functions of a supervisory authority for both personal data protection and free access to information. Its competences in matters of data protection include monitoring the implementation of the MDPL 2008 and providing opinions on its implementation.[734] Furthermore, the Agency is responsible for receiving and handling data subject complaints ("request for protection of rights").[735] Notably, the Agency does not have the right of legislative initiative, but it may make proposals for assessment of constitutionality of the laws.[736] Additionally, trade associations and other bodies representing "special categories of controllers"[737] must submit their rules of work and conduct, as well as acts on the basis of which they process personal data, to the Agency for approval and assessment of compliance with the law.[738]

2 Independence

The MDPL 2008 states that the Agency is autonomous and independent in performing its tasks.[739] The Agency is comprised of the Council and the Director.[740] The Council consists of a President and two members who are appointed and dismissed by the Parliament of Montenegro.[741] The MDPL 2008 sets out the requirements for appointing a Director, who must be a Montenegrin citizen with a university degree and at least five years of experience in the field of human rights and freedoms.[742] Additionally, the Director or member of the Council may not

---

734 Art. 50 MDPL 2008.
735 Art. 50(2) MDPL 2008.
736 Art. 50(11) MDPL 2008.
737 Special categories of controllers are not defined in the MDPL 2008.
738 Art. 73(a) MDPL 2008.
739 Art. 49(2) MDPL 2008.
740 Art. 52(1) MDPL 2008.
741 Art. 52(2) MDPL 2008.
742 Art. 53 MDPL 2008.

be a member of the government or parliament, an official of a political party, or legally convicted of a criminal offense prosecuted ex officio.[743]

The Agency is required to submit regular annual reports on the state of personal data protection to the Parliament of Montenegro.[744] The Agency may also submit a special report to the Parliament if requested or if the Agency deems that there are special reasons for doing so.[745] The Agency's funding primarily comes from the government budget, though other sources are permitted by law.[746]

3 Powers

The Agency performs the tasks of a supervisory authority as prescribed by the MDPL 2008, with powers that can be categorised as supervisory[747], advisory[748] and corrective powers.[749] As part of its supervisory powers, the Agency conducts investigations into the processing activities of controllers and processors.[750] In order to exercise this power, the Agency has a right of access to files and other documentation related to the processing of personal data, including means of electronic processing of personal data, regardless of the degree of confidentiality.[751] In carrying out its supervisory function, the Agency is authorised to issue corrective measures, such as orders to eliminate irregularities in the processing of personal data within a specified timeframe, temporary prohibition of processing personal data that are processed contrary to the law, ordering the deletion of personal data collected without a legal basis, prohibiting the transfer of personal data from Montenegro, and prohibiting the entrustment of personal data processing tasks to a processor that does not meet the requirements regarding the protection of personal data.[752] The decisions of the Agency are not subject to appeal by controllers, but an administrative dispute may be filed against them.[753] It is important to note, however, that the Agency does not have the power to impose fines on data

743 Art. 54 MDPL 2008.
744 Art. 62(1) MDPL 2008.
745 Art. 62(2) MDPL 2008.
746 Art. 63 MDPL 2008.
747 Art. 65 MDPL 2008.
748 Art. 50 MDPL 2008.
749 Art. 71 MDPL 2008.
750 Chapter VII MDPL 2008.
751 Art. 66 MDPL 2008.
752 Art. 71 MDPL 2008.
753 Art. 72 MDPL 2008.

controllers. The sanctions provided for by the MDPL 2008 can only be imposed before the competent courts.[754]

4 Challenges

The enforcement powers of the Agency under the MDPL 2008 differ significantly from those conferred upon supervisory authorities under the GDPR. Furthermore, the MDPL 2008 lacks additional provisions that would ensure the independence of the Agency, a similar issue to that found in the BDPL 2006.[755] The challenges currently confronting the Agency may be classified into several key areas, as explained below.

a) Lack of Enforcement Powers

The MDPL 2008 grants limited enforcement powers to the Agency, as it is not authorised to directly impose fines on data controllers and processors. The lack of such powers not only diminishes the Agency's independence but also undermines its ability to effectively enforce data protection standards and promote public awareness. Resorting to court proceedings may not be a practical solution, as they can be lengthy and time-consuming, and data subjects may lack the necessary incentives to pursue such remedies. This is evidenced by the fact that only one case was resolved in 2022, related to the disclosure of personal data of individuals infected with Covid-19,[756] a case that attracted a lot of public attention in 2020, as explained further.

b) Understaffing

In addition to the aforementioned challenge of the lack of enforcement powers, the Agency faces a serious obstacle in the form of understaffing. In 2022, the total number of staff employed by the Agency was 33.[757] Considering that the Agency has a double competence, namely the protection of personal data and the freedom of access to information of public interest, this number seems clearly insufficient to cover all the activities that the Agency is tasked to carry out. This

---

754 Art. 69(2) MDPL 2008.

755 Chapter 4, B.III.4.

756 The case no P. 33/2022, (22.04.2022), Basic Court of Pljevljna, in Montenegrin available at the following link <https://sudovi.me/ospv/odluka/474169> (accessed on 30.04.2023).

757 Information available from the Agency's website – The Document "List of employees in the Agency for 2022", in Montenegrin, available at the following link <https://www.azlp.me/storage/docs/zajednicka/Proaktivan%20pristup/Spisak%20zaposlenih%20septembar%202022.pdf> (accessed on 20.01.2023).

has been confirmed by the RCC Report as well, which indicated that the number of staff assigned to the supervision of the MDPL 2008 (inspections) is also insufficient (only four of them out of the total number of stuff).[758] The EU Commission has also been critical of the Agency's capacity, emphasising that it needs to be further strengthened.[759]

c) Political Influence

The Covid-19 pandemic has revealed the vulnerability of the Agency's independence to political influence. A significant data breach occurred when lists of individuals in mandatory self-isolation upon their return from abroad were published on the government's website. The lists contained sensitive personal data, including names, surnames, dates of entry into self-isolation, and home addresses, divided by municipality.[760] The National Coordination Council (hereinafter: "NCT"), a body established by the government to coordinate infectious disease control measures, decided to publish the lists in March 2020. Beforehand, on the same day, the NCT requested and received approval from the Agency to publish this list.[761] The Prime Minister's statement "we assessed that the right to health and life is above the right to unconditional protection of personal data [...] this is not the time for legal nuances, but for saving human lives"[762] suggests that political pressure had been exerted on the Agency to grant the permission.

The case drew significant attention and criticism from NGOs and the Ombudsman of Montenegro.[763] Consequently, the Montenegrin government agreed to pay

---

758 RCC Report 2020, p. 115 (n. 18).

759 EU Commission Report for Montenegro 2022, SWD(2022) 335 final (12.10.2022) p. 35 available at the following link <https://neighbourhood-enlargement.ec.europa.eu/system/files/2022-10/Montenegro%20Report%202022.pdf>, and EU Commission Report for Montenegro 2021, SWD(2021) 293 final/2 (19.10.2021), p. 30 <https://neighbourhood-enlargement.ec.europa.eu/system/files/2021-10/Montenegro%202021%20report.PDF> (both accessed on 22.05.2023).

760 The Government's press release with statement of former prime minister "Prime Minister Duško Marković: We are taking measures to protect citizens, there will be no forgiveness for disobeying the rules", published on 22.03.2020, available at the following link in Montenegrin <https://www.gov.me/clanak/223147--premijer-dusko-markovic-mjere-donosimo-da-zastitimo-gradane-nece-biti-prastanja-za-nepostovanje-pravila>; Article "Montenegro published personal data of people in isolation", (22.03.2022), published by BDK Advokati, Lexology, available at the following link <https://www.lexology.com/library/detail.aspx?g=b8e27d04-9836-4ed4-a949-025557b61f4c> (both accessed on 21.01.2023).

761 *Ibid.*

762 Statement of former Prime Minister Duško Marković (n. 760).

763 For example, the NGO CGO launched an initiative with the Agency regarding the mobile phone apps created after the publication of the personal data, which made it possible to track the

€300 in compensation to each person on the list, as they had threatened to sue the government.[764] A year later, following the scandal, the Parliament dismissed two of the Agency's employees (the Chairman of the Agency's Council and another Council member).[765] The Agency responded by claiming that the decision to dismiss them was entirely politically motivated, illegal and jeopardised the functioning of the Agency.[766] The Agency even approached the Delegation of the EU in Montenegro pointing out an inadequate reaction of the Parliament.[767]

5 Conclusion to III

The supervisory authority in Montenegro does not have the adequate enforcement powers, as it does not possess the authority to impose fines. Additionally, the absence of a right to judicial remedy for data subjects, who may only complain to the Agency or seek compensation for damages, undermines the effectiveness of the overall redress mechanism in Montenegro. Furthermore, the Agency's insufficient staffing and resources compound these issues, particularly as the Agency is tasked with multiple responsibilities, including maintaining register of records of personal data filing systems. As such, there are concerns as to whether the authority can operate independently. Finally, the Director and Council, as well as other members, are not prohibited from being members of political parties by the MDPL 2008.[768] Collectively, these shortcomings lead to the conclusion that the present institutional set-up, as provided for by the MDPL 2008, does not satisfy the criteria for an independent supervisory authority under the GDPR.

movements of people who were ordered to be in self-isolation, see the Report on the supervision of the Agency no. 05–29–500602/20 (22.07.2020) available in Montenegrin at the following link <https://media.cgo-cce.org/2020/09/AZLP-04.08.2020..pdf>; Reaction of the Ombudsman, (02.04.2020) <https://www.ombudsman.co.me/34348.news.html> (both accessed on 21.01.2023).

764 Article "300 euros each to citizens of Montenegro from the public list of 'covid isolated" published by Radio Free Europe (24.12.2021), available in Montenegrin at the following link <https://www.slobodnaevropa.org/a/obestecenje-crna-gora-spisak-kovid-samoizolacija/31624362.html> (accessed on 21.01.2023).

765 Press release of the Parliament (29.12.2021), available at the following link <https://www.skupstina.me/me/clanci/zavrsena-treca-sjednica-drugog-redovnog-zasijedanja-u-2021-godini> (accessed on 21.03.2023).

766 Agency's reaction available at the following link <https://www.azlp.me/me/agencija/20080> (accessed on 21.01.2023).

767 *Ibid.*

768 The GDPR does not include this as a criterion, but it could be a challenge for WB6 supervisory authorities, as these countries face particular problems of corruption.

IV Draft Law

As previously mentioned, Montenegro commenced the harmonisation process of the MDPL 2008 with the GDPR, which is still ongoing. For the implementation of this task, the Ministry of Internal Affairs, as the proposer of the law, formed a working group in 2018, the members of which included two representatives of the Agency.[769] Although a Draft was scheduled to be adopted in 2021, its adoption has been delayed, as also highlighted in the Report on the Implementation of the Programme for the Accession of Montenegro to the European Union 2021–2023.[770]

1 Overview of the Draft Law

The Draft mirrors the provisions of the GDPR. As with other WB6 legislation, the Draft does not include the GDPR's Recitals. Aside from that, the Draft does not fully replicate the GDPR text, and its structure differs from the GDPR. Instead, the Draft retains the structure of the MDPL 2008, appearing to be more of an amending law rather than a direct replication of the GDPR.

The Draft incorporates the definition of personal data (Art. 12 (1)), special categories of personal data (Art. 17) and legal grounds for data processing (Art. 13). Moreover, it mirrors the provision on the rights of data subject,[771] including consent as a legal basis for exceptions to the right not to be subject to a decision based solely on automated processing, including profiling.[772] While the Draft maintains the specific security measures obligation from the MDPL 2008 (elaborated in Section II (9)) and it also incorporates the security measures set out in Artt. 32–36 GDPR (notification of data breaches and DPIA).[773] It also adopts provisions related to appointment of a DPO[774] and code of conduct and certification.[775] Notably, the Draft replaces the general notification obligation of each data processing with the

769 Report on the state of protection of personal data for 2021, p. 9, available at the following link <https://www.azlp.me/me/izvjestaji> (accessed on 05.05.2023).

770 Izvještaj o realizaciji Programa pristupanja Crne Gore Evropskoj uniji 2021–2023, za 2021. godinu (Eng. Report on the implementation of the Program for the Accession of Montenegro to the European Union 2021–2023, for the year 2021), published on 26.01.2022, available in Montenegrin at the following link <https://www.gov.me/dokumenta/a4fb6c49-bdc4-4880-b978-4b92805d859a> (accessed on 30.04.2023).

771 Chapter III Draft.

772 Art. 44 (2)(3) Draft.

773 Artt. 55–59 Draft.

774 Artt. 60–63 Draft.

775 Chapter IX Draft.

requirement to keep records on data processing as outlined in Art. 30 GDPR.[776] Lastly, the Draft keeps the provisions related to fines as stipulated by the MDPL 2008, including the amount of the fines.[777]

2 Particularities

While the Draft aligns with the GDPR to a great extent, there are considerable divergences, resulting from inaccuracies in translating GDPR provisions. In contrast to other WB6 GDPR-like laws or draft laws, the Draft adopts provisions from the GDPR while retaining the specific provisions of the previous legislation, namely the MDPL 2008. This Section outlines the principal differences between the MDPL 2008 and the Draft resulting from the incorporation of the GDPR. Consequently, it serves as an overview of the key distinctions between the Draft and the GDPR.

a) Scope

The Draft goes beyond incorporating provisions from the GDPR, but also includes the provisions reflecting the LED, which extends the law's scope to the processing of personal data by competent law enforcement authorities for 'criminal matters'.[778] The provisions relating to these authorities are not confined to a single chapter, but rather are interwoven with the general provisions reflecting the GDPR.

The Draft law also seeks to amend the current provisions on material and territorial scope to align them with the GDPR. Regarding territorial scope, the legislator has chosen to combine the solutions provided in both the GDPR and the MDPL 2008.[779] Specifically, Art. 10 Draft retains the provisions of Art. 5 MDPL 2008 (which corresponds to Art. 10 DPD), while Art. 11 Draft incorporates a similar solution as provided by Art. 3(2) of the GDPR.[780] As a result, the Draft recognises exterritorial scope provided by both the DPD and the GDPR. Moreover, neither of the extraterritorial solutions cover data processors. This represents a significant oversight in the alignment of Montenegrin data protection legislation with the GDPR and should be amended to apply to data processors as well. It is also unclear why the territorial scope from the MDPL 2008 provided by Art. 10 Draft would still

776 Art. 52 Draft.
777 Art. 100 Draft.
778 Art. 2(1) Draft.
779 Previous Art. 4 MDPL 2008.
780 However, Art. 11 does not include the extraterritorial reach provided in Art. 3(1) GDPR (establishment context).

remain in force, as the GDPR amended this provision to clarify the territorial scope, which was previously ambiguous under the DPD.

b) Rights of Data Subject

The Draft law transposes the data subject's rights from the GDPR,[781] but fails to include the right to data portability. The right to data portability was neither mentioned in the Report on the public discussion regarding the Draft.[782] Furthermore, in the provisions on the right to be forgotten defined by the Draft[783] there is a provision which is significantly different compared to Art. 17 GDPR. Specifically, Art. 24(3)(5) Draft replicates from Art. 17(3)(e) GDPR the exceptions from granting the right to be forgotten by controllers, but with a significant difference. Art. 2(3)(5) envisages an exemption for "processing is necessary for legal interests" whereas according to the Art. 17(3)(e) GDPR the exemption is only possible "for the establishment, exercise or defence of legal claims". There is even a reference in the Draft to the fact that this provision Art. 24(3)(5) has been brought into line with Art. 17 GDPR, even though it continues to differ from the latter. It is not clear whether this is an error resulting from a mistaken literal transposition of the GDPR's text or if it was the intention of the Montenegrin legislator to make such a difference.

c) Lawfulness of Processing

The Draft proposes amendments to Art. 10 MDPL 2008 to align it with the GDPR.[784] Yet, the legal ground which is defined by the MDPL 2008 as a 'law-based interest' of the controller is now replaced with "for the purposes of exercising the powers of controller or processor, unless these interests are overridden by interests or fundamental rights of data subject".[785] The wording seems to refer to the legitimate interest defined by 6 (1)(f) GDPR, but with two notable differences. First, Art. 6 (1)(f) GDPR does not include the processor's legitimate interest but refers to "legitimate interests pursued by the controller or by a third party." Permitting the legitimate interest of a processor is contradictory, considering the role of the processor who shall processes the personal data only on instructions from the

---

781 Art. 22 Draft.

782 Report on the public discussion regarding the Draft Law on the Protection of Personal Data (10.07.2019), available at the following link <https://www.gov.me/dokumenta/6c2470bc-aeee-4281-95de-3c40c591bb94> (accessed on 10.05.2023).

783 Art. 24 Draft.

784 Art. 13 Draft.

785 Art. 13(6) Draft.

controller[786] as also stipulated by the Draft.[787] Second, the Draft uses the term 'powers' (in Montenegrin: 'ovlašćenja'), which is different from 'legitimate interest' and can be understood as if the legitimate interest must be based on the law or some other regulation. This formulation is very imprecise and vague. There has already been criticism of the legitimate interest as defined by the GDPR, that a loose application of the legitimate interest ground provision could lead to uncertainty and potentially be a 'tool for circumvention' of the legal protection offered to individuals.[788] Some authors even state that the legitimate interest is a 'loophole' in the protection of personal data.[789] Therefore, an even broader formulation of legitimate interest, as currently provided for in the Draft, could affect the protection of personal data or compliance with the EU acquis.

d) Consent

The Draft introduces more stringent rules for obtaining consent, including some aspects of Art. 7 GDPR, such as the rule that the controller must be able to prove that the data subject has given consent.[790] However, the Draft law still creates a legal vacuum with regard to consent requirements. It does not set out the rules governing the manner in which consent must be given, such as the requirement for an intelligible and easily accessible form, using clear and plain language. Beyond that, there are no further rules that would provide more guidance on the voluntary nature of consent.[791] Consent as regulated by the GDPR has already been criticised for not reflecting a conscious, free and informed decision by the data subject.[792] Critics point out that in many cases, consent is reduced to a

---

786 Also, in the "WP29 Opinion 06/2014 on the notion of legitimate interests of the data controller under Art. 7 of Directive 95/46/EC, WP 217", there is no reference to the use of the legitimate interests of the data processor.

787 Art. 50(2) Draft.

788 Balboni, Paolo, Daniel Cooper, Rosario Imperiali, and Milda Macenaite "Legitimate interest of the data controller. New data protection paradigm: legitimacy grounded on appropriate protection", International Data Privacy Law: ipt019, (2018), p. 247.

789 Irene Kamara and Paul De Hert, "Understanding the Balancing Act behind the Legitimate Interest of the Controller Ground: A Pragmatic Approach", Brussels Privacy Hub, Vol. 4, No. 12, (August 2018), p. 8.

790 Art. 15 Draft.

791 The Draft fails to include Art. 7 (4) GDPR, which regulates the assessment of the voluntariness of consent.

792 Buchner/Kühling "Art. 7 DS-GVO Bedingungen für die Einwilligung" para 10 (n. 350); Bart W. Schermer, Bart Custers and Simone van der Hof, "The crisis of consent: how stronger legal protection may lead to weaker consent in data protection", Ethics Inf. Technol. 16, 171–182 (2014); Bergemann, B.: Der "informed consent" im Datenschutz: Eine politikwissenschaftliche Analyse,

mere 'fiction', and that the legal requirements for effectiveness in everyday data processing are reduced to mere formalism – in the form of pre-formulated consent clauses –over-long privacy statements and supposed choices à la 'take it or leave it'.[793] As a result, the lack of minimum requirements for consent means that the Draft is out of step with the GDPR and fails to provide sufficient guidance to data controllers or sufficiently protect the rights of data subject. Therefore, it is crucial for the Draft to include specific requirements for obtaining valid consent.

e) Redress Rights

The Draft does not include Chapter 8 GDPR and instead maintains the provisions of the MDPL 2008. As a consequence, data subjects will not have the right to judicial protection against data controllers and processors, but only the right to make a 'request for protection of rights' to the Agency.[794] Furthermore, the Draft does not explicitly mention the right to compensation, which is present in the MDPL 2008.[795] This is a significant omission that must be remedied in the Draft in order for Montenegro to be in compliance with the requirements for the adoption of an adequacy decision. According to the WP29, the level of data protection in third countries must be assessed in part by the availability of "effective administrative and judicial redress, including for compensation for damages as a result of the unlawful processing."[796] The WP29 also notes that this is a key element which must involve a system of independent adjudication or arbitration that allows for the payment of compensation and the imposition of sanctions where necessary.[797]

f) Personal Scope

The Draft introduces the concept of joint controllership, which has been derived from the GDPR. Furthermore, the Draft also incorporates the provisions of Art. 26(2) GDPR, which requires that the essence of the agreement between joint controllers shall be made available to the data subject.[798] In fact, the Draft goes further than the GDPR, by obliging the joint controllers to publish their

Master thesis. Freie Universität Berlin (2017); Benjamin Bergemann, "The consent paradox: Accounting for the prominent role of consent in data protection", IFIP International Summer School on Privacy and Identity Management. Springer, Cham, (2017).

793 Buchner/Kühling "Art. 7 DS-GVO Bedingungen für die Einwilligung" paras. 10–12 (n. 350).

794 Art. 22(1)(10) Draft.

795 Art. 48 MDPL 2008.

796 WP29 Adequacy Referential, p. 8 (n. 155).

797 *Ibid.*

798 Art. 26(2) GDPR.

agreement on their website, thereby ensuring transparency.[799] Additionally, the Draft addresses the gaps in the MDPL 2008 and incorporates the GDPR provisions on the processor. This includes the mandatory content of the agreement between the controller and the processor[800] and the requirement that the processor may not engage another sub-processor without prior written consent of the controller.[801]

g) Data Transfers

The Draft sets out specific rules for data transfers, which draw from a combination of GDPR and MDPL 2008 provisions, including three different solutions for data transfers to third countries. Firstly, the Draft shall give the right to the supervisory authority to decide if the country provides adequate measures for processing of personal data.[802] The criteria for adopting adequacy decisions are derived from Art. 45 (2) GDPR,[803] but the procedure differs. Unlike the adequacy decisions under the GDPR, it appears that the supervisory authority does not adopt the 'adequacy list' in advance, but only grants prior approval at the request of the data controller.[804] Once the approval is granted, the decision shall be valid for 4 years.[805] However, it is unclear whether data controllers must still request prior approval if there is already an 'approval decision' for a certain country. The absence of requests for data transfers in 2020 to the supervisory authority[806] raises doubts about the viability of this solution. As the GDPR's adequacy mechanism is the preferred method for data transfers, with no other requirements, it would be practical for the Draft to follow Art. 45 GDPR and facilitate the Agency's administration. Secondly, the Draft incorporates the provisions of Art. 46 GDPR on transfers subject to appropriate safeguards, which represent the second stream of data transfers. This stream allows for data transfers without approval if the data controller has taken 'adequate protection measures' which are taken over from Art. 46 (2)(3) GDPR. Lastly, the Draft incorporates the provisions of Art. 49

799 Art. 48(3) Draft.
800 Art. 50(2) Draft.
801 Art. 50(1) Draft.
802 Art. 38(6) Draft.
803 Art. 38(2) Draft.
804 *Ibid.*
805 Art. 38(3) Draft.
806 Agency's Report on the state of personal data protection for 2020, p. 49, available at the following link <https://www.azlp.me/docs/zajednicka/izvjestaj_o_stanju/IZVJESTAJ%202020%20final.pdf> (accessed on 08.06.2023).

GDPR, which provide for exceptions for specific situations, in the third stream of data transfers.[807]

h) Supervisory Authority – Agency

The provisions regarding the appointment of the Director and Council remain unchanged from those stipulated in the MDPL 2008. However, with regards to the competence and powers of the Agency, the Draft law incorporates mostly the provisions of the GDPR, providing the Agency with greater enforcement powers. Nonetheless, the Draft uses a different wording when stating that the Agency has the power "to issue a misdemeanour order", whereas Art. 58 GDPR concerning corrective powers of the supervisory authority clearly states that each supervisory authority has the power "to impose an administrative fine". As such, it remains unclear whether a misdemeanour order carries the same meaning as an administrative fine under the GDPR. Additionally, the Draft lacks further rules on imposing fines. For instance, Art. 100 Draft only lists the infringements but does not provide guidance on the rules for imposing fines, such as those outlined in Art. 83 GDPR, which also specify factors to be considered when determining the amount of the fine.[808]

3 Conclusion to IV

Compared to other WB6 laws aimed at aligning with the GDPR, the Draft is not a mere replica of the GDPR. While it incorporates most of the GDPR provisions, it also retains some provisions of the current legislation – MDPL 2008. Consequently, the Draft appears complicated to comprehend and leads to inconsistencies, as seen in the unclear extraterritorial effect, where solutions of exterritorial scope from both GDPR and MDPL 2008 are provided. Furthermore, the Draft fails to include significant provisions from the GDPR, such as redress rights and requirements for valid consent. Additionally, some translation errors in interpreting the GDPR are evident, such as the use of legitimate interest as one of the legal grounds for processing personal data. Also, it still remains unclear whether the Agency has the authority to impose fines, while the amount of fines remains the same as under old legislation. Hence, the Draft requires further amendments

---

807 Art. 41 Draft.

808 According to Art. 83 GDPR the circumstances on deciding whether to impose an administrative fine and deciding on the amount of the administrative fine in each individual case include, among others, the nature, gravity and duration of the infringement, intentional or negligent character, the degree of responsibility etc.

to address these shortcomings and align it better with the GDPR, enabling it to provide an adequate level of data protection.

V Case Law and Enforcement

As for adoption of an adequacy decision, the EU Commission must also assess the enforcement of data protection legislation in a third country, this Section will look at the activities of the Agency in enforcing the MDPL 2008 and will also provide an overview of cases both before the Agency and the competent courts.

1 Activities of the Supervisory Authority

Compared to other supervisory institutions in the WB6 countries, the Agency appears to be less proactive in publishing guidelines, recommendations and other relevant information for controllers, processors, and data subjects. One of the reasons for this may be the Agency's lack of authority to issue bylaws.[809] The government has only adopted two bylaws, namely the Rulebook on the Manner of Marking and Protection of Special Categories of Personal Data[810] and the Rulebook on the Form and Manner of Keeping Record of Personal Databases[811] which are addressed to the controllers. Other than that, the Agency has published the templates for the request for protection of rights and for the request to initiate the supervisory procedure. It is also evident that the Agency's recommendations and opinions are rare and primarily focused on video surveillance, with the most recent publication dating back to 2019. This may be due to the Agency's understaffing (whereas the Agency has the double authority – free access to public information and data protection), and the dismissal of the Agency's Council, including the President, in December 2021, with a new President appointed only in August 2022.[812]

---

809 Most statutes are enacted by the government, e.g. Art. 13(3) MDPL 2008 or Art. 26(3) MDPL 2008.

810 Rulebook on the Manner of Marking and Protection of Special Categories of Personal Data (2011) in Montenegrin, available on the website of the Agency at the following link <http://www.azlp.me/me/propisi> (accessed on 01.05.2023).

811 Rulebook on the Form and Manner of Keeping Record of Personal Databases (2010) available on the website of the Agency at the following link <http://www.azlp.me/me/propisi> (accessed on 01.05.2023).

812 Report on the State of Protection of Personal Data and Access to Information for 2022, p. 5, in Montenegrin, available on the website of the Agency at the following link <https://www.azlp.me/me/izvjestaji> (accessed on 01.05.2023).

2 Complaints and Investigations Before the Supervisory Authority

The Agency has the authority to perform inspections (regular and irregular upon the request to initiate the supervisory procedure under Art. 65) over the activities of data controllers and processors. Moreover, the Agency has the authority to address the data subjects' request for protection of rights under Art. 47. The annual reports of the Agency indicate a slight increase in the number of requests for protection of rights and requests to initiate the supervisory procedure received over the years, with 215 requests registered in 2022[813] compared to only 47 requests in 2015.[814] This trend may indicate a slight improvement in privacy awareness. However, while the EU Commission noted that the number of complaints is increasing, it stated that the overall awareness on personal data protection issues in Montenegro remains low.[815] With the increasing of complaints the Agency's capacity to conduct ordinary inspections has been affected, as demonstrated by the declining numbers of such inspections over time. In 2022 for instance out of the 127 performed inspections, none were ordinary inspections.[816] Similarly, in 2020, only 5 out of the 68 inspections were regular,[817] whereas in 2015, 39 inspections out of 86 total were ordinary inspections.[818]

Case law before the Agency reveals a variety of issues but primarily concerning video surveillance, non-compliance with the principle of data minimisation in ID card processing, direct marketing, data breaches in employment law, failure to implement adequate personal data security measures. The case law also indicates a prevalent lack of awareness regarding the principles of minimisation and privacy by design and default, in particular when requesting the 'JMBG' number.

3 Court Cases

With regard to the current case law before the courts, as discussed above, data subjects do not have the right to an effective judicial remedy against controllers and processors under the MDPL 2008.[819] As a result, the case law is not very ex-

813 *Ibid*, p. 8.

814 Report on the State of Protection of Personal Data and Access to Information for 2015, pp. 29–30, in Montenegrin, available on the website of the Agency at the following link <https://www.azlp.me/me/izvjestaji> (accessed on 01.05.2023).

815 EU Commission Report 2022, p. 35 and EU Commission Report 2021, p. 30, (n. 759).

816 Annual Report 2022, p. 13 (n. 812).

817 Report on the State of Protection of Personal Data and Access to Information for 2020, p. 33, in Montenegrin, available at the following link <https://www.azlp.me/me/izvjestaji> (accessed on 01.05.2023).

818 Annual Report 2015, p. 25 (n. 814).

819 This right is provided by Art. 79 GDPR.

tensive, and most of the court cases concern challenges to the decisions of the Agency before the administrative court, as well as claims for damages resulting from violations of the MDPL 2008. Video surveillance is a frequent issue in such cases, with one instance resulting in the ECtHR finding a violation of Art. 8 ECHR due to the introduction of video surveillance in contravention of the MDPL 2008.[820] In this particular case, a university recorded lectures without the consent of the professors, who subsequently complained to the Agency and the courts seeking compensation for damages due to the violation of their right to privacy.[821] The national courts initially found that video surveillance in public places, such as universities, could not violate the data subjects' right to respect for their private life, as the data collected could not be considered personal data.[822] Furthermore, recent cases have been related to measures taken during the Covid-19 pandemic, with the majority of cases involving compensation for damages resulting from a decision of the government[823] to publish lists of individuals in mandatory self-isolation upon their return from abroad on the government's website, which the Constitutional Court in Montenegro abolished and declared unconstitutional.[824] In 2020, there were 18 court decisions on this topic, representing the only court decisions related to the protection of personal data.[825] By way of comparison, in 2021, there were two cases related to privacy violations resulting from the same data breach[826] and in 2022, there was only one such case.[827] Other court decisions are primarily related to access to public information, in which in-

820 Antović and Mirković v. Montenegro, application no. 70838/13 (ECtHR, 28.11.2017).

821 *Ibid*, para 6–9.

822 *Ibid*, para 14.

823 Decision of the National Coordinating Body for Infectious Diseases on publishing the names of persons in self-isolation, no. 8–501-/20–129 (21.04.2020), in Montenegrin, available at the following link <https://www.gov.me/clanak/223143--nkt-za-zarazne-bolesti-pocinje-objavljivanje-identiteta-lica-u-samoizolaciji-zastita-zdravlja-i-zivot-gradana-nas-najvisi-priori> (accessed on 01.05.2023).

824 Decision of the Constitutional Court of Montenegro on revoking the decision of the National Coordinating Body for Infectious Diseases on publishing the names of persons in self-isolation, U-II no. 22/20, in Montenegrin, available at the following link <https://www.ustavnisud.me/ustavnisud/skladiste/blog_4/objava_181/fajlovi/Odluka%20USCG,%20predmet%20U_II%20br%2022_20.pdf > (accessed on 02.05.2023).

825 Information from the official website of the Portal of Courts in Montenegro, available at the following link <https://sudovi.me/sdvi/odluke> (accessed on 01.05.2023).

826 Basic Court in Nikšić, case no. P 1411/2021, (04.04.2021) and Basic court Nikšić, case no. P 150/2021 (08.12.2021), available in Montenegrin at the following link <https://sudovi.me/sdvi/odluke> (accessed on 01.05.2023).

827 Basic Court in Pljevlja, case no. P 33/2022 (22.03.2022), available at the following link <https://sudovi.me/sdvi/odluke> (accessed on 01.05.2023).

dividuals have challenged decisions rejecting requests for information on the grounds of the protection of personal data.[828]

4 Conclusion to V

Data subjects in Montenegro only have the option to file their complaints before the Agency, resulting in the majority of cases being dealt with by this institution (apart from claims for compensation for damages). The recent increase in complaints submitted to the supervisory authority may reflect a positive impact of the GDPR and improved public awareness of data protection. However, as the supervisory authority lacks adequate resources to handle data subjects' complaints and exercise its powers, such as investigations, the current redress mechanism may not effectively safeguard data protection rights. Additionally, there is still a low level of public awareness regarding data protection among data controllers and public institutions, as evidenced by the government's decision to publicly disclose lists of individuals infected with Covid-19. Furthermore, the current Draft of the proposed new legislation does not offer improved redress mechanisms, such as the right to effective judicial remedy. These issues could pose significant challenges not only to the enforcement of the MDPL 2008, but also to the proposed new legislation, if they are not addressed. Higher standards for ensuring the independence of the supervisory authority and redress mechanisms aligned with the GDPR are therefore essential.

VI Conclusion to D

Despite being a frontrunner in the EU accession process, Montenegro appears to be lagging behind other WB6 countries in terms of data protection legislation. The current legislation is reflective of the DPD, the predecessor of the GDPR. The introduction of the new data protection law, aimed at aligning the legislation with the GDPR, has been slow, with the harmonisation process commencing in 2018 and the final draft still to be finalised.

Furthermore, Montenegro has not developed a data protection strategy prioritising this issue. Unlike other countries (e. g. Albania, North Macedonia and Serbia) that have set goals to be included in the EU Commission's adequacy decision list,

828 E. g. Administrative Court of Montenegro, case no. In 1586/2017; Supreme Court of Montenegro, case no. Uvp 353/2022 (26.05.2022); Supreme Court of Montenegro case no. Uvp 268/2022 (11.05.2022), available at the following link <https://sudovi.me/sdvi/odluke> (accessed on 01.05.2023).

Montenegro has not established any such targets. However, the country is obliged under the SAA to align its legislation.

The implementation of the current legislation, the MDPL 2008, has demonstrated that public awareness of data protection remains low, with data subjects having only the supervisory authority as a point of contact for violations of their rights. The Draft still falls short of fully addressing the issues identified in the implementation of the MDPL 2008, as well as important aspects of the GDPR, such as the extraterritorial effect, the low level of fines, and the lack of consent requirements. It is therefore necessary for Montenegro to amend the Draft to ensure compliance with the most important concepts of the GDPR and to bring its data protection regime in line with EU standards, thus increasing the possibility of being placed on the EU Commission's adequacy list.

E North Macedonia

North Macedonia is recognised as a candidate country for the EU. In April 2001, North Macedonia signed an SAA[829] and submitted its application for EU membership in 2004.[830] In March 2020, the members of the European Council endorsed the decision of the General Affairs Council to open accession negotiations with North Macedonia.[831] In July 2020, the draft negotiating framework was presented to the Member States, and the EU Commission commenced the screening process.[832] As part of its obligations under the SAA, North Macedonia has already aligned its national data protection legislation with the GDPR in 2020.[833] Until it meets the criteria to join the EU, the country is determined to be recognised by the EU Commission as providing an adequate level of data protection, and has set ambitious goals accordingly.[834]

---

829 Stabilisation and Association Agreement between the European Communities and their Member States, of the one part, and the Republic of North Macedonia, of the other part, OJ L 84, (20.3.2004) p. 13, available at the following link <https://eur-lex.europa.eu/legal-content/EN/TXT/PDF/?uri=CELEX:02004A0320(03)-20210909&from=EN> (accessed on 16.04.2023).

830 Information from the EU Commission's website: European Neighbourhood Policy and Enlargement Negotiations (DG NEAR), North Macedonia, available at the following link <https://neighbourhood-enlargement.ec.europa.eu/enlargement-policy/north-macedonia_en> (accessed on 15.04.2023).

831 *Ibid.*

832 *Ibid.*

833 Art. 68 SAA North Macedonia (n. 829).

834 Strategic Goal 1 "Republic of Macedonia is recognized as a country providing adequate level of personal data Protection" defined in the Strategy on Personal Data Protection in North

This Chapter provides an overview of the Macedonian data protection legal framework, including the constitutional provisions on data protection and privacy, as well as cases illustrating the level of compliance with the previous and current data protection legislation.

I Constitutional Parameters and International Commitments

The Constitution of North Macedonia[835] guarantees the protection of both privacy and personal data. The right to privacy as a fundamental right includes safeguarding the personal and family life, dignity, and reputation of individuals, in a manner similar to that guaranteed by the ECHR.[836] Data protection, as established under Art. 18 of the Constitution of North Macedonia, provides protection against violations of personal integrity resulting from the registration of personal information through automatic and non-automatic data processing.

Protection of human rights in North Macedonia, including privacy and data protection, is also provided by respecting and upholding the international agreements adopted globally by the UN as well as regionally, particularly by the CoE. North Macedonia has also signed the Convention 108[837] and the Additional Protocol (CETS no. 223) – Convention 108+.[838]

Regarding the status of international agreements in the legal system, North Macedonia recognises the importance of international agreements in protecting human rights, including privacy and data protection. International agreements ratified in accordance with the Constitution form part of the internal legal order and cannot be changed by law, as stated in Art. 118. Moreover, courts in North Macedonia base their decisions on the Constitution, laws, and international agreements ratified in accordance with the Constitution.[839]

Macedonia, 2017–2022, available at the following link <https://azlp.mk/en/library/> (accessed on 10.10.2022).

835 Constitution of North Macedonia (no 08–4642/1 17 November 1991).

836 Art. 25 Constitution of North Macedonia.

837 Law on Ratification of the Convention for Protection of Individuals Against Automatic Data Processing (Official Gazette of the Republic of Macedonia, no. 7/05) and Law on Ratification of the Additional Protocol to the Convention for Protection of Individuals Against Automatic Personal Data Processing, with Respect to the Supervisory Bodies and the Cross-border Transfer (Official Gazette of the Republic of Macedonia, no. 103/08).

838 CoE Newsroom, "North Macedonia signs Convention 108+", (05.12.2019), available at the following link <https://www.coe.int/en/web/data-protection/-/north-macedonia-signs-convention-108-> (accessed on 05.10.2022).

839 Amendment XXV to the Constitution.

1 Conclusion to I

The safeguarding of data protection and privacy is entrenched as a fundamental right in the Constitution of North Macedonia. In addition to constitutional protections, North Macedonia, as a signatory to various international instruments, is also bound by the provisions of these instruments, including those relating to data protection as guaranteed by the ECHR. Consequently, individuals in North Macedonia are entitled to challenge decisions made by national authorities and seek redress from the ECtHR.

II Data Protection Legislation

The origins of data protection law in North Macedonia can be traced back to the draft of law on personal data protection proposed in 1994,[840] which aimed to establish standards for safeguarding personal data. However, this proposal was not adopted, and it was not until 2005 that the first legislation on personal data, the Law on Personal Data Protection (hereinafter: "MDPL 2005"),[841] was enacted upon the recommendation of the EU.[842] The MDPL 2005 introduced for the first time a supervisory authority for data protection – the Directorate for data protection.[843] This law was in effect for over 15 years, until North Macedonia replaced it with a new comprehensive piece of legislation, akin to the GDPR. The new data protection law adopted in 2020 (hereinafter: "MDPL 2020")[844] comprehensively covers data protection in North Macedonia and outlines principles to which all sectoral legislation should adhere. In contrast to other WB6 new data protection laws or draft laws, the MDPL 2020 does not include the provisions from the LED and focuses only on the provisions of the GDPR.[845] Further, the

840 Draft of Law on Personal Data Protection from 1994 (Official Gazette of the Republic of Macedonia, no. 12/94).

841 Law on Personal Data Protection (Official Gazette of the Republic of Macedonia, no. 7/2005, 103/2008, 124/10, 135/11, 43/14, 153/15, 99/16 and 64/18).

842 Elena Stojanovska and Jovana Ananievska, "Privacy, information, and the public interest: the right to privacy versus the right of the public to know", School of Journalism and Public Relations, Institute for Communication Studies, (2016) p. 62.

843 Art. 51 MDPL 2005.

844 Law on Protection of Personal Data (Official Gazette of the Republic of North Macedonia, no. 42/20) (hereinafter: "MDPL 2020"), Eng. Translation: <https://www.refworld.org/pdfid/6290d1814.pdf> (accessed on 21.03.2023).

845 According to the supervisory authority's 2022 Annual Report, alignment with the LED is still ongoing. Supervisory Authority's Annual Report for 2022, (in Macedonian) p. 5 <https://azlp.mk/wp content/uploads/2023/03/Годишен-извештај-за-2022-година.pdf> (accessed on 21.04.2023).

MDPL 2020 provided a 'grace period' until 24 August 2021 for controllers and processors to comply with the new change.[846] Additionally, the supervisory authority allowed an informal six-month period in which it decided not to impose fines but to require only corrective measures.[847] This leniency was intended to give companies sufficient time to rectify any irregularities within a given deadline.[848]

1 Status Quo of GDPR Alignment

The MDPL 2020 transposes the GDPR provisions, while incorporating certain variations that either define the opening clauses outlined in the GDPR or impose stricter requirements for handling personal data in certain circumstance, particularly concerning data transfers. One of the most significant differences in comparison to the GDPR is the lack of explanations that are provided by the Recitals of the GDPR. Given that the MDPL 2020 introduced significant changes to the Macedonian data protection legislation, this can be particularly challenging for effective implementation.

In December 2021, amendments to the MDPL 2020 were introduced for the purpose of clarifying some definitions, without introducing substantial modifications.[849] However, the supervisory authority introduced its proposals for further amendments in 2022 due to various reasons.[850] Among the main reasons cited by the supervisory authorities is that the MDPL 2020 has not fully implemented the solutions necessary to ensure that the supervisory authority has all the resources needed to execute its functions and powers effectively.[851] Additionally, another significant reason is to align the MDPL 2020 with EU regulations regarding the transfer of personal data, particularly the EDPB recommendations concerning the European essential guarantees and transfer measures. Nevertheless, these amendments have not yet been adopted.[852] Lastly, it is noteworthy that in October 2022, the supervisory authority successfully completed the implementation of the twinning project "Support in the implementation of the modernized national pro-

---

846 Art. 120 MDPL 2020.

847 Karanovic & Partners, "Additional Period for Ensuring Data Protection Compliance in North Macedonia", CEE Legal Matters, (09.09.2021), available at the following link <https://ceelegalmatters.com/macedonia/17809-additional-period-for-ensuring-data-protection-compliance-in-north-macedonia> (accessed on 21.04.2023).

848 *Ibid.*

849 Law amending and supplementing the Data Protection Law (RSM, Official Gazette, No 294, 27.12.2021).

850 Annual Report North Macedonia 2022 pp. 10–11 (n. 845).

851 *Ibid.*

852 *Ibid.*

tection framework of personal data", financed by the EU.[853] The project's primary aim was to enhance North Macedonia's personal data protection framework in line with EU legislation standards.

Given that the MDPL 2020 provisions are based on the GDPR, this Chapter will only present the exceptions from the GDPR, as well as a comparison of the MDPL 2020 with the former data protection legislation, the MDPL 2005, to identify the significant changes influenced by the GDPR.

2 Overview of the MDPL 2020

MDPL 2020 consists of nine parts. Part 1 encompasses the general provisions, which include the scope of the law and definitions (first chapter). Part 2 outlines the principles of data processing and provides a definition of special categories of personal data (second chapter). Part 3 defines rights of data subject (third chapter). Part 4 governs data controllers and processors, including their obligations related to security of data processing (fourth chapter). Part 5 defines rules on international data transfers (chapter five). Part 6 clarifies the role of the supervisory authority and its functions and powers (chapter six). Part 7 stipulates the provisions relating to specific processing situations (chapter seven). In part 8 judicial remedy and liability is defined, together with the rules on supervision and enforcement of the data protection legislation, including penalties (chapter eight, nine and ten). Finally, Part 9 contains transitional and final provisions (chapter eleven).

3 Scope of the MDPL 2020

The territorial scope of the MDPL 2020 (Art. 3) is entirely replicated from Art. 3 GDPR. Consequently, it also has an extraterritorial effect and applies to the processing of personal data when "the controller or processor is established on the territory of the Republic of North Macedonia, regardless of whether the processing takes place on the territory of the Republic of North Macedonia or not."[854] Additionally, it applies to the processing of personal data of "data subjects from North Macedonia" by a "controller or processor not established in North Macedo-

853 The project was done with the cooperation of the Agency for the Protection of Personal Data (AZOP) from the Republic of Croatia and the German Foundation for International Legal Cooperation (IRZ) from the Federal Republic of Germany. Additional information can be found at the following link <https://azlp.mk/en/support-in-the-implementation-of-the-modernized-national-framework-for-the-protection-of-personal-data/> (accessed on 21.04.2023).
854 Art. 3(1) MDPL 2020.

nia, if processing activities are related to 1) the offering of goods or budgets [*sic*][855], irrespective of whether a payment of the data subject from the Republic of North Macedonia is required, 2) or the monitoring of the data subject behaviour as far as their behaviour takes place in the Republic of North Macedonia."[856] Considering this, international companies with pan-European operations would potentially need to comply with both the GDPR and the MDPL 2020, if the conditions set by Art. 3 MDPL 2020 apply. However, the MDPL 2020 does not provide a definition of an establishment, which could lead to complications in understanding its territorial scope. The interpretation of Art. 3 GDPR has already generated substantial debate regarding the circumstances in which an extraterritorial scope may apply, not only in cases where the GDPR applies to non-EU entities (Art. 3(2)) but also in cases of entities with an establishment in the EU (Art. 3(1)), as the notion of 'establishment' has a broader context according to CJEU jurisprudence.[857]

4 Data Protection Principles

MDPL 2020 prescribes the same data protection principles along with two new principles – the accountability principle[858] and privacy-by-design and default[859] – as new principles explicitly introduced by the MDPL 2020. Given that these principles were relatively new in all WB6 data protection legislation, the supervisory authority was preparing for their implementation for longer time.[860] The accountability principle is not completely new in the Macedonian legislation. The MDPL 2005 already provided that data protection controllers and processors must maintain documentation that serves as evidence of the implementation of appropriate TOMs.[861]

855 The officially published English version of the MDPL 2020 uses the term 'budgets', but the official Macedonian version of the MDPL uses the term 'services', which is in line with the term used in Art. 3(2) GDPR.

856 Art. 3(2) MDPL 2020.

857 This exterritorial scope of the GDPR has been elaborated in Chapter 3.

858 Art. 9(2) MDPL 2020.

859 Art. 29 MDPL 2020.

860 The supervisory authority recognised already in its annual report in 2014 that privacy-by-design and default and shared responsibility of the data processors are novelties that have to be incorporated into the national legislation, Supervisory Authority's Annual Report for 2014, (in Macedonian) available at the following link <https://www.dzlp.mk/sites/default/files/doc.1a_en.pdf> (accessed on 30.03.2021).

861 Art. 23(4) MDPL 2005; See also Gunderman Lukas, "Law on personal data protection with comment", Direction for personal data protection (2010), available at the following link <https://www.dzlp.mk/sites/default/files/283.pdf> (accessed on 30.03.2021).

5 Lawfulness of Processing

The MDPL 2020 provides legal grounds for data processing that are consistent with those of the GDPR (consent, performance of the contract, legal obligation, legitimate interests, protecting vital interests etc.).[862] The MDPL 2020 also indicates that, when the legal basis for processing personal data is compliance with a legal obligation to which the controller is subject, or when processing is necessary for the performance of a task carried out in the public interest or in the exercise of official authority vested in the controller, the legal basis shall be established by that law.[863] The MDPL 2020 further stipulates the mandatory provisions which the national laws should contain.[864] This implies that many sector-specific laws would need to be revised to ensure that data controllers and processors comply with the MDPL 2020. In line with this, in early 2022 the supervisory authority adopted the Decision on determining the methodology for the harmonisation of the sectoral legislation (hereinafter: "Harmonisation Decision").[865] This Harmonisation Decision contains guidelines that regulate the procedure of the ministries in the processes of harmonisation of sectoral legislation, including the process of reviewing existing laws, as well as the process of implementation assessment of the impact of laws from the perspective of personal data protection.[866] These guidelines are based on positive experiences from the practice of the EU and its Member States, as well as their legislation.[867] However, no specific deadline is envisaged by the Harmonisation Decision, while according to the Art. 120 MDPL 2020 all laws have to be aligned within 18 months from the day of entry into force of the MDPL 2020.

---

862 Art. 10(1) MDPL 2020.

863 Art. 10(3) MDPL 2020.

864 Under Art. 10(2) MDPL 2020 the sector law shall include the general conditions governing the lawfulness of processing by the controller, purposes of the processing, the categories of data which are subject to the processing; categories of data subjects, the entities to, and the purposes for which, the personal data may be disclosed, the purpose limitation, storage periods, processing operations and processing procedures, including measures to ensure lawful and fair processing, in order to meet an objective of public interest and be proportionate to the legitimate aim pursued. The mentioned 'law' must also contain data protection impact assessment for the cases provided by the law.

865 Decision on determining the methodology for the harmonisation of the sectoral legislation (Official Gazette of the Republic of North Macedonia no. 38/22), available in Macedonian <https://azlp.mk/wp-content/uploads/2022/11/be389c475ea244fdbe2abd9632ac3647.pdf> (accessed on 21.04.2023).

866 Art. 2 Decision on determining the methodology for the harmonisation of the sectoral legislation (n. 865).

867 As noted by the supervisory authority in its Annual Report North Macedonia 2022, p. 5 (n. 845).

6 Special Categories of Personal Data

The MDPL 2020 recognises special categories of personal data.[868] Their definition and further rules on their processing is mostly aligned with GDPR rules. Special categories of personal data encompass data that reveal racial or ethnic origin, political opinions, religious or philosophical beliefs, trade union membership, genetic data, biometric data, data concerning health, and data concerning a natural person's sex life or sexual orientation.[869] In contrast to the MDPL 2005, which recognised only so-called particularly sensitive data, the MDPL 2020 identifies a wider range of special categories of personal data. Specifically, the MDPL 2005 did not include political opinions, religious and philosophical beliefs, trade union memberships, and data concerning a natural person's sex life or sexual orientation as particularly sensitive.[870]

One significant difference between the MDPL 2020 and the GDPR concerns the regulation of special categories of personal data. Under the MDPL 2020, certain categories of data, such as health data, genetic data (except when the processing is carried out by medical professionals for preventive medicine, medical diagnosis, or care and therapy of the data subject), and biometric data, can only be processed with prior written approval from the supervisory authority.[871] Except this case, a prior approval of the supervisory authority is necessary for a systematic and extensive processing of the national identification number of the citizens.[872]

7 Rights of Data Subject

The rights of data subject are the same as under the GDPR. The MDPL 2020 contains the same enhanced data subject rights as the GDPR and defines the same rules for exercising those rights, including the restrictions.[873] Most of the rights of data subject were already recognised by the MDPL 2005, such as the right to be informed (both when data is collected from the data subject directly of from the third party),[874] the right to access,[875] the right to object[876] and the right to supplement, amend, delete or prevent the use of the personal data.[877] However, the

868 Art. 13 MDPL 2020.
869 Art. 4(1)(13) MDPL 2020.
870 Art. 29 MDPL 2005.
871 Art. 84 MDPL 2020.
872 Art. 83 MDPL 2020.
873 Chapter III MDPL 2020.
874 Artt. 10–11 MDPL 2005.
875 Art. 12 MDPL 2005.
876 Art. 13 MDPL 2005.
877 Art. 13 MDPL 2005.

MDPL 2020 also introduces some entirely new rights, such as the right to data portability[878] and the right to object to automated individual decision making, including profiling.[879]

8 Redress Mechanism

The redress mechanisms are set out in the eighth chapter of the MDPL 2020. This chapter is fully modelled on the provisions of the GDPR. This includes the right of data subjects to 'submit a request'[880] to the supervisory authority in the event of a violation of their rights, without prejudice to any other administrative or judicial remedy.[881] The supervisory authority is also required to publish a template for such a request, in order to facilitate the submission of requests by data subjects.[882] Moreover, data subjects are entitled to an effective judicial remedy against decisions of the supervisory authority,[883] and against a controller or processor in case their rights have been violated.[884] Lastly, data subjects have the right to compensation for any material or non-material damage suffered as a result of a breach of the MDPL 2020.[885]

9 Personal Scope

MDPL 2020 acknowledges the key data protection entities, namely the controller and the processor, whose respective roles and responsibilities align with those prescribed by the GDPR.[886] Data subjects also have the same meaning as foreseen by Art. 4(1) GDPR. Moreover, the MDPL 2020 introduces the concept of joint controllers,[887] a novel construct emulated from the GDPR, who are beholden to identical obligations and liabilities as per the GDPR. Concepts such as DPIA,[888] notification of data breaches,[889] code of conducts[890] and certifications[891] were incorporated by the MDPL 2020 into the national legislation.

878 Art. 24 MDPL 2020.
879 Artt. 25–25 MDPL 2020.
880 The English translation of the MDPL 2020 uses the term 'request', but this term is identical with the term 'complaint' under Art. 77 GDPR.
881 Art. 97 MDPL 2020.
882 Art. 97(3) MDPL 2020.
883 Art. 98 MDPL 2020.
884 Art. 99 MDPL 2020.
885 Art. 101 MDPL 2020.
886 Chapter IV MDPL 2020.
887 Art. 30 MDPL 2020.
888 Art. 39 MDPL 2020.
889 Artt. 37–38 MDPL 2020.

a) Specific Security Obligations

Similar to the provision of GDPR (Art. 30), both data processors and data controllers are obliged to maintain a record of processing activities.[892] However, the MDPL 2020 distinguishes from the GDPR by imposing this duty on entities with fewer than 50 employees, whereas the GDPR sets the threshold at 250 persons.[893] As a result, even smaller companies must comply with this obligation, potentially providing the supervisory authority with greater insight into data protection practices across a wider range of organisations than might be possible in other EU countries.[894] The MDPL 2020 lays down some additional security measures for the protection of personal data not envisaged by the GDPR.

b) High-risk Filing Systems

A high-risk filing system concept was introduced by Art. 71 MDPL 2002. This safeguard measure stems from the MDPL 2005, under which companies were required to inform the supervisory authority prior to any processing of personal data.[895] The supervisory authority maintained a so-called 'central registry' of these notifications.[896] Some controllers were exempted from this obligation, e.g., companies that employed fewer than ten employees.[897]

With the introduction of the MDPL 2020, the central registry underwent modification and now operates as an electronic 'record of high-risk filing system', operated by the supervisory authority.[898] In accordance with this development, controllers are now obligated to notify the supervisory authority if "the use of new technologies for a specific type of processing, taking into account the nature, scope, context and purposes of the processing of personal data, raises the possibility of a high risk for the rights and freedoms of natural persons."[899] The supervisory authority published the Guidelines regarding the notification of processing

890 Artt. 44–45 MDPL 2020.
891 Artt. 46, 67 MDPL 2020.
892 Art. 34 MDPL 2020.
893 Art. 34(5) MDPL 2020.
894 For example, the German Federal Data Protection Act (BDSG) in Art. 30 (5) prescribes that the obligation to maintain a record of processing activities does not apply to companies or institutions employing less than 250 employees or the Croatian Implementation Act of the EU General Data Protection Regulation no. 42/18 which implements the GDPR, provides for the same rule.
895 Art. 27 MDPL 2005.
896 *Ibid.*
897 Art. 28 MDPL 2005.
898 Art. 71(3) MDPL 2020.
899 Art. 71(1) MDPL 2020.

of personal data that will result in high risk.[900] In these guidelines, the authority also clarified the relationship between the high-risk data processing and the duty to perform the DPIA (a concept taken from the GDPR). The assessment which is a matter of high-risk personal data processing refers to the already established collections or records of personal data, which controllers already managed – within their scope of work – before the adoption of the MDPL 2020, whereas the DPIA is needed only for each new personal data processing process. The guidelines suggest a three-step process to evaluate whether the processing of personal data presents a high risk to data subjects. Firstly, data controllers need to assess whether they use technological solutions such as software solutions to make personal data available and usable to authorised parties.[901] If this is the case, the second step is to evaluate the nature of the personal data being processed. Finally, the third step involves assessing whether the personal data processing operations are extensive by taking into account factors such as the number of affected data subjects, the volume and types of data being processed, the duration and continuity of the processing, and the geographical scope of the personal data processing activities.[902] The supervisory authority has also adopted a separate Rulebook on reporting personal data processing of high risk,[903] which offers guidance on technical steps for reporting high risk data processing to the supervisory authority and the requisite information to be included, such as an assessment of risk data processing activities, TOMs and information on data transfers, if applicable.[904] Thus, this concept is very much similar to the DPIA introduced by the GDPR,[905] with a difference that it applies to the already established processing activities, whereas the obligation to perform a DPIA (concept introduced by the MDPL 2020) applies to the new processing activities. Interestingly, the MDPL 2020 also incorporates a clause which state that after North Macedonia's accession to the EU, records of filing systems of personal data with high risk cease to apply.[906]

---

900 Guidelines for notifying high risk processing of personal data, available at the following link <https://azlp.mk/en/guidelines-regarding-the-notification-of-processing-of-personal-data-that-will-result-in-high-risk/> (accessed on 21.04.2023).

901 *Ibid.*

902 *Ibid.*

903 Rulebook on reporting personal data processing of high risk (Official Gazette of the Republic of North Macedonia no. 42/20), available at the following link <https://azlp.mk/wp-content/uploads/2022/12/Rulebook-on-Reporting-High-Risk-Data-Processing.pdf> (accessed on 21.04.2023).

904 Art. 2 Rulebook on reporting personal data processing of high risk (n. 903).

905 The factors which are assessed for the high-risk assessments are also provided by the WP29 Guidelines on Data Protection Impact Assessment (DPIA) and determining whether processing is "likely to result in a high risk" for the purposes of Regulation 2016/679, wp248rev.01 (04.04.2017).

906 Art. 122 MDPL 2020.

c) DPIA

As previously noted, the MDPL 2020 introduces the obligation for data controllers to perform a DPIA, where a type of processing "in particular using new technologies [...] is likely to result in a high risk to the rights and freedoms of natural persons".[907] This obligation is separate from a "high-risk filing system", as explained above.

The MDPL 2020 stipulates that the supervisory authority must establish and publish a list of processing operations subject to the DPIA requirement or for which no DPIA is required.[908] In line with this, the supervisory authority has adopted a Rulebook on the process for data protection impact assessment.[909] The cases prescribed by the rulebook generally align with the GDPR and the WP29 Guidelines on Data Protection Impact Assessment (hereinafter: "DPIA Guidelines").[910] However, there are some additional cases not envisaged by the DPIA Guidelines, such as the processing of personal data in a manner that includes monitoring the location or behaviour of individuals through systematic processing of communication data generated by the use of telephone, internet, or other communication channels, such as GSM, GPS, and Wi-Fi, for monitoring and processing of location data.[911] Additionally, processing of personal data through the use of devices and technologies that may endanger the health of one or more individuals in the event of an incident and processing of special categories of personal data of employees used for unique identification by the employer or through the use of an application or system for monitoring their work are also included.[912] This example shows that the supervisory authority has a stricter approach to the processing of personal data by technological means compared to the time before adoption of the MDPL 2020.

Further, regarding the prior consultation with the supervisory authority, the GDPR leaves it open to Member States' controllers to consult with, and obtain prior authorisation from, the supervisory authority in relation to processing by a controller for the performance of a task carried out by the controller in the public interest, including processing in relation to social protection and public

---

907 Art. 39(1) MDPL 2020.

908 Art. 39(4) MDPL 2020.

909 Rulebook on the process for data protection impact assessment (Official Gazette of the Republic of North Macedonia no. 122/20), available at the following link <https://azlp.mk/wp-content/uploads/2022/12/Rulebook-Impact-Assessment.pdf> (accessed on 21.04.2023).

910 WP29 Guidelines on DPIA (n. 905).

911 Art. 3 Rulebook on the process for data protection impact assessment (n. 909).

912 *Ibid.*

health.[913] The MDPL 2020 specifies this provision by requiring controllers who process personal data for tasks in the public interest, including processing related to social protection and public health, to consult with and seek prior authorisation from the supervisory authority in certain cases. Specifically, this applies when (a) the controller's core activities involve large-scale processing operations that require regular and systematic monitoring of data subjects, (b) the controller's core activities involve large-scale processing of special categories of data and personal data relating to criminal convictions and offences, or (c) there is systematic monitoring of areas on a large scale.[914]

d) DPO

The role of a DPO is not a new concept in Macedonian legislation. The MDPL 2005 mandated the appointment of a DPO by (only) controllers obligated to notify the supervisory authority of data processing.[915] Therefore, the concept of a DPO was in many respects similar to the concept of a DPO prescribed by the GDPR, albeit with a different scope.[916]

The MDPL 2020 has incorporated Art. 37 GDPR, with some novelties introduced.[917] Firstly, Art. 41 MDPL 2020 elaborates on the provisions of the GDPR with regard to the criteria for the appointment of the DPO and stipulates that a person may be appointed as a DPO if they meet specific conditions, including an active command of the Macedonian language, a clean criminal record, higher education, and have acquired knowledge and skills regarding the practices and regulations for personal data protection.[918] These conditions for the appointment of the DPO are not only more detailed than the Art. 37(5) GDPR, but also make the appointment of foreigners as DPOs more difficult (in particular active command of the Macedonian language). The Macedonian legislator has in this way prevented that some companies choose a foreign employee who is part of the company's international group and who already has a proven knowledge of data protection matters. Secondly, under the new legislation the supervisory authority is entrusted with providing trainings for DPOs and employees and issues certificates of

---

913 Art. 36(5) GDPR.

914 Art. 40(5)(6) MDPL 2020.

915 Art. 26-a MDPL 2005.

916 The controllers were not obliged to appoint a DPO, if the personal data are part of publicly available collections based on a law.

917 Art. 41 MDPL 2020.

918 Art. 41(5) MDPL 2020.

completion of training, with the aim of educating and developing their ability to perform their duties under the MDPL 2020.[919]

Thus, these provisions of the MDPL 2020 for the DPO are a positive example of taking into account the development of the law by providing provisions that are related to the specific legal system, rather than blindly copying provisions from the GDPR.

e) Representatives

As under the GDPR, the MDPL 2020 requires foreign controllers and processors to designate a representative in cases where Art. 3 (2) MDPL 2020 applies. This is an innovation that did not exist in the MDPL 2005.

f) Codes of Conduct

The MDPL 2020 introduces provisions for establishing codes of conduct and certification, modelled upon those stipulated by the GDPR. Companies wishing to create a code of conduct, or amend or extend an existing code, must submit the draft, amendment or extension to the supervisory authority, which gives an opinion and approves the draft, amendment or extension if it finds that it contains sufficient appropriate safeguards.[920] The supervisory authority also registers and publishes approved codes and maintains a register of all approved codes, amendments and extensions.[921] Further, the MDPL 2020 provides that the monitoring of codes of conduct may be carried out by a body which has an appropriate level of expertise and is accredited for that purpose by the supervisory authority.[922]

g) Certifications

Certifications shall be issued by the supervisory authority or by the certification bodies.[923] Regarding the issuance of certifications by certification bodies, the MDPL 2020 provides that the certification bodies shall be accredited by the Institute for Accreditation of North Macedonia (hereinafter: "Institute").[924] However, it appears that the supervisory authority is not empowered to fully control certifica-

---

919 Art. 69 MDPL 2020.
920 Art. 44(3) MDPL 2020.
921 Art. 44(5) MDPL 2020.
922 Art. 45(1) MDPL 2020.
923 Art. 46(4) MDPL 2020.
924 Art. 47(2) MDPL 2020.

tions performed by the special certification bodies.[925] By contrast, the GDPR stipulates that Member States must ensure that certification bodies receive accreditation from either the supervisory authority or the national accreditation body, with additional requirements established by the supervisory authority.[926] The EDPB Guidelines[927] provide further detail on the GDPR's provisions, stating that certification bodies must demonstrate their independence and expertise to the satisfaction of the competent supervisory authority.[928] These additional requirements established by the supervisory authority should define specific requirements to facilitate the assessment of certification bodies' independence and data protection expertise.[929] In contrast, the MDPL 2020 only requires certification bodies to demonstrate their independence and expertise to the satisfaction of the Institute, rather than the supervisory authority.[930] This suggests that the Institute, not the supervisory authority, will assess certification bodies' independence and expertise. This reduces the supervisory authority's power to monitor and inspect the new instruments in North Macedonia's legislation. Lastly, it seems that technical standards and norms for certification have not yet been prescribed by the supervisory authority.[931]

10 Transfer of Personal Data

The biggest differences from the GDPR are the rules on the transfer of personal data. The MDPL 2020 sets forth more stringent conditions for the transfer of personal data compared to the GDPR. Particularly, the MDPL 2020 imposes several changes in comparison to the GDPR.

First of all, as a general principle the MDPL 2020 states that "any transfer of personal data [...] to a third country or to an international organisation shall take place only if the conditions laid down in this law are fulfilled [...], including for onward transfers [...] in order to ensure that the level of protection of natural per-

925 This issue was also recognised by the NGO Civil Rights Defenders in their Report "Effectiveness of NHRIs in Western Balkan countries Albania, Bosnia and Herzegovina, Kosovo, Montenegro, North Macedonia, Serbia" available at the following link <https://indexnhri.org/> (accessed on 21.02.2022).

926 Art. 42(5)(a) GDPR.

927 EDPB Guidelines 4/2018 on the accreditation of certification bodies under Article 43 of the General Data Protection Regulation (2016/679), version 3 (04.06.2019).

928 This is also provided by the Art. 43(2)a GDPR.

929 EDPB Guidelines 4/2018 (n. 927).

930 Art. 47(2)(a) MDPL 2020.

931 No information is available on the website of the supervisory authority regarding the certification under Artt. 46–47 MDPL 2020.

sons [...] is not undermined."[932] Secondly, the MDPL 2020 privileges data transfers from North Macedonia to the EU or EEA by according these countries a special status, under which the restrictions for data transfers to these countries do not apply.[933] However, despite the exemption from transfer restrictions for data transfers from North Macedonia to EU/EEA member countries, companies are still required to notify the supervisory authority of each data transfer to the EU/EEA.[934] Thirdly, transfers from North Macedonia to third countries which do not include EU or EEA are subject to stricter rules. These rules correspond to the GDPR provisions, and include transfers based on an adequacy decision,[935] transfers subject to appropriate safeguards,[936] transfers or disclosures of personal data based on an international agreement[937] and derogations.[938]

a) Adequacy Decisions

The MDPL 2020 is not the first legislation in North Macedonia to introduce provisions related to data transfers based on an adequacy decision. Provisions on restricting data transfers, including transfers based on an adequacy decision, derived from the DPD were also included in the MDPL 2005.[939] Interestingly, the MDPL 2005, by replicating Art. 25 DPD, required the supervisory authority to notify the EU Commission if it found that a third country did not provide an adequate level of protection for personal data,[940] although Art. 25 DPD applied only to EU Member States. This illustrates the legislator's tendency, even before the adoption of the GDPR, to incorporate articles of EU data protection legislation directly into domestic law.

Under MDPL 2020, the transfer of personal data to third countries or international organisations beyond the EU or EEA may take place if the supervisory authority determines that the third country or international organisation guarantees an adequate level of data protection.[941] In the context of granting an adequacy decision, data protection legislation (including bylaws) incorporates similar provisions as the GDPR, with three major variations. Firstly, it does not allow for the

932 Art. 48(1) MDPL 2020.
933 Art. 48(2) MDPL 2020.
934 *Ibid.*
935 Art. 49 MDPL 2020.
936 Art. 50 MDPL 2020.
937 Art. 52 MDPL 2020.
938 Art. 53 MDPL 2020.
939 Art. 31 MDPL 2005.
940 Art. 31(5) MDPL 2005.
941 Art. 49(1) MDPL 2020.

determination that a territory or one or more specific sectors in a third country or an international organisation ensure an adequate level of protection.[942] As a result, an adequacy decision encompasses the entirety of a country or international organisation. Secondly, even in case the supervisory authority assesses a third country as providing an adequate level, controllers and processors are still required to submit a request for approval of such transfer.[943] Thirdly, the legislation lacks a mechanism for the regular evaluation of adequacy decisions.[944]

The list of countries offering an adequate level of data protection has not yet been made available. However, the supervisory authority has released the Rulebook on Data Transfers, which provides guidelines on the matter.[945] Under Art. 3 of this rulebook, the supervisory authority "when taking an adequacy decision, shall make due consideration of decisions taken by the European Union wherein it is established that certain third countries guarantee an adequate level of personal data protection and whether concerned third countries are signatories to the Council of Europe's Convention 108". This suggests that the supervisory authority will follow the EU Commission's adequacy decisions. Furthermore, the Rulebook on Data Transfers outlines the requirements for notifying the supervisory authority of any personal data transfer to the EU or EEA and the procedures for seeking approval for data transfers to countries with adequate data protection.[946] The purpose of an adequacy decision under the GDPR is to allow the free flow of personal data to countries ensuring adequate protection, which raises questions why the Macedonian legislature chose to impose additional requirements for authorising such transfers. Moreover, if the law already grants privileged status to EU/EEA countries, it is unclear why data controllers should still be required to notify supervisory authorities of such transfers. These additional bureaucratic requirements imposed on companies create a significant burden for companies that may lack the necessary resources or have to incur additional costs to meet the requirements.

942 Art. 49(1) MDPL 2020 states "A transfer of personal data to a third country or an international organisation may take place where the Agency has decided that the third country or the international organisation in question ensures an adequate level of protection".

943 This obligation is not specified by the MDPL 2020, but by the bylaw: Rulebook on Data Transfers (Official Gazette of RNM, no. 122 from 12.5.2020).

944 Neither the MDPL 2020 nor the Rulebook on Data Transfers (n. 943) provide for such a rule.

945 Rulebook on Data Transfers (n. 943).

946 Art. 3 Rulebook on Data Transfers (n. 943).

b) Transfers Based on Safeguards

Similar to the GDPR, the MDPL 2020 stipulates that if there is no adequacy decision, a controller or processor may only transfer personal data to a third country or international organisation if appropriate safeguards have been established, and data subjects have access to enforceable rights and effective legal remedies.[947] The safeguards standards have been copied from the Art. 46 GDPR.[948] In this regard, it should be noted that the MDPL 2020 itself does not require a special transfer approval from the supervisory authority if the safeguards are provided or if the adequacy decision exists. However, the Rulebook on Data Transfers imposes this obligation and the supervisory authority has already confirmed that transfer approval will be necessary for cross-border/boundary data transfers to countries outside EU/EEA.[949]

c) Derogations

Following Art. 49 GDPR, the MDPL 2020 provides a list of exemptions for specific situations where a lawful data transfer outside of North Macedonia is not subject to a transfer approval (e. g. consent of the data subject, enforcement of a contract between a data subject and a data controller, etc.).[950] However, the supervisory authority has taken a very conservative approach, insisting that even in such cases a transfer authorisation must be obtained.[951]

---

947 Art. 50 MDPL 2020.

948 Under Art. 50 MDPL 2020 safeguards include (a) legally binding and enforceable instruments between public authorities or bodies; (b) binding corporate rules in accordance with Article 51; (c) standard data protection clauses adopted by the supervisory authority or approved by the EU Commission; (d) an approved code of conduct pursuant to Art. 44 together with binding and enforceable commitments of the controller or processor in the third country to apply the appropriate safeguards, including as regards data subjects' rights; or (f) an approved certification mechanism pursuant to Art. 46. Further, subject to the authorisation from the supervisory authority, the appropriate safeguards may also be provided for, in particular, by: (a) contractual clauses between the controller or processor and the controller, processor or the recipient of the personal data in the third country or international organisation; or (b) provisions to be inserted into administrative arrangements between public authorities or bodies which include enforceable and effective data subject rights.

949 The Agency confirmed in the communication with the RCC (RCC Report 2020, pp. 134–135 (n. 18)) that they will have a rather conservative approach towards data transfers outside of the EU/EEA and require always a prior approval before commencing such a data transfer. See also Karanovic & Partners "North Macedonia: Informal Requirement for Transfer Impact Assessments in the New Yea", Lexicology (15. 12. 2021) available at the following link <https://www.lexology.com/library/detail.aspx?g=a36a570d-5777-45a8-89a3-e19e4356b7ef> (accessed on 28. 05. 2023).

950 Art. 53 MDPL 2020.

951 RCC Report 2020, pp. 134–135 (n. 18).

d) Data Transfers in Practice

At the outset of the implementation of the MDPL 2020 the number of data transfers from North Macedonia to other countries was low. As per the supervisory authority's annual report in 2020,[952] a total of seven notifications for the transfer of personal data to EU and EEA and nine requests for transfer to third countries requiring prior approval were processed. However, in 2022, these numbers increased, with sixty-six applications for the transfer of personal data to EU and EEA countries and sixteen requests for transfer to third countries requiring supervisory authority approval.[953] The most common reasons for data transfers include the fulfilment of contractual obligations, collaboration with external partners, customers and suppliers, backup and cloud services, and the support of human resources management processes in companies that are part of international groupings (personal data of employees, job candidates, external collaborators, clients, suppliers, etc.).[954]

11 Penalties

The MDPL 2020 introduces more significant fines exampled by the GDPR, with controllers and processors facing fines of up to 2% and 4% of their total annual turnover from the preceding financial year for non-compliance with the law.[955] However, the fines are only defined in %, which differs from the GDPR, which provides for fines up to a maximum fixed amount or 2%/4%, whichever is higher. Additionally, the MDPL 2020 imposes fines of between €300 and €500 on responsible persons within legal entities and between €100 and €250 on officials within state administrative bodies.[956] Also, natural persons who are considered as controllers or processors are also facing fines in amount between €100 and €250.[957] Therefore, the MDPL 2020 not only establishes fines for responsible persons but also differentiates between the accountability of natural persons, the controller or processor, and provides for lower fines for them. This distinction is not provided for in the GDPR.

---

952 Supervisory Authority's Annual Report for 2020, available in Macedonian at the following link <https://www.dzlp.mk/sites/default/files/pdf-azlp-godisen_izvestaj_za_2020_mk.pdf>, p. 21 (accessed on 21.04.2023).

953 Annual Report North Macedonia 2022 (n. 845).

954 Information from the Supervisory Authority's Annual Report for 2018, available in Macedonian at the following link <https://www.dzlp.mk/sites/default/files/annual_report_dpdp_2018_en.pdf>, p. 15 (accessed on 21.04.2023) and Annual Report North Macedonia 2020 p. 21 (n. 952).

955 The MDPL 2020 provides two categories of fines in the same way as the GDPR (Artt. 110–111).

956 Art. 110(7) MDPL 2020.

957 Art. 110(5) MDPL 2020.

The range of fines under the MDPL 2020 is now more aligned with the EU Acquis. The penalties under the MDPL 2005 were significantly lower. For example, penalties ranged up to €2,000 for a legal entity-controller, up to €1,250 for a legal entity-processor, and up to €600 for the entity's responsible person.[958] Such low fines under the old legislation were also criticised as insufficient to ensure effective compliance.[959]

The rules governing the imposition of fines, as well as the factors to be taken into account when determining the fine amount, are derived from the GDPR.[960] The supervisory authority is vested with the authority to impose fines, which is executed through a misdemeanour body charged with commencing and imposing misdemeanour procedures and sanctions.[961] Decisions delivered by the misdemeanour body may be contested in accordance with the Macedonian Law on Misdemeanours.[962]

12 Specific Processing Situations

The GDPR provides a margin of manoeuvre for Member States to set out the circumstances for specific processing situations related to their national legal system ('opening clauses'), including determining more precisely the conditions under which the processing of personal data is lawful.[963] Some of these specific processing situations are listed in Chapter IX GDPR. The opening clauses could pose a challenge to third countries, which will have to adapt these provisions to their national legal order, while ensuring that the level of protection of personal data is 'equivalent' to that in the EU, as already explained in Part A (in relation to Albania).

MDPL 2020 provides several specific processing situations in chapter seven, which include processing and freedom of expression and information (Art. 81), processing and public access to official documents (Art. 82), processing citizen's national identification number (Art. 83), processing for which prior approval is necessary (Art. 84), processing in the context of employment (Art. 85), processing for archiving purposes in the public interest, scientific or historical research purposes or statistical purposes (Art. 86), processing of personal data by churches, religious communities or religious groups (Art. 87), processing data of deceased per-

958 Art. 49 MDPL 2005.
959 Nora Osmani (n. 13).
960 Artt. 113, 114 MDPL 2020.
961 Art. 114 MDPL 2020.
962 Art. 115 MDPL 2020.
963 Recital 10 GDPR.

sons (Art. 88), video surveillance (Art. 89), providing personal data to recipients (Art. 94) and direct marketing (Art. 96).

Hence, the MDPL 2020 contains certain provisions outside of the scope of the GDPR, including the most detailed and specific rules on video surveillance. This part focuses only on those provisions that are not covered by the GDPR, or that have been further elaborated by the MDPL 2020.

a) Processing and Freedom of Expression and Information (Art. 81)

The MDPL 2020 specifies the provisions on criteria which shall apply when reconciling the right to personal data protection with the freedom of expression and information, in line with Art. 85(1) GDPR. These criteria encompass a range of considerations, including the nature of personal data, circumstances in which data are obtained, the impact of the published information on the discussion on public interest, how renowned is the physical person concerned and the subject-matter of the information, prior conduct of the physical person concerned, prior consent of the physical person concerned and content, form and consequences of publishing of this information.[964]

b) Processing of Citizens' National Identification Number (Art. 83)

The national identification number of a citizen (ID number) may be processed only upon prior consent of the data subject, for the exercise of legally binding rights or responsibilities of the data subject and the controller, and in other cases stipulated by law.[965] In cases the law is a legal base for the processing of an ID number, such law must contain safeguards and other measures for protection of the rights and freedoms of data subjects.[966] Further, in case of a systematic and extensive processing of the national identification numbers, the prior approval from the supervisory authority is required.[967] Lastly, the MDPL 2020 obliges controller and processor to ensure that the ID number is not unduly made visible, printed or extracted from a filing system.[968] Such strong rules may come from the fact that the ID number is particularly sensitive data in North Macedonia. The ID number (in Macedonian "Матичен број") is not the typical ID number which is changing every time a new identity card is issued, but it is a number that

---

964 Art. 81(4) MDPL 2020.
965 Art. 83(1) MDPL 2020.
966 Art. 83(3) MDPL 2020.
967 Art. 83(2) MDPL 2020.
968 Art. 83(6) MDPL 2020.

all citizens receive at birth and that never changes, for which reason it is highly sensitive data and can be misused in many situations.[969]

c) Prior Approval(s)

The MDPL 2020 envisages provisions which mandate that certain types of personal data can only be processed with the prior approval of the supervisory authority. Such provisions are not contemplated by the GDPR. The prior approval of the supervisory authority is necessary before processing personal data falling within the following categories: health data, genetic data (except where processing is carried out by specialists for the purposes of preventive medicine, medical diagnosis, or care and treatment of the data subject) and biometric data.[970] Nonetheless, this approval shall not be required where the processing of personal data is governed by a law that contains appropriate safeguards and measures to safeguard the rights and freedoms of data subjects.[971]

Moreover, the MDPL 2020 stipulates that approval must be obtained if the processing of special categories of personal data is carried out subsequent to explicit consent from the data subject.[972] This represents a more stringent approach to regulating special categories of personal data in comparison to the GDPR, which does not necessitate approval in cases where such data is processed pursuant to the data subject's consent.[973]

d) Deceased Persons

While the GDPR does not extend to the personal data of deceased individuals, it provides that Member States may stipulate specific rules regarding the processing

969 The former Yugoslavia adopted a law on the unique identification number (JMBG) in 1976, and the law was subsequently adopted by all republics. Date of birth, region of birth, serial number and gender are encoded in the JMBG. For data protection reasons Croatia adopted a Law on the Termination of the Law on Personal Identification Number (NN 10/2023) in 2023 to end the validity of this unique identification number.

970 Art. 84(1) MDPL 2020.

971 Art. 84(3) MDPL 2020.

972 Art. 84(2) MDPL 2020.

973 Art. 9(2)(a) GDPR pertains to the processing of special categories of personal data with explicit consent from the data subject. The article does not require prior approval from the supervisory authority for such processing. However, the article stipulates that special categories of personal data may not be processed based on the data subject's consent where Union or Member State law provides for a prohibition on lifting the prohibition of processing such data by the data subject.

of personal data of deceased persons.[974] The regulation of this matter differs across various Member States, with the majority of them not regulating it.[975] The MDPL 2020 introduces unique regulations pertaining to the processing of personal data of deceased persons. Pursuant to the Art. 88 MDPL 2020, the controller may only disclose the personal data of deceased individuals to authorised recipients.[976] Authorised recipients are considered to be the legal successors of the deceased or any other person who processes the data for scientific or historical research or for statistical purposes, unless the deceased persons have prohibited in writing the disclosure of their personal data.[977]

e) Direct Marketing

According to the WP29 Guidelines "additional content principles to be applied in specific situations of processing" are relevant for the assessment of the level of data protection in third countries, including also where data is processed for direct marketing.[978] Therefore, third country legislation must include provisions on direct marketing which are in accordance with the GDPR.

The MDPL 2020, in addition to the right to object at any time to the processing of personal data for the purposes of direct marketing,[979] also governs direct marketing in its provisions on specific situations of processing. The processing of personal data for the purpose of direct marketing, which includes profiling to the extent that it is related to direct marketing, is permitted only with the explicit consent of the data subject.[980]

f) Video Surveillance

The MDPL 2020 incorporates extensive and comprehensive provisions pertaining to video surveillance, which may be uncharacteristic for data protection laws meant to provide the basic principles and guidelines for sectoral laws.[981] While

974 Recital 27 GDPR.

975 See an overview of national laws in the EU regulating personal data of deceased persons: Bird & Bird, Personal data of deceased persons (n. 660).

976 Art. 88(1) MDPL 2020.

977 Art. 88(2) MDPL 2020.

978 WP29 Adequacy Referential, p. 7 (n. 155).

979 Art. 25(2) MDPL 2020.

980 Art. 96 MDPL 2020.

981 The German Federal Data Protection Act (BDSG), for example, only regulates video surveillance of publicly accessible areas in its Section 4, but not video surveillance of private areas, nor does it contain such detailed provisions. Instead, video surveillance is provided for in other laws.

the GDPR does not encompass provisions governing video surveillance, the WP29 Guidelines 3/2019 provide further detail on the matter.[982] This could be seen a positive and proactive approach of Macedonian legislator, given that some WB6 legislation do not regulate the video surveillance at all.[983] Furthermore, instances of personal data breaches via video surveillance have been prevalent in the WB6 case law.[984]

Under Art. 89 provisions of the MDPL 2020 apply to all processing of personal data by video surveillance, unless the processing of personal data is performed by a natural person solely for the purpose of domestic activities.[985] The law sets forth general principles and obligations for data controllers, including the requirement to publish a clear, visible, and publicly accessible notice regarding the presence of video surveillance,[986] limiting the scope of the surveillance to the necessary extent,[987] storing video surveillance recordings for a maximum of 30 days,[988] and implementing other specific security measures to safeguard the rights and freedoms of data subjects.[989] It also contains some specific provisions on video surveillance in official or business premises,[990] in employment context[991] and in single unit and multi-unit residential buildings.[992] Moreover, the additional safeguards to protect the rights and freedoms of data subjects include carrying out "an anal-

982 EDPB Guidelines 3/2019 on processing of personal data through video devices, version 2 (29.01.2020).
983 The Serbian legal system for example, see Chapter 4, F.
984 For example, the Serbian supervisory authority initiated proceedings against the company Bershka in 2021 for allegedly illegally carrying out video surveillance in changing rooms; See Commissioner's statement on initiation of proceeding for invasion of privacy of shopping mall visitors (02.06.2021), available in Serbian at the following link <https://www.poverenik.rs/sr-yu/saopstenja/3561-кршење-приватности-посетилаца-тржног-ц%25> (accessed on 18.05.2022). See also Part IV, 4 (Court Cases) of this Section and the case of Montenegro in Section D, V, 3.
985 Art. 89(1)(2) MDPL 2020.
986 Art. 89(3)(4) MDPL 2020.
987 Art. 89(6) MDPL 2020.
988 Art. 89(8) MDPL 2020.
989 Artt. 92–93 MDPL 2020.
990 Under Art. 90 MDPL 2020 the controller may conduct video surveillance of official or business premises if deemed necessary for protection of lives or health of people, protection of ownership, protection of lives and health of employees, due to the nature of work, or controlling the movement in and out of official or business premises. Further, Art. 90(3) specifically prohibits video surveillance in changing rooms, dressing rooms, toilets and similar rooms.
991 Art. 89(7) MDPL 2020.
992 Art. 91 MDPL 2020.

ysis of the goals of the video surveillance prior to the installation process"[993] and a "periodical assessment" which shall be performed every two-year.[994]

g) Recipients

The MDPL 2020 also governs the provision of personal data to third parties as part of specific processing situations. The controller may disclose personal data to recipients "based on a written request of the recipient, in case the recipient is authorised to process that personal data".[995] The written request shall include the reasons, legal grounds for the use of personal data, a category of data subjects and categories of personal data requested.[996] Yet, in case the obligation for providing personal data to a recipient is "laid down by law and takes place with the planned dynamics" the recipient is not obliged to submit a written request to the controller.[997] Moreover, the MDPL 2020 prohibits the provision of personal data to recipients whose processing is not conducted in accordance with the principle of lawfulness and provisions regulating special categories of personal data.[998] In addition, personal data cannot be made available if the purpose for which the data is requested violates purpose limitation.[999] Data controllers are also required to maintain separate records of personal data provided to recipients, including the details of data recipient, the category of data subjects, the legal grounds and reasons for which the personal data have been disclosed to the recipient.[1000] These measures contain more stringent requirements compared to the GDPR, as the records of data activities do not have to contain such detailed information, nor is there a specific obligation to maintain separate records on recipients.[1001] However, under the latest CJEU decision from 2023, data controllers are also required to provide data subjects with the actual identity of the recipients

993 Under Art. 92(1) MDPL 2020 the analysis needs to indicate the reasons of the video surveillance explaining the reasons for fulfilment of the aim (protection of lives or health of people; protection of ownership; protection of lives and health of employees, due to the nature of work, controlling the movement in and out of official or business premises), as well as a description of movable and immovable assets, the premises which will be protected by installing the video surveillance.
994 Art. 92(3) MDPL 2020.
995 Art. 94(1) MDPL 2020.
996 Art. 94(3) MDPL 2020.
997 Art. 94(2) MDPL 2020.
998 Art. 94(5) MDPL 2020.
999 *Ibid.*
1000 Art. 94(7) MDPL 2020.
1001 Art. 30 GDPR.

when possible,[1002] which means that controllers would have to have special records on the recipients. These additional provisions on records on data recipients provided by the MDPL 2020 may not only conform with the latest CJEU case law, but also provide a solid additional safeguard mechanism, especially in relation to the government's access rights, as the controllers would have to document each time they disclose the data to government authorities, which ensures better transparency for the data subjects.

13 Conclusion to II

The MDPL 2020 was enacted by North Macedonia in response to the adoption of the GDPR in the EU. As an EU candidate country, North Macedonia was required to update its data protection framework to align with the GDPR. In addition, in order to facilitate cross-border data transfers with EU Member States without restrictions, the country is seeking to meet the criteria for the adoption of an adequacy decision.

The MDPL 2020 largely mirrors the GDPR, with the same principles, almost identical provisions and a very similar structure, but also a key difference, illustrated by the lack of Recitals provided in the GDPR preamble. The MDPL 2020 has not only replicated the GDPR but has also concretised the opening clauses of the GDPR, particularly in the seventh chapter defining provisions relating to specific processing situations. In the absence of further explanation from the Recitals, this shall provide greater clarity and specificity in the application of the MDPL 2020.

However, the MDPL 2020 also introduced very bureaucratic provisions, including obtaining prior authorisations or notifications to the supervisory authority, especially in the part regulating data transfers and processing of special categories of personal data. The rationale for such stringent provisions may be to offer additional safeguards and to strengthen North Macedonia's negotiating position in potential adequacy decisions with the EU Commission. For example, granting a privileged position to Member States with regard to data transfers, while imposing overly strict rules for transfers to other countries (such as prior authorisation by the supervisory authority even if adequate safeguards are in place) is aimed at ensuring the safeguards in 'onward transfer' of personal data transferred from the EU to North Macedonia. Nonetheless, imposing excessively

---

1002 The CJEU noted in the case Österreichische Post (n. 694) "that every person has the right to know to whom his or her personal data have been disclosed", see the press release no 4/23 CJEU (12.01.2023) <https://curia.europa.eu/jcms/upload/docs/application/pdf/2023-01/cp230004en.pdf> (accessed on 21.04.2023).

strict rules may not be conducive to ensure a 'good level of compliance'[1003] in the country as companies may lack the incentive to comply with such regulations.

III Supervisory Authority

The Personal Data Protection Agency (hereinafter: "PDPA") is the designated supervisory authority with exclusive competence in the field of personal data protection. The PDPA was established by the MDPL 2005 under the name of the Directorate for Personal Data Protection, whose mandate was subsequently revoked and revised by the 2020 MDPL. Prior to the establishment of the PDPA, there was no comparable supervisory authority in North Macedonia.

1 General Functions

The PDPA's functions are defined as competences, tasks, and powers,[1004] as also set out in Chapter 6 GDPR. The role of the PDPA is to promote compliance with the MDPL 2020 and to raise public awareness of personal data protection[1005] among data controllers, processors, and data subjects, including providing training on personal data.[1006] The PDPA is also vested with the responsibility of enforcing compliance with the MDPL 2020, which includes conducting investigations, imposing fines, and handling data subjects' complaints.[1007] Alongside these monitoring and enforcement powers, the PDPA's tasks include advising the Parliament of North Macedonia, the Government, and other institutions and bodies on legislative and administrative measures concerning the processing of personal data.[1008] In addition, the PDPA has the power to initiate amendments to laws and challenge them before the Constitutional Court to ensure harmonisation with the MDPL 2020.[1009]

2 Independence

By virtue of Art. 58 MDPL 2020, the PDPA is an autonomous and independent body of the state administration, responsible for overseeing the lawfulness of personal

---

1003 Term used by the WP29.
1004 Artt. 65, 67 MDPL 2020.
1005 Art. 65(1)(a)(b) MDPL 2020.
1006 Art. 65(1)(u) MDPL 2020.
1007 Art. 65(1)(f)(h) MDPL 2020.
1008 Art. 65(5) MDPL 2020.
1009 *Ibid.*

data processing activities within the territory of North Macedonia, as well as safeguarding the fundamental rights and freedoms of individuals in relation to the processing of their personal data.[1010] According to the MDPL 2020, PDPA's independence must be respected and protected at all times, and no entity or individual may influence its members in the exercise of their powers and duties.[1011]

The PDPA's director and its deputy are appointed and dismissed by the Parliament.[1012] The PDPA is also accountable for its work before the Parliament.[1013] The MDPL 2020 establishes criteria for the election of the PDPA's director, including a clean criminal record, higher education, at least ten years of work experience, and a minimum of five years of experience in the field of data protection, as well as an official English language certification.[1014] The MDPL 2020 also prohibits the director and deputy director from engaging in incompatible functions or affiliations with political parties or workplaces, and imposes a duty of professional secrecy upon them.[1015] It should be noted that these rules on refraining from incompatible functions and the duty of professional secrecy only apply to the office of the director and deputy director, and not to other members of the PDPA.[1016]

3 Powers

The MDPL 2020 sets out the investigative,[1017] corrective,[1018] and advisory competencies[1019] of the PDPA, which correspond to those established by the GDPR. The investigative powers are regulated in a separate chapter "Supervision of Data Protection" (chapter nine), largely devoted to defining the rules of investigations, which include regular, irregular and control investigations, as well as the possibility of electronic supervision.[1020] Furthermore, this chapter regulates the rights of inspectors[1021] and the obligation of controllers and processors to cooperate with them and give them access to all relevant documents.[1022] Finally, on the

1010 Art. 57 MDPL 2020.
1011 Art. 58(4) MDPL 2020.
1012 Art. 59(1)(4) MDPL 2020.
1013 Art. 59(11) MDPL 2020.
1014 Art. 60 MDPL 2020.
1015 Art. 62 MDPL 2020.
1016 Art. 62 MDPL 2020 which regulates 'incompatibility of office and confidentiality', mentions only 'the office of director and/or deputy director'.
1017 Art. 66(1) MDPL 2020.
1018 Art. 66(2) MDPL 2020.
1019 *Ibid.*
1020 Art. 104 MDPL 2020.
1021 Art. 105 MDPL 2020.
1022 Art. 106 MDPL 2020.

basis of the results of the inspections, the inspectors have the right to initiate the misdemeanour procedure before the Misdemeanour Commission, which is part of the organisation of the PDPA.[1023]

a) Cooperation with State Administration Bodies

The MDPL 2020 provides special rules for the cooperation of the PDPA with state administration bodies, not provided by the GDPR. According to Art. 67(1) state administration bodies are obligated to cooperate with the PDPA and inform the authority of all measures taken to implement the PDPA's requests, proposals and opinions. If a state authority fails to notify the PDPA or does not act on its recommendations, the PDPA shall "inform of this the direct superior body, the managing official of that body of North Macedonia, that is, the Government or Parliament of North Macedonia."[1024] Upon receiving a 'special report on non-compliance' by the PDPA the Parliament or Government must deliberate and take a position in a session attended by the official managing the state administration body referred to in the special report. They must also propose provisional measures and notify the PDPA of the measures taken within the deadline specified in the special report.[1025]

While this provides an additional accountability mechanism for state administration bodies, it may also undermine the independence of the PDPA. Indeed, the MDPL 2020 appears to allow measures for non-compliance by administration bodies to be proposed by government or parliament, rather than the PDPA itself. Art. 67(2) MDPL 2020 mentions a 'special report on non-compliance' that the PDPA must provide to the superiors of the administration bodies, but it is not clear what the special report should include. Additionally, the MDPL 2020 does not specify what will happen if the PDPA is dissatisfied with the measures proposed by parliament or government. This lack of clarity may result in uncertainty and potential challenges to the independence and effectiveness of the PDPA. Thus, clarity surrounding the roles and responsibilities of all parties involved would be beneficial to ensure the effective functioning of the PDPA enforcing data protection on state authorities in North Macedonia.

4 Challenges

Under Art. 52(5) GDPR each Member State "shall ensure that each supervisory authority chooses and has its own staff which shall be subject to the exclusive direc-

1023 Art. 109 MDPL 2020.
1024 Art. 67(2) MDPL 2020.
1025 Art. 67(3) MDPL 2020.

tion of the member or members of the supervisory authority concerned".[1026] Additionally, Member States must ensure that each supervisory authority is "subject to financial control which does not affect its independence."[1027] Despite the MDPL 2020 stipulating that the PDPA "has full political, financial and functional independence",[1028] it is not completely functionally independent in reality.[1029] Instead, employment of the PDPA's staff involves the approval by the Ministry of Information Society and Administration,[1030] as well as the approval of the PDPA's budget for employment by the Ministry of Finance.[1031] The initial draft law for personal data protection included comprehensive rules on the employment of PDPA staff.[1032] Art. 106(5) of the draft law envisioned that the director of the PDPA would have complete decision-making power over employment and promotion, within the financial resources provided in the budget of North Macedonia, without prior approvals as required by the current MDPL 2020. The PDPA's conditionality in this area poses a challenge to its independence, particularly with regard to its supervisory powers over public institutions, as it is subject to recruitment processes overseen by the very institutions it is supposed to supervise. The PDPA itself also recognised this as a big burden for the authority in its annual reports and proposed the amendments of the MDPL 2020.[1033] Moreover, these challenges were also recognised by the EU Commission in its 2021 Report,[1034] where it was stated that the PDPA overall functioning "depends largely on the Ministry of Finance [...]. This undermines, to a certain extent, the Agency's ability to perform effectively and fully independently." These challenges are also reflected in the number of members of the PDPA. By the end of 2022, the PDPA had a total of only 22 employees, which represents 42 % of filled positions given that the internal

1026 Art. 52(5) GDPR.
1027 Art. 52(6) GDPR.
1028 Art. 58(1) MDPL 2020.
1029 This issue has been also reported by the RCC Report 2020 (n. 18) and by the NGO Civil Rights Defenders' report, p. 31 (n. 925).
1030 Rulebook on internal organizational structure and job systematization states in Art. 16 that the prior approval of the Ministry of Information Society and Administration is needed for the adoption of the rulebook, available in Macedonian at the following link <https://azlp.mk/wp-content/uploads/2022/11/pravilnik_za_vnatreshna_organizacija.pdf> (accessed on 17.04.2023).
1031 Pursuant to Art. 82(2) MDPL 2020, the Ministry of Finance approves the budget of the PDPA.
1032 Initial draft Law for Protection of Personal Data 2018, available in Macedonian at the following link <https://ener.gov.mk/Default.aspx?item=pub_regulation&subitem=view_reg_detail&itemid=49944> (accessed on 31.03.2021).
1033 Also explained in Chapter 4, E.II.1. Annual Reports available in Macedonian at the following link <https://azlp.mk/azlp/propisi-i-dokumenti/годишни-извештаи/> (accessed on 18.04.2023).
1034 EU Commission Report for North Macedonia 2021, SWD(2021) 294 final (19.10.2021) p. 28.

systematisation foresees 46 positions with a total of 50 employees.[1035] The PDPA thus had a significant lack of human resources.

Moreover, political influence seems to also have an impact on the PDPA independence. According to Bertelsmann Stiftung's Transformation Index, the PDPA has been staffed by party members who remain loyal to their political parties.[1036] Further, while the MDPL 2020 defines that all PDPA members are obliged to pay attention to possible conflict of interests and must not be guided by personal, family, religious, political and ethnic interests, nor from pressures and promises from a superior or other person, there is no provision stating that one of the requirements for employees is non-membership in a political party.[1037] Art. 62 MDPL 2020 states that only the office of director and/or deputy director shall be incompatible with other public functions as well as with the exercise of function in a political party or workplace.

5 Conclusion to III

The MDPL 2020 has given the PDPA a number of new roles and responsibilities, such as advising the parliament in the legislative process, managing a new register of high-risk processing by data controllers, providing training, monitoring and approving codes of conduct and certification, managing data breach notifications, enforcing higher penalties, etc. The PDPA, thus, has the same powers and responsibilities as the independent data protection authorities in the EU. This is a positive point compared to the MDPL 2005. However, it is questionable whether the PDPA will be able to carry out such new tasks due to the lack of sufficient human and other resources. It may not receive the same financial support in carrying out its new tasks, nor the same support in the form of guidelines and opinions (such as EDPB's guidelines and opinions), compared to the EU data protection authorities. In the course of the EU Twinning project,[1038] it was recognised that the inability of the PDPA to fully exercise its competences under the new law could jeopardise the whole national data protection system. Therefore, this seems to be of great importance for compliance with the EU acquis and could be one of the main obstacles to an adequacy decision.

1035 PDPA's Annual Report for 2022, p. 8, available in Macedonian at the following link <https://azlp.mk/годишен-извештај-за-работата-на-азлп-за/> (accessed on 20.04.2023).

1036 Bertelsmann Stiftung's Transformation Index (BTI) Report for North Macedonia from 2020, p. 14 <https://bti-project.org/fileadmin/api/content/en/downloads/reports/country_report_2020_MKD.pdf> (accessed on 21.04.2023).

1037 Art. 58(3) MDPL 2020.

1038 Twinning project "Support to the Implementation of the Modernised Data Protection Legal Framework in North Macedonia" (n. 853).

IV Case Law and Enforcement

In order for an adequacy decision to be issued, it is not sufficient that the third country has equivalent data protection principles and standards as those provided for by the GDPR, but the whole "data protection system must ensure a good level of compliance".[1039] Art. 45(2)(a) GDPR explicitly refers to the EU Commission, taking into account in particular "respect for human rights and fundamental freedoms" and "case-law as well as effective and enforceable data subject rights".

There is a substantial amount of case law in North Macedonia, not solely stemming from data subjects' exertion of their rights but also from data controllers and processors' insufficient accountability, particularly in the public sector. In its annual reports the PDPA also confirmed that the controllers from public sector do not comply with the obligations deriving from the PDPA's decisions or recommendations.[1040] This Section will provide an overview of the PDPA's activities in enforcing the MDPL 2020. Additionally, it delves into significant data breaches that have captured public attention and offers a short overview of pertinent cases adjudicated by national courts.

1 Activities of the Supervisory Authority

According to Art. 66(1) MDPL 2020 the PDPA has investigative powers similar to Art. 58(1) GDPR. Yet, as discussed in the preceding Section, a significant concern in the operations of the PDPA pertains to the issue of insufficient autonomy within the scope of its employment. There has been a notable trend of PDPA's employees leaving their posts to pursue more favourable employment opportunities in the private sector.[1041] In its annual report for 2022, the PDPA reported the departure of two supervisors that year and projected that only five supervisors would remain in their positions by the end of 2023.[1042] This reduction in personnel capacity compromises the PDPA's ability to effectively carry out supervisory tasks. This trend is also reflected in the declining number of supervisions carried out by the PDPA, as there were only 170 supervisions conducted[1043] in total[1044]compared

---

1039 WP29 Adequacy Referential, p. 7 (n. 155).

1040 PDPA's Annual Report for 2020, p. 25 and Annual Report for 2010, p. 26, available <https://www.dzlp.mk/sites/default/files/292.pdf> (accessed on 16.05.2021).

1041 PDPA's Annual Report for 2022, p. 11 (n. 1035).

1042 *Ibid.*

1043 102 ordinary, 48 extraordinary and 20 control supervisions, PDPA's Annual Report for 2022, p. 13 (n. 1035).

1044 According to Art. 44-b MDPL 2020, regular inspections are carried out on an annual basis program adopted by the director, extraordinary inspections at the initiative of a legal or natural

to the 304 supervisions in 2021.[1045] The PDPA identified staffing shortages as one of the factors contributing to this trend. Another factor was that in 2022 the PDPA focused on the regular inspections of the public institutions authorised to carry out interception of communications, which are inherently complex by their nature.[1046]

The PDPA's inspections revealed that these institutions were not fully compliant with all the obligations arising from the MDPL 2020.[1047] In the private sector, the most common irregularities found by the PDPA were the absence of privacy policies on websites, the lack of consent for cookies in accordance with the Law on Electronic Communications, the absence of TOMs, the processing of personal data in violation of direct marketing rules, and the lack of appointment of a DPO.[1048]

Pursuant to Art. 37 MDPL 2020 the controllers are obliged to notify the PDPA of any data breaches that occur. In the course of 2022, the PDPA received a total of 19 notifications of data breaches, with 14 coming from the private sector and 5 from the public sector.[1049] This represents an increase in the number of data breach notifications compared to 2020, the initial year of implementing the MDPL 2020, wherein only eight notifications were submitted.[1050] In 2021, the number increased slightly to 9 notifications.[1051] The PDPA also noted that, in 2022, the number of data breach notifications from public sector controllers had increased in comparison to previous years of the MDPL 2020's implementation (with only one notification received in 2021).[1052] Additionally, four of the private sector controllers who submitted a notification were foreign legal entities based in the United States.[1053]

Acting on the cases the PDPA discovered that controllers have not established a complete system for documenting and reporting on data breaches.[1054] Beside lacking of a fully established documentation system for reporting personal data

---

person or state authority, and the control inspections after the expiration of the deadline for removing the deficiencies determined by the decision.

1045 180 ordinary, 88 extraordinary and 30 control supervisions, PDPA's Annual Report for 2021, pp. 11–22, available at the following link <https://azlp.mk/biblioteka/> (accessed on 16.05.2023).

1046 PDPA's Annual Report for 2022, p. 12 (n. 1035).

1047 See for more PDPA's Annual Report for 2022, pp. 36–37 (n. 1035).

1048 *Ibid*, pp. 12–13 and PDPA's Annual Report for 2021 pp. 12–15 (n. 1045).

1049 PDPA's Annual Report for 2020, p. 14 (n. 1040).

1050 PDPA's Annual Report for 2020 p. 15 (n. 1040).

1051 PDPA's Annual Report for 2021, pp. 15–16 (n. 1045).

1052 PDPA's Annual Report for 2022, p. 14 (n. 1035).

1053 *Ibid.*

1054 *Ibid.*

security breaches, the PDPA noted that controllers do not distinguish between an incident and a disturbance, or between probable risk to the controller and probable risk to the rights and freedoms of the subject of personal data.[1055] Furthermore, they may also hesitate to notify the PDPA of personal data security violations, even though they are legally obligated to do so.[1056]

2 Data Subjects' Complaints Before the PDPA

According to Art. 97 MDPL 2020, data subjects are entitled to submit requests to the PDPA. Following the implementation of the MDPL 2020, there has been a modest increase in the number of requests received by the PDPA. Specifically, in 2020, the PDPA received 418 requests, while in 2021, the number rose to 506.[1057] However, in 2022, the total number of requests decreased to 300.[1058] The major number of the requests is related to abuses of social networks.[1059] Other reasons include complaints related to direct marketing, inability to withdraw consent, failure to facilitate the exercise of data subjects' rights, particularly the right of access, correction, or deletion of personal data, processing of personal data through video surveillance systems, and failure to provide prior information to data subjects regarding the collection, processing, and storage of personal data.[1060]

3 Data Breach 'Scandals'

Several major data breaches occurred in North Macedonia both before and after the adoption of the MDPL 2020. These incidents underscored the necessity of strengthening the enforcement capacities of the PDPA and improving public awareness of data protection regulations. This part will highlight three notable cases of data leaks that occurred in the last years.

1055 *Ibid.*

1056 *Ibid.*

1057 Information from PDPA's Annual Report for 2020 (n. 1040) and Annual Report for 2021 (n. 1045). In comparison in 2019 there were 356 requests (PDPA's Annual Report for 2019, p. 13) and in 2018 there were 396 requests (PDPA's Annual Report for 2018, p. 13), both available in Macedonian at the following link <https://azlp.mk/biblioteka/> (accessed on 21.05.2023).

1058 PDPA's Annual Report for 2022, p. 17 (n. 1035).

1059 According to PDPA's Annual Reports in 2022: 77% of requests related to abuse of data subjects' rights on social media (n. 1035); in 2021: 45% (n. 1045); and in 2020: 65% (n. 1040).

1060 *Ibid.*

a) Wiretapping

In North Macedonia, similarly as in Albania, political scandals have been associated with violations of privacy and data protection. In 2015, the opposition party (Social Democratic Union of Macedonia, SDSM) disclosed a series of wiretapped conversations involving mass surveillance of thousands of Macedonian citizens, including government officials, journalists, and even foreign individuals.[1061] This incident highlighted the issue of personal communication privacy in North Macedonia. In response to the massive surveillance, the EU Commission commissioned a group of independent senior rule of law experts to conduct a rapid analysis of the situation, known as the "Priebe Report."[1062] The group concluded that the laws regulating interception for security purposes did not ensure complete protection and were not in line with EU standards.[1063] The group also found that the data protection authority at that time, operated generally well and with a high degree of professionalism.[1064] However, the group expressed concern that the director of the supervisory authority was not sufficiently engaged in investigating the apparent lack of data protection, the potential improper and uncontrolled registration of telephone numbers, and the invasion of privacy resulting from unauthorised surveillance.[1065] Notably, this case occurred before North Macedonia reformed the Agency for National Security's work, as explained further in Chapter 5.

b) State Election Commission

One of the recent cases which shocked the public in the country was the breach of the safety of personal data processed by the State Election Commission (hereinafter: "SEC"), following an incident on the SEC website on the election day (15

1061 United States Department of State, Bureau of Democracy, "Human Rights and Labor: 2016 Country Report on Human Rights Practices Macedonia", p. 1, available at the following link <https://www.state.gov/wp-content/uploads/2019/01/Macedonia-1.pdf> (accessed on 20.05.2023).

1062 The EU gathered a group of independent experts, led by a retired European Commission director Reinhard Priebe and tasked to identify systemic Rule of Law issues in the country. This endeavour resulted in the so called Priebe Report.

1063 The Recommendations of the Senior Experts' Group on systemic Rule of Law issues relating to the communications interception revealed in spring 2015 (June 2015), available at the following link <https://ec.europa.eu/neighbourhoodenlargement/sites/near/files/news_corner/news/newsfiles/20150619_recommendations_of_the_senior_experts_group.pdf> (accessed on 12.02.2023).

1064 *Ibid.*

1065 *Ibid.*

July 2020).[1066] The SEC, by virtue of its mandate, processes a voluminous amount of personal data pertaining to various categories in connection with the electoral process, some of which are available in electronic format. The PDPA identified numerous violations, including a lack of appropriate TOMs regarding the protection of websites and information infrastructure to ensure a level of security appropriate to the risk of failure to assess commissioned data processors, failure to conduct a DPIA, transferring data to third countries without a legal base, not fulfilling the obligation to report a breach of the security of personal data processing to the PDPA, not appointing a DPO and several other breaches.[1067] The PDPA reacted by only issuing corrective measures and deadlines for elimination of the identified violations.[1068]

c) Stop Corona App

Another issue related to personal data protection was the introduction of the 'StopKorona!' mobile app, introduced by the Macedonian government to track COVID-19 infections, exchanges data via Bluetooth and follows user location. While the government guaranteed data safety, opposition members and IT experts raised concerns.[1069] Following scrutiny of PDPA, the Ministry of Health was obliged to take several measures, which were missing, such as to set deadlines for storage of personal data, to perform encrypted measures, to determine the authorised persons who should have access to the 'StopKorona!' application, to conclude contracts with the processors and to perform a DPIA.[1070]

4 Court Cases

Data subjects in North Macedonia have a right to an effective judicial remedy against a controller or processor who violates their rights without prejudice to any available administrative or non-judicial remedy.[1071] Besides that, decisions

1066 Bojan Stojkovski, "North Macedonia Probes Election Day Cyber Attacks", BIRN, (17.07.2020), available at the following link <https://balkaninsight.com/2020/07/17/north-macedonia-probes-election-day-cyber-attacks/> (accessed on 14.05.2021).

1067 Findings from the supervision of the SEC are available at PDPA's website, in Macedonian at the following link <https://azlp.mk/mk/content/> (accessed on 14.05.2021).

1068 *Ibid.*

1069 Bojan Stojkovski, "North Macedonia Leads Region in COVID-19 Tracing App", BIRN, (16.04.2020), available at the following link <https://balkaninsight.com/2020/04/16/north-macedonia-leads-region-in-covid-19-tracing-app/> (accessed on 15.06.2021).

1070 Annual Report 2020, pp. 31–32, available at the following link <https://azlp.mk/wp-content/uploads/2022/12/pdf-azlp-godisen_izvestaj_za_2020_mk-1.pdf> (accessed on 1 9.04.203).

1071 Art. 99 MDPL 2020.

of the PDPA may be challenged by lodging an administrative dispute with the administrative court within 30 days of receiving the decision.[1072]

The case law of the Macedonian courts shows an extensive body of precedent vis-à-vis other WB6 jurisdictions, with a pronounced focus on violations concerning the processing of personal data in employment, video surveillance, processing of personal identification numbers and media contexts.[1073] Within this legal landscape, certain judicial decisions evince a proclivity for overturning determinations rendered by the PDPA that establish instances of personal data violation. An illustrative case exemplifying this trend involves a dispute brought before the Administrative court where the Administrative court found no violation of personal data published by Macedonian newspapers without the consent of the data subject.[1074] The newspapers had published the personal data of a data subject who sued the newspaper for copyright infringement.[1075] The newspapers later published an article claiming the lawsuit was fraudulent and disclosed a photo of the lawsuit with full personal data.[1076] The court ruled that the published personal data did not meet the legal definition of personal data as it lacked unique identifiers or characteristics specific to the data subject's identity, thereby not violating their right to personal data protection, despite the decision of the PDPA[1077] that the newspapers could have achieved the same purpose without processing the personal data of the data subject, by for example anonymising data.[1078] In another case[1079], a complaint filed by the PDPA was deemed unfounded. The PDPA alleged a violation of personal data protection rights of an individual (M.G.) by a financial association that disclosed incomplete, inaccurate, and outdated personal data to third parties, contrary to Art. 14 MDPL 2005.[1080] The court ruled that the personal data had been lawfully processed by the financial association, as the transfer of data to third

---

1072 Art. 98 MDPL 2020.

1073 E. g., Supreme Administrative Court case no. UŽ-1–500/20 (violation of personal data protection rights by disclosing the personal data of employees to third parties without a legal basis), Administrative Court Case No. U-6.бр. 900/2020 (violation of personal data protection rights by publishing on a notice board, visible to anyone entering the employer's premises, the decision to terminate the employment contract of an employee, including the employee's name, surname, personal identification number).

1074 Administrative Court of North Macedonia no. UŽ-z. 1452/2019 (09.06.2020).

1075 *Ibid.*

1076 *Ibid.*

1077 At that time the MDPL 2005 was in force the PDPA had a different name – the Directorate for Data Protection.

1078 Administrative Court of North Macedonia no. UŽ-z 1452/2019 (09.06.2020).

1079 Supreme Administrative Court of North Macedonia no. UŽ-3–1389/19 (06.11.2020).

1080 *Ibid.*

party was in line with the legal obligation of the financial association as a financial entity, without requiring specific consent from the data subject.[1081] The court also found that the personal data provided by the data subject were incomplete and were therefore transferred to the third party as such.[1082] Similarly, in another case, the administrative court found that the PDPA had applied data protection rules too broadly when it required a transport company that had collected personal data from audio recordings without obtaining consent to remedy the breaches found.[1083]

5 Conclusion to IV

The case law in North Macedonia indicates that there is still a significant lack of awareness among public authorities and companies regarding their duties and responsibilities under the data protection laws. This has been evidenced by several high-profile data protection violations, which have mainly been committed by political parties or government authorities. Such breaches not only jeopardize the fundamental right to personal data protection but also undermine the public's trust in the ability of these entities to safeguard personal data.

In contrast, the increasing number of court cases and requests made to the PDPA demonstrates that data subjects do have a certain degree of familiarity with their legal rights and remedies and are willing to utilise them. A matter of concern is the trend of employees leaving the PDPA, which may have a significant impact on the PDPA's competence to conduct investigations and respond to data subject requests. The PDPA plays a critical role in ensuring that data protection laws are effectively enforced, and that data subjects' rights are protected. Therefore, steps must be taken to ensure that the PDPA is adequately staffed with knowledgeable and experienced personnel who can competently fulfil their duties and obligations under the data protection laws.

V Conclusion to E

North Macedonia enacted a GDPR-like law in 2020, the MDPL 2020, which came into force at the end of 2021. The MDPL 2020 incorporates all the principles and concepts established by the GDPR, with the exception of the GDPR's Recitals, and also elaborates on certain provisions copied from the GDPR. In particular,

1081 *Ibid.*
1082 *Ibid.*
1083 Administrative Court of North Macedonia no. U-5. 1249/2020.

the MDPL 2020 contains stricter criteria than the GDPR for data transfers, special categories of personal data and specific obligations for data controllers to obtain authorisations for the processing of personal data.

The supervisory authority's powers have also been extended, including the imposition of significant fines compared to the previous legislation. However, the supervisory authority faces a challenge of limited independence in recruiting new staff, as it requires prior approval from the Ministry of Finance and the Ministry of Information Society and Administration.

Despite these challenges, the supervisory authority has demonstrated reasonable activity in conducting investigations into MDPL 2020 compliance. However, corrective measures appear to be more frequently imposed than high fines. Notwithstanding, proposed amendments to the MDPL 2020 seek to enhance the supervisory authority's employment competence, which is crucial since the EU Commission regards the independence of supervisory authorities as a critical criterion in deciding on granting an adequacy decision.

F Serbia

Serbia was designated as a potential candidate for EU membership already in 2003.[1084] In March 2012, Serbia was granted EU candidate status[1085] and in 2013, a SAA between the EU and Serbia entered into force.[1086] Presently, 22 out of the 35 chapters outlined in the SAA have been opened for negotiations, with two chapters provisionally concluded.[1087] The two most important chapters 23 – Judiciary and Fundamental Rights and 24 – Justice, Freedom and Security were opened in 2016, but remain pending closure.[1088] Art. 81 SAA sets forth provisions on protec-

1084 Information from the EU Commission's website: European Neighbourhood Policy and Enlargement Negotiations, Serbia, available at the following link <https://neighbourhood-enlargement.ec.europa.eu/enlargement-policy/serbia_en> (accessed on 24.01.2022).

1085 European Council, 9 December 2011, Conclusions, EUCO 139/1/11, REV 1, Brussels, (25.01.2012), available at the following link <https://data.consilium.europa.eu/doc/document/ST-139-2011-REV-1/en/pdf> (accessed on 24.01.2023).

1086 Stabilisation and Association Agreement between the EU and Serbia, Official Journal of the European Union, L 278, Entry into force (01.09.2013).

1087 The status of all chapters is available on the website of the EU Delegation to the Republic of Serbia at this link <https://europa.rs/chapters-opened-and-closed/?lang=en> (accessed on 24.01.2023).

1088 Council of the EU Press release 18 July 2016, Third meeting of the Accession Conference with Serbia at Ministerial level, available at the following link <https://www.consilium.europa.eu/en/press/press-releases/2016/07/18/fac-serbia-accession-conference/> (accessed on 24.01.2023).

tion of personal data and commits Serbia to harmonise its legislation with EU and international data protection legislation and to establish independent supervisory authorities with sufficient financial and human resources to effectively monitor and ensure the enforcement of national legislation on the protection of personal data.

I Constitutional Parameters and International Commitments

Chapter 2 of the Serbian Constitution deals extensively with human and minority rights and freedoms and contains a total of 63 articles.[1089] Art. 42 of the Constitution guarantees the protection of personal data and defines it in detail, inter alia, by stating that the collection, storage, processing and use of personal data must be regulated by law, and that the use of personal data outside the purpose for which it was collected is prohibited (except for the purpose of conducting criminal proceedings or protecting the security of Serbia).[1090] In addition, according to Art. 42(4) everyone has the right to be informed about the collection of their personal data, in accordance with the law, and everyone has the right to judicial protection in case of their misuse.

Moreover, Art. 18 of the Constitution establishes the direct applicability of human and minority rights enshrined in universally recognised principles of international law and affirmed by international treaties. Serbia is also a signatory to the ECHR and to Convention 108+.[1091] However, the question of the hierarchy of international law and treaties remains inconsistent.[1092] On the one hand, the constitution states that generally recognised rules of international law and international treaties ratified by Serbia are part of the legal order.[1093] On the other hand Art. 16(1) stipulates that ratified international treaties are subject to constitutional review.[1094] Nevertheless, the Constitution provides that the judicial sys-

1089 Artt. 18–81 Serbian Constitution.

1090 Art. 42(3) Serbian Constitution.

1091 The supervisory authority's announcement "Protocol CETS No.223 was ratified in 2020", (29.05.2020), available in Serbian at the following link <https://www.poverenik.rs/sr-yu/saopstenja/3352-србија-ратификовала-протокол-којим-се-мења-конвенција-о-заштити-лица-у-односу-на-аутоматску-обраду-личних-података.html> (accessed on 15.05.2023).

1092 Prof. Dr. Marijana Pajvančić, "Commentary on the Constitution of the Republic of Serbia", Konrad Adenauer Stiftung, (2009), pp. 27–28.

1093 Art. 16(1) Serbian Constitution.

1094 *Ibid.*

tem should rule on the basis of the constitution, laws, generally recognised rules of international law and confirmed international agreements.[1095]

The Constitutional Court also affirmed that a constitutional appeal safeguards all human and minority rights and freedoms guaranteed by the Constitution, regardless of their systematic placement or explicit incorporation within the Constitution or their implementation through ratified international treaties.[1096] In their decision-making process, the courts in Serbia have already interpreted and applied international treaties.[1097]

1 Conclusion to I

Data protection and the right to judicial protection in the event of data protection violations are guaranteed on the constitutional level in Serbia. Moreover, Serbia is signatory to significant international conventions on human rights, including the ECHR and Convention 108+. The constitution recognises the direct applicability of human and minority rights based on universally recognised principles of international law and international conventions. Although the hierarchy of international law and treaties remains inconsistent, judiciary in Serbia has interpreted and applied international treaties in their decision-making processes.

II Data Protection Legislation

The first law in Serbia, the Law on Personal Data Protection, was adopted in 2008 and subsequently underwent multiple amendments, with the last amendment in 2012[1098] (hereinafter: "SDPL 2008"). This law replaced the FRY DPL.[1099] It also established an independent supervisory authority, the Data Protection and Information Commissioner (hereinafter: "DPC"), as a central state body responsible for

1095 Art. 142(2) Serbian Constitution.

1096 See the position of the Constitutional Court, which was adopted at the sessions of October 30, 2008 and April 2, 2009, available in Serbian at the following link <http://www.ustavni.sud.rs/page/view/163-100890/stavovi-suda> (accessed on 10.05.2023).

1097 E. g., the first decision in which the Constitutional Court mentioned the ECHR was Decision of the Constitutional Court no. Už-306/2008 (25.95.2008); See also Nataša Plavšić, "Primena prakse Evropskog suda za ljudska prava od strane Ustavnog suda u postupcima po ustavnim žalbama" (Eng. The Jurisdiction of the European Court of Human Rights in the Constitutional Complaint Proceedings before the Constitutional Court), Fondacija Centar za javno pravo, (2019).

1098 Law on Personal Data Protection (Official Gazette of RS, No. 97/2008, 104/2009 – other law, 68/2012 – decision of CC and 107/2012).

1099 FRY DPL (n. 70).

overseeing the implementation of the SDPL 2008. When it was enacted, the SDPL 2008 mirrored the provisions of the DPD, which was then the prevailing data protection law in the EU. However, the SDPL 2008 faced criticism shortly after its adoption. One of the main points of criticism was its inherently abstract nature.[1100] This, combined with a lack of knowledge and a lack of defined democratic standards in practice, led to problems in understanding and accepting the legal norms and their underlying standards.[1101] Consequently, the need for new legislation arose not only due to the implementation of the GDPR in the EU but also to address the shortcomings of the existing legislation. The SDPL 2008 remained in effect until August 2019 when a new law similar to the GDPR was introduced.

This part will provide an overview of the current data protection legislation framework and the process of harmonising it with the GDPR. The harmonisation process led to the adoption of a GDPR-like law in 2018, which subsequently came into effect in 2019.

1 Status Quo of GDPR Alignment

Since 2014, there have been several efforts at adopting new data protection legislation, aimed at addressing growing technological capabilities and improving current data protection standards. At that time, the Serbian government formed an inter-ministerial working group to prepare a new data protection law. However, the work of this working group did not produce any results. In an attempt to help, the DPC prepared a complete model of the new law (hereinafter: "First DPC Draft") and submitted it to the government.[1102] In the Action Plan for Chapter 23 of the EU accession process, the government announced that the new law would be adopted by the end of 2015,[1103] but this never happened. A few years later, after the adoption of the GDPR, the DPC prepared a second model of the new law (hereinafter: "Second DPC draft") in 2017, as the First DPC Draft did not comply with the current EU acquis standards anymore.[1104] However, this draft was never considered as a foundation for the drafting of a new law. In a letter to the Serbian Prime Minister, the former head of the DPC therefore expressed

1100 Nataša Pirc Musar, Guide to the Law on Personal Data Protection (n. 73).
1101 *Ibid.*
1102 Press release of the DPC, available at the following link <https://www.poverenik.rs/sr-yu/%D0%B0rhiva/model-zakona-arhiva.html> (accessed on 16.03.2022).
1103 Republic of Serbia, Negotiation group for chapter 23, Action plan for chapter 23, August 2014, available at the following link <https://eupregovori.bos.rs/progovori-opregovorima/uploaded/Action%20Plan%20AP23eng.1.9..pdf> p. 213 (accessed on 16.03.2023).
1104 Press release of the DPC (2017), (in Serbian) <https://www.poverenik.rs/sr-yu/%D0%B0rhiva/model-zakona-arhiva.html> (accessed on 16.03.2021).

his disappointment and fear that the preparation of the new draft law would not be successful without the involvement of the DPC.[1105]

In November 2017, the Ministry of Justice (hereinafter: "MOJ") again published a new draft (hereinafter: "Third Draft"), which had been prepared without the assistance of the DPC. The public debate on the Third Draft was relatively short, from 1 December 2017 to 15 January 2018.[1106] After the public debate, the text of the law ("Final Draft") was finalised after incorporating only a few proposals and comments from the DPC, NGOs, lawyers and businesses.[1107] However, the Final Draft received a lot of criticism as many proposals and comments were not accepted. The DPC[1108] and some NGOs[1109] assessed the Final Draft as a non-functional document that did not take into account the specificities of the Serbian legal system. Another point of criticism was that the LED was incorporated together with the provisions which relate to the GDPR, whereas the LED by its very nature is not a directly applicable legal instrument.[1110] In this respect, the critics stated

---

1105 Letter from the DPC, No: 073 – 14 – 1289/2017– 01, (28.08.2017), available at the following link <https://www.poverenik.rs/images/stories/dokumentacija-nova/pismaorganima/2017/vlada28.8.2017.pdf> (accessed on 16.03.2023).

1106 The Article "Mišljenje EK o Nacrtu zakona o zaštiti podataka o ličnosti – dokument za koji je Ministarstvo mesecima tvrdilo da ne postoji" (Eng. The opinion of the EU Commission on the Draft Law on the Protection of Personal Data – a document that the Ministry claimed for months did not exist), Insajder, (15.08.2018), available at the following link <https://insajder.net/arhiva/vesti/misljenje-ek-o-nacrtu-zakona-o-zastiti-podataka-o-licnosti-dokument-za-koji-je-ministarstvo-mesecima-tvrdilo-da-ne-postoji> (accessed on 17.01.2021).

1107 Report on the public debate on the text of the Draft Law on Personal Data Protection (02.03.2018), available at the following link <https://www.mpravde.gov.rs/sekcija/53/radne-verzije-propisa.php> (accessed on 13.03.2023).

1108 The Article "Nacrt Zakona o zaštiti podataka o ličnosti: Poverenik navodi da je Nacrt zakona koncepcijski i sadržinski znatno ispod nužnog nivoa" (Eng. Draft Law on the Protection of Personal Data: The Commissioner states that the Draft Law is far below the necessary level in terms of concept and content), Paragraf Lex *d.o.o.*, (26.01.2018), available at the following link <https://paragraflex.rs/dnevne-vesti/290118/290118-vest11.html> (accessed on 17.03.2021).

1109 Commentary on the draft law on personal data protection, SHARE, (January 2018), available at the following link <https://resursi.sharefoundation.info/wp-content/uploads/2018/01/Komentari-na-Nacrt-ZZPL-SHARE-Fondacija.pdf> (accessed on 17.03.2023); The Article "Nacrtom zakona o zaštiti podataka o ličnosti Srbija samo formalno ispunjava evropski standard, upitna njegova primena" (Eng. Serbia's draft law on personal data protection only formally meets European standards; its implementation is questionable), Insajder, (02.03.2018), <https://insajder.net/arhiva/tema/nacrtom-zakona-o-zastiti-podataka-o-licnosti-srbija-samo-formalno-ispunjava-evropski-standard-upitna-njegova-primena> (accessed on 17.03.2021).

1110 Article "Zabrinjavajuće stanje i loš nacrt zakona o zaštiti ličnih podataka" (Eng. Worrying situation and bad draft law on personal data protection), Glas Amerike, (27.01.2018), available at

that it does not present a concise text with a clear structure, but is full of references and unclear norms.[1111] Further, the head of the DPC also expressed his concern that many parts regulating the processing of personal data under the LED are excluded from the general protection regime.[1112]

In November 2018, the Parliament adopted the Final Draft enacting the Data Protection Law which provided for a nine-month grace period for companies to prepare for the new changes and became applicable in August 2019 (hereinafter: "SDPL 2019"). Due to the relatively short grace period, the DPC sent an official letter to the president of the parliament, in August 2019, requesting that the entry into force be postponed for another year, until 1 September 2020.[1113] The DPC explained that the public institutions, controllers and processors were 'not ready' for the SDPL 2019 and that the DPC was understaffed which could affect the training of all entities that would have to comply with the new legislation. Yet, parliament did not accept these arguments and the SDPL 2019 became applicable in August 2019.

The SDPL 2019 is an 'umbrella regulation' in the field of protection of personal data. Therefore, the general principles set out apply to all forms of personal data processing, including interception of communications and electronic marketing. While the SDPL 2019 largely mirrors the provisions of the GDPR, certain distinctions do exist. Firstly, it does not incorporate the explanatory Recitals of the GDPR, as previously mentioned. Secondly, the SDPL 2019 includes provisions from the LED in addition to the articles adapted from the GDPR. These LED and GDPR provisions are interconnected, necessitating the reader to differentiate between those relating to the general data protection provisions under the GDPR and those relating to the LED. This poses a particular challenge as the SDPL 2019 is the primary legislation governing data protection as a fundamental human right and therefore should be understandable to the general public. Recognising the need to address these shortcomings, amendments to the SDPL 2019 have been announced in the Data Protection Strategy Proposal for 2023–2030 (hereinafter: "Strategy Proposal").[1114] These amendments shall address existing defi-

---

the following link <https://www.glasamerike.net/a/zabrinajvajuce-stanje-i-los-nacrt-zakona-o-zasti ti-licnih-podataka/4228354.html> (accessed on 17.03.2021).

1111 *Ibid.*

1112 *Ibid.*

1113 Press release by the DPC (02.08.2019), available in Serbian at the following link <https://www.poverenik.rs/sr-yu/arhiva/saopštenja-arhiva/3147-повереник-затражио-одлагање-примене-новог-закона-о-заштити-података-о-личности.html> (accessed on 18.03.2021).

1114 See Data Protection Strategy Proposal for 2023–2030, available in Serbian at the website of MoJ at the following link <https://www.mpravde.gov.rs/sekcija/53/radne-verzije-propisa.php> (ac-

ciencies and improve the effectiveness and clarity of the data protection framework in Serbia.[1115]

This Section will only examine the articles in the SDPL 2019 that relate to the GDPR, excluding provisions related to the LED. Given that a significant number of articles in the SDPL 2019 are taken directly from the GDPR, the analysis will primarily focus on identifying any missing or different provisions compared to the GDPR. In addition, a comparison will be made with the old legislation in order to have a better understanding of the GDPR's impact.

a) The EU Commission Assessment

The EU Commission assessed both the Third Draft and the SDPL 2019. The EU Commission's first assessment took place in 2018.[1116] The EU Commission, inter alia, criticised the structure of the Third Draft as difficult to read,[1117] which was also criticised by the DPC. The EU Commission pointed out some of the important missing parts, such as explanations of the institutes which are contained in the Recitals of the GDPR. The Serbian legislator adopted many of the EU Commission proposals, but not all of them, as explained later.

The second time, the EU Commission provided an assessment study of the SDPL 2019, with the aim to assess its alignment with the EU acquis.[1118] The EU Commission found that the vast majority of the provisions are in line with the provisions of the GDPR. Nevertheless, several key criticisms were identified, including a lack of additional explanations, particularly concerning the principles,

---

cessed on 15.05.2023). See also the summary of Data Protection Strategy Proposal for 2023–2030, Ivan Milošević, Partner, JPM, "Data Protection Strategy Proposal for 2023–2030", available at the following link <https://www.jpm.law/wp-content/uploads/2023/03/Serbia-%E2%80%93-Data-Protection-Strategy-Proposal-for-2023-2030.pdf> (accessed on 30.03.2023).

1115 Data Protection Strategy Proposal for 2023–2030, pp. 31–32 (n. 1114).

1116 Partners for Democratic Change received the European Commission's comments on the Third Draft on the protection of personal data in August 2018 from the Ministry for EU Integration after the Ministry of Justice had claimed in June 2018 that no such document existed. See the statement of Partners for Democratic Change at the following link <https://www.partners-serbia.org/post?id=43> (accessed on 13.03.2023).

1117 The EU Commission General Assessment from 2018, available at the following link <https://insajder.net/attachment/201/20180423-DP-law-Serbia-General-EC-JUST-comments.pdf?g_download=1> and the EU Commission Detailed Assessment from 2018 <https://insajder.net/attachment/202/LAW-PDP-FINAL-20_02-FOR-EC-edited-JUST-comments.pdf?g_download=1> (both accessed on 13.03.2023).

1118 EU Commission, Assessment of the Draft Law on Personal Data Protection of Serbia, TAIEX mission 30066, (May 2019), available the following link <https://www.poverenik.rs/images/stories/dokumentacija-nova/Publikacije/engEKStudija.pdf> (accessed on 12.02.2023).

institutions, and solutions expounded in the preamble of the GDPR, which contributes to difficulties in understanding of the SDPL 2019, as well as the limitations of the data subject's rights and the provisions on data transfers. The EU Commission's detailed assessment and its proposed amendments will be thoroughly examined in the respective sections analysing the data protection concepts within the SDPL 2019 individually.

2 Overview of the SDPL 2019

The SDPL 2019 consists of ten chapters. Chapter 1 defines the general provisions, including the scope of the law and definitions. Chapter 2 outlines the principles of data processing and provides a definition of special categories of personal data. Chapter 3 envisages the rights of data subject. Chapter 4 governs data controllers and processors, including their obligations related to security of data processing. Chapter 5 sets out the rules on international data transfers. Chapter 6 clarifies the role of the supervisory authority and its functions and powers. In chapter 7 redress rights are defined. Chapter 8 stipulates the provisions relating to specific processing situations. Chapter 9 imposes misdemeanour provisions. Finally, Chapter 10 contains transitional and final provisions.

3 Scope of the SDPL 2019

The SDPL 2019 aligns its material and territorial scope with that of the GDPR. However, there are some differences in regulation of exterritorial scope. Specifically, Art. 3 SDPL 2019 does not use the term 'establishment' from the analogous provision in Art. 3(1) GDPR.[1119] Instead, it employs the concepts of 'business seat' (for legal entities) and 'residence' (for natural persons).[1120] The difference in the wording appears to be due to the lack of a suitable translation for 'establishment' in the Serbian language, rather than to any intention on the part of the legislature to regulate the question of jurisdiction differently from the GDPR.[1121]

Consequently, the DPC recognised the necessity to interpret the notion of 'business seat' or 'residence' as corresponding to the concept of establishment in the GDPR, given that the provisions of the SDPL 2019 alone lack the necessary precision for practical application of Art. 3 SDPL 2019. The DPC expressed its opinion that, in order to ensure the effective protection of personal data, the term

---

1119 The term 'establishment' under Art. 3(1) GDPR has been already discussed in Chapter 3, A.I.
1120 BDK Advokati, "Q&A: the data protection legal framework in Serbia", Lexology, (August, 2018), available at the following link <https://www.lexology.com/library/detail.aspx?g=fcad4a22-1dca-4c3a-8390-11f315d9933d> (accessed on 04.04.2021).
1121 *Ibid.*

'business seat', as employed in the SDPL 2019, should be interpreted in accordance with the provisions of the GDPR.[1122] To support its interpretation, the DPC referred to Recital 22 GDPR and the EDPB guidelines.[1123] This means that the DPC applies the provisions of the GDPR when interpreting the SDPL 2019, even though the GDPR is not directly applicable in Serbia as a non-EU country.

4 Data Protection Principles

The SDPL 2019 defines the same data processing principles as the GDPR. The previous SDPL 2008 already recognised some of the data protection principles, as lawfulness, purpose limitation, accuracy and data minimisation.[1124] The SDPL 2019 introduced, for the first time in Serbian legislation, the principles of fairness and transparency, storage limitation, accountability, integrity, and confidentiality.[1125] A significant issue in the SDPL 2008 was the absence of provisions regarding storage limitation. The determination of retention periods was entirely entrusted to sectoral laws or bylaws, resulting in numerous inconsistencies. For instance, the Law on Records in the Field of Labour, enacted during the validity of the SDPL 2008, allows for the indefinite retention of certain personal data pertaining to employees.[1126] Consequently, there was a pressing need to introduce and strengthen data protection principles.

5 Lawfulness of Processing

The legal grounds provided by the SDPL 2019 are similar with the legal grounds of the GDPR.[1127] Nevertheless, while the SDPL 2019 introduced legal grounds that are generally comparable with the GDPR, there are concerns that the conditions for lawful data processing may not be met in practice. In particular, the SDPL 2019 requires that processing for the purpose of performing tasks in the public interest or exercising the legally prescribed powers of controllers must be established by law.[1128] It also prescribes additional conditions and safeguards to be included in

---

1122 DPC, Publication no. 6 – Data protection "Publikacija br. 6 – Zaštita podataka – Stavovi i mišljenja Poverenika", (Eng. Positions and opinions of the Commissioner), pp. 15–16.

1123 EDPB, Guidelines 3/2018 (Article 3) (n. 119).

1124 Art. 8 SDPL 2008.

1125 Art. 5 SDPL 2019.

1126 E.g., Artt. 25(3), 43(2) Law on Records in the Field of Labour (Serb. Zakon o Evidencijama u Oblasti Rada (Sl. list SRJ, br. 46/96 i Sl. glasnik RS, br. 101/2005 – dr. zakon i 36/2009 – dr. zakon). This law is still in force.

1127 Art. 12 SDPL 2019.

1128 Art. 14 SDPL 2019.

sectoral laws. However, in order for these restrictions to be effectively implemented, sectoral laws that allow data collection in the public interest or for the exercise of legal powers need to be harmonised with the SDPL 2019, which has not yet been achieved.[1129]

Moreover, the SDPL 2019 broadened the legal grounds for processing personal data compared to the previous legislation by introducing the concept of legitimate interest.[1130] Legitimate interest as a legal ground is a completely new concept in Serbian legislation and, as such, may present practical challenges, given that many data controllers might use this legal ground without carrying out the so-called balancing test, which compares on the one hand the legitimate interests of the controller (which must prevail) with the interests and freedoms of the data subject (which must not be prejudiced). Recognising this as a significant challenge, the DPC issued a model framework for assessing legitimate interest. This framework entails a three-step process for evaluating legitimate interest, after which the controller should decide whether or not the specific conditions for the application of legitimate interest are met.[1131] However, the SDPL 2019 and other accompanying bylaws do not provide further guidance or examples regarding the circumstances in which legitimate interest might apply, as outlined in the Recitals of the GDPR.

Therefore, lawyers and NGOs have pro-actively sought to interpret legitimate interest.[1132] For example, an article published in the Serbian Institute of Comparative Law seeks to further explain legitimate interest using examples provided in the preamble of the GDPR.[1133] The author also notes that the legal formulation of legitimate interest in the SDPL 2019 "causes headaches for anyone trying to inter-

1129 Nevertheless, the Data Protection Strategy Proposal for 2023–2030, pp. 32–33 (n. 1114) recognises the failure to harmonise the sector legislation and announces that it must be achieved.

1130 Art. 12(1)(6) SDPL 2019.

1131 The DPC's Guidance on Legitimate Interest, available in Serbian on the following link <https://www.poverenik.rs/sr-yu/zaštita-podataka/легитимни-интерес.htmll>, (accessed on 05.05.2022).

1132 Article "The controller's legitimate interest as a legal basis for personal data processing – can you apply it correctly?", published by the PR legal (15.08.2021), available at the following link <https://www.prlegal.rs/sr/legitimni-interes-rukovaoca-kao-pravni-osnov-obrade-podataka-o-licnosti-da-li-umete-da-ga-pravilno-primenite/> (accessed on 27.01.2022); Dubravka Dolenc, "Legitimni interes kao pravni osnov obrade osobnih podataka (Eng. Legitimate interest as legal basis of processing personal data), Bankarstvo, 2020, vol. 49, br. 3, (26.08.2020); SHARE, "Rečnik pojmova o zaštiti podataka" (Eng. Glossary of Personal Data protection), (2021); Dragan Milić, pp. 50–59 (n. 13).

1133 Dragan Milić, pp. 50–59 (n. 13).

pret and apply it", due to its broadness, lack of definitions, and absence of examples provided in the legislation's preamble.[1134]

While the legal basis in the SDPL 2019 initially appears to be in line with the GDPR there are concerns regarding its interpretation in practice. Relying solely on the text of the SDPL 2019 would not be sufficient and would require reliance on the guidance and practices established by the EU supervisory authorities and EDPB.

6 Special Categories of Personal Data

The definition and further rules on processing of special categories of personal data correspond to the respective GDPR rules.[1135] In comparison to the SDPL 2008 (which recognised 'sensitive data'), biometric and genetic data are completely new types of personal data which are now defined as special categories of persona data.

The SDPL 2008 provided for a number of additional safeguards for the processing of sensitive personal data, which, however, have never been implemented in practice. For example, any processing of sensitive data had to be specifically identified and protected by security measures (in the sense that these measures should be stricter than those applicable to the processing of 'regular' personal data).[1136] It was also stipulated that these measures should be determined by the Serbian government after prior consultation of the DPC.[1137] However, such measures were never established (i. e. the government never issued a regulation/rulebook on the subject), and consequently the relevant legal obligation to apply special security measures when processing sensitive data remained relevant only in theory. Apart from that, the sensitive data could only have been processed if 1) there was specific consent and 2) it was required by law.[1138] Hence, no further derogations existed. Moreover, the specific consent for the processing of sensitive personal data could only be obtained in writing on paper (an online form was not allowed).[1139] The introduction of the SDPL 2019 has therefore had a positive impact by removing such bureaucratic measures that are out of touch with the realities of modern technology and everyday life.

1134 *Ibid.*
1135 Art. 17(1) SDPL 2019.
1136 Art. 16(1) SDPL 2008.
1137 Art. 16(4)(5) SDPL 2008.
1138 Art. 16(1)(2) SDPL 2008.
1139 Art. 17 SDPL 2008.

7 Rights of Data Subject

Most of the data subject's rights were already recognised in the SDPL 2008 (e.g. right of access, right of copy, right of erasure, right of rectification),[1140] but some were only introduced by the SDPL 2019 – the right to data portability[1141] and automated individual decision making, including profiling.[1142] Another innovation is the obligation for the data controller to provide information to the data subject if personal data was not collected from them.[1143]

While the provisions regarding data subjects' rights in the SDPL 2019 are generally consistent with those outlined in the GDPR, certain inconsistencies arise as a consequence of the copy-paste approach used during the drafting process, without including the Recitals of the GDPR.

a) Art. 21 – Transparent Information

The requirements for the exercise of data subjects' rights set out in Art. 12 GDPR are missing in Art. 21 SDPL 2019, in particular the procedural requirements or practice with regard to standardised icons.[1144] This is particularly problematic, as these rules affect the right to informational self-determination which is established in the GDPR and according to which substantive rights of data subject can only serve their purpose when supported by clear information as well as proportionate and effective procedure.[1145] The EU Commission criticised this issue, including the lack of sanctions for breach of Art. 21, which is a more serious breach under the GDPR.[1146]

b) Art. 30 – Right to be Forgotten

Art. 30 SDPL 2019, which regulates the right to be forgotten, contains a paragraph not provided for by Art. 17 GDPR. Art. 30(4) SDPL 2019 limits the data subject's right to request erasure to be addressed solely to controllers without stating that this request might be directed to processors. The EU Commission criticised

1140 Chapter 3 SDPL 2008.
1141 Art. 36 SDPL 2019.
1142 Art. 38 SDPL 2019.
1143 Art. 24 SDPL 2019.
1144 EU Commission's Assessment 2019, p. 8 (n. 1118).
1145 See also Boris P. Paal, in Paal/Pauly, DS-GVO Art. 12 Transparente Information, Kommunikation und Modalitäten für die Ausübung der Rechte der betroffenen Person, DS-GVO BDSG (3rd eds, C.H. Beck 2021); Florent Thouvenin, "Informational Self-Determination: A Convincing Rationale for Data Protection Law?", 12 J. Intell. Prop. Info. Tech. & Elec. Com. L. 246 (2021).
1146 EU Commission's Assessment 2019, p. 8 (n. 1118).

this as it could affect the processor's obligation to assist the controller in the fulfilment of the controller's obligation to respond to a data subject's request.[1147] In practice, there are many situations where data subjects have direct communication with the processors and may send their requests to the processor. With this provision, processors could easily and possibly lawfully, as the EU Commission noted, refuse the data subject's request. The EU Commission stated that this could be in contradiction with the GDPR.[1148]

c) Art. 38 – Automated Individual Decision-Making, Including Profiling

The right not to be subject to a decision based solely on automated processing, including profiling, is regulated differently compared to the GDPR. While Art. 22 GDPR defines that "the data subject shall have the right not to be subject to a decision based solely on automated processing [...] which produces *legal effects* or *similarly significantly affects*," Art. 38 SDPL 2019 defines that the "data subject has the right not to be subject [...] if that decision *may produce legal effects* or *the decision significantly affects his or her position.*" First of all, the GDPR does not use the term "may produce legal effect" but "produces legal effect". Second, the GDPR does not recognise the term "significantly affects" but rather "similarly significantly affects". Hence, according to the GDPR a decision-making process that does not have a direct effect on people's legal rights could still fall within the scope of Art. 22 GDPR if it produces an effect that is equivalent or similarly significant in its impact.[1149] The GDPR introduced the word "similarly" (which was not present in Art. 15 DPD) to the phrase "significantly affects".[1150]

The EU Commission criticised this approach taken by Art. 38 SDPL 2019, as it fails to reflect both concepts of legal effect and similarly significant effect established by the GDPR.[1151] In particular, the wording "may produce legal effect" is too vague and may result in lowering the standard for protecting personal data. Further, the SDPL 2019 does not provide any examples of the legal effects, which are included in the Recital 71 GDPR (such as automatic refusal of an online credit application, e-recruiting practices without any human intervention).

1147 *Ibid*, p. 9.

1148 *Ibid.*

1149 WP29 Guidelines on Automated individual decision-making and Profiling for the purposes of Regulation, pp. 21–22 (n. 367).

1150 *Ibid.*

1151 EU Commission's Assessment 2019, p. 10 (n. 1118).

d) Art. 40 – Restrictions and Controversy

The SDPL 2019 adopts the grounds for restricting the rights of data subject from the GDPR.[1152] Although Art. 40 SDPL 2019 states that "rights may only be restricted if the restrictions do not affect the core of fundamental rights and freedoms and if it is necessary and proportionate in a democratic society", it does not provide that such a restriction may only be made by a legislative measure. Before being finalised, an earlier draft had asserted that restrictions could only be imposed by law.[1153] SHARE expressed its concerns as well but noted that Art. 42 of the constitution provides that the processing of personal data must be regulated by a law, from which one could assume the restriction of data protection rights must also be regulated by law.[1154] Noteworthy, the Constitutional Court decided in 2012 that part of the SDPL 2008 was not constitutional because it gave the possibility of limiting the rights of citizens on the basis of a 'bylaw regulation'.[1155] Further, as the ECHR is directly applicable in Serbia, the standards on the limitations of the ECtHR apply as well. Therefore, it remains unclear why Art. 40(2) SDPL 2019 fails to include the requirement for restricting rights only by legislative measure.

In this context, the DPC, still led by the former commissioner,[1156] sent a letter to the Parliament expressing its reservations regarding the controversial Art. 40.[1157] The DPC warned the MPs that such a solution would lead to a "drastic collapse of the legal system, which is in complete contradiction with the Serbian Constitution and international documents and conventions, and seriously violates the principle of the rule of law".[1158] The DPC's criticism was not alone in its criticism, as the EU Commission also denounced the legislature's failure to align Art. 40 with the EU acquis.[1159]

1152 Art. 40(1) SDPL 2019.

1153 DPC, "Nedostaci Predloga zakona o zaštiti podataka o ličnosti" (Eng. Shortcomings of the Draft Law on the Protection of Personal Data) (23.10.20218), available the following link <https://www.pravniportal.com/nedostaci-predloga-zakona-o-zastiti-podataka-o-licnosti/> (accessed on 12.02.2023).

1154 SHARE, Guide on the Law on Data Protection and GDPR, p. 77 (n. 19).

1155 Decision of the Constitutional Court, IUz No. 41/2010 of May 30, 2012, published in the Official Gazette of RS, no. 68/2012 (18.07.2012).

1156 Mr. Roduljub Šabić, who was very critical of the government compared to the current commissioner. More on this in part III of this Chapter.

1157 The Commissioner's letter to the parliament, no. 073–14–1602/2018–01 (22.10.2018), available at the following link <https://www.poverenik.rs/images/stories/dokumentacija-nova/pismaorganima/pismoposlanicimaZZPLCL40.pdf> (accessed on 12.02.2023).

1158 *Ibid.*

1159 EU Commission's Assessment 2019, p. 11 (n. 1118).

8 Redress Mechanism

The SDPL 2019 provides several ways for data subjects to exercise their rights – through a complaint to the DPC (which does not affect the right to initiate other administrative or judicial protection procedures),[1160] judicial redress against the DPC's decisions,[1161] judicial redress against a controller and processor[1162] and the right to compensation.[1163] Although the SDPL 2019 mirrors the provisions of the GDPR when defining the right to judicial protection, there have been some critics to the copy-past approach of these provisions without properly adapting it to the characteristics of the national legal system by the DPC.[1164] The DPC stated that the procedural provisions according to which the data subject has the right to file a complaint with the DPC, while the right to initiate other administrative or judicial proceedings for data protection remains unaffected, are not appropriate for the Serbian legal system. The problem of applying the principle of "ne bis in idem" arises because the authorities before which proceedings can be brought (DPC, Administrative Court, Civil Court, Supreme Court) have no mutual obligation to inform each other or to check whether any proceedings are being conducted by another body. This means that legal certainty is called into question in any procedure in which several mechanisms for the protection of personal rights are involved. The DPC is of the opinion that amendments to the SDPL 2019 are necessary as the effective implementation of the SDPL 2019 will be difficult.[1165] The Strategy Proposal recognises this as well and announced amendments of the law in this respect. Moreover, it is worth mentioning that in the Strategy Proposal and Action Plan for Strategy implementation, the Serbian Government announced to introduce the possibility to electronically submit and track data subject's complaints.[1166] This shall promote and empower individuals to report the breaches of their personal data.

9 Personal Scope

The SDPL 2019, similarly to the previous law, recognises the roles of data controllers and data processors. Notwithstanding, the SDPL 2019 introduces the con-

1160 Art. 82 SDPL 2019.
1161 Art. 83 SDPL 2019.
1162 Artt. 83–84 SDPL 2019.
1163 Art. 86 SDPL 2019.
1164 The DPC's Annual Report for 2021, p. 39, available at the following link <https://www.poverenik.rs/images/stories/dokumentacijanova/izvestajiPoverenika/2021/Izve%C5%A1ta2021CIRfinal.pdf> (accessed on 13.02.2023).
1165 *Ibid.*
1166 Ivan Milošević, Partner, JPM, Data Protection Strategy Proposal for 2023–2030 (n. 1114).

cept of 'joint controllers',[1167] stemming from the GDPR. Provisions for the appointment of processors and sub-processors, as well as the rules for concluding a data processing agreement governing their relationship, were copied from the GDPR.[1168] Moreover, the SDPL 2019 imposes a broader range of obligations and higher liability on data processors compared to the SDPL 2008.[1169] For example, under the SDPL 2019 both data controllers and data processors have the obligation to conduct ROPAs, whereas the SDPL 2008 imposed a similar obligation only for the controller.[1170]

a) Security of Personal Data

Under the SDPL 2019, both data controllers and data processors are responsible for ensuring that they take all necessary technical, organisational and staffing measures to comply with the law.[1171] Art. 41 adds the word "staffing" which is not envisaged by the 24 GDPR. The EU Commission noted that this is not logical, as the "personnel measures" are already included in the term "organisational measures", and this definition could imply that personnel measures are of higher importance than other measures.[1172]

The SDPL 2019 promotes the use of technological achievements in the same way as in Art. 32 GDPR (e.g., pseudonymisation measures).[1173] However, the SDPL 2019, similar to the GDPR, does not provide in-depth detail, such as state of the art, or comprehensive guidance on pseudonymisation or anonymisation. In fact, the SDPL 2019 provides even less information, given that it does not incorporate the GDPR's Recitals which would provide additional guidance.[1174] Therefore, companies would need to rely on the guidance published by the DPC, or guidance of the EU supervisory authorities.

Moreover, the SDPL 2019 introduced some new concepts into the legislation relevant to the security of personal data, such as the obligation to notify data breaches[1175] and the data protection impact assessment.[1176] The DPC drew up

1167 Art. 43 SDPL 2019.
1168 Art. 45 SDPL 2019.
1169 See also SHARE, Guide on the Law on Data Protection and GDPR (n. 19).
1170 Art. 48 SDPL 2008.
1171 Artt. 41, 45 SDPL 2019.
1172 EU Commission's Assessment 2019, p. 11 (n. 1118).
1173 Art. 50 SDPL 2019.
1174 E.g., Recitals 28–29, 77 and 78 GDPR.
1175 Artt. 52–53 SDPL 2019.
1176 Artt. 54–55 SDPL 2019.

and published a list[1177] of processing operations for which this assessment is required including cases which align with the WP29 Guidelines on Data Protection Impact Assessment.[1178]

Finally, one of the improvements which the GDPR has brought to data protection legal framework in Serbia is the elimination of the burdensome requirement for data controllers to register their data processing activities with the DPC every time they initiate processing of personal data processing,[1179] (a legacy of the DPD) which ceased to exist with the adoption of the GDPR.[1180] Instead, the SDPL 2019 adopts the obligation for both data controllers and processors to conduct ROPA from Art. 30 GDPR.[1181]

b) DPO

Under the SDPL 2019, data controllers and data processors are obliged to appoint a DPO in the same cases as provided by Art. 37 GDPR.[1182] However, the SDPL 2019 contains several specifications. The first specification in the national legislation is that there is an obligation for companies to provide the DPC with the contact details of the DPO.[1183] The DPC keeps a record of all DPOs with their contact details.[1184] Another difference is that the DPC has interpreted the role of a DPO in a way that only a natural person can be appointed as a DPO.[1185] The GDPR, on the other hand, does not specify this, while the Guidance of the Working Party states

1177 DPC, Decision on the list of types of personal data processing actions for which an assessment of the impact on the protection of personal data must be carried out and the opinion of the Commissioner must be sought, (Official Gazette of the RS, no. 45/2019).

1178 WP29 Guidelines on DPIA (n. 905).

1179 Art. 98 SDPL 2019.

1180 Recital 89 GDPR states that DPD's general obligation to notify the processing of personal data to the supervisory authorities produced administrative and financial burdens, it did not in all cases contribute to improving the protection of personal data.

1181 Art. 47 SDPL 2019.

1182 Artt. 56–57 SDPL 2019.

1183 While Art. 37(7) GDPR states that controllers and processors shall communicate the details of the DPO to the supervisory authority, there is no specific requirement for the supervisory authority to publish the list of all 'registered' DPOs.

1184 Art. 56(10) SDPL 2019.

1185 Information available on the DPC's website, in the rubric "Data Protection Officer" where it is stated that each of the controllers or processors who are obliged or want to designate a person for the protection of personal data – designate only one, and not several natural persons"; See also DPC's Q&A, available in Serbian at the following link <https://www.poverenik.rs/images/stories/dokumentacijanova/Publikacije/Publikacija_Lica_za_zastitu/PublikacijaLiceza zastitu.pdf> (accessed on 02.05.2023).

that a DPO can also be an external organisation with a team under the responsibility of a designated lead contact for the client.[1186] The EU Commission website also states: "a DPO may be an individual or an organisation".[1187] In this regard, the DPC promotes the appointment of individuals as DPOs. It is also worth nothing, there are no restrictions in the SDPL 2019 that would prevent a foreign natural person from being appointed as a DPO,[1188] which is more liberal compared to certain other national legislations, such as in North Macedonia.[1189]

Regarding the education and qualifications of DPOs, the SDPL 2019 does not contain specific requirements. It reiterates the provision of the GDPR, which states that the DPO should be appointed based on their professional qualities and expertise.[1190] It also provides for the criterion of independence of the DPO.[1191]

c) Representatives of Foreign Entities

Like the GDPR, the SDPL 2019 introduces the position of the representative of controllers and processors not established in Serbia, a new institution in Serbian national legislation. In particular, when the SDPL 2019 applies to foreign controllers or processors (under the extraterritorial effect envisaged by Art. 3 SDPL 2019), these foreign entities are obliged to appoint their representative for the Serbian territory.[1192] The DPC publishes a list of appointed representatives of foreign entities on its website. So far, around 40 companies (e.g. Google, Netflix, Alibaba) have appointed representatives, and all of them have appointed only law firms (the largest Serbian law firms such as Karanović Partners, BDK advokati or Živković Samardžić).[1193]

1186 WP29 Guidelines on Data Protection Officers ('DPOs') WP 243 rev.01, (Dec 2016).

1187 See website of the EU Commission, "Does my company/organisation need to have a Data Protection Officer (DPO)?" available at the following link <https://commission.europa.eu/law/law-topic/data-protection/reform/rules-business-andorganisations/obligations/data-protection-officers/does-my-companyorganisation-need-have-data protection-officer-dpo_en> (accessed on 28.01. 2023).

1188 This Opinion that a foreign national can be appointed as a DPO is confirmed by the DPC in its Publication no. 6 "Data protection – Attitudes and opinions of the Commissioner", Publisher Commissioner for Information of Public Importance and personal data protection, Belgrade, 2021, p. 62.

1189 Art. 41(5) MDPL 2020. See also the Section E.II of this Chapter.

1190 Art. 56(8) SDPL 2019.

1191 Art. 57(3) SDPL 2019.

1192 Art. 44 SDPL 2019.

1193 The list of representatives available at the DPC website at the following link <https://www.poverenik.rs/sr-yu/zaštita-podataka/представници-страних-привредних-друштава-у-складу-са-законом-о-заштити-података-о-личности.html> (accessed on 26.11.2021).

One of the great achievements of the DPC has been to encourage the big tech companies to appoint their representatives, for example in the case of Google and Facebook. The DPC's efforts to motivate large tech companies to appoint their representative are important, as the penalties foreseen in the SDPL 2019 are unlikely to be an incentive. The DPC contacted Google and Facebook in 2019 to encourage them to appoint a representative in Serbia, after SHARE filed misdemeanour charges against Google LLC and Facebook Inc.[1194] However, Facebook has not responded to the DPC's communication and has yet to appoint a local representative in Serbia.[1195]

In turn, Google engaged in discussions with the DPC, ultimately leading to their appointment of a representative in Serbia after an extended dialogue and thorough investigation of the case by the DPC.[1196] Google's position was that it was already 'established' in Serbia through its subsidiary Google d.o.o. Belgrade and that it was therefore not obliged to appoint a representative.[1197] However, the DPC found that although Google d.o.o. Belgrade was established in 2007 and registered with the Serbian Agency for Business Registration (hereinafter: "APR"), it did not constitute an establishment in terms of the SDPL 2019 for several reasons: 1) The representatives of Google d.o.o. were US citizens registered with the APR. 2) The address at which Google d.o.o. Belgrade was registered was a private residence belonging to a natural person. 3) A DPC employee himself went to the registered address, where no one answered the doorbell and where there was only "a piece of paper stuck to the door with transparent adhesive tape, which read Google doo". 4) No letters could be delivered to the registered address for a longer period. 5) The last activity in the APR dated back to 2016. 6) The telephone number registered at the APR did not exist. 7) Google d.o.o. Belgrade neither provided the DPC with the contact details of a DPO nor published them on its website.

1194 SHARE files complaints against Facebook and Google, article published by SHARE, 05.12. 2019, available at the following link <https://www.sharefoundation.info/en/share-files-complaints-against-facebook-and-google/> (accessed on 21.02.2022).

1195 Facebook's representative cannot be found on the list of representatives available at the DPC website, available at the following link <https://www.poverenik.rs/sr-yu/zaštita-podataka/представници-страних-привредних-друштава-у-складу-са-законом-о-заштити-података-о-личности.html> (accessed on 26.11.2021).

1196 DPC's List of representatives (n. 1193).

1197 The letter from Google LLC to the DPC, (4 February 2022). This letter is not publicly available and was provided to the author by the DPC using the right to request information from the DPC, file number 073–06–4170/2022–07 (02.12.2022).

8) Google d.o.o. Belgrade was not mentioned as a subsidiary in the privacy policy of Google LLC.[1198]

The DPC concluded that the lack of 'real contact' with Google d.o.o. Belgrade prevented data subjects in Serbia from exercising their rights under the SDPL 2019. Therefore, Art. 44 SDPL 2019, which refers to Serbian representatives of foreign entities, is applicable in this case.[1199] As a result, Google LLC decided to appoint a local representative on 21 May 2020.[1200]

d) Codes of Conduct and Certification

The SDPL 2019 introduced entirely new institutes of semi-self-regulation modelled on the GDPR, namely codes of conduct (Artt. 59–50), certifications (Artt. 61–62) and BCRs (Art. 67). Nevertheless, due to the copy-paste-approach, misunderstandings may occur, as some words may have a different meaning in terms of Serbian legislation. SHARE expressed its concern that a potential problem may arise in determining who can develop a code of conduct.[1201] Under the SDPL 2019, these can be drafted by associations and other entities (a similar wording as provided by the GDPR).[1202] However, this may lead to the incorrect interpretation that a code of conduct can be created by an association as a separate legal entity established under the Serbian Law on Associations. The English word 'association' has a different meaning from the word 'association' (Serbian 'udruženja') in the Serbian legal system.[1203] The logic of the GDPR is that these associations and other organisations are categories of data controllers or data processors that are representative vis-à-vis the controllers/processors of the relevant sector/industry.[1204] The main concept refers therefore to the common processing activities within a given economic sector/industry. In contrast, the 'association' in the sense of the

---

1198 Email by the DPC delivered to Google LCC (26.02.2020). This email is not publicly available and was provided to the author by the DPC using the right to request information from the Commission (n. 1197).
1199 *Ibid.*
1200 *Ibid.*
1201 SHARE, Guide on the Law on Data Protection and GDPR, p. 67 (n. 19).
1202 Art. 59(1) SDPL 2019.
1203 Association, in the sense of Art. 2 the Serbian Law on Associations, is a voluntary and non-governmental non-profit organisation based on the freedom of association of several natural or legal persons, established for the purpose of achieving and promoting a certain common or general goal and interest, which are not prohibited by the constitution or the law.
1204 EDPB Guidelines 1/2018 on certification and identifying certification criteria in accordance with Articles 42 and 43 of the Regulation 2016/679.

Serbian legislation is a general term, referring to a single non-profit entity established under the Serbian Law on Associations.

Also, it appears that the provisions on code of conducts and certification have not yet been established in practice. There are no adopted criteria for issuing certification, nor are there any approved codes of conduct available and published on the DPC website.[1205] Indeed, as there is not much practice in this area even in the EU,[1206] it is possible that the DPC is waiting for more activity from data protection authorities in EU countries.

10 Transfers of Personal Data

Under the SDPL 2008, the key question was whether a country to which the data were to be transferred was a member of Convention 108.[1207] If a third country was a member of Convention 108, a data transfer was free in the sense that no prior approval of the DPC was required (hereinafter: "Transfer Approval").[1208] If not, the only way to ensure a lawful data transfer from Serbia was to obtain a Transfer Approval prior to commencing the transfer. This stricter approach was very burdensome for companies, as it was a lengthy and complicated procedure with no alternative.

The SDPL 2019 introduces a set of mechanisms on the basis of which a legitimate transfer of data out of Serbia is possible, providing other alternatives where a Transfer Approval would not be required. This means that the SDPL 2019, like the GDPR, tends to allow the legitimate transfer of personal data whenever there are legitimate safeguards for the data transfer. Yet, this part of the SDPL 2019 differs significantly from the GDPR. The specific data transfer mechanisms will be detailed below.

a) Art. 64 – Adequacy Decisions

The transfer of personal data to third countries is allowed without any additional requirements if an adequacy decision has been issued, following the approach set

1205 Artt. 59(5), 61(9) SDPL 2019 require both codes of conduct and certifications to be published on the Commissioner's website.

1206 E.g., The first certification mechanism was adopted by the Luxemburg National Data Protection Commission (CNPD) only in June 2022; See EDPB news "The CNPD adopts the certification mechanism GDPR-CARPA", available at the following link <https://edpb.europa.eu/news/national-news/2022/cnpd-adopts-certification-mechanism-gdpr-carpa_en> (accessed on 21.04.2023).

1207 Art. 54(1) SDPL 2008.

1208 Art. 54(3) SDPL 2008.

out in the GDPR. However, there are significant differences between the two in this regard.

Firstly, the SDPL 2019 incorporates a provision whereby an adequate level of protection is automatically deemed to be provided in countries and international organisations that are members of Convention 108 and countries which are already listed on the EU Commission's adequacy list.[1209] This is a carry-over from the SDPL 2008 and represents a more permissive approach compared to the current practices outlined in the GDPR.

Secondly, the SDPL 2019 contains a 'negative definition' whereby the government may determine that a country does not provide an adequate level of protection with the exemption of countries which are members of Convention 108.[1210] The decision-making criteria are taken from the GDPR.[1211] However, such a solution is not consistent with the GDPR, given that countries that are members of Convention 108 are exempt from the rule that the government can decide that the country no longer provides an adequate level of data protection.[1212] In addition to the members of Convention 108 and countries featured on the EU Commission's adequacy list, the government's adequacy decisions include the US in the catalogue of countries that are considered to provide an adequate level of protection for personal data.[1213] The fact that the government decides solely on the adequacy decisions may undermine the DPC's position, as the government will likely look for its political and economic advantages and not for the best data protection guaranties. Although the GDPR does not assign the power to decide on adequacy decisions to the independent supervisory authorities, the process of adoption of an adequacy decision provides for a much higher level of independent control than it is foreseen by the SDPL 2019. As explained in Chapter 3 of this study, the EU Commission does not have a stand-alone role in taking the adequacy decision. The EDPB, as a central data protection authority, needs to give an opinion to an adequacy decision, and the EU countries representatives must give an ap-

1209 Art. 64(2) SDPL 2019.

1210 Art. 64(3) SDPL 2019.

1211 *Ibid.*

1212 *Ibid.*

1213 Decision on the list of states, parts of their territories or one or more sectors of certain activities in those states and international organisations in which an appropriate level of personal data protection is considered to be ensured (Official Gazette of RS, no. 55/2019), available in Serbian at the following link <https://www.poverenik.rs/en/подзаконски-акти4/3127-одлука-о-листи-врста-радњи-обраде-података-о-личности-за-које-се-мора-извршити-процена-утицаја-на-заштиту-података-о-личности-и-тражити-мишљење-повереника.html#> (accessed on 23.04.2022).

proval.[1214] In addition, the European Parliament has a right of scrutiny over adequacy decisions. For instance, the European Parliament adopted a resolution on the adequacy of the protection afforded by the EU-US Data Privacy Framework in which it concluded that the EU-US Data Privacy Framework fails to create essential equivalence in the level of protection.[1215] The Serbian adequacy decision making, for its part, gives full power to the Serbian government, without any additional checks and balances. Given the centralisation of power in Serbia this is a matter of concern.[1216] It is also worth mentioning that other WB6 countries' GDPR-like laws have interpreted this provision differently, giving the supervisory authority the power to decide on the adequacy list based on the legal criteria, while the laws do not automatically include countries that have signed Convention 108 as countries providing adequate level of data protection.[1217]

Thirdly, within the SDPL 2019 there is no mechanism for a periodic review of adequacy decisions. From the wording of the law, it appears that the government will continuously monitor the situation of personal data in the respective countries.[1218] However, no specific deadline or timeframe is stipulated for this monitoring process.

Finally, an adequate level of protection is deemed to exist if an international agreement on the transfer of personal data has been concluded with another country or an international organisation. Although the same rules apply to assess whether these countries provide an adequate level of data protection, the monitoring of the situation of personal data in these countries is not foreseen.[1219] This aspect has already drawn criticism from the EU Commission as it deviates from the requirements of the GDPR.[1220] According to the EU Commission's per-

1214 WP29 Adequacy Referential, p. 4 (n. 155).

1215 European Parliament resolution on the adequacy of the protection afforded by the EU-US Data Privacy Framework (2023/2501(RSP)) (11.05. 2023).

1216 EU Commission Report for Serbia 2022, SWD(2022) 338 final (12.10.2022) states that the political and media landscapes remained polarised and continued to be dominated by the Serbian Progressive Party (SNS) and the incumbent President. Political influence on human rights and data protection rights is elaborated in more detail in Chapter 6.

1217 Kosovo and Macedonian data protection GDPR-like laws (Chapter 4, C.II and E.II).

1218 Art. 64(6) SDPL 2019.

1219 Art. 64(5) provides that in the process of ratification of an international agreement, the fulfilment of the conditions set out in paragraph 3 of this article shall be specifically determined. However, paragraph 3 only refers to the conditions for assessing the adequate level, not to the monitoring of the personal data situation.

1220 EU Commission's Assessment 2019, p. 15 (n. 1118).

spective, Serbia will have to amend this provision in order to ensure alignment with the EU acquis.[1221]

This approach to adequacy decisions may be a major obstacle for Serbia to obtain an adequacy decision from the EU Commission. Looking at other third countries that already have an adequacy decision from the EU Commission, it seems that they always follow the approach of the EU Commission for fear of losing their privileged status.[1222]

b) Adequate Safeguards

If a country to which data is to be transferred is not on the adequacy list, a transfer is still possible without a Transfer Approval if adequate data protection measures are undertaken. These measures align with those outlined in the GDPR (e.g., SCC, BCR, Codes of Conduct, Certificates) (hereinafter: "Adequate Safeguards"). However, it should be noted that transfers from Serbia to EU countries may be subject to additional administrative burdens, as the SDPL 2019 does not provide 'by default' recognition of appropriate safeguards approved by the EU authorities.

aa) SCCs

Controllers and processors in Serbia have the option to transfer personal data to a third country by adopting the SCCs issued by the DPC. However, the SDPL 2019 does not address the situation concerning data transfers with the EU. For instance, if an EU-based controller engages a Serbian-based processor, it could not rely only on the SCCs adopted by the EU Commission (hereinafter: "EU SCCs"), as that would not satisfy the criteria of Art. 56(2) SDPL 2019. The EU Commission expressed its concern that in such a case it can occur that transfers from the EU to Serbia that depend only on the EU SCC will be in violation of the SDPL 2019. This could lead to EU companies to be discouraged from such business activities including data transfers with Serbia due to the additional administrative obstacles.[1223] Such a dichotomy would have been easy to overcome if the SDPL 2019 recognised the use of EU SCCs, as does the data protection law of North Macedonia.

1221 *Ibid.*

1222 E.g., Swiss Federal Data Protection Authority removed the US from its list of adequate countries. See also Daniela Fábián Masoch "Swiss Data Protection Authority considers the CH-US Privacy Shield no longer adequate – Swiss companies must act now" Lexology (11.09.2020), available at the following link <https://www.lexology.com/library/detail.aspx?g=2ddd0dd2-e345-4a61-b77a-54ca57bfd78a> (accessed on 17.05.2023).

1223 EU Commission's Assessment 2019, p. 15 (n. 1118).

Further, the SCCs adopted by the DPC do not have the same modular approach as the EU SCCs. While the new EU SCCs have several models 1) controller to controller 2) controller to processor 3) processor to processor and 4) processor to controller, the SCCs adopted by the DPC contain only one model: controller to processor. Considering that the Serbian legislator has not adopted the new EU SCCs, for any such transfers not covered by the DPC's SCCs – most notably the intra-group controller-to-controller transfers – local companies would need to rely on other safeguards available under SDPL 2019 or, in their absence, on the administratively-burdensome approval of the DPC.

bb) BCR

The definition of the BCR rules under the SDPL 2019 is seemingly different from the definition established by the GDPR Art. 4(21) SDPL 2019 defines them as binding "internal policies [...] for the purpose of regulating the transfer [...] within a multinational company or group of economic entities", while Art. 4(20) GDPR defines them as "data protection policies [...] for transfers or a set of transfers [...] within a group of undertakings, or group of enterprises engaged in a joint economic activity". Consequently, in the Serbian legal system, BCRs seem to refer to internal company policies, whereas under the GDPR, BCRs typically refer to agreements signed between legally separate entities.[1224] The EU Commission advised aligning the definitions with the wording of the GDPR to prevent potential issues where the DPC might not approve BCRs approved by the lead supervisory authority in the EU due to the differing legal treatment of BCR rules.[1225] This has particular relevance as the SDPL 2019 does not recognise by default the EU data transfer instruments.

c) DPC's Approval

In addition to the Adequate Safeguards mentioned above, the DPC may grant an authorisation in two cases where it is considered that Adequate Safeguards are in place: a) contractual clauses between the controller or processor and the controller or recipient in another country or international organisation or b) provisions included in the agreement between the authorities, which ensure effective and enforceable protection of the rights of data subject.[1226] This solution is aligned

1224 See also WP29 Working Document Setting Forth a Co-Operation Procedure for the approval of "Binding Corporate Rules" for controllers and processors under the GDPR (WP263 rev.01) (11.04.2018); Also noted in the EU Commission Assessment 2019, p. 5 (n. 1118).
1225 EU Commission's Assessment 2019, p. 5 (n. 1118).
1226 Art. 65(3) SDPL 2019.

with Art. 46(3) GDPR. Although these types of data transfers are not common in the EU, they have a higher relevance in Serbia due to the lack of other modules of the SCCs (except for the model of controller to processor). Considering that the idea of the EU SCCs is to facilitate data transfers to third countries with the four models of SCCs, such high bureaucratic hurdles are not logical from the perspective of the Serbian legislator. Serbia would benefit more if it had easier rules for data transfers from the EU and vice versa (via recognising by default the EU transfer instruments), considering that most investors and companies in Serbia are EU companies.

d) Special Cases

Even if there are no Adequate Safeguards, there are still certain exceptional circumstances in which personal data can be transferred without the need for a Transfer Approval. These special situations are explicitly prescribed by the SDPL 2019,[1227] similar to the provisions outlined in Art. 49 GDPR.

11 Penalties

The penal policy in the Serbian legal framework on data protection is one of its most significant differences from GDPR provisions. Firstly, in contrast to the very strict penalty policy and high fines introduced by the GDPR, the SDPL 2019 maintains a very lenient penalty policy. Specifically, it provides for tort liability for violations of the SDPL 2019, with maximum fines for such violations of RSD 2 million (approximately up to €17,000) for a legal person[1228] and RSD 150,000 (approximately up to €1,300) for the representative of a legal person or a natural person per violation.[1229] In addition to fines envisaged by the SDPL 2019, the Law on General Administrative Procedure allows for the imposition of fines of up to 10 % of the entity's annual turnover achieved in Serbia in the preceding year for failure to comply with an injunction issued by a public body, including the DPC.[1230] However, the practical application of this remedy remains uncertain as the law is relatively new and there is limited case law on its implementation.[1231] It should also be noted that the DPC does not have the power to impose all types of fines. The SDPL 2019 only empowers the DPC to impose fines for specific breaches where

1227 Art. 69 SDPL 2019.
1228 Art. 95(1) SDPL 2019.
1229 Art. 95(4) SDPL 2019.
1230 Art. 198(2) Law on General Administrative Procedure (Official Gazette of RS, no. 18/2016, 95/2018 – authentic interpretation and 2/2023 – US decision).
1231 RCC Report 2020, pp. 172–173 (n. 18).

a fixed fine is provided, such as continuing processing for direct marketing purposes despite objection from the data subject, failure to maintain ROPAs and failure to publish and submit the contact details of the DPO to the DPC.[1232]

Another notable deficiency in the SDPL 2019 is the absence of sanctions for several provisions within the law itself. One significant omission is the lack of a penalty for processing personal data without a legal basis (Art. 12 SDPL 2019). The SDPL 2019 only provides for sanctions in cases of processing based on invalid consent (Art. 15 SDPL 2019).[1233]

Finally, criminal liability is also regulated in the relevant Serbian legislation. The Serbian Criminal Code includes the offence of unauthorised collection of personal data, which is punishable by a fine (determined by the court) or imprisonment for up to three years.[1234] However, criminal liability remains more of a theoretical possibility, as prosecution in such cases is relatively rare.[1235]

12 Specific Processing Situations

The SDPL 2019 recognises several specific processing situations, including processing and freedom of expression and information (Art. 88), processing and free access to information of public importance (Art. 89), processing of the unique identity number of citizens (Art. 90), processing in the context of labour and employment (Art. 91), protection measures and limitation of the application of the law on processing for the purposes of archiving in the public interest, for the purposes of scientific or historical research or for statistical purposes (Art. 92), processing by the church and religious communities (Art. 93) and processing for humanitarian purposes by public authorities (Art. 94). The above specific processing situations are mostly in line with the GDPR, with a few exemptions.

a) Processing in the Field of Labour and Employment

The first exemption is found in Art. Art. 91(1) SDPL 2019 regulating processing of personal data for employment purposes. This article stipulates that the "provisions of the law regulating work and employment and collective agreements are applied to processing in the field of work and employment, *along with the application* of this law." This provision is significantly different from Art. 88(1) GDPR which stipulates that "Member States may, by law or by collective agreements,

1232 Art. 79(1)(9) SDPL 2019.
1233 Art. 79(1)(5) SDPL 2019.
1234 Art. 146 Criminal Code of Serbia (Official Gazette of RS, no. 85/2005, 88/2005 – corrected, 107/2005 – corrected, 72/2009, 111/2009, 121/2012, 104/2013, 108/2014, 94/ 2016 and 35/2019).
1235 RCC Report 2020, p. 173 (n. 18).

provide for more specific rules to ensure the protection of the rights and freedoms". Therefore, the purpose of Art. 88 GDPR is to provide for more specific rules to ensure the protection of personal data, while it serves a minimum standard for data protection. The wording of Art. 91(1) in the SDPL 2019 raises concerns that it may undermine or supersede the requirements set forth in the law itself. The EU Commission expressed criticism regarding this provision and recommended amending the phrase 'along with' to 'in accordance with this law'.[1236] Such an amendment would ensure that the provisions of the SDPL 2019 take precedence and are not overshadowed by other laws and agreements pertaining to work and employment.

b) Processing for Humanitarian Purposes by the Public Authorities

The second difference with the GDPR is the specific processing situation defined in Art. 94 –processing for humanitarian purposes by public authorities – which does not exist at all in the GDPR. During the public debate surrounding the legislation, numerous proposals were submitted advocating for the removal of this exception.[1237] Despite these proposals, the government decided to retain the provision, arguing that processing for the mentioned humanitarian purposes was already permitted under the previous legislation (SDPL 2008) and that it has widespread practical application.[1238]

The EU Commission raised concerns and criticism regarding this provision as well. It noted that such a general provision allowing public bodies to use personal data for fundraising purposes is not in conformity the GDPR.[1239] The EU Commission also referred to Recital 46 GDPR, which regulates the processing of personal data for protection of an interest which is essential for the life of the data subject or that of another natural person. As stated by the EU Commission this legal basis should only be used exceptionally and not as a matter of course.[1240] It further stated that raising funds for humanitarian purposes does not have the same purpose as Recital 46 (i. e., cannot serve es an important public interest or the vital interest of the data subject) and recommended amending Art. 94 SDPL 2019 to align it with the provisions of Recital 46 GDPR.[1241]

1236 EU Commission's Assessment 2019, p. 18 (n. 1118).

1237 Report on the public debate on the text of the Draft Law on Personal Data Protection (March 2018), p. 4, available in Serbian at the following link <https://www.mpravde.gov.rs/sekcija/53/radne-verzije-propisa.php> (accessed on 21.03.2022).

1238 *Ibid.*

1239 EU Commission's Assessment 2019, p. 19 (n. 1118).

1240 *Ibid.*

1241 *Ibid.*

13 Conclusion to II

The SDPL 2019 has been largely replicated from the GDPR. This replication process resulted in numerous inconsistencies within the law. Furthermore, the inclusion of the LED Directive in the SDPL 2019 has further complicated its interpretation and implementation. One of the most controversial aspects of the SDPL 2019 is the absence of a provision explicitly stating that the rights of data subject can only be restricted by legislative measures. However, the established constitutional practice asserts that restrictions on human rights are permissible solely through the means of law.

Moreover, the prescribed penal policy within the SDPL 2019 falls significantly short of the penal provisions established by the GDPR, potentially hindering the enforcement of data protection standards in Serbia. Additionally, the provisions regarding data transfers are not in alignment with the GDPR. The adequacy list adopted by the Serbian government includes all countries that are members of the Convention 108. This liberal approach may pose challenges when considering a potential adequacy decision for Serbia. Notably, data transfers from the EU to Serbia may face particular difficulties, as the Serbian system does not recognise the EU SCCs.

The EU Commission assessed the SDPL 2019 and put forth proposals for necessary amendments. This evaluation acknowledges the need for improvements and adjustments to align the Serbian legislation with European standards and best practices in data protection. In response to these identified flaws, Serbia has taken steps towards rectifying the situation. The country prepared the Strategy Proposal, which acknowledges the existing deficiencies and commits to harmonising sector laws, enhancing redress rights, and refining penal policies. This proactive approach demonstrates Serbia's commitment to addressing the issues within the data protection framework and striving towards a more robust and comprehensive system. Finally, one of the primary objectives of the Strategy Proposal is to attain adequacy decisions from the EU Commission. To achieve this, Serbia must address the identified flaws within the SDPL 2019.

III Supervisory Authority

The DPC, Commissioner for Information of Public Importance and Protection of Personal Data (in Serbian: "Poverenik za informacije od javnog značaja i zaštitu podataka o ličnosti"), is a supervisory authority for the protection of personal data in accordance with Serbian legislation. The DPC has a crucial role in safeguarding data subjects' rights and promoting implementation of the data protection standards in Serbia.

1 General Functions

The DPC is an authority with a dual competence, including protection of personal data and ensuring access to public information in accordance with relevant legislation, similar to the supervisory authority in Kosovo. In terms of its data protection competence, the SDPL 2019 introduced new functions of the DPC. Under the SDPL 2019, the DPC's fulfils several key functions, including overseeing the implementation of the SDPL 2019, promoting the right to data protection, and raising public awareness about the protection of personal data.[1242] The DPC is also empowered to conduct investigations, handle complaints from data subjects[1243] and impose fines.[1244] In addition to these functions, the DPC's tasks include advising the parliament, the government, and other institutions and bodies on legislative and administrative measures concerning the processing of personal data.[1245] The DPC is also responsible for monitoring the development of information and communication technologies, as well as business and other practices relevant to the protection of personal data.[1246]

2 Independence

In accordance with the SDPL 2019, the DPC is an independent authority free from any form of direct or indirect external influence.[1247] To ensure the effective exercise of its competences, the DPC shall have at its disposal the necessary financial resources, working space and the necessary technical and organisational conditions.[1248] Additionally, the DPC shall be independent in the selection of its staff and in their management.[1249] As a public authority, the DPC's activities are funded through the state budget in accordance with the provisions of the Budget Act, the Public Administration Act, and the Civil Service Act.[1250] Furthermore, the DPC is required to prepare an annual report on its activities, which is submitted to the Parliament and the Government.[1251]

The DPC is headed by the commissioner, who is supported by two deputies, two advisors, and a team of experts who provide the necessary assistance to fulfil

1242 Art. 78 SDPL 2019.
1243 *Ibid.*
1244 Art. 79(1)(9) SDPL 2019.
1245 Art. 78 SDPL 2019.
1246 *Ibid.*
1247 Art. 74(1) SDPL 2019.
1248 Art. 74(3) SDPL 2019.
1249 Art. 74(4) SDPL 2019.
1250 Art. 74(3) SDPL 2019.
1251 Art. 81 SDPL 2019.

its responsibilities and exercise its powers.[1252] The SDPL 2019 does not provide specific regulations regarding the appointment of the commissioner, but refers to the law governing access to public information and specifies that the commissioner must possess the requisite professional knowledge and experience in the field of personal data protection.[1253] Under this law governing access to public information the commissioner is elected and dismissed by the parliament.[1254] It is also important to note that compared to other WB6 supervisors, the Serbian DPC has the most resources and personnel to carry out its responsibilities under the SDPL 2019.[1255]

3 Powers

The tasks of the DPC are in general in line with Art. 78 GDPR. The powers of the DPC are divided into investigative, corrective, authorisation and advisory powers reflecting the scope of Art. 78 GDPR. However, as highlighted earlier[1256] the DPC is limited to imposing fines with a fixed amount. This is the key difference compared to the powers of the EU supervisory authorities, who are authorised to impose substantial fines on controllers and processors. Nonetheless, this represents a noteworthy improvement since under the SDPL 2008 the DPC did not possess the power to impose fines.[1257] Instead, the DPC could only submit an infringement complaint, and the final decision on fines rested with the courts.[1258]

4 Challenges

Despite the expanded powers granted to the DPC by the SDPL 2019, which enable it to exercise its supervisory role in ensuring compliance with data protection laws, the institution continues to face a variety of challenges. In particular, the independent functioning of the DPC has become vulnerable to significant political pressure, which has manifested itself both before and after the adoption of the SDPL 2019. This part highlights two cases that serve to illustrate this prevalent issue.

1252 RCC Report 2020 p. 178 (n. 18).

1253 Art. 75 SDPL 2019.

1254 Artt. 30–31 Law on the free access to public information (Official Gazette RS no. 120/04).

1255 SHARE, Comparative Analysis, p 5. (n. 20).

1256 Chapter 4, F.II.14.

1257 Art. 56 SDPL 2008.

1258 *Ibid.*

a) Election of DPC's Head and Controversy

The former commissioner, Mr. Šabić, played an active role in his position, often offering critical perspectives on the government's actions and assisting NGOs and independent media in their investigations related to data protection and the right to public information issues.[1259] However, his mandate ended with the adoption of the SDPL 2019. The appointment of the new commissioner took a long time, and for a while (December 2018 – July 2019) the DPC did not have a commissioner. In December 2018, approximately 80 NGOs submitted an initiative to the Parliament, proposing specific criteria for the appointment of the new commissioner.[1260] They argued that both the former SDPL 2008 and the SDPL 2019 had overly broad criteria for the selection of the commissioner, necessitating more specific criteria to ensure a suitable candidate.[1261] Later, in June 2019, NGOs called on the Parliament to withdraw the controversial condition that the nominated candidate should not be employed in another government institution at the time of nomination (the criterion which is not even required by the SDPL 2019).[1262] They contended that this condition was a disqualifying factor for all candidates currently working in government agencies, including the office of the DPC.[1263] Excluding these experienced professionals could rose the suspicion that government preferred to install a less critical commissioner than the previous one.[1264]

1259 E.g. the cases of "Aunts from Canada", "Savamala" or "President's letters to pensioners", see also "Otkrića do kojih je Krik došao uz pomoć Poverenika" (Eng. Discoveries made by Krik with the help of the Commissioner) available at the following link <https://www.krik.rs/otkrica-do-kojih-je-krik-dosao-uz-pomoc-poverenika-sabica/> and <https://www.slobodnaevropa.org/a/29604307.html> (both accessed on 12.02.2023).

1260 The initiative "Hoću Poverenika, a ne poslušnika!" (Eng. I want a commissioner, not a yes-man), available at the following link <https://srbijadoinformacija.rs/poverenik/> (accessed on 12.03.2023).

1261 The criteria included: the candidate did not violate the laws, professional standards and rules of the profession, has not been associated with a political party in the last three years, specific competencies and integrity criteria together with the criteria for the selection process. See the proposal at the following link <http://crta.rs/wp-content/uploads/2018/12/Kriterijumi-za-izbor-kandidata-za-Poverenika-za-informacije-od-javnog-zna%C4%8Daja-i-za%C5%A1titu-podataka-o-li%C4%8Dnosti.pdf> (accessed on 13.05.2023).

1262 Article published by CRTA, "The Assembly should withdraw the questionable criterion for selection of the new Commissioner", (15.06.2019), available at the following link <https://crta.rs/en/the-assembly-should-withdraw-the-questionable-criterion-for-selection-of-the-new-commissioner/> (accessed on 13.05.2023).

1263 *Ibid.*

1264 For instance, the former leader of the SNS parliamentary group, Aleksandar Martinović, said in January 2019 that "Šabić was an opposition politician disguised by the function of com-

Finally, in July 2019, three candidates were proposed. The Parliament voted in favour of the candidate proposed by the parliamentary group of the ruling Serbian Progressive Party (hereinafter: “SNS”), while the candidate nominated by certain opposition parties and supported by nearly 80 NGOs received only one vote.[1265] The process revealed the pressure exerted by the government to appoint a candidate that was likely to be less critical than the former head of the DPC, without consulting or taking into consideration the proposals tabled by the NGOs.

b) President’s Son’s Wine Shop Case

In November 2021 (during the mandate of a new commissioner), the DPC conducted an ordinary inspection in line with Art. 79 SDPL 2019 at an online wine shop allegedly owned by the son of the President of Serbia. The inspection was carried out in accordance with the inspection plan published on the DPC’s website and it was announced to the controller in advance.[1266] Following the inspection, several articles with sensationalist headlines were published by pro-government media, such as “Special war against Vučić [president]! Inspectors inspected the wine shop where the president’s son Danilo works!”[1267] or “We are investigating! What is really hidden behind the ‘commissioner’ affair? They wanted to falsely accuse Danilo of money laundering?!?”.[1268] Subsequently, a televised debate took place where the commissioner had to explain over the phone the purpose of the inspection to a guest on the program, who expressed doubt and disbelief re-

missioner and that the SNS proposal for a new Commissioner will be the exact opposite of Šabić”, see article published by Krik (28.01.2019) available in Serbian at the following link <https://www.krik.rs/martinovic-kandidat-za-poverenika-bice-susta-suprotnost-sabicu/> (accessed on 12.02.2023).

1265 See for more information the article published in Krik “Odbor podržao Milana Marinovića kao kandidata za poverenika za informacije od javnog značaja” (Eng. the competent parliamentary committee supported Milan Marinović as a candidate for commissioner for information of public importance) (01.07.2019) available in Serbian at the following link <https://insajder.net/arhiva/vesti/odbor-podrzao-milana-marinovica-kao-kandidata-za-poverenika-za-informacije-od-javnog-znacaja> (accessed on 12.02.2023).

1266 The DPC’s plan on the inspections in 2021 available in Serbian at the following link <https://www.poverenik.rs/images/stories/dokumentacija-nova/akti-oradusluzbe/2021/plan_inspekcijskog_nadzora_2021.pdf> (accessed on 12.02.2023).

1267 Article published in Informer (11.11.2021) available at the following link <https://informer.rs/vesti/politika/651187/specijalni-rat-protiv-vucica-inspektori-proveravali-vinoteku-kojoj-radi pred sednikov-sin-danilo> (accessed on 12.02.2023).

1268 Article published in Informer (13.11.2021), available at the following link <https://informer.rs/vesti/politika/651558/sta-krije-iza-afere-poverenik> (accessed on 12.02.2023).

garding the intentions behind the DPC's inspection.[1269] The lack of understanding of the DPC's jurisdiction and of the principles of personal data protection was evident during the debate.

Even the Prime Minister publicly accused the DPC of 'abusing its position to go after Danilo'[1270] and questioned the DPC's authority to carry out such inspections, suggesting that the DPC might have been influenced by opposition parties, stating: "Are we so well regulated in the field of personal data protection that the DPC should go to the shops to inspect them, or should they say that they have been instrumentalised by the opposition so that we will harass the people where Danilo Vučić works?"[1271] In response to these allegations, the DPC issued an official statement clarifying that the inspection had been a regular and pre-announced procedure, conducted in accordance with the provisions of the SDPL 2019. The DPC categorically denied the accusations made against them and affirmed their commitment to upholding the principles of data protection within the scope of its powers.[1272]

5 Conclusion to III

While the powers of the DPC are largely in line with the GDPR, except for the limited power to impose fines, the criteria for an independent supervisory authority may not be met given the political pressure put on the DPC. Although Art. 74(1) SDPL 2019 states that the DPC is completely independent, free from any direct

---

1269 The video is available at the following link (in Serbian) <https://informer.rs/vesti/politika/651558/sta-krije-iza-afere-poverenik> (accessed on 12.02.2023).

1270 The prime minister's statements were published in several media (in Serbian), e.g. in Danas (13.11.2021), available at the following link < https://www.danas.rs/vesti/politika/brnabic-tvrdi-da-je-zloupotrebljena-funkcija-poverenika-za-zastitu-podataka-o-licnosti/>; in N1 (13.11.2021), available at the following link <https://n1info.rs/vesti/brnabic-poverenik-kontrolom-vinoteke-zloupotrebio-svoju-funkciju/> (accessed on 12.02.2023); In Vesti.rs (13.11.2021), available at the following link <https://www.vesti.rs/Novi-Sad/Brnabic-Poverenik-zloupotrebio-funkciju-kada-je-kontrolisao-vinoteku-u-kojoj-radi-Danilo-Vucic.html> (all accessed on 12.02.2023).

1271 *Ibid.*

1272 Statement of the DPC on the occasion of the regular inspection of the implementation of the SDPL 2019 by the controller whose activities include the online sale of wine, performed on November 10, 2021, according to the Inspection Plan for 2021, (12.11.2021), available in Serbian at the following link <https://www.poverenik.rs/sr-yu/arhiva/saopštenja-arhiva/3682-саопштење-повереника-за-информације-од-јавног-значаја-и-заштиту-података-о-личности поводом-извршеног-редовног-теренског-инспекцијског-надзора-над-спровођењем-закона-о-заштити-података-о-личности-од-стране-једног-руковаоца-—-односно-надзираног-субјекта,-којем-је-једна-од-делатности-online-продаја-вина,-дана-10-11-2021-године-према-плану-инспекцијског-надзора-за-2021-годину-од-31-3-2021-године.html> (accessed on 03.05.2022).

or indirect external influence and cannot seek or receive orders from anyone, indirect influence from the government has been obvious – from the appointment of the commissioner to the subsequent pressure on the newly appointed commissioner and a smear campaign against the DPC. Such cases seriously weaken the independent position of the DPC, which is also one of the key conditions for the adoption of an adequacy decision by the EU Commission. Unfortunately, the mentioned cases are just some of the examples. The institution of the DPC has repeatedly been the subject of campaigns and criticism by politicians who attacked the commissioner(s) as a person and/or the DPC as a supervisory authority.[1273] Nevertheless, it is important to note that so far these pressures have not led to a visible reduction of the commissioner's or the DPC's activities.[1274]

IV Case Law and Enforcement

This Section outlines the DPC's activities to enforce the SDPL 2019 and summarises some relevant cases filed with DPC and competent courts.

1 Activities of the Supervisory Authority

The DPC has been commendably effective in the implementation of the SDPL 2019 and the publication of guidelines for data controllers and data processors. The

1273 E. g. Nebojša Bakarec, "Commissioner's affair – new findings!", published in Informer (16.11.2021), available at the following link <https://informer.rs/vesti/politika/652339/nebojsa-bakarec-afera-poverenik-nova-saznanja>; Official response of the DPC to a PM' parliamentary question "Which provisions of the law allow the commissioner to abuse its position?" no. 073/24/1524/2018–01 (10.10.2018), available in Serbian at the following link <https://www.poverenik.rs/images/stories/dokumentacija-nova/pismaorganima/2018/Markovic.A.poslanicko.p.pdf>; Public announcement of the DPC "Continuity of the state's irresponsible attitude towards the protection of personal data" after the prime minister sent a letter to the DPC expressing her dissatisfaction with the commissioner's criticism of the data protection draft, (30.08.2017), available in Serbian at the following link <https://www.poverenik.rs/sr-yu/arhiva/saopštenja-arhiva/2645-kontinuitet-neodgovornog-odnosa-države-prema-zaštiti-podataka-o-ličnosti.html> (all accessed on 01.04.2022).

1274 For example, under the mandate of the new Commissioner, the DPC opened a new regional office in the city of Novi Sad for the first time, organised a number of conferences on data protection, conducted inspections of public authorities, etc. See the 'Announcements' section of the DPC website <https://www.poverenik.rs/sr-yu/saopstenja.html>, where the DPC publishes regular updates on its activities. The activities of the DPC are also further analysed in Chapter 4, F.IV.

DPC has enacted multiple bylaws, including the Decision on the SCCs,[1275] a Rulebook on the form and manner of keeping records of DPOs,[1276] a Rulebook outlining the complaint submission process,[1277] a Rulebook detailing the format for data breach notifications,[1278] and the Decision pertaining to performing a DPIA.[1279] In addition, the DPC has issued numerous recommendations and Frequently Asked Questions (FAQs) concerning the effective implementation of the SDPL 2019.[1280] These guidelines cover various aspects, including consent requirements, the role of DPOs, legitimate interests, and obligations for both data controllers and processors. Furthermore, the DPC has published an FAQ document specifically addressing the interpretation of the GDPR's provisions.[1281] Within this GDPR FAQ, the DPC acknowledges that since the GDPR's enactment, the institution has been receiving a significant number of inquiries concerning the GDPR's application within Serbia and the alignment of the national legal system with the EU's legal acquis.[1282] Last but not least, the DPC also conducts regular training sessions

---

1275 Odluka o utvrđivanju standardnih ugovornih klauzula (Službeni glasnik RS, broj 5/2020) (Eng. Decision on establishing standard contractual clauses, Official Gazette of RS, no. 5/2020).

1276 Pravilnik o obrascu i načinu vođenja evidencije lica za zaštitu podataka o ličnosti (Službeni glasnik RS, broj 40/2019) (Eng. Rulebook on the form and method of keeping records of persons for the protection of personal data, Official Gazette of RS, no. 40/2019).

1277 Pravilnik o obrascu pritužbe (Službeni glasnik RS, broj 40/2019) (Eng. Rulebook on the complaint form, Official Gazette of RS, no. 40/2019).

1278 Pravilnik o obrascu obaveštenja o povredi podataka o ličnosti i načinu obaveštavanja Poverenika za informacije od javnog značaja i zaštitu podataka o ličnosti o povredi podataka o ličnosti (Službeni glasnik RS, broj 40/2019) (Eng. Rulebook on the form of notification of a breach of personal data and the method of notifying the Commissioner for Information of Public Importance and Protection of Personal Data of a breach of personal data, Official Gazette of the RS, no. 40/2019).

1279 Odluka o listi vrsta radnji obrade podataka o ličnosti za koje se mora izvršiti procena uticaja na zaštitu podataka o ličnosti i tražiti mišljenje Poverenika za informacije od javnog značaja i zaštitu podataka o ličnosti (Službeni glasnik RS, br. 45/2019 i 112/2020) (Eng. Decision on the list of types of personal data processing actions for which an impact assessment on personal data protection must be carried out and the opinion of the Commissioner for Information of Public Importance and Personal Data Protection must be sought, Official Gazette of the RS, no. 45/2019 and 112/ 2020).

1280 All recommendations and FAQ are available online on the DPC's website (in Serbian) <https://www.poverenik.rs/sr-yu/zaštita-podataka/најчешће-постављена-питања-у-вези-са-заштитом-података-о-личности.html> (accessed on 13.05.2023).

1281 DPC, "Najčešće postavljana pitanja u vezi sa primenom Opšte uredbe o Zaštita podataka (GDPR)" (Eng. FAQ on GDPR) available at the following link <https://www.poverenik.rs/images/stories/dokumentacija-nova/ZZPLnajcescapitanja/GDPRQA.pdf> (accessed on 14.05.2023).

1282 *Ibid.*, p 1.

on data protection.[1283] In particular, an important project is the cooperation between the DPC and the Faculty of Security of the University of Belgrade. These two institutions have launched a specialised training programme for 'data protection managers'.[1284] The programme lasts six months and ends with exams organised by a special committee.[1285]

These activities undertaken by the DPC are crucial, given that the SDPL 2019 essentially replicates the provisions of the GDPR without incorporating additional explanations from the GDPR's preamble.

2 Cases Before the Supervisory Authority

Given that under the SDPL 2008 the data subject did not have a judicial remedy against controllers and processors, most cases were brought before the DPC. This trend seems to have continued also after the adoption of the SDPL 2019. According to the DPC's activity reports, there has been a significant increase in the number of complaints and cases brought before the DPC in recent years. In 2010, the first cases on data protection issues were filed with the DPC (250), while in 2022 the number of cases relating to personal data protection exceeded 5000.[1286] Interestingly, the highest numbers of cases brought before the DPC was in 2018 (8749) and 2019 (7229), after the GDPR entered into force in the EU.[1287] The cases cover a wide range of personal data breaches, in particular the misuse of ID numbers (JMBG), the use of video surveillance, special categories

1283 The DPC has a dedicated section on its website on the data protection trainings available at the following link <https://www.poverenik.rs/sr-yu/za%C5%A1tita-podataka/obuke-iz-za%C5%A1tite-podataka-o-li%C4%8Dnosti-koje-dr%C5%BEi-poverenik.html> (accessed on 14.05.2023).

1284 Faculty of Security of the University of Belgrade, "Personal Data Protection Manager Training – officially registered and approved the first short study program in the field of personal data protection in the domestic education system" (21.06.2020), available at the following link <https://fb.bg.ac.rs/2020/06/21/obuka-menadzera-za-zastitu-podataka-o-licnosti-zvanicno-evidentiran-i-odobren-prvi-kratak-program-studija-u-oblasti-zastite-podataka-o-licnosti-u-domacem-obrazovnom-sistemu/> (accessed on 124.05.2023).

1285 *Ibid.*

1286 In 2022, the DPC received a total of 18,701 cases, of which 13.285 related to freedom of access to information, 4.116 to the protection of personal data and 1.300 to both areas of the DPC's activities, according to the DPC's Activity Report 2022, p. 54, available at the following link <https://www.poverenik.rs/images/stories/dokumentacija-nova/izvestajiPoverenika/2022/Godi%C5%A1nji_izve%C5%A1taj_2022_-_16_03_2023_LAT.pdf> (accessed on 14.05.2022).

1287 *Ibid.*

of personal data, the right to be forgotten, the right of access and the right of rectification.[1288]

In terms of the DPC's inspections, since the enactment of the SDPL 2019, the primary subjects of supervision procedures have been private companies, with the primary concern being the security of personal data.[1289] On the other hand, the majority of data subject complaints were against public authorities, such as police authorities, health authorities and government ministries.[1290]

Some cases before the DPC attracted a lot of public attention and mostly involved data breaches by public authorities and political parties. The following examples, which include the mass collection of personal data, illustrate the lack of awareness of the protection of personal data, even among high-level public figures and public authorities.

a) The President's Letters

One of the cases that caused significant public attention was the mass distribution of letters to all pensioners by the President of Serbia in his capacity as the President of the SNS (ruling party) in 2018. On this occasion, the DPC initiated a supervisory procedure (still under the SDPL 2008) against the Republic Fund for Pension and Disability Insurance (hereinafter: "Fund"), the President's office and SNS political party.[1291] In the course of its investigation, the DPC requested information on the legal basis and the purpose of the disclosure of the personal data which included name, surname, and address.[1292] Since none of the parties provided a satisfactory explanation regarding the purpose and legal basis for the data disclosure, the DPC filed a criminal complaint against an official of the Fund for having unauthorisedly disclosed personal data of pension beneficiaries to the SNS Party, on suspicion of the official having committed a crime under Art. 146 of the Criminal Code.[1293]

1288 DPC's activity reports for 2019, 2020, 2021 and 2022, all reports available at the following link <https://www.poverenik.rs/sr-yu/o-nama/godisnji-izvestaji.html> (accessed on 02.03.2023).

1289 *Ibid.*

1290 DPC's activity report for 2022, p. 101 (n. 1286).

1291 The DPC's official statement (16.11.2018) available in Serbian at the following link <htttps://www.poverenik.rs/sr-yu/arhiva/saopštenja-arhiva/2966-повереник-покренуо-поступак-надзора-поводом-обраде-личних-података-пензионера.html> (accessed on 20.03.2022).

1292 *Ibid.*

1293 The DPC's official statement, (03.12.2018), available in Serbian at the following link (accessed on 20.03.2022) <https://www.poverenik.rs/sr-yu/arhiva/saopštenja-arhiva/2974-поводом-писма-пензионерима-повереник-поднео-кривичну-пријаву-против-нн-лица-из-фонда-пио.html>.

While the case was still pending, in 2020 (when SDPL 2019 came into force), the President once again sent letters to pension beneficiaries on behalf of his political party, expressing gratitude for their adherence to the COVID-19 measures and announcing financial compensation.[1294] As a result, the DPC informed the Public Prosecutor's Office that the President sent a new letter to the pension beneficiaries, potentially in a repeated violation of the Criminal Code.[1295] However, no further information regarding the outcome of this case is currently available.

b) Senior Cards

The case of 'senior cards' is another case involving the misuse of personal data for political gains. These cards, issued by the City of Belgrade, offered discounts on various purchases to elderly individuals. However, in order to obtain such a card, applicants were required to complete a form that included optional data fields, namely the personal identification number (JMBG) and date of birth, contrary to the principle of data minimisation.[1296] Upon conducting an inspection under the SDPL 2008, the DPC found that the City of Belgrade collected the personal data for various incompatible purposes (e.g. marketing purposes to send birthday wishes), in violation of the purpose limitation principle.[1297] Further, the DPC found that a formal decision of the City of Belgrade, which would define in a precise and unambiguous manner all relevant issues related to the processing of personal data, was missing.[1298] Consequently, it remained unclear who would be responsible for collecting the personal data, particularly given media reports suggesting that these cards could be obtained from various locations such as city councils, elderly care facilities, shopping centres, street stalls, markets, and

1294 Article "Poverenik: Obavestićemo tužilaštvo da je predsednik SNS poslao novo pismo penzionerima, nemamo informacije šta je s prethodnim postupkom" (Eng. Commissioner: We will inform the prosecution that the SNS president sent a new letter to pensioners, we have no information about the previous procedure), published by Insajder (25.05.2020), available at the following link <https://insajder.net/arhiva/vesti/poverenik-obavesticemo-tuzilastvo-da-je-predsednik-sns-poslao-novo-pismo-penzionerima-nemamo-informacije-sta-je-s-prethodnim-postupkom> (accessed on 12.05.2023).

1295 *Ibid.*

1296 DPC's RECORDS on the performed supervision on the city of Belgrade, no. 072–04–3576/2017–07, (28.11.2017), available in Serbian at the following link <https://www.poverenik.rs/sr-yu/arhiva/saopštenja-arhiva/2744-окончан-надзор-у-случају-београдске-сениор-картице.html> (accessed on 12.05.2023).

1297 *Ibid.*

1298 The DPC's official decision no 072–04–3576/2017–07, (14.12.2017), available in Serbian at the following link <https://www.poverenik.rs/sr-yu/arhiva/saopštenja-arhiva/2744-окончан-надзор-у-случају-београдске-сениор-картице.html> (accessed on 12.05.2023).

health centres.[1299] In the DPC's view, the security measures in place for personal data were therefore inadequate.[1300] Following the DPC's inspection and its decisions, the City of Belgrade anonymised the personal identification numbers and changed the form for issuing new senior citizen cards.[1301] This case brought to light the failure of the government to explore alternative means of providing benefits to pension beneficiaries and to avoid the creation of new databases based on extensive collections of personal data. Instead, the government opted for a method of processing personal data that served their own marketing purposes.

Interestingly, the government recently announced its intention to reintroduce senior citizen cards in 2023, making it available nationwide.[1302] However, the revised approach involves electronic issuance of such cards, with individuals registering online at the Fund's website and providing their personal data.[1303] According to the available privacy policy and the registration form on the Fund's website, the data collected includes the individual's personal identification number (JMBG), ID number, email address, and telephone number.[1304] Additionally, based on a previously given consent, data from the fiscal account for paid goods and services will be submitted by the Tax Administration to the Fund.[1305] While there has been no official reaction from the DPC to this development so far, the former head of the DPC questioned the rationale behind this collection of personal data, especially considering that the Fund already has the necessary personal data to issue the senior cards.[1306]

3 Court Cases

The jurisprudence on data protection issues before the courts is not very extensive in Serbia. Nevertheless, this Section aims to provide a summarised overview of

1299 *Ibid.*
1300 *Ibid.*
1301 *Ibid.*
1302 Article "Objavljeno uputstvo za prijavu za penzionerske kartice: Na kom linku se možete prijaviti?" (Eng. Published instructions for applying for pension cards: On which link can you apply?) published in Danas (15.03.2023), available at the following link <https://www.danas.rs/vesti/ekonomija/prijava-za-penzionerske-kartice-uputstvo-link/> (accessed on 14.05.2023).
1303 *Ibid.*
1304 Registration form and privacy policy available of the Fund website, available at in Serbian at the following link <https://zpk.trezor.gov.rs./prijava> (accessed on 14.05.2023).
1305 *Ibid.*
1306 Rodoljub Šabić "Penzionerske Kartice", (Eng. "Pension Cards") published in Peščanik (20.03.2023), available in Serbian at the following link <https://pescanik.net/penzionerske-kartice/> (accessed on 14.05.2023).

the cases before the competent courts, covering both the period when the previous legislation was in force and the implementation of the SDPL 2019.

a) SDPL 2008

As mentioned above, under the previous legislation, the DPC had no authority to impose fines on data controllers and data processors.[1307] The data subject had the right to complain exclusively to the DPC, without the right to effective judicial remedy.[1308] The only way to challenge the decisions of the DPC was to bring an administrative action before the competent courts.[1309] In addition, the DPC was obliged to file a misdemeanour complaint in the event of violations of the provisions of the SDPL 2008.[1310] This legal framework did not prove to be effective in practice. The number of cases brought before administrative courts was very low.[1311]

b) Criminal Complaints (Art. 146 Criminal Code)

Meanwhile, looking at the case law based on the Art. 146 Criminal Code, between 2015 and 2020 the number of cases brought before the courts responsible for criminal matters was slightly higher – twenty-eight (28).[1312] Only two out of 28 total cases have resulted in a conviction.[1313] Moreover, only two cases were initiated through the indictment proposed by the prosecution and the rest were initiated by a private criminal complaint.[1314] The number of criminal complaints filed by the DPC between 2015–2020 (both based on the SDPL 2008 and SDPL 2019) was 17, and not a single criminal complaint received its epilogue. They ended by

1307 Under Art. 56 SDPL 2008, the DPC could only 1) order the correction of irregularities within a certain period of time, 2) temporarily prohibit the processing of personal data and 3) order the deletion of personal data collected without a legal basis.

1308 Artt. 42, 56(3) SDPL 2008.

1309 Art. 56 SDPL 2008.

1310 Art. 56(4) SDPL 2008.

1311 For instance, between 2015 and 2019 (prior to the adoption of the SDPL 2019), according to the information available on the website of the Ministry of Justice of Serbia the following link <https://www.sudskapraksa.sud.rs/sudska-praksa> (accessed on 05.06.2023), there were less than 5 cases resolved by data subjects before the administrative courts: decisions no. I-2 U 13549/15, (23/10/2015); no. I-1 U 5390/1, (09/06/2016); no. 2 U 2350/17, (02/2021) and no. Gž 3189/2019 (22/08/2019).

1312 Partners for Democrats changes Serbia, "Privatnost i zaštita podataka o ličnosti u Srbiji" (Eng. Privacy and protection of personal data in Serbia), (March 2021), p. 11.

1313 *Ibid.*, p. 13.

1314 *Ibid.*

being rejected, or by not bringing forward an indictment proposal by the prosecution authorities.[1315]

c) SDPL 2019

Looking at the court cases after the adoption of the new GDPR-like legislation, between 2020–2023 it is evident that there has been a slightly higher number of cases brought before administrative courts.[1316] Moreover, it has been observed that data subjects are more likely to exercise their rights under the SDPL 2019 (e.g. right to access or obtain a copy of their data from data controllers – mostly public data controllers), especially in cases where access to personal data or a copy of it can be used for private purposes, that may not necessarily be related to the right to data protection.[1317] Further, only one case involved the right to be forgotten, where the data subject requested the deletion of their medical data from medical records.[1318] Similarly, only one case concerned the unlawful processing of data through video surveillance.[1319] Interestingly, the competent court in this case did not rely on the SDPL 2019 which lacks provisions on video surveillance. Instead, the court based its decision on Art. 8 ECHR.[1320]

4 SHARE as Data Privacy Watchdog in the WB6

One of the key players in raising awareness for data protection and data protection laws enforcement in Serbia is SHARE. A non-profit organisation, SHARE was established in 2012 with the aim of promoting human rights and freedoms, focusing on freedom of expression on the internet, data protection, digital security and

1315 *Ibid.*, p. 25.

1316 From the online search of the judicial portal, about ten cases were solved between 2020 and 2023, available at the following link <https://www.sudskapraksa.sud.rs/sudska-praksa> (accessed on 05.06.2023).

1317 E.g., in the case no. U 14837/2019 (18/11/2019) before the Administrative Court, the data subject's claim was rejected as the access to personal data did not concern the personal data of the data subject, but of the family member. In the case no. I-3 U 7406/20, (28/08/2020) before the Administrative court division in Kragujevac, the data subject's claim was rejected as the right of access was not within the meaning of Art. 4 SDPL 2019, but with the aim of obtaining information on the reasons for the decision to reject the data subject's criminal complaint. In the case no. U 9228/2017 (12/08/2020) before the Administrative Court, the data subject claim was rejected because the right of access to personal data was not in accordance with Art. 4 (the requested personal data related to a third party and not to the data subject).

1318 Judgment no. U 715/2019 (07/22/2020).

1319 Judgment no. Gž 1676/2021 (17/06/2021.)

1320 *Ibid.*

free access to knowledge.[1321] One could compare SHARE to the Austrian organisation None of Your Business (hereinafter: "NOYB"), which was founded in 2019, in the context of acting as a watchdog.[1322] However, the scope of SHARE's work goes beyond that of NOYB, covering a broader range of areas and concerns. SHARE is active not only in Serbia, but also in other WB6 countries. In cooperation with another NGO – Balkan Investigative Reporting Network (hereinafter: "BIRN"), SHARE has set up a database to monitor digital rights violations in Southern and Eastern Europe.[1323] Besides organising conferences, workshops and monitoring personal data abuses, SHARE publishes very useful guidelines on privacy and other laws affecting human rights and freedoms online.[1324]

Like NOYB, SHARE actively monitors the activities of major tech companies in the area of personal data. For example, in October 2020, SHARE filed a misdemeanour complaint to the DPC against 16 global tech companies for failing to comply with their obligation under the SDPL 2019 to designate a representative in Serbia.[1325] As a result, Google LC appointed a representative with the help of the DPC, as explained in part II of this Section.[1326] This allowed data subjects to invoke the right to be forgotten for the first time against a big tech company in Serbia, and SHARE's legal team helped data subjects win this fight against YouTube (a company owned by Google).[1327]

SHARE's advocacy efforts extend beyond confronting big tech companies, they also combat state abuse of privacy rights. One of SHARE's most significant legal battles involves massive video surveillance in Belgrade using Chinese technology,

1321 See for more information at the following link <https://www.sharefoundation.info/en/about-us/> (accessed on 14.05.2023).

1322 NOYB Statutes (November 2019), available at the following link <https://noyb.eu/en/our-detailed-concept> (accessed on 14.05.2023).

1323 These countries include Bosnia and Herzegovina, Croatia, North Macedonia, Serbia, Hungary and Romania.

1324 SHARE has so far published a number of useful guidance on the GDPR and SDPL 2019, such as the SHARE's Guide on data protection (n. 19), the Guide for Media Protection of Personal Data and Journalists' Exemption, 2018, the Guide to Improving Advertisements on the Internet, June 2019 etc., all publications available at the following link <https://www.sharefoundation.info/sr/category/publikacije/page/2/> (accessed on 14.05.2023).

1325 The misdemeanour complaint is available on the SHARE website (in Serbian) <https://www.sharefoundation.info/wp-content/uploads/SHARE-Fondacija-Prekrsajna-prijava-1.10.2020.pdf> (accessed on 14.05.2023).

1326 Chapter 4, II.9.

1327 SHARE, "Internet ipak može da zaboravi: kako je izbrisan jedan YouTube kanal" (Eng. The internet can still forget: How a YouTube channel was deleted) (24.09.2020), available at the following link < https://www.sharefoundation.info/sr/internet-ipak-moze-da-zaboravi/> (accessed on 02.05.2023).

as explained later in Chapter 6. In addition, SHARE has often campaigned to raise public awareness about the misuse of personal data by politicians and political parties.[1328] Also worth noting, similar to NOYB[1329], SHARE conducts assessments of websites with the objective of evaluating their security standards and the usage of cookies.[1330] However, SHARE has primarily focused on assessing public authorities' websites, revealing that 80 % of public authorities lack both a privacy policy and proper cookie settings.[1331] Finally, the SHARE 's dedication to promoting digital rights was recognised by the DPC in January 2017, when SHARE was awarded a "Certificate of Gratitude" for its outstanding contribution to promoting the right to the protection of personal data.[1332]

5 Conclusion to IV

Current case law in Serbia highlights several key points in relation to data protection. Firstly, it is evident that public authorities account for the majority of violations of data protection laws, often misusing personal data for their own purposes. This highlights the need for greater accountability and adherence to data protection obligations among these actors. Secondly, there is still a lack of awareness among data controllers and processors regarding their obligations under the SDPL 2019. This knowledge gap emphasizes the necessity for enhanced education and training initiatives to ensure proper compliance with data protection laws. Thirdly, the DPC has demonstrated active engagement and effectiveness in carrying out its responsibilities. The DPC's efforts play a significant role in safeguarding data protection rights and enforcing compliance, especially in light of the new changes introduced by the SDPL 2019. However, although public awareness has increased since the adoption of the SDPL 2019 (looking at the submitted complains to the DPC), it is noteworthy that the majority of cases are still handled by the DPC

1328 SHARE publishes cases of misuse of personal data on its 'Monitoring Platform', e. g., the case of politician Miša Vacić, who had access to personal data of citizens during the election campaign in Medveđa, or politician Goran Vesić, who published on his Facebook page official emails from the correspondence of N1 journalists containing their personal data, etc. The Monitoring Platform is available at the following link <https://monitoring.bird.tools/> (accessed on 17.05.2023).

1329 NOYB, "226 complaints lodged against deceptive cookie banners that are still not complying with GDPR requirements" (09.08.2022).

1330 SHARE, "Analiza sajtova beogradskih javnih preduzeca i službi" (Eng. Analysis of websites of Belgrade public companies and services), (02.11.2022), available at the following link <https://www.sharefoundation.info/wp-content/uploads/BG-sajtovi-analiza.pdf> (accessed on 02.05.2023).

1331 *Ibid.*

1332 Information provided on the SHARE website at the following link <https://www.sharefoundation.info/en/about-us/> (accessed on 01.05.2023).

without the power to impose significant fines. This suggests a limitation in the enforcement mechanisms, which may warrant further attention and potential reforms.

Additionally, the contributions of NGOs like SHARE have been instrumental in promoting data protection awareness and advocating for individuals' rights. Such organisations are an important stakeholder in the shaping of the data protection landscape in Serbia and the whole region.

In conclusion, while some progress has been made in data protection in Serbia, ongoing efforts are needed to strengthen compliance among public authorities, improve understanding among data controllers and processors, empower the DPC with greater enforcement capabilities, and sustain public awareness and engagement in data protection matters.

V Conclusion to F

Serbia took the lead among the WB6 countries by being the first to adopt a new data protection law in 2018, with the main objective of aligning it with the provisions of the GDPR. The law became applicable in 2019, after a nine-month grace period (SDPL 2019). The process of adopting the new data protection law, was rapid, characterised by a short period of public debate and the lack of involvement of the DPC (supervisory authority). The new data protection law, SDPL 2019, closely mirrors the provisions of the GDPR, but lacks the explanations which are found in the Recitals of the GDPR. Moreover, the SDPL 2019 also introduced provisions from the LED. However, in comparison to other data protection laws in the WB6 region, the SDPL 2019 exhibits a higher number of irregularities that occurred during the transposition process of the GDPR provisions. This fact, combined with the lack of explanation in the Recitals of the GDPR and LED provisions, has resulted in a complex legal framework that is difficult to comprehend.

One of the key concerns pertains to the liberal approach adopted in relation to data transfer rules. Under the SDPL 2019, all countries that are parties to Convention 108 are automatically deemed to have an adequate level of data protection, as determined by the Serbian Government. This leaves no room for individual assessments of level of data protection in these countries. Such an approach raises questions about the level of protection afforded to personal data during the onward international transfers of personal data.

The EU Commission assessed the SDPL 2019 and provided recommendations for amending specific articles to enhance alignment with the GDPR. In response, Serbia is also preparing a new Strategy Proposal under which the country puts an ambitious goal of obtaining an adequacy decision from the EU Commission. The country has also announced its intent to amend the SDPL 2019, addressing the identified shortcomings and working towards obtaining an adequacy decision from the EU Commission. However, it remains uncertain whether amending the SDPL 2019 alone will be sufficient to achieve the desired privileged status of an adequacy decision, considering the level of enforcement of data protection standards. In particular, it is evident that government authorities are lacking the level of data protection awareness of basic data protection principles. Additionally, the DPC does not possess the authority to impose significant fines, thereby placing the burden on data subjects to seek redress through the courts. However, available case law suggests that judicial redress is not commonly employed by data subjects as a means of seeking redress, highlighting potential deficiencies in the existing redress mechanism before the DPC.

G Conclusion to Chapter 4

The WB6 countries have made progress in aligning their national data protection laws with the acquis communautaire and in fulfilling their obligations under the SAAs signed with the EU. When it comes to progress on legislative alignment the WB6 countries can be divided into two groups.

Albania, Kosovo, North Macedonia and Serbia have already adopted new laws similar to the GDPR. However, Serbia and North Macedonia have recognised the need to amend their recently implemented data protection laws due to challenges stemming from a copy-paste approach that hinders effective implementation. In particular, Serbia's law has been identified by the EU Commission as having significant shortcomings (although it is not publicly known whether the EU Commission has produced similar reports for other WB6 data protection laws).

In comparison to this first group of countries, BiH and Montenegro are lacking behind in the process of legal harmonisation. Despite having published draft laws similar to the GDPR-like legislation adopted by the first group, they have experienced delays in adopting this harmonised legislation. These delays pose challenges in terms of maintaining data protection standards and aligning with the GDPR. It is essential for this second group to expedite the adoption process to ensure a robust and harmonised data protection framework.

Awareness of data protection among both the public and relevant stakeholders is a crucial aspect for all WB6 countries. While there is a visible trend of improved awareness, overall awareness remains relatively low. Public education campaigns, training programs, and raising awareness about data protection rights and obligations are necessary to foster a culture of data privacy and security.

Obtaining an adequacy decision from the EU Commission should be the ultimate goal for all WB6 countries. Their legal systems are formally already largely aligned with the EU framework, which shall facilitate compliance with most of the adequacy criteria introduced by the GDPR. By closing the remaining legal gaps and ensuring proper implementation they can – as discussed in detail in this Chapter – strengthen their data protection regimes and pave the way for closer integration with the EU's digital single market.

In essence this means in some cases expediting the adoption of legislation that is in line with the GDPR standards, in other cases amending existing laws where necessary and, in all cases, improving awareness programmes and securing enforcement of data protection legislations.

Chapter 5 – Government Access to Personal Data in the WB6

While the data protection and constitutional framework have already been analysed in Chapter 4, this Chapter focuses on the essential access of personal data transferred from the EU to the WB6 countries by public authorities of these countries. The Chapter offers an overview of the provisions governing public authorities' right of access in the WB6 countries to provide context for determining the adequacy level.

For the adoption of an adequacy decision, the limitations and safeguards for government access to personal data are of crucial importance. In the adequacy decisions which the EU Commission has adopted so far, it mostly focused on two main aspects: 1) rules applying to the processing of personal data, where the EU Commission took into account the constitutional framework, international instruments and data protection framework together with oversight and enforcement of the supervisory authority and 2) access and use of personal data transferred from the EU to the third country by public authorities.

Following the Schrems II judgement, the issue of access to personal data transferred from the EU to non-EU countries by public bodies, especially intelligence agencies, in the recipient non-EU countries have become crucial to the adequacy assessment. This underlines the importance of this aspect when assessing the level of the data protection framework in WB6 countries. The structure of this Chapter and analysis of each country follows the pattern of analysis used by the EU Commission in the sections regulating access and use of personal data by public authorities in its adequacy decisions, and looks both at the law enforcement and intelligence sector.

A Criteria

The EU Commission is checking the 'essential equivalence' test pursuant to Art. 45(1) GDPR when assessing the conditions under which government can access the data transferred to a third country. Art. 45(2)(a) GDPR requires the EU Commission to take into account the relevant legislation "concerning public security, defence, national security and criminal law and the access of public authorities to personal data". The EU Commission is also taking the criteria interpreted by the CJEU in light of the Charter of Fundamental Rights. The EDPB has adopted the Recommendations on the European Essential Guarantees for Surveillance

https://doi.org/10.1515/9783112221013-007

Measures in 2020[1333] (hereinafter: "EEGSM"), following the Schrems judgments. The guarantees included in the EEGSM do not aim on their own at defining all the elements which are necessary to consider that a third country provides a level of protection in accordance with Art. 45 GDPR,[1334] but serve as an assessment in order to determine whether a third country provides a level of protection essentially equivalent to that guaranteed within the EU.[1335] It should be stressed out that the EEGSM are primarily based on the jurisprudence of the CJEU and the ECtHR.[1336] Following the assessment of the jurisprudence (Schrems decisions), WP29 came to the conclusion that the requirements can be summarised in four essential guarantees that "need to be respected for access to data, whether for national security purposes or law enforcement purposes, by all third countries [...] to be considered adequate".[1337] First, data processing "should be based on clear, precise and accessible rules". Second, "the necessity and proportionality with regard to the legitimate objectives pursued need to be demonstrated". Third, data processing must be subject to "an independent oversight mechanism". Lastly, and importantly, "effective remedies need to be available to the individual".[1338] Indeed, the EEGSM should be taken into consideration, as they are a fair translation of the core of the rights that a third country should ensure to be declared adequate.

Under the first guarantee it is important to note that any limitation to the right to the protection of personal data must be provided for by law.[1339] Further, the legal basis must itself define the scope of the limitation on the exercise of the right concerned.[1340] Under the second guarantee the legislation needs to fulfil the requirement of proportionality. The limitations to the protection of personal data must apply only in so far as is strictly necessary.[1341] This means that the legislation of the third country must lay down clear and precise rules governing the scope and application of the measures in question and impose minimum safeguards on the transferred data. Under the third guarantee any interference with the right to privacy and data protection should be subject to an effective, independent and impartial oversight system that must be provided for either by a

1333 EDPB, Recommendations 02/2020 on the European Essential Guarantees for surveillance measures (10.11.2020).
1334 *Ibid.*, para 8.
1335 *Ibid.*
1336 WP29 Adequacy Referential, (n. 155).
1337 *Ibid.*
1338 *Ibid.*
1339 Schrems II, para 173 (n. 143).
1340 EPDB, Essential Guarantees for surveillance measures, para 26 (n. 1333).
1341 *Ibid.*, para 35.

judge or by another independent body.[1342] The ECtHR has expressed its preference for a judge to be responsible to maintain oversight.[1343] Finally, the last guarantee is related to the redress rights of the individual. The CJEU, in the context of the Schrems II judgment when assessing the adequacy of the level of protection of a third country, has reiterated that "data subjects must have the possibility of bringing legal action before an independent and impartial court in order to have access to their personal data, or to obtain the rectification or erasure of such data".[1344] For the ECtHR, as well, the question of an effective remedy is inextricably linked to the notification of a surveillance measure to the individual once the surveillance is over.[1345] The ECtHR thus acknowledged that in some cases there might be no notification, however an effective remedy must be provided.[1346]

Art. 8 ECHR provides that any interference with privacy must be in accordance with the law, in the interests of one of the aims set out in Art. 8(2) ECHR, and proportionate to the aim pursued. Art. 8 ECHR also requires that the interference is 'foreseeable', i.e. has a clear, accessible basis in law, and that the law contains appropriate safeguards to prevent abuse.

Moreover, adequacy decisions have been criticised for assessing the level of equivalence with the EU acquis, despite the broad rights of access to personal data granted to the government by the third country's laws.[1347]

The ECHR safeguards apply in all WB6 countries, except Kosovo,[1348] as also explained in Chapters 4 and 7. WB6 countries, by virtue of their membership in the CoE, are bound by the ECHR and subject to a range of obligations enshrined in international law. In the UK Adequacy Decision, the EU Commission acknowledged that direct application of ECHR safeguards brings the system of government access on the basis of principles, safeguards and individual rights similar to those guaranteed under EU law and applicable to the Member States.[1349]

In addition to the national mechanisms for oversight and control of institutions authorised to access data, the WB6 countries also comply with international standards recommended by the CoE. The Venice Commission, the Parliamentary Assembly of the CoE, and the Commissariat for Human Rights of the CoE oversee

1342 *Ibid.*, para 39.
1343 *Ibid.*, para 47.
1344 Schrems II, para 194 (n. 143).
1345 EPDB, Essential Guarantees for surveillance measures, para 45 (n. 1333).
1346 *Ibid.*
1347 Laura Drechsler (n. 10).
1348 Kosovo is not yet member of Council of Europe, explained more in Chapter 3.C.I. and Chapter 7.A.I.
1349 UK Adequacy Decision, para. 120 (n. 248).

the law enforcement of special investigative measures and the powers of law enforcement agencies. Specifically, the Venice Commission plays an important role in securing democratic control over security services and ensuring their compliance with the law.

B Challenges in Aligning Government Access Legislation

Despite the general criteria set out in Article 45(2) GDPR, a significant challenge for the WB6 countries in aligning their legal frameworks – particularly in relation to access to personal data by law enforcement and national security authorities – lies in the lack of clarity surrounding the interpretation of Article 45(2)(a) GDPR. Within the EU, a definitive consensus on the rules governing government access to personal data remains elusive.[1350] Over the past two decades, the issue of data retention has been the subject of recurrent debates at both national and EU level.[1351] This lack of consensus hampers the ability of the WB6 countries in the process of EU accession to harmonise their national laws, as they lack clear guidance in this regard. Also, no similar requirements for law enforcement and national security access have been introduced in any international treaty in the context of data export.[1352] Consequently, there is little opportunity to draw on international or foreign legal standards to interpret this provision, further complicating the alignment process.[1353]

Nevertheless, experience from past adequacy negotiations illustrates that legal convergence is not always a prerequisite at the outset. Negotiations and concessions during the adequacy process, as exemplified by the case of Japan, demonstrate the potential for improving data protection standards through dialogue. In its effort to obtain an adequacy decision, Japan adopted Supplementary Rules to address gaps identified by the EU Commission, most notably ensuring that "data subject rights would apply to all personal data transferred from the EU, regardless

1350 EU Data Retention Directive 2006/24/EC which regulated access to personal data was annulled by the CJEU in 2014 in its decision Digital Rights Ireland and Seitlinger (Joined Cases C-293/12 and C-594/12, 08.04.2014). Since then, only the jurisprudence of the CJEU provides guidance on the limits and rules for EU government access to personal data. See also Adam Juszczak and Elisa Sason, "Recalibrating Data Retention in the EU. The Jurisprudence of the Court of Justice of the EU on Data Retention – Is this the End or is this the Beginning?", EUCRIM (2021), pp. 238–266.

1351 See also Alena Birrer, Danya He and Natascha Just, "The state is watching you – A cross-national comparison of data retention in Europe", Telecommunications Policy, Volume 47, Issue 4, 2023.

1352 Julian Wagner (2018), p. 332 (n. 10).

1353 *Ibid.*

of the retention period", even though Japanese law does not provide such protections.[1354]

C Albania

In Albania no specific legislation on the interception of telecommunications existed until 1995. The Code of the Penal Procedure (hereinafter: "ACPP") approved in 1995 provided for the first time the procedure for carrying out judicial interceptions. However, it was not until 2003 that legislation was adopted to regulate lawful interceptions for collecting intelligence or security-related information. It is important to note that the Albanian Constitution establishes the rule that the limitation of rights and freedoms may be established by law only in the public interest or for the protection of the rights of others.[1355] In this sense, a limitation must be proportionate to the situation that has dictated it and cannot violate the essence of rights and freedoms and must not exceed the limitations provided by the ECHR.

Finally, the Albanian Constitution also provides that human rights are applicable to foreigners on the territory of Albania, with only a few special rights reserved for Albanian citizens. Therefore, all human rights envisaged by the Albanian Constitution would also apply to EU citizens.

I Criminal Law Enforcement Purposes

In Albania, lawful interceptions for law enforcement purposes are governed by the ACPP. The ACPP specifically regulates interception during criminal proceedings, while 'preventive interceptions' for national security purposes are regulated by a special law and cannot be used as evidence in criminal proceedings. The ACPP sets out general rules regarding the authorities responsible for applying for and issuing interception warrants, the grounds for interception approval, and the duration and renewal of warrants.

1354 Opinion 28/2018 regarding the European Commission Draft Implementing Decision on the adequate protection of personal data in Japan (05.12.2018), par. 9; See also. Flora Y. Wang, "Cooperative Data Privacy: The Japanese Model of Data Privacy and the EU-Japan GDPR Adequacy Agreement" Harvard Journal of Law & Technology, Volume 33, Number 2 (2020), p. 672.
1355 Art. 17(1) Albanian Constitution.

1 Rules for Authorising and Limiting Interception Measures

The ACPP provides detailed rules on the issuance of authorisation for interception measures, allowing interception only if authorised by the court upon request from the prosecutor. The court may authorise interception if there is "reasonable doubt" and "enough evidence for a charge to be filed" against the person who committed a criminal offense listed in Art. 122(1) ACPP. The interception decision must also indicate the method and time limit for execution. However, the duration of the interception is a subject of controversy, as it is limited to fifteen days, but the court may extend it for another fifteen days upon the reasoned request of the prosecutor "whenever it is necessary", implying that no maximum limit on interception measures exists.

The ACPP regulates the limits of authorisation by specifying the cases in which interception measures may be performed. The interception of communications is allowed only for special types of crimes (e. g. international crimes committed by telecommunication means, anti-corruption and organised crimes) and against a limited number of persons (e. g. a suspect for a criminal offence, a person who is believed receiving or transmitting communications to the suspect person, a person who takes part in transactions with the suspect, a person whose surveillance may lead to the discovery of the location or the suspect identity). The ACPP also allows interception without a court warrant in emergency situations, provided that the prosecutor informs the court immediately, but no later than twenty-four hours from the decision, and reasonable grounds exist to believe that a delay may result in serious damage to the investigation, and the conditions for conducting interception are met.

Regarding the methods used for interception, the ACPP specifies that interception operations can only be carried out using equipment installed in designated locations authorised and controlled by the public prosecutor. Therefore, the ACPP does not allow the authorities to order operators to intercept data for criminal purposes. As a result, since this type of interception is limited to criminal proceedings and the methods used do not allow access to companies that may store personal data of EU citizens, it may not have a significant impact on personal data transferred from the EU to Albania.

2 Redress

Oversight mechanisms play a crucial role in ensuring that the interception measures carried out by Albanian public authorities are conducted lawfully and do not violate the rights of individuals. In Albanian legislation, mechanisms for redress are available under both the ACPP and the general provisions on data protection. The ACPP stipulates that defence lawyers or representatives of the parties in criminal proceedings shall be immediately informed once the interception has been concluded. Additionally, the ACPP allows for appeals against the decision authorising an interception within ten days from the date the interested party learns about the interception, thereby affording data subjects the right to challenge interception measures.

Another avenue for redress is provided by the data protection legislation – ADPL 2024 – as elaborated in Chapter 4.[1356] Moreover, according to the Albanian Constitution, the data subject has the right to know what data has been collected about them, unless otherwise provided by law.[1357] Everyone also has the right to request the rectification or deletion of data that is untrue, incomplete, or collected in violation of the law.[1358] Finally, it should be noted that unlawful interception is treated as a criminal offense under the Albanian Penal Code (hereinafter: "APC").[1359] The interception of telephone communications or any other means of communication is punishable with a prison sentence of up to two years or a financial penalty.[1360]

3 Oversight

In Albania, criminal enforcement authorities are subject to oversight and control by various institutions, including those from the executive, judiciary, and Parliament. The executive branch exercises control and oversight over the work and functionality of the enforcement authorities primarily through the Minister of the Interior.[1361] In addition, the Parliament has established three permanent commissions – the National Security Committee, the Committee on Legal Matters, Public Administration and Human Rights, and the Committee on Economy and Finances – that are responsible for conducting oversight and control.[1362] These commissions act as a means of ensuring accountability and transparency in the functioning of the enforcement authorities.

In addition to the parliamentary commissions, independent institutions such as the Ombudsperson and the Commissioner for Protection against Discrimination exert oversight over the police. Finally, law enforcement agencies are over-

1356 See Chapter 4, Section A.II.9 for a detailed explanation of the redress mechanisms provided under the ADPL 2024.

1357 Art. 35 Albanian Constitution.

1358 *Ibid.*

1359 Artt. 121, 123 APC.

1360 Art. 123 APC.

1361 Art. 7 Law no. 108/2014 on the State Police.

1362 Mentor Beqa, "Law Enforcement and Equal Treatment of Citizens in Albania", CSDG, (November 2021), p. 19.

seen by the judiciary via Constitutional court and special oversight institutions introduced by the judiciary reforms in Albania.[1363] However, judiciary has been criticised as ineffective in practice.[1364]

II National Security Purposes

In 2003, the Albanian Parliament enacted the Law on the Interception of Electronic Communications (hereinafter: "AIEC")[1365] as a requirement for compliance with the ECHR.[1366] The AIEC provides a legal framework for the use of interception measures in Albania. The State Intelligence Service (hereinafter: "SIS"), established under the Law on the Organisation of the National Intelligence Service in 1991 (hereinafter: "LSIS"), is responsible for protecting national security in Albania. The SIS uses several interception techniques such as physical control, electronic control, postal control, telecommunication interception, and recording.[1367]

In addition to SIS, several other intelligence agencies are also authorised to perform data interception.[1368] The state police, SIS, and other intelligence and security agencies under the Ministries of Interior, Defence, Finance, and Justice are authorised to intercept telecommunications under the AIEC.[1369]

1363 Geron Kamberi and Erdi Memaj, "The Albanian Public's Trust in Security: Stumbling Blocks to EU Negotiations", Center for the Study of Democracy and Governance, (2020), p. 28

1364 In particular, the length of trials and the backlog of cases, as well as the independence and political influence on the judiciary, remain a challenge. See Geron Kamberi and Erdi Memaj, (2020), (n. 1500) and 2024 Rule of Law Report; Country Chapter on the rule of law situation in Albania, SWD(2024) 828 (24.7.2024).

1365 AIEC No. 9157 of 4.12.2003 available at the following link <https://www.euralius.eu/index.php/en/library/albanian-legislation?task=download.send&id=214&catid=112&m=0> (accessed on 12.02.2023).

1366 Arjan Dyrmishi, "Strengthening Intelligence Governance in the Western Balkans – Intelligence Governance in Albania", DCAF, Centre for Security, development and the Rule of Law (2018).

1367 Information available from the SIS's website at the following link <https://shish.gov.al/en/pages/transparency/transparency.html> (accessed on 12.02.2023). The English version of the Law on the Organization of the National Intelligence Service is not available and therefore not part of the analyses.

1368 Other intelligence agencies are: DISA – Defence Intelligence and Security Agency, SICMI – Service of Internal Control in the Ministry of the Interior, SICPS – Service of Internal Control in the Prisons System, FIU – Financial Intelligence Unit, OID/GD – The Operational and Investigative Department in the General Directorate of the Customs, DTI/GDT – the Directorate on Tax Investigations in the General Directorate of Taxation.

1369 Arjan Dyrmishi, Intelligence Governance in Albania, pp. 7–10 (n. 1366).

Initially, only the Ministry of Interior and the Ministry of Defence were authorised to carry out interceptions, but the AIEC has been amended several times since its adoption.[1370] After amendments in 2008 and 2009, the Ministries of Finance and Justice were allowed to use interceptions as well.[1371] This is a fairly extensive list of state institutions that are allowed to intercept citizens' communications. This expanded list of institutions allowed to intercept communications has been criticised.[1372] One of the major issues with the current setting of security agencies in Albania is the allocation of intelligence collection roles to a series of other agencies where the distinction between the intelligence and law enforcement has been eroded and there is no clear division or roles between the two. While SIS has no enforcement powers, other intelligence agencies have also some powers which are more related to the criminal enforcement powers, which when combined can create really powerful institutions.[1373] Moreover, some of these agencies are not established by an 'organic' law and most of their powers are allocated by governmental decisions rather than by laws adopted by the parliament.[1374] However, under AIEC the powers of the intelligence authorities shall be limited, as none of them have the right to submit a request for interception for matters or activities that are not foreseen by the law as subject-matter of their informative-tracing activity.[1375]

1 Rules for Authorising Interception Measures

The AIEC lays down the rules governing the scope and application of the interception measures by all security agencies, as well as the specific limitations, which seem not conform completely with the EU acquis. On a positive note, since 2017 (when the AIEC was amended again) the use of interception measures is allowed only if authorised by competent courts. The authority for approving the interception warrants has been transferred from the Prosecutor to the Chief of the Appellate court on Anti-Corruption and Organised Crime, which was part of the justice reform.[1376] This aligns with the ECtHR practice, as the ECtHR held that in the case of Popescu v. Romania, that the Romanian authority which ordered the intercep-

---

1370 *Ibid.*

1371 *Ibid.*

1372 *Ibid.*

1373 Arjan Dyrmishi and Besjana Kuci, Policy Paper "Security Management Network: The need to reform the intelligence system in Albania", Institute for Democracy and Mediation Centre for European and Security Affairs (2011), pp. 7–9.

1374 *Ibid.*

1375 Art. 6(2) AIEC.

1376 Arjan Dyrmishi, Intelligence Governance in Albania, p. 8 (n. 1366).

tion (the prosecutor) was not independent from the executive power.[1377] Therefore the decision on the interception under AIEC is adopted by the Court of Appeal against Corruption and Organised Crime.[1378] The request for interception, as well as all data collected by interception is confidential.[1379] The warrant for the interception of electronic communications is valid for up to three months, and it can be extended for another three months without limitations on how many times, which poses certain concerns related to the limitation of such interceptions.[1380]

Electronic communication operators in Albania could be requested to take the necessary steps in order to facilitate the interceptions under Art. 22 AEIC.[1381] The operator receives a copy of the warrant, containing an abbreviated content without data that may affect the intelligence-tracking process, and a time limit within which they must provide the necessary identification elements.[1382]

2 Limits and Safeguards

The AIEC defines the core principles for interception of electronic communications which include respect for fundamental human rights and freedoms, necessity and proportionality, secrecy, and objectivity.[1383] The AIEC does provide 'limitations on interception' in Art. 16, but this article only provides that the authorities in charge with interception are forbidden to diffuse or utilise the data acquired contrary to the law and intercept without authorisation or outside the procedure's setup by the law. The AIEC only provides a general rule for the interception of individuals suspected of serious crimes without specifying the categories of persons or types of offenses that may be intercepted,[1384] nor does it set limits on the duration of interception.[1385] The lack of specific rules on the supervision and compliance with data protection laws, as well as the absence of regular

1377 Dumitru Popescu V. Romania, applications nos. 49234/99 and 71525/01. (ECtHR, 26.4.2007).
1378 Art. 9(1) AIEC.
1379 Art. 9(2) AIEC.
1380 Art. 14(1) AIEC.
1381 Art. 22 AEIC.
1382 *Ibid.*
1383 Art. 4 AIEC.
1384 Art. 3(8) AIEC.
1385 Art. 14(1)(3) AIEC – the interception decisions are valid for a period of 3 months and any extensions is limited to further 3 months, but there are no limits on how many extensions are possible under the law.

reporting to the Ombudsman or data protection authority, have been criticised for not conforming to EU and ECtHR minimum standards.[1386]

Despite the lack of explicit reference to data protection or privacy, the AIEC requires the respect of human rights and freedoms, which are subject to specific data protection safeguards defined by the data protection legislation.[1387]

The material obtained through preventive interception of electronic communications must be destroyed within 10 days after the expiration of the interception time limit,[1388] with few exceptions when the interception material may be stored for longer period.[1389] However, the AEIC does not provide a specific time limit in such a case.

3 Redress

In terms of redress, the AIEC falls short in providing effective remedies for individuals. While individuals have the right to file a request for information,[1390] the competent authorities are not obliged to inform the person once the interception measures have ended. Furthermore, the responsible state institution may refuse to provide information if it could jeopardize the institution's tasks, endanger the safety of another person, or if the content of the intercepted communication constitutes a state secret and could harm national security or interests.[1391] These grounds are very broad and might not aligned with the criteria for effective remedy established by the ECHR and Schrems decisions. Additional redress mechanisms may be available as mentioned above.[1392]

4 Oversight

Regarding oversight, SIS underwent reforms in 1998 that allowed for parliamentary oversight. Today, external oversight of SIS is vested in several authorities, in-

1386 See for more information: Arjan Dyrmishi and Mandrit Kamolli, "Albania's approaches in security provision and accountability of security institutions: the need for further efforts to converge with the EU policy, legislation and practices," Friedrich-Ebert-Stiftung Office (December 2018).

1387 See ADPL 2024, Part III – *Personal Data Processing by Competent Public Authorities for National Security and Authorities for the Prevention and Prosecution of Criminal Offences* (Artt. 47–74).

1388 Art. 20(1) AEIC.

1389 Under Art. 20 AEIC if it is likely to be important for the protection of life, national security, public order or the prevention of serious crimes.

1390 Art. 20/1 AEIC.

1391 *Ibid.*

1392 Chapter 5, B.I.

cluding: a) Legislative – Parliament[1393] b) Executive – Prime Minister[1394] or other ministers and c) Judiciary[1395] – including Constitutional court.[1396] In general, on other service agencies the same external oversight applies, whereas only SIS directly reports to the Parliament, and all other intelligence agencies report to Parliament through their respective ministers.[1397] As noted above, Parliament has several commissions through which it exercises oversight of the security sector. In addition, the LSIS provides for the establishment of a permanent sub-committee within the National Security Commission of Parliament to report on all matters relating to its activities.[1398] The Director of the SIS reports to the National Security Commission at least once a year.[1399] However, oversight has been criticised for not being very effective in practice.[1400] The SIS has also been accused of being in the front line of political control and lacking transparency.[1401]

III Conclusion to C

Based on the analysis of the Albanian legislation on interception for criminal and national security purposes, it is evident that some progress has been made to meet the country's obligations under the ECHR and improve rule of law as part of the EU negotiations. However, the legislation still lacks some of the minimum safeguards defined by the ECHR.

In particular, the AIEC lacks limitations on the nature of offenses, categories of persons, remedies, and effective independent oversight. Moreover, the AIEC does not provide specific rules on the supervision and assessment of compliance with data protection laws by the data protection authority, which is also a requirement under EU standards. It also lacks provisions on regular reporting to the Ombudsman or the data protection authority. Regarding redress mechanisms, the AIEC only provides the right to file a request for information, but competent authorities are not obliged to inform the person after the interception measures

1393 Art. 80 Albanian Constitution.
1394 Art. 102 Albanian Constitution.
1395 Artt. 18, 135–147 Albanian Constitution.
1396 Art. 80 Albanian Constitution.
1397 Arjan Dyrmishi, Intelligence Governance in Albania, p. 17 (n. 1366).
1398 Geron Kamberi, Erdi Memaj, "The Albanian public's trust in security: Stumbling blocks to EU negotiations," CSDG, November 2020, pp. 30–31.
1399 *Ibid.*
1400 Arjan Dyrmishi, Intelligence Governance in Albania, pp. 12–22 (n. 1366).
1401 Geron Kamberi, Erdi Memaj, pp. 30–31 (n. 1398).

have ended. The grounds for rejecting a citizen's request for information are also very broad.

In conclusion, while the Albanian legislation on interception has improved in recent years, it still falls short of the minimum standards defined by the ECHR. Therefore, it is recommended that Albania adopts additional measures to align its legislation with the relevant international standards and improve its oversight mechanism to ensure effective compliance with the legislation.

D Bosnia and Herzegovina

The law enforcement system in BiH is unique due to the conflicts of the 1990s, culminating in the Dayton Agreement[1402] The need for police reform in BiH to align with internationally recognised standards was enshrined in Annex 11 Dayton Agreement, which established the International Police Task Force (hereinafter: "IPTF").[1403] Within this context, the UN took over the task of police reform in the period 1995–2002. The EU followed-on after UN's departure in 2003.[1404] The EU Police Mission in BiH (hereinafter: "EUPM") was a non-executive mission, providing advisory support to local authorities over the course of nearly a decade, until the conclusion of its mandate in 2012.[1405] During its tenure, the EUPM was tasked with reforming the enforcement system, including legislative support, and aligning it with EU standards.[1406] Following the conclusion of the EUPM's mandate, the Office of the High Representative (hereinafter: "OHR") remained as an international institution charged with aligning the rule of law in BiH.[1407]

1402 Dayton Agreement (n. 324). Already discussed in Chapter 4, A.II.

1403 Blaustein, Jarrett, "Reforming the Police in Bosnia and Herzegovina', Speaking Truths to Power: Policy Ethnography and Police Reform in Bosnia and Herzegovina", Clarendon Studies in Criminology (Oxford, 2015; online edn, Oxford Academic, 21 May 2015), pp. 55–74.

1404 Amelia Padurariu, "The Implementation of Police Reform in Bosnia and Herzegovina: Analysing UN and EU Efforts", Stability – International Journal of Security & Development, (2014), pp. 1–18.

1405 *Ibid.*

1406 EUPM, EU Institute for Security Studies, Joint Report: "Ten years after: Lessons from the EUPM in Bosnia and Herzegovina 2002–2012", (January 2013), pp. 68–70, available at the following link <https://www.iss.europa.eu/sites/default/files/EUISSFiles/EUPM_report_0.pdf> (accessed on 12.03.2023).

1407 OHR was established by the Dayton Agreement (n. 324) as an ad hoc institution to oversee implementation of the civilian component of the agreement and is accountable to the Peace Implementation Council (PIC). With the appointment of Mr. Paddy Ashdown as High Representative in 2002, the High Representative also became the EU Special Representative in Bosnia and Herzegovina.

I Criminal Law Enforcement Purposes

Access to personal data for criminal law enforcement purposes in BiH is governed by the Criminal Procedure Law (hereinafter: "BCPL"). The BCPL provides for special investigative measures that restrict the privacy rights of data subject. Firstly, among other actions aimed at obtaining the evidence,[1408] These measures, inter alia, include two types of access to personal data that can be ordered for any criminal offense if it is useful in a criminal case, namely "Seizure of Mail and Telegrams and other Consignments"[1409] and "Order to the Telecommunication Operator"[1410] (hereinafter: "Investigative Measures"). Secondly, the BCPL provides in chapter IX for special investigative actions, which may be used only if evidence cannot be obtained in another way or its obtaining would be accompanied by disproportional difficulties.[1411] This means that such measures shall not be used per se in line with the principle of proportionality. They include, inter alia, surveillance and technical recording of telecommunications[1412] and access to the computer systems and computerised data processing[1413] (hereinafter: "Surveillance Measures").

1 Rules for Authorising and Limiting Interception Measures

Under the BCPL, a warrant for both Investigative Measures and Surveillance Measures must be issued by the investigative judge on the motion of the Prosecutor.[1414] The BCPL also sets out the details that each warrant must contain.[1415] With regard to the time limits of Investigative Measures, the seizure of mail, telegrams and other communications provided for in Art. 67 may not exceed six months in total, while the BCPL does not provide for any time limits for the measures – order to the telecommunications operator.

1408 Chapter VIII BCPL regulates the actions aimed at obtaining evidence.

1409 Art. 67 BCPL.

1410 Art. 72a BCPL.

1411 Art. 116(1) BCPL.

1412 Art. 116(2)(a) BCPL.

1413 Art. 116(2)(b) BCPL.

1414 Art. 67(3) BCPL (Seizure of Mail and Telegrams and other Consignments) and Art. 72a(1) (Order to the Telecommunication Operator).

1415 Under Art. 65 (3) BCPL, a warrant needs to contain the name of the court, the legal grounds for taking the measure, an indication of the objects to be seized, the names of the persons from whom the objects are to be seized, the place where the objects are to be seized and the period within which the objects are to be seized.

In terms of Surveillance Measures, the BCPL provides numerous limits for allowing Surveillance Measures. It regulates for which specifies types of criminal acts the measures may be ordered,[1416] to which persons,[1417] time limits,[1418] redress and the procedure for obtaining a warrant. The Surveillance Measures may only be authorised by the competent judge.[1419] Exceptionally, if a written order cannot be received in due time and if delay poses a risk, the execution of Surveillance Measures may commence on the basis of a verbal order pronounced by the investigative judge.[1420] The written order of the court must be obtained within 24 hours following the issue of the verbal order.[1421]

Regarding time limits, the Surveillance Measures may last up to one month, while on account of particularly important reasons the duration of such measures may upon the properly reasoned motion of the prosecutor be prolonged for a term of another month, provided that the measures referred to last up to six months in total.[1422] Upon the completion of the Surveillance Measures, all information and data as well as a report must be submitted by police authorities to the prosecutor.[1423] If the data obtained from the Surveillance Measures is not needed for the criminal proceedings, they shall be destroyed under the supervision of the preliminary proceedings judge.[1424] If the data is still needed it shall be stored and kept as long as the court file is being kept.[1425] The BCPL further states that 'incidental findings' cannot be used as evidence if they are not related to a special criminal offense.[1426] Further, if Surveillance Measures have been undertaken without the order of the preliminary proceedings judge the national courts cannot base its decision on the data or evidence thereby obtained.[1427]

1416 Other criminal acts are: Criminal offenses against the integrity of Bosnia and Herzegovina: criminal offenses against humanity and values protected under international law and criminal offenses for which, pursuant to the law, a prison sentence of three (3) years or more may be pronounced.
1417 Art. 116(1)(3) BCPL.
1418 Art. 188(3) BCPL.
1419 Art. 118(1) BCPL.
1420 Art. 118(2) BCPL.
1421 Art. 118(2) BCPL.
1422 Art. 118(3) BCPL.
1423 Art. 119(1) BCPL.
1424 Art. 119(2) BCPL.
1425 Art. 119(4) BCPL.
1426 Art. 120 BCPL.
1427 Art. 121 BCPL.

2 Redress

Redress options are available to individuals who are subject to investigative and surveillance measures in BiH. In cases of investigative measures, individuals can appeal to the panel of the court's criminal division consisting of three judges under Art. 69 BCPL. In regard to Surveillance Measures, if the measures were undertaken without sufficient grounds for criminal prosecution, the person against whom they were taken shall be notified and can request a review of the legality of the order and its enforcement.[1428]

Further, individuals have the rights under the data protection legislation (BDPL 2006) as explained in Chapter 4.[1429] More importantly, individuals have the right to file a complaint to the data protection authority and demand that the controller or processor refrains from such actions and corrects the factual situation caused by those actions or demand corrections and deletion of data.[1430] Also, individuals have the right to file a complaint to the Ombudsman of BiH independently of their nationality or citizenship.[1431] Finally, the right to file an constitutional appeal is guaranteed by the Rules of the Constitutional Court of BiH[1432] in case of serious violations of rights and fundamental freedoms protected by the BiH Constitution or international conventions applied in BiH.[1433]

3 Oversight

Oversight of criminal enforcement authorities is complex in BiH, as they are divided between cantons. The oversight of the criminal enforcement authorities on the federation level is provided by special committees of the Parliament, including the Independent committee and the Committee for Citizen Complaints on the Work of Police Officers.[1434] Further, there are other institutions[1435] which monitor the

1428 119(2)(3) BCPL.

1429 Chapter 4, B.II.9.

1430 Art. 30 BDPL 2006.

1431 Art. 18 Law on Human Rights Ombudsman of BiH (Official Gazette of Bosnia and Herzegovina, no. 19/2002, 35/2004, 32/2006, 38/2006 – amended and 50/2008 – other laws).

1432 Art. 21(2)(4) Rules of the Constitutional Court of BiH.

1433 Art. 18 Rules of the Constitutional Court of BiH.

1434 The work of both committees is regulated by the Law on Independent and Supervisory Bodies of the Police Structure of Bosnia and Herzegovina (Official Gazette of Bosnia and Herzegovina, no. 36/08).

1435 For more information on the external controller of law enforcement agencies, see Alma Kovačević, Hamza Visca, "Evaluation Integrity Police in Bosnia and Herzegovina", Beogradski centar za bezbednosnu politiku, (2015), available at the following link <http://css.ba/wp-content/uploads/2011/06/Assessment-of-police-integrity-in-Bosnia-and-Herzegovina-BHS-web.pdf> (accessed on 03.04.2023).

work of the enforcement bodies, but most importantly, the BA (supervisory authority[1436] and Ombudsman.[1437]

II National Security Purposes

The primary intelligence agency of (BiH is the Intelligence-Security Agency of BiH (hereinafter: “ISA”), commonly referred to as OSA-OBA BiH.[1438] The establishment of ISA was authorised by the Law on the Intelligence and Security Agency of Bosnia and Herzegovina in March 2004 (hereinafter: “LISA”), which merged the prior entity intelligence services into one comprehensive intelligence service.[1439] The consolidation of the intelligence services was a critical requirement for the initiation of negotiations between BiH and the EU in connection with the conclusion of the SAA.[1440] A fundamental aspect of the reform was the creation of a single intelligence institution that possessed jurisdiction over the entire BiH entity in order to better control the work of the intelligence sector.[1441] Beyond this, it is noteworthy that the BiH Constitution safeguards human rights to “all individuals on the BiH territory” without any reservations to nationality.[1442]

As per the LISA, the ISA has the primary responsibility of collecting intelligence relating to security threats to BiH. Additionally, the ISA is tasked with collecting, analysing, and disseminating intelligence for the purpose of providing assistance to authorised officials, as defined by the BCPL, and other competent bodies in BiH, when necessary to prevent threats to the security of BiH. In the pursuit of its authorised activities, the ISA is entitled to collect information from other bodies and institutions in BiH and through electronic surveillance, including from telecommunication service providers.[1443]

1436 Already discussed in Chapter 4, B.III.
1437 Art. 25 Law on Human Rights Ombudsman of BiH.
1438 Official website of the OSA-OBA-BIH available at the following link <https://www.osa-oba.gov.ba/pnadze.html> (accessed on 12.02.2023).
1439 Official Gazette of BiH, No. 12/04, available at the following link <https://www.osa-oba.gov.ba/norme.html> (accessed on 12.02.2023).
1440 Bob de Graaf and James M. Nyce with Chelsea Locke, “The Handbook of European Intelligence Cultures”, the Rowman & Littlefield Publishing group, Inc, 2016, p. 49.
1441 Speech by Deputy Head of the Rule of Law Pillar Bill Potter at the seminar “Draft Law on the Intelligence and Security Agency”, available at the following link <http://www.ohr.int/speech-by-deputy-head-of-the-rule-of-law-pillar-bill-potter-at-the-seminar-draft-law-on-the-intelligence-and-security-agency/?print=pdf> (accessed on 12.02.2023).
1442 Art. 3 BiH Constitution.
1443 Artt. 74, 77 LISA.

1 Rules for Authorising Interception Measures

The rules governing the authorisation and limitations of electronic surveillance stipulate that such surveillance may only be utilised following prior authorisation by the president of the court or a designated judge.[1444] The LISA provides detailed rules for obtaining authorisation[1445] and the content of the warrant.[1446] However, the duration of the warrant has been the subject of controversy. The LISA originally allowed for a maximum period of sixty days. Since its adoption, the LISA was amended several times, allowing in justified cases, that the judge may extend the validity of the warrant for additional periods of 30 days if convinced that the order is still needed.[1447] However, the Constitutional court found this provision unconstitutional and relayed on the ECtHR practice (Art. 8), as it did not ensure that surveillance measures would not be introduced accidentally or without proper consideration.[1448] Subsequently, the LISA has to be amended again. The new amendment proposal was to allow for a maximum period of 48 months, which could be repeated. However, this proposal was met with criticism from the BA,

1444 Art. 77(1) LISA.

1445 According to Art. 77(3) LISA, the Director-General shall make a written application to the judge, which must include the following: 1) The type of communication for which it is proposed to use eavesdropping measures, the type of information, records, documents or things that are proposed to be collected, and the means that will be used for that purpose; 2) The name of the person or persons proposed as the subject of monitoring or search; 3) General description of the place or places proposed for monitoring or search, if it is possible to give a general description of such a place; 4) Information justifying the application of monitoring or search measures in order to enable the Agency to conduct an investigation into the threat to the security of Bosnia and Herzegovina; 5) Statement that the requested information cannot be collected in the required time period in any other way; 6) The period not exceeding 60 days for which the validity of the order is requested; 7) Information on all previous requests that were submitted in connection with the person or place that is the subject of monitoring or search, the date when the request was submitted, the name of the judge to whom it was addressed and the judge's decision on the request.

1446 According to Art. 78(1) LISA The warrant must contain: a) the type of communication that is intended to be intercepted, the type of information, records, documents or things that must be collected, and the powers that will be applied for these purposes; b) names of the person or persons for whose monitoring the order was issued; c) a general description of the place or places where the order should be executed if such a description can be given; and d) validity period of the order.

1447 Art. 78(3), this version of LISA available at the following link <https://www.paragraf.ba/propisi/bih/zakon-o-obavjestajno-bezbjednosnoj-agenciji-bosne-i-hercegovine.html> (accessed on 12.03.2023).

1448 The BiH Constitutional Court, decision no. U-21/16, date 01.06.2017, Official Gazette of BiH 43/17, 16.06.201.

which found it to be imprecise and lacking in proportionality.[1449] The BA noted that such a long and radical intrusion into the privacy of individuals is difficult to explain in the light of the concrete threats to the security of BiH, where it is difficult to make a professional and argumentative case for the thesis that a serious threat can last for eight years without being eliminated.[1450] Consequently, the proposal was not adopted,[1451] and currently, the duration of surveillance measures may last up to 60 days.

Furthermore, the BiH Law on Communication (hereinafter: "BLC") requires all telecommunication service providers to ensure maintenance of the function of legal interception of telecommunications.[1452] However, the detailed rules on interception of telecommunications and the obligations of the service providers to provide the access to personal data is not regulated by the BLC. Instead, the Council of Ministers, at the proposal of the Ministry of Security, is tasked with defining these rules.[1453] This solution has been criticised by the BA, stating that it represents a threat to the protection of personal data and is therefore unacceptable, as limitations on human rights shall be limited only by the law.[1454] Further, in its activity reports, the BiH Data Protection Agency has also noted that this is not in line with the EU acquis, and particularly the ePrivacy Directive 2009/136/EC.[1455]

Apart from the BLC, BiH does not have a law which regulates electronic communication and media. The EU has acknowledged the need for BiH to develop and adopt laws on electronic communications and electronic media, as well as on elec-

1449 Annual Report 2020, pp. 41–42 (n. 336).

1450 *Ibid.*

1451 Information available from the website of BiH Parliament, see available in Bosnian at the following link <https://parlament.ba/olaw/OLawDetails?lawId=61312> (accessed 04.03.2023).

1452 Art. 3 Law on Communication from 2003 and last time amended in 2012 (BLC) available in Bosnian at the following link <http://legalist.ba/wp-content/uploads/2014/02/Zakon-o-komunikacijama-BiH-nesluzbeni-precisceni-tekst.pdf> (accessed on 04.03.2023).

1453 *Ibid.*

1454 Interview with the former Director, Petar Kovačević, of the Agency for the Protection of Personal Data of Bosnia and Herzegovina "Izgleda da nikoga u BiH ne zanima nezakonito prisluškivanje!" (Eng. It seems that nobody in BiH is interested in illegal wiretapping!) Dnevni Nalaz, (2014), available at the following link <https://avaz.ba/vijesti/127943/izgleda-da-nikoga-u-bih-ne-zanima-nezakonito-prisluskivanje> (accessed on 12.03.2023).

1455 Report on data protection for 2014, no. 01–37–6–585–1/14, (09.06.2014) pp. 3–5, available in Bosnian at the following link <http://www.azlp.ba/publikacije/Archive.aspx?langTag=bs-BA&template_id=149&pageIndex=1> (accessed on 12.03.2023).

tronic identity and trust services in line with the EU acquis, as outlined in its report for 2021.[1456]

2 Limits and Safeguards

The ISA is bound by various limitations that dictate the scope and nature of its activities, as per LISA. The ISA must operate in accordance with the provisions of the Constitution and laws of BiH, including the provisions of the ECHR and its protocols, as well as international treaties and agreements signed or acceded to by BiH.[1457] The ISA can only collect information as can reasonably be assumed to be necessary for the performance of its duties.[1458] Further, in carrying out surveillance, the ISA shall use the least intrusive techniques reasonably available.[1459] The LISA also provides the limitation regarding in which situations the surveillance might be allowed, meaning that the ISA may engage in surveillance only in situations where it is necessary to prevent threats to the security of the country, such as terrorism, espionage, and acts punishable under international humanitarian law.[1460]

The LISA stipulates the obligation to terminate the secret surveillance immediately if the objective set forth in the warrant has been achieved, if no further results can be expected, if the deadline has expired without extension, or if the covert information gathering is unlawful for any reason.[1461] Further, the data obtained in a manner inconsistent with the LISA must be immediately destroyed.[1462]

Moreover, as defined by LISA, the ISA must operate in an apolitical manner, free from involvement in political activities or the furthering, protecting, or undermining of the interests of any political party or organisation.[1463] The employees of ISA cannot be members of the political parties, nor shall they take instructions from political parties or perform any remunerative activity or other public or professional duties incompatible with work in the ISA.[1464] These limitations shall ensure that the ISA operates within legal and ethical boundaries, protecting

1456 The EU Commission Report for BiH 2021, SWD(2021) 291 final /2 (19.10.202), available at the following link <https://neighbourhoodenlargement.ec.europa.eu/system/files/202110/Bosnia%20and%20Herzegovina%202021%20report.PDF> (accessed on 03.02.2023).

1457 Art. 2 LISA.

1458 Art. 73 LISA.

1459 Art. 77(7) LISA.

1460 Art. 5 LISA.

1461 Art. 79 LISA.

1462 Art. 79 LISA.

1463 Art. 62 LISA.

1464 Artt. 36(1)(c), 45 LISA.

also the rights and privacy of individuals while fulfilling its duties to prevent threats to the security of BiH.

The ISA is authorised to collect, analyse, keep and disseminate intelligence information in compliance with the Constitution of BiH, the LISA, and other relevant national legislation. However, the BDPL 2006 does not apply to personal data collected and processed by the ISA.[1465] This sets BiH apart from other WB6 countries.[1466] Also, looking at the comparative law, it seems that authorities responsible for security are obliged to respect data protection laws, including countries which obtained an adequacy decision.[1467]

Nonetheless, the BA is authorised to supervise the work of telecommunication service providers and the lawful interception of data for criminal law enforcement purposes. The BA has in its practice performed such inspections to ensure that telecommunication service providers respect data subjects' rights and freedoms when cooperating with police authorities.[1468] Yet, BA's inspections are limited to cases where telecommunication service providers cooperate with the ISA.

Nevertheless, the LISA provides its own provisions related to personal data protection. The LISA defines the principle of personal data protection, including purpose limitation, accuracy, storage limitation, data minimisation and the disseminated of information on a 'need-to-know' basis only as provided for by the LISA.[1469] Furthermore, the LISA prohibits the collection of information on individuals based solely on their ethnic or racial origin, religious convictions, sexual behaviour, political opinions, or membership in particular movements or organisations not prescribed by law.[1470]

Moreover, the LISA provides several safeguards for personal data and privacy. These include the implementation of appropriate security measures to protect in-

---

1465 Art. 81 LISA.

1466 In all other WB6 general data protection law applies to security sector, yet with certain limitation where not all obligations applicable for data controllers apply to them, e.g. obligations related to information and access to personal data.

1467 For instance, in Germany according to the Art. 3(1) Law on the Federal Intelligence Service (BNDG) intelligence service may process the necessary information, including personal data, unless the applicable provisions of the Federal Data Protection Act or special regulations in the law conflict therewith. Moreover, in other adequacy decisions adopted by the EU Commission there were no such restrictions found (e.g., Japan adequacy decision, para 118, South Korea Adequacy decision para 147, UK Adequacy Decision para 121).

1468 BA's Annual Report on Data Protection for 2013 no. 01–37–6–585–1/14, p. 3, available in Bosnian at the following link <http://www.azlp.ba/publikacije/default.aspx?id=936&langTag=bs-BA> (accessed on 01.03.2023).

1469 Artt. 82, 85 LISA.

1470 Art. 83 LISA.

telligence information related to identifiable persons stored in automated data files, as well as limitations on disclosure of collected information classified as confidential or secret.[1471] Disclosure is only authorised if expressly foreseen by law or if one of several conditions is fulfilled.[1472] For example, disclosure may be necessary in the vital interest of the person concerned or because of overriding public interests that fall under the responsibilities of the ISA.[1473] More importantly, the ISA is required to inform citizens, upon their written request, whether data collection measures have been instituted against them and whether there is a record of their personal data.[1474] The ISA must also make such records available to citizens upon their request. The ISA must provide the required information within 60 days of receiving the access request, except when such information would jeopardize the ISA's tasks or endanger the safety of a source or another person.[1475] Individuals may appeal against a decision that rejects access requests in accordance with the Law on Freedom of Access to Information.[1476]

3 Redress

The LISA contains certain provisions on redress mechanisms, including the right to be informed of the completion of surveillance or interception measures, the right to obtain information on whether such measures have been carried out and the right to judicial redress.

Firstly, the LISA stipulates that a BiH citizen who was a subject to surveillance or interception should be, after the termination of surveillance or interception, informed on the applied measures within 30 days at the latest upon the termination of the procedure. However, there is no rule on other citizens (foreigners). Secondly, under Art. 68 LISA any individual who feels that their rights have been violated by acts or omissions of the ISA can seek judicial redress before a competent court, without any reference to BiH citizenship, implying that foreigners also have this right.[1477] Thirdly, according to the Art. 68 (2) LISA "any person in Bosnia and Herzegovina" may raise a complaint with the Director-General regarding actions of the ISA.

1471 Art. 84 LISA.
1472 Art. 84 LISA.
1473 Art. 87 LISA.
1474 Art. 91 LISA.
1475 Art. 91(2) LISA.
1476 Art. 91(4) LISA.
1477 Art. 68 LISA.

More importantly, any individual may request obtaining information whether they were subject to surveillance measures.[1478] If such request is refused, they have the right to an appeal against a rejection decision in accordance with the Law on Freedom of Access to Information.[1479] Finally, there is a redress mechanism facilitated by the Ombudsman and the BA.[1480]

4 Oversight

The LISA establishes a detailed framework for external oversight of the ISA. The ISA is externally supervised by several institutions, including the Presidency, Council of Ministers, Parliament and courts. The Chair of the Council of Ministers has a significant role in overseeing the ISA's work and coordinating its activities, which includes ensuring its lawful performance, providing an annual briefing on ISA activities to the Presidency and Parliament, reviewing and approving all requests for intelligence support, and bearing political responsibility for the ISA's work.[1481] Parliamentary supervision is embodied in the Joint Security and Intelligence Commission for the Oversight of the ISA, which requires the House of Representatives and the House of Peoples to jointly establish the Security and Intelligence Oversight Commission.[1482] The LISA also defines the control role of judicial bodies in several articles.[1483] Thus, the courts have a dual role: they are part of the security system insofar they authorise the surveillance measures and at the same time they have the oversight control.

Despite the detailed framework, the external oversight of the ISA has faced criticism for being ineffective in practice. In particular, control by Parliament and the Council of Ministers is lacking.[1484] Judicial oversight by the Public Prosecutor's Office has not been successful either, as investigations have generally not resulted in any judicial follow-up in terms of sanctions for acts for which the Public Prosecutor's Office is responsible.[1485] The EU Commission has also noted that

1478 Art. 68 LISA.
1479 Art. 91(2) LISA.
1480 Chapter 5, B.I.3.
1481 Artt. 9–10 LISA.
1482 Art. 18 LISA.
1483 Artt. 77–78, 80 LISA.
1484 Predrag Ćeranić, Duško Baškalo, "The question of control of the civilian intelligence service in Bosnia and Herzegovina, University of Banja Luka, Faculty of Security Sciences", Journal of Security and Criminalistics 2021, vol. 3, no. 2, p. 23–33.
1485 *Ibid.*

the professionalism and accountability of law enforcement agencies needs to be significantly improved.[1486]

III Conclusion to D

The legal framework in BiH governing the interception of personal data by public authorities for criminal law enforcement and national security purposes incorporates several limitations and safeguards. While the overall legal framework enabling access to personal data for criminal law enforcement purposes establishes a robust system for restricting such measures, the specific legal framework governing access to personal data for enforcement purposes raises concerns. The LISA was amended several times with the aim to extend the duration of warrants for the implementation of interception measures. These amendments have led the BA, the supervisory authority, to express serious concerns about the restrictions on individuals' privacy.[1487] This raises further concerns about the adequacy of limitations on authorities' access to personal data for national security purposes. The EU Commission has already expressed its concerns and highlighted the need to ensure better accountability of the law enforcement sector.[1488]

E Kosovo

In Kosovo, access to personal data is granted to authorities for both law enforcement and national security purposes. The applicable legislation outlines several limitations and includes oversight and redress mechanisms. While Kosovo is not yet a member of the CoE, its Constitution includes provisions for the direct application of international human rights conventions and instruments, such as the UDHR and the ECHR and its protocols.[1489] More importantly, the Constitution establishes a rule that limits on rights and freedoms may only be imposed by law and only to the extent necessary to achieve the aim for which the limitation is permitted in an open and democratic society.[1490] In cases of limitations of human rights and freedoms, public authorities and the courts must take into account various factors, including the importance of the aim pursued, the nature of the re-

1486 EU Commission Report for BiH 2022, SWD(2022) 336 final (12.10.2022), p. 38.
1487 Chapter 5, C.II.1.
1488 EU Commission Report BiH, p. 38 (n. 1486).
1489 Art. 22 Constitution of Kosovo. See also Chapter 4.C.I.
1490 Art. 55(1)(2) Constitution of Kosovo.

striction and its relationship to the aim sought, and the possibility of attaining the aim through less restrictive means.[1491] These provisions underscore the commitment of Kosovo to uphold human rights and freedoms in its legal framework.

I Criminal Law Enforcement Purposes

In Kosovo, significant changes have been made to criminal procedural rules in recent years, with the introduction of the Criminal Procedure Core of Kosovo (hereinafter: "KCPC") in 2013.[1492] The KCPC introduced a shift from the primarily inquisitorial system in place until 2013 to a system principally characterised as an adversarial one.

The KCPC recognises several measures which may interfere with the privacy of individuals, which, inter alia, include, 1) covert monitoring of conversations, interception of telecommunications and use of an international mobile service identification 'IMSI Catcher'[1493] and 2) interception of communications by a computer network (together: "Surveillance Measures").[1494] While the KCPC does not provide further specifications on the mentioned terms, it does define the term 'interception of telecommunications' which under the Art. 87(1)(5) means the interception of voice communications, text communications or other communications through fix or mobile telephone networks, including any similar technological device or system that carries information that is normally intended to be private.

Besides the KCPC, the Law on Interception of Electronic Communications (hereinafter: "KIEC")[1495] regulates the interception of electronic communications for both criminal enforcement and national security purposes.[1496] Prior to the adoption of the KIEC in 2015, there was a lack of standard definition and safeguards for interception of telecommunications, which created confusion and uncertainty in this area.[1497] The adoption of the KIEC represents an important step towards greater transparency and stronger protections for electronic communications in Kosovo.

1491 Art. 55(4) Constitution of Kosovo.
1492 KCPC (Criminal Procedure Law no. 04/L-123).
1493 Art. 87(1)(1.4.) KCPC.
1494 Art. 87(1)(1.5) KCPC.
1495 KIEC (Law on Interception of Electronic Communications no. 05/030).
1496 Art. 1(1) KIEC.
1497 Criminal Code no 06/L-074 of Kosovo. See also Shpend Kursani, "Lawful Interception of Telecommunications in Kosovo: Security Implications", Kosovar Centre for Security Studies (27.10.2011).

1 Rules for Authorising and Limiting Interception Measures

The authorisation and use of interception measures for criminal law enforcement purposes are regulated by the KCPC. The KCPC outlines the circumstances under which the Surveillance Measures, such as 'covert monitoring of conversations' and 'interception of telecommunications', may be ordered. The Surveillance Measures are only allowed if there is reasonable suspicion that they will provide crucial evidence that cannot be obtained by other investigative means without unreasonable difficulty or potential danger to others and only for certain suspected criminal offences defined by the Art. 90 Criminal Code.[1498]

The Surveillance Measures must be authorised, by eighter the state prosecutor or a judge. They are generally issued by a pre-trial judge on the basis of an application by a state prosecutor.[1499] The state prosecutor may also issue a provisional warrant only in special cases, e. g. in emergency criminal cases.[1500] In the event that the state prosecutor issue provisional warrants, they shall cease to have effect if not confirmed in writing by a pre-trial judge within three days of issuance.[1501] When confirming the provisional order of a state prosecutor, the pre-trial judge shall make a written determination as to its lawfulness ex officio.[1502]

The KCPC also provides the detailed provision on the content of a warrant.[1503] There is a general rule that the ordered Surveillance Measures shall not exceed sixty days.[1504] However, exceptions are made for covert monitoring of conversations[1505] and interception of communications by a computer network, which can be extended for up to 360 days.[1506]

In terms of storage limitations, Art. 85 KCPC defines that a file on data collected through Surveillance Measures must be sealed for no longer than twelve months, or until the initiation of the investigative stage, at which point the court registrar must unseal the file. Exceptions may be made for an additional six months, but only if authorised by a pre-trial judge, if public knowledge of the preliminary investigation could interfere with the investigation or pose a dan-

1498 Such criminal offences induce serios crimes e. g. sabotage, espionage, terrorism, humanity and war crimes, torture etc., but also some other crimes related to election rights, like violation of the right to be a candidate, threat to the candidate, abuse of official duty during elections, falsification of voting results and fraud and tax related crimes.

1499 Art. 91(2) KCPC.

1500 Art. 91(1) KCPC.

1501 *Ibid.*

1502 *Ibid.*

1503 Art. 92 KCPC.

1504 Art. 92 KCPC.

1505 Covert monitoring is only one part of measure defined by Art. 87(1)(1.4.) KCPC.

1506 Art. 94(2) KCPC.

ger to witnesses or investigators.[1507] Also, personal data which was collected by means of Surveillance Measures need to be labelled accordingly.[1508]

2 Redress

Regarding redress for data processing by law enforcement authorities, a number of legal remedies are available, including the ones guaranteed by the KCPC (which also includes the right to compensation), KDPL 2019 (data protection law), the law on the Ombudsperson, and the Constitution.

Firstly, the KCPC provides that the individuals who were targeted or significantly affected by Surveillance Measures shall be notified as soon as possible according to the Art. 96(5) KCPC. If the person is not notified withing twelve months after the completion of the Surveillance Measure, any further deferral of notification shall be subject to the approval of the court.[1509] Individuals who believe they have been unlawfully targeted may submit a complaint to the President of the Basic Court, who may appoint a Surveillance and Investigation Review Panel (hereinafter: "SIR Panel") for adjudication.[1510] The individuals also have the right to compensation in case the SIR Panel finds that a Surveillance Measure was unlawful.[1511] Secondly, the individuals have the rights under the applicable data protection legislation.[1512] Thirdly, the individuals have the right to initiate the procedure before the Ombudsman of Kosovo in case they believe that their rights and freedoms are violated by any law, action or inaction or maladministration of authorities.[1513] Finally, the Constitution of Kosovo provides by Art. 54 guarantees everyone the right to judicial protection of rights, including the right to effective legal remedy in the event of a violation.

3 Oversight

In terms of oversight, various bodies are performing oversight of criminal law enforcement, including the government via the Ministry of Internal Affairs, Parliament and other institutions, such as the data protection authority and Ombudsperson. Parliament is responsible for controlling the government and

1507 Art. 85(4) KCPC.
1508 Art. 96(3) KCPC.
1509 Art. 96(6) KCPC.
1510 Art. 98(5) KCPC.
1511 Art. 98(1) KCPC.
1512 Chapter 4, C.II.13.
1513 Art. 19 Law on Ombudsperson, no 05/L-019.

enforcement authorities and fostering good cooperation.[1514] The Ombudsperson is also empowered to investigate any violation of human rights committed by state authorities, as provided for by the Constitution, laws and other legal acts, as well as international human rights instruments, in particular the ECHR.[1515] Further, the data protection authority has the right to supervise the activities of the enforcement authorities, in line with the KDPL 2019.[1516]

Last, but not least, oversight is also provided by chapter 5 KIEC. The KIEC introduced the mechanism of Commissioner for Oversight of Interception of Communication (hereinafter: "COIC").[1517] The COIC is a mechanism functioning within the institutional structure of the Kosovo Judicial Council and conducts yearly control of the lawfulness of interception of communications over all the authorities (including the authorities for national security) authorised to intercept data. The COIC reports to the Kosovo Judicial Council and to the State Prosecutor and respective parliamentary Committees of the Parliament on annual basis on identified possible violations.[1518]

II National Security Purposes

In Kosovo, national security is safeguarded primarily by the Kosovo Intelligence Agency (hereinafter: "KIA"), established under the Law on the Kosovo Intelligence Agency (hereinafter: "LKIA").[1519] The KIA gathers information concerning threats to the security of Kosovo. A threat to the security of Kosovo is defined by Art. 2 LKIA and includes threats like terrorism and espionage. In order to carry out its mandate, the KIA is authorised to employ various measures, including, inter alia, 1) mobile and static surveillance, 2) technical surveillance, such as listening devices, interception and tracking and 3) gathering of confidential data, such as from banks, ports and telephone (all together: "Interception Measures").[1520]

1514 For more information on this topic see Florian Qehaja, "Strengthening Intelligence Governance in the Western Balkans: Kosovo", DCAF (31.12.2012).
1515 Art. 16 Law on Ombudsperson.
1516 Chapter 4, C.II.
1517 Art. 32 KIEC.
1518 Art. 32(2) KIEC.
1519 LKIA (Law on the Kosovo Intelligence Agency No. 03/L-063).
1520 Art. 2(2.2) LKIA.

1 Rules for Authorising Interception Measures

The legal framework for the authorisation and use of Interception Measures in Kosovo is set out in the LKIA and the KIEC. The LKIA provides that Interception measures may only be authorised by a Supreme Court Judge, based on a written application from the KIA that demonstrates a reasonable need for interception in furtherance of its investigative mandate.[1521] The authorisation must include specific details, such as the scope and duration of the interception (60 days) and a declaration that less intrusive techniques cannot reasonably achieve the same results.[1522] The use of Interception measures shall be immediately terminated if the objectives set forth in the judge's order are achieved or if no further results can be expected from its continued use.[1523] Exceptionally, in cases where there is insufficient time to prepare a request in writing, a Supreme Court Judge can authorise the Interception measures verbally, which needs to be confirmed in writing within 48 hours – the so-called "emergency warrant".[1524]

The KIA may also request the access to personal data held by a third party, whereas the third-party may comply with the requirements of the prescribed notice but is under no obligation to do so.[1525] On the other hand, business operators are obliged to provide the access to data if requested by KIA.[1526] In order to facilitate this, network operators are permitted to retain meta-data for a maximum period of nine calendar months, after which period data shall be deleted.[1527] Regarding the retention of intercepted data from the network operators, the KIEC provides that data shall be permanently destroyed by the director of the KIA within one calendar month after fulfilling the purpose of interception.[1528] In exceptional cases, the data may be stored for nine months.[1529]

2 Limits and Safeguards

As part of the safeguards set out in the LKIA, all KIA's activities must comply with the principles of legality, proportionality, and necessity.[1530] In addition to compliance with these principles, all KIA activities must be undertaken only in further-

1521 Art. 28.3 LKIA.
1522 Art. 28.4 LKIA.
1523 Art. 28.8 LKIA.
1524 Art. 29 LKIA.
1525 Art. 30 LKIA.
1526 Art. 19 KIEC.
1527 Art. 30 KIEC.
1528 Art. 29(2) KIEC.
1529 Art. 29(2) KIEC.
1530 Art. 23 LKIA.

ance of national security and comply with internationally recognised human rights instruments, including the ECHR.[1531] The techniques of interception must be designed to minimise collection, retention, and dissemination of irrelevant information.[1532]

The LKIA imposes a legal obligation on the KIA to safeguard personal data. Personal data collected through interception measures must be used only for specified and lawful purposes, and not in any way that is incompatible with those purposes.[1533] Furthermore, the KIA is only permitted to retain such data for as long as it is necessary to accomplish its tasks. Once the purpose for which the personal data was collected has been achieved, the KIA shall destroy it in accordance with its internal procedures.[1534]

In addition, the KIEC also provides for a number of limitations and safeguards. Firstly, it sets out the basic principles governing interception, including respect for human rights and fundamental freedoms (under the Constitution and the ECHR) and the prohibition of interception without a court order.[1535] Moreover, when taking the decision on interception, the competent court is obliged to take into account, in particular, the essence of rights and freedoms, the principle of proportionality and necessity, the extent of interception, the relationship between the aim to be achieved and the possibility of achieving it through employing other investigative methods, as well as secrecy and objectivity in the process of interception.[1536] Further, KIEC defines the specific obligations and responsibilities of the public institutions authorised to order Interception measures to network operators, which include the obligation of retention and destruction of data,[1537] security measures[1538] and principle of confidentiality.[1539] Moreover, it stipulates various obligations of network operators regarding the handling of intercepted data.[1540]

However, despite the comprehensive legal framework provided by the KIEC, concerns have been raised about the actual enforcement of the limitations and safeguards imposed. Some organisations have expressed concerns, "that human rights are routinely violated when it comes to surveillance of persons suspected

1531 Art. 2(5) LKIA.
1532 Art. 28.5 LKIA.
1533 Art. 31 LKIA.
1534 Art. 31 LKIA.
1535 Art. 4 KIEC.
1536 Art. 4 KIEC.
1537 Artt. 26–20 KIEC.
1538 Artt. 21, 25 KIEC.
1539 Art. 20 KIEC.
1540 Art. 30 KIEC.

of being a national security threat, or of committing terrorism, for example – especially if no cases has been initiated by the prosecution, or the suspect has been acquitted by the court" [*sic*].[1541] This highlights challenges about the effective enforcement of the limitations envisaged by the KIEC and requires further attention.

3 Redress

In terms of redress, individuals have the right of complaint against the KIA to the Ombudsperson.[1542] However, any complaint submitted to the Ombudsperson shall not prejudice the right of an individual, institution or third party to seek adjudication from a court.[1543] Additionally, the LKIA stipulates that the Government of Kosovo is liable for damages incurred on individuals or legal entities resulting from Interception measures.[1544] Lastly, the individuals have redress rights under the KDPL 2019 and the Constitution, as explained above in part regarding law enforcement purposes.

4 Oversight

The LKIA outlines the scope of oversight over the KIA, which includes only parliamentary and judicial oversight. If the KIA is suspected of acting unlawfully, inappropriately, or unprofessionally, Parliament may conduct an inquiry to question KIA employees and review relevant documents.[1545] Judicial oversight is ensured through individuals' right to file complaints against the KIA before competent courts in Kosovo.[1546] Furthermore, the data protection authority has the power to oversee the KIA and network operators.

Oversight mechanism is also provided through the institution of the COIC, within the institutional structure of the Kosovo Judicial Council, as mentioned above in part focusing on criminal law enforcement purposes. As part of the monitoring, network operators are required to provide not only to the data protection

---

1541 Xhorxhina Bami, "Kosovo Surveillance Build-up Raises Privacy Concerns", BIRN (31.12.2021), <https://balkaninsight.com/2021/12/31/kosovo-surveillance-build-up-raises-privacy-concerns/> (accessed on 21.05.2023).
1542 Art. 39 LKIA.
1543 Art. 39 LKIA.
1544 Art. 3(3.3) LKIA.
1545 Art. 31 LKIA.
1546 Art. 39.3 LKIA.

authority, but also the COIC with reports on the quantity and type of interception data that they have destroyed on a six-monthly basis.[1547]

III Conclusion to E

The legal framework in Kosovo governing the interception of personal data by public authorities for criminal law enforcement and national security purposes incorporates a range of limitations and safeguards. The primary legislation, KIEC, establishes fundamental principles that emphasise the protection of human rights and fundamental freedoms as enshrined in the Constitution and the ECHR (although applied unitarily as explained in Chapter 4). Notably, the KIEC strictly prohibits interception without a court order, ensuring a necessary legal basis for such actions. Furthermore, the KIEC delineates the specific obligations and responsibilities of authorised public institutions in relation to network operators with regards to interception measures. These obligations encompass data retention and destruction, implementation of security measures, and adherence to the principle of confidentiality.

Moreover, the legal framework in Kosovo encompasses a comprehensive redress mechanism. Individuals affected by Surveillance Measures have recourse to the rights granted by data protection legislation, including the right to seek compensation in cases of unlawful surveillance. Additionally, individuals possess the right to initiate proceedings before the Ombudsman of Kosovo. Lastly, the Constitution of Kosovo, specifically through Art. 54, guarantees everyone the right to judicial protection of their rights, ensuring access to effective legal remedies in the event of violations.

However, despite this comprehensive legal framework, there are concerns about the practical enforcement of these restrictions. It appears that the envisaged safeguards are not always respected in case of communication interception measures. It is therefore important to address these challenges in order to ensure effective protection of individual rights and to maintain the integrity of interception operations.

1547 Art. 30(4) LKIA.

F Montenegro

The access to personal data by public authorities for the purpose of criminal law enforcement and national security is subject to regulation under various legal frameworks. While these laws do provide a degree of limitation and safeguards, there exist certain deficiencies and controversies, as explained below. Some important safeguards are also provided by the Constitution of Montenegro. The Constitution of Montenegro stipulates that human rights and freedoms may only be restricted in a manner that is permissible under the Constitution or national law and necessary to achieve a lawful objective in a democratic society.[1548] Moreover, Art. 43(3) Constitution guarantees individuals the right to access and review their collected personal data, as well as the right to seek judicial redress in the event of abuse. The Criminal code of Montenegro (hereinafter: "MCC") also criminalises unauthorised wiretapping and recording[1549] and unauthorised collection and use of personal data.[1550]

I Criminal Law Enforcement Purposes

Access and utilisation of personal data by Montenegro public authorities for criminal law enforcement purposes is based on the Criminal Procedure Code of Montenegro (hereinafter: "MCPC"), which defines the secret surveillance measures, including secret surveillance and recording of telephone conversations and other remote communications[1551] and interception, collection and recording of computer data[1552] (together "Surveillance Measures"). Surveillance Measures may only be ordered in specific cases involving serious criminal acts as defined by Art. 158 MCPC.[1553] Postal and other communication companies registered for the transmis-

1548 Art. 24 Constitution of Montenegro.
1549 Art. 173 MCC.
1550 Art. 176 MCC.
1551 Art. 157(1)(2) MCPC.
1552 Art. 157(1)(2) MCPC.
1553 Interception measures may be ordered for criminal acts: 1) for which a prison sentence of ten years or a heavier sentence may be imposed; 2) with elements of organized crime; 3) causing false bankruptcy, abuse of assessment, accepting bribes, giving bribes, illegal influence, abuse of official position, as well as abuse of authority in the economy and fraud in the service for which a prison sentence of eight years or a heavier sentence is prescribed; 4) kidnapping, extortion, blackmail, intermediation in the performance of prostitution, showing pornographic material, bribery, evasion of taxes and contributions, smuggling, illegal processing, disposal and storage of dangerous substances, attack on an official in the performance of official duties, prevention of

sion of information are obligated under the MCPC and Law on Electronic Communications (hereinafter: "MLEC") to enable authorised police officers to carry out interception measures.[1554]

1 Rules for Authorising and Limiting Interception Measures

Rules for the authorisation of Surveillance Measures and limitations are established by the MCPC. Only a written order by an investigating judge based on a reasoned proposal by a public prosecutor may authorise a Surveillance Measure. The MCPC defines the information that must be included in the authorisation decision and the prosecutor's proposal.[1555] Exceptionally, if the written order cannot be issued on time, and there is a risk of delay, the Surveillance Measures may be initiated based on the oral order of the investigating judge or the state prosecutor. In that case, the written order must be obtained within twelve hours of issuing the verbal order.[1556] The Surveillance Measures may last up to four months.[1557] For justified reasons, the measures can be extended against the same person and for the same criminal offense for a maximum of 18 months.[1558] The MCPC also provides the rules on handling with the intercepted data, i. e. the special protection measures and rules on retention and deletion of data.[1559] Lastly, the MLEC provides additional safeguards, which is explained in the next part II.

2 Redress

Individuals subject to surveillance must be informed that a measure has been taken against them. Prior to the destruction of the material obtained as a result of Surveillance Measures, the investigating judge shall inform the person con-

evidence, criminal association, disclosure of secret information, violation of procedural secrecy, money laundering, forgery of money, forgery of documents, forgery of official documents, making, procuring and giving to others means and materials for forgery, participation in foreign armed formations, fixing the outcome of competitions, illegal possession of weapons and explosive materials, illegal crossing of the state border and people smuggling; 5) against the security of computer data.

1554 Art. 159(9) MCPC.

1555 Under Art. 159 MCPC the decision on the authorization of the interception must include: type of measure, information about the person against whom the measure is being implemented, if that person is known, reasons for suspicion, method of execution of the measure, its goal, scope and duration.

1556 Art. 159(3) MCPC.

1557 Art. 159(4) MCPC.

1558 Art. 159(4) MCPC.

1559 Artt. 159(10), 160(7) MCPC.

cerned and allow them to inspect the material collected.[1560] However, the judge may decide not to inform the person against whom the measure was taken only if there is a well-founded fear that notifying the person referred or viewing the obtained material could represent a serious danger to the life and health of people or could endanger one of the ongoing investigations or for other justified reasons.[1561]

Moreover, individuals have the right to complaints envisaged by the MDPL 2008 (data protection law)[1562] and Law on the Ombudsperson of Human Rights and Freedoms.[1563] Finally, the Constitution of Montenegro defines the right to legal remedy to any individual against a decision that determines their rights or interests based on law.[1564]

3 Oversight

The external supervision of law enforcement authorities is exercised by the Parliament, according to the Law on Parliamentary Oversight in the Field of Security and Defence.[1565] Parliamentary oversight is performed directly by the Parliament and through the Committee on Security and Defence.[1566] In addition to parliamentary oversight, there are other bodies that exercise oversight over the work of law enforcement agencies. The Ombudsperson for Human Rights and Freedoms has the power to investigate complaints related to human rights violations by state authorities, including law enforcement bodies. The Agency oversees the implementation of MDPL 2008, including those related to the handling of personal data by law enforcement bodies. Finally, the judiciary also plays an important role in oversight of law enforcement bodies. In particular, the investigating judge who authorises Surveillance Measures must ensure that the measures are justified, and that they are conducted in accordance with the law. The judiciary also exercises its oversight via the available legal remedies.

1560 Art. 162(1) MCPC.

1561 Art. 162(2) MCPC.

1562 Art. 2 Law on Parliamentary Oversight in the Field of Security and Defence (Official Gazette of Montenegro, no. 80/10).

1563 Art. 28 Law on the Ombudsperson of Human Rights and Freedoms (12.01.2012).

1564 Art. 20 Constitution of Montenegro.

1565 Law on Parliamentary Oversight in the Field of Security and Defence, no. 01–2653/2 (27.12.2010).

1566 Art. 2 Law on Parliamentary Oversight in the Field of Security and Defence.

II National Security Purposes

Access and use by Montenegrin public authorities for national security purposes is based on the Law on the National Security Agency in Montenegro (hereinafter: "LMNSA")[1567] and MLEC. The MLEC requires operators to enable the interception of communications for national security purposes by providing the necessary technical and organisational conditions.[1568] The National Security Agency in Montenegro (hereinafter: "MNSA") is the authority with intelligence and security powers for protection of national security.

1 Rules for Authorising Interception Measures

In 2015 Montenegro adopted new amendments to the LMNSA,[1569] which has been subject to criticism due to the broad powers given to the MNSA in terms of access to personal data.[1570] Under the amended LMNSA, there are two modalities by which the MNSA can have access to personal data. The first involves mandatory cooperation with public institutions and businesses, and the second involves covert interception. The first modality does not require a judicial authorisation, and the MNSA can access all databases in Montenegro by presenting their official identification cards.[1571] According to Art. 8 LMNSA, not only the state institutions, but also all legal entities in Montenegro that keep registers of data collection are obliged to provide access to data. However, the MNSA may access data electronically only on the basis of a written agreement concluded with the responsible person in the legal entity.[1572] The conclusion of such an agreement can be carried out only with the prior opinion of the administrative body responsible for the protection of secret data and the Agency.[1573] The second modality involves the covert interceptions, where the MNSA can conduct the covert interception of electronic commu-

1567 LMNSA (Law on the National Security Agency, Official Gazette of the Republic of Montenegro, no. 28/2005 and Official Gazette of Montenegro, no. 86/2009 – second law, 20/2011 and 8/2015).

1568 Art. 180 LMNSA.

1569 Amendments no. 08–1373/6 (17.06.2014), available in Montenegrin at the following link <https://zakoni.skupstina.me/zakoni/web/dokumenta/zakoni-i-drugi-akti/548/612-3950-00-38-14-1.PDF> (accessed on 10.03.2023).

1570 Dušica Tomović, "Montenegro Adopts Controversial Surveillance Law", Balkan Insight (18.02.2015), available at the following link <https://balkaninsight.com/2015/02/18/montenegoro-s-parliament-adopts-controversial-spying-law/> (accessed on 08.03.2023).

1571 Art. 8(3)(5) LMNSA.

1572 Art. 8(7) LMNSA.

1573 Art. 8(8) LMNSA.

nications, including a) content of electronic communication, b) data on traffic, c) location data related to the user, d) content and type of a postal item, i. e. service.[1574]

There is indeed some kind of authorisation mechanism for conducting interception measures, but not for the access to all types of personal data. In general, interception measures can be carried out on the basis of an order issued by the Director of the MNSA[1575] with the approval of the President of the Supreme Court of Montenegro.[1576] The order which authorises covert interception must contain data on the identity of the person to whom this order refers, the type of technical means used, the duration, as well as the validity of the reasons for the application of monitoring and interception.[1577] However, the interception of location data does not require the approval of the President of the Supreme Court and can be issued solely on the basis of the decision of the MNSA's Director.[1578]

2 Limits and Safeguards

Limitations on data collection and processing are set forth by the LMNSA and MLEC. Data collection is limited to only what is necessary and proportionate for the exercise of competence and execution of prescribed tasks of the MNSA, as established by the LMNSA.[1579] The LMNSA provides specific instances where the MNSA has the power to collect data, such as the prevention of activities directed against the territorial integrity, defence, security and legal order or the prevention of serious crimes, e. g. organised crime, crimes against humanity, but also for the "prevention of other possible threats to national security".[1580] Leaving much room for interpretation, this definition is quite broad. In the case of secret interception of electronic communication, the MNSA is only permitted to conduct such measure in special cases defined by Art. 14 LMNSA, which must be specific threats to national security and not based on general provisions,[1581] except for the location data, for which there are not specific limits.[1582]

1574 Art. 9(1)(4) LMNSA.
1575 Art. 14(1) LMNSA.
1576 Art. 14(3) LMNSA.
1577 Art. 11(2) LMNSA.
1578 Art. 14(3) LMNSA.
1579 Art. 7 LMNSA.
1580 Art. 6 LMNSA.
1581 Art. 14(1) LMNSA.
1582 Art. 14(4) LMNSA.

Under the MLEC, all forms of interception, taping, or storage of communications content and data and without consent from user is prohibited,[1583] except for interception of data necessary, appropriate, and proportional to protect national security and enforce criminal measures.[1584] Operators are obliged to enable interception of communications to the MNSA.[1585] This also means that they have the obligation to retain particular data on traffic and location, and relevant data required for identification and registration of subscribers, of both legal and natural persons.[1586] Yet, the data revealing the content of electronic communications is excluded from this obligation,[1587] unless defined by the Government otherwise.[1588] The period for retaining these types of data shall not be shorter than six months nor longer than two years from the date of communication.[1589]

Data protection rules are also established under the LMNSA and MLEC, in addition to general data protection framework.[1590] The MNSA is obliged to keep records on the personal data, which have the status of secret data under the law regulating secret data.[1591] Also, the LMNSA stipulates rules for the destruction of data collected through interception of electronic communication.[1592]

According to the MLEC, the provisions of the data protection law apply to the data processed by the operators.[1593] The MLEC also provides for several obligations related to protection of personal data. Considering that Montenegro still has not adopted the new GDPR-like law, this is a positive solution, as the additional obligations for the protection of personal data under MLEC include institutes which are not regulated by the MDPL 2008 (data protection law). In line with this, operators are required to appoint a person responsible for data protection, similar to a DPO under the GDPR.[1594] Further, the operators have the obligation

---

1583 Art. 172(2) MLEC.

1584 Art. 172(5) MLEC.

1585 Artt. 180–181 MLEC.

1586 Art. 181 MLEC.

1587 Under Artt. 181–182 MLEC the types of data include the data necessary for tracing and identifying the source and destination of communication; identifying location of parties to communication; identifying date, time and duration of communication; identifying type of communication; identifying communication equipment of user or equipment used for the purpose of communication; identifying location of mobile communications equipment.

1588 Art. 182(2) MLEC.

1589 Art. 181(6) MLEC.

1590 According to Art. 17 LMNS, the MDPL 2008 applies directly to the work of MNSA.

1591 Art. 16 LMNSA.

1592 Art. 16 LMNSA.

1593 Art. 147(4) MLEC.

1594 Art. 169(1) MLEC.

to report any data breach to the Electronic Communications and Postal Agency (hereinafter: "ECPSA") and the Agency and to keep records on data breaches.[1595] They must also implement appropriate technical and organisational measures to ensure the integrity and protection of electronic communications networks and services[1596] Additionally, the MLEC defines the obligation to implement 'safety measures' for personal data which also include the implementation of basic data protection principles such as purpose limitation, access limitation and storage limitation.[1597]

3 Redress

With regards to redress, Montenegrin citizens have the right to request information about whether the MNSA has collected data about them and to receive documents on the collected data.[1598] However, this right is limited only to Montenegrin citizens. Given that citizens only receive information upon their request, in most cases they will not learn about the interception of their electronic communications and access to their personal data. Moreover, the MNSA is not obliged to respond to the requests, if it would be difficult or impossible to carry out the MNSA's work or it could lead to endangering the safety of another person.[1599] Nevertheless, the individuals have access to the redress mechanism explained above in the part discussing access to personal data for criminal law enforcement purposes.

4 Oversight

Despite the existence of both internal and external oversight mechanisms, the effectiveness of oversight over the MNSA remains uncertain as shown in the practice.[1600] The internal control is executed by the Inspector General, appointed and

1595 Art. 170 MLEC.
1596 Art. 168(1) MLEC.
1597 Art. 183 MLEC.
1598 Art. 18(1) LMNSA.
1599 Art. 18(3) LMNSA.
1600 Article "Za prisluškivanje građana 1.400 naloga" (in English: 1,400 orders for wiretapping citizens) published in Sjever Cne Gore in which NGOs expressed concern that the laws governing the interception of communications were not being respected (24.04.2021) available at the following link <https://www.sjevercg.me/za-prisluskivanje-gradjana-1-400-naloga/> (accessed on 21.05.2023); See also Dina Bajramspahić, Marko Sošić, Monitoring report, "Law on Parliamentary Oversight of Security and Defense Sector" DCAF (2013) available at the following link <https://media.institut-alternativa.org/2013/03/law-on-parliamentary-oversight-of-security-and-defense-sector.pdf> (accessed on 21.05.2023).

dismissed by the Government.[1601] The General Inspector submits a report to the Director of the MNSA on all matters of importance for the work of the Agency, violations of laws and other regulations, as well as on other findings obtained during the control and makes recommendations and sets a deadline for eliminating deficiencies.[1602] External oversight is provided by the Parliament of Montenegro. Parliamentary control is carried out through the competent working body of parliament – the Committee for Security and Defence.[1603] Moreover, the Agency is authorised to perform oversight with the MDPL 2008 over the operators who may be requested to perform communication interception for government institutions under MLEC and over the LMNSA.[1604] Furthermore, the ECPSA is empowered to supervise whether the operators are complying with their obligation to ensure the confidentiality of communications as defined by Art. 172 MLEC.[1605]

III Conclusion to F

The legal framework in Montenegro establishes limitations on access to personal data by public authorities for criminal and national security purposes. Interception measures for criminal purposes are permissible only upon a written order issued by an investigating authority. However, the restrictions concerning national security purposes remain a subject of controversy. With the adoption of the new amendments to the LMNSA in 2015, a provision was introduced that allows intelligence officers to access all databases in Montenegro by presenting their official identification cards, without the requirement of obtaining a court order, except in cases of covert interception. This provision raises concerns regarding the potential infringement on privacy rights and the lack of sufficient judicial oversight.

Nevertheless, the MLEC provides additional criteria for the protection of personal data in the case of interception. In accordance with the MLEC, operators that are obliged to cooperate with authorities are required to designate a person responsible for data protection, similar to a DPO under the GDPR. In addition, operators are required to report any data breaches to the ECPSA and the Agency and are also required to keep records of such breaches.

Taking into account the aforementioned legal framework, it is evident that Montenegro has taken steps to regulate access to personal data for criminal

1601 Art. 40 LMNSA.
1602 Art. 41 LMNSA.
1603 Art. 43 LMNSA.
1604 Art. 183(2) MLEC.
1605 Art. 189(1)(6) MLEC.

and national security purposes. However, the controversial provisions concerning interception measures for national security raise concerns about the potential impact on rights of data subject in Montenegro, and in particular, in case of data transferred from the EU to Montenegro. Striking a balance between national security interests and the protection of privacy remains an ongoing challenge that Montenegro needs to address to ensure the adequate safeguarding of personal data within its legal framework including for the purpose of meeting the adequacy requirements assessed by the EU Commission.

G North Macedonia

According to the Constitution of North Macedonia, the freedoms and rights of individuals can only be restricted in cases stipulated by the Constitution.[1606] Unlike with other WB6 countries, there are no provisions in the Constitution of North Macedonia stating that such limitations can only be regulated by the law. However, the limitations to the rights for the purposes of law enforcement and national security are set out in the MDPL 2020 (data protection legislation). Under Art. 27(2) MDPL 2020, the rights of data subject may only be restricted by the legislative measures, which must contain specific provisions, as also set out in Art. 32(2) GDPR. The Constitution also stipulates that the confidentiality of communication and correspondence can only be restricted by a court decision, in cases where it is indispensable to a criminal investigation or required in the interests of the defence of the country.[1607] Moreover, regarding the redress rights, the Constitution provides that "every citizen may invoke the protection of freedoms and rights determined by the Constitution before the regular courts, as well as before the Constitutional Court of Macedonia [...]. Judicial protection of the legality of individual acts of state administration [...] is guaranteed. A citizen has the right to be informed on human rights and basic freedoms [...]."[1608] Yet, it is not clear if the term 'every citizen' would also apply to foreigners.[1609] Nonetheless, the Constitution does provide for foreign subjects to enjoy the freedoms and rights guaranteed

1606 Art. 54 Constitution of North Macedonia.
1607 Art. 17 Constitution of North Macedonia.
1608 Art. 50 Constitution of North Macedonia.
1609 The Constitution of North Macedonia uses different terms such as 'everyone' (e.g. Art. 44 – right to education), 'every citizen' (e.g. Art. 22 – right to vote), 'citizen' (e.g. Art. 20 – right to freedom of association) 'person' (e.g. Art. 14 – Nulla poena sine lege), 'citizen of North Macedonia' (e.g. Art. 27 – freedom of movement).

by the Constitution, subject to conditions established by law and international agreements.[1610]

I Criminal Law Enforcement Purposes

Macedonian public authorities are granted access to personal data and may use certain investigative measures for criminal law enforcement purposes, as provided for under the Art. 252 Criminal Procedure Law of North Macedonia (hereinafter: "NMCPL"). These measures include 1) monitoring and recording of the telephone and other electronic communications, 2) secret access and search of computer systems, 3) automatic or in other way searching and comparing personal data of citizens and 4) access to telephone or other electronic communications, all together (all together: "Investigative Measures"). The NMCPL obliges 'database controllers', which are considered to be all entities and natural persons involved in the processing of personal data, to provide access to data for the purpose of carrying out Investigative Measure of automatic or other searches and comparisons of personal data of citizens.[1611] However, this measure only refers to citizens of North Macedonia and it is not clear whether it would also affect EU residents.

Further, the Law on Interception of Communications of North Macedonia (hereinafter: "NMLIC")[1612] adopted in 2018 regulates the secret interception of communications, distinguishing between two types of interception: (1) the interception of communications as a special investigative measure, used by law enforcement in order to collect evidence in criminal proceedings,[1613] and (2) the implementation of measures for interception of communications for the purpose of protecting the interests of security and defence of the state (all together: "Interception Measures").[1614]

1 Rules for Authorising and Limiting Interception Measures

Authorisation for Interception and Investigative measures is subject to specific rules under both the NMCPL and NMLIC. Under both laws, these measures may only be ordered by a competent judicial body, by means of a written order. The authorisation for imposing Investigative Measures under NMCPL is granted by

1610 Art. 29 Constitution of North Macedonia.
1611 Art. 266 NMCPL.
1612 Law on Interception of Communications, no. 71/2018.
1613 Art. 8 NMLIC.
1614 Art. 29 NMLIC.

the preliminary investigation judge upon a substantiated request by the public prosecutor, except for the measure "access to telephone or other electronic communications", which may be ordered by the public prosecutor by means of a written order without the need for authorisation by the preliminary investigation judge.[1615] The NMCPL also provides the provisions on the content of the warrant, which inter alia, has to contain an explanation on the reasons due to which the data or evidence cannot be collected otherwise.[1616]

To limit the scope of Investigative Measures, the NMCPL provides for safeguards aimed at ensuring legality and proportionality, restricting the limitation of freedoms and rights of the defendant and other persons to only what is necessary, under circumstances as provided for in the Constitution, ratified international agreements, and the provisions of the NMCPL.[1617] The Investigative Measures have a special purpose and may be authorised only for specific criminal acts[1618] and individuals.[1619]

When it comes to the duration of the Investigative Measures, they must immediately be discontinued once they are no longer necessary, while any measure cannot last longer than four months, with a maximum limit of then months.[1620] The NMCPL also outlines provisions for the retention of material obtained through investigative measures, mandating that all collected data be erased or destroyed under the supervision of the preliminary procedure judge, the public prosecutor, and a representative from the data protection authority, if no criminal procedure is instigated within 15 months after the completion of the measure, whereas the public prosecutor shall be obliged to compile a report accordingly.[1621] As an additional safeguard, NMCPL defines that any person who, in any way, learns about information that is related to or results from the application of Investigative measures, shall be obliged to keep it as an official secret.[1622] Furthermore, any data obtained in violation of the NMCPL cannot be used as the basis for a court decision.[1623]

1615 Art. 256 NMCPL.
1616 Art. 257 NMCPL.
1617 Artt. 252–271 NMCPL.
1618 Art. 253 NMCPL.
1619 Art. 255 NMCPL.
1620 Art. 260 NMCPL.
1621 Art. 267 NMCPL.
1622 Art. 264 NMCPL.
1623 Art. 259(5) NMCPL.

2 Redress

The NMCPL establishes an obligation to provide a written order for investigative measures upon request of the person concerned, provided that such a request does not prejudice the ongoing proceedings.[1624] However, it is not entirely clear how a person who is subject to such measures would become aware of them and be able to challenge them, as no obligation to notify individuals is defined. Additionally, under Art. 290 NMCPL any person who considers that their rights have been violated by any of the measures taken may file a complaint with the judge of the preliminary proceedings, who is obliged to rule on the legality of the action or measure, without prejudice to the person's right to seek legal protection by other means.[1625]

On the other hand, the NMLIC guarantees the person whose data has been intercepted the right to be informed and provided with the material.[1626] The person whose communication has been intercepted contrary to the provisions of the NMLIC may claim for compensation.[1627]

Apart from these two laws, the Constitution also provides for redress mechanisms. Art. 15 of the Constitution allows for the right to appeal against individual legal acts by a court, administrative body, organisation, or other institution carrying out public mandates. Also, the MDPL 2020 provides individuals with a redress mechanism as explained in Chapter 4, Section E. Finally, the individuals have the right to file a complaint with the Ombudsman of North Macedonia.[1628]

3 Oversight

The NMCPL imposes specific record-keeping and transparency requirements to enhance accountability and oversight. In particular, the police shall produce a report during the execution of the Investigative Measure that is going to be submitted to the public prosecutor, upon the completion of the measures.[1629] Such reports are then delivered to the judge of the preliminary procedure.[1630] Furthermore, the Chief Public Prosecutor is required to submit an annual report on the special investigative measures requested during the previous calendar year

1624 Art. 262 NMCPL.
1625 Art. 290 NMCPL.
1626 Art. 24 NMLIC.
1627 Art. 28 NMLIC.
1628 Art. 13 Law on the Ombudsman (Official Gazette of the Republic of Macedonia nos. 60/2003, 114/2009, 181/2016, 189/2016 and 35/2018).
1629 Art. 258 NMCPL.
1630 Art. 258 NMCPL.

to the parliament.[1631] These provisions shall ensure that the public authorities are accountable to the legislative branch of government, and that the parliament is able to provide additional oversight over the use of these measures. The external oversight of interception of communications is also regulated by the NMLIC which defines the parliamentary oversight, through a special parliamentary committee.[1632] Further, the external oversight is performed by the data protection authority and ombudsman.[1633]

II National Security Purposes

Interception measures for national security purposes in North Macedonia are regulated by the NMLIC. The NMLIC covers all types of telephone and other electronic communications such as internet protocol, speech through internet protocol, website, and e-mail (hereinafter: "Interception Measures").[1634] Defined like this, the interception of communications covers communications via internet apps for transfer of voice, video and other content (for example: Skype, Viber, Snapchat, WhatsApp, FaceTime).[1635]Moreover, the Law on Electronic Communications (hereinafter: "NMLEC") obliges all operators to retain meta data for 12 months[1636] and allow interception of communications as per the NMLIC.[1637]

The authorised bodies for implementation of Interception Measures in order to protect the interests of the security and defence of the state are: the National Security Agency (hereinafter: "NSA"), the Military Security and Intelligence Service and the Centre for Electronic Reconnaissance of the Army which are designated for the needs of the defence.[1638] The NSA is the main authority responsible for protecting the national security of North Macedonia, established by the Law on the Agency for National Security (hereinafter: "LNSA"). It replaced the Administra-

1631 Art. 271 NMCPL.
1632 Art. 36 NMLIC.
1633 Art. 11 Law on the Ombudsman.
1634 Art. 4 NMLIC.
1635 Aleksandar Nikolov, "Analysis of the Legal Framework for Interception of Communications and Implementation thereof", Foundation for Internet and Society, Metamorphosis, and Association for Progressive Communications (APC), (2019), available at the following link <https://metamorphosis.org.mk/wp-content/uploads/2019/08/Legal-framework-on-interception-of-communication_eng.pdf> (accessed on 20.01.2023).
1636 Art. 178 NMLEC.
1637 Art. 175 NMLEC.
1638 See also Eta Bardjieva Miovska, "The use of special investigative measures in the Republic of North Macedonia – legal provisions and human rights aspects" (2022).

tion for Security and Counterintelligence which was dissolved following the adoption of the LNSA as part of the reforms of the intelligence system.[1639] This authority was reformed in 2019 after the EU criticised the independence of the intelligence institutions.[1640] Unlike its predecessor, the NSA is not a part of the Ministry of Interior, but an independent legal entity, and it holds no police powers.[1641] Its main tasks are counterintelligence, anti-terrorism and the protection of the constitutional order. North Macedonia had to adapt to European standards and best practices as a candidate for EU accession, but also as part of the preparation for full NATO membership (which was completed in March 2020).[1642]

1 Rules for Authorising Interception Measures

The Supreme court is authorised to issue an order for Interception Measures, upon the request of the Minister of Interior or the Minister of Defence.[1643] As provided by the NMLIC, the Supreme court may order the interception of communications of a person for whom there is a reasonable suspicion that they are preparing to commit a criminal act against the state, armed forces or against humanity and international law.[1644] The Interception Measure may last up to 90 days, but can be extended for a year at most upon the authorisation of the Supreme court.[1645] These provisions have been criticised for being overly broad.[1646]

Personal data collected during the enforcement of the court order for Interception Measures are kept in the Ministry of Interior or Ministry of Defence under a special regime, for a period no longer than one year following the expiry of the term determined in the order.[1647] Following the expiry of the term, the data shall be destroyed under the surveillance of the judge who established the order.[1648] If it is acknowledged that the person is a perpetrator of a certain criminal act, the procedure of interception of communications may continue according to

1639 See also more information on intelligence sector reform in North Macedonia explained in the EU Commission Report for North Macedonia 2020, (6.10.2020), SWD(2020) 351 final, pp. 3–4.

1640 *Ibid.*

1641 DCAF, Guidelines for intelligence oversight for parliamentary committees in the Assembly of the Republic of North Macedonia (January 2021), p. 21.

1642 *Ibid.*

1643 Artt. 30–31 NMLIC.

1644 Art. 29(1) NMLIC.

1645 Art. 33 NMLIC.

1646 See also on the criticism of interception measures in North Macedonia, Aleksandar Nikolov (n. 1635).

1647 Art. 34(1) NMLIC.

1648 Art. 34(2) NMLIC.

the conditions of Art. 8 NMLIC which regulates the interception for criminal purposes.[1649]

In addition to the interception rules regulated by NMLIC, the LNSA regulates other measures which include use of special techniques for interceptions without the operators acting as intermediaries. Such measures for interception under LNSA include 1) secret monitoring of communications for the purpose of protecting the interest of the security, (Art. 24) 2) monitoring and recording of international telecommunications (Art. 25) and monitoring and recording of telephone and other electronic communications (Art. 26) (all together: "Interception Measures"). Interception Measures must be approved by the competent courts, while the measure under Art. 24 NMLIC has to be approved by the Supreme Court.[1650] The competent courts issue a written order, with the defined content as provided by the Art. 37 LNSA. The secret surveillance under Art. 24 LNSA may last only up to 6 months,[1651] while other Interception Measures may last up to 2 years.[1652] Interception Measures can be performed only in specific cases, regulated by Art. 34(2), when the data cannot be obtained in another way.[1653] Once the goal of the Interception Measures have been reached, the competent judge immediately submits the order to stop the measure.[1654]

2 Limits and Safeguards

The NSA collects, processes, uses and protects personal and other data and information relating to matters under the competence of the NSA, in accordance with the MDPL 2020.[1655] The data collected and processed by the execution of the Interception Measure for secret collection of data are stored withing the NSA in accordance with the MDPL 2020 and classified information, for a period of maximum three years.[1656] After the expiration of the term, the data and all materials related

---

1649 Art. 39(3) NMLIC.

1650 Art. 32(1) LNSA.

1651 Art. 38(1) LNSA.

1652 Art. 38(2) LNSA.

1653 These include the purpose of preventive action against individuals who incite, organize or participate in an armed attack against North Macedonia or in disabling its security system to carry out its own functions, as well as for preventive action in relation to criminal acts of the Criminal Code: terrorist organization (Art. 394a), terrorism (Art. 394-b) and financing of terrorism (Art. 394-c).

1654 Art. 39 LNSA.

1655 Art. 49(1) LNSA.

1656 Art. 44(1) LNSA.

to the execution of the order to implement secret measures is deleted under the supervision of a judge from the Supreme Court.[1657]

In order to ensure confidentiality and protection of personal data, the NSA is obliged to apply appropriate technical and organisational measures to protect against accidental or illegal destruction, loss, impersonation, unauthorised disclosure, or access of personal data.[1658] Further, the NSA also has transparency standards, by virtue of LNSA, which mandates the publication of "relevant regulations of the importance of the work, organisational structure of the Agency, and an annual work report" on its website.[1659]

Moreover, the NMLIC defines basic principles including 1) respect for human freedoms and rights[1660] and 2) prohibition to monitor communications without a court order.[1661] Also, the NMLEC provides several obligations in terms of obligations of the operators to respect the confidentiality of communication and protection of data.[1662]

3 Redress

The LNSA provides the right to access, meaning that upon the request of an individual there is an obligation to provide information whether Interception Measures have been taken against them and provide the relevant documents on the intercepted data.[1663] Further, under Art. 6 NMLIC any individual whose communication was intercepted has the right to challenge the authenticity of the data collected and the legality of the procedure of interception of their communications. Also, the NMLIC stipulates the right to judicial protection and compensation to 1) a person whose data was collected by implementing measures for monitoring communications and exposed to the public 2) any person whose communication was monitored contrary to the provisions of the law.[1664] Lastly, the individuals have the redress rights under the Constitution and data protection authority mechanism.[1665]

1657 Art. 44(3) LNSA.
1658 Art. 49(2) LNSA.
1659 Art. 64 LNSA.
1660 Art. 5 NMLIC.
1661 Art. 3 NMLIC.
1662 Artt. 168, 177 NMLEC.
1663 Art. 52 LNSA.
1664 Art. 23 NMLIC.
1665 Chapter 5, F.II.3.

4 Oversight

External supervision over the Interception and Interception Measures of communications is performed by several institutions, including the Parliament via its special committees (e.g., Committee on Oversight of the Implementation of Measures for Interception of Communications), Council for Civil Control, Directorate for Security of Classified Information, PDPA and Ombudsman.[1666] Specifically for data protection, the PDPA has the possibility to conduct an audit (which may be regular, extraordinary or for control purposes) of the NSA's work.[1667] The obligation of the NSA is to enable full implementation of the audit without obstructing or concealing, changing, or disabling the audit and handling of certain personal data.[1668]

III Conclusion to G

North Macedonia has a legal framework which regulates the limitations of interception of communications for criminal and national security purposes. The adoption of the NMLIC in 2018 marked a crucial milestone in the reform process, which was undertaken as part of the country's efforts to join the EU.[1669] The NMLIC serves as the primary legislation governing the interception of communication and aims to strike a balance between the needs of law enforcement and national security agencies, and the protection of individual rights to privacy and data protection. It sets forth several limitations and safeguards to prevent abuse of interception powers and provides legal remedies for individuals whose communications have been intercepted. The need for such comprehensive legislation became evident in the wake of a major scandal that unfolded in the country, where wiretapped conversations involving mass surveillance of Macedonian citizens, including foreign individuals, were revealed.[1670] This scandal prompted a thorough examination of the intelligence sector and led to the production of the

1666 See also DCAF Guidelines (n. 1641).

1667 Zlate Dimovski, "Analysis of the Content and Practical Implementation of the Law on the National Security Agency and Law for Coordination of the Security and Intelligence Community in the Republic of North Macedonia, Skopje", DCAF, (February 202) p. 20.

1668 *Ibid.*

1669 See also DCAF Geneva Centre for Security Sector Governance, "Intelligence and Security Sector Reform Program in the Republic of North Macedonia (2021–2026)" Newsletter No. 2, (2 October-December 2021), <https://aidstream.org/files/documents/North_Macedonia_Newsletter_EN_OCT-DEC_2021-(final) 20230124110112.pdf> (accessed on 12.03.2023).

1670 This case been discussed in Chapter 3, F.IV.3.

EU Commission's 'Priebe Report', which shed light on the deficiencies and shortcomings in the existing legal framework.[1671] While the reform of the intelligence sector and the adoption of the NMLIC represent important steps forward, challenges remain in ensuring the integrity of the intelligence sector and upholding the privacy rights of individuals.[1672] The EU Commission also recognised the results of the reform of the intelligence sector, but stated that the country needs to strengthen the capacity for parliamentary oversight over the intelligence services.[1673]

H Serbia

In Serbia, government authorities possess the legal authority to access personal data for both law enforcement and national security purposes. Such access rights and safeguards for individuals are regulated by the respective legislation, as explained below. Additionally, the Serbian Constitution upholds the fundamental principle that human and minority rights guaranteed by the Constitution may only be restricted by law if permitted by the Constitution, and solely for ends allowed by the Constitution.[1674] The Constitutional Court has already issued see principle of necessity[1675] and proportionality,[1676] mandating all state bodies, particularly the courts, to consider the substance of the restricted right, the relevance of the restriction, the nature and extent of the restriction, the relation of the restriction and its purpose, and the possibility of achieving the restriction's purpose with less restrictive measures with regard to human and minority rights.[1677] Notably, the Constitutional Court has already issued several decisions that overturned restrictions on human rights, which allowed restrictions to be imposed by statute rather than by law.[1678] More importantly, the Constitution guarantees that, in accordance with international treaties, foreigners in Serbia shall enjoy

1671 Priebe Report (n. 1591).
1672 E.g., Justifications for the interception of data is too broad, meta data of all citizens are stored for one year by the business operators, without any limitations etc. See also Aleksandar Nikolov (n. 1635).
1673 EU Commission Report North Macedonia 2020 (n. 1639).
1674 Art. 20(1) Serbian Constitution.
1675 This principle is regulated by Art. 52(1), first sentence CFR.
1676 This principle is regulated by Art. 52(1), second sentence CFR.
1677 Art. 20(3) Serbian Constitution.
1678 E.g., Decision of the Constitutional Court (Official Gazette of Republic of Serbia, no. 60/2013).

all the rights guaranteed by the Constitution and the law,[1679] with the exception of the rights exclusively reserved for Serbian citizens, such as the right to vote.[1680]

Regarding redress mechanisms, the Serbian Constitution provides any person, including foreign nationals, the right to judicial protection when a human or minority right guaranteed by the Constitution is violated or denied, as well as the right to seek remedy for the effects of such violation.[1681] Furthermore, individuals may seek to assert their rights and freedoms before the Constitutional Court by filing a constitutional complaint against an individual act or an act of a state authority or organisation entrusted with public authority, when these remedies have been exhausted, when no other remedy is provided for, or when the right to judicial protection is excluded by law.[1682]

It is important to note that in its Strategy Proposal, the Serbian government set an ambitious goal: harmonisation of data protection legislation with the acquis communautaire resulting in obtaining an EU decision on the adequate protection of personal data and resulting in a free flow of personal data with the EU.[1683] For this, data protection laws are not the only ones to be harmonised, but also the respective laws which are relevant to government's access to personal data transferred from the EU to Serbia.

I Criminal Law Enforcement Purposes

Regarding the utilisation of Investigative measures for criminal law enforcement purposes the Serbian Criminal Procedure Code (hereinafter: "SCPC") contains relevant articles that regulate various special evidentiary measures, including secret surveillance of communication[1684] and computer data search[1685] (all together: "Investigative Measures"). Pursuant to the principle of lawfulness guaranteed under Art. 12 SDPL 2019, such measures may be applied only if certain material and formal conditions defined by the SCPC are met: 1) the necessity of the existence of grounds for suspicion that any of the offenses referred to in Art. 162 SCPC has

1679 Art. 17 Serbian Constitution.
1680 Art. 52 Serbian Constitution.
1681 Art. 22 Serbian Constitution.
1682 Art. 82 Law on the Constitution Court, (Official Gazette of RS, no. 109/2007, 99/2011, 18/2013 – US decision, 103/2015 and 40/2015 – other laws).
1683 Ivan Milošević, Partner, JPM, Data Protection Strategy Proposal for 2023–2030 (n. 114).
1684 Art. 166 SCPC.
1685 Art. 178 SCPC.

been committed,[1686] and (2) a requirement that the special investigative measures are to be imposed as a kind of evidence ultima ratio, meaning that otherwise evidence for prosecution cannot be collected or it would otherwise be significantly more difficult.[1687] It is essential to note that secret interception is not allowed for criminal enforcement purposes.

When determining the application and duration of Investigative Measures, the competent authority must consider proportionality and determine whether the same outcome could be achieved using less restrictive measures.[1688]

1 Rules for Authorising and Limiting Interception Measures

Investigative Measures may be imposed on a person against whom there are predefined grounds for suspicion, but only on the basis of a court decision.[1689] This warrant must be accompanied by an explanatory statement, which is particularly important because it encroaches on privacy and the judge is obliged to explain the reasons that justify the use of these special Investigative Measures. The court order must contain available data on the person against whom the Investigative Measures are imposed, the classification of the criminal offense, the known telephone number or address of the suspect, the types of data subject to computer search, the reasons for suspicion, the method of implementation, and the scope and duration of the special evidentiary action.[1690] In order to facilitate application of the surveillance, the postal, telegraphic and other business operators registered for transmission of information are obliged to assist the authorities who execute the Investigative Measures by enabling the implementation of surveillance and recording of communications.[1691] However, this applies only on the measure of secret surveillance of communication.

The SCPC states that the measure of secret surveillance of communication may be implemented not only by the police belonging to the enforcement system but also by other secret surveillance agencies,[1692] and its definition indicates that the measure refers only to the monitoring of the content of communications.[1693] The EU Commission criticised this and noted that a clear separation needs to be made between the remits and regulations for criminal investigation and

1686 Art. 162 SCPC.
1687 Art. 161(3) SCPC.
1688 Art. 161(3) SCPC.
1689 Art. 167(1) SCPC.
1690 Art. 167(2) SCPC.
1691 Art. 168 SCPC.
1692 Secret surveillance agencies are explained bellow in Section II.
1693 Art. 173 SCPC.

those for security purposes and questioned whether this is in line with EU standards and best practice.[1694] This is particularly problematic given that secret surveillance agencies have more extensive interception powers, which may not always respect the limits imposed by the SCPC in cases where such agencies carry Investigative Measures for the purposes of prosecution under the SCPC.

Secret surveillance of communication can last for three months, and due to the necessity of further evidence gathering, it can be extended by a maximum of three months.[1695] The same applies to the computer search, with the difference that it can be extended by a maximum of two months.[1696] With regard to the treatment of the collected material, if the public prosecutor does not initiate criminal proceedings within six months from the day of the introduction of the material collected by means of Investigative Measures, or if they declare that it will not be used in the proceedings, or that they do not require proceedings against the suspect, the judge of the preliminary proceedings is expected to issue a decision on the destruction of the collected material.[1697]

Considering that the Investigative Measures under SCPC include actions such as monitoring and recording of communication by telephone or other technical means as well as surveillance of electronic or other address of the suspect and the seizure of letters and other consignments in the course of criminal investigations (but neither of emails nor other messages transmitted using electronic communications services),[1698] their impact on the transferred data from the EU to Serbia may be limited.

2 Redress

The judge for preliminary proceedings has the discretion to inform the subject of surveillance measures, provided their identity is established during the implementation of such actions and informing them would not undermine the possibility of conducting criminal proceedings.[1699] Hence, this is not an absolute obligation, as the law employs the term 'may' rather than 'shall' or 'must'.[1700]

1694 EU Commission Report Serbia, p. 50 (n. 1216).

1695 Art. 167(3) SCPC.

1696 Art. 179(3) SCPC.

1697 Art. 163(1) SCPC.

1698 Milana Pisarić, "Surveillance of Electronic Communications in Republic of Serbia", in Berendt, B., Engel, T., Ikonomou, D., Le Métayer, D., Schiffner, S. (eds) Privacy Technologies and Policy, Lecture Notes in Computer Science, vol 9484. Springer, Cham. (2016).

1699 Art. 163(2) SCPC.

1700 According to Art. 163(2) SCPC "The judge for preliminary proceedings may inform the person against whom a special evidentiary action from article 166 of this Code has been conducted about

In addition, individuals have the right to apply for protection of legality under the SCPC.[1701] An application for the protection of legality may be filed against a legally binding decision or against violations of criminal procedure provisions if: 1) there has been a violation of the law; 2) a law has been applied which, according to the decision of the Constitutional Court, is inconsistent with the Constitution, generally recognised rules of international law and confirmed international treaties or 3) if, as established by a decision of the Constitutional Court or the ECtHR, the human rights and freedoms (guaranteed by the Constitution or the ECHR and its additional protocols) have been violated or denied to the defendant or other participants in the proceedings.[1702] Additionally, the individuals have the complaint rights under the SDPL 2019,[1703] and under Constitution as already mentioned above. Lastly, any individual, regardless of nationality, who believes that their human or minority rights and freedoms have been violated by an act, action, or inaction of an administrative body has the right to complain to the Ombudsman.[1704] It is noteworthy also that the data collected cannot be a base for a judicial decision if authorities acted contrary to the provisions of the SCPC or court order when conducting the Investigative Measures.[1705]

3 Oversight

External work control of enforcement bodies is carried out by: 1) Parliament; 2) assemblies of units of provincial autonomy or units of local self-government, including city municipalities; 3) judicial authorities; and 4) independent state bodies responsible for supervision and other authorised state bodies and bodies. The external oversight of enforcement bodies is executed by Parliament through its Committee on Defence and Security.[1706] Moreover, the external control of enforcement bodies is foreseen by several institutions, but in particular relevant for the data protection, via the Ombudsman[1707] and the DPC.[1708]

---

the decision referred to in paragraph 1 of this article, if his identity has been established during the conduct of the action and if this would not jeopardise the possibility of conducting criminal proceedings[...]".

1701 Art. 482 SCPC.

1702 Art. 486 SCPC.

1703 Already discussed in Chapter 4, E.II.15.

1704 Art. 28 Law on the Ombudsman (Official Gazette of RS, No. 105/2021).

1705 Art. 163(3) SCPC.

1706 Art. 222 Law on the Police (Official Gazette of RS, no. 6/2016, 24/2018 and 87/2018).

1707 In accordance with Art. 19 Law on the Ombudsman the Ombudsman is authorized to control the legality and regularity of the work of administrative bodies, in order to determine whether their acts, actions or inaction have violated the rights of citizens guaranteed by the Constitution,

II National Security Purposes

In Serbia, certain institutions are authorised to access personal data for national security purposes. The main security intelligence institutions are Security Information Agency (known as "BIA" and hereinafter: "BIA"), Military Security Agency (hereinafter: "MSA") and Military Intelligence Agency (hereinafter: "MIA") all together "Secret Agencies".

The work of the BIA is governed by the Law on Security Information Agency (hereinafter: "LSIA"),[1709] which sets out specific measures that can be taken to derogate from the confidentiality of letters and other means of communication. These measures are regulated by Art. 13 LSIA and include, among others, 1) secret monitoring and recording of communications, regardless of the form and technical means used, 2) statistical electronic monitoring of communication and information systems with the aim of obtaining data on communications or the location of mobile devices used, and 3) computer searches of already processed personal data and their comparison with other data collected in accordance with Art. 13 LSIA.

The other two agencies, MSA and MIA, are both regulated by the Law on Military Security Agency and Military Intelligence Agency (hereinafter: "LMSIA").[1710] Among other special procedures and measures, MSA may apply covert secret surveillance of the content of letters and other means of communication, including secret electronic surveillance of the content of telecommunications and information systems (hereinafter: "covert ECS").[1711] Additionally, MSA may use covert electronic surveillance of telecommunications and information systems in order to collect the retained data on telecommunications traffic, without insight into their content[1712] (hereinafter: "covert STI"). Both MSA and MIA can collect data from the business operators[1713] and apply secret data collection to counter threats to the Ministry of Defence and the Serbian Army and cooperate with the police or

---

confirmed international treaties, generally accepted rules of international law, laws, other regulations and general acts of the Republic of Serbia.

1708 In accordance with Art. 78 and 79 DPL the DPC has several inspection and related powers vis-à-vis controllers.

1709 Law on the Security-Information Agency (Official Gazette of RS, no. 42/2002, 111/2009, 65/2014 – decision US, 66/2014 and 36/2018).

1710 Law on Military Security Agency and Military Intelligence Agency (Official Gazette of RS, no. 88/2009, 55/2012 – decision US and 17/2013).

1711 Art. 12(1)(7).

1712 Art. 12(1)(5).

1713 Artt. 16, 26 LMSIA.

the BIA in executing the secret data collection.[1714] The MIA may also apply some secret surveillance measures, which do not include surveillance of the electronic communication explicitly, but the "secret cooperation with the legal and natural entities".[1715]

1 Rules for Authorising Interception Measures

The relevant legislation sets out the rules on who is authorised to order surveillance measures and which court has jurisdiction over each of these actors. Under the LMSIA, a proposal is made by the MSA's Director and the jurisdiction to authorise the special measures lies either on the judges of the Supreme Court of Cassation[1716] or the judges of the competent Higher court[1717] depending on the special measure. On behalf of the BIA, the proposal for the application of special measures can only be made by the Director of the BIA and the authorisation is given by the President or the authorised judge of the Special Department (for organised crime) of the High Court in Belgrade.[1718] If the Court accepts the proposal to impose a special measure, it shall issue a written order with an explanation.[1719] The order imposing a special measure shall include the title of the special measure, the available data on the person, group or organisation against whom it is to be applied, the reasons for considering that the conditions of the LSIA are met, the manner of application, the extent and the duration of the special measure.[1720]

Furthermore, the BIA may request and receive information, data, and professional assistance from state authorities and legal entities, but this is based on voluntary disclosure of data. The LSIA lays down the rule that no one can be forced to provide assistance and information, but withholding or refusing assistance, or information must be based on reasons established by law.[1721]

1714 Art. 10 LMSIA.
1715 Art. 27 LMSIA.
1716 Art. 14 LMSIA.
1717 Art. 13a LMSIA – for the covert electronic STI the authorisation is required from the judges of Higher courts, and not the Supreme court.
1718 Art. 15(3) LSIA.
1719 Art. 15a(1) LSIA.
1720 Art. 15a(2) LSIA.
1721 Art. 10 LSIA.

2 Limits and Safeguards

The surveillance measures under the LSIA may be used only in specific situations, with the aim to eliminate and prevent activities aimed at undermining or destroying the constitutional order of Serbia and jeopardizing security in the country and the circumstances of the case indicate that such acts could not otherwise be detected, prevented or proven, or would cause disproportionate hardship or great danger.[1722] While deliberating on the prescription and duration of special measures, the BIA shall particularly consider whether the same result could be acquired in a manner less restrictive for citizens' rights, in a volume necessary for fulfilling the purpose of limitation in a democratic society.[1723] Special measures under LSIA may be in effect for three months and may be prolonged not more than three times, each time for a three-month period.[1724] Application of the special measures shall be discontinued when reasons for its application cease to exist.[1725]

Another law which regulates data interception of communication is the Law on Electronic Communications (hereinafter: "SLEC").[1726] Business operators are required to retain data on electronic communication, which may only be accessed with the user's consent or a court decision, if it is necessary for conducting criminal proceedings (in accordance with the SCPC) or protecting the security of Serbia (in accordance with the LMSIA and LSIA).[1727] The operators are obliged to keep the retained data for 12 months from the day of communication.[1728] The rule that the operators may provide the access to personal data to the competent authorities only based on a court decision was introduced in 2014, after the Constitutional Court declared unconstitutional the previous solution of Art. 128 SLEC under which operators had to give access to retained data to the competent authority without a prior court decision.[1729] This was not in line with the right to confidentiality of communication of the users of electronic communications.

The SLEC lays down several rules for protection of retained data. The business operator is obliged, in terms of the protection of retained data, to ensure in particular that 1) the retained data is of the same quality and subjected to the same security and protection measures as the data in the operator's electronic commu-

---

1722 Art. 14 LSIA.
1723 Art. 14(2) LSIA.
1724 Art. 15a LSIA.
1725 *Ibid.*
1726 Art. 127 SLEC.
1727 Art. 128 SLEC.
1728 Art. 128(6) SLEC.
1729 Decision of the Constitutional Court (Official Gazette of Republic of Serbia, No. 60/2013).

nication network; 2) that the retained data is protected in an appropriate manner against accidental or unauthorised destruction, accidental loss or alteration, unauthorised or illegal storage, processing, access or disclosure, in accordance with SDPL 2019 (the law governing the protection secret data; 3) the access to the data is limited and 4) the data is destroyed after 12 months, except for the data that has been saved and submitted to the police or secret agencies. In order to prove that the protection measures are in place, the operator is obliged to create the necessary technical and organisational conditions and to provide evidence of this to the Regulatory Authority for Electronic Communications and Postal Services.[1730]

a) Challenges

Despite the reforming of legislation, concerns remain about lawful interception of communication and access to stored electronic data. Firstly, the legislation does not provide clear rules on whether the competent authorities can directly intercept communications and access stored data, even without the knowledge of the operator.[1731] It seems that the wording of the SLEC leaves the possibility of direct interceptions as the competent authority requests the operator only "when they are unable to obtain the access to retained data without access to the premises, network, associated facilities or equipment operators".[1732] In fact, this seems to be much more common in practice, as the reports submitted by some operators to the DPC[1733] do not contain any requests for access to retained data by security services.[1734] The EU Commission also noted in its reports that the potential for abuse of interception of communications needs to be addressed and that a law on access to state security communications still needs to be adopted.[1735] Secondly, safeguards and limitations rules are mostly regulated by bylaws instead of laws. For example, one of the crucial problems is the failure to define by laws detailed procedures and technical requirements for the implementation of interception actions.[1736] In this respect, the government adopted the Rulebook on Requirements and Program Support for the Lawful Interception of Electronic Communications

1730 Art. 130(2) SLEC.
1731 Milana Pisarić, p. 170 (n. 1698).
1732 Art. 128(9) SLEC.
1733 According to Art. 128 SLEC, the operators are obliged to keep the records upon the request of the competent state authorities for access to the retained data, as explained below in part II.
1734 Predrag Petrović, Katarina Đokic "Slippery Slopes in the Reform of Serbian Security Services" Belgrade Centre for Security Policy (2017), p. 15.
1735 EU Commission Report for Serbia, SWD(2016) 361 final (9.11.2016) p. 71.
1736 Milana Pisarić, p. 170 (n. 1698).

and Technical Requirements for the Fulfilment of the Obligation of Electronic Communications Data Retention,[1737] which stipulates additional safeguards. However, according to the Constitution, any restriction on human rights can only be regulated by law, and not by ordinance. Further, there is no provision in the respective laws on how BIA and MSA store and destroy data legally collected by special measures in order to protect national security.[1738] This is also regulated by secondary legal acts and internal rules.[1739]

In February 2023, the government passed a new law on electronic communications (hereinafter: "New SLEC").[1740] However, this law does not regulate the interception of communications. Instead, the law stipulates in its Art. 40 that legal interception of data shall be regulated by another special law. The transitional provisions of the New SLEC provide that the former SLEC shall continue to apply for the purpose of interception of communications.[1741] This solution is therefore foreseen until Serbia adopts the new legislation on lawful interception. The New SLEC only provides that the storage and any form of interception or surveillance of electronic communications and related traffic data shall be prohibited in order to ensure its confidentiality.[1742] It remains to be seen whether the new law on lawful interception will resolve outstanding issues and impose stricter rules and limits on interception measures by Security Agencies.

4 Redress

Serbia's legal system provides various avenues for obtaining redress in the area of national security, similar to the area of criminal enforcement law. Firstly, under the SDPL 2019, individuals have the right to access, correction, deletion of personal data, and have the right to complaint to the DPC and to the competent authorities, as explained in Chapter 4.[1743] Secondly, as announced in the Strategy Proposal data subjects might have even easier ways to assert their rights.[1744] Thirdly,

1737 Rulebook on Requirements and Program Support for the Lawful Interception of Electronic Communications and Technical Requirements for the Fulfilment of the Obligation of Electronic Communications Data Retention (Official Gazette of the RS, 88/2015 of 23.10.2015).

1738 See more critics on this topic Jelena Pejić, "Who is our Interceptor? How does interception of electronic communications and access to stored electronic data work in Serbia?" Belgrade Centre for Security Policy, Belgrade (2014).

1739 Art. 32 LMSIA.

1740 Law on Electronic Communications (Official Gazette of RS, no. 35/2023).

1741 Art. 180 New SLEC.

1742 Art. 160 New SLEC.

1743 Chapter 4, F.II.15.

1744 Ivan Milošević, Partner, JPM, Data Protection Strategy Proposal for 2023–2030 (n. 1114).

they have a right to complain to the Ombudsman.[1745] Finally, they have the right to a constitutional claim, as explained above.

5 Oversight

The oversight of security institutions such as BIA, MSA, and MSI is established through external supervision by the Parliament[1746] and the Government, specifically the Ministry of Defence and the General Inspector in the case of MSA and MSI.[1747] The Parliamentary control is exercised through the Committee on Defence and Security.[1748] Additionally, the BIA is obliged to submit a report twice a year on the its work to the Parliament and the Government.[1749] However, it seems that MSA and MIA do not have such obligation, as neither the LSIA nor LMSIA provides specific further rules on their external oversight.

Additionally, the Ombudsman and the DPC may utilise their powers to oversee these institutions. The Ombudsman has played a crucial role in supervising security services, which has led to improvements in their activities after investigations.[1750] The DPC is empowered to supervise the execution of business operators' obligations arising from SLEC.[1751] More importantly, the DPC has established the regular oversight of the access to retained data, in accordance with amendments to SLEC in 2014. Both operators and the Security Agencies, are obliged to keep records of requests for access to retained data during one calendar year.[1752] The record contains information on: 1) the number of requests for access to retained data; 2) the number of fulfilled requests for access to retained data; 3) the time elapsed from the day the data was retained to the day when access to the data was requested. The records cannot contain personal data. There is also the obligation of the operators and Secret Agencies and the police authorities to submit such records to the DPC by January 31 of the previous calendar year at the latest.[1753]

1745 Chapter 4, G.I.3.
1746 Art. 52 LMSIA, Art. 17 LSIA.
1747 Artt. 53–54 LMSIA, Art. 17 LSIA.
1748 See more on the parliamentary control over security services: Luka Glušac, "National Human Rights Institutions and Oversight of the Security Services", Journal of Human Rights Practice 10:1, (2018), pp. 58–82.
1749 Art. 17 LSIA.
1750 Read more about the oversight of security intelligence Predrag Petrović, p. 24 (n. 1734).
1751 Art. 130(3) SLEC.
1752 Art. 130a(1) SLEC.
1753 Art. 130a(3) SLEC.

III Conclusion to H

The Serbian data protection framework limits government access to personal data for both law enforcement and national security purposes. Despite this, the legal framework does not appear to be effectively enforced. Criticism refers in particular to the inefficiency of the security services' supervision.[1754] The work of the BIA has also been much criticised as a political institution serving the government and politicians.[1755] Both the Ombudsman and the DPC have been prevented from exercising their powers of control over the security institutions in practice.[1756] This means that even if there are legal criteria for the definition of external supervision, it is not effective in practice. Another fundamental flaw remains in the lack of clear rules on whether the competent authorities can directly intercept communications and access stored data, even without the knowledge of the operator.[1757] Yet, the Strategy Proposal recognises the need to reform the applicable Serbian regulations governing data protection enforcement and sectorial laws subject to the protection of personal data.[1758]

IV Conclusion to Chapter 5

All WB6 countries have either adopted or drafted GDPR replica laws. However, in order to achieve complete alignment with GDPR standards they also need to thoroughly revise their relevant sectoral legislation in particular by reforming their national frameworks in the areas of enforcement and national security. In light of the Schrems rulings, the EU Commission has intensified its scrutiny of surveillance laws to guarantee that personal data transferred from the EU to third countries is safeguarded against clandestine interception and other privacy violations. The EU Commission, when it comes to possible adequacy decisions, will therefore particularly focus on the access rights of the government to the personal data transferred from the EU to WB6. The EU Commission has a good basis to assess these standards through the EU's annual reports that evaluate the WB6 countries' alignment with the EU acquis.

1754 Predrag Petrović, p. 24 (n. 1734).
1755 Predrag Petrović and Katarina Djokic "State Capture and Security Intelligence Agencies in Serbia", Belgrade: Belgrade Centre for Security Policy (2017).
1756 Predrag Petrović, pp. 67–75 (n. 1734).
1757 Milana Pisarić, p. 170 (n. 1698).
1758 Ivan Milošević, Partner, JPM, Data Protection Strategy Proposal for 2023–2030 (n. 1114).

General limitations and safeguards exist in the WB6 legal framework. Yet, there are many shortcomings, for example, where national data protection law does not apply to the processing of personal data by national security agencies, such as in BiH. Another case of particular concern is Serbia, where some types of covert interception measures remain unregulated, even though they are carried out by security agencies.

On a positive note, the WB6 countries do not differentiate between their own citizens and EU citizens in terms of data protection rights. Their constitutions ensure that human rights, including data protection rights, also apply to foreigners, contrary to the US as outlined in Schrems II.[1759] In all the WB6 legal systems guarantee judicial protections, including protection provided by an Ombudsman.[1760] Moreover, in all the WB6 there are several oversight authorities for both law enforcement and intelligence sector. However, the main problem remains with the existing legislation enforcement.

Nonetheless, the WB6, as aspiring members of the EU, must exhibit their commitment to upholding the GDPR's stringent personal data protection standards, including the ECHR standards. The EU Commission possesses the power to motivate these countries to reform their legal systems, but the challenge lies in ensuring that laws governing criminal enforcement and national security activities are effectively implemented and respected. Although data protection authorities have demonstrated dedication to enforcing data protection laws, other national institutions may not consistently adhere to these regulations. By addressing the identified shortcomings (as detailed separately for each country) in their criminal enforcement and national security laws, the WB6 countries can pave the way for a more secure digital environment that respects the privacy rights of individuals and would potentially ensure the free flow of data between their borders and the EU.

1759 Section 702 of the FISA was passed in 2008 and allows the National Security Agency to collect intelligence on foreign targets located abroad from 'electronic communication service provider[s]' under a 'certification' that the Foreign Intelligence Surveillance Court must approve annually. The certification must specify targeting, querying and data collection procedures that ensure only non-U.S. persons are targeted, minimize the capture of information about U.S. persons and ensure a 'significant purpose of the acquisition is to obtain foreign intelligence information'. See also Joseph Liss, David Peloquin, Mark Barnes, and Barbara E Bierer, "Demystifying Schrems II for the cross-border transfer of clinical research data", J Law Biosci, (Jul-Dec 2021).
1760 In Schrems II decision, the ECJU concluded that the Privacy Shield Ombudsperson is not a tribunal within the meaning of Article 47 of the CFR. See para 65 Schrems II.

Chapter 6 – Privacy-Infringing Technologies in the WB6

The WB6 countries in recent years have displayed a proclivity towards utilising cutting-edge technologies. The concern that these technologies may compromise the privacy of citizens is less of a hindrance in this region than within the EU. The WB6 governments also exhibit a tendency to employ technology as a means of achieving their policy objectives. This tendency was particularly evident during the Covid-19 pandemic, during which time the governments demonstrated a decreased regard for privacy. For instance, during a press conference on March 19, 2020, Aleksandar Vučić, the President of Serbia and leader of the ruling political party SNS, announced that the police were monitoring the movements of individuals with 'Italian phone numbers', referencing the fact that a large number of Serbian citizens returned to the country from Italy on the brink of the pandemic.[1761] Additionally, he alluded to the utilisation of 'another method' to track the movements of individuals who had left their phones behind, though he did not elaborate on what this method entailed.[1762]

It is worth noting that the WB6 countries are not alone in this approach within the Western Balkans. Croatia, for instance, nearly passed contentious legislative changes that would have enabled the tracking of individuals' mobile phone locations, although these changes were ultimately put on hold.[1763] Croatia also employed drones to detect violations of state measures during the Covid-19 pandemic, particularly those pertaining to the prohibition of public gatherings.[1764] Nonetheless, Serbia appears to be a frontrunner among the WB6 countries in this regard, as evidenced by the significant 'Safe City' project with Chinese company Huawei, which will be discussed in greater detail later in this Chapter.

This Chapter will focus on the challenges that arise regarding the privacy of individuals within the WB6 region due to the implementation of privacy-invasive technologies by WB6 governments. Furthermore, the resulting obstacles to the

---

1761 Danilo Krivokapić, Bojan Perkov and Davor Marko, "State of pandemonium: Digital rights in the Western Balkans and COVID-19", Global Campus of Human Rights, Policy Brief, (2020) p. 5.
1762 *Ibid.*
1763 Melita Vrsaljko, "Pracenje mobitela stavljeno na čekanje" (Eng. Tracking mobile phones put on hold) Al Jazeera Balkans, (published on 10.04.2020) <http://balkans.aljazeera.net/vijesti/pracenje-mobitela-stavljeno-na-cekanje> (accessed 29.03.2023).
1764 Katja Miličić, "Vukovar police using drones to enforce social-distancing measures", The Voice of Croatia (14.04.2020) <https://glashrvatske.hrt.hr/en/news/domestic/vukovar-police-using-drones-to-enforce-social-distancing-measures> (accessed 29.03.2023).

https://doi.org/10.1515/9783112221013-008

adoption of a potential adequacy decisions by the EU Commission will be examined. This aspect is also germane to adequacy decisions regarding the onward transfer of personal data, as the limitations on such transfers constitute an integral component of the EU Commission's evaluation.

A The Beijing Effect

The concept of the "Beijing Effect" has been discussed by scholars Matthew S. Erie and Thomas Streinz.[1765] They observed that this term was inspired by Anu Bradford's "Brussels Effect"[1766] which serves as a prevailing theory for understanding how laws may have regulatory effects beyond its jurisdiction of origin.[1767] Erie and Streinz argue that, unlike the Brussels Effect where legislative power drives influence, the Beijing Effect emerges through China's export of digital infrastructure.[1768] Other scholars also refer to this phenomenon as 'digital authoritarianism', a phenomenon through which China not only exports its technology but also its values and governance system to third countries.[1769] Lawrence Lessig argued with the notion "Code is Law" that the design of software and digital architecture inherently regulate behaviour much like traditional legal framework.[1770] This notion resonates with the Beijing Effect, as Chinese technology – ranging from surveillance tools to censorship mechanisms – carries with it a regulatory logic that can shape the digital, social, and political landscapes of third countries. When nations adopt these systems, they may inadvertently adopt restrictions on speech, privacy, and political expression similar to those prevalent in China, ulti-

1765 Matthew s. Erie and Thomas Streinz, "The Beijing Effect: China's 'Digital Silk Road' as Transnational Data Governance", 54 New York University Journal of International Law and Politics (2021), pp. 1–92.

1766 Already discussed in Chapter 3, B.I.

1767 Matthew S. Erie and Thomas Streinz, pp. 1–5 (n. 1765).

1768 *Ibid*, p. 14.

1769 See also Monique Taylor, "China's Digital Authoritarianism A Governance Perspective," Part of the book series: Politics and Development of Contemporary China (PDCC) (2022); Khalil, Lydia, "Digital Authoritarianism, China and COVID", Lowy Institute For International Policy (2020); The new big brother-China and digital authoritarianism: a minority staff report, United States. Congress. Senate. Committee on Foreign Relations (2020); Dimitar Ilkov, "Made in China: Tackling Digital Authoritarianism", European View, 2020, Vol. 19(1) 110 (April 2020).

1770 Lawrence Lessig, "Law Regulating Code Regulating Law." Loyola University Chicago Law Journal, vol. 35, no. 1, Fall 2003, pp. 1–14.

mately enhancing state control, disseminating propaganda, and prioritising economic gains over liberal human rights.[1771]

Data protection law regulation is rather complex in China. China has recently adopted comprehensive legislation on data protection called the Personal Information Protection Law (hereinafter: "PIPL"), which seems to emulate the goals of the GDPR.[1772] At first sight it incorporates several GDPR concepts, such as purpose limitation (Art. 6 PIPL), the lawfulness of processing (Art. 13 PIPL), special provisions on sensitive personal information (Section II PIPL) and rules on the cross-border provisions (Chapter III PIPL).[1773] The PIPL should be understood to be entirely connected with the idea that the scope of data sovereignty should be extended.[1774] Through PIPL, China seeks to establish a functioning data flow order for Chinese private firms with globally integrated operations, and it serves as a critical component in the local and extraterritorial design of China's model of cross-border data access.[1775] Also, the PIPL was mainly introduced due to the state's concern about uncontrolled mass data collection by private companies, which takes place beyond state control.[1776] Moreover, similar data protection rules to those in the EU can help Chinese technology companies to better adapt to them, but also help to convince companies from the EU to do business with them.[1777]

Despite China's adoption of a comprehensive data protection law, it conceptually differs from the European (and WB6) foundations by not recognising privacy as a fundamental right.[1778] Most importantly, the PIPL largely leaves the power of government bodies untouched, as it does not restrict their power to collect and process data.[1779] This lack of constraint is complemented by the Chinese state's

1771 Monique Taylor, p. 31 (n. 1769); Matthew s. Erie and Thomas Streinz, p. 10 (n. 1765).

1772 The PIPL is effective from 1 November 2021.

1773 For a detailed overview see also: Rogier Creemers, "China's Emerging Data Protection Framework", Cyber Policy Center, Leiden Institute for Area Studies, (November, 2021); Ra Paul C. Johannes, "China, Kurzsynopse der Regelungsinhalte des neuen chinesischen Datenschutzgesetzes PIPL zur DS-GVO", ZD-Aktuell 05455 (2021).

1774 Igor Calzada, "Citizens' Data Privacy in China: The State of the Art of the Personal Information Protection Law (PIPL)" Smart Cities (2022), pp. 1131–1132.

1775 *Ibid.*

1776 Rogier Creemers, pp. 7–9 (n. 1773).

1777 See also Chi Chen and Leo Zhou, "How China's data privacy and security rules could impact your business", Partner, Forensic & Integrity Services, Ernst & Young (18.07.2022) <https://www.ey.com/en_kw/forensic-integrity-services/how-chinas-data-privacy-and-security-rules-could-impact-your-business> (accessed on 03.05.2023).

1778 Rogier Creemers, p. 19 (n. 1773).

1779 *Ibid.*

broad access rights to data held by companies, which are justified by national security concerns or the Social Credit System.[1780]

I Beijing Technologies in the WB6

The WB6 occupy a unique geopolitical position as they are influenced by both Western and Asian countries. This results in a variety of foreign companies with diverse data protection cultures investing and utilising their technologies in the region. China, in particular, is a relatively new but rapidly growing player in the WB6, with an expanding economic footprint and investment potential.[1781] Since the launch of its Belt and Road Initiative (hereinafter: "BRI") in 2013,[1782] China has financed a number of notable construction projects in the WB6,[1783] but also some other significant technology related projects. Some researchers argue that the EU's ambivalent approach to the WB6's EU accession perspective over the past decade has created a vacuum that Beijing has quickly and willingly filled.[1784] This has deepened the challenges faced by WB6 countries to integrate

---

1780 See also Yongxi Chen and Anne Sy Cheung, "The Transparent Self under Big Data Profiling: Privacy and Chinese Legislation on the Social Credit System", Vol. 12, No. 2, The Journal of Comparative Law (2017), pp. 356–378.

1781 Henrik Boesen Lindbo Larsen, "The Western Balkans between the EU, NATO, Russia and China", CSS Analyses in Security Policy 263, ETH Zurich Research Collection, (May 2020).

1782 The Belt and Road Initiative (BRI) serves as the main framework for expanding China's economic presence in the WB6 and enables it to access key land and maritime routes.

1783 China earmarked more than six billion Euro worth of loans for the Western Balkans, which mostly targeted the energy and transportation sectors. Among them, Serbia stands out as the prime destination of Chinese investments. For an overview about the China influence in the WB6 countries see: Branislav Stanicek with Simona Tarpova, "China's strategic interests in the Western Balkans", Members' Research Service, PE 733.558 European Parliament, (2022).

1784 Simona Tarpova, "China's investments in the West Balkans: gaining a foothold in Europe. Is Beijing set to replace the EU in shaping the region's future?" published in The Gaudie, (02.11.021), available at the following link <https://www.gaudie.co.uk/post/china-s-investments-in-the-west-balkans-gaining-a-foothold-in-europe> (accessed on 15.05.2023); Danijela Jaćimović, Nikola Milović, Tanja Miščević and Marta Radenović, "Does China Challenge Integration Perspective of the Western Balkan Countries?", 12th SCF International Conference on Contemporary Issues in Social Sciences (October 202); Wendy Robinson, "The Trojan Dragon Comes to the Balkans", The Fletcher Forum of World Affairs , SUMMER 2020, Vol. 44, No. 2, A Return to Great Power Competition (SUMMER 2020), The Fletcher School of Law and Diplomacy; Loïc Poulain, "China's New Balkan Strategy", SCIS, Volume 1, Number (02.11.2021), pp. 29–44.

into the EU and slowed or even reversed the comprehensive reform process necessary for eventual EU accession.[1785]

An integral part of the BRI and China's strategy in Southeast Europe is the promotion and integration of technological products.[1786] One major initiative for the Digital Silk Road, another component and objective of the BRI, has been the development of 5G wireless networks and supportive technology, which promises 5G to smartphones and other digital platforms to achieve quicker downloads and to become the foundation for gleaming futuristic cities.[1787] Huawei is a Chinese telecommunications giant that is leading the charge on cutting-edge 5G technology and technology equipment. However, the company has been heavily criticised for its close ties with the Beijing government, which raise concerns that Huawei may be compelled to cooperate with Chinese intelligence services, potentially compromising sensitive data and information.[1788] Moreover, Huawei has received a special status from the Chinese government and military, earning the title of a 'national champion', which is granted to companies that support China's broader geopolitical objectives.[1789] In mid-2019, Huawei drafted a legal report claiming that the company would not be coerced into espionage due to a vague Chinese espionage law that supposedly does not mandate Chinese businesses to hand over sensitive corporate information to Chinese intelligence.[1790] Nevertheless, lawyers in China and abroad have challenged the validity and actual position of this law.[1791]

1785 Henrik Boesen Lindbo Larsen (n. 1781).

1786 Philippe Le Corre, "On Chinese Investment and Influence in Europe," Carnegie Endowment for International Peace, (23.05.2018), available at the following link <https://carnegieendowment.org/2018/05/23/on-chinese-investment-and-influence-in-europe-pub-76467> (accessed 11.05.2020).

1787 Lindsay Maizland and Andrew Chatzky, "Huawei: China's Controversial Tech Giant," Council on Foreign Relations, (12.06.2019) <https://www.cfr.org/backgrounder/huawei-chinas-controversial-tech-giant> (accessed on 11.05.2023).

1788 See also Elena Boldyreva, Finn Stam, and Natalia Grishina, "EU Concerns About Security, 5G and Huawei" in, *et al.* Proceedings of Topical Issues in International Political Geography. TIPG 2021, Springer Geography, Springer, Cham (02.01.2023); Álvaro Artigas, "Surveillance, Smart technologies and the development of Safe City solutions: the case of Chinese ICT firms and their international expansion to emerging markets", Institut Barcelona d'Estudis Internacionals (IBEI) (2017).

1789 Lindsay Maizland and Andrew Chatzky, p. 32 (n. 1787).

1790 *Ibid.*

1791 *Ibid.*

Despite these controversies, almost all countries in the WB6,[1792] with the exception of Kosovo,[1793] are signing up for joint ventures with Chinese companies that make temptingly innovative and seemingly financially-savvy offers. This is most prominent in the case of Serbia and BiH. Serbia has already partnered with Huawei on several projects, including the Safe City project[1794] and opening a centre for innovation and digitalisation development.[1795] BiH followed Serbia's path by signing a Safe City agreement with Huawei.[1796] Huawei already cooperates with Bosnia's two major carriers, HT Eronet and M:Tel.[1797] The third big player in BiH, BH Telekom, did not rule out the opportunity of cooperating with Huawei on rolling out 5G in the future.[1798] Huawei has also launched a development programme for Bosnian IT professionals, Seeds for the Future, that aims to share its knowledge on 5G and artificial intelligence.[1799] The same programme was also extended to IT professionals from Serbia and North Macedonia.[1800]

1792 For an overview of Chinese investments in each WB6 countries see W Zweers V. Shopov, F. Van der Putten, M. Petkova, & M. Lemstra, "China and the EU in the Western Balkans" Clingendael Report, 8. (2020)

1793 Kosovo has not been included in China's strategy as China does not recognize the Kosovo's sovereignty from Serbia, see Philippe Le Corre and Vuk Vuksanovic, "Serbia: China's Open Door to the Balkans," Carnegie Endowment for International Peace, available at the following link <https://carnegieendowment.org/2019/01/01/serbia-china-s-open-door-to-balkans-pub-78054> (accessed 01.04.2023).

1794 The Safe City project will be explained further in the next part.

1795 Mila Djurić, "Srbija i Huawei: Intenziviranje saradnje uprkos sporazumu iz Vašingtona" (Eng. Serbia and Huawei: Intensification of cooperation despite the agreement from Washington), published in Radio Free Europe / Radio Liberty, available at the following link <https://www.slobodnaevropa.org/a/srbija-i-huawei-intenziviranje-saradnje-uprkos-sporazumu-iz-va%C5%A1ington a/30840366.html> (accessed on 02.04.2023).

1796 See more on cooperation between BiH and Huawai "Bosnia and Herzegovina Safe & Smart City", Balkaninsight, (07.11.2018), available at the following link <https://china.balkaninsight.com/node/4071> (accessed on 02.04.2023)

1797 Stefan Vladisavljev, "Policy Paper: China's 'Digital Silk Road' Enters the Western Balkans", Association for International Affairs (AMO), June 2021, p. 14.

1798 *Ibid.*

1799 See article "Po prvi put u Bosni i Hercegovini – uspješno održan prvi program za mlade talente kompanije Huawei Technologies", (Eng. For the first time in Bosnia and Herzegovina – the first program for young talents of Huawei Technologies was successfully held) published A&S Adria, (16.11.2020), available at the following link <https://www.asadria.com/po-prvi-put-u-bosni-i-hercegovini-uspjesno-odrzan-prvi-program-za-mlade-talente-kompanije-huawei-technologies/> (accessed on 02.04.2023).

1800 Gent Salihu "The US–China 5G Race in Europe's Western Balkans", in: Berghofer, J., Futter, A., Häusler, C., Hoell, M., Nosál, J. (eds) The Implications of Emerging Technologies in the Euro-Atlantic Space. Palgrave Macmillan, Cham (07.03.2023), pp. 43–55.

1 Safe City Projects

The concept of the Safe City emerged from the Smart City concept,[1801] with the aim to enhance public safety and security by deploying advanced digital technologies such as facial recognition, surveillance cameras, and big data analytics. Huawei has been the front runner in deploying such technologies. One of the cornerstones of Huawei's project, is the Smart Cities initiative, which develops cities structured around liveable, workable, and sustainable technology and the use of 5G networks is touted as an affordable means to increase efficiency.[1802] Huawei is utilising this same network of connected devices, or Internet of Things (IOT), to afford governments new tools to improve public services such as crime-fighting, and to keep an eye on what is going on generally.[1803]

Safe City projects have raised significant privacy concerns, with critics arguing that they could lead to violations of civil liberties and human rights. One of the concerns is that the vast amounts of data collected from different devices and shared among various individuals and groups could be used by government intelligence agencies to gain access to sensitive personal data.[1804] In this context it is therefore even more crucial, for governments to implement robust data protection measures and ensure that privacy rights of individuals are respected in the development and deployment of safe city technologies. However as previous Chapters 4 and 5 of this study have shown there is both a limited level of data protection awareness, deficits in the legal framework and the enforcement of data protection rules in the WB6. Combined with the use of potentially privacy-infringing technologies this raises additional doubts whether the WB6 governments are genuinely committed to protecting the privacy and personal data of their citizens. This is an important consideration for the adequacy decision regarding the transfer of data from the EU to the WB6. Currently, among the WB6 countries, Serbia and BiH have initiated cooperation with Huawei on the deployment of 5G networks and safe city projects.

1801 For an overview of smart cities see: Sarah Murray "Safe Cities Index 2017. Security in a Rapidly Urbanising World," *Report from The Economist Intelligence Unit*, (2017) available at the following link <https://dkf1ato8y5dsg.cloudfront.net/uploads/5/82/safe-cities-index-eng-web.pdf> (accessed on 12.04.2023).

1802 Fortune Editors, "How Smart Cities and Homes Will Take China Into the Future," Fortune, November 7, 2019, <https://fortune.com/2019/11/07/china-smart-cities/> (accessed on 11.05.2020).

1803 Álvaro Artigas (n. 1788).

1804 Kelsey Finch and Omer Tene, "Smart cities: Privacy, transparency, and community", In Cambridge Handbook of Consumer Privacy (2018), pp. 1125–144.

a) Safe Society Project in Serbia

In early 2019, the Serbian Ministry of Interior and the Serbian Police announced that Belgrade will receive "a thousand" smart surveillance cameras with face and license plate recognition capabilities, supplied by Huawei as part of the project 'Safe Society in Serbia'.[1805] Not long after this announcement, the Ministry of Interior of Serbia started with installing cameras for the recognition of persons' faces and analysis of the movements of persons moving through the streets of Belgrade.[1806] Huawei had stated in its case study that video materials and received data will be kept on an advanced storage device called 'OceanStore', which provides a number of options, such as data analysis and big data analysis, while the retention period of received data is limited to one year.[1807] The Ministry of Interior of Serbia was obliged by the SDPL 2019 (data protection law) to conduct a DPIA of the new smart surveillance system, but it failed so far twice to fulfil the legal requirements, as warned by the DPC.[1808] In its latest opinion the DPC stated that the submitted DPIA on using the video surveillance system is not made in accordance with the SDPL 2019 because, among other things, it still does not provide an appropriate legal basis for the intended processing of biometric data and warned Ministry of the Interior that the intended processing may violate the provisions of the Serbian Law.[1809]

1805 SHARE, "hiljade.kamera.rs: Community Strikes Back Against Mass Surveillance", (19.05. 2020), available at the following link <https://www.sharefoundation.info/en/hiljade-kamera-rs-community-strikes-back/> (accessed on 01.04.2023).

1806 SHARE "Huawei knows everything about cameras in Belgrade – and they are glad to share!" (29.03.2019), available at the following link <https://www.sharefoundation.info/en/huawei-knows-everything-about-cameras-in-belgrade-and-they-are-glad-to-share/> (accessed on 07.12.2021).

1807 Huawei case study for video surveillance in Belgrade was removed from the official website of Huawei. The archived version of the case study is available at the following link <https://archive.li/pZ9HO> (accessed on 21.02.2021).

1808 The Ministry of Interior has so far drafted two DPIAs because the first one was not accepted for the following reasons: it was impossible to determine which specific video surveillance systems is used, the legal basis for the surveillance was not provided, planned processing operations were missing, nor were the risks for the rights and freedoms of data subjects assessed, and consequently, it was not possible to determine whether the controller properly assessed the risks to the data subjects and whether it provided appropriate measures to mitigate them. The first Serbian Commissioner's Opinion on the conducted DPIA no. 073–15–1741/2019–02 (12.11. 2019), available in Serbian the following link <https://praksa.poverenik.rs/predmet/detalji/FB967E2A-AE57-4B2C-8F11-D2739FD85A9B> (accessed on 21.02.2021).

1809 The Second Serbian Commissioner's opinion no. 073–15–1253/2020–02 (29.5.2022), available in Serbian at the following link <https://www.sharefoundation.info/Documents/Mi%c5%a1ljenje_Poverenika_2_0.pdf> (accessed on 21.02.2021).

According to the Art. 9(1) GDPR, the processing of biometric data for the sole purpose of identifying a natural person is generally prohibited, except under specific conditions. In particular, under the Art. 9(2) GDPR, such processing can only take place for a limited number of reasons. According to Art. 9(2)(i), biometric data could be processed for archiving purposes in the public interest, in which case the processing must take place on the basis of EU or national law, subject to the requirements of proportionality, respect for the essence of the right to data protection and appropriate safeguards.[1810] A similar provision is prescribed by Art. 17 SDPL 2019.[1811] However, at present, there is no such law in the valid legal framework of Serbia that would allow mass biometric processing to meet all the requirements. The Serbian Government attempted several times to pass controversial Laws on Internal Affairs to enable the implementation of the Safe City project. The most recent attempt to impose a controversial Law on Internal Affairs was in late 2022. The Government had to withdraw from the legislative procedure in December 2022, after civil organisations and citizens expressed big concerns in the public.[1812] At the same time, the Serbian government announced 'broad consultations' in further work on the draft of this regulation, with the aim "to clarify all doubts in the public and for everyone to understand the intention of the law, which is of particular importance for the safety of all citizens of the Republic of Serbia."[1813]

Despite the absence of a legal basis to install cameras and the two negative opinions by the DPC, the Serbian Ministry of Interior installed already thousands of Huawei cameras in Belgrade, causing negative reactions from the civil sector and citizens in Serbia, but also a concern by the Serbian DPC.[1814] Information regarding the employment of Huawei cameras has been shrouded in secrecy, as the

---

1810 Art. 9 GDPR.

1811 Art. 17(2)(7): processing is necessary in order to achieve a significant public interest determined by national law, if such processing is proportionate to achieving the goal, while respecting the essence of the right to protection of personal data and if the application of appropriate and special measures to protect basic rights and interests of data subjects is provided.

1812 See for the detail overview "SHARE Foundation's Position after the Proposed Draft Laws", (12.12.2022), available at the following link <https://www.sharefoundation.info/wp-content/uploads/SHARE_Position_Paper_BMS.pdf> (accessed on 21.02.2021).

1813 Hiljadekamera, "Round two of the battle against mass biometric surveillance", (10.01.2023), available at the following link <https://hiljade.kamera.rs/en/news/round-two-of-the-battle-against-mass-biometric-surveillance/>, (accessed on 01.04.2023).

1814 Interview with Serbia's Personal Data Commissioner: "Huawei Cameras a 'Dangerous' Decision", Balkan Insight, (18.12.2021) available at the following link <https://balkaninsight.com/2021/12/28/serbias-personal-data-commissioner-huawei-cameras-a-dangerous-decision/> (accessed on 02.04.2023).

public was kept in the dark on the most important aspects of this state-led project.[1815] As a reaction to the deployment of state-of-the-art facial recognition surveillance technology in Belgrade, Serbian citizens launched a website called "hiljade.kamera.rs", which allows people to check the location of detected cameras.[1816] Civil sector and general public were not the only ones who expressed their worries, the members of the European Delegation to the EU–Serbia Stabilisation and Association Parliamentary Committee reacted over such 'invasive' technology, raising concerns over democratic governance, personal data protection, and human rights.[1817] More importantly, European Parliamentarians also expressed their concerns over the attempt to impose the controversial law which would allow systematic surveillance using biometric technologies.[1818]

b) Huawei in BiH

Serbia is not the only one to implement the "Safe City" project. In 2018, the government of BiH entered into a collaboration with Huawei to support the development of Smart City and Safe City projects in the country as well.[1819] Under the same framework, the City of Sarajevo and Huawei signed a cooperation agreement for the implementation of Smart City solutions in the country's capital.[1820] Further, recently, in March 2023, one of Bosnia's entities, Republika Srpska, signed a Memorandum of Understanding with Huawei on digital transformation in the economy of the entity.[1821] The Minister of Economy of Republika Srpska empha-

---

1815 SHARE, "hiljade.kamera.rs: Community Strikes Back Against Mass Surveillance", (19.05.2020) available at the following link <https://www.sharefoundation.info/en/hiljade-kamera-rs-community-strikes-back/> (accessed on 01.04.2023).

1816 Website 'hiljadekamera' available at the following link <https://hiljade.kamera.rs/sr/pocetna/> (accessed on 14.05.2023).

1817 Viola von Cramon, "Use of mass surveillance in Belgrade", (29.09.2021) available at the following link <https://violavoncramon.eu/en/news/content/use-of-mass-surveillance-in-belgrade/> (accessed on 01.04.2023).

1818 See the "Letter from MEPs on new Draft Laws on Internal Affairs & biometric surveillance in Serbia" published by hiljadekamera, (December 2022), available at the following link <https://hiljade.kamera.rs/wp-content/uploads/Letter_from_MEPs_on_new_Draft_Laws_on_Internal_Affairs.pdf> (accessed on 01.04.2023).

1819 Article "Sarajevo innovation conference explores China-CEEC cooperation opportunities", published in Xinhua, (17.11.2018) available at the following link <http://www.xinhuanet.com/english/2018-11/07/c_137587059.htm> (accessed on 01.04.2023).

1820 Article "Huawei aids Bosnia and Herzegovina in building smart city", published by Xinhua, (07.11.2018) <https://en.imsilkroad.com/p/118790.html> (accessed on 01.04.2023).

1821 Article "Huawei i RS potpisali Memorandum o razumijevanju u vezi sa digitalnom transformacijom", (Eng. Huawei and RS signed a Memorandum of Understanding regarding digital

sised that this Memorandum formalises the framework for the Ministry to implement activities aimed at achieving digital transformation in the economy of the entity, with Huawei providing its expertise and skills.[1822] The Memorandum also allows for the "transfer of Huawei's experiences and innovations to Republika Srpska, which could benefit both the public and private sectors".[1823]

The implementation of both the agreements on state and on entity level seems to be much less advanced than in the case of Serbia and so is the level of public scrutiny in a country struggling with a variety of stability challenges.

II Developments in the EU

The Beijing effect is not only evident in the WB6, but also in the EU. Chinese foreign investments have been increasing in the EU in the last decade, a trend that mirrors the growing influence of Chinese digital infrastructure in global markets.[1824] Huawei's network has been active in several EU Member States, and this has contributed to an internal lack of consensus among EU members on a variety of China-related issues, including a discussion on the potential ban of Huawei's networks.[1825] In light of mounting controversy over the use of Chinese telecommunications technology, some countries, like Germany and France, have called for a more meticulous screening of foreign investments, whereas other countries like Italy have done little to obstruct Huawei's construction of 5G networks in the country.[1826] Despite these divergences in national policies towards China, scepticism towards foreign digital influences is overall prevalent in the EU approach, with a special focus on data protection and national security.

On a community level, EU and China signed a so-called "milestone agreement," committing to joint research and development of 5G technologies as well

---

transformation) published in Akta, (23.03.2023) available at the following link <https://www.akta.ba/vijesti/bih/160506/huawei-i-rs-potpisali-memorandum-o-razumijevanju-u-vezi-sa-digitalnom-transforma> (accessed 01.04.2023).

1822 *Ibid.*

1823 *Ibid.*

1824 Frank Bickenbach and Wan-Hsin Liu, "Chinese Direct Investment in Europe – Challenges for EU FDI Policy", CESifo Forum, ifo Institut – Leibniz-Institut für Wirtschaftsforschung an der Universität München, München, Vol. 19, Iss. 4, pp. 15–22 (2018).

1825 Wendy Robinson, p. 37 (n. 1784).

1826 Jodi Xu Klein, "Around the World, Doors Are Shutting on Chinese Investment," South China Morning Post, (14.09.2018), available at the following link (accessed 22.04.2023) <https://www.scmp.com/business/ banking-finance/article/2163974/its-not-just-us-around-world-doors-are-shutting-chinese>.

as reciprocal open market access.[1827] In 2019, the European Parliament published a report "Security Threats Connected with the Rising Chinese Technological Presence in the EU and Possible Action on the EU Level to Reduce Them."[1828] This document served as a catalyst for extensive debates on 5G security, with sustained concerns regarding the risks associated with foreign vendors. By 2023, the EU Commission had classified Chinese companies Huawei and ZTE as "high-risk suppliers", a designation that has provided a basis for enacting restrictions and contemplating the exclusion of their products and services from the EU market.[1829] The EU Commission further articulated its intention to minimise exposure to Huawei and ZTE within the EU telecommunications sector, with proposals for an EU-wide mandatory ban on Huawei's infrastructure products and services remaining under consideration.[1830]

III Conclusion to A

Governments in the WB6 region have shown a propensity to use cutting-edge technologies to support their policy objectives. Although aspiring to EU membership, they are also subject to the influence of various global actors, including China. As a result, the region is attracting investment and technology use from foreign companies with different privacy cultures. In particular, China has developed a relatively new but rapidly expanding presence in the WB6, with a significant economic footprint and investment potential, particularly through projects such as the BRI. The cooperation between WB6 countries and Huawei in the implementation of the Safe City and Smart City projects raises concerns over data privacy and human rights violations. In Serbia, the government installed Huawei's advanced surveillance cameras without an appropriate legal basis and failed to conduct a valid DPIA. The government has faced strong opposition from civil society and

---

1827 EU Commission, "The EU and China signed a key partnership on 5G, our tomorrow's communication networks" (28.9.2015), available at the following link <https://ec.europa.eu/commission/presscorner/detail/cs/ip_15_5715> (accessed on 02.02.2025).

1828 European Parliament resolution of 12 March 2019 on security threats connected with the rising Chinese technological presence in the EU and possible action on the EU level to reduce them (2019/2575(RSP) (12.03.2019).

1829 T. Breton, "5G Security: The EU Case for Banning High-Risk Suppliers: Statement by Commissioner Thierry Breton". available at <https://ec.europa.eu/commission/presscorner/api/files/document/print/en/statement_23_3312/STATEMENT_23_3312_EN.pdf> (2023), (accessed on 23.02.2025)

1830 J Espinoza and A. Gross, "EU considers mandatory ban on using Huawei to build 5G", Financial Times. Available at https://www.ft.com/content/a6900b0f-08d5-433d-bfb0-f57b6041e381 (accessed on 24.02.2025) (2023).

EU officials. Similarly, in BiH, the government signed agreements with Huawei for technical support in implementing the Smart City and Safe City projects. The recent signing of a Memorandum of Understanding with Huawei by the Minister of Economy in Republika Srpska for digital transformation in the economy further raises concerns over potential risks to data privacy and security.

B Challenges for the Adoption of Adequacy Decisions

The EDPB prepared a study on "Government access to data in third countries" in which it analysed three countries: China, India, and Russia.[1831] The study found that China does not constitute a democratic or liberal state and lacks adherence to the rule of law, which is why "it cannot be considered as having the ability to provide people with the protection of personal data equivalent to the EU".[1832] The study argued that "Chinese secondary laws should be interpreted with an eye on China's political system and Constitution".[1833] According to the EDPB "substantial protection of personal data against government access does not exist in China".[1834] On Russia, the study found that, while the legislative framework seems comprehensive, "the enforcement and application of the legislation shows the weaknesses of data protection in Russia" and that "the right to privacy is strongly limited when interests of national security are at stake."[1835] The study argues that the law is used "as an instrument to enforce political aspirations, resulting in legitimisation of new types of surveillance and censorship to control the flow of information in the country."[1836]

These assessments present a challenge for the WB6, as their particular reliance on Chinese technology and investment could hinder their ability to meet EU data protection standards and gain adequacy status. Despite civil society and development grant-focused programs offered by the EU, China's offers of money and advanced technology, with less restrictive oversight, have allowed China to better capitalize on WB6 vulnerabilities.[1837] In some countries, notably Serbia, institutionalised ties with the EU are also increasingly paired with econom-

1831 EPDB, Study on the Government access to data in third countries, Milieu Consulting Brussels, EDPS/2019/02–13 (November 2021).
1832 *Ibid*, pp. 24–25.
1833 *Ibid*, p. 5.
1834 *Ibid.*
1835 *Ibid.*
1836 *Ibid*, p. 52.
1837 Wendy Robinson, p. 30 (n. 1784).

ic and political ties with China. At one point, the Serbian president went as far as saying: "China has no more reliable partner and sincere friend than Serbia."[1838] While data protection legislation in Serbia does not put China on the 'adequacy list', legislation provides for easier data transfer rules, which opens up the possibility to easily transfer data to China.[1839] The Serbian government decides which countries shall be put on the adequacy list without any consultations with the data protection authority, making such adequacy decisions solely political.[1840] For instance, Russia is found on the country's adequacy list despite the concerns expressed by the EDPB.

WB6 governments' projects involving mass video surveillance raise questions regarding compatibility with EU standards on privacy and data protection, as enshrined in the GDPR.[1841] Serbia has recently, for the fourth year in a row, been qualified as a 'hybrid regime' in the Nations in Transit report from Freedom House and such mass video surveillance is feared as a way to suppress civil liberties, including the right to privacy.[1842] Along with the complications for the EU accession process, the close ties between Chinese companies and the WB6 countries could have significant implications for the adoption of an adequacy decision by the EU. Concerns have been raised by the EU regarding the potential links between Chinese corporations and Chinese intelligence sector, which could pose a threat to privacy and sensitive data access in Europe.[1843] Some of the EU Member States have even gone so far as to ban use of Chinese apps like TikTok in certain areas due to these concerns.[1844]

1838 President's statement published on the website of the Ministry of Defence (21.09.2019), available in Serbian at the following link <https://www.mod.gov.rs/lat/14451/predsednik-vucic-kina-nema-pouzdanijeg-partnera-i-iskrenijeg-prijatelja-od-srbije-14451> (accessed on 01.04.2023).

1839 See Chapter 4, B.II.12.

1840 *Ibid.*

1841 See also Report: "China and the EU in the Western Balkans. A zero-sum game?", Clingendael Institute, (2020), available at the following link <https://www.clingendael.org/sites/default/files/2020-08/china-and-the-eu-in-the-western-balkans.pdf> (accessed on 02.04.2023).

1842 Freedom House, "Nations in Transit: Dropping the Democratic Façade", (2020) available at the following link <ahttps://freedomhouse.org/sites/default/files/2020-04/05062020_FH_NIT2020_vfinal.pdf> p. 3 (accessed on 02.04.2023).

1843 Sandra Kalniete, "Report on foreign interference in all democratic processes in the European Union, including disinformation", Special Committee on Foreign Interference in all Democratic Processes in the European Union, including Disinformation, (2020/2268(INI)), (8.2.2022), available the following link <https://www.europarl.europa.eu/doceo/document/A-9-2022-0022_EN.html> (accessed on 02.04.2023).

1844 Article "European Commission bans TikTok on staff devices", published in BBC (23.02.2023), available at the following link <https://www.bbc.com/news/technology-64743991>, Article "Belgium bans TikTok from government phones after U.S. and E.U.", published in Nbcnews, (11.03.2023),

I Conclusion to B

The influence exerted by countries like China into employing cutting edge technologies withing the WB6 may be an obstacle for adequacy decisions. This potential obstacle is additionally worrying as some of the tech infrastructure acquired from China is cost-intensive and will likely not be replaced in the foreseeable future.

This problem arises not only due to the EU Commission's evaluation of regulations governing the onward transfer of personal data belonging to EU citizens but also because Chinese companies have already established data processing regimes within the WB6. Even if the WB6 countries were to establish a comprehensive data protection frameworks and establish robust mechanisms for EU data subjects to seek redress, these safeguards could be undermined by the concurrent use of surveillance technologies and permissive rules on onward data transfers. Specifically, permitting personal data to be transferred to jurisdictions that, in the EU Commission's assessment, either lack legal frameworks governing access to personal data or fail to enforce such frameworks effectively would significantly diminish the protections afforded by the WB6's data protection laws. This would not only result in the WB6 countries remaining ineligible for EU membership until the issue is addressed but could also pose a challenge to the EU Commission's assessment of the adequacy and effectiveness of the data protection measures in place.

II Conclusion to Chapter 6

The EU Commission employs a rigorous evaluation process to determine the level of data protection in a country prior to granting an adequacy decision. This assessment encompasses various factors, including the adherence to the rule of law, regulations governing government access to personal data, and rules pertaining to onward transfers of personal data of EU citizens. The cooperation with Chinese companies like Huawei in the WB6 raises questions over the established data protection framework in this region and onward transfers of personal data to China, but also other countries like Russia, in the case of Serbia.[1845] These factors could have significant implications for the WB6 countries' chances for the adoption of

available at the following link <https://www.nbcnews.com/news/world/tiktok-ban-belgium-government-phones-us-europe-bytedance-rcna74468> (both accessed on 05.04.2023).

1845 The Russian Federation is listed in Serbia as having an equivalent level of data protection under the Government's adequacy list (n. 1213).

an adequacy decision by the EU. While China is developing its own standards for data protection and privacy,[1846] its standards allow governments to build backdoors into software for reasons of public security.[1847] Although there is no clear policy in the EU itself on the use of Huawei technologies, the EDPB has taken a firm stance that China does not offer an equivalent level of data protection as compared to the EU. Similar concerns exist regarding the Russian data protection framework.

Despite the fact that certain EU countries collaborate with Huawei and other Chinese companies, the EU will likely take a stricter stance on WB6 countries' activities on the road to EU accession. If these concerns are not adequately addressed, WB6 countries may face challenges both in their efforts to become part of the EU's digital single market and in their aim to benefit from free flow of personal data.

1846 See Chapter 6, A.
1847 Emmanuel Pernot-Leplay, "Data Privacy Law in China: Comparison with the EU and US Approaches" Journal of Law & International Affairs, Volume 8 no. 1 (2020).

Chapter 7 – Towards Adequacy Decision(s): Prospects for the WB6

The GDPR foresees some high-level criteria for the adoption of adequacy decisions in Art. 45(2) as already discussed in Chapter 3. These criteria have been examined more thoroughly by the CJEU in the Schrems decisions, as well as by the EU Commission in various adequacy decisions.[1848] While the CJEU did not provide a detailed set of requirements for assessing third countries' data protection, it highlighted specific aspects and factors that the third country's legislation must provide to ensure an adequate level of protection.[1849] In Schrems II the CJEU referred to the provisions on the independent supervisory authority (Artt. 51–58 GDPR), the right to lodge a complaint with a supervisory authority (Art. 77 GDPR) and the right to an effective judicial remedy against a supervisory authority (Art. 78 GDPR).[1850]

Following the adoption of the GDPR in the EU, the WB6 countries have encountered new challenges in aligning their legislation, primarily due to their obligations arising from the signed SAAs. Not being placed on the EU Commission's list of adequacy decisions, the transfer of data from the EU to the WB6 is restricted to additional requirements as per Art. 46 GDPR. Furthermore, as the WB6 countries have commenced the process of transposing and interpreting the provisions of the GDPR in their own manner, data transfers from the EU to the WB6 and vice versa have become even more complex, necessitating compliance with both national laws of the WB6 countries and the GDPR to facilitate the data transfers. Although the criteria for the adoption of adequacy decisions remain somewhat ambiguous, it is crucial for the WB6 countries to obtain such decisions due to their geographical and economic ties with the EU.

The aim of this Chapter is to summarise the current situation regarding the harmonisation of data protection legislation with the GDPR and the fulfilment criteria for adequacy decisions in the WB6 countries, and shed light on the possible

1848 The EU Commission has so far recognised Andorra, Argentina, Canada (commercial organisations), Faroe Islands, Guernsey, Israel, Isle of Man, Japan, Jersey, New Zealand, Republic of Korea, Switzerland, the United Kingdom under the GDPR and the LED, and Uruguay as providing adequate protection. EU Commission, Adequacy Decisons, available at the following link <https://ec.europa.eu/info/law/law-topic/data-protection/international-dimension-data-protection/adequacy-decisions_en> (accessed on 29.05.2023).

1849 The criteria for adopting adequacy decisions by the EU Commission have been already discussed in Chapter 3, B.I.1.

1850 Schrems II, paras 16–23, 108–109, para 141 (n. 143).

https://doi.org/10.1515/9783112221013-009

future development. Building on this summary the Chapter will examine in how far a copy-paste approach of the GDPR appears to be the best solution for the WB6 countries' data protection frameworks and potential EU Commissions' adequacy decisions. In addition, and assuming that EU accession is most likely not to be achieved in the short and medium term, this Chapter will look at alternatives to this approach and provide recommendations on the most promising avenues to be taken both to have a better regulated data protection regime throughout the region and to achieve adequacy decisions for the WB6 countries.

A Current Developments in the WB6

As already mentioned in previous chapters, the WB6 have commenced the process of harmonising their respective data protection laws with the GDPR, but they are not at the same stage in this endeavour. Nevertheless, amendments and reforms to the laws are already being announced, even in countries that have adopted new data protection laws (e.g. North Macedonia and Serbia). Despite the different levels of alignment with the GDPR, common challenges have been identified across all WB6 countries. These challenges include difficulties in comprehending laws mainly due to a copy-paste approach that fails to implement the Recitals of the GDPR (or draft laws in case of BiH and Montenegro) and limited support from governments to enforce applicable data protection laws. In addition, lower penalties and limited resources for supervisory authorities are prevalent issues in these countries.

This Section aims to provide an overview of the current developments both in the countries that have already adopted GDPR-like legislation, and in those that have yet to enact the necessary legislation. Examining these developments will help to understand the progress made and the challenges faced.

I Countries with Adopted GDPR-like Laws

Albania is the country with the most recent adopted law on data protection – ADPL 2024. Its adoption received support from the EU through a twinning project.[1851] However, this law was adopted with significant delays, as the National Plan for European Integration outlined the approval of the new draft law on per-

1851 Twinning Project, Albania – Italy – Austria (n. 216).

sonal data protection in the fourth quarter of 2021.[1852] Nevertheless, the supervisory authority in Albania had taken steps to align with the GDPR even before the adoption of the new law, through the publication of various bylaws, such as Instruction no.47 and Instruction no.22 which regulate security obligations for "large and small controllers".[1853] While the adoption of the ADPL 2024 marks a significant milestone in the Albanian data protection landscape, the practical impact of the new legislation remains to be observed. Future assessments will be crucial to determine its effectiveness in enforcement, its uptake by data controllers and processors, and its potential impact on Albania's prospects of obtaining an adequacy decision from the EU Commission.

Process of aligning Kosovo's data protection legislation with the GDPR was initiated immediately after the adoption of the GDPR in 2016, supported by an EU-funded project.[1854] Notably, the KDPL 2019 introduces certain departures from the GDPR, particularly in relation to stricter rules on data transfers and a more lenient approach to penalties.[1855] It is worth noting that Kosovo does not currently recognise other WB6 countries as providing an adequate level of data protection. This strict position can be attributed to Kosovo's efforts to fully align with the EU data protection framework. However, unlike certain other countries such as Albania and North Macedonia, Kosovo has not yet formulated a data protection strategy that explicitly sets the goal of obtaining an adequacy decision from the EU Commission. In addition, there have been no official announcements of new amendments to the KDPL 2019. Nevertheless, Kosovo has made efforts to promote regional cooperation in the field of personal data protection.[1856] This is evidenced by the organisation of regional conferences aimed at facilitating the exchange of best practices, addressing common challenges in the area of personal data protection, and promoting cooperation between institutions in the region.[1857]

North Macedonia has adopted a law, the MDPL 2020, similar to the GDPR in 2020. In December 2021, the MDPL 2020 underwent amendments aimed at providing clarification on certain definitions, without introducing substantial modifica-

1852 The AC's Annual Report 2021, pp. 28–29 (n. 217).

1853 Instruction no. 47 and Instruction no. 22 (n. 235).

1854 Njomëza Zejnullahu, p. 309 (n. 14).

1855 KDPL 2019 has been the subject of detailed discussion in Chapter 4, F.II.

1856 The conference was organised with Montenegro and North Macedonia.

1857 IPA's website, "News: For the first time in Kosovo, a Regional Conference on Personal Data Protection is being organized", (28.06.2022), available at the following link <https://aip.rks-gov.net/en/for-the-first-time-in-kosovo-a-regional-conference-on-personal-data-protection-is-being-organized/> (accessed on 27.05.2023).

tions.[1858] However, the supervisory authority introduced its proposals for further amendments in 2022 due to various reasons.[1859] One of the key reasons for the proposed amendments is the need to ensure that the MDPL 2020 contains the necessary provisions to ensure that the supervisory authority has adequate resources to effectively carry out its functions and powers effectively.[1860] Another notable rationale for these amendments is to align the MDPL 2020 with EU rules on the transfer of personal data, particularly with the EDPB recommendations concerning the European essential guarantees and transfer measures. Nevertheless, these amendments have not yet been adopted.[1861] Moreover, in October 2022, the supervisory authority successfully concluded the implementation of the twinning project "Support in the implementation of the modernized national protection framework of personal data", financed by the EU.[1862] The primary objective of this project was to enhance North Macedonia's framework for personal data protection in accordance with the standards set forth in EU legislation. The European Data Protection Supervisor (hereinafter: "EDPS") acknowledged the country's progress towards alignment with the EU acquis in a letter, highlighting achievements such as increased public awareness, as well as reforms and modernisation of the supervisory authority.[1863]

Nonetheless, achieving full harmonisation is impeded primarily by the sector legislation. At the onset of 2023, the Director of the PDPA accentuated the lack of notable progress in the harmonisation process of the sectoral legislation with the MDPL 2020.[1864] This deficit stems from the inconsistent application of the provisions set forth in the Rules of Procedure of the Government of North Macedonia, specifically pertaining to the non-compliance with the obligation of proponents

1858 Law amending and supplementing the Data Protection Law (RNM, Official Gazette, no 294, 27.12.2021), available in Macedonian at the following link <https://azlp.mk/wpcontent/uploads/2022/11/57d665472d164493815e8b3bdcf8e2a1.pdf> (accessed on 21.04.2023).

1859 PDPA's Annual Report for 2022, pp. 10–11 (n. 1035).

1860 *Ibid.*

1861 *Ibid.*

1862 The project was done with the cooperation of the Agency for the Protection of Personal Data (AZOP) from the Republic of Croatia and the German Foundation for International Legal Cooperation (IRZ) from the Federal Republic of Germany, more information available at the following link <https://azlp.mk/en/support-in-the-implementation-of-the-modernized-national-framework-for-the-protection-of-personal-data/> (accessed on 21.04.2023).

1863 Letter from the European Data Protection Supervisor (07.10.2022), available at the following link <https://azlp.mk/en/letter-from-the-european-data-protection-supervisor/> (accessed on 27.05.2023).

1864 Conference "Заедно за заштита на личните податоци" (Eng. Together for the protection of personal data) held on 27.01.2023, more information available at the following link <https://azlp.mk/конференција-на-тема-заедно-за-зашти/> (accessed on 27.05.2023).

(ministries and other authorities) to submit materials, draft laws, by-laws, and other regulations relevant to the safeguarding of personal data to the PDPA.[1865] Another concern are the limited sources of the PDPA, necessitating the forthcoming amendment of the MDPL 2020. Stefan Hudolin, the Head of the Cooperation Department at the Delegation of the EU in North Macedonia, also stressed the imperative need for the comprehensive implementation of provisions concerning adequate resources allocated to the PDPA.[1866] According to him, the PDPA should be actively involved in all consultations and negotiations regarding personal data protection, highlighting that the recent report from the EU Commission regarding the country's progress in this domain recognised the commitment and efforts of this institution as well as the advancements made towards harmonisation with the EU's personal data protection standards.[1867] North Macedonia adopted a data protection strategy in 2017, the first objective of which is to obtain an adequacy decision from the EU Commission.[1868] In January 2023, the director of the PDPA announced that the PDPA, with the support of the EU, will engage in the development of a new ten-year strategy for the protection of personal data.[1869]

In Serbia, the enactment of the new data protection law, SDPL 2019, took place in 2018 with enforcement beginning in August 2019. The SDPL 2019 presents comprehensive challenges due to its approach of direct copying and pasting without adapting the provisions to the specificities of the Serbian legal system, as discussed in Chapter 4. Notably, one of the significant obstacles relates to the permissive regulations on onward data transfers and the complexities surrounding data transfer rules with the EU.[1870] The safeguards envisaged by the GDPR are not directly recognised in Serbia, which means that both SDPL 2019 and the GDPR need to be respected in parallel. The country has identified these challenges and is already preparing a new data protection strategy.[1871] The Strategy Proposal highlights that "the main obstacles in realising the right to protection of personal data are the numerous shortcomings of the SDPL 2019, which primarily relate to unclear provisions and overwritten mechanisms that do not exist in the domes-

---

1865 *Ibid.*
1866 *Ibid.*
1867 *Ibid.*
1868 Strategy on Personal Data Protection in North Macedonia (2017–2022) (n. 834).
1869 Conference "Заедно за заштита на личните податоци" (n. 1864).
1870 According to the SDPL 2019, all countries that are signatories to Convention 108 are deemed to provide an equivalent level of data protection where no additional requirements apply. Also discussed in Chapter 4, F.II.12.
1871 Data Protection Strategy Proposal for 2023–2030, p. 30 (n. 1114).

tic legal system, which calls into question its applicability."[1872] Moreover, the Strategy Proposal states that "the text of the SDPL 2019 to the greatest extent represents an adapted translation of the GDPR. However, the Preamble, which is an integral part and a necessary starting point for the interpretation of regulations, is not included in the law".[1873] Furthermore, the Strategy Proposal acknowledges that certain matters remain unregulated or inadequately addressed within the current framework. It highlights the presence of numerous articles containing an excessive number of provisions and an overwhelming number of cases exempt from the application of the SDPL 2019.[1874] Consequently, the effective implementation of the SDPL 2019 is challenging, necessitating a revision and supplementation of its provisions. Regarding the permissive approach in governing international data transfers, the Strategy Proposal does not explicitly mention the harmonisation of the Government adequacy list with the EU Commission adequacy list, but it does announce forthcoming amendments aimed at facilitating the transfer of personal data between the EU and Serbia, eliminating the need for additional administrative obligations.[1875]

II Countries without Adopted GDPR-like Laws

Countries which have not adopted new data protection laws are BiH and Montenegro.

In BiH efforts have been made by the supervisory authority to develop a new data protection law. In 2018 the supervisory authority prepared and published for consultation a draft law.[1876] Nevertheless, it appears that the proposed law did not gain acceptance due to numerous objections and suggestions raised by the Ministry of Justice. This information was obtained in late 2021 directly from the Civil Ministry, which served as the official proponent of the new data protection law.[1877] In early 2023, the director of the supervisory authority also noted "that a new law had been drafted but had yet to be adopted,[1878] without providing more

1872 *Ibid*, pp. 31–33.
1873 *Ibid.*
1874 *Ibid.*
1875 *Ibid*, p. 31.
1876 See for the detailed overview of the draft law in Chapter 2, IV.
1877 *Ibid.*
1878 Dragoljub Reljić, "Potrebno usvajanje novog zakona o zaštiti ličnih podataka" (Eng: The adoption of a new law on the protection of personal data is necessary) published in TRT Balkan,

information. This suggests that the adoption of a new data protection law aligned with the GDPR is not currently a top priority in political and legislative decision-making. The complicated political situation in the country and the lack of functionality within the Parliament may contribute to this state of affairs.[1879] It is worth noting that BiH has not yet adopted a specific data protection strategy. However, the supervisory authority has published a Medium-Term Plan for 2023–2025 in September 2022, wherein the harmonisation of the data protection framework with the EU acquis is identified as the primary objective.[1880]

A similar situation is found in Montenegro. The proposal for a new data protection law was published by the Montenegrin Ministry of Interior already in April 2019, but it has not yet been adopted.[1881] Following its publication, a public hearing was conducted in July 2019, during which several objections to the draft law were raised.[1882] However, the consolidated version of the draft law after the public hearing has not been made publicly available. According to the latest publicly available information, the new law was expected to be adopted in the first half of 2023.[1883] In January 2023, when a request for access to public information was made to ascertain the existence of a consolidated version of the draft law, the supervisory authority responded by stating that it was solely responsible for the supervision of data protection laws and that such a request should be submitted to the Ministry of the Interior, as the formal proposer of the law.[1884] Subsequently, in early May 2023, a request for this information was submitted to the Ministry of the Interior. However, despite the expiration of the legal deadline for providing the requested information, no reply has been received thus far.[1885]

(27.02.2023), available at the following link <https://bhsc.trtbalkan.com/region/bih-potrebno-usvajanje-novog-zakona-o-zastiti-licnih-podataka-11841199> (accessed on 22.04.2023).

1879 See also Article "Grupa parlamentaraca traži hitnu sjednicu zbog 'blokade' Parlamenta BiH" (Eng. A group of parliamentarians is demanding an urgent session due to the 'blockade' of the BiH Parliament) published in Slobodna Evropa, (November 2021), available in Bosnian at the following link <https://www.slobodnaevropa.org/a/parlament-bosna-hercegovina-blokada/31573330.html> (accessed on 28.05.2023).

1880 Medium Term Work Plan of the Personal Data Protection Agency in Bosnia and Herzegovina for the Period 2023–2025 (September 2022), p. 6, available in Bosnian at the following link <http://www.azlp.ba/publikacije/Archive.aspx?langTag=bs-BA&template_id=149&pageIndex=1> (accessed on 28.05.2023).

1881 The Draft law (n. 642).

1882 Report on the public discussion (n. 643).

1883 One trust, Montenegro – Data Protection Overview (n. 646).

1884 The official answer of the Agency no. 06–29/1186102/22 (26.01.2023).

1885 The request was formally submitted to the Ministry of Internal Affairs on 03.05.2023. The deadline for providing information is 15 days according to the Guide on Access to Information of

III Regional Initiatives and State of Play of Mutual Recognition of Adequacy

Regional cooperation among the WB6 countries concerning data protection laws appears to be limited. Despite facing similar challenges, there seems to be insufficient collaboration among these countries to effectively address them. Nevertheless, there are some initiatives, such as "Initiative 20i7" between BiH, Croatia, Kosovo, North Macedonia, Montenegro, Serbia and Slovenia. "Initiative 20i7" was established in 2017 and "follows the example of similar informal cooperation between the data protection authorities of the Nordic countries, which also share a historical, cultural and legal background".[1886] The primary objective of the "Initiative 20i7" is to combine the collective efforts of all supervisory authorities in the region, recognising their shared challenges and technical issues.[1887] It was also recognised that numerous companies and organisations from the public sector in the region exchange and transfer personal data across the border, highlighting the need to harmonise the interpretation of data protection standards and guarantee effective protection of personal data in the region, as an important economic gain for all countries.[1888] However, it appears that this initiative has not been highly active, as the most recent meeting was held in 2021.[1889] Additionally, it should be noted that Albania is not part of this cooperation framework.

The main initiative within the WB6 countries concerning regional economic cooperation is known as the "Common Regional Market". Launched in November 2020 in the framework of the so-called "Berlin Process"[1890], this initiative is based on the four freedoms: the free movement of goods, services, capital, and people, while also covering aspects of digital, investment, innovation and industry poli-

the Ministry of Interior no. 037/21–8985/1 (21.04.2021) and the Law on Free Access to Information (Official Gazette of Montenegro, no. 44/12 and 30/17).

1886 Information from the Bosnian supervisory authority "Zajedničko saopćenje za javnost sa prvog sastanka "Inicijativa 20i7", Bled, Slovenija 15.5.2017" <http://azlp.ba/saopstenja/default.aspx?id=1790&langTag=bs-BA&template_id=149&pageIndex=1> (accessed on 29.05.2023).

1887 *Ibid.*

1888 *Ibid.*

1889 Information from the Croatian supervisory authority "Četvrti sastanak "Inicijative 20i7", 28.5.2021" available at the following link <https://azop.hr/cetvrti-sastanak-inicijative-20i7-28-5-2021/> (accessed on 29.05.2023).

1890 The 'Berlin Process', launched in 2014, is an initiative to foster regional co-operation in the Western Balkans. At the summit held on November 2020, the leaders of the WB6 countries agreed to launch the 'Common Regional Market' and reaffirmed this in the Chair's Conclusions. Conclusions available at the following link <https://www.wb6cif.eu/wp-content/uploads/2021/09/Chairs-Conclusions_Sofia-2020.pdf> (accessed on 29.05.2023).

cy.[1891] The Common Regional Market represents a stepping-stone to integrate the region more closely with the EU Single Market already before EU accession. The underlying rationale is that this initiative, in conjunction with the accession process and gradual alignment with the EU acquis, would enhance intra-regional integration.

However, despite mentioned regional cooperation efforts, some of the WB6 countries do not recognise one another as countries providing an adequate level of data protection. Specifically, at the moment Albania[1892] and Serbia[1893] recognise the WB6 countries as countries providing adequate level of data protection. BiH does not provide direct recognition, but instead assesses the adequacy of data transfers on a case-by-case basis for third countries. Nevertheless, the supervisory authority in BiH has expressed the opinion that countries that are signatories to Convention 108 provide an adequate level of data protection.[1894] Consequently, all WB6 countries, except Kosovo, would be indirectly recognised as adequate.

Other WB6 countries do not recognise the WB6 region as providing an adequate level of data protection. In particular, Kosovo does not recognise the WB6 countries as countries with an adequate level of data protection and instead follows the decisions of the EU Commission.[1895] The same is the case with the Montenegrin data protection law (MDPL 2008).[1896] North Macedonia adopts a very strict position regarding the transfer of personal data, where on the one hand only the EU Member States and EEA countries are considered to provide an adequate level of data protection, but still even in these cases data transfers must be notified to the supervisory authority. On the other hand, the WB6 countries are

1891 Western Balkans Leaders Declaration on Common Regional Market: A catalyst for deeper regional economic integration and a stepping stone towards EU Single Market, CRM 2021–2024 AP(1), available at the following link <https://www.rcc.int/docs/544/declaration-on-common-regional-market> (accessed on 28.05.2023).

1892 Decision no. 8 dated 31/ 10/ 2016 (n. 256).

1893 Art. 64(2) SDPL 2019. See also Chapter 4, E.II.12.

1894 Decision on the transfer of personal data abroad for the purpose of the transmission of penalty notices (14.05.2018). In this decision, which ruled on the data subject's complaint about the transfer of personal data to the United Kingdom, the supervisory authority found that the United Kingdom, a signatory to Convention 108, provided an adequate level of data protection and therefore this aspect of the law was not violated.

1895 Decision on the countries providing an adequate level of data protection, no. 11/2021 (n. 553); See also Chapter 4, C.II.12.

1896 See Chapter 4, D.II.11.

not recognised as 'adequate' by North Macedonia, necessitating even a prior approval for data transfers to these countries.[1897]

In summary it can be concluded that the WB6 countries amongst each other's apply different standards when it comes to accepting their respective levels of data protection as adequate. For some of them – Albania, Serbia and BiH – the guiding principle seems to be to ensure a free flow of personal data in the region, which is why they accept their neighbours' data protection provisions as adequate.[1898] For the other three – Kosovo, Montenegro and North Macedonia – the intention to align with the EU approach and adhere to the EU acquis seems to be the guiding principle which is why they do not accept their neighbours as adequate. In practice however, in a region so closely interconnected, data transfers may frequently occur despite the restrictions imposed by data protection laws.

IV Conclusion to A

In the region, some countries have adopted GDPR-like legislation, while others have yet to follow suit. In their pursuit of the common goal of harmonisation with the GDPR, the WB6 countries face similar challenges arising from a 'copy-paste' legislative approach and insufficient resources allocated to their respective data protection authorities. This approach has led to complications, such as the non-recognition of each other's data protection standards, resulting in restricted data flows within the region. Additional country-specific challenges further complicate the regional landscape. For example, Serbia continues to face the issue of non-recognition of EU data transfer mechanisms, resulting in a dual compliance burden under both Serbian and EU data transfer rules. In jurisdictions where data protection legislation remains outdated, the lack of political will and governmental prioritisation exacerbates legal uncertainty and undermines the development of a coherent regulatory framework. Moreover, the absence of strong regional cooperation further impedes the effective harmonisation and enforcement of data protection standards across the WB6. Notably, even those countries that have recently adopted new legislation have acknowledged the necessity of subsequent amendments to address persisting deficiencies. Whether these reforms will ultimately bring the region's legal frameworks closer to meeting the requirements for an adequacy decision under EU law remains an open question.

1897 See Chapter 4, E.II.9.

1898 However, only Serbia has adopted a new GDPR-aligned law. It remains to be seen whether Albania and BiH will continue with this approach once they have adopted new GDPR like laws.

B Current State of Play: Fulfilment of Art. 45(2) GDPR?

The criteria established under Art. 45(2) GDPR were analysed in Chapter 3. This Section provides a concise evaluation and systematic comparison of how these criteria are fulfilled across the six WB6 countries. While Chapters 4 and 5 offer a detailed examination of each country's data protection framework, this Section adopts a broader comparative approach. It assesses the extent to which the WB6 countries meet the adequacy criteria set out in Art. 45(2) GDPR, focusing on key aspects such as data protection legislation, constitutional safeguards, rule of law considerations, redress mechanisms, supervisory authorities, and relevant international agreements applicable in the region.

I Rule of Law

When assessing the possibility of an adequacy decision, the EU Commission considers the rule of law as a fundamental criterion. Similarly, the Copenhagen criteria establish the rule of law as one of the key requirements for candidate countries seeking EU membership, making it a central pillar of the accession process.[1899] Despite formal advancements in the EU accession process, numerous studies indicate that most governments in the WB6 region have become increasingly authoritarian over the past decade. These governments have managed to maintain a rhetorical commitment to democracy and EU integration while simultaneously engaging in informal authoritarian practices.[1900] In fact, Freedom House in its annual report of the status of democracy, considers all WB6 countries transitional or hybrid regimes, on a stable or even declining trend.[1901] Among them, Serbia has experienced the most significant democratic backsliding.[1902] The key concerns are related to political interference and political pressure on the judicia-

---

1899 Accession criteria (Copenhagen criteria) (n. 79).

1900 Marko Kmezić, "EU Rule of Law Conditionality: Democracy or 'Stabilitocracy' Promotion in the Western Balkans?" in: Džankić, J., Keil, S., Kmezić, M. (eds) The Europeanisation of the Western Balkans. New Perspectives on South-East Europe. Palgrave Macmillan (2019).

1901 European Court of Auditors, Special Report: Rule of Law in Western Balkans, despite efforts, fundamental problems persist (2022), available at the following link <https://op.europa.eu/webpub/eca/special-reports/eu-support-to-the-rule-of-law-in-Western-Balkans-01–2022/en/> (accessed on 01.03.2025).

1902 European Western Balkans, "Freedom House: Democracy deteriorates in the Western Balkans, Serbia faces the strongest decline," published on 11.04.2024, <https://europeanwesternbalkans.com/2024/04/11/freedom-house-democracy-deteriorates-in-the-western-balkans-serbia-faces-the-strongest-decline/> (accessed on 03.03.2025).

ry as well as corruption which undermine the independence of the judiciary, but also affect its effectiveness in processing the cases and most important decrease the quality of the work of the judicial system.[1903]

II Legislation

The EU Commission assesses both general and sectoral legislation when determining the adequacy of a third country's data protection framework, including its implantation. Moreover, 'legislation' goes beyond specific data protection laws and explicitly covers the legislation concerning public security, defence, national security, and criminal law.[1904] The WP29 has provided detailed guidelines on the essential elements that third-country data protection laws should contain, including, inter alia, principles of lawfulness, fundamental data protection principles, restrictions on onward transfers, special categories of personal data, direct marketing, and provisions on automated decision-making.[1905]

1 Constitutional Provisions

The constitutions of the WB6 countries guarantee the right to privacy and data protection to varying degrees, with the exception of BiH, which only provides for the right to privacy. This can be attributed to the fact that BiH has a unique constitution – Annex 4 of the Dayton Agreement – which offers only general provisions and is less detailed compared to the other WB6 countries.[1906] Notably, the constitutions of Kosovo, Montenegro, and Serbia provide for the restriction of privacy only by court decision. The Serbian constitution offers the most comprehensive protection of data, including provisions for lawfulness of processing, purpose limitation, the right to be informed, and court protection. Similarly, the Montenegrin constitution provides for the right to be informed and court protection as part of its constitutional data protection guarantees. The following table provides an overview of the constitutional parameters in the WB6.

1903 Aleksandar Lj. Spasov, "The European Integration of the Western Balkans and the Rule of Law (Current Situation and Challenges)", 15 Iustinianus Primus L. Rev. 1 (2024).

1904 Leonie Wittershagen, "The Transfer of Personal Data from the European Union to the United Kingdom post-Brexit", Volume 1 in the series Global and Comparative Data Law, (2023), p. 58.

1905 WP29 Adequacy Referential (n. 155).

1906 Dayton Agreement (n. 324).

Table 2: Overview of Constitutional Parameters on Privacy and Data Protection in the WB6

Country	Right to Data Protection	Right to Privacy
Albania	Art. 35 "No one may be obliged [...] law requires it, to make public personal data [...] The collection, use and making public of personal data is done with consent, except for the cases provided by law. Everyone has the right to become acquainted [...], except for the cases provided by law. Everyone has the right to request the correction or expunging of untrue or incomplete data or data collected in violation of law."	Art. 36 "The freedom and secrecy of correspondence or any other means of communication are guaranteed."
BiH	x	Art. II 3. (f) "The right to private and family life, home, and correspondence."
Kosovo	Art. 36 par. 4 "Every person enjoys the right of protection of personal data. Collection, preservation, access, correction and use of personal data are regulated by law."	Art. 36 par 1 and 3 1. "Everyone enjoys [...] private and family life {...} the inviolability of {...} confidentiality of correspondence, telecommunication [...]. 3. Secrecy of correspondence, telephony and other communication is an inviolable right. This right may only be limited temporarily by court decision if it is necessary for criminal proceedings or defense of the country as defined by law."
Montenegro	Art. 43 "The protection of personal data shall be guaranteed. It is prohibited to use personal data for purposes other than those for which they were collected. Everyone shall have the right to be informed about the personal data collected about him or her and the right to court protection in case of abuse."	Art. 42 "Confidentiality of [...] communication shall be inviolable. The principle of inviolability of confidentiality [...] communication shall be deviated from only on the basis of a court decision, if so required for the purposes of conducting criminal proceedings or for the security of Montenegro."
North Macedonia	Art. 18 "The security and confidentiality of personal information are guaranteed. Citizens are guaranteed protection from any violation of their personal integrity deriving	Art. 25 "Each citizen is guaranteed the respect and protection of the privacy of his/her personal and family life and of his/her dignity and repute."

Table 2 *(Continued)*

Country	Right to Data Protection	Right to Privacy
	from the registration of personal information through data processing."	
Serbia	Art. 42 "Protection of personal data shall be guaranteed. Collecting, keeping, processing and using of personal data shall be regulated by the law. Use of personal data for any the purpose [...] shall be prohibited [...], unless this is necessary to conduct criminal proceedings or protect safety of the Republic of Serbia, [...] Everyone shall have the right to be informed about personal data collected about him, in accordance with the law, and the right to court protection in case of their abuse."	Art. 41 "Confidentiality of letters and other means of communication shall be inviolable. Derogation shall be allowed only for a specified period of time and based on decision of the court if necessary to conduct criminal proceedings or protect the safety of the Republic of Serbia, in a manner stipulated by the law."

2 Data Protection Laws

As explored in detail in Chapter 4, the WB6 countries are currently at different stages of the harmonisation process with the GDPR. In particular, Kosovo, North Macedonia, and Serbia have demonstrated a rapid response to the GDPR by enacting GDPR-like laws. Albania also adopted a new data protection legislation in December 2024. Conversely, BiH, and Montenegro have yet to adopt new data protection laws that adhere to the GDPR. The following table offers a concise overview of the relevant laws applicable in the WB6 countries and announced amendments:

Table 3: Overview of the Data Protection Laws and Their Status in the WB6

Country	Data Protection Law	GDPR-like Law	Draft Law or Amendment on Data Protection Introduced	Status
Albania	Law on personal data protection no. 124/2024 dated 19.12.2024.	Yes	2024	–
BiH	Personal Data Protection Law (Official Gazette of Bosnia and	No	2020	The law has been drafted; the further

Table 3 *(Continued)*

Country	Data Protection Law	GDPR-like Law	Draft Law or Amendment on Data Protection Introduced	Status
	Herzegovina, n. 49/2006, 76/2011 and 89/2011 – correction)			legislative procedure is still pending.
Kosovo	Law 06/L-082 on Personal Data Protection	Yes	–	–
Montenegro	Personal Data Protection Law (Official Gazette of Montenegro, no. 079/08 dated 23.12.2008, 070/09 dated 21.10.2009, 044/12 dated 09.08.2012, 022/17 dated 03.04.2017)	No	2019	Public consultation finalised.
North Macedonia	Law on Personal Data Protection (Official Gazette of the Republic of North Macedonia, no. 42/20 and 294/21)	Yes	2021	Amendments announced.
Serbia	Law on Personal Data Protection (Official Gazette of RS, no. 87/2018)	Yes	2022	Amendments announced.

As analysed in individual chapters on the WB6 countries, all jurisdictions in the region incorporate basic data protection concepts and principles in their respective data protection laws. However, in BiH and Montenegro, certain provisions remain absent or do not correspond to the GDPR provisions, as their legislative frameworks are still modelled on the DPD. For instance, in BiH, the BDPL 2006 recognises the legitimate interest of political parties as a basis for lawful processing, which raises concerns regarding its compatibility with the GDPR's lawfulness criteria.[1907] Additionally, BiH data protection law mandates that consent for processing special categories of personal data must be provided in writing and bear the data subject's signature, an outdated approach that does not reflect the modern technological advancements and the increasing digitisation of data processing.[1908] In Montenegrin data protection law the definition of personal data does

1907 See Chapter 4, B.II.5.
1908 See Chapter 4, B.II.6.

not include location data, genetic data, or online identifiers[1909] – an omission that may pose challenges for obtaining an adequacy decision, given the GDPR's broader scope of personal data protection.

The lack of equivalent data protection standards is not confined to countries that have yet to update their legislation. In Serbia, for example, provisions on automated decision-making diverge from the GDPR's definition, thereby reducing the level of protection afforded to data subjects – a factor that is crucial in adequacy assessments.[1910] Similarly, restrictions on onward data transfers present another challenge in the WB6. Under the principle that the level of protection must not be undermined by subsequent transfers, the Serbian adequacy decision permits data transfers to countries that the EU Commission itself has not recognised as adequate, raising potential concerns.[1911] Furthermore, in BiH and Kosovo, data protection laws do not provide for transfers subject to appropriate safeguards, which exist under Art. 46 GDPR.[1912] The absence of such provisions limits the options available to data controllers for onward transfers and could weaken the protection of transferred data.

3 Essential Guarantees National Security and Criminal Laws

With regard to legislation governing national security and criminal law, as analysed in Chapter 5, general legal frameworks exist that provide essential guarantees to regulate law enforcement and national security access while limiting interferences with fundamental rights. However, these frameworks contain certain limitations and ambiguities. Each country within the WB6 has an Ombudsman institution and judicial mechanisms to address complaints related to such interferences. Nevertheless, in some jurisdictions, legal provisions governing state access to personal data are overly broad or lack sufficient clarity, raising concerns about potential overreach.[1913] Furthermore, given the broader challenges related to the rule of law in the region, the practical enforceability of these legal guarantees remains uncertain, as their effectiveness is contingent upon independent judicial oversight and institutional capacity to ensure compliance.

1909 See Chapter 4, D.II.4.
1910 See Chapter 4, F.II.7 (c).
1911 See Chapter 4, F.II.10.
1912 See Chapter 4, Sections B.10 and C.11.
1913 See for example the case of Albania, Chapter 5, B.II or case of Serbia, Chapter 5, G.II.

4 Implementation of Legislation

Concerning the implementation of the legislation, particular attention should be given to the theory and practice of the adoption of the EU acquis in the accession countries. While the majority of these countries have made substantial progress with regard to the adoption of the EU acquis, its implementation and enforcement are still highly insufficient and problematic.[1914] This is the case with the WB6 countries who struggle with the implementation of the new legislation aligned with the EU acquis. Some of them have a special fast track procedure for adopting new laws with the purpose of harmonisation with the EU acquis.[1915] This option gives them the possibility to adopt 'express laws' without actually incorporating them into their specific national legal system. This has already been criticised by the EU Commission and consequently remains one of the major obstacles for the harmonisation with the EU acquis.[1916] Additionally, some critics argue that the EU's enlargement policy toward the WB6 has been largely stagnant over the past fifteen years, with the accession process increasingly perceived as a bureaucratic "box-ticking" exercise rather than a substantive commitment to reform.[1917] This broader context is also relevant when assessing the feasibility of potential adequacy decisions, as the rule of law and effective implementation of legal frameworks play a crucial role in determining whether a third country meets the necessary standards for data protection adequacy.

1914 Tanja Marktler, (2006), (n. 153).

1915 See more on "Urgent Procedure" in Serbia <http://www.parlament.gov.rs/acts/birth-of-a-law.664.html?action=print>; See more on "Urgent Procedure" in Kosovo: BPRG, "Skupština Kosova: Povećanje Delotvornosti Putem Poboljšanja Poslovnika o Radu" (in Eng: "Parliament of Kosovo: Increase efficiency through Improvements of the Rules of Procedure") (April 2020) <https://balkansgroup.org/wp-content/uploads/2020/04/Skup%C5%A1tina-Kosova_Pove%C4%87anje-delotvornosti-putem-poboljs%C5%A1anja-Poslovnika-o-radu_web-1.pdf?>, pp. 21–23; See more on "Urgent Procedure" in North Macedonia, website of Macedonian parliament (in Macedonian) <https://www.sobranie.mk/zakonodavna-postapka.nspx> (all accessed on 22.02.2022).

1916 EU Commission Report for Serbia 2019, <https://ec.europa.eu/neighbourhood-enlargement/system/files/2019-05/20190529-serbia-report.pdf> pp. 8, 21–24; EU Commission Report for Serbia 2019 Albania <https://ec.europa.eu/neighbourhood-enlargement/system/files/2019-07/20190529-albania-report.pdf>, p. 8.

1917 Andi Hoxhaj, "The EU Rule of Law Initiative Towards the Western Balkans", Hague J Rule Law, pp. 143–172 (2021).

III Case Law

Under Art. 45(2)(a) GDPR case law, effective and enforceable data subjects' rights as well as effective administrative and judicial redress are crucial criteria. Case law seems to be rather limited on data protection issues. Most court case law is evident in case of North Macedonia.[1918] Private enforcement seems to be sparse, as the data subjects might not have the right awareness. Available case law is usually related to state authorities not respecting data protection laws, which leads to 'data scandals' as evaluated in the cases of Albania[1919] and Serbia[1920] in particular. Finally, it is also important to note that the rule of law issues also affect the effectiveness of available redress mechanisms in these countries. Many years of neglect and underinvestment have undermined judicial efficiency and access to justice in the WB6. In most countries, there are long court delays and a high backlog of cases.[1921] The WP29 also emphasised that efficient enforcement mechanisms are of "paramount importance" when assessing the adequate level of personal data protection.[1922] Thus, this last criterion will be of significant importance for the WB6 countries.

IV Effective Redress

In each WB6 country, data subjects have varying mechanisms for enforcing their rights under national data protection legislation. The means of seeking redress differ across jurisdictions. In countries that have adopted GDPR-inspired laws – Albania, Kosovo, North Macedonia, and Serbia – data subjects have multiple avenues for redress, including the right to file a complaint with the supervisory authority, judicial redress against the supervisory authority's decisions, judicial redress against a controller and processor, and the right to seek compensation.[1923] In the case of BiH, data subjects have the right to lodge a complaint with the supervisory authority and, if dissatisfied with its decision, to initiate an administra-

1918 Especially court case law is more evident in North Macedonia, compared to other WB6 countries, see Chapter 4, D.IV.4.

1919 Chapter 4, A.IV.2.

1920 Chapter 4, F.IV.2.

1921 Huma Haider, "Rule of law challenges in the Western Balkans", Institute of Development Studies Brighton, UK (2018).

1922 WP29, Working Document on Adequacy Referential 18/EN, WP 254rev.01, February 2018, p. 3.

1923 See Chapter 4, parts 'Redress Rights' in the Sections A, C, E and F.

tive dispute before the competent courts.[1924] Additionally, they are entitled to claim compensation for both material and non-material damage resulting from a breach of their right to privacy.[1925] In Montenegro, data subjects may submit a "request for protection of rights" to the supervisory authority and pursue an administrative dispute before the competent court.[1926] While data subjects in Montenegro also have the right to compensation, this right is not explicitly regulated under data protection law but instead falls under a separate legal framework.[1927]

Beyond data protection legislation, data subjects in WB6 countries also benefit from rights enshrined in constitutional, criminal and civil laws. Furthermore, as all WB6 countries – except Kosovo – are signatories to the ECHR, data subjects have the right to submit complaints to the ECtHR as a final instance.[1928]

Despite the existence of these legal safeguards, concerns persist regarding the effectiveness of data subject rights in practice. As analysed in Chapter 4, supervisory authorities generally provide a quicker and more effective means of redress compared to the judiciary. However, judicial protection presents certain challenges. Courts often issue decisions that diverge from those of supervisory authorities, and judicial proceedings tend to be prolonged, reflecting broader inefficiencies within the WB6 judicial systems.[1929] These delays and inconsistencies undermine the overall effectiveness of data protection enforcement in the region.

V International Instruments

The adherence of third countries to international obligations is a key factor in determining adequacy decisions.[1930] Recital 105 GDPR emphasises that the EU Commission should consider the third country's adherence to Convention 108 and its Additional Protocol, among other factors, when assessing adequacy decisions. All WB6 except Kosovo are signatories to the ECHR and Convention 108. However, Kosovo's statehood is not universally recognised, which limits its ability to sign international instruments. Additionally, Montenegro has yet to sign and ratify Protocol no. 223. It is crucial to emphasize that adherence to ratified international instruments is vital for ensuring data protection standards in third countries. The

1924 Chapter 4, B.II.8.
1925 *Ibid.*
1926 Chapter 4, D.II.9.
1927 *Ibid.*
1928 See table 4 – Overview of International Instruments in the WB6.
1929 See the case of BiH, Chapter 4, B.III.4 or case of Montenegro, Chapter 4, D.III.4.
1930 WP29 Adequacy Referential, p. 4 (n. 155).

EU Commission takes into account international commitments of the third country when assessing adequacy decisions, as already elaborated in Chapter 3. Thus, this plays also a crucial factor for determining potential adequacy decisions in the WB6.

Table 4: Overview of International Instruments in the WB6

Country	ECHR (signed and ratified)	Convention 108 (signed and ratified)	Protocol no. 223 signed	Protocol no. 223 ratified
Albania	✓	✓	✓	✓
BIH	✓	✓	✓	✓
Kosovo	×	×	×	×
Montenegro	✓	✓	×	×
North Macedonia	✓	✓	✓	✓
Serbia	✓	✓	✓	✓

VI Supervisory Authorities

Art. 45(2)(b) GDPR sets out the general criteria for determining whether the third country supervisory authority has the necessary independence required for an adequacy decision. The presence of an independent supervisory authority, equipped with the necessary powers to monitor and enforce compliance with data protection rules, is crucial for ensuring that an adequate level of data protection is practically guaranteed.[1931] In its guidance,[1932] WP29 emphasizes the importance of complete independence and impartiality of the supervisory authority in performing its duties and exercising its powers, without seeking or accepting instructions. Additionally, the supervisory authority must have all the necessary powers and resources to ensure compliance with data protection rights and promote awareness, including considerations of staffing and budget.[1933]

The GDPR provides detailed requirements for independent supervisory authorities in EU Member States, as stated in Artt. 51–29. Art. 52 GDPR specifically addresses independence, stating that members of the supervisory authority must be free from outside influence when making decisions. Direct supervision

1931 Recital 6 UK Adequacy Decision, (n. 248).
1932 WP29 Adequacy Referential, pp. 7–9 (n. 155).
1933 *Ibid.*, p. 7.

of a personal data protection authority by a government minister responsible for the administrative department, including personal data protection, would likely contravene EU law.[1934]

All WB6 countries have supervisory authorities responsible for monitoring national data protection legislation, with varying forms of organisation. Most of them have a dual function and monitor both data protection laws and laws on freedom of access to information, with the exception of BiH and North Macedonia, which only monitor data protection laws. All supervisory authorities are subordinate to their respective national parliaments, while the Serbian authority is also subordinate to the Government. The Serbian authority currently has the greatest capacity and the highest number of staff, compared to the other authorities in the region. However, there are many challenges related to the independence of data protection authorities. In practice, these authorities have not always been able to exercise their powers. For example, in BiH, the data protection law does not apply at all to national security authorities.[1935] In Serbia, the data protection authority has also been prevented from exercising its investigative powers over the national security agency, as the Serbian government tends to label its documents as secret and prevent the authority from gaining access to relevant documents.[1936] Thus, the WB6 data protection authorities are not completely free from the respective government's influence and political pressures.[1937]

1934 Pawel Hajduk, "The Powers of the Supervisory Body in the GDPR as a Basis for Shaping the Practices of Personal Data Processing", Review of European and Comparative Law (RECoL), HeinOnline 45 (2021), pp. 57–76.

1935 See Chapter 5, Section D.II.4.

1936 E. g., The former DPC, Rodoljub Šabić, has not received the security certificate to gain the access to labeled documents relevant for performance of investigation in 2018; see Interview with the former Commission "Šabić: Opstrukcija Poverenika i zakona" (Eng. Obstruction of the Commissioner and the law), published in Danas (13.05.2018), available at the following link <https://www.danas.rs/vesti/drustvo/sabic-opstrukcija-poverenika-i-zakona/?fbclid=IwAR0mkFZ2DAQ_SAxJ7J6mdNOGvN4QnP4WWTTj-nIk_-vFnbzmtmuA9CcGoRI> (accessed on 07.04.2023).

1937 These challenges have been addressed in Chapter 4 and 5 in sections focusing on respective countries.

Table 5: Overview of Supervisory Authorities in the WB6

Country	Supervisory authority	Jurisdiction	Supervised by	Number of employees[1938]
Albania	Information and Data Protection Commissioner	Data protection and free access to information	Parliament	44
BiH	Personal Data Protection Agency	Data protection	Parliament	26
Kosovo	Information and Privacy Agency	Data protection and free access to information	Parliament	34
Montenegro	Agency for Personal Data Protection and Free Access to Information	Data protection and free access to information	Parliament	29
North Macedonia	Personal Data Protection Agency	Data protection	Parliament	22
Serbia	Commissioner for Public Information and Data Protection	Data protection and free access to information	Parliament and Government	105

VII Conclusion to B

The WB6 countries have shown varying degrees of readiness to align their data protection frameworks with the GDPR, and consequently meeting the adequacy criteria. While Albania, Kosovo, North Macedonia and Serbia have been relatively quick to adopt legislation similar to the GDPR, BiH and Montenegro are lagging

1938 Albania: "Annual Report for 2022", available at the following link <https://www.idp.al/wp-content/uploads/2016/11/ENGLISH_Raporti-Vjetor-2022_21_MARS_-Rev01_29_Mars_rishikuar_Rev01_5-4-2023.pdf>, p. 43; BiH, Information from the website of the supervisory authority, available at the following link <http://www.azlp.ba/o_agenciji/organizaciona_struktura/Default.aspx?id=455&langTag=bs-BA&template_id=149&pageIndex=1>; Kosovo, Performance Plan of the Information and Privacy Agency 2020, available at the following link: <https://www.azlp.ba/o_agenciji/organizaciona_struktura/Default.aspx?id=455&langTag=bs-BA&template_id=149&pageIndex=1>; Montenegro, Annual Report 22, p. 65, (n. 970); North Macedonia, available at the website of the supervisory authority at the following link <https://azlp.mk/en/pdpa/organization/>; Serbia, DPC's activity report for 2022, p. 146 (n. 1286); For a similar overview see also SHARE, Comparative Analysis (n. 20) (all accessed on 05.06.2023).

behind in adopting comparable legislation which would address the novelties introduced by the GDPR. Except for Kosovo, the WB6 are parties to important international treaties such as the ECHR and Convention 108, and they also have modern constitutions that recognise the right to data protection and privacy, with the exception of BiH, which only recognises the right to privacy. Despite legislative efforts to approximate GDPR standards, persistent challenges related to the rule of law and the effective implementation of data protection laws remain significant barriers to achieving an adequacy decision. Moreover, although all WB6 countries have established data protection authorities, these institutions face varying degrees of operational challenges, including resource constraints and limitations in enforcement capacity.

The diversity of legal and institutional frameworks across the WB6 underscores the complexity of the region's data protection landscape. While notable progress has been made, significant challenges remain in fully harmonising national data protection laws with the EU acquis and ensuring the level of protection required for an adequacy decision. Addressing these structural and institutional shortcomings will be essential for advancing data protection standards and facilitating future adequacy assessments.

C Beyond EU Accession: Possible Adequacy Decision(s) for the WB6?

Although all the WB6 countries are in the process of implementing the GDPR into their national legislation, to date it is unknown whether there are concrete plans for adequacy talks between the EU Commission and the WB6 countries. According to the estimation of local experts on the EU integration process, there is also the possibility that the EU Commission could adopt only a single decision for all WB6 countries jointly.[1939] However, this approach might not be conducive, as this would take considerably longer time before WB6 countries are on the EU Commission's

1939 In the sixth panel of the series "Data Protection Laws in the Western Balkans: Let's Talk about Adequacy!", organised by the author in cooperation with the Research Centre for Law and Digitisation ("FREDI") of the Faculty of Law at the University of Passau and Prof. Dr. Moritz Hennemann, one of the panellists mentioned the possibility of a joint adequacy decision by the EU Commission. Further information on the sixth panel of the series can be found on the University of Passau website at the following link <https://www.jura.uni-passau.de/aktuelles/meldung/diskussionsreihe-zum-datenschutz-im-westlichen-balkan> (accessed on 13.02.2023).

list of countries that offer an adequate level of data protection, due to their varying levels of alignment with the GDPR.[1940]

While the strategy of direct adoption of GDPR provisions by the WB6 countries has its own challenges and their data protection frameworks in the WB6 may not yet be ready to meet the criteria for an adequacy decision, as also discussed previously in this Chapter, it shall not stop these countries in leveraging their status as candidates or potential candidates for EU membership. The opening of adequacy discussions with the WB6 countries could motivate these countries to work on further harmonisation with the GDPR standards and fulfilling adequacy criteria. Once the WB6 countries become member of the EU, these issues will belong to the past and data can flow freely amongst all Member States. However, as this membership depends on a wide range of reforms and political decisions and there is no timeframe to complete the EU accession process, the adoption of an adequacy decision in the meantime would be of significant importance for the WB6 countries.

Moreover, they might be already in a better position than most other third countries, as their legal order is directed towards meeting EU standards. The WB6 countries are considered 'third countries' in terms of the GDPR, but they are not in the same position as other 'third countries' due to their EU assession process. The WB6 countries are already for a long time in the 'waiting room' for the EU and have started aligning their national data protection laws with the EU acquis around twenty years ago.[1941] Considering that there are other countries outside the European continent with a very different legal framework that have become 'adequate' in terms of data protection, such as Japan or South Korea, obtaining an adequacy decision for WB6 countries shall not be a 'mission impossible'. Their constitutions acknowledge data protection as a fundamental human right, similar as in the EU. Moreover, the concepts and norms are very similar to those in the EU due to the accession process, in contrast to countries with different legal traditions for which adequacy decisions have been adopted (e.g. Japan).[1942] As Moritz Hennemann points out, a regulatory approach often expresses specific (legal) cultural experiences and (legal) traditions which shape the spe-

---

1940 As mentioned in the previous Chapters, Kosovo, North Macedonia and Serbia have adopted a GDPR replica law, while Albania, BiH and Montenegro are preparing to adopt the new law.
1941 The Stabilisation and Association Process (SAP) was launched in June 1999 and strengthened at on the EU- Western Balkans Summit Thessaloniki in 2003, when the EU reiterated its support to the EU perspective of the WB6.
1942 Read more about the different privacy and data protection regimes in Japan and EU: Flora Y. Wang, pp. 670–679 (n. 1354).

cific application of certain norms or form the basis for their acceptance.[1943] Considering that the WB6 countries have continuously harmonised their laws with EU trends, and are signatories to Convention 108 and the ECHR,[1944] there is in general a lower (but not none) risk that any 'import' of EU laws into their legal system would likely have a different 'effect' than in the legal system of the EU.[1945] Of course, since these systems are still very unique compared to the EU, this does not mean that any 'import' of the GDPR concept into their national laws would per se be appropriate, as discussed below.[1946] In particular, the low enforcement level of the legal transplants coming from the EU accession process has been a subject of critics.

Moreover, it is important to state that the EU Commission is following the WB6 individual progress on their path towards EU accession on a yearly basis and is publishing reports with the state of play on harmonisation including giving opinions and recommendations. Through this mechanism, the EU Commission already has a very good overview of the rule of law and data protection regulations in the WB6 countries, which makes the assessment of an adequacy decision much easier compared to other countries. Moreover, the language barriers are not the same as it was the case with other countries (e.g. Japan or South Korea), considering that some EU countries speak a very similar language as most of the WB6 countries.

This Section will explore the difficulties encountered by the WB6 countries in striving for an adequacy decision, and it will cite instances of other countries that have successfully attained 'adequacy status' from the EU Commission. Furthermore, this discussion will offer guidance designed to guide the WB6 countries in tailoring their legislation to meet adequacy criteria, while also considering their unique economic and political contexts. Additionally, it aims to advise the EU Commission on factors to consider when evaluating their laws and engaging in adequacy negotiations.

1943 Moritz Hennemann, "Exportbeschränkungen für den Datenschutz?", Frankfurter Allgemeine Tageszeitung, Einspruch (01.10.2020).

1944 Except Kosovo; see Chapter 7, A.I.

1945 Moritz Hennemann notes that 'import' into another legal system does not necessarily have to, but will usually have a different "effect" than in the legal system of origin; Moritz Hennemann, Wettbewerb der Datenschutzrechtsordnungen?, p. 890. (n. 2).

1946 E.g., In case of Serbia the import of the concept of 'code of conduct' has raised the questions of the correct interpretation of this concept. See Chapter 4, F.II.9 (d).

I Challenges

The adoption of an adequacy decision may take a long time. There are increasing complaints about the adequacy decision process for taking such a long period.[1947] Only 13 countries have received an adequacy decision in the 26 years since the DPD entered into force in 1995.[1948] So far, only Japan, South Korea, the UK and the United States (for commercial organisations participating in the EU-US Data Privacy Framework) have obtained an adequacy decision since the introduction of the GDPR.[1949] Critics also argue that the decision making process on adequacy by the EU Commission is lacking transparency,[1950] especially in cases where the EU Commission has not published the reasons why a third country does not meet the criteria for an adequacy decision.[1951] It is important not to forget that the adequacy assessments are also influenced by political and economic motivations.[1952] There are critics who argue that the EU applies its privacy principles and the limits of the adequacy-based data transfer approach inconsistently.[1953] Some authors argue that this has been reflected in the case of Argentina, where the decision was granted despite the WP29 expressing concerns about weaknesses in Argentinian data protection laws.[1954] Similarly, in the case of Israel, Douwe Korff critically assesses whether the Israeli data protection framework aligns

1947 Graham Greenleaf (2012), pp. 68–92 (n. 146).
1948 See also Leonie Wittershagen, p. 316 (n. 151).
1949 *Ibid.* See also the list of adequacy decisions available on the EU Commission website <https://commission.europa.eu/law/law-topic/data-protection/international-dimension-data-protection/adequacy-decisions_en> (accessed on 05.03.2025).
1950 Vincent Manancourt, "Why Brussels Went Easy on Britain in Its Data Deal" published in Politico (30.06.2021), available at the following link <https://www.politico.eu/article/why-brussels-went-easy-on-britain-in-data-adequacy-deal/> (accessed on 10.06.2023).; Graham Greenleaf (2012), p. 15 (n. 146).
1951 E.g., Morocco requested an adequacy recognition decision from the EU Commission as early as 2009 and this request is still pending: see the article "Moroccan data protection law: Moving to align with EU data protection?" IAPP (11.09.2018) available at the following link <https://iapp.org/news/a/moroccan-data-protection-law-moving-to-align-with-eu-data-protection/> (accessed on 29.05.2023); See also Graham Greenleaf (2012), p. 15 (n. 146) and Leonie Wittershagen, p. 316 (n. 151).
1952 See Chapter 3, B.I.
1953 Information Technology & Innovation Foundation, "Response to the Consultation of the EU Commission on Transfers of Personal Data to Third Countries and Cooperation between Data Protection Authorities" (2020), available at the following link <https://www2.itif.org/2020-gdpr-two-year-review.pdf> (accessed on 10.06.2023).
1954 *Ibid*, p. 3.

with the adequacy criteria stipulated in Art. 45 GDPR.[1955] In addition, a dialogue with Eastern and South-Eastern key trading partners of the EU, including India, as well as with Latin American countries on adequacy decisions was announced by the EU Commission.[1956]

Although the WB6 countries are economically and geographically linked to the EU, it seems that they are not as appealing to the EU for an adequacy decision as these countries are no major investors in the EU, but rather beneficiaries of EU investments.[1957] The EU Commission nevertheless announced a dialogue with countries in "the European neighbourhood which have expressed an interest in obtaining an adequacy finding", in 2017.[1958] However, no further concrete steps towards such a dialogue have been announced.

II Transplantation Approach and Dilemmas

The use of comparative law while drafting new legislation is as old as the phenomenon of statutory law itself.[1959] The reception of foreign legal transplants in most of the WB6 countries began in the period when the region was under Habsburg rule.[1960] According to leading comparative law scholars, the Austrian Civil Code (ABGB) was 'exported' to countries in Southeast Europe.[1961]

1955 Douwe Korff, "Update on the Opinion on the future of personal data transfers from the EU/EEA to Israel & the Occupied Territories", available at the following link <https://www.ianbrown.tech/wp-content/uploads/2022/02/KORFF-Opinion-update-EU-Israel-data-transfers-final220223-2.pdf> (accessed on 29.05.2023); See also bellow in Section III.1. a deeper analysis of Israel data protection framework.

1956 EU Commission, Exchanging and Protecting Personal Data in a Globalised World, p. 8 (n. 186).

1957 For more information see Infographic, "The EU: main trade partner and investor for the Western Balkan Council of Europe, General Secretariat", available at the following link <https://www.consilium.europa.eu/en/infographics/the-eu-main-trade-partner-and-investor-for-the-western-balkans/> (03.06.2023).

1958 EU Commission, Exchanging and Protecting Personal Data in a Globalised World, p. 8 (n. 186).

1959 Jan M. Smits, "Comparative Law and its Influence on National Legal Systems", The Oxford Handbook of Comparative Law (2nd edn) (2019), p. 505.

1960 Lana Bubalo, An Introduction to the Legal Cultures of Bosnia and Herzegovina, Croatia, and Serbia (Western Balkan)", Koch, S., Kjølstad, M.M. (eds) Handbook on Legal Cultures. Springer, Cham (2023), p. 174.

1961 Konrad Zweigert and Hein Kötz, "An Introduction to Comparative Law", Clarendon Press, Oxford (1998), p. 166.

Several factors motivate countries to embrace foreign legal solutions. One compelling reason is the practicality of adopting a solution already in operation elsewhere, which saves time and resources.[1962] Additionally, the adoption of foreign law can enhance a country's reputation on the global stage.[1963] The most important reason for a country to take over foreign law, however, is that it is often more or less compelled to do so,[1964] as is the case with the WB6 countries on the EU integration path. Legal transplants in WB6 were and are still used as a method for legal evolution and the development of legal culture.[1965] They are seen as a faster, cheaper, and useful source of new law.[1966] Not rarely are they a signal to foreign investors that the national law is familiar with Western legal standards.[1967]

Scholars have raised doubts about the practical effectiveness of incorporating foreign laws, often referred to as legal transplants.[1968] There are a couple of key reasons for these doubts. First of all, the transfer of law across linguistic borders is inextricably bound up with massive translation efforts.[1969] They often lead to the introduction of a new vocabulary and concepts.[1970] For example, the accession of several Central and Eastern European countries to the EU required the translation of the EU acquis into Slavic languages, a formidable challenge in its own right.[1971] Unfortunately, translations can sometimes lead to misunderstandings or incorrect interpretations, as seen in the case of translating GDPR articles into the national legislation of the WB6 countries.[1972] Secondly, it has been argued that legal transplants cannot succeed or even be possible because "at best, what can be transferred from one jurisdiction to another is, literally, a meaningless form of words".[1973] Yet, as Uwe Kischel states, such arguments do not establish the impos-

---

1962 Jan M. Smits, p. 517 (n. 1959).

1963 *Ibid.*

1964 *Ibid.*

1965 Lana Bubalo, p. 174 (n. 1960).

1966 *Ibid.*

1967 Daniel Berkowitz, Katharina Pistor, Jean-Francois Richard, "The transplant effect", Am J Comp Law 51(1):16–204, (2003), p. 164.

1968 The term legal transplant was created in the 1970s by the Scottish legal scholar Alan Watson to describe the transfer of a rule or system of law from one country to another: Alan Watson, "Legal Transplants: An Approach to Comparative Law", University Press of Virginia (1974).

1969 Michele Graziadei, "Comparative Law, Transplants, and Receptions", The Oxford Handbook of Comparative Law (2nd edn) (2019), p. 457.

1970 *Ibid.*

1971 *Ibid.*

1972 See for more information Chapter 4 and analyses of each country's profile.

1973 Pierre Legrand, "What 'Legal Transplants'?", in David Nelken and Joachim Feest (eds), Adapting Legal Cultures (2001), p. 59.

sibility of legal transplants, but rather simply raise one already familiar issue: the question of how and to what extent legal rules are changed by transplantation.[1974]

In recent times, the EU has played a prominent role in encouraging the adoption of its legislative models by many other countries.[1975] This is especially true for the GDPR. The GDPR, a seminal EU data protection framework, has served as a source of inspiration for numerous countries outside of the EU looking to develop their own data protection regulations using the GDPR as a benchmark. Within the WB6 countries, the GDPR not only served as a source of inspiration but was taken as a fundamental blueprint. With minimal to almost no adaptations to their unique legal systems and cultural contexts, these countries opted for a comprehensive incorporation of the GDPR provisions into their national legal frameworks.

Despite the fact that legal transplants are a common feature in other countries, in the WB6 it has been evident that the cut-and-paste practice functions poorly in an environment with weak institutions.[1976] Moreover, lawyers not familiar with the foreign rules and principles of transplanted laws have avoided using the new concepts, which has prevented many of these transplants from fully coming to life.[1977] For legal transplants to succeed and be correctly accepted, there is a need for a further development of legal concepts through comparative legal analysis, which will make these transplanted concepts more understandable and approachable.[1978]

III Evaluating Alternatives to GDPR Transplantation: Lessons and Models

The GDPR has undoubtedly set a high standard. That does, however, not mean that the GDPR has set the most innovative standard.[1979] Significant doubts have been raised whether the GDPR actually fosters competition and innovation.[1980]

1974 Uwe Kischel, "Comparative Law", Oxford University Press (April 2019), p. 63.

1975 European Commission, A European Strategy for Data, COM(2020) 66 final, p. 24. See also Patricia Boshe and Moritz Hennemann, and Ricarda von Meding, "African Data Protection Laws – Current Regulatory Approaches, Policy Initiatives, and the Way Forward" Global Privacy Law Review (2022), p. 4.

1976 Lana Bubalo, p. 177 (n. 1960).

1977 *Ibid.*, p. 174.

1978 Mirjana Radović, "Utjecaj anglosaksonskog prava na srpsko kompanijsko pravo" (Eng: The influence of Anglo-Saxon law on Serbian company law), Strani pravni život 63(2), pp. 33–44 (2019).

1979 Patricia Boshe, Moritz Hennemann, and Ricarda von Meding, p. 30 (n. 1975).

It is questionable whether a 'one size fits all' approach is a sound approach to data protection regulation.[1981] The GDPR in particular has raised concerns in Europe (and elsewhere) of overregulating small businesses by subjecting them to excessive requirements (and corresponding fines).[1982] Furthermore, the 'success' of the GDPR transplanting European-style legislation – and thereby European values – to the 'importing' states has been questioned.[1983] That is to say that the GDPR might not be the most suitable standard in every cultural context.[1984] One might even frame this process as a 'data imperialism'[1985] or 'legal imperialism'.[1986] As Uwe Kischel explained, legal imperialism entails a simplistic belief that one's native legal system simply does a better job in regulating various aspects of life.[1987] In the case of the WB6 countries, this translated into a belief that a straightforward copy-and-paste of GDPR provisions would lead to better results than developing their own customised legislation. However, this approach disregards the need for nuanced legal adaptations to suit the specific needs and characteristics of each jurisdiction. While the WB6 have an obligation to align their national legislation with the EU acquis, this obligation does not mean that the WB6 need to copy-paste GDPR articles,[1988] nor does Art. 45 GDPR state that for

1980 Michal Gal and Oshritviv *Aviv*, "The Competitive Effects of the GDPR", Journal of Competition Law and Economics (2020), p. 349.

1981 Moritz Zimmermann, "The GDPR two years on: Time for the EU to go after privacy violations by big tech", article published by European Digital SM Alliance (24.06.2020) available at the following link <https://www.digitalsme.eu/the-gdpr-two-years-on-time-for-the-eu-to-go-after-privacy-violations-by-big-tech/> (accessed on 01.12.2023); Maria Tzanou, Addressing Big Data and AI Challenges: A Taxonomy and Why the GDPR Cannot Provide a One-size-fits-all Solution (17.07.2020).

1982 Dror Liwer, GDPR: one size does not fit all, CSO-US 2018, available at the following link <https://www.csoonline.com/article/3269570/gdpr-one-size-does-not-fit-all.html> (accessed on 01.12.2023).

1983 Patricia Boshe, Moritz Hennemann, and Ricarda von Meding, p. 31 (n. 1975).

1984 Moritz Hennemann, Wettbewerb der Datenschutzrechtsordnungen, p. 865 (n. 2).

1985 Scott and Cerulus in Politico wrote, for example, that: "the upcoming data protection changes risks being viewed as yet another diktat handed down by former colonial powers in a form of 'data imperialism'; Marc Scott and Laurens Cerulus, "Europe's new data protection rules export privacy standards worldwide", Politico (31.01.2018), <https://www.politico.eu/article/europe-data-protection-privacy-standards-gdpr-general-protection-data-regulation/> (accessed on 06.11.2023).

1986 Uwe Kischel, p. 48 (n. 1974).

1987 *Ibid.*

1988 Art. 70 SAAs with Albania and BiH states that the county shall endeavour to ensure that its existing laws and future legislation shall be gradually made 'compatible' with the Community acquis. The same applies to the other WB6 countries (Art. 74 SAA with Kosovo, Art. 68 SAA with North Macedonia and Art. 72 SAA with Serbia).

adoption of an adequacy decision, third countries have to make copies of the GDPR.[1989]

1 Other Adequacy Decisions

A look at other third countries that have received an adequacy decision confirms this, as will be shown below using the cases of Israel, Japan, South Korea and Hungary (before it joined the EU). The three examples of Israel, Japan and South Korea seem to be particularly worthwhile to look at because – other than e.g. in the case of the United Kingdom – they have different legal backgrounds than the EU and still managed to obtain adequacy decisions. Moreover, adequacy decisions for Japan and South Korea have been adopted recently, after the adoption of the GDPR and the EU Commission assessments are far more detailed in these two cases. Lastly, the look at Hungary will evaluate that even for countries on the EU membership path, it makes sense to obtain an adequacy decision and not wait until joining the EU.

a) Israel's Adequacy Decision

The adequacy decision for Israel was adopted under the DPD, before the implementation of the GDPR, and it continues to be valid.[1990] Israel serves as an example wherein a non-EU country does not need to replicate EU data protection legislation to obtain 'adequacy status'. Israel and the EU have different starting points for their data protection regulations, but they have similar legal mechanisms by prioritising individual rights over public goods such as democracy and national security.[1991] Israeli data protection law is a subsystem of the Israeli privacy protection regime whereas the right to privacy is derived from human dignity.[1992] The legal standards for the protection of personal data in Israel are laid down in the Privacy Protection Act 5741–1981.[1993] Not confined to a singular statutory law, data protection legislation is supplemented by governmental decisions addressing the implementation of the Privacy Protection Act and the organisation

1989 Schrems II, paras 94–105 (n. 143).

1990 EU Commission Decision 2011/61/EU pursuant to Directive 95/46/EC of the European Parliament and of the Council on the adequate protection of personal data by the State of Israel with regard to automated processing of personal data L 27/39 (01.02.2011).

1991 Soren Zimmermann, "The Legal Framework of Data Protection in Israel: A European Perspective", 5 Eur. Data Prot. L. Rev. 246 (2019).

1992 *Ibid.*, p. 248.

1993 Privacy Protection Act 5741–1981, available at the following link <https://www.gov.il/en/Departments/legalInfo/legislation> (accessed on 01.12.2023).

and functioning of the supervisory authority.[1994] Moreover, case law in Israel, which is primarily based on the Israeli Supreme Court, is of significant importance.[1995] For instance, the main principle of informed consent has been a result of case law.[1996] However, when the adequacy decision for Israel was adopted, it was challenged for perceived shortcomings in the protection of personal data compared to the EU's higher standards.[1997] In 2010, even the Irish Minister of Justice formally objected to a favourable WP29 adequacy report[1998] on the basis that Israeli officials could not be trusted with Europeans' personal data.[1999] Despite this, Israel retained the adequacy decision by reforming its data protection framework. In 2023, Israel enacted "Privacy Protection Regulations (Instructions Regarding Data Transfers from the European Economic Area to Israel), 5783–2023" specifically addressing the protection of personal data transferred from the EU,[2000] thereby preserving its adequacy status.[2001]

1994 Israel Adequacy decision, para. 7.

1995 Soren Zimmermann, The Legal Framework of Data Protection in Israel: A European Perspective, 5 Eur. Data Prot. L. Rev. 246 (2019).

1996 Ruth Levush, "Israel. Online Privacy Law" in Ethan P William (ed.), Online Privacy Laws European Union & select foreign countries (Nova Science 2013) p. 81; Soren Zimmermann, The Legal Framework of Data Protection in Israel: A European Perspective, 5 Eur. Data Prot. L. Rev. 246 (2019), p. 251.

1997 Omer Tene, Is Israeli Data Protection Law 'Adequate' Under Article 25? (November 2, 2008). Privacy and Data Protection, Vol. 8, No. 5, pp. 9–13 (2008).

1998 WP29, Opinion 6/2009 on the level of protection of personal data in Israel, 02316/09/EN WP 165 (01.12.2009).

1999 John Ihle, "Ireland blocks EU data sharing with Israel", (8 July 2010) Jewish Telegraphic Agency <www.jta.org/2010/07/08/news-opinion/world/ ireland-blocks-eu-data-sharing-with-israel> (accessed on 01.12.2023).

2000 One Trust Data Guidance, Israel: Privacy protection regulations on transfers from the EEA published in final form (09.05.2023) <https://www.dataguidance.com/news/israel-privacy-protection-regulations-transfers-eea > (accessed on 01.12.2023). Regulations available at the following link <https://www.gov.il/BlobFolder/legalinfo/datatransferredisrael2023/en/Privacy%20Protection%20Regulations%20(Instructions%20for%20Data%20that%20was%20transferred%20to%20Israel%20from%20the%20European%20Economic%20Area).pdf > (accessed on 01.12.2023).

2001 The Israeli Ministry of Justice initiated the draft of regulations in light of a review process the EU Commission is conducting for the purpose of considering if to reaffirm its adequacy decision. See for more information: Area Barnea Jaffa Lande, "New Israeli Privacy Protection Regulations for European Citizens' Data", Lexology (13.12.2023), available at the following link <https://www.lexology.com/library/detail.aspx?g=11147a9b-cc22-4f59-917c-785fd72b5bca> (accessed on 03.01.2024).

b) Japan's Adequacy Decision

The adequacy decision for Japan holds significant importance, representing not only the first adequacy agreement post-GDPR implementation but also the first mutual adequacy agreement between the EU and a non-EU country.[2002] This landmark decision is seen as important because Japan's cooperative but restrictive approach in response to the Brussels effect can serve as a model for other countries.[2003] The adequacy decision covers the public sector, but it does not cover the public sector.[2004]

The most significant difference between the EU approach and the Japanese approach to privacy is that the EU considers data protection and privacy to be fundamental rights, viewing those rights as a more dominant rationale for regulation than economic incentives.[2005] The Japanese Act on the Protection of Personal Information (hereinafter: "APPI") protects 'personal information', which provides a narrower scope of protection than a general right to data protection under the GDPR.[2006] Also, the APPI distinguishes between 'personal information 'and 'personal data', where 'personal data' is defined as "personal information constituting a personal information database".[2007] This distinction between personal information and personal data is relevant because such information may not always be part of a 'personal information database' and therefore those provisions of the APPI that only relate to personal data will not apply.[2008] The EU Commission, however, stated that this distinction will not be relevant for personal data imported from the EU to Japan on the basis of an adequacy decision, as such data will typically be transferred by electronic means and hence become part of the data importer's electronic filing system, such EU data will fall into the category of personal data under the APPI.[2009] Furthermore, notable differences exist in the

2002 Flora Y. Wang, p. 663 (n. 1354).

2003 *Ibid.*, p. 664.

2004 EU Commission Implementing Decision (EU) 2019/419 C/2019/304/ pursuant to Regulation (EU) 2016/679 of the European Parliament and of the Council on the adequate protection of personal data by Japan under the Act on the Protection of Personal Information, OJ L 76, (19.03. 2019), para. 10.

2005 William McGeveran, "Friending the Privacy Regulators", 58 ARIz. L. REV. p. 967 (2016).

2006 Art. 2(1) APPI. The scope of protected data for personal information is limited to "information relating to a living individual […] such as "name, date of birth, or other descriptions […] which can be used to identify a specific individual […] or those containing an individual identification code." The GDPR on the other hand defines personal data as "any information relating to an identified or identifiable natural person".

2007 Art. 16(3) APPI.

2008 Recital 21 Japan Adequacy Decision, (n. 2004).

2009 *Ibid.*, Recital 22.

enforceability of 'guidelines'. From the EU perspective, the common understanding of guidelines is that they "are just guidelines, they are not mandated", while under the APPI guidelines are considered to be binding when they say that a business 'must' or 'should not' undertake certain actions as outlined in the guidelines, with non-compliance constituting a violation of the law.[2010] Despite initial concerns that the Japan's guidelines were not legally binding, the EU Commission seems to have acknowledged the PPC's explanation, indicating that Japanese courts treat the guidelines as effectively binding.[2011]

Despite the differences between the Japanese legal system and the GDPR, the EU Commission recognised the Japanese legal framework as offering sufficient protection, proving that these differences do not prevent obtaining an adequacy decision. Yet, in order to meet the EU's adequacy criteria, Japan made two important concessions in the supplementary rules. First, Japan agreed to begin classifying sexual orientation and trade union membership status as special categories of personal data (sensitive data), contrary to prior practice.[2012] Second, the Supplementary Rules "ensure that data subject rights will apply to all personal data transferred from the EU, irrespective of their retention period", even though Japanese law does not provide such protections.[2013] These supplementary rules adopted by Japan were specifically designed to enhance the protection of personal information transferred from the EU to Japan.[2014]

In 2023, the EU Commission performed the first assessment of the mutual adequacy decision, and noted an increased level of alignment between the data protection frameworks in the EU and Japan and welcomed the establishment of contact points for EU individuals regarding data processing in Japan, as well as the extension of safeguards to academic and the public sector, which may even pave the way for an extension of the adequacy decision beyond commercial exchanges.[2015]

Japan's example demonstrates that states do not have to copy GDPR articles to comply with Art. 45(2) GDPR. According to Flora Y. Wang "the unique Japanese model suggests that countries can pursue a cooperative approach to data privacy

2010 Flora Y. Wang, p. 676 (n. 1354).

2011 Recital 16 Japan Adequacy Decision, (n. 2004).

2012 EDPB, Opinion 28/2018 Regarding the European Commission Draft Implementing Decision on the Adequate Protection of Personal Data in Japan, (05.12.2018), para. 9.

2013 *Ibid.*

2014 Nick Blue, "Spirited away: The EU's Adequacy Decision for Japan as a Roadmap for U.S. Privacy Law after Schrems II", 21 Wash. U. GLOBAL Stud. L. REV. 437 (2022), p. 453.

2015 Report from the EU Commission to the European Parliament and the Council on the first review of the functioning of the adequacy decision for Japan SWD(2023) 75 final (03.04.2023).

that maintains domestic values, culture, and identity – all while also benefiting economically from data flows".[2016] This dual objective illustrates a strategic balance that the Japanese system seeks to achieve: strategic alignment with EU data protection law while simultaneously reforming the data protection framework to accommodate its own legal cultural and economic considerations.

c) South Korea's Adequacy Decision

The EU Commission's adequacy decision concerning South Korea was the third such decision under the GDPR. It follows those concerning Japan (2019) and the United Kingdom (2021). The scope of this adequacy decision is broad, covering all information controllers in South Korea bound by the Personal Information Protection Act (hereinafter: "PIPA"), with the exception of missionary activities, political party nominations, and most credit transactions.[2017]

South Korea announced that it wished to obtain an adequacy assessment from the EU, and took the novel approach of preparing a detailed self-assessment report on the strengths and remaining weaknesses of Korea's data protection regime, which it presented to the EU in 2016.[2018] In 2017 South Korea updated this self-assessment report, and the EU stated that this is one of the adequacy assessments to which it is giving priority.[2019]

As a part of its ongoing adequacy negotiations with the EU, South Korea conducted numerous reforms to its data protection laws.[2020] Two reforms can be considered to be the most significant ones. Firstly, South Korea had to introduce additional safeguards in relation to Personal Information Protection Commission (hereinafter: "PIPC") to ensure that this institution has more equivalent power and competencies as the data protection authorities in the EU and the second one was related to criminal law and national security matters ('government ac-

---

2016 Flora Y. Wang, p. 665 (n. 1354).

2017 For more detailed overview see Graham Greenleaf, "The draft Korea adequacy Decision: Submission to European Union authorities", UNSW Sydney (16.08.2021).

2018 Graham Greenleaf, "Update to Graham Greenleaf's Asian Data Privacy Laws – Trade and Human Rights Perspectives" UNSW Law Research Paper no. 17–47 (12.07.2017). p. 12.

2019 *Ibid.*

2020 Daniel R. Stoller, "South Korea Privacy Law Changes May Help EU Data Transfer Talks", BLOOMBERG L. (22.02.2019) available at the following link <https://news.bloomberglaw.com/privacy-and-data-security/south-korea-privacy-law-changes-may-help-eu-data-transfer-talks> (accessed on 02.12.2023); see also European Commission Press Statement 17/4739 by Commissioner Wra Jourova, Mr. Lee Hyo-seong, Chairman of the Korea Communications Commission and Mr. Jeong Hyun-cheol, Vice President of the Korea Internet & Security Agency, European Commission (20.11.2017).

cess').[2021] Despite these legal reforms, South Korea did not transplant the whole GDPR into its national legislation,[2022] although its legislation seems to be more similar to the GDPR compared to the one of Japan.[2023] For example, automated decision making processing protection is not envisaged by the PIPA,[2024] while data portability is provided by another law.[2025]

d) Hungary

The adequacy decision for Hungary was adopted in 2000, prior to the country's accession to the EU.[2026] This decision is notably shorter than the previously analysed adequacy decisions. The decision affirmed that Hungary's legal framework encompasses all fundamental principles necessary to ensure an adequate level of protection for natural persons.[2027] Furthermore, it confirmed that these legal standards are upheld through judicial remedies and independent supervisory mechanisms.[2028] Importantly, this decision demonstrates a precedent in which the EU Commission assessed the data protection framework of a country that was already engaged in EU accession negotiations. Hungary commenced negotia-

2021 Daniel R. Stoller (n. 2020).

2022 For example, the PIPA doesn't use the terms 'controller' and 'processor', but rather 'personal information controllers'. See the detailed analyses of South Korea data protection framework in the Opinion 32/2021 regarding the European Commission Draft Implementing Decision pursuant to Regulation (EU) 2016/679 on the adequate protection of personal data in the Republic of Korea Version 1.0 (24.09.2021).

2023 For a better overview of the comparison between Japan's and South Korea's reforms of data protection law see Graham Greenleaf, "Japan and Korea: Different Paths to EU Adequacy" 156 Privacy Laws & Business International Report, pp. 9–11 (2018).

2024 Recital 81 South Korea Adequacy Decision (n. 2022); The EU Commission stated in its adequacy decision that as regards personal data that has been collected in the EU, any decision based on automated processing will typically be taken by the controller in the EU (which has a direct relationship with the concerned data subject) and is thus subject to GDPR, therefore the absence of specific rules on automated decision-making in the PIPA is unlikely to affect the level of protection of the personal data transferred under the adequacy decision.

2025 Act on the Use and Protection of Credit Information, see Recital 110 South Korea Adequacy Decision, (n. 2022).

2026 2000/519/EC: Commission Decision of 26 July 2000 pursuant to Directive 95/46/EC of the European Parliament and of the Council on the adequate protection of personal data provided in Hungary (notified under document number C(2000) 2305), Official Journal L 215 , 25/08/2000 P. 0004–0006 (Hungarian Adequacy Decision).

2027 Para 8 Hungarian Adequacy Decision.

2028 *Ibid.*

tions for EU membership (or, at the time, accession to the European Communities) in 1991[2029] and formally joined the EU in 2004.[2030]

2 A Unique Solution for the WB6?

The prevailing emphasis in current academic literature lies in the imperative for the WB6 countries to align their domestic data protection legislation with the GDPR.[2031] However this mainstream research focus gives little attention to the idea of developing own data protection laws of the WB6 that are both appropriate to their legal systems and their particular position in the 'EU waiting room'. While the WB6 countries are already very much aligning their national legislation with the EU acquis, it could be argued that legal transplants and mere 'copies' of the GDPR are not appropriate for these countries and that it is crucial to reflect not only on the legal culture and economic position of the WB6, but also on the previous experience of unsuccessful legal transplants in the WB6.[2032] On this basis, one might then examine a framework (potentially) more suitable for them.

Considering that the GDPR is not very friendly towards small and mid-size companies (hereinafter: "SMEs") due to its 'one size fits all' approach and significantly high fines, one could challenge the reason behind WB6 countries to adopt such approach instead of focusing on their economies and legal culture. In this respect, Nelken emphasizes that privacy is not only culturally sensitive but also socially revealing[2033] rather than a perceived universality. Speaking through the lens of Luhmann's Systemtheorie, law must be *umweltsensibel,* sensible for its 'surroundings'.[2034] A good example are Albania and Kosovo who while mostly coping the EU way of regulation data protection, opted for a more unique way of regulating protection of data based on the size and nature of companies.[2035] Even

2029 Europe Agreement establishing an association between the European Communities and their Member States and Hungary (16/12/1991)

2030 Treaty of Accession of the Czech Republic, Estonia, Cyprus, Latvia, Lithuania, Hungary, Malta, Poland, Slovenia and Slovakia was finalised in 2003 OJ L 236, 23.9.2003 and Hungary joined the EU in 2004 after the referendum. Y.V. Tverdova, C.J. Anderson, Choosing the West? Referendum choices on EU membership in east-central Europe, Electoral Studies, Volume 23, Issue 2 (2004).

2031 Chapter 1, C.

2032 As explained above in this Chapter 7, C.II.

2033 David Nelken, "Adapting Legal Cultures", Towards a Sociology of Legal Adaptation in Nelken/Feest, Oxford – Portland Oregon (2001), pp. 25.

2034 Niklas Luhmann, "Das Recht der Gesellschaft", Suhrkamp (1993), p. 441.

2035 While the current data protection law follows the 'one size fits all' approach, Albanian data protection authority has adopted two (Instruction no.47 and Instruction no. 22) which differentiate obligations of controllers depending on their size, see for more Chapter 4, A.II. Kosovo data protection authority has adopted a special Rulebook no. 05/2022 on Security Measures to regulate

countries that have been granted adequacy decisions, such as the UK, are considering a more balanced approach to the alignment of their national legislation with the GDPR. For example, the UK's Secretary of State for Digital, Culture, Media and Sport, Oliver Dowden MP, emphasised that the UK does not need to replicate the EU's rules word-for-word, citing examples of countries like Israel and Uruguay that achieved adequacy decisions while having their own personal data regulation regimes.[2036] He also stressed out the importance of encouraging businesses to embrace innovation, public service enhancement, and scientific discoveries.[2037]

a) Specifics of the WB6's Legal Systems

When considering the legal framework of the WB6 countries, several distinctive factors shall be taken into account. First and foremost, their legal systems adhere mostly to the European-continental legal family,[2038] primarily founded on statutory law, a strict hierarchy of norms and the prevalence of positivism in law, also referred as to 'legal formalism'.[2039] Their legal cultures do not recognise the concept of judicial precedent as part of the accepted mechanisms of norm production, and legal practice is not a formal source of law, where judges are not bound by the decisions of higher courts and do not have the power to authoritatively interpret and modify them.[2040] Even though WB6 countries for a while were classified as a third (socialist) legal family, they are today referred to as 'legal cultures in

in more detail the obligations of data controllers and processors, based on their nature of business, differentiating between low-risk and high-risk data controllers, see for more Chapter 4, C.II.

2036 Oliver Dowden, "New approach to data is a great opportunity for the UK post-Brexit", Financial Times (27.02.2021), <https://www.ft.com/content/ac1cbaef-d8bf-49b4-b11d-1fcc96dde0e1> (accessed on 12.11.2023). However, the UK Adequacy Decision (Art. 4), is subject to a time limit, a 'sunset clause', with the intention to observe the reforms of the UK data protection framework (n. 248); See also See also Leonie Wittershagen, pp. 214–215 (n. 151).

2037 *Ibid.*

2038 For an overview see Lana Bubalo (n. 1960); Марија Амповска, and Ристо Илиоски, "The Process of Civil Law Codification in Western Balkans", Macedonian Yearbook-Faculty of Law (2013).

2039 In the context of the socialist legal culture (which was dominant in the WB6 countries), characterised by a predominant emphasis on the concept of 'written law' or 'legal formalism', the primary judicial strategy was to make decisions on formal grounds and not to delve into substantive considerations. Legal formalism emphasises the importance of strict adherence to the letter of the law, with a tendency for public bodies to adopt restrictive interpretations, focusing primarily on grammatical aspects, when analysing legal norms; See also Fikret Karčić, "A study on legal formalism in the former Yugoslavia and its successor states", CIDS report no. 1 (2020).

2040 Lana Bubalo, p. 169 (n. 1960).

transition'.[2041] These legal cultures are characterised by the introduction of pluralistic democracy, rule of law, legal formalism, as well as legal transplants from Western countries.[2042] The following paragraphs will describe more in detail this particular legal environment in the WB6 that needs to be taken account in order to determine which is the best approach to regulate data protection in this region.

Firstly, in contrast to the EU, where recent years have witnessed an increasing influence of common law principles through the jurisprudence of the ECJU,[2043] the WB6 region has not seen a comparable elaboration of data protection mechanisms and standards.[2044] Instead, their data protection frameworks predominantly rely on legal provisions and soft law, such as recommendations issued by data protection authorities. Yet, it is noteworthy to acknowledge a subtle departure from this approach, facilitated by the application of the ECHR.[2045] Although it remains a fact that case law does not have the binding force of precedent, the jurisprudence of ECtHR, but also of the ECJU is taken into account by national courts in the WB6.[2046] What more, according to the harmonisation clause in the SAAs with the EU, the courts are to be guided by the practice of the ECJU.[2047]

Secondly, the enforcement mechanisms within the WB6 countries diverge significantly from those in the EU. The EU benefits from a more robust enforcement system compared to the WB6 countries, supported by institutions like the ECJU.[2048] In contrast, the WB6 depend primarily on their domestic courts and legal apparatus for the enforcement of legal provisions, a situation that is at times hindered by issues related to corruption.[2049] Moreover, the WB6 countries have undergone a profound transition from socialist legal systems to market-oriented economies

2041 *Ibid.* p. 152

2042 *Ibid.*

2043 The CJEU has developed and interpreted several principles in its case law; See also Maja Brkan, "The Essence of the Fundamental Rights to Privacy and Data Protection: Finding the Way Through the Maze of the CJEU's Constitutional Reasoning", German Law Journal (2019).

2044 As analysed in Chapter 4 for each country separately.

2045 For example, the Constitutional Court of Serbia refers to the ECHR in its decisions. See Chapter, 4.F.I (n. 1097).

2046 Lana Bubalo, p. 166. (n. 1960).

2047 Art. 70(1) SAAs with Albania and BiH, Art. 74(1) SAA with Kosovo, Art. 68(1) SAA with North Macedonia and Art. 72(1) SAA with Serbia.

2048 See more about enforcement system in the EU: Jonas Tallberg, "Paths to Compliance: Enforcement, Management, and the European Union", Cambridge University Press (2003).

2049 Corruption has been seen as one of the most common challenges for the rule of law from the EU Commission reports.

and democratic governance, necessitating substantial legal reforms.[2050] This transformation has engendered enduring challenges, particularly evident within the judiciary, encompassing issues related to the rule of law and the autonomy of the judiciary.[2051] One of the most common critiques of the WB6 countries legal systems in the post-transition period is that there are many good and modern laws but there is a low level of enforcement and effective implementation in practice.[2052] Although these challenges are the subject of ongoing reform efforts in the context of the accession process, they represent formidable hurdles. This is underscored by the fact that courts, public institutions and legal professionals are compelled to adapt to the new legal frameworks and practices emanating from the EU as part of the process of aligning with the acquis communautaire. The complexity is compounded by the relative lack of support and guidance available to these stakeholders in the WB6 countries compared to their counterparts in the EU.

Last, but not least a comprehensive evaluation of the WB6 region necessitates an examination of its economic landscape. Notably, a majority of businesses within this region are characterised as SMEs, with microenterprises accounting for the vast majority.[2053] With significant EU business presence and investment, particularly in the manufacturing sector,[2054] the alignment of data protection laws with familiar EU standards is logical. However, a critical assessment is required to determine the suitability of uniform application of all GDPR provisions within the unique economic landscape of WB6. For example, the GDPR's penalty structure may prove excessively burdensome for the WB6's smaller-scale economies, which some of the WB6 countries already recognised.

2050 See also Alan Uzelac, "A Survival of the third legal tradition?", Supreme Court Law Rev SCLR 49(2d) p. 378 (2014).

2051 This has also been noted in the reports of the EU Commission; For example, the EU Commission Reports for Albania and North Macedonia 2023 noted that corruption remains prevalent in many areas and is an issue of concern. Albania, <https://neighbourhood-enlargement.ec.europa.eu/system/files/2023-11/SWD_2023_690%20Albania%20report.pdf> and North Macedonia <https://neighbourhood-enlargement.ec.europa.eu/system/files/2023-11/SWD_2023_693%20North%20Macedonia%20report.pdf> (accessed on 05.01.2024). The situation is similar in the other WB6 countries.

2052 Lana Bubalo, p. 169 (n. 1960).

2053 Up to 99% of all companies in the WB6 countries are small or medium-sized according to the European Investment Bank (EIB); see "The EIB Group's support for SMEs in the Western Balkans", the publication available on the following link <https://www.eib.org/en/publications/the-eib-group-support-for-smes-in-the-western-balkans> (accessed on 11.11.2023).

2054 See the "Infographic – The EU: main investor, donor and trade partner for the Western Balkans", available at the following link <https://www.consilium.europa.eu/en/infographics/the-eu-main-trade-partner-and-investor-for-the-western-balkans/> (accessed on 20.01.2024).

Looking at the current statutory fine frameworks in the region, two trends are already clearly visible. On the one hand, in the jurisdictions which have incorporated the GDPR-like laws, the only provisions that have not been fully replicated from GDPR are the penalty provisions. Moreover, it appears that in these jurisdictions, milder measures such as warnings are still preferred to the imposition of higher fines, which casts doubt on the effectiveness of the legal sanctions.[2055] On the other hand, in jurisdictions that have not yet adopted legislation akin to the GDPR, statutory fines are generally considered insufficiently significant and not well enforced.[2056] Therefore, WB6 countries should consider whether other provisions also merit a modified approach, as their organisations may have limited resources to fully comply with the obligations 'imported' from the GDPR. As declining trust in the rule of law is a major challenge for businesses in the region,[2057] it is important to address these concerns and improve the compliance with data protection rules in order to facilitate investment. Developing digital infrastructure and strengthening data protection laws could not only boost investor confidence, but also enable WB6 countries to transition from their traditional low value-added 'factory economy'[2058] model to a more technologically advanced and digitally orientated economic landscape.

b) Shift from a 'One Size Fits All' to a 'Risk Based' Approach?

Looking at the socio-economic characteristics of the WB6 as outlined above it seems worthwhile to look deeper into the question whether the overall 'one size fits all' approach of the GDPR is an appropriate model for this region or whether elements of a 'risk based approach' in which data protection varies according to the level of threat in stake or the actors involved, would be more conducive.[2059] While GDPR has few elements of a risk-based approach to data protection, it places the onus on data controllers to assess the potential risks associated with data processing and their impact on the rights and freedoms of data subjects,

2055 See Chapter 4 for individual country section.

2056 *Ibid.*

2057 Matteo Rivellini, "What will it take for Western Balkan economies to scale up?" (06.10.2023), available at the following link <https://www.euractiv.com/section/economy-jobs/opinion/what-will-it-take-for-western-balkan-economies-to-scale-up/> (accessed on 20.01.204).

2058 WB6 countries are often specialised in lower value-added economic sectors and are in a functional 'specialisation trap', serving more as 'factory economies' in European production networks, as opposed to the 'headquarters economies' of Western Europe; see Richard Baldwin, "The Great Convergence: Information technology and the new globalization", Harvard University Press, Cambridge, MA (14.11.2016).

2059 Patricia Boshe, Moritz Hennemann, and Ricarda von Meding, p. 39 (n. 1975).

through tools like DPIAs.[2060] Nevertheless, this model assumes that companies bear sole responsibility for such assessments. In WB6 countries, where there is generally a lower level of compliance with data protection laws and a lower level of awareness of data controllers of their data protection obligations,[2061] this approach may prove insufficient. Instead, the WB6 countries may consider introducing data protection rules which would apply differently to data controllers depending to levels of threats at stake or the actors involved (e.g. health sector, sensitive data, public vs private sector, big corporations vs SMEs). While some countries already show the tendency not to completely abide by the one size fits all approach (but only via soft law) like Albania and Kosovo, all the WB6 countries could consider if a risk-based approach would be a more adequate one. There are two main options one could consider.

First, a regulatory approach based on data controllers' size is worth considering. Their SMEs may not have sufficient resources to meet all the obligations of the GDPR or have in-house compliance and data protection teams to work on data protection programmes compared to the SMEs in the EU.[2062] Provisions could be considered that would differentiate controllers' obligations according to their size.

Secondly, a sector-specific approach could be considered. The prevalence of a low rule of law and evident corruption in WB6 countries necessitates a nuanced strategy targeting data controllers exhibiting lower compliance levels. Public institutions and political bodies frequently emerge as primary offenders in data protection breaches.[2063] Accordingly, imposing more stringent obligations on public institutions and political organisations is recommended to address the unique challenges posed by specific sectors and enhance overall data protection compliance. This should be followed by concrete recommendations from data protection authorities that would be of assistance to companies in the management of their risks.

2060 Maria Eduarda Gonçalves, "The Risk-Based Approach Under the New EU Data Protection Regulation: A Critical Perspective", Journal of Risk Research, 23:2, 139–152 (2020); Raphaël Gellert, "Understanding the Notion of Risk in the General Data Protection Regulation", Computer Law & Security Review, Volume 34, Issue 2 (2018).

2061 As elaborated for each country separately in Chapters 4 and 5.

2062 RCC Report 2020, p. 145 (n. 18).

2063 See for example cases of Albania: Chapter 4, A.II, cases of North Macedonia: Chapter 4, E.III and cases of Serbia, Chapter 4, F.III.

c) Strengthening Enforcement

As outlined in Chapters 4 and 5, a striking problem is the lack of enforcement mechanisms in the WB6 countries. Chapter 4 highlights the low prevalence of court case law in the WB6, even though in some countries only courts can decide on data subjects' complaints.[2064] This disparity can be attributed to both the weakness of the rule of law and the lack of expertise in data protection compared to specialised data protection authorities. Strengthening the powers of data protection authorities is therefore imperative. These authorities, possessing more adequate expertise, should play a pivotal role in enforcing data protection laws, as courts may lack comparable legal knowledge and resources. This concern is particularly pronounced in Montenegro, where the data protection authority does not have the power to impose fines.[2065] However, this problem is not unique to Montenegro and can also be observed in other countries, where courts tend to impose lower fines or overlook decisions taken by data protection authorities. Strengthening the powers of data protection authorities is therefore essential to promote a more robust and effective data protection framework. The Serbian data protection authority's assertive stance against Meta underscores the effectiveness of proactive authorities in enhancing trust in enforcement systems.[2066]

In addition, it is imperative for these jurisdictions to consider the integration of complementary soft law provisions and the strengthening of case law. The implementation of the GDPR provisions in WB6 jurisdictions is proving challenging, given its reliance on detailed legal provisions. As the GDPR does not comprehensively address all possible scenarios, there is a need to move away from a strictly legal, formalistic approach. Soft law provisions play a crucial role in clarifying the evolving legal framework, contributing to a better understanding among businesses and promoting compliance with national legislation. While alignment with the established practice of the ECJU is important, it is equally important for these jurisdictions to develop their own body of case law. This dual approach not only ensures compatibility with EU standards, but also enables the development of a set of legal precedents and interpretations specific to their own legal context.

d) Amending the Legal Framework to Strengthen Data Protection Compliance

In seeking to align their domestic legal frameworks with the GDPR, the WB6 countries should consider to avoid mere replication and instead adopt a nuanced ap-

2064 E. g. Montenegro, see Chapter 4, D.III.
2065 See Chapter 4, D.III.
2066 See Chapter 4, F.II.9(c).

proach. As noted above, the implementation of legal transplants in the WB6 has not proven very effective in practice. Lana Bubalo observes that legal practitioners unfamiliar with foreign rules and principles embedded in transplanted laws tend to avoid adopting new concepts, thereby preventing many of these legal transplants coming fully to life.[2067]

The experience of Serbia, which directly transcribed GDPR articles into its legislation, highlights the practical limitations of this copy-paste approach. Within a few years, it became evident that the SDPL 2019 faced significant challenges in its application, which primarily relate to unclear provisions and copied GDPR formulations. While Serbia has announced the amendment of the SDPL 2019 to correct this issue, it remains to be seen how the new amendments will improve legal clarity. Other WB6 countries should consider following suit. Additionally, they should correct any legal loopholes and uncertainties created by the literal translation of the GDPR.

It is noteworthy that the EU Commission, in its assessment of the SDPL 2019 alignment with the GDPR, refrained from commenting on the practice of copy-pasting articles of the GDPR, but only focused on flaws in the translation of the GDPR.[2068] Instead of following this formalistic approach, the EU Commission should have a closer look at the actual enforcement of such laws and critically assess whether the direct verbal replication of GDPR provisions is a good solution for countries that are still in the (long) process of EU accession.

The emphasis of legal reforms should be on drafting rules that are easily understandable and feasible for compliance, not only for companies, but also to individuals. The goal shall be to avoid the encumbrance of additional administrative burdens, such as the dual requirement of adhering to both EU SCCs and local SCCs observed in Serbia, or the prerequisite for entities in North Macedonia to notify data transfers to the EU to their data protection authortiy, notwithstanding the recognition of EU Member States as countries providing adequate level of data protection in North Macedonia. The overarching aim must be to emphasize the robust enforcement of data protection principles rather than the simple replication

2067 Lana Bubalo, p. 169 (n. 1960).

2068 The EU Commission noted only that "it is not in contradiction to GDPR to also regulate certain areas that are not included in the scope of the GDPR with the national law [...] video surveillance, biometrics, records of entry to and exit from premises [...]", but did not explicitly emphasise the possibility for WB6 countries to tailor other provisions to their specific needs beyond the 'opening clauses'. This approach can be understood as the EU Commission's assessment was framed in the context of the WB6 countries' prospective EU accession, see EU Commission's Assessment 2019 p. 2 (n. 1118).

of legislative texts, especially when such replication results in practical ineffectiveness.

e) Enhancing Regional Cooperation to Obtain Adequacy Decision(s)

Enhancing collaborative efforts in data protection is imperative for WB6 countries. While some recent regional collaboration with EU data protection authorities has been observed,[2069] the WB6 countries' independent initiatives in regional cooperation remain rather limited. Beyond the inherent benefits of sharing best practices within the region and fostering cooperation with neighbouring EU-affiliated countries, a concerted collaboration in negotiations with the EU Commission is of paramount importance. In pursuit of effective enhancement, the WB6 countries can draw inspiration from successful models, such as the proactive engagement demonstrated by South Korea in identifying and addressing areas for improvement and presenting it to the EU Commission.[2070]

Moreover, the WB6 countries, bound by their SAAs, are obligated to fortify regional cooperation. This commitment extends to the possibility of concluding bilateral or regional agreements on regional collaboration, particularly in domains like justice and free trade.[2071] Consequently, considerations should be given to establishing comprehensive data protection agreements. Such agreements could regulate the cross-border transfer of data and outline shared goals and necessary steps towards obtaining an adequacy decision from the EU Commission.

In the context of the Berlin Process framework, the RCC, acting as the secretariat alongside the EU Commission, has the potential to develop a strategic plan aimed at aligning the data protection approaches of the WB6 countries with a step-by-step alignment with the GDPR. Through the Berlin Process the WB6 countries have already reached several agreements, such as the free movement

2069 Co-created by SIGMA Programme, Eastern Partnership Regional Fund for Public Administration Reforms (GIZ), Regional Cooperation Council (RCC) and ReSPA, the high-level exchange and learning week aims to tackle key challenges for both the Western Balkans and Eastern Partnership Region and express the true willingness from the EU to support the data-protection (22.09.2023) available at the following link <https://www.respaweb.eu/0/events/374/data-protection-in-the-western-balkans-and-eastern-partnership-region>; EDPS, "International cooperation in data protection: not an option, but vital to our tasks", (20.09.2023) available at the following link <https://edps.europa.eu/press-publications/press-news/blog/international-cooperation-data-protection-not-option-vital-our-tasks_en> (accessed on 12.12.2023).

2070 Graham Greenleaf, Update to Graham Greenleaf's Asian Data Privacy Laws, p. 12 (n. 2018).

2071 Art. 15 SAA for Albania and Serbia, Art. 14 for BiH, Art. 17 for Kosovo.

throughout the region.[2072] While the RCC has initiated some efforts in analysing data protection in the WB6 countries,[2073] it has not yet accorded the necessary political priority to push this matter forward and put closer the WB6 region and the EU Commission in addressing it. As part of the Berlin Process, there are annual meetings of the interior ministers of the WB6 region with the interior ministers of the EU member states and the EU Commission.[2074] Within this framework they could bring this topic to a political level and create understanding for the fact that it is better for the WB6 countries to not only individually copy-paste the GDPR but to have a two-fold approach of setting up a regional data protection scheme that can be gradually brought in line with EU legislation and enforced in practice.

Lastly, the Western Balkans Investment Framework (hereinafter: "WBIH") emphasizes the importance of regional cooperation in aligning national data protection laws with the GDPR. In its call for investment grants, the WBIH stresses that projects in the digital sector must align with EU rules related to data protection and that such interventions have to be part of "broader strategies at regional and or country level".[2075] This underscores the vital role of regional cooperation for the WB6 countries, not only in facilitating the alignment of national data protection laws with the EU acquis, but also in promoting a unified front. This unity is critical in demonstrating to potential investors that the region is committed to robust data protection standards, thereby creating an environment conducive to attracting investment in the digital sector.

f) Regional Approach Versus the 'Regatta Principle'

Despite the position of the WB6 as countries on the EU path, there is no information available on ongoing adequacy talks with the WB6 countries, or on concrete steps for the WB6 countries to achieve an equivalent level of data protection and be placed on the EU Commission's adequacy list. The EU Commission could wait

---

2072 Euractiv, Western Balkans sign landmark agreements in Berlin ahead of December summit (03.11.2022), available at the following link <https://www.euractiv.com/section/enlargement/news/western-balkans-sign-landmark-agreements-in-berlin-ahead-of-december-summit/> (accessed on 25.07.2023).

2073 RCC Report 2020 (n. 155).

2074 See for more information on the organisation structure of Berlin Process at the official website of the Berlin Process, available at the following link <https://www.berlinprocess.de/en/how-does-it-work> (accessed on 05.01.2024).

2075 WBIF, 26th Call for Technical Assistance and Extension of 6th Call for Investment Grants, (14.06.2021), available at the following link <https://www.wbif.eu/news-details/26th-call-technical-assistance-and-extension-6th-call-investment-grants> (accessed on 18.12.2023).

for all WB6 countries to align with the GDPR in order to start negotiations on adequacy talks and issue a single decision for the WB6 countries, which would not raise additional issues for transfers of personal data between the WB6 countries.

However, this approach may not be the best as it could take a very long time. In contrast, the 'regatta principle' also known as 'principle of own merits' may be a better solution for adequacy decisions for the WB6 countries. The regatta principle is the underlying principle of the EU assession process formulated at the EU-Western Balkans Summit in Thessaloniki. According to this principle, progress of each country towards the EU depends on its own merits in meeting the Copenhagen criteria and the conditions set for the SAP.[2076] Yet, this principle has also been criticised in the context of the EU accession process.[2077] Due to this approach, the WB6 countries have not been inspired to put maximum efforts into fostering regional cooperation and have rather looked towards their individual progress towards EU accession, without taking into account their neighbours' progress, which has weakened the joint bargaining power of the countries of the region.[2078]

If the EU Commission were to initiate simultaneous but individual negotiations with all WB6 countries and formulate a comprehensive plan to address their needs for further improvements and harmonisation, it would facilitate better assistance in their efforts to align with the GDPR. In accordance with the regatta principle, the first WB6 country to align its data protection framework with the EU's would be included in the EU Commission's adequacy list. However, this would also mean that this country would have to restrict the transfers with other WB6 countries due to the strict rules on onward transfers. As already explained, some of the WB6 countries are strictly following the EU Commission's adequacy decisions countries list due to this reason, without taking into account their neighbouring countries and not subjecting them to their own adequacy decisions. Therefore, though a strict implementation of the regatta principle the flow of personal data would be newly restricted in the WB6 countries, despite the close trade relationships in the region and the emerging Common Regional Market.

However, there might be an acceptable solution to this problem, combining both the incentive for WB6 countries to achieve an individual EU adequacy decision and the goal to foster regional co-operation. The EDPB upholds the importance of aligning third country's rules on data transfers including the third coun-

---

2076 EU-Western Balkans Summit Thessaloniki, 21 June 2003 Declaration, C/03/163 (21.06.2003), para 4.

2077 Christophe Solioz, "The EU: wider and deeper with the Balkans", Open Democracy (08.10.2014), available at the following link <https://www.opendemocracy.net/en/can-europe-make-it/eu-wider-and-deeper-with-balkans/> (accessed on 28.05.2023).

2078 *Ibid.*

try's adequacy decisions in order to ensure that the level of data protection under the GDPR is maintained in case of onward transfers.[2079] However, the EU Commission has already adopted adequacy decisions for countries who do not have the exact same rules for international transfers as the EU. For example, the EU Commission 'overlooked' the fact that – unlike the EU – the UK held the territory of Gibraltar to have an adequate level of protection.[2080] Moreover, in August 2021 the UK Government announced that it is working in partnership with a number of priority destinations which may be the subject of adequacy regulations in the future, although not all of them are included in the EU Commission's adequacy list.[2081] This shows that there has been some margin of manoeuvre in accepting a certain temporary deviation from EU rules for international transfers and still granting adequacy status according to the GDPR. Christian Schröder noted that the purpose of giving the EU Commission, as a political authority, some leeway in assessing the adequacy of the level of protection in third countries, is in line with economic policy and entrepreneurial freedoms.[2082] Therefore, the EU Commission could explore alternative, more flexible approaches to adequacy decisions for the WB6 countries, which would not restrict data transfers within the region at least for a certain grace period. Previous successful experiences with flexibility and negotiations in granting adequacy decisions to other countries support this possibility.[2083]

2079 Opinion 28/2018 regarding the European Commission Draft Implementing Decision on the adequate protection of personal data in Japan, para 17 (n. 1354).

2080 See the adequacy regulations applicable in the UK explained in the ICO's guide to international transfers, available at the following link <https://ico.org.uk/for-organisations/uk-gdpr-guidance-and-resources/international-transfers/international-transfers-a-guide/> (accessed on 29.05.2023). See also Leonie Wittershagen (n. 151).

2081 These countries include Australia, Brazil, Colombia, The Dubai International Financial Centre, India, Indonesia, Kenya, The Republic of Korea, Singapore and The United States of America; See UK Government Publication "Guidance International data transfers: building trust, delivering growth and firing up innovation" (26.08.2021), available at the following link <https://www.gov.uk/government/publications/uk-approach-to-international-data-transfers> (accessed on 29.05.2023).

2082 Christian Schröder, "Art. 45 DS-GVO", in Jürgen Kühling and Benedikt Buchner (eds), Datenschutz-Grundverordnung, Bundesdatenschutzgesetz: DS-GVO/BDSG (3rd edn, C.H. Beck 2020), para 11.

2083 For example, in the adequacy decision for Japan, the use of the word 'guidelines' to describe the new legal regime became "one of the most difficult problems" during the negotiations. The main source of confusion stems from the difference between Western and Japanese perspectives on the enforceability of 'guidelines'. Despite initial concerns that the guidelines lacked sufficient force, the European Commission appears to have accepted the PPC's explanation that the guidelines have been treated as effectively binding by Japanese courts, as it decided to include

The EU Commission could therefore grant an adequacy decision to the WB6 country which would first meet the adequacy criteria without the need for this country to restrict necessary transfers of personal data to other WB6 countries. The imposition of a 'sunset clause'[2084] which would limit the validity of the regional exemption and during which the EU Commission could monitor the legal situation and possible deviations with regard to the level of data protection in the WB6 countries could be one of the possible modalities for them. Offering such a model could inspire WB6 countries to align with the EU acquis in terms of data protection more quickly.

IV Conclusion to C

While the current data protection frameworks within the WB6 may not yet meet the criteria for an adequacy decision, the initiation of adequacy discussions could serve as a catalyst for these countries to pursue further harmonisation and alignment with EU rules. Although the WB6 are obliged to align their legislation with the EU acquis, this obligation does not require the wholesale transplantation of GDPR provisions. It has been shown that the conventional practice of 'copy-paste' legal transplants is not effective within the WB6, where the rule of law is comparatively weaker than in the EU. This approach fails to recognise the need for nuanced legal adaptations tailored to the specific needs of each WB6 jurisdiction. Consequently, these countries should take into account the nuances of their legal systems, and the EU Commission should also take these factors into account in any potential adequacy negotiations with the WB6 countries. In addition, in the event of opening adequacy negotiations with the region, the EU Commission should promote an approach that encourages, rather than restricts, enhanced regional cooperation within the WB6 countries.

---

their language in the adequacy decision; Opinion 28/2018 regarding the European Commission Draft Implementing Decision on the adequate protection of personal data in Japan, paras. 48–56 (n. 1354).

2084 During the discussion of the draft of the GDPR, the European Parliament tried to insert a 'sunset clause', common in US law, according to which adequacy decisions would automatically expire after five years if they were not confirmed or amended by another positive act of the Commission. This request was rejected by the Council, so that only the review obligation under para. 4 GDPR remained: Christopher Kuner, Lee A Bygrave, Christopher Docksey, "Background and Evolution of the EU General Data Protection Regulation (GDPR) (February 2020) in Christopher Kuner and others (eds), the EU General Data Protection Regulation (GDPR): A Commentary. Yet, this sunset clause has been used in the UK Adequacy Decision (n. 248).

D Conclusion to Chapter 7

The WB6 countries have started the process of harmonising their data protection regimes with the GDPR, in order to align with the EU acquis. However, they are not at the same stage of harmonisation. Although the WB6 countries still face certain challenges and none of them may yet fully meet all adequacy criteria, their legal systems have already achieved a significant level of alignment with GDPR standards due to their EU accession process, which can be relevant for assessing the adequacy of the level of data protection in these countries.

Efforts to harmonise with the EU acquis, in particular the GDPR, have had different consequences across the WB6 region. One of the most visible consequences has been the issue of importing legal transplants into their national legislation, with difficulties to be effectively implemented. Instead of simply copying the GDPR texts, this study analysed what other alternative options or methods the WB6 countries could use to align their national legislation with the GDPR. The analysis considers several focal points, including prioritising the enforcement of data protection legislation, considering a shift to risk-based legislation, focusing on the actors that deserve stricter regulation due to potentially higher risks, and the specificities of the regional economic context. These points should also be given greater emphasis by the EU Commission when assessing the alignment of WB6 countries' data protection legislation with the GDPR. The fact that these countries do not fully recognise each other as countries where personal data flows freely is an illustrative case of the impracticality of direct implementation of the GDPR. Some WB6 countries, seeking to align more closely with EU standards, restrict data transfers to other WB6 countries, while others take a more liberal approach. A more permissive approach to onward transfers is beneficial for regional cooperation, but could of course be an obstacle to obtaining an adequacy decision.

The process of adopting adequacy decisions by the EU Commission as such lacks transparency and shows inconsistencies in the application of strict criteria. Although the WB6 countries have been aligning their legal systems with the EU for several years, the EU Commission does not appear to prioritise the adoption of adequacy decisions for these countries. Given the limited likelihood of these countries joining the EU in the near future, the EU Commission should start negotiations on adequacy decisions with the WB6 countries. Such decisions would bring significant benefits to both the region and the EU, given their status as trading partners.[2085] It would also remove further restrictions on data transfers between WB6 countries.

In case the EU Commission would finally embark on issuing adequacy decisions for the WB6 countries, it could either opt for a single decision covering the entire region or for strictly applying the regatta principle, whereby the first country to meet the criteria receives the adequacy decision, regardless of where the rest of the region stands in the process.

This study finds that a middle way between these two options would likely be most efficient and expedient. While granting the adequacy status to the first country that fulfils the criteria, the region should be held together by not imposing the obligation to restrict onward data transfers for a certain grace period. Like this the EU Commission could strike a balance that respects the 'own merits principle' and at the same time ensures cooperation within the region and avoids undue restrictions on data transfers. Initialising such a process is overdue to encourage further alignment of the WB6 countries with EU data protection standards, thereby benefiting the overall WB6 EU accession process.

2085 In 2007, the Western Balkan economies and the Republic of Moldova ratified the new Central European Free Trade Agreement (CEFTA) 2006; See also a brochure "Implementing the CEFTA 2006 Agreement: Reaping the benefits of trade and investment integration in South East Europe", available at the following link <https://www.oecd.org/global-relations/Reaping_the_benefits_of_trade_and_investment.pdf> (accessed on 29.05.2023).

Chapter 8 – Conclusion

The EU has played a pioneering role in the development of data protection standards. From the EU's perspective, data protection is considered a fundamental right, safeguarded and upheld through provisions such as Art. 7 and Art. 8 CFR, as well as the GDPR.[2086] Similarly, the WB6 countries have enshrined data protection as a constitutional guarantee.[2087] The GDPR has significantly expanded its global impact (Brussels effect) through mechanisms such as its extraterritorial effect (Art. 3) and the adequacy decisions (Art. 45).[2088] Given their geopolitical position and aspirations for EU accession, the WB6 countries have traditionally followed the EU's lead in matters of data protection. Rather than developing their own unique data protection rules, they have largely transposed EU standards, both under the DPD and the GDPR.[2089] Four countries in the region – Albania, Kosovo, North Macedonia and Serbia – have already adopted new data protection laws aimed at aligning with the GDPR. The remaining two countries – Bosnia and Herzegovina and Montenegro – have initiated the harmonisation process, and their new data protection laws are expected to be enacted soon.[2090] However, specific deadlines for their adoption are currently unknown, as some have already been missed.[2091]

To date, the WB6 countries have not been included in the EU Commission's adequacy list, nor are any concrete plans for negotiations with them known in this regard. However, in 2017, the EU Commission mentioned the possibility of engaging in a dialogue on adequacy decisions with countries in "the European neighbourhood which have expressed an interest in obtaining an adequacy finding".[2092] Although it is uncertain whether each WB6 government is actively pursuing this goal, some national data protection strategies within the WB6 countries, namely in Serbia[2093] and Albania,[2094] have outlined this objective. What is clear, however, is that all WB6 countries– given their strategic goal of becoming EU members – need to continue aligning with the EU acquis also with regard to their national

2086 Chapter 2, A.
2087 Chapter 2, B.
2088 Chapter 3.
2089 Chapter 2, B, Chapter 4.
2090 Chapter 4, Chapter 7, A.
2091 *Ibid.*
2092 EU Commission, Exchanging and Protecting Personal Data in a Globalised World, p. 8 (n. 186).
2093 Data Protection Strategy Proposal for 2023–2030, p. 31 (n. 1114).
2094 AC's Institutional Strategy 2022–2025 (n. 218).

https://doi.org/10.1515/9783112221013-010

data protection laws and all of them would benefit from obtaining an adequacy decision. This is not only because of their aspirations for EU membership, but also because of their significant economic dependence on investment from the EU.

Although the EU is known for having a strict approach when evaluating the adequacy of data protection standards in third countries, the procedure and the logic of adequacy decisions have not always been transparent.[2095] In addition, the EU has been criticised for treating third countries differently, often favouring its main trading partners.[2096]

WB6 countries would likely not meet the strict adequacy criteria at the moment for a number of reasons. Firstly, not all of the WB6 countries have adopted new data protection legislation that meets the requirements of the GDPR. Secondly, even those countries that have enacted GDPR-like legislation have not achieved a level of harmonisation that can be considered 'equivalent'. They have essentially copied the articles of the GDPR omitting the Recitals of GDPR and failing to take into account the specifics of their own unique legal systems, which makes their laws difficult to interpret and apply in practice. In particular, the new Serbian data protection law contains various shortcomings resulting from this copy-paste approach,[2097] which has been criticised by the EU Commission as well.[2098] Thirdly, the rules governing international data transfers vary across the WB6 countries. For instance, Serbia has adopted more permissive rules[2099], while North Macedonia has implemented overly restrictive rules that may not encourage companies to comply with such burdensome requirements.[2100] Fourthly, while the WB6 countries have focused on harmonising their data protection laws, there still appears to be a lack of harmonisation in sector-specific legislation. The EU Commission will also assess the laws on government access to personal data in these countries. Although progress has been made to align these laws with the GDPR, some challenges remain that need careful evaluation for the purpose of adequacy decisions.[2101] Sixthly, some of the WB6 countries are influenced by regimes beyond Brussels, such as the 'Beijing effect' (e.g., Serbia and BiH). These countries have employed advanced technologies for extensive surveillance practices, which raises additional concerns and has been criticised by the NGO

2095 Chapter 7, C.I.
2096 Chapter 7, C.I. and C.III.
2097 Chapter 4, F. II, Chapter 7, A.I.
2098 EU Commission's Assessment 2019 (n. 1118).
2099 Chapter 4, F.II.10, Chapter 7, A.III.
2100 Chapter 4, E.II.10, Chapter 7, A.III.
2101 Chapter 4, Chapter 7, B.

sector in the region.[2102] Seventhly and finally, issues persist with the availability of sufficient resources for independent supervisory authorities to enforce data protection laws and establish adequate mechanisms for redress.[2103] The lack of resources primarily stems from a lack of political will within the WB6 countries to invest in these institutions.

Despite all these challenges, discussed in detail in Chapters 4, 5, 6 and 7, the WB6 countries have achieved a solid level of alignment on data protection rules (at least formally) when compared to other world regions. Over the course of decades, they have consistently aligned their legal systems with those of the EU and have become signatories to key conventions, including Convention 108 and the ECHR.[2104] Having in mind that these countries are an integral part of Europe where the flow of personal data shall be facilitated, the EU Commission should therefore at least initiate concrete and result-oriented negotiations on possible adequacy decisions with the WB6 countries. Waiting for the WB6 eventual EU accession, which would automatically allow personal data to flow freely, does not seem to be a good approach, given the political uncertainties of this comprehensive process.[2105] In contrast, engaging in such adequacy discussions would ultimately contribute to the overall EU accession process of the WB6 countries, as countries would have to align their laws with the EU standards, ultimately bringing them one step closer to EU membership.

When it comes to how to concretely achieve such adequacy decisions, this study finds the working hypothesis of Chapter 1 confirmed that the standard approach of copying-and-pasting the GDPR in each WB6 country without taking into consideration the regional dimension should not be completely overthrown but modified. As elaborated in Chapter 7, the WB6 and the EU Commission should reconsider their mainstream approach of such a mere word-by-word transposition of GDPR rules into the national legal frameworks of the WB6 countries. Although the WB6 are required to harmonise their national legislation with the EU acquis, this obligation does not entail a strict copy-and-paste of the GDPR's articles. Similarly, Art. 45 GDPR does not mandate third countries to replicate the GDPR verbatim in order to obtain an adequacy decision, as also shown by other countries who successfully obtained adequacy decisions.[2106] The need to avoid simple replication of foreign (EU) law is demonstrated by the experience of difficulties in enforcing legal transplants in the WB6 countries due to their unique legal systems,

2102 Chapter 6.
2103 *Ibid.*
2104 Chapter 7, B.V.
2105 Chapter 7, C.
2106 Chapter 7, C.III.1.

often described as 'legal cultures in transition'.[2107] The aim of establishing data protection regimes that integrate well into the specifics of the transforming economies of the WB6, are enforceable in practice, and can at the same time be considered adequate according to Art. 45 GDPR standards seems to be better achievable with a more tailor-made approach. This approach could include, inter alia, implementing a risk-based rather than a one-size-fits-all strategy and strengthening the enforcement elements of data protection regimes.

Finally, in order to ensure that adequacy decisions for the countries of the WB6 both serve the interest of facilitating a safe transfer of data with the EU and do not lead to a new 'data transfer divide' in the region, it is advisable for the EU to take a balanced approach: Motivating the countries individually to fulfil the GDPR criteria and then taking adequacy decisions one-by-one but allowing for a grace period for onward data transfers within the region.

With such an approach, the EU commission could achieve within a relatively short period of time that the hole in the regime for safe transfers of personal data in the Southeast flank of the EU can be closed. As a wanted side-effect this development would likely also contribute to bringing this region closer to fulfilling the criteria for EU accession.

2107 Chapter 7, C.III.2.

Tables

Table of Cases

1 Montenegro

Administrative Court of Montenegro, case no. 1586/2017
Basic Court in Nikšić, case no. P 1411/2021, (04.04.2021)
Basic court Nikšić, case no. P 150/2021 (08.12.2021)
Basic Court in Pljevlja, case no. P 33/2022 (22.03.2022)
Basic Court of Pljevljna, case no P. 33/2022, (22.04.2022)
Supreme Court of Montenegro, case no. Uvp 353/2022 (26.05.2022)
Supreme Court of Montenegro case no. Uvp 268/2022 (11.05.2022)

2 North Macedonia

Administrative Court, case no. U-6.6p. 900/2020
Administrative Court of North Macedonia, case no. U-5.no. 1249/2020
Administrative Court of North Macedonia, case no. UŽ-z. 1452/2019 (09.06.2020)
Administrative Court of North Macedonia, case no. UŽ-z no. 1452/2019 (09.06.2020)
Supreme Administrative Court of North Macedonia, case no. UŽ-1 – 500/20
Supreme Administrative Court of North Macedonia, case no. UŽ-3 – 1389/19 (06.11.2020)

3 Serbia

Administrative Court, case no. I-2 U 13549/15, (23/10/2015);
Administrative Court, case no. U 715/2019 (07/22/2020)
Administrative Court, case no. U 14837/2019 (18/11/2019)
Administrative Court, division in Kragujevac, case no. I-3 U 7406/20, (28/08/2020)
Administrative Court, case no. Gž 1676/2021 (17/06/2021.)
Administrative Court, case no. 2 U 2350/17, (02/2021)
Administrative Court, case no. Gž 3189/2019 (22/08/2019).
Administrative Court, case no. I-1 U. 5390/1, (09/06/2016);
Administrative Court, case no. U 9228/2017 (12/08/2020)
Decision of the Constitutional Court (Official Gazette of Republic of Serbia, no. 60/2013)
Decision of the Constitutional Court, case no. Už-306/2008 (25.95.2008)
Decision of the Constitutional Court, case no. IUz 41/2010 of May 30, 2012, (Official Gazette of RS, no. 68/2012) (18.07.2012)

https://doi.org/10.1515/9783112221013-011

4 CJEU Cases

Google Spain SL and Google Inc. v Agencia Española de Protección de Datos (AEPD) and Mario Costeja González, C-131/12, EU:C:2014:317 (13.05.2014)
RW v Österreichische Post, CJEU C-154/21, ECLI:EU:C:2023:3 (12.01.2023)
Weltimmo s.r.o. v Nemzeti Adatvédelmi és Információszabadság Hatóság, C-230/14, EU: C:2015:639 (01.10.2015)
Satakunnan Markkinapörssi Oy and Satamedia Oy v Finland [GC], no 931/13, 27 June 2017 Data Protection Commissioner v Facebook Ireland Limited and Maximilian Schrems, C-311/18, EU: C:2020:559 (16.07.2020)
Maximilian Schrems v Data Protection Commissioner, C-362/14, EU:C:2015:66 (06.10.2015)
La Quadrature du Net and Others v Premier ministre and Others, C-511/18, C-512/8 and C - 520/18, EU:C:2020:791 (06.10.2020)
Privacy International v Secretary of State for Foreign and Commonwealth Affairs and Others, C 623/17, EU:C:2020:790 (06.10.2020)

5 ECtHR

Antović and Mirković v. Montenegro, application no. 70838/13 (ECtHR, 28.11.2017)
Big Brother Watch, applications nos. 58170/13, 62322/14, and 24960/15 (ECtHR 13.09.2018)
Dumitru Popescu V. Romania, applications nos. 49234/99 and 71525/01. (ECtHR, 26.4.2007)
Szabo´and Vissy v Hungary, application no. 37138/14 (ECtHR 12.12.2016)

Table of Legislation

1 Albania Legislation

Decision no. 8, dated 31.10.2016 on Determining Sates that ensure an Adequate Level of Personal Data Protection, available at following link <https://www.idp.al/wp-content/uploads/2020/10/Decision_no_8.pdf> accessed on 10.04.2023
Instruction no. 19 on the regulation of the relationship between the controller and the processor in the event of delegation of the processing of personal data and the form of the framework agreement for such legal agreements
Instruction no. 22, dated 18.10.2012 on determining rules for safeguarding personal data processed by small controllers
Instruction no. 41, dated 13.06.2014 on allowing certain categories of international transfers of personal data in a country with no adequate level of personal data protection
Instruction no. 47, dated 14.09.2018 on determining rules for safeguarding personal data processed by large controllers
Law no. 108/2014 on the State Police
Law no. 8517 of 1999 on the Right to Information and Protection of Personal Data, 1 June 1999,
Law no. 9157, date 4.12.2003 on Interception of Electronic Communications
Law on personal data protection no. 124/2024 dated 19 December 2024
Law on the protection of personal data no. 9887/2008 dated 10.03.2008 (with amendments).

Law on the protection of personal data, amendments no. 120 of 18 September 2014
Proposed new data protection law (December 2021) <https://www.idp.al/projekt-akte-te-zyres-se-komisionerit/> accessed on 01.07.2022

2 Bosnia and Herzegovina Legislation

Amendments on Law on Personal Data Protection (Official Gazette of Bosnia and Herzegovina, no. 76/2011 and 89/2011 – corrected)
Amendments on Law on Personal Data Protection (Official Gazette of BiH 49/06)
Constitution of BiH no. 327/09, 26 March 2009
Constitution of Republika Srpska (Official Gazette of the Republic of Srpska, no. 21/92 – revised text, 28/94, 8/96, 13/96, 15/96, 16/96, 21/96, 21/02, 26/02, 30/02, 31/02, 69/02, 31/03, 98/03, 115/05, 117/05)
Constitution of the Federation of Bosnia and Herzegovina (Official Gazette of FBiH, no. 1/1994, 1/1994 – Amendment I, 13/1997 – Amendments II-XXIV, 13/1997 – Amendments XXV and XXVI, 16/2002 – Amendments XXVII -LIV, 22/2002 – Amendments LVI-LXIII, 52/2002 – Amendments LXIV-LXXXVII, 60/2002 – Amendment LXXXI, 18/2003 – Amendment LXXXVIII, 63/2003 – Amendments LXXXIX-XCIV, 9/2004 – Amendments XCV-CII, 32/2007 – corr., 20/2004 – Amendments CIII and CIV, 33/2004 – Amendment CV, 71/2005 – Amendments CVI-CVIII, 72/2005 – Amendment CVI, 88/2008 – Amendment CIX , 79/2022 – Amendments CX-CXXX, 80/2022 – correction and 31/2023 – Amendment CXXXI)
Dayton Peace Agreement. Annex 11: Agreement on International Police Force (1995)
Decision on the Formation of the Interdepartmental Working Group for Drafting the Draft Law on the Protection of Personal Data (Official Gazette of Bosnia and Herzegovina, number 49/18), <http://www.sluzbenilist.ba/page/akt/zAxqEkGJ7Uc=> accessed on 23.04.2023
Law on Amendments to the Law on the Protection of Personal Data, no: 01,02-02-1-2/11 (September 14, 2011)
Law on Civil Service in the Institutions (Official Gazette of BiH, no. 12/2002, 19/2002, 8/2003, 35/2003, 4/2004, 17/2004, 26/2004, 37/2004, 48/2005, 2/2006, 50/2008 – other laws, 43/2009, 8/2010, 40/2012 and 93/2017)
Law on Communication from 2003 and last time amended in 2012
Law on Human Rights Ombudsman of BiH (Official Gazette of Bosnia and Herzegovina, no. 19/2002, 35/2004, 32/2006, 38/2006 – amended and 50/2008 – other laws)
Law on Independent and Supervisory Bodies of the Police Structure of Bosnia and Herzegovina (Official Gazette of Bosnia and Herzegovina, number 36/08)
Law on Personal Data Protection (Official Gazette of BiH, no. 32/01)
Law on the intelligence and security agency (Official Gazette of Bosnia and Herzegovina, no. 12/2004, 20/2004, 56/2006, 50/2008 – other laws and 12/2009)
Personal Data Protection Law (Official Gazette of Bosnia and Herzegovina, no. 49/2006, 76/2011 and 89/2011 – correction)
Personal Data Protection Law (Official Gazette of Bosnia and Herzegovina, no. 32/01)
Rulebook on Supervision Inspection Regarding Personal Data Protection (Official Gazette of Bosnia and Herzegovina no. 32/02)
Rulebook on the Procedure for Complaints by Data Subjects before the Personal Protection Agency in Bosnia and Herzegovina (Official Gazette of Bosnia and Herzegovina no. 32/02)
Rules of the Constitutional Court of BiH

3 Kosovo Legislation

Constitution of Kosovo 2008
Criminal Procedure Law no. 04/L-123
Criminal Code no. 06/L-074
Decision on the countries providing an adequate level of data protection, no. 11/2021 (13.09.2021)
Guidelines for political parties during the election campaign MDHP Guidelines (15.09.2021) available at the following link <https://aip.rks-gov.net/mbrojtja-e-te-dhenave-personale/mbrojtja-e-te-dhenave-personale/> accessed on 30.05.2023
Guidelines for the Processing of Personal Data for Direct Marketing Purposes MDHP Guidelines (24.05.2022), <https://aip.rks-gov.net/mbrojtja-e-te-dhenave-personale/mbrojtja-e-te-dhenave-personale/> accessed on 30.05.2023
Guidelines for Using the Camera Surveillance System for Data Controllers MDHP Guidelines (30.03.2022) available at the following link <https://aip.rks-gov.net/mbrojtja-e-te-dhenave-personale/mbrojtja-e-te-dhenave-personale/> accessed on 30.05.2023
Kosovo Information and Privacy Agency, Guidelines for the Processing of Personal Data for Direct Marketing Purposes MDHP Guidelines (24.05.2022)
Law no. 02/L-37 of 2006 on the Use of Languages 26 July 2006
Law no. 03/L-172 on the Protection of Personal Data
Law on Interception of Electronic Communications no. 05/030
Law on Ombudsperson, no. 05/L-019
Rulebook no. 05/2022 on Security Measures in the Course of Personal Data Processing (27.09.2022)
Universal Declaration on Human Rights

4 Montenegro Legislation

Agency for Personal Data Protection and Free Access to Information, Rulebook on the Manner of Marking and Protection of Special Categories of Personal Data (2011)
Agency for Personal Data Protection and Free Access to Information, Rulebook on the Form and Manner of Keeping Record of Personal Databases (2010)
Amendments on Law on Personal Data Protection (Official Gazette of Montenegro, no. 22/2017)
Constitution of Montenegro (Official Gazette of Montenegro, no. 1/2007 and 38/2013 – Amendments I-XVI)
Decision of the Constitutional Court of Montenegro on revoking the decision of the National Coordinating Body for Infectious Diseases on publishing the names of persons in self-isolation, U-II no. 22/20
Decision of the National Coordinating Body for Infectious Diseases on publishing the names of persons in self-isolation, no. 8-501-/20 – 129 (21.04.2020)
Law on Electronic Communications no. 40/2013
Law on Interception of Communications, no. 71/2018.
Law on Parliamentary Oversight in the Field of Security and Defence (Official Gazette of Montenegro, no. 80/10)
Law on Parliamentary Oversight in the Field of Security and Defence, no. 01 – 2653/2 (27.12.2010)
Law on Personal Data Protection (Official Gazette of Montenegro, no. 079/08 dated 23.12.2008, 070/09 dated 21.10.2009, 044/12 dated 09.08.2012, 022/17 dated 03.04.2017)

Law on the National Security Agency Official Gazette of the Republic of Montenegro, no. 28/2005 and Official Gazette of Montenegro, no. 86/2009 – second law, 20/2011 and 8/2015)
Law on the Ombudsman (Official Gazette of the Republic of Macedonia" nos. 60/2003, 114/2009, 181/2016, 189/2016 and 35/2018)
Law on the Ombudsperson of Human Rights and Freedoms (12.01.2012)
Montenegrin Criminal Code (Official Gazette of the Republic of Montenegro, no. 70/2003, 13/2004 – corrected and 47/2006 and Official Gazette of the Republic of Montenegro, no. 40/2008, 25/2010, 32/2011, 64/2011 40/2013, 56/2013 – amended, 14/2015, 42/2015, 58/2015 – Law, 44/2017, 49/2018 and 3/2020)
Report on the public discussion regarding the Draft Law on the Protection of Personal Data (published on 10.07.2019) <https://www.gov.me/dokumenta/6c2470bc-aeee-4281-95de-3c40c591bb94> accessed on 29.04.2023
The Draft law on Personal Data Protection (published on 10.04.2019) <https://www.gov.me/dokumenta/2ca5b30b-16ef-4fcf-a043-c05e2afa8fe6> accessed on 29.04.2023

5 North Macedonia Legislation

Constitution of North Macedonia (no. 08 – 4642/1 17 November 1991)
Decision on Determining the Methodology for the Harmonisation of the Sectoral Legislation (Official Gazette of the Republic of North Macedonia no. 38/22)
Draft of Law on Personal Data Protection from 1994 (Official Gazette of the Republic of Macedonia, no. 12/94)
Guidelines for Notifying High Risk Processing of Personal Data <https://azlp.mk/en/guidelines-regarding-the-notification-of-processing-of-personal-data-that-will-result-in-high-risk/> accessed on 21.04.2023
Initial draft Law for Protection of Personal Data 2018, <https://ener.gov.mk/Default.aspx?item=pub_regulation&subitem=view_reg_detail&itemid=49944>, accessed on 31.03.2021
Law amending and supplementing the Data Protection Law (RNM, Official Gazette, no. 294, 27.12.2021), available in Macedonian at the following link <https://azlp.mk/wpcontent/uploads/2022/11/57d665472d164493815e8b3bdcf8e2a1.pdf> accessed on 21.04.2023
Law amending and supplementing the Data Protection Law (RSM, Official Gazette, no. 294, 27.12.2021)
Law on Personal Data Protection (Official Gazette of the Republic of Macedonia no. 7/2005)
Law on Personal Data Protection (Official Gazette of the Republic of Macedonia no. 7/2005, 103/2008, 124/10, 135/11, 43/14, 153/15, 99/16 and 64/18)
Law on Personal Data Protection (Official Gazette of the Republic of Macedonia no. 7/2005, 103/2008, 124/10, 135/11, 43/14, 153/15, 99/16 and 64/18)
Law on Personal Data Protection (Official Gazette of the Republic of North Macedonia, no. 42/20 and 294/21
Law on Personal Data Protection (Official Gazette of the Republic of North Macedonia, no. 42/20 and 294/21
Law on Protection of Personal Data (Official Gazette of the Republic of North Macedonia, no. 42/20), Eng. Translation: <https://www.refworld.org/pdfid/6290d1814.pdf> accessed on 21.03.2023
Law on Ratification of the Convention for Protection of Individuals Against Automatic Data Processing (Official Gazette of the Republic of Macedonia, no. 7/05) and Law on Ratification

of the Additional Protocol to the Convention for Protection of Individuals Against Automatic Personal Data Processing, with Respect to the Supervisory Bodies and the Cross-border Transfer (Official Gazette of the Republic of Macedonia, no. 103/08)

Report on the public discussion regarding the Draft Law on the Protection of Personal Data (10. 07. 2019), <https://www.gov.me/dokumenta/6c2470bc-aeee-4281-95de-3c40c591bb94> accessed on 10. 05. 2023

Rulebook on Data Transfers (Official Gazette of RNM, no. 122 from 12. 5. 2020)

Rulebook on Internal Organizational Structure and Job Systematization states 01/1407/1 (2020) <https://azlp.mk/wp-content/uploads/2022/11/pravilnik_za_vnatreshna_organizacija.pdf> accessed on 17. 04. 2023

Rulebook on reporting personal data processing of high risk (Official Gazette of the Republic of North Macedonia no. 42/20),

Rulebook on the Process for Data Protection Impact Assessment (Official Gazette of the Republic of North Macedonia no. 122/20), available at the following link <https://azlp.mk/wp-content/uploads/2022/12/Rulebook-Impact-Assessment.pdf> accessed on 21. 04. 2023

Strategy on Personal Data Protection in North Macedonia, 2017 – 2022, n. 14752 (May 2017)

6 Serbia Legislation

Commissioner for Information of Public Importance and Protection of Personal Data, Rulebook on the Form of Notification of a Breach of Personal Data and the Method of Notifying the of a Breach of Personal Data (Official Gazette of RS, no. 40/2019)

Commissioner for Information of Public Importance and Protection of Personal Data, Guidance on Legitimate Interest, <https://www.poverenik.rs/sr-yu/zaštita-podataka/легитимни-интерес.htmll> accessed on 05. 05. 2022

Commissioner for Public Information and Data Protection, Decision on the list of types of personal data processing actions for which an assessment of the impact on the protection of personal data must be carried out and the opinion of the Commissioner must be sought, (Official Gazette of the RS, no. 45/2019)

Criminal Code of Serbia (Official Gazette of RS, no. 85/2005, 88/2005 – corrected, 107/2005 – corrected, 72/2009, 111/2009, 121/2012, 104/2013, 108/2014, 94/ 2016 and 35/2019)

Data Protection Strategy Proposal for 2023 – 2030, <https://www.mpravde.gov.rs/sekcija/53/radne-verzije-propisa.php> accessed on 15. 05. 2023

Decision on the Determination of Standard Contractual Clauses (Official Gazette of RS, no. 5/2020)

Decision on the list of states, parts of their territories or one or more sectors of certain activities in those states and international organisations in which an appropriate level of personal data protection is considered to be ensured (Official Gazette of RS, no. 55/2019)

Decision on the List of Types of Personal Data Processing Activities Requiring an Assessment of Impact on the Protection of Personal Data and the Requirement to Seek the Opinion of the Commissioner for Information of Public Importance and Protection of Personal Data (Official Gazette of RS, no. 45/2019 and 112/2020)

Law on Electronic Communications (Official Gazette of RS, no. 35/2023)

Law on General Administrative Procedure (Official Gazette of RS, no. 18/2016, 95/2018 – authentic interpretation and 2/2023 – US decision)

Law on Military Security Agency and Military Intelligence Agency (Official Gazette of RS", no. 88/ 2009, 55/2012 – decision US and 17/2013)

Law on Personal Data Protection (Official Gazette of RS, no. 87/2018)
Law on Personal Data Protection (Official Gazette of RS, no. 97/2008, 104/2009 – other law, 68/2012 – decision of CC and 107/2012)
Law on Personal Data Protection (Official Gazette of RS, no. 97/2008, 104/2009 – other law, 68/2012 – decision of CC and 107/2012
Law on Records in the Field of Labour (Official Gazette of SRJ, br. 46/96 and Official Gazette of RS, no 101/2005 – other law and 36/2009 – other law)
Law on the Constitution Court, (Official Gazette of RS, no. 109/2007, 99/2011, 18/2013 – US decision, 103/2015 and 40/2015 – other laws)
Law on the free access to public information (Official Gazette RS no. 120/04)
Law on the Security-Information Agency (Official Gazette of RS, no. 42/2002, 111/2009, 65/2014 – decision US, 66/2014 and 36/2018)
Report on the public debate on the text of the Draft Law on Personal Data Protection (02. 03. 2018), <https://www.mpravde.gov.rs/sekcija/53/radne-verzije-propisa.php> accessed on 13. 03. 2023
Rulebook on Requirements and Program Support for the Lawful Interception of Electronic Communications and Technical Requirements for the Fulfilment of the Obligation of Electronic Communications Data Retention (Official Gazette of the RS, 88/2015 of 23.10.2015)
Rulebook on the Complaint Form (Official Gazette of RS, no. 40/2019)
Rulebook on the Form and Method of Keeping Records of Persons for the Protection of Personal Data (Official Gazette of RS, no. 40/2019)

7 EU Legislation

Charter of Fundamental Rights of the European Union (2000/C 364/01)
Commission Implementing Decision (EU) 2021/914 on standard contractual clauses for the transfer of personal data to third countries pursuant to Regulation (EU) 2016/679 of the Directive 2006/24/EC of the European Parliament and of the Council on the retention of data generated or processed in connection with the provision of publicly available electronic communications services or of public communications networks and amending Directive 2002/58/EC (2006) OJ L 105/54
Directive 2009/136/EC of the European Parliament and of the Council of 25 November 2009 amending Directive 2002/22/EC on universal service and users' rights relating to electronic communications networks and services, Directive 2002/58/EC concerning the processing of personal data and the protection of privacy in the electronic communications sector and Regulation (EC) No 2006/2004 on cooperation between national authorities responsible for the enforcement of consumer protection laws (2009) OJ L 337
EU Commission Implementing Decision 2019/419 pursuant to Regulation (EU) 2016/679 of the EU Parliament and of the Council on the adequate protection of personal data by Japan under the Act on the Protection of Personal Information (2019) OJ L 76/
EU Commission Implementing Decision 2021/1772 pursuant to Regulation (EU) 2016/679 of the European Parliament and of the Council on the adequate protection of personal data by the United Kingdom [2021] OJ L 360/1
EU Commission Implementing Decision 2021/1773 pursuant to Directive (EU) 2016/680 of the European Parliament and of the Council on the adequate protection of personal data by the United Kingdom [2021] OJ L 360/69

European Parliament and of the Council [2021] OJ L 199/13 Commission Implementing Decision pursuant to Regulation (EU) 2016/679 of the European Parliament and of the Council on the adequate protection of personal data by the Republic of Korea under the Personal Information Protection Act, C(2021) 4800 final

Regulation 2016/679 of the European Parliament and of the Council on the protection of natural persons with regard to the processing of personal data and on the free movement of such data, and repealing Directive 95/46/EC (General Data Protection Regulation) [2016] OJ L 119/1

8 Council of Europe

Additional Protocol to the Convention for the Protection of Individuals with regard to Automatic Processing of Personal Data, regarding supervisory authorities and transborder data flows, no. 181, 8 November 2001

Convention for the Protection of Individuals with Regard to Automatic Processing of Personal Data, no. 108, 28 January 1981

European Convention on Human Rights 1950

Protocol amending the Convention for the Protection of Individuals with regard to Automatic Processing of Personal Data, no. 233, 18 May 2018

9 Other Jurisdictions

Austrian Federal Act Concerning the Protection of Personal Data

Constitution of the Federal Republic of Yugoslavia (1992)

Croatian Implementation Act of the EU General Data Protection Regulation no. 42/18

German Federal Data Protection Act (15.11.2006)

German Federal Data Protection Act (30.06.2017)

Hessian Data Protection Act, GVBI. II 300 – 20, (October 1970)

Law on Personal Data Protection (Official Gazette of the FRY, no. 24/98 and 26/98)

Law on Ratification of the Convention on Automatic Processing of Personal Data (Official Gazette of the FRY – International Agreements, no. 1/92)

Law on the Termination of the Law on Personal Identification Number (NN 10/2023)

Section 702 of the Foreign Intelligence Surveillance Act (FISA)

UN's Universal Declaration of Human Rights of 1948

Israel Privacy Protection Act 5741 – 1981

South Korean Act on the Use and Protection of Credit Information 2009

Japanese Act no. 57 of 2003 on the Protection of Personal Information

Table of Interview, Panel, and Accessed Public Information

Official Answer of the Personal Data Protection Agency Bosnia and Herzegovina, no. 04 – 02 – 1 – 1042 – 3/21, 24.11.2021

Serbian Commissioner for Public Information and Data Protection, 'The letter from Google LLC to the DPC', (21.05.2022) file no. 073-06-4170/2022-07

Serbian Commissioner for Public Information and Data Protection, 'The letter from Google LLC to the DPC', (4 February 2022), file no. 073-06-4170/2022-07

Official answer of the Montenegro Agency for Personal Data Protection and Free Access to Information no. 06-29/1186102/22 (26.01.2023)

The sixth panel of the series "Data Protection Laws in the Western Balkans: Let's Talk about Adequacy!", organised by Sofija Rasic in cooperation with the Research Centre for Law and Digitisation ("FREDI") of the Faculty of Law at the University of Passau and Moritz Hennemann, further information can be found on the University of Passau website at the following link <https://www.jura.uni-passau.de/aktuelles/meldung/diskussionsreihe-zum-datenschutz-im-westlichen-balkan> accessed on 13.02.2023

Interview with Erida Skendaj, Executive Director of the Albanian Helsinki Committee, Conducted via Email Communication in December 2021

Email by the DPC delivered to the Google LCC (26.02.2020). This email is not publicly available and was provided to the author by the DPC using the right to request information from the Commission, file no. 073-06-4170/2022-07.

Table of Activity Reports on Data Protection in the WB6

Albanian Office of the Information and Data Protection Commissioner, Annual Report 2018, <https://www.idp.al/wpcontent/uploads/2019/03/ENGLISH_Annual_Report_2018_KDIMDP.p>, accessed on 20.03.2023

Albanian Office of the Information Data Protection Commissioner, Annual Report 2021 <https://www.idp.al/wp-content/uploads/2016/11/Annual-report-2021.pdf> accessed on 22.04.2023

Bosnian Personal Data Protection Agency, Medium Term Work Plan of the for the Period 2023-2025 (September 2022) <http://www.azlp.ba/publikacije/Archive.aspx?langTag=bsBA&template_id=149&pageIndex=1> accessed on 28.05.2023

Bosnian Personal Data Protection Agency, Annual Report on Data Protection for 2013 no. 01-37-6-585-1/14, <http://www.azlp.ba/publikacije/default.aspx?id=936&langTag=bs-BA> accessed on 01.03.2023

Bosnian Personal Data Protection Agency, Annual Report on Data Protection for 2020, no. 01-02-4-661-1/21 (04.06.2021)

Bosnian Personal Data Protection Agency, Annual Report on Data Protection for 2021, no. 01-02-4-489-1/22 (22.06.2022)

Bosnian Personal Data Protection Agency, Annual Report on Data Protection for 2019, no. 01-02-4-568-1/20, (27.07.2020)

Bosnian Personal Data Protection Agency, Annual Report on Data Protection for 2014, no. 01-37-6-585-1/14 (09.06.2014)

Kosovo Information and Privacy Agency, General Overview of the Activities for 2022, <https://aip.rks-gov.net/bs/opsti-prgled-aktivnosti-agencije-za-informacije-i-privatnost-za-2022-godinu/> accessed on 08.05.2023

Kosovo Information and Privacy Agency, Media report for 2021 (30.12.2021) <https://aip.rks-gov.net/download/raporti-mediatik-per-vitin-2021-i-agjencise-per-informim-dhe-privatesi/> accessed on 03.04.2023

Montenegro Agency for Personal Data Protection and Free Access to Information, Annual Report for 2020, <https://www.dzlp.mk/sites/default/files/pdf-azlp-godisen_izvestaj_za_2020_mk.pdf> accessed on 21.04.2023

Montenegro Agency for Personal Data Protection and Free Access to Information, Report on the State of Protection of Personal Data and Access to Information for 2022 <https://www.azlp.me/me/izvjestaji> accessed on 01.05.2023

Montenegro Agency for Personal Data Protection and Free Access to Information, Report on the State of Protection of Personal Data and Access to Information for 2015, <https://www.azlp.me/me/izvjestaji> accessed on 01.05.2023

Montenegro Agency for Personal Data Protection and Free Access to Information no. 05 – 29 – 500602/20 (22.07.2020) <https://media.cgo-cce.org/2020/09/AZLP-04.08.2020..pdf>; accessed on 01.05.2023

North Macedonia Personal Data Protection Agency Annual Report for 2021 <https://azlp.mk/biblioteka/> accessed on 16.05.2023

North Macedonia Personal Data Protection Agency, Annual Report for 2018 <https://www.dzlp.mk/sites/default/files/annual_report_dpdp_2018_en.pdf> accessed on 21.04.2023

North Macedonia Personal Data Protection Agency, Annual Report for 2022, <https://azlp.mk/годишен-извештај-за-работата-на-азлп-за/ > accessed on 20.04.2023

North Macedonia Personal Data Protection Agency, Annual Report for 2020 <https://www.dzlp.mk/sites/default/files/292.pdf > accessed on 16.05.2021

North Macedonia Personal Data Protection Agency, Annual Report for 2010 <https://www.dzlp.mk/sites/default/files/292.pdf > accessed on 16.05.2021

North Macedonia Personal Data Protection Agency, Annual Report for 2014 available at the following link <https://www.dzlp.mk/sites/default/files/doc.1a_en.pdf> accessed on 30.03.2021

Serbian Commissioner for Public Information and Data Protection, Activity Report for 2021, <https://www.poverenik.rs/images/stories/dokumentacijanova/izvestajiPoverenika/2021/Izve%C5%A1ta2021CIRfinal.pdf> accessed on 13.02.2023

Serbian Commissioner for Public Information and Data Protection, Activity Report 2022, <hytps://www.poverenik.rs/images/stories/dokumentacijanova/izvestajiPoverenika/2022/Godišnji_izveštaj_2022_-_16_03_2023_LAT.pdf> accessed on 14.05.2022

Serbian Commissioner for Public Information and Data Protection, Activity Report for 2019, <https://www.poverenik.rs/sr-yu/o-nama/godisnji-izvestaji.html> accessed on 02.03.2023

Serbian Commissioner for Public Information and Data Protection, Activity Report for 2020, <https://www.poverenik.rs/sr-yu/o-nama/godisnji-izvestaji.html> accessed on 02.03.2023

Table of WB6 Supervisory Authorities' Decisions

Albanian Data Protection Commissioner, 'Recommendation no. 44 to Socialist Party of Albania' (19.08.2021) <https://www.idp.al/rekomandime-2021/> accessed on 02.09.2022

Albanian Office of the Information and Data Protection Commissioner, 'Institutional Strategy 2022 – 2025, <https://www.idp.al/wp-content/uploads/2016/11/ENGLISH_Strategjia-Institucionale-2022 – 2025_revised.pdf> accessed on 20.05.2023

Bosnian Personal Data Protection Agency, 'Decision on the transfer of personal data abroad for the purpose of the transmission of penalty notices' (14.05.2018).

Kosovo Information and Privacy Agency, 'Decision on the authorisation of personal data transfer on behalf of FINCA to the USA no. 03/2021 (9.11.202)

Serbian Commissioner for Public Information and Data Protection, Official decision no. 072–04–3576/2017–07 (14.12.2017) <https://www.poverenik.rs/sr-yu/arhiva/saopštenja-arhiva/2744-окончан-надзор-у-случају-београдске-сениор-картице.html> accessed on 12.05.2023

Serbian Commissioner for Public Information and Data Protection, Records on the performed supervision on the city of Belgrade, no. 072–04–3576/2017–07 (28.11.2017) <https://www.poverenik.rs/sr-yu/arhiva/saopštenja-arhiva/2744-окончан-надзор-у-случају-београдске-сениор-картице.html> accessed on 12.05.2023

Bibliography

A&S Adria, 'Po prvi put u Bosni i Hercegovini – uspješno održan prvi program za mlade talente kompanije Huawei Technologies' (16.11.2020) <https://www.asadria.com/po-prvi-put- u-bosni-i-hercegovini-uspjesno-odrzan-prvi-program-za-mlade-talente-kompanije-huawei-technologies/> accessed on 02.04.2023

Abdurrahmani B, 'Data Protection in Albania: A Challenge Towards Improving Legislation on the Way to EU Integration', Aleksandër Moisiu University, Durrës (2022)

Akta, 'Huawei i RS potpisali Memorandum o razumijevanju u vezi sa digitalnom transformacijom' (23.03.2023) <https://www.akta.ba/vijesti/bih/160506/huawei-i-rs-potpisali-memorandum-o-razumijevanju-u-vezi-sa-digitalnom-transforma> accessed on 01.04.2023

Alsenoy B V and Koekkoek M, 'Internet and jurisdiction after Google Spain: the extraterritorial reach of the right to be delisted', International Data Privacy Law, Volume 5, Issue 2, (May 2015)

Andonović S and Prlja, D, 'The Basics of Personal Data Protection Rights', Institute of Comparative Law, Belgrade (2020)

Area Barnea Jaffa Lande, 'New Israeli Privacy Protection Regulations for European Citizens' Data' Lexology (13.12.2023), <https://www.lexology.com/library/detail.aspx?g=11147a9b-cc22-4f59-917c-785fd72b5bca> accessed on 03.01.2024

Art. 29 Data Protection Working Party 'Document on Biometrics 2003' WP80 (2003)

Art. 29 Data Protection Working Party 'Guidelines on Automated individual decision-making and Profiling for the purposes of Regulation' WP251rev.01 (2018)

Art. 29 Data Protection Working Party 'Guidelines on Data Protection Impact Assessment (DPIA) and determining whether processing is "likely to result in a high risk" for the purposes of Regulation 2016/679' WP248rev.01 (2017)

Art. 29 Data Protection Working Party 'Working Document Setting Forth a Co-Operation Procedure for the approval of "Binding Corporate Rules" for controllers and processors under the GDPR' WP263 rev.01 (2018)

Art. 29 Data Protection Working Party Opinion '06/2014 on the notion of legitimate interests of the data controller under Article 7 of Directive 95/46/EC, WP 217 (2014)

Art. 29 Data Protection Working Party, 'Guidelines on Consent under Regulation 2016/679' WP259 rev.01 (2018)

Art. 29 Data Protection Working Party, 'Guidelines on Data Protection Officers' WP243 rev.01 (2017)

Art. 29 Data Protection Working Party, 'Opinion 1/2010 on the Concepts of "Controller" and "Processor"' WP 169 (2010)

Art. 29 Data Protection Working Party, 'Opinion 4/2007 on the concept of personal data', WP 136 (2007)

Art. 29 Data Protection Working Party, 'Working Document: Transfers of personal data to third countries: Applying Articles 25 and 26 of the EU data protection directive' WP 12 (1998)

Art. 29 Data Protection Working Party, First Orientations on Transfers of Personal Data to Third Countries – Possible Ways Forward in Assessing Adequacy, XV D/5020/97-EN Final (26.06.1997)

Art. 29 Data Protection Working Party, Opinion 6/2009 on the level of protection of personal data in Israel, 02316/09/EN WP 165 (01.12.2009)

https://doi.org/10.1515/9783112221013-012

Artigas Á, 'Surveillance, Smart technologies and the development of Safe City solutions: the case of Chinese ICT firms and their international expansion to emerging markets', Institut Barcelona d'Estudis Internacionals (IBEI) (2017)

B. Stanic M, 'Election of Members of the Supervisory Body for Personal Data Protection as a Guarantee of Their Independence – Examples of Albania, Bosnia and Herzegovina, Montenegro and North Macedonia', Foreign Legal Life (2020)

Bajramspahić D and Sošić M, 'Monitoring report: Law on Parliamentary Oversight of Security and Defense Sector" DCAF (2013) <https://media.institut-alternativa.org/2013/03/law-on-parliamentary-oversight-of-security-and-defense-sector.pdf> accessed on 21.05.2023

Balboni P and others, 'Legitimate interest of the data controller. New data protection paradigm: legitimacy grounded on appropriate protection' International Data Privacy Law (2013)

Baldwin R, 'The Great Convergence: Information technology and the new globalization', Harvard University Press, Cambridge, MA 14.11.2016

Balkaninsight, 'Bosnia and Herzegovina Safe & Smart City' (07.11.2018) <https://china.balkaninsight.com/node/4071> accessed on 02.04.2023

Balkaninsight, Analysis 'Police, Soldiers among Albanian Ruling Party's Voter Tracking 'Army' (21.04.2021) <https://balkaninsight.com/2021/04/21/police-soldiers-among-albanian-ruling-partys-voter-tracking-army/> accessed on 28.08.2022

Balkaninsight, Interview with Serbia's Personal Data Commissioner: 'Huawei Cameras a 'Dangerous' Decision' (18.12.2021) <https://balkaninsight.com/2021/12/28/serbias-personal-data-commissioner-huawei-cameras-a-dangerous-decision/> accessed on 02.04.2023

Bami X, 'Kosovo Surveillance Build-up Raises Privacy Concerns', published BIRN (31.12.2021), <https://balkaninsight.com/2021/12/31/kosovo-surveillance-build-up-raises-privacy-concerns/> accessed on 21.05.2023

Bami X, Analysis 'Kosovo Lawmakers Play Politics with Personal Data', published by BIRN, (21.09.2021) <https://balkaninsight.com/2020/09/21/kosovo-lawmakers-play-politics-with-personal-data/> accessed on 07.05.2023

BBC, 'European Commission bans TikTok on staff devices' (23.02.2023) <https://www.bbc.com/news/technology-64743991> accessed on 04.04.2021

BDK Advokati, 'Montenegro published personal data of people in isolation', (22.03.2022), published by Lexology <https://www.lexology.com/library/detail.aspx?g=b8e27d04-9836-4ed4-a949-025557b61f4c> accessed on 21.01.2023

BDK Advokati, 'Q&A: the data protection legal framework in Serbia', Lexology (August, 2018), <https://www.lexology.com/library/detail.aspx?g=fcad4a22-1dca-4c3a-8390-11f315d9933d> accessed on 04.04.2021

Beogradski centar za bezbednosnu politiku and other NGOs, 'Predlog članovima Odbora za kulturu i informisanje Narodne skupštine Republike Srbije Kriterijumi za izbor kandidata za Poverenika za informacije od javnog značaja i zaštitu podataka o ličnosti' (2018) <http://crta.rs/wp-content/uploads/2018/12/Kriterijumi-za-izbor-kandidata-za-Poverenika-za-informacije-od-javnog-zna%C4%8Daja-i-za%C5%A1titu-podataka-o-li%C4%8Dnosti.pdf> accessed on 13.05.2023

Beqa M, 'Law Enforcement and Equal Treatment Of Citizens In Albania', CSDG (November 2021)

Bergemann B, 'Der "informed consent" im Datenschutz: Eine politikwissenschaftliche Analyse', Freie Universität Berlin (2017)

Bergemann B, 'The consent paradox: Accounting for the prominent role of consent in data protection' IFIP International Summer School on Privacy and Identity Management, Springer, Cham (2017)

Berkowitz D, Pistor K and Richard J F, 'The transplant effect', Am J Comp Law 51(1):16–204, (2003)

Bertelsmann Stiftung's 'Transformation Index (BTI) Report for North Macedonia' (2020) <https://btiproject.org/fileadmin/api/content/en/downloads/reports/country_report_2020_MKD.pdf> accessed on 21.04.2023

Bickenbach F and Liu Wan-Hsin, 'Chinese Direct Investment in Europe – Challenges for EU FDI Policy', CESifo Forum, ifo Institut – Leibniz-Institut für Wirtschaftsforschung an der Universität München, München, Vol. 19, Iss. 4

Bieker F, 'Enforcing Data Protection Law – The Role of the Supervisory Authorities in Theory and Practice', In: Lehmann, A., Whitehouse, D., Fischer-Hübner, S., Fritsch, L., Raab, C. (eds) Privacy and Identity Management. Facing up to Next Steps. Privacy and Identity 2016. IFIP Advances in Information and Communication Technology, vol 498. Springer, Cham. (2017)

Bird & Bird 'Personal data of deceased persons', <https://www.twobirds.com/en/capabilities/practices/privacy-and-data-protection/general-data-protection-regulation/gdpr-tracker/deceased-persons> accessed on 30.12.2022

BIRN, 'In Kosovo and Albania, Personal Data Up for Grabs', (14.11.2022) <https://balkaninsight.com/2022/11/14/in-kosovo-and-albania-personal-data-up-for-grabs/> accessed on 04.03.2023

Birrer A and other, 'The state is watching you—A cross-national comparison of data retention in Europe', Telecommunications Policy, Volume 47, Issue 4, 2023

Blaustein J, 'Reforming the Police in Bosnia and Herzegovina: Speaking Truths to Power: Policy Ethnography and Police Reform in Bosnia and Herzegovina', Clarendon Studies in Criminology, Oxford Academic (21.05.2015)

Blue N, 'Spirited away: The EU's Adequacy Decision for Japan as a Roadmap for U.S. Privacy Law after Schrems II', 21 Wash. U. GLOBAL Stud. L. REV. 437 (2022)

Boga & Associates, 'Proposed amendments to the Law on Protection of Personal Data and Law on the Right to Information', Lexicology, (December 2021), <https://www.lexology.com/library/detail.aspx?g=d39443f1-01b7-4b88-b2ad-884b5bdeacd5> accessed on 10.04.2023

Boldyreva E and others, 'EU Concerns About Security, 5G and Huawei' in, et al. Proceedings of Topical Issues in International Political Geography. TIPG 2021, Springer Geography, Springer, Cham (02.01.2023)

Boshe P, Hennemann M and Meding R von, 'African Data Protection Laws – Current Regulatory Approaches, Policy Initiatives, and the Way Forward' (2022), Global Privacy Law Review (2022)

Bosnian Personal Data Protection Agency's Opinion on Application of the Personal Data Protection Law to a Controller not based in Bosnia and Herzegovina" (07.04.2021) <http://www.azlp.ba/misljenja/Archive.aspx?langTag=bs-BA&template_id=149&pageIndex=1>, accessed on 22.04.2023

Bosnian supervisory authority 'Zajedničko saopćenje za javnost sa prvog sastanka "Inicijativa 20i7", Bled, Slovenija (15.5.2017) <http://azlp.ba/saopstenja/default.aspx?id=1790&langTag=bsBA&template_id=149&pageIndex=1> accessed on 29.05.2023

Bradford A, 'The Brussels Effect', Northwestern University Law Review, Vol. 107, No. 1, 2012, Columbia Law and Economics Working Paper No. 533 (2012)

Breton T, '5G Security: The EU Case for Banning High-Risk Suppliers: Statement by Commissioner Thierry Breton', (2023) available at <https://ec.europa.eu/commission/presscorner/api/files/document/print/en/statement_23_3312/STATEMENT_23_3312_EN.pdf> accessed on 23.02.2025

Brkan M, 'The Essence of the Fundamental Rights to Privacy and Data Protection: Finding the Way Through the Maze of the CJEU's Constitutional Reasoning', Cambridge University Press, (2019)

Bubalo L, 'An Introduction to the Legal Cultures of Bosnia and Herzegovina, Croatia, and Serbia (Western Balkan), Koch, S., Kjølstad, M.M. (eds) Handbook on Legal Cultures. Springer, Cham (2023)

Budak E and others, 'Privacy Concern in Western Balkan Countries: Developing a Typology of Citizens', Working Papers 1402, The Institute of Economics, Zagreb (2014)

Bygrave Lee A, 'Data Protection Law, Approaching its Rationale, Logic and Limits', Kluwer Law International (2002)

Bygrave Lee A, 'The 'Strasbourg Effect' on data protection in light of the 'Brussels Effect': Logic, mechanics and prospects', Computer Law & Security Review (2021)

C Hillion, 'The Copenhagen Criteria and Their Progeny', (ed), EU enlargement, Oxford, Hart Publishing (2004)

Calzada I, 'Citizens' Data Privacy in China: The State of the Art of the Personal Information Protection Law (PIPL)' Smart Cities (2022),

Cate F H, Kuner C, Millard C, Svantesson D J B and Lynskey O, 'Risk Management in Data Protection', International Data Privacy Law (2015)

CEFTA, 'Implementing the CEFTA 2006 Agreement: Reaping the benefits of trade and investment integration in South East Europe' <https://www.oecd.org/global-relations/Reaping_the_benefits_of_trade_and_investment.pdf> accessed on 29.05.2025

Çeloaliaj M, 'Commissioner of the Right to Information and Personal Data Protection, Department of Legal Affairs, Albania, Knowledge, General Regulation on Personal Data Protection, Certain Aspects of the GDPR's Impact on Legal Entities in the Republic of Albania', International Journal, Vol.34.5 (September 2019)

Çeloaliaj M, 'General Regulation on Personal Data Potection: Certain Aspects of the GDPR's Impact on Legal Entities in the Republic of Albania', International Journal, Vol.34.5 (September 2019)

Center for Democracy and Human Rights (CEDEM) and AIRE CENTER, 'The right to privacy in Montenegrin legislation and European practice' (March 2012) <http://www.cedem.me/publikacije/studije-i-javne-politike/send/69-studije-i-javne-politike/678-policy-paperpravo-na-privatnost> accessed on 04.06.2023

Centre for Security Studies and the Geneva Centre for Democratic Control of Armed Forces, Speech by Deputy Head of the Rule of Law Pillar Bill Potter at the seminar 'Draft Law on the Intelligence and Security Agency' <http://www.ohr.int/speech-by-deputy-head-of-the-rule-of-law-pillar-bill-potter-at-the-seminar-draft-law-on-the-intelligence-and-security-agency/?print=pdf> accessed on 12.02.2023

Ćeranić P and Baškalo D, 'The question of control of the civilian intelligence service in Bosnia and Herzegovina, University of Banja Luka, Faculty of Security Sciences', Journal of Security and Criminalistics vol. 3, no. 2 (2021)

Chair's Conclusions on Common Regional Market (2020) <https://www.wb6cif.eu/wp-content/uploads/2021/09/Chairs-Conclusions_Sofia-2020.pdf> accessed on 29.05.2023

Chart of signatures and ratifications of Treaty 108, Convention for the Protection of Individuals with regard to Automatic Processing of Personal Data (ETS No. 108), status as of 19.05.2023

Chen C and Leo Z, 'How China's data privacy and security rules could impact your business', published by EY (18.07.2022) <https://www.ey.com/en_kw/forensic-integrity-services/how-chinas-data-privacy-and-security-rules-could-impact-your-business> accessed on 03.05.2023

Chen Y and Cheung A. S, 'The Transparent Self under Big Data Profiling: Privacy and Chinese Legislation on the Social Credit System', Vol. 12, No. 2, The Journal of Comparative Law (2017)

Christakis T, 'Schrems III"? First Thoughts on the EDPB post-Schrems II Recommendations on International Data Transfers (Part 1)" European Law Blog, (13.11.2020) <https://europeanlawblog.eu/2020/11/13/schrems-iii-first-thoughts-on-the-edpb-post-schrems-ii-recommendations-on-international-data-transfers-part-1/> accessed on 22.01.2023

Cimpanu C, 'Personal and salary data for 637,138 Albanian citizens leaks online', published on The Record, (23.12.2021), <https://therecord.media/personal-and-salary-data-for-637138-albanian-citizens-leaks-online> accessed on 02.09.2022

Civil Rights Defenders, Report 'Effectiveness of NHRIs in Western Balkan countries Albania, Bosnia and Herzegovina, Kosovo, Montenegro, North Macedonia, Serbia' <https://indexnhri.org/> accessed on 21.02.2022

Civil Rights Defenders, Report: 'Effectiveness of NHRIs in Western Balkan countries Albania, Bosnia and Herzegovina, Kosovo, Montenegro, North Macedonia, Serbia' <https://indexnhri.org/> accessed on 21.02.2022

CJEU Fact sheet on Protection of personal data (March 2021) <https://curia.europa.eu/jcms/upload/docs/application/pdf/2018-10/fiche_thematique_-_donnees_personnelles_-_en.pdf> accessed on 05.02.2022

Clingendael Institute, Report: 'China and the EU in the Western Balkans. A zero-sum game?' (August 2020), <https://www.clingendael.org/sites/default/files/2020-08/china-and-the-eu-in-the-western-balkans.pdf> accessed on 02.04.2023

Committee on Foreign Relations United States Senate, A Democratic Staff Report 'The new big brother-China and digital authoritarianism' (2020)

Coppel P KC, 'Information Rights: A Practitioner's Guide to Data Protection, Freedom of Information and other Information Rights', Bloomsbury Publishing (2020)

Council of Europe, Treaty list for a specific State or International Organisation: Montenegro <https://www.coe.int/en/web/conventions/by-non-member-states-of-the-coe-or-the-european-union?module=treaties-full-list-signature&CodePays=MOT> accessed on 29.04.2023

Council of Europe's Newsroom, 'Argentina becomes the 23rd state to ratify Convention 108+ on data protection' (published 17.04.2023) <https://www.coe.int/en/web/human-rights-rule-of-law/-/argentina-ratifies-convention-108-during-the-privacy-symposium> accessed on 19.05.2023

Council of Europe's Newsroom, 'North Macedonia signs Convention 108+', (05.12.2019) <https://www.coe.int/en/web/data-protection/-/north-macedonia-signs-convention-108-> accessed on 05.10.2022

Council of Europe's Newsroom, 'With Albania Convention 108+ reaches half the needed ratifications', (22.07.2022) <https://www.coe.int/en/web/data-protection/-/with-albania-convention-108-reaches-half-the-needed-ratifications> accessed on 02.09.2022

Council of Europe's Newsroom, Bosnia and Herzegovina and Malta, two new signatures for Convention 108+ <https://www.coe.int/en/web/data-protection/-/bosnia-and-herzegovina-and-malta-two-new-signatures-for-convention-108-> accessed on 22.04.2023

Council of the EU Press release, 'Third meeting of the Accession Conference with Serbia at Ministerial level' (18.07.2016) <https://www.consilium.europa.eu/en/press/press-releases/2016/07/18/fac-serbia-accession-conference/> accessed on 24.01.2023

Council of the European Union Enlargement and Stabilisation and Association Process, 15935/22, 13 December 2022, paras. 82–86 <https://www.consilium.europa.eu/media/60797/st15935-en22.pdf> accessed on 22.04.2023

Creemers R, 'China's Emerging Data Protection Framework', Cyber Policy Center, Leiden Institute for Area Studies, (November, 2021)

Croatian supervisory authority 'Četvrti sastanak "Inicijative 20i7", 28.5.202' <https://azop.hr/cetvrti-sastanak-inicijative-20i7-28-5-2021/> accessed on 29.05.2023

CRTA, 'The Assembly should withdraw the questionable criterion for selection of the new Commissioner', (15.06.2019) <https://crta.rs/en/the-assembly-should-withdraw-the-questionable-criterion-for-selection-of-the-new-commissioner/> accessed on 13.05.2023

Dahsyla E, 'Political League: NGOs Demand Cancellation of selection of the Information and Privacy Commissioner', < https:// kallxo.com/shkurt/lidhja-politike-ojq-te-kerkojne-anulimin-e-perzgjedhjes-se-komisionerit-per-informim-dhe-privatesi/> accessed on 12.01.2023

Dallmann M and Busse P, 'Verarbeitung von öffentlich zugänglichen personenbezogenen Daten', ZD (2019)

Danas, 'Objavljeno uputstvo za prijavu za penzionerske kartice: Na kom linku se možete prijaviti?' <https://www.danas.rs/vesti/ekonomija/prijava-za-penzionerske-kartice-uputstvo-link/> accessed on 14.05.2023

Danas, Interview with the former Commission 'Šabić: Opstrukcija Poverenika i zakona' (13.05.2018) <https://www.danas.rs/vesti/drustvo/sabic-opstrukcija-poverenika-izakona/?fbclid=IwAR0mkFZ2DAQ_SAxJ7J6mdNOGvN4QnP4WWTTj-nIk_-vFnbzmtmuA9CcGoRI> accessed on 07.04.2023

Danas, the Serbian prime minister's statement 'Brnabić tvrdi da je zloupotrebljena funkcija poverenika za zaštitu podataka o ličnosti'(13.11.2021) <https://www.danas.rs/vesti/politika/brnabic-tvrdi-da-je-zloupotrebljena-funkcija-poverenika-za-zastitu-podataka-o-licnosti/> accessed on 01.02.2023

DCAF, Guidelines for intelligence oversight for parliamentary committees in the Assembly of the Republic of North Macedonia (January 2021)

De Hert P, and Gutwirth S, 'Privacy, Data Protection and Law Enforcement. Opacity of the individual and transparency of power', in Erik Claes and others (eds), Privacy and the Criminal Law (2006)

De Hert Paul and Korenica F, 'The New Kosovo Constitution and Its Relationship with the European Convention on Human Rights: Constitutionalization "Without" Ratification in Post-Conflict Societies', Max-Planck-Institut für ausländisches öffentliches Recht und Völkerrecht (2016)

Diligenski A, Prlja D and Cerović D, 'Data Protection Law, GDPR', Institute of Comparative Law, Belgrade (2020)

DIlkov D, 'Made in China: Tackling Digital Authoritarianism', European View 020, Vol. 19(1) 110 (April 2020)

Dimovski Z, 'Analysis of the Content and Practical Implementation of the Law on the National Security Agency and Law for Coordination of the Security and Intelligence Community in the Republic of North Macedonia, Skopje', DCAF (February 202)

DiploFoundation Cybersecurity in the Western Balkans 'Policy gaps and cooperation opportunities Research report under the project Cybersecurity Capacity Building and Research Programme for South-Eastern Europe' (September 2016)

Djurić M, 'Srbija i Huawei: Intenziviranje saradnje uprkos sporazumu iz Vašingtona' published in Radio Free Europe / Radio Liberty <https://www.slobodnaevropa.org/a/srbija-i-huawei-intenziviranje-saradnje-uprkos-sporazumu-iz-va%C5%A1ingtona/30840366.html> accessed on 02.04.2023

Dnevni Nalaz, Interview with the former Director, Petar Kovačević, of the Agency for the Protection of Personal Data of Bosnia and Herzegovina 'Izgleda da nikoga u BiH ne zanima nezakonito prisluškivanje!'<https://avaz.ba/vijesti/127943/izgleda-da-nikoga-u-bih-ne-zanima-nezakonito-prisluskivanje> accessed on 12.03.2023

Dolenc D, 'Legitimni interes kao pravni osnov obrade osobnih podataka'Bankarstvo, 2020, vol. 49, br. 3, author (26.08.2020)

Dowden O, 'New approach to data is a great opportunity for the UK post-Brexit', Financial Times (27.02.2021), <https://www.ft.com/content/ac1cbaef-d8bf-49b4-b11d-1fcc96dde0e1> accessed on 12.11.2023

Drechsler L, 'What Is Equivalent? A Probe into GDPR Adequacy Based on EU Fundamental Rights' Jusletter IT (21.02.2019)

Dyrmishi A and Kamolli M, 'Albania's approaches in security provision and accountability of security institutions: the need for further efforts to converge with the EU policy, legislation and practices', Friedrich-Ebert-Stiftung Office (December 2018)

Dyrmishi A and Kuci B, Policy Paper 'Security Management Network: The need to reform the intelligence system in Albania', Institute for Democracy and Mediation Centre for European and Security Affairs (2011)

Dyrmishi A, 'Strengthening Intelligence Governance in the Western Balkans – Intelligence Governance in Albania', DCAF (Centre for Security, development and the Rule of Law) (2018)

EDPB, 'Guidelines 1/2018 on certification and identifying certification criteria in accordance with Articles 42 and 43 of the Regulation 2016/679' (30.05.2018)

EDPB, 'Guidelines 3/2018 on the Territorial Scope of the GDPR (Article 3)' (2019)

EDPB, 'Guidelines 3/2019 on processing of personal data through video devices, version 2' (29.01.2020)

EDPB, 'Opinion 28/2018 regarding the European Commission Draft Implementing Decision on the adequate protection of personal data in Japan' (05.12.2018)

EDPB, 'Recommendations 01/2020 on measures that supplement transfer tools to ensure compliance with the EU level of protection of personal data (R01/2020)' (11.11.2020)

EDPB, Opinion 28/2018 Regarding the European Commission Draft Implementing Decision on the Adequate Protection of Personal Data in Japan (05.12.2018)

EDPB's news 'State Commissioner for Data Protection in Lower Saxony imposes € 10.4 million fine against notebooksbilliger.de' <https://edpb.europa.eu/news/national-news/2021/state-commissioner-data-protection-lower-saxony-imposes-eu-104-million-fine_en> accessed on 18.05.2022

EDPB's news, 'The CNPD adopts the certification mechanism GDPR-CARPA', <https://edpb.europa.eu/news/national-news/2022/cnpd-adopts-certification-mechanism-gdpr-carpa_en> accessed on 21.04.2023

EDPS, 'International cooperation in data protection: not an option, but vital to our tasks', (20.09.2023) <https://edps.europa.eu/press-publications/press-news/blog/international-cooperation-data-protection-not-option-vital-our-tasks_en> accessed on 12.12.2023

Eduarda Gonçalves M, 'The Risk-Based Approach Under the New EU Data Protection Regulation: A Critical Perspective', Journal of Risk Research, 23:2, 139–152 (2020)

Eduart H, 'Commissioner Asked to Close Probe on Salaries, Plates Data Leak Scandal', (02.05.2022), <https://albaniandailynews.com/news/commissioner-asked-to-close-probe-on-salaries-plates-data-leak-scandal> accessed on 02.09.2022

EPDB, 'Study on the Government access to data in third countries, Milieu Consulting Brussels', EDPS/2019/02–13 (November 2021)

Erebara G, 'Albania Prosecutors Investigate Socialists' Big-Brother-Style Database, Balkan Insight (16.04.2021) <https://balkaninsight.com/2021/04/16/albania-prosecutors-investigate-over-socialist-party-big-brother/> accessed on 02.09.2022

Erie M s. and Streinz T, 'The Beijing Effect: China's "Digital Silk Road" as Transnational Data Governance', 54 New York University Journal of International Law and Politics (2021)

Erlbacher F, 'Article 49 TEU', in Manuel Kellerbauer, Marcus Klamert, and Jonathan Tomkin (eds), The EU Treaties and the Charter of Fundamental Rights: A Commentary, online edn, Oxford Academic, (2019)

Ernst S, 'Art. 3 DS-GVO' in Boris P Paal and Daniel A Pauly (eds), Datenschutz- Grundverordnung. Bundesdatenschutzgesetz: DS-GVO BDSG (3rd edn, C.H. Beck 2021)

EU Commission – Press release, 'Commission starts process to adopt adequacy decision for safe data flows with the US'(13.12.2022)

EU Commission Adequacy Decision C(2021) 4800 final (28.6.2021)

EU Commission Decision 2011/61/EU pursuant to Directive 95/46/EC of the European Parliament and of the Council on the adequate protection of personal data by the State of Israel with regard to automated processing of personal data L 27/39 (01.02.2011)

EU Commission Detailed Assessment on Serbian Data Protection Law (2018) <https://insajder.net/attachment/202/LAW-PDP-FINAL-20_02-FOR-EC-edited-JUST-comments.pdf?g_download=1> accessed on 13.03.2023

EU Commission General Assessment on Serbian Data Protection Draft Law (2018), available at the following link <https://insajder.net/attachment/201/20180423-DP-law-Serbia-General-EC-JUST-comments.pdf?g_download=1> accessed on 13.03.2023

EU Commission Implementing Decision (EU) 2019/419 C/2019/304/ pursuant to Regulation (EU) 2016/679 of the European Parliament and of the Council on the adequate protection of personal data by Japan under the Act on the Protection of Personal Information, OJ L 76, (19.03.2019)

EU Commission Opinion on Bosnia and Herzegovina's application for membership of the European Union, 29.5.2019 {SWD(2019) 222 final}

EU Commission Press Statement 17/4739 by Commissioner Wra Jourova, Mr. Lee Hyo-seong, Chairman of the Korea Communications Commission and Mr. Jeong Hyun-cheol, Vice President of the Korea Internet & Security Agency, European Commission (20.11.2017).

EU Commission Report for Albania 2019, SWD(2019) 215 final (29.05.2019)

EU Commission Report for Albania 2021, SWD(2021) 289 final (19.10.2021)

EU Commission Report for Albania 2023, SWD(2023) 690 final (8.11.2023)

EU Commission Report for Albania SWD(2023) 690 final (08.11.2023)

EU Commission Report for Bosnia and Herzegovina 2021, SWD(2021) 291 final /2 (19.10.2021)

EU Commission Report for Bosnia and Herzegovina 2022, SWD(2022) 336 final (12.10.2022)

EU Commission Report for Kosovo 2020, SWD(2022) 334 final (12.10.2022)

EU Commission Report for Montenegro 2012, SWD(2012) 331 final (10.10.2012)

EU Commission Report for Montenegro 2020, SWD(2020) 353 final, (06.10.2020)

EU Commission Report for Montenegro for 2021, SWD(2021) 293 final/2 (19.10.2021)

EU Commission Report for Montenegro for 2022, SWD(2022) 335 final (12.10.2022)
EU Commission Report for North Macedonia 2020, SWD(2020) 351 final (6.10.2020)
EU Commission Report for North Macedonia 2021, SWD(2021) 294 final (19.10.2021)
EU Commission Report for North Macedonia SWD (2023) 693 final (08.11.2023)
EU Commission Report for Serbia 2019, SWD(2019) 219 final, (25.09.2019)
EU Commission Report for Serbia, SWD(2016) 361 final (09.11.2016)
EU Commission, 'Communication from the Commission to the European Parliament and Council. Exchanging and Protecting Personal Data in a Globalised World' COM (2017) 7 final (10.01.2017)
EU Commission, 'Data protection as a pillar of citizens' empowerment and the EU's approach to the digital transition – two years of application of the General Data Protection Regulation', no. 264, (2020)
EU Commission, 'Does my company/organisation need to have a Data Protection Officer (DPO)?' <https://commission.europa.eu/law/law-topic/data-protection/reform/rules-business-and organisations/obligations/data-protection-officers/does-my-companyorganisation-need-have-data-protection-officer-dpo_en> accessed on 28.01.2023
EU Commission, 'The EU and China signed a key partnership on 5G, our tomorrow's communication networks' (28.9.2015), available at the following link <https://ec.europa.eu/commission/presscorner/detail/cs/ip_15_5715> accessed on 02.02.2025
EU Commission, 'The Recommendations of the Senior Experts' Group on systemic Rule of Law issues relating to the communications interception revealed in Spring 2015' (June 2015)
EU Commission, Assessment of the Draft Law on Personal Data Protection of Serbia, TAIEX mission 30066 (May 2019) <https://www.poverenik.rs/images/stories/dokumentacija-nova/Publikacije/engEKStudija.pdf> accessed on 12.02.2023
EU Commission, European Neighbourhood Policy and Enlargement Negotiations: Serbia <https://neighbourhood-enlargement.ec.europa.eu/enlargement-policy/serbia_en> accessed on 24.01.2022
EU Commission, MOTION FOR A EUROPEAN PARLIAMENT RESOLUTION on the 2019–2020 Commission Reports on Montenegro, (20.04.2021), 2019/2173(INI)
EU Commission, Stabilisation and Association Agreement between the European Union and Kosovo, 10728/1/15 REV 1
EU Commission, Stabilisation and Association Agreement between the European Communities and their Member States, of the one part, and Montenegro, of the other part (2010) O.J. (L 108)
EU Commission, Stabilisation and Association Agreement between the European Communities and their Member States, of the one part, and the Republic of North Macedonia, of the other part (OJ L 84, 20.3.2004)
EU Commission, Stabilisation and Association Agreement between the EU and Serbia, Official Journal of the European Union, L 278 (01.09.2013)
EU Commission's website: 'European Neighbourhood Policy and Enlargement Negotiations (DG NEAR), North Macedonia'
EU Council Decision (EU) 2015/997 of 16 June 2008 on the signing on behalf of the European Community of the Stabilisation and Association Agreement between the European Communities and their Member States, of the one part, and Bosnia and Herzegovina, of the other part, 2015, O.J. (L164)
EU Commission Report 2022 for Serbia SWD(2022) 338 final (12.10.2022)

EU Project 'Support to Kosovo institutions in the field of Protection of Personal Data' EuropeAid/133806/C/SER/XK, (31.01.2016)

EU website, 'The EU and the Western Balkans: towards a common future' <https://www.eeas.europa.eu/eeas/eu-and-western-balkans-towards-common-future_en> accessed on 21.12.2020

EUPM, EU Institute for Security Studies, Joint Report: 'Ten years after: Lessons from the EUPM in Bosnia and Herzegovina 2002–2012' (January 2013), <https://www.iss.europa.eu/sites/default/files/EUISSFiles/EUPM_report_0.pdf> accessed on 12.03.2023

Euractiv, 'Western Balkans sign landmark agreements in Berlin ahead of December summit' (03.11.2022), <https://www.euractiv.com/section/enlargement/news/western-balkans-sign-landmark-agreements-in-berlin-ahead-of-december-summit/> accessed on 25.07.2023

Eurasia, 'Soldiers among Albanian Ruling Party's Voter Tracking 'Army' <https://eurasia.ro/2021/04/23/police-soldiers-among-albanian-ruling-partys-voter-tracking-army/> accessed on 28.08.2022

Europe Agreement establishing an association between the European Communities and their Member States and Hungary (16/12/1991)

European Council, Conclusions, EUCO 139/1/11, REV 1, Brussels, (25.01.2012) <https://data.consilium.europa.eu/doc/document/ST-139-2011-REV-1/en/pdf> accessed on 24.01.2023

European Council, Infographic 'The EU: main investor, donor and trade partner for the Western Balkans' <https://www.consilium.europa.eu/en/infographics/the-eu-main-trade-partner-and-investor-for-the-western-balkans/> accessed on 20.01.2024

European Court of Auditors, Special Report: Rule of Law in Western Balkans, despite efforts, fundamental problems persist (2022), available at the following link <https://op.europa.eu/webpub/eca/special-reports/eu-support-to-the-rule-of-law-in-Western-Balkans-01–2022/en/> accessed on 01.03.2025

European Data Protection Supervisor, 'Letter to the participants of the closing conference: Support to the implementation of the modernized data protection legal framework' (07.10.2022) <https://azlp.mk/en/letter-from-the-european-data-protection-supervisor/> accessed on 27.05.2023

European Neighbourhood Policy and Enlargement Negotiations, Negotiation Status of Albania, <https://ec.europa.eu/neighbourhood-enlargement/enlargement-policy/negotiations-status/albania_en> accessed on 17.06.2022

European Neighbourhood Policy and Enlargement Negotiations: Bosnia and Herzegovina <https://neighbourhood-enlargement.ec.europa.eu/enlargement-policy/bosnia-and-herzegovina_en> accessed on 22.04.2023

European Parliament resolution of 12 March 2019 on security threats connected with the rising Chinese technological presence in the EU and possible action on the EU level to reduce them (2019/2575(RSP) (12.03.2019)

European Parliament resolution on the adequacy of the protection afforded by the EU-US Data Privacy Framework (2023/2501(RSP)) (11.05.2023)

European Parliament, 'Report on foreign interference in all democratic processes in the European Union, including disinformation, Special Committee on Foreign Interference in all Democratic Processes in the European Union, including Disinformation, Rapporteur: Sandra Kalniete' (2020/2268(INI)) (8.2.2022) <https://www.europarl.europa.eu/doceo/document/A-9-2022-0022_EN.html> accessed on 02.04.2023

European Parliament's Committee on Civil Liberties, Justice and Home Affairs, 'Draft motion for a resolution 2023/2501 (RSP)' (March 2023) <https://www.europarl.europa.eu/doceo/document/LIBE-RD-740749_EN.pdf> accessed on 12.05.2023

European Treaty Series – No. 108, Explanatory Report to the Convention for the Protection of Individuals with regard to Automatic Processing of Personal Data, Strasbourg, (28.01.1981)
EU-Western Balkans Summit Thessaloniki, 'Final Declaration' C/03/163 (21.06.2003)
Exit news, 'ECHR Ruling in Privacy Case Shows Similarities to Albania's Massive Data Leak' <https://exit.al/en/echr-ruling-in-privacy-case-shows-similarities-to-albanias-massive-data-leak/> accessed at 02.09.2022
Fabbrini F, 'Five Years of Legally Binding Charter of Fundamental Rights' (Oxford, Hart Publishing, 2015)
Faculty of Security of the University of Belgrade, 'PERSONAL DATA PROTECTION MANAGER TRAINING – officially registered and approved the first short study program in the field of personal data protection in the domestic education system' (21.06.2020), <https://fb.bg.ac.rs/2020/06/21/obuka-menadzera-za-zastitu-podataka-o-licnosti-zvanicno-evidentiran-i-odobren-prvi-kratak-program-studija-u-oblasti-zastite-podataka-o-licnosti-u-domacem-obrazovnom-sistemu/> accessed on 124.05.2023
Fahey E and Mancini I, 'The EU as an Intentional or Accidental Convergence Actor? Learning from the EU-Japan Data Adequacy Negotiations', International Trade Law and Regulation 2020 Volume 2, (2020)
Fennessy C, 'A breakdown of EDPB's recommendations for data transfers post-'Schrems II' (International Association of Privacy Professionals, 11 November 2020) accessed on 12.12.2020
Finch K and Tene O, 'Smart cities: Privacy, transparency, and community', In Cambridge Handbook of Consumer Privacy (2018)
Foityik P, 'Publicly available data under the GDPR: Main considerations', IAPP (28.05.2019) <https://iapp.org/news/a/publicly-available-data-under-gdpr-main-considerations/> accessed on 12.02.2023
Fortune Editors, 'How Smart Cities and Homes Will Take China into the Future', Fortune, (07.11.2019) <https://fortune.com/2019/11/07/china-smart-cities/> accessed 11.05.2020
Freedom House, 'Nations in Transit: Dropping the Democratic Façade', (2020) <https://freedomhouse.org/sites/default/files/2020-04/05062020_FH_NIT2020_vfinal.pdf> accessed on 02.04.2023
Freedom House, European Western Balkans, 'Freedom House: Democracy deteriorates in the Western Balkans, Serbia faces the strongest decline', published on 11.04.2024, <https://europeanwesternbalkans.com/2024/04/11/freedom-house-democracy-deteriorates-in-the-western-balkans-serbia-faces-the-strongest-decline/> accessed on 03.03.2025
Fuster G G and Gellert R, 'The fundamental right of data protection in the European Union: in search of an uncharted right', International Review of Law, Computers & Technology (2012)
Gal M and O Aviv, 'The Competitive Effects of the GDPR', Journal of Competition Law and Economics (2020)
Gellert R, 'Understanding the Notion of Risk in the General Data Protection Regulation', Computer Law & Security Review, Volume 34, Issue 2 (2018)
Geneva Centre for Security Sector Governance 'Intelligence and Security Sector Reform Program in the Republic of North Macedonia (2021–2026)' Newsletter No. 2, DCAF (2 October – December 2021), <https://aidstream.org/files/documents/North_Macedonia_Newsletter_EN_OCT-DEC_2021-(final)-20230124110112.pdf> accessed on 12.03.2023
German Data Protection Conference ('DSK'), Orientierungshilfe der Aufsichtsbehörden zur Verarbeitung von personenbezogenen Daten für Zwecke der Direktwerbung unter Geltung der Datenschutz-Grundverordnung (DSGVO)

GIZ, Achieving progress on Albania's pathway to EU accession (February 2023), <https://www.giz.de/en/worldwide/120333.html> accessed on 09.04.2023

Glas Amerike, 'Zabrinjavajuće stanje i loš nacrt zakona o zaštiti ličnih podataka' (27.01.2018) <https://www.glasamerike.net/a/zabrinajvajuce-stanje-i-los-nacrt-zakona-o-zastiti-licnih-podataka/4228354.html> accessed on 17.03.2021

Glušac L, 'National Human Rights Institutions and Oversight of the Security Services', Journal of Human Rights Practice 10:1 (2018)

Gola P and Heckmann D, 'Art. 3 Räumlicher Anwendungsbereich', Datenschutz-Grundverordnung – Bundesdatenschutzgesetz, (3th edn. C.H. Beck. 2022)

Gola P, 'Das Internet als Quelle von Bewerberdaten', NZA (2019)

Golland A, 'Der räumliche Anwendungsbereich der DS-GVO', Datenschutz Datensich (2018),

González Fuster, G and Gellert, R 'The fundamental right of data protection in the European Union: in search of an uncharted right', International Review of Law, Computers & Technology (2012).

González Fuster, G, 'The Emergence of Personal Data Protection as a Fundamental Right of the EU', Law, Governance and Technology Series 16. Springer (2014)

Graaf B de and others, 'The Handbook of European Intelligence Cultures', the Rowman & Littlefield Publishing group, Inc (2016)

Graziadei M, 'Comparative Law, Transplants, and Receptions', The Oxford Handbook of Comparative Law (2nd edn) (2019)

Greenleaf G 'The draft Korea adequacy Decision: Submission to European Union authorities', UNSW Sydney (16.08.2021)

Greenleaf G, 'Japan and Korea: Different Paths to EU Adequacy' 156 Privacy Laws & Business International Report, (2018)

Greenleaf G, 'Japan and Korea: Different Paths to EU Adequacy', Privacy Laws & Business 156 International Report (10.12.2018)

Greenleaf G, 'The influence of European data privacy standards outside Europe: implications for globalization of Convention 108', International Data Privacy Law, Volume 2, Issue 2 (May 2012)

Greenleaf G, 'Update to Graham Greenleaf's Asian Data Privacy Laws – Trade and Human Rights Perspectives' UNSW Law Research Paper no. 17–47 (12.07.2017)

Greze B, 'The extra-territorial enforcement of the GDPR: a genuine issue and the quest for alternatives', International Data Privacy Law, Volume 9, Issue 2 (May 2019)

Gstrein OJ and Zwitter A, 'Extraterritorial Application of the GDPR: Promoting European Values or Power?' Internet Policy Review, Volume 10 Issue 3 (September 30, 2021)

Guide to the Case-Law of the of the European Court of Human Rights Data protection (31.08.2022) <https://www.echr.coe.int/Documents/Guide_Data_protection_ENG.pdf> accessed on 05.05.2023

Gulczyńska Z, 'A certain standard of protection for international transfers of personal data under the GDPR, International Data Privacy Law', Volume 11, Issue 4 (November 2021)

Haider H, 'Rule of law challenges in the Western Balkans', Institute of Development Studies Brighton, UK (2018)

Hajdari P, Nimani P, Hebibi D and Maloku A, 'Implementation of the right to privacy in the Republic of Kosovo, International Journal of Health Sciences' (2022)

Hajduk P, 'The Powers of the Supervisory Body in the GDPR as a Basis for Shaping the Practices of Personal Data Processing' Review of European and Comparative Law (RECoL), HeinOnline 45, (2021), pp. 57–76.

Hajduk P, 'The Powers of the Supervisory Body in the GDPR as a Basis for Shaping the Practices of Personal Data Processing', Review of European and Comparative Law (RECoL), HeinOnline (2021)

Hennemann M, 'Das Schweizer Datenschutzrecht im Wettbewerb der Rechtsordnungen' in Festschrift für Werner F. Ebke zum 70. Geburtstag, Paal, Boris P. and Poelzig, Dörte and Fehrenbacher, Oliver, Eds. München C.H. Beck (2021)

Hennemann M, 'Exportbeschränkungen für den Datenschutz?', Frankfurter Allgemeine Tageszeitung Einspruch (01.10.2020)

Hennemann M, 'Wettbewerb der Datenschutzrechtsordnungen? – Zur Rezeption Der Datenschutz-Grundverordnung' RabelsZ, vol. 84 (2020)

Hert P De and Czerniawski M, 'Expanding the European Data Protection Scope Beyond Territory: Article 3 of the General Data Protection Regulation in its Wider Context' International Data Privacy Law, Volume 6, Issue 3, (August 2016)

Hert P De and Papakonstatinou V, 'The proposed data protection Regulation replacing Directive 95/46/EC: A sound system for the protection of individuals', Computer Law & Security Review, Volume 28, Issue 2 (2012)

Hiljadekamera, 'Letter from MEPs on new Draft Laws on Internal Affairs & biometric surveillance in Serbia' (December 2022) <https://hiljade.kamera.rs/wp-content/uploads/Letter_from_MEPs_on_new_Draft_Laws_on_Internal_Affairs.pdf> accessed on 01.04.2023

Hiljadekamera, 'Round two of the battle against mass biometric surveillance', (10.01.2023) <https://hiljade.kamera.rs/en/news/round-two-of-the-battle-against-mass-biometric-surveillance/> accessed on 01.04.2023

Hillion C, 'The Copenhagen Criteria and Their Progeny' (2014), in C. Hillion (ed), EU enlargement, Oxford, Hart Publishing (2004)

Hustin P, 'EU Data Protection Law: The Review of Directive 95/46/EC and the Proposed General Data Protection Regulation' (September 2014)

IAPP, 'Moroccan data protection law: Moving to align with EU data protection?' (11.09.2018) <https://iapp.org/news/a/moroccan-data-protection-law-moving-to-align-with-eu-data-protection/> accessed on 29.05.2023

IAPP, European Data Protection: Law and Practice, Second Edition, International Association of Privacy Professionals (01.01.2018)

ICO, Guidance on direct marketing using electronic mail <https://ico.org.uk/for-organisations/guide-to-pecr/guidance-on-direct-marketing-using-electronic-mail/how-do-we-comply-with-the-rules-on-sending-marketing-by-electronic-mail/#howdoweusesoft> accessed on 08.05.2023

ICO, Guide to international transfers <https://ico.org.uk/for-organisations/uk-gdpr-guidance-and-resources/international-transfers/international-transfers-a-guide/> accessed on 29.05.2023

Ihle J, 'Ireland blocks EU data sharing with Israel' Jewish Telegraphic Agency (08.07.2010), available at the following link <www.jta.org/2010/07/08/news-opinion/world/ ireland-blocks-eu-data-sharing-with-israel> accessed on 15.12.2023

Infographic, 'The EU: main trade partner and investor for the Western Balkan Council of Europe, General Secretariat' <https://www.consilium.europa.eu/en/infographics/the-eu-main-trade-partner-and-investor-for-the-western-balkans/> accessed on 03.06.2023

Information Technology & Innovation Foundation, 'Response to the Consultation of the EU Commission on Transfers of Personal Data to Third Countries and Cooperation between Data Protection Authorities' (2020) <https://www2.itif.org/2020-gdpr-two-year-review.pdf> accessed on 06.04.2023

Informer, 'ISTRAŽUJEMO! ŠTA SE ZAPRAVO KRIJE IZA AFERE "POVERENIK"? Hteli su da Danila lažno optuže za pranje para?!?' (13.11.2021) <https://informer.rs/vesti/politika/651558/sta-krije-iza-afere-poverenik> accessed on 12.02.2023

Informer, 'SPECIJALNI RAT PROTIV VUČIĆA! Inspektori proveravali vinoteku u kojoj radi predsednikov sin Danilo!' (11.11.2021) <https://informer.rs/vesti/politika/651187/specijalni-rat-protiv-vucica-inspektori-proveravali-vinoteku-kojoj-radi-predsednikov-sin-danilo> accessed on 12.02.2023

Informer, Bakarec Nebojša: 'Nebojša Bakarec: Afera "Poverenik" – nova saznanja!!', (16.11.2021) <https://informer.rs/vesti/politika/652339/nebojsa-bakarec-afera-poverenik-nova-saznanja> accessed on 03.01.2023

Insajder, 'Nacrtom zakona o zaštiti podataka o ličnosti Srbija samo formalno ispunjava evropski standard, upitna njegova primena' (02.03.2018) <https://insajder.net/arhiva/tema/nacrtom-zakona-o-zastiti-podataka-o-licnosti-srbija-samo-formalno-ispunjava-evropski-standard-upitna-njegova-primena> accessed on 17.03.2021

Insajder, 'Mišljenje EK o Nacrtu zakona o zaštiti podataka o ličnosti – dokument za koji je Ministarstvo mesecima tvrdilo da ne postoji' (15.08.2018) <https://insajder.net/arhiva/vesti/misljenje-ek-o-nacrtu-zakona-o-zastiti-podataka-o-licnosti-dokument-za-koji-je-ministarstvo-mesecima-tvrdilo-da-ne-postoji> accessed on 17.01.2021

Insajder, 'Poverenik: Obavestićemo tužilaštvo da je predsednik SNS poslao novo pismo penzionerima, nemamo informacije šta je s prethodnim postupkom' (25.05.2020) <https://insajder.net/arhiva/vesti/poverenik-obavesticemo-tuzilastvo-da-je-predsednik-sns-poslao novo-pismo-penzionerima-nemamo-informacije-sta-je-s-prethodnim-postupkom> accessed on 12.05.2023

Jaćimović D and others, 'Does China Challenge Integration Perspective of the Western Balkan Countries?', 12th SCF International Conference on "Contemporary Issues in Social Sciences" (October 2020)

Johannes RA PC, 'China, Kurzsynopse der Regelungsinhalte des neuen chinesischen Datenschutzgesetzes PIPL zur DS-GVO', ZD-Aktuell 05455 (2021)

Juszczak A and Sason E, 'Recalibrating Data Retention in the EU The Jurisprudence of the Court of Justice of the EU on Data Retention – Is this the End or is this the Beginning?', EUCRIM (2021)

Kamara I and Hert P De, 'Understanding the Balancing Act behind the Legitimate Interest of the Controller Ground: A Pragmatic Approach', Brussels Privacy Hub, Vol. 4, No. 12 (August 2018)

Kamberi G and Memaj E, 'The Albanian Public's Trust in Security: Stumbling Blocks to EU Negotiations' Friedrich Ebert Stiftung (November 2020)

Kamberi G and Memaj E, 'The Albanian Public's Trust in Security: Stumbling Blocks to EU Negotiations', Center for the Study of Democracy and Governance (2020)

Karanovic & Partners, 'Additional Period for Ensuring Data Protection Compliance in North Macedonia', CEE Lelgal Matters (09.09.2021) <https://ceelegalmatters.com/macedonia/17809-additional-period-for-ensuring-data-protection-compliance-in-north-macedonia> accessed on 21.04.2023

Karanovic & Partners, 'North Macedonia: Informal Requirement for Transfer Impact Assessments in the New Yea', Lexicology (15.12.2021) <https://www.lexology.com/library/detail.aspx?g=a36a570d-5777-45a8-89a3-e19e4356b7ef> accessed on 28.05.2023

Karčić F, 'A study on legal formalism in the former Yugoslavia and its successor states', CIDS report no. 1 (2020)

Khalil L, 'Digital Authoritarianism, China and COVID', Lowy Institute for International Policy (2020)

Kischel U, 'Comparative Law', Oxford University Press (April 2019)

Klein J Xu, 'Around the World, Doors Are Shutting on Chinese Investment', South China Morning Post, (14.09.2018), available at the following link <https://www.scmp.com/business/ banking-finance/article/2163974/its-not-just-us-around-world-doors-are-shutting-chinese> accessed 22.04.2023

Kloth A, 'One law to rule them all – On the extraterritorial applicability of the new EU General Data Protection Regulation' Völkerrechtsblog (05 February 2018)

Kmezić M, 'EU Rule of Law Conditionality: Democracy or 'Stabilitocracy' Promotion in the Western Balkans?', in: Džankić, J., Keil, S., Kmezić, M. (eds), The Europeanisation of the Western Balkans. New Perspectives on South-East Europe. Palgrave Macmillan (2019)

Kochenov D, 'The Acquis and Its Principles: The Enforcement of the 'Law' versus the Enforcement of 'Values' in the European Union', A. Jakab and D. Kochenov (eds.), The Enforcement of EU Law and Values University of Groningen Faculty of Law Research Paper, (2018)

Kokott J and Sobotta C, 'The distinction between privacy and data protection in the jurisprudence of the CJEU and the ECtHR', International Data Privacy Law 3(4) (2013)

Korff D, 'EC Study on Implementation of Data Protection Directive, Comparative Summary of National Laws', Cambridge, (Study Contract ETD/2001/B5 – 3001/A/49) (September 2002)

Korff D, 'Update on the Opinion on the future of personal data transfers from the EU/EEA to Israel & the Occupied Territories' (23.02.2023) <https://www.ianbrown.tech/wp-content/uploads/2022/02/KORFF-Opinion-update-EU-Israel-data-transfers-final220223-2.pdf>, accessed on 29.05.2023

Kosovo IPA, 'For the first time in Kosovo, a Regional Conference on Personal Data Protection is being organized' (28.06.2022), <https://aip.rks-gov.net/en/for-the-first-time-in-kosovo-a-regional-conference-on-personal-data-protection-is-being-organized/> accessed on 27.05.2023

Kosta E, 'A divided European data protection framework: A critical reflection on the choices of the European legislator post-Lisbon', in E. Kosta, R. Leenes, & I. Kamara (Eds.), Research handbook on EU data protection law (2022)

Kostanica M, 'Data Protection Regulation in the Republic of Kosovo and Compliance by the Companies: A Proposed Model for Kosovo', International In-House Counsel Journal, Vol. 2, Issue 8 (Summer 2009)

Kovačević A and Visca H, 'Evaluation Integrity Police in Bosnia and Herzegovina', Beogradski centar za bezbednosnu politiku (2015) <http://css.ba/wp-content/uploads/2011/06/Assessment-of-police-integrity-in-Bosnia-and-Herzegovina-BHS-web.pdf> accessed on 03.04.2023

Krik, 'Martinović: Kandidat za Poverenika biće sušta suprotnost Šabiću' (28.01.2019) <https://www.krik.rs/martinovic-kandidat-za-poverenika-bice-susta-suprotnost-sabicu/> accessed on 12.02.2023

Krik, 'Odbor podržao Milana Marinovića kao kandidata za poverenika za informacije od javnog značaja' (01.07.2019) <https://insajder.net/arhiva/vesti/odbor-podrzao-milana-marinovica-kao-kandidata-za-poverenika-za-informacije-od-javnog-znacaja> accessed on 12.02.2023

Krik, 'Otkrića do kojih je KRIK došao uz pomoć poverenika Šabića' (21. 12. 2018) <https://www.krik.rs/otkrica-do-kojih-je-krik-dosao-uz-pomoc-poverenika-sabica/> accessed on 03. 03. 2022

Krivokapić D and others, 'State of pandemonium: Digital rights in the Western Balkans and COVID-19', Global Campus of Human Rights, Policy Brief (2020)

Krzysztofek M and Kluwer W, 'General Data Protection Regulation (EU) 2016/679: Post-reform Personal Data Protection in the European Union', Band 107 von European monographs, (2019)

Kühling B and Buchner B, 'Art. 7 DS-GVO Bedingungen für die Einwilligung' in Jürgen Kühling and Benedikt Buchner, Datenschutz-Grundverordnung, Bundesdatenschutzgesetz: DS-GVO/BDSG (3rd edn, C.H. Beck 2020)

Kuner C and others, 'Background and Evolution of the EU General Data Protection Regulation (GDPR)' in Christopher Kuner and others (eds) (February 2020)

Kuner C and others, 'The GDPR as a chance to break down borders', International Data Privacy Law, Volume 7, Issue 4, (November 2017)

Kuner C, 'Article 45 Transfers on the basis of an adequacy decision', The EU General Data Protection Regulation (GDPR): A Commentary, Oxford University Press (2020)

Kuner C, 'International Regulation of Transborder Data Flows', Transborder Data Flows and Data Privacy Law, Oxford Academic (2013)

Kuner C, 'Protecting EU data outside EU borders under the GDPR', Common Market Law Review, Volume 60, Issue 1 (2023)

Kurir, 'ISTRAŽUJEMO! ŠTA SE ZAPRAVO KRIJE IZA AFERE "POVERENIK"? Hteli su da Danila lažno optuže za pranje para?!?' (13. 11. 2021) <https://informer.rs/vesti/politika/651558/sta-krije-iza-afere-poverenik> accessed on 03. 03. 2022

Kursani S, 'Lawful Interception of Telecommunications in Kosovo: Security Implications' Kosovar Center for Security Studies (27. 10. 2011)

L Cerulus S and Kayali L, 'Six months in, Europe's privacy revolution favors Google, Facebook', in Politicopro <https://www.politico.eu/article/gdpr-facebook-google-privacy-data-6-months-in-europes-privacy-revolution-favors-google-facebook/> accessed on 12. 08. 2022

Larsen H, 'The Western Balkans between the EU, NATO, Russia and China', CSS Analyses in Security Policy 263, ETH Zurich Research Collection (May 2020)

Laue P and Kremer S, 'Das neue Datenschutzrecht in der betrieblichen Praxis' (2nd edn, C.H. Beck 2019)

Le Corre P and Vuksanovic V, 'Serbia: China's Open Door to the Balkans', Carnegie Endowment for International Peace <https://carnegieendowment.org/2019/01/01/serbia-china-s-open-door-to-balkans-pub-78054> accessed 01. 04. 2023

Le Corre P, 'On Chinese Investment and Influence in Europe', Carnegie Endowment for International Peace, (23. 05. 2018) <https://carnegieendowment. org/2018/05/23/on-chinese-investment-and-influence-in-europe-pub-76467> accessed 11. 05. 2020

Legrand P, 'What 'Legal Transplants'?', in David Nelken and Joachim Feest (eds), Adapting Legal Cultures (2001)

Lessig L, 'Law Regulating Code Regulating Law', Loyola University Chicago Law Journal, vol. 35, no. 1, (2003)

Levush R, 'Israel. Online Privacy Law' in Ethan P William (ed.), Online Privacy Laws European Union & select foreign countries, Nova Science (2013)

Lindqvist J, 'New challenges to personal data processing agreements: is the GDPR fit to deal with contract, accountability and liability in a world of the Internet of Things?', International Journal of Law and Information Technology, Volume 26, Issue 1, Spring 2018

Liss J and others, 'Demystifying Schrems II for the cross-border transfer of clinical research data', J Law Biosci (Jul-Dec 2021)

Liwer D, GDPR: one size does not fit all, CSO-US 2018, <https://www.csoonline.com/article/3269570/gdpr-one-size-does-not-fit-all.html> accessed on 01.12.2023

Luhmann N, 'Das Recht der Gesellschaft', Suhrkamp (1993)

Luzha D, 'Krenare Sogojeva-Dërmaku zgjidhet komisionere e Agjencisë për Informim dhe Privatësi' <https://kallxo.com/lajm/krenare-sogojeva-dermaku-zgjidhet-komisionere-e-agjencise-per-informim-dhe-privatesi/> accessed on 16.06.2022

Lynskey O, 'The Foundations of EU Data Protection Law', Oxford University Press (November 2015)

Lynskey O, Deconstructing Data Protection 'The 'Added-Value' of a Right To Data Protection in the EU Legal Order', International and Comparative Law Quarterly, 63(3) (2014)

Maizland L, and Chatzky, A 'Huawei: China's Controversial Tech Giant', Council on Foreign Relations, (12.06.2019) <https://www.cfr.org/backgrounder/huawei-chinas-controversial-tech-giant> accessed on 11.05.2023

Manancourt V, 'Why Brussels Went Easy on Britain in Its Data Deal', published in Politico (30.06.2021), <https://www.politico.eu/article/why-brussels-went-easy-on-britain-in-data-adequacy-deal/> accessed on 23.03.2023

Marktler T, 'The Power of the Copenhagen Criteria' 2 Croatian Yearbook of European Law and Policy (2006) pp. 343–348

Masoch F D, 'Swiss Data Protection Authority considers the CH-US Privacy Shield no longer adequate – Swiss companies must act now' Lexology (11.09.2020) <https://www.lexology.com/library/detail.aspx?g=2ddd0dd2-e345-4a61-b77a54ca57bfd78a> accessed on 17.05.2023

Mc Cullagh K, Tambou O and Bourton S, 'National Adaptations of the GDPR', Collection Open Access Book, Blogdroiteuropeen, Luxembourg (February 2019)

McGeveran W, 'Friending the Privacy Regulators', 58 ARIz. L. REV (2016)

Merlin G, 'The new territorial scope of EU data protection law: Deconstructing a revolutionary achievement', 54, Common Market Law Review, Issue 2 (2017)

Michael D B, 'The EU Data Protection Directive: An engine of a global regime', Computer Law & Security Review, Volume 24, Issue 6 (2008)

Milić D, 'Legitimni interes kao osnov obrade podataka o ličnosti', The Personal Data Protection Rights in Serbia (2020), Serbian Institute of Comparative Law, pp. 50–59.

Miličić K, 'Vukovar police using drones to enforce social-distancing measures', The Voice of Croatia (14.04.2020) <https://glashrvatske.hrt.hr/en/news/domestic/vukovar-police-using-drones-to-enforce-social-distancing-measures> accessed 29.03.2023

Milošević I, Data Protection Strategy Proposal for 2023–2030, JPM <https://www.jpm.law/wp-content/uploads/2023/03/Serbia-%E2%80%93-Data-Protection-Strategy-Proposal-for-2023-2030.pdf> accessed on 30.03.2023

Miovska L B, 'The use of special investigative measures in the Republic of North Macedonia – legal provisions and human rights aspects', ROCZNIK ADMINISTRACJI PUBLICZNEJ 2022 (8)

Moere L, 'The long arm of EU data protection law: Does the Data Protection Directive apply to processing of personal data of EU citizens by websites worldwide?', International Data Privacy Law, Vol. 1, No. 1 (2011)

Moniz G C, 'The risk-based approach in the GDPR and the 'two-step test' within Article 44', International Data Privacy Law, Volume 14, Issue 2, (May 2024)

Montenegrin Agency for Personal Data Protection and Free Access to Information, the document 'List of employees in the Agency for 2022' <https://www.azlp.me/storage/docs/zajednicka/

Proaktivan%20pristup/Spisak%20zaposlenih%20septembar%202022.pdf> accessed on 20.01.2023

Montenegrin Government, Report on the implementation of the Program for the Accession of Montenegro to the European Union 2021–2023 (26.01.2022), <https://www.gov.me/dokumenta/a4fb6c49-bdc4-4880-b978-4b92805d859a> accessed on 30.04.2023

Montenegrin Government's press release with statement of former prime minister 'Premijer Duško Marković: Mjere donosimo da zaštitimo građane, neće biti praštanja za nepoštovanje pravila', (22.03.2020) <https://www.gov.me/clanak/223147--premijer-dusko-markovic-mjere-donosimo-da-zastitimo-gradane-nece-biti-prastanja-za-nepostovanje-pravila> accessed on 01.02.2022

Montenegrin Ombudsman, 'Osuda objavljivanja ličnih podataka zaraženih građana' (03.04.2020) <https://www.ombudsman.co.me/34348.news.html> accessed on 12.03.2023

Murray P J, 'The Adequacy Standard under Directive 95/46/EC: Does U.S. Data Protection Meet This Standard', McGill Guide 9th ed. (1998)

Murray S, 'Safe Cities Index 2017. Security in a Rapidly Urbanising World' Report from The Economist Intelligence Unit, (2017) <https://dkf1ato8y5dsg.cloudfront.net/uploads/5/82/safe-cities-index-eng-web.pdf> accessed om 12.04.2023

Murtezić A, 'Opšta Uredba o Zaštiti podataka: Odnos Prava na Privatnost i Zaštite Ličnih Podataka s osvrtom na Bosnu i Hercegovinu', Anali Pravnog fakulteta Univerziteta u Zenici, ISSN 1986–5791 (2019)

Musar P N, 'Vodič kroz Zakon o Zaštiti Podataka o Ličnosti' Publisher Commissioner for Information of Public Importance and Personal Data Protection, Belgrade, (May 2009)

N1, 'Brnabić: Poverenik kontrolom vinoteke zloupotrebio svoju funkciju' (13.11.2021) <https://n1info.rs/vesti/brnabic-poverenik-kontrolom-vinoteke-zloupotrebio-svoju-funkciju/> accessed on 12.02.2023

Nadezhda P, 'The law of everything. Broad concept of personal data and future of EU data protection law', Law, Innovation and Technology (2018)

National Council for European Integration, Report: Thematic Roundtable on Justice, Freedom and Security (2020) <https://president-ksgov.net/repository/docs/TRT_2_ENG.pdf> accessed on 30.05.2023

Nbcnews, 'Belgium bans TikTok from government phones after U.S. and E.U.', (11.03.2023), <https://www.nbcnews.com/news/world/tiktok-ban-belgium-government-phones-us-europe-bytedance-rcna74468> accessed on 05.04.2023

Nelken D, 'Towards a Sociology of Legal Adaptation', Adapting Legal Cultures in David Nelken and Joachim Feest (eds), Oxford – Portland Oregon (2001)

Nikolov A, 'Analysis of the Legal Framework for Interception of Communications and Implementation thereof', Foundation for Internet and Society, Metamorphosis, and Association for Progressive Communications (APC), (2019) <https://metamorphosis.org.mk/wp-content/uploads/2019/08/Legal-framework-on-interception-of-communication_eng.pdf> accessed on 20.01.2023

NOYB, '226 complaints lodged against deceptive cookie banners that are still not complying with GDPR requirements' (09.08.2022) <https://noyb.eu/en/226-complaints-lodged-against-deceptive-cookie-banners> accessed on 02.02.2023

Nuredini B, Xhafaj J and Paukovska Dodevska V, 'A Comparative Overview of Data Protection in e-Commerce in the European Union, the United States of America, the Republic of North Macedonia, and Albania: Models and Specifics', Studia Iuridica Lubliensia, Vo 31, No 3 (2022)

OECD, 'Guidelines on the Protection of Privacy and Transborder Flows of Personal Data' (2013)

OECD, 'Original Explanatory Memorandum to the OECD Privacy Guidelines (OECD, Paris 1980)' in OECD (ed), The OECD Privacy Framework (2013)

One Trust, 'Israel: Privacy protection regulations on transfers from the EEA published in final form' (09. 05. 2023), <https://www.dataguidance.com/news/israel-privacy-protection-regulations-transfers-eea> accessed on 01. 12. 2023

One Trust, Montenegro – Data Protection Overview (December 2022), available at the following link <https://www.dataguidance.com/notes/montenegro-data-protection-overview> accessed on 20. 01. 2023

Opinion 32/2021 regarding the European Commission Draft Implementing Decision pursuant to Regulation (EU) 2016/679 on the adequate protection of personal data in the Republic of Korea Version 1.0 (24. 09. 2021)

Osmani N, 'Privacy and data protection: Legal aspects in the Republic of Macedonia', Information Technology Law,Ss. Cyril and Methodius University, Skopje, Republic of Macedonia (2016)

Paal BP and Hennemann M, 'DS-GVO Art. 14 Informationspflicht, wenn die personenbezogenen Daten nicht bei der betroffenen Person erhoben wurden', in Boris P Paal and Daniel A Pauly (eds), Datenschutz-Grundverordnung. Bundesdatenschutzgesetz: DS-GVO BDSG (3rd edn, C.H. Beck 2021)

Paal BP and Pauly DA, 'DS-GVO Art. 12 Transparente Information, Kommunikation und Modalitäten für die Ausübung der Rechte der betroffenen Person', in Boris P Paal and Daniel A Pauly (eds), Datenschutz-Grundverordnung. Bundesdatenschutzgesetz: DS-GVO BDSG (3rd edn, C.H. Beck 2021)

Padurariu A, 'The Implementation of Police Reform in Bosnia and Herzegovina: Analysing UN and EU Efforts. Stability', International Journal of Security & Development, (2014)

Pajvančić M, 'Commentary on the Constitution of the Republic of Serbia", Konrad Adenauer Stiftung, (2009)

Paragraf Lex d.o.o., The Article 'Nacrt Zakona o zaštiti podataka o ličnosti: Poverenik navodi da je Nacrt zakona koncepcijski i sadržinski znatno ispod nužnog nivoa' (26. 01. 2018) <https://paragraflex.rs/dnevne-vesti/290118/290118-vest11.html> accessed on 17. 03. 2021

Parliament and of the Council on the adequate protection of personal data provided in Hungary (notified under document number C(2000) 2305), Official Journal L 215 , 25/08/2000 P. 0004 – 0006

Partners for Democratic Change, 'Komentari Evropske komisije o Nacrtu Zakona o zaštiti podataka o ličnosti konačno dostupni javnosti' (15. 08. 2018) <https://www.partners-serbia.org/post?id=43> accessed on 13. 03. 2023

Partners for Democrats changes Serbia, 'Privatnost i zaštita podataka o ličnosti u Srbiji' (March 2021)

Pauly DA, 'Art. 44 DS-GVO' in Boris P Paal and Daniel A Pauly (eds), Datenschutz-Grundverordnung. Bundesdatenschutzgesetz: DS-GVO BDSG (3rd edn, C.H. Beck 2021)

Pauly DA, 'Art. 45 DS-GVO' in Boris P Paal and Daniel A Pauly (eds), Datenschutz-Grundverordnung. Bundesdatenschutzgesetz: DS-GVO BDSG (3rd edn, C.H. Beck 2021)

Pauly DA, 'Art. 46 DS-GVO' in Boris P Paal and Daniel A Pauly (eds), Datenschutz-Grundverordnung. Bundesdatenschutzgesetz: DS-GVO BDSG (3rd edn, C.H. Beck 2021)

Pauly DA, 'Art. 47 DS-GVO' in Boris P Paal and Daniel A Pauly (eds), Datenschutz-Grundverordnung. Bundesdatenschutzgesetz: DS-GVO BDSG (3rd edn, C.H. Beck 2021)

Pauly DA, 'Art. 49 DS-GVO' in Boris P Paal and Daniel A Pauly (eds), Datenschutz-Grundverordnung. Bundesdatenschutzgesetz: DS-GVO BDSG (3rd edn, C.H. Beck 2021)

Pech L, 'A Union Founded on the Rule of Law: Meaning and Reality of the Rule of Law as a Constitutional Principle of EU Law' (2010) 6(3) European Constitutional Law Review Vol. 6, pp. 359–396, (January 2011)
Peers S, Hervey T, Kenner J and Ward A, 'The EU Charter of Fundamental Rights', Nomos, Second Edition (2022)
Pejić J, 'WHO IS OUR INTERCEPTOR? How does interception of electronic communications and access to stored electronic data work in Serbia?' Belgrade Center for Security Policy, Belgrade (2014)
Pernot-Leplay E, 'Data Privacy Law in China: Comparison with the EU and US Approaches'; Journal of Law & International Affairs, Volume 8 no. 1 (2020)
Petrović P and Djokic K, 'State Capture and Security Intelligence Agencies in Serbia', Belgrade Centre for Security Policy (2017)
Petrović P and Đokic K, 'Slippery Slopes in the Reform of Serbian Security Services' Belgrade Centre for Security Policy (2017)
Piltz C, 'DS-GVO Art. 20 Recht auf Datenübertragbarkeit', in Gola/Heckmann, Datenschutz-Grundverordnung, Bundesdatenschutzgesetz (3d edn, C.H. Beck 2022)
Pisarić M, 'Surveillance of Electronic Communications in Republic of Serbia', in Berendt, B., Engel, T., Ikonomou, D., Le Métayer, D., Schiffner, S. (eds) Privacy Technologies and Policy. APF 2015. Lecture Notes in Computer Science(), vol 9484. Springer, Cham. (2016)
Plavšić N, 'Primena prakse Evropskog suda za ljudska prava od strane Ustavnog suda u postupcima po ustavnim žalbama' Fondacija Centar za javno pravo (2019)
Poulain L, 'China's New Balkan Strategy', SCIS, Volume 1, Number (02.11.2021)
PR legal, 'Legitimate Interest of Controller as a Legal Basis for Personal Data Processing – Do You Know How to Apply it Properly?' (15.08.2021) <https://www.prlegal.rs/legitimate-interest-of-controller-as-a-legal-basis-for-personal-data-processing-do-you-know-how-to-apply-it-properly> accessed on 27.01.2022
Qehaja F, 'Strengthening Intelligence Governance in the Western Balkans: Kosovo', DCAF (31.12.2012)
Radio Free Europe, 'Po 300 eura građanima Crne Gore sa javne liste 'kovid izolovanih'' (24.12.2021), <https://www.slobodnaevropa.org/a/obestecenje-crna-gora-spisak-kovid-samoizolacija/31624362.html> accessed on 21.01.2023
Radio Slobodna Evropa, 'Poverenik pokrenuo postupak zbog Vučićevih pisama penzionerima' (16.11.2018) <https://www.slobodnaevropa.org/a/29604307.html> accessed on 03.04.2022
Radović M, 'Utjecaj anglosaksonskog prava na srpsko kompanijsko pravo', Strani pravni život 63(2):33–44 (2019)
Recio M, 'The Key Figure to Ensure Data Protection and Accountability', 3 Eur. Data Prot. L. Rev. 114 (2017)
Regional Cooperation Council, Compliance of Legal Framework in the Western Balkans Economies with the General Data Protection Regulation (GDPR) Requirements (December 2020)
Reljić D, 'Potrebno usvajanje novog zakona o zaštiti ličnih podataka' TRT Balkan, (27.02.2023) <https://bhsc.trtbalkan.com/region/bih-potrebno-usvajanje-novog-zakona-o-zastiti-licnih-podataka-11841199> accessed on 22.04.2023
Report from the EU Commission to the European Parliament and the Council on the first review of the functioning of the adequacy decision for Japan SWD(2023) 75 final (03.04.2023)

Rivellini M, 'What will it take for Western Balkan economies to scale up?' (06.10.2023), <https://www.euractiv.com/section/economy-jobs/opinion/what-will-it-take-for-western-balkan-economies-to-scale-up/> accessed on 20.01.204

Riza G, 'GDPR and personal data protection in non- EU countries: Albanian case of data protection legislation'; University of Tirana, Faculty of Economics, Tirana, Albania, RTA-CSIT (May 2021)

Robinson N and others, 'Review of the European Data Protection Directive', Information Commissioner's Office (ICO) (May 2009);

Robinson W, 'The Trojan Dragon Comes to the Balkans', The Fletcher Forum of World Affairs; Medford Vol. 44, Iss. 2 (2020)

Rodoljub Š, 'Penzionerske Kartice', Peščanik (20.03.2023) <https://pescanik.net/penzionerske-kartice/> accessed on 14.05.2023

Rodotà S, 'Data Protection as a Fundamental Right', in Gutwirth, S., Poullet, Y., De Hert, P., de Terwangne, C., Nouwt, S. (eds) Reinventing Data Protection?. Springer, Dordrecht (2009)

Rubinstein I and Petkova B, 'The International Impact of the General Data Protection Regulation' Commentary on the General Data Protection Regulation, Marc Cole and Franziska Boehm, Edward Elgar (2018)

Rustad M L, and H Koenig T, 'Towards a Global Data Privacy Standard', Florida Law Review, vol. 71, no. 2 (March 2019)

Ružić N, 'Nationalising the General Data Protection Regulation in Western Balkan', Regional L. Rev. 313 (2021)

Ryngaert C and Zoetekouw M, 'The End of Territory? The Re-Emergence of Community as a Principle of Jurisdictional Order in the Internet Era' (October 2014)

Salihu G, 'The US–China 5G Race in Europe's Western Balkans', in: Berghofer, J., Futter, A., Häusler, C., Hoell, M., Nosál, J. (eds) The Implications of Emerging Technologies in the Euro-Atlantic Space. Palgrave Macmillan, Cham (07.03.2023)

Sandfuchs B, 'The Future of Data Transfers to Third Countries in Light of the CJEU's Judgment C-311/18 – Schrems II', GRUR Int. (2021)

Schantz P, 'DSGVO Art. 49 Ausnahmen für bestimmte Fälle', in Simitis/Hornung/Spiecker gen. Döhmann, Data Protection Law (1st edn, C.H. Beck 2021)

Schermer B and others 'The crisis of consent: how stronger legal protection may lead to weaker consent in data protection', Springer (May 2014)

Schröder C, 'Art. 45 DS-GVO', in Jürgen Kühling and Benedikt Buchner (eds), Datenschutz-Grundverordnung, Bundesdatenschutzgesetz: DS-GVO/BDSG (3rd edn, C.H. Beck 2020)

Scott L C and Overly S, 'How Silicon Valley gamed Europe's privacy rules', Politico.eu, (22.05.2019) <https://www.politico.eu/article/europe-data-protection-gdpr-general-data-protection-regulation-facebook-google/> accessed on 05.03.2022

Scott M and Cerulus L, 'Europe's new data protection rules export privacy standards worldwide', Politico (31.01.2018), <https://www.politico.eu/article/europe-data-protection-privacy-standards-gdpr-general-protection-data-regulation/> accessed on 06.11.2023

Serbian Commissioner for Public Information and Data Protection – Publication no. 6 – Data protection – Attitudes and opinions of the Commissioner, Publisher Commissioner for Information of Public Importance and personal data protection, for the publisher Milan Marinovic, Editor Gordana Mohorović, Belgrade (2021)

Serbian Commissioner for Public Information and Data Protection announcement 'Protocol CETSNo.223 was ratified in 2020', (29.05.2020) <https://www.poverenik.rs/sr-yu/saopstenja/

3352-србија-ратификовала-протокол-којим-се-мења-конвенција-о-заштити-лица-у-односу-на-аутоматску-обраду-личних-података.html> accessed on 15.05.2023

Serbian Commissioner for Public Information and Data Protection Press (02.08.2019), <https://www.poverenik.rs/sr-yu/arhiva/saopštenja-arhiva/3147-повереник-затражио-одлагање-примене-новог-закона-о-заштити-података-о-личности.html> accessed on 18.03.2021

Serbian Commissioner for Public Information and Data Protection Plan on the inspections in 2021 <https://www.poverenik.rs/images/stories/dokumentacija-nova/akti-o-radusluzbe/2021/plan_inspekcijskog_nadzora_2021.pdf > accessed on 12.02.2023

Serbian Commissioner for Public Information and Data Protection Q&A <https://www.poverenik.rs/images/stories/dokumentacija-nova/Publikacije/Publikacija_Lica_za_zastitu/PublikacijaLicezazastitu.pdf> accessed on 02.05.2023

Serbian Commissioner for Public Information and Data Protection, Statement on initiation of proceeding for invasion of privacy of shopping mall visitors (02.06.2021) <https://www.poverenik.rs/sr-yu/saopstenja/3561-кршење-приватности-посетилаца-тржног-ц%25> accessed on 18.05.2022

Serbian Commissioner for Public Information and Data Protection, 'Najčešće postavljana pitanja u vezi sa primenom Opšte uredbe o Zaštita podataka (GDPR)' <https://www.poverenik.rs/images/stories/dokumentacijanova/ZZPLnajcescapitanja/GDPRQA.pdf> accessed on 14.05.2023

Serbian Commissioner for Public Information and Data Protection, 'The list of representatives available at the DPC website at the following link' <https://www.poverenik.rs/sr-yu/zaštita-podataka/представници-страних-привредних-друштава-у-складу-са-законом-о-заштити-података-о-личности.html> accessed on 26.11.2021

Serbian Commissioner for Public Information and Data Protection's official response to a PM' parliamentary question 'Which provisions of the law allow the commissioner to abuse its position?' no. 073/24/1524/2018 – 01 (10.10.2018), <https://www.poverenik.rs/images/stories/dokumentacija-nova/pismaorganima/2018/Markovic.A.poslanicko.p.pdf> accessed on 01.02.2022

Serbian Commissioner for Public Information and Data Protection's opinion no. 073 – 15 – 1253/2020 – 02 (29.5.2022) <https://www.sharefoundation.info/Documents/Mi%c5%a1ljenje_Poverenika_2_0.pdf> accessed on 21.02.2021

Serbian Commissioner for Public Information and Data Protection's Announcment 'Kontinuitet neodgovornog odnosa države prema zaštiti podataka o ličnosti' (30.08.2017), <ps://www.poverenik.rs/sr-yu/arhiva/saopštenja-arhiva/2645-kontinuitet-neodgovornog-odnosa-države-prema-zaštiti-podataka-o-ličnosti.html> accessed on 01.04.2022

Serbian Commissioner for Public Information and Data Protection's Opinion on the conducted DPIA no. 073 – 15 – 1741/2019 – 02 (12.11.2019) <https://praksa.poverenik.rs/predmet/detalji/FB967E2A-AE57-4B2C8F11D2739FD85A9B> accessed on 21.02.2021

Serbian Commissioner for Public Information and Data Protection's Statement (12.11.2021) <ps://www.poverenik.rs/sr-yu/arhiva/saopštenja-arhiva/3682-саопштење-повереника-за-информације-од-јавног-значаја-и-заштиту-података-о-личности поводом-извршеног-редовног-теренског-инспекцијског-надзора-над-спровођењем-закона-о-заштити-података-о-личности-од-стране-једног-руковаоца-–-односно-надзираног-субјекта,-којем-је-једна-од-делатности-online-продаја-вина,-дана-10-11-2021-године-према-плану-инспекцијског-надзора-за-2021-годину-од-31-3-2021-године.html> accessed on 03.05.2022

Serbian Commissioner for Public Information and Data Protection's letter to the parliament, no. 073 – 14 – 1602/2018 – 01, (22.10.2018), <https://www.poverenik.rs/images/stories/dokumentacijanova/pismaorganima/pismoposlanicimaZZPLCL40.pdf> accessed on 12.02.2023
Serbian Commissioner for Public Information and Data Protection's official statement (16.11.2018) <htttps://www.poverenik.rs/sr-yu/arhiva/saopštenja-arhiva/2966-повереник-покренуо-поступак-надзора-поводом-обраде-личних-података-пензионера.html> accessed on 20.03.2022
Serbian Commissioner for Public Information and Data Protection's official statement, (03.12.2018) <https://www.poverenik.rs/sr-yu/arhiva/saopštenja-arhiva/2974-поводом-писма-пензионерима-повереник-поднео-кривичну-пријаву-против-нн-лица-из-фонда-пио.html> accessed on 20.03.2022
Serbian Commissioner for Public Information and Data Protection's letter, no. 073 – 14 – 1289/2017 – 01, (28.08.2017) <https://www.poverenik.rs/images/stories/dokumentacija-nova/pismaorganima/2017/vlada28.8.2017.pdf> accessed on 16.03.2023
Serbian DPC, 'Nedostaci Predloga zakona o zaštiti podataka o ličnosti' (23.10.20218) <https://www.pravniportal.com/nedostaci-predloga-zakona-o-zastiti-podataka-o-licnosti/> accessed on 12.02.2023
Serbian Government, 'Negotiation group for chapter 23, Action plan for chapter 23', (August 2014) <https://eupregovori.bos.rs/progovori-opregovorima/uploaded/Action%20Plan%20AP23eng.1.9..pdf> accessed on 16.03.2023
Serbian Ministry of Defence, President's statement published on the website of the Ministry of Defence (21.09.2019) <https://www.mod.gov.rs/lat/14451/predsednik-vucic-kina-nema-pouzdanijeg-partnera-i-iskrenijeg-prijatelja-od-srbije-14451> accessed on 01.04.2023
SHARE Foundation, 'Opšti komentar na nacrt Zakona' (January 2018), <https://resursi.sharefoundation.info/wp-content/uploads/2018/01/Komentari-na-Nacrt-ZZPL-SHARE-Fondacija.pdf> accessed on 17.03.2023
SHARE Foundation, 'Analiza sajtova beogradskih javnih preduzeca i službi' (02.11.2022) <https://www.sharefoundation.info/wp-content/uploads/BG-sajtovi-analiza.pdf> accessed on 02.05.2023
SHARE Foundation, 'Files complaints against Facebook and Google' (05.12.2019) <https://www.sharefoundation.info/en/share-files-complaints-against-facebook-and-google/> accessed on 21.02.2022
SHARE Foundation, 'hiljade.kamera.rs: Community Strikes Back Against Mass Surveillance', (19.05.2020) <https://www.sharefoundation.info/en/hiljade-kamera-rs-community-strikes-back/> accessed on 01.04.2023
SHARE Foundation, 'Huawei case study for video surveillance in Belgrade' <https://archive.li/pZ9HO> accessed on 21.02.2021
SHARE Foundation, 'Huawei knows everything about cameras in Belgrade – and they are glad to share!' (29.03.2019), <https://www.sharefoundation.info/en/huawei-knows-everything-about-cameras-in-belgrade-and-they-are-glad-to-share/> accessed on 07.12.2021
SHARE Foundation, 'Internet ipak može da zaboravi: kako je izbrisan jedan YouTube kanal' (24.09.2020), <https://www.sharefoundation.info/sr/internet-ipak-moze-da-zaboravi/> accessed on 02.05.2023
SHARE Foundation, 'Position Paper after the Proposed Draft Laws', (12.12.2022), <https://www.sharefoundation.info/wp-content/uploads/SHARE_Position_Paper_BMS.pdf> accessed on 21.02.2021

SHARE Foundation, 'Prekršajne prijave protiv internacionalih kompanija' (2020) <https://www.sharefoundation.info/wp-content/uploads/SHARE-FondacijaPrekrsajnaprijava-1.10.2020..pdf> accessed on 14.05.2023)

SHARE Foundation, 'Rečnik pojmova o zaštiti podataka' (2021)

SHARE Foundation, 'Regulatory Framework in the field of Digital Rights, Comparative Analysis: Albania, Bosnia and Herzegovina, Kosovo, Montenegro, North Macedonia, Serbia' (December 2021)

SHARE Foundation, 'Vodič kroz zakon o zaštiti podataka o ličnosti i GDPR: Tumačenje novog pravnog okvira' (2018)

Sjever Crne Gore, 'Za prisluškivanje građana 1.400 naloga' (24.04.2021) <https://www.sjevercg.me/za-prisluskivanje-gradjana-1-400-naloga/> accessed on 21.05.2023

Skapi A, 'The law of treaties and its implementation in Albania, Pillar 1 Albanian Legislation', Law Journal ISSN 2523–1766, (November 2017) <https://www.lawjournal.al/sites/default/files/Pillar%20I%2C%20ALJ%20No.%204%20-%20ENGL.pdf> accessed on 18.05.2022

Slobodna Evropa, 'Grupa parlamentaraca traži hitnu sjednicu zbog 'blokade' Parlamenta BiH' (November 2021) <https://www.slobodnaevropa.org/a/parlament-bosna-hercegovina-blokada/31573330.html> accessed on 28.05.2023

Smits J, 'Comparative Law and its Influence on National Legal Systems', The Oxford Handbook of Comparative Law (2nd edn) (2019)

Solioz C, 'The EU: wider and deeper with the Balkans', Open Democracy (08.10.2014) <https://www.opendemocracy.net/en/can-europe-make-it/eu-wider-and-deeper-with-balkans/> accessed on 28.05.2023

Spasov A Lj, 'The European Integration of the Western Balkans and the Rule of Law (Current Situation and Challenges)', 15 Iustinianus Primus L. Rev. 1 (2024)

Stanicek B and Tarpova S, 'China's strategic interests in the Western Balkans', Members' Research Service, PE 733.558 European Parliament, (2022)

Stojanovska E and Ananievska J, 'Privacy, information, and the public interest: the right to privacy versus the right of the public to know', School of Journalism and Public Relations, Institute for Communication Studies, (2016)

Stojkovski B, 'North Macedonia Leads Region in COVID-19 Tracing App', BIRN, (16.04.2020) <https://balkaninsight.com/2020/04/16/north-macedonia-leads-region-in-covid-19-tracing-app/> accessed on 15.06.2021

Stojkovski B, 'North Macedonia Probes Election Day Cyber Attacks', BIRN, (17.07.2020), <https://balkaninsight.com/2020/07/17/north-macedonia-probes-election-day-cyber-attacks/> accessed on 14.05.2021

Stoller R D, 'South Korea Privacy Law Changes May Help EU Data Transfer Talks', BLOOMBERG L. (22.02.2019) <https://news.bloomberglaw.com/privacy-and-data-security/south-korea-privacy-law-changes-may-help-eu-data-transfer-talks> accessed on 02.12.2023

Svantesson D and Jerker B, 'Extraterritoriality and targeting in EU data privacy law: the weak spot undermining the regulation,' International Data Privacy Law, Volume 5, Issue 4, November 2015

Svantesson D, 'The Regulation of Cross-Border Data Flows' (2011) 1(3) International Data Privacy Law

Switzerland Federal Data Protection and Information Commissioner, 'Policy paper on the transfer of personal data to the USA and other countries lacking an adequate level of data protection within the meaning of Art. 6 Para. 1 Swiss Federal Act on Data Protection' <https://www.newsd.admin.ch/newsd/message/attachments/64261.pdf> accessed on 23.04.2023

Taeger J and Gabel D, 'DS-GVO Art. 44 Allgemeine Grundsätze der Datenübermittlung, in Taeger/Gabel, DSGVO – BDSG – TTDSG, Deutscher Fachverlag GmbH, Fachmedien Recht und Wirtschaft, (4th eds 2022)

Tallberg J, 'Paths to Compliance: Enforcement, Management, and the European Union', Cambridge University Press (2003)

Tarpova S, 'China's investments in the West Balkans: gaining a foothold in Europe. Is Beijing set to replace the EU in shaping the region's future?' published in the Gaudie (02.11.021) <https://www.gaudie.co.uk/post/china-s-investments-in-the-west-balkans-gaining-a-foothold-in-europe> accessed on 15.05.2023

Taylor M, 'China's Digital Authoritarianism A Governance Perspective', Part of the book series: Politics and Development of Contemporary China (PDCC) (2022)

Taylor M, 'Permissions and prohibitions in data protection jurisprudence' Vol. 2, Brussels Privacy Hub Working Paper, (May 2016)

Tene M, 'Is Israeli Data Protection Law 'Adequate' Under Article 25?', Privacy and Data Protection, Vol. 8, No. 5, pp. 9–13 (2008)

Tene O and Wolf C, White Paper 'Overextended: Jurisdiction and Applicable Law under the EU General Data Protection Regulation', The Future of Privacy Forum White Paper (January 2013)

The EIB Group's support for SMEs in the Western Balkans' <https://www.eib.org/en/publications/the-eib-group-support-for-smes-in-the-westernbalkans> accessed on 11.11.2023

The Fletcher Forum of World Affairs, 'A Return to Great Power Competition', Vol. 44, No. 2, The Fletcher School of Law and Diplomacy (2020)

The initiative 'Hoću Poverenika, a ne poslušnika!' <https://srbijadoinformacija.rs/poverenik/> accessed on 12.03.2023

The New York Times, 'G.D.P.R., a New Privacy Law, Makes Europe World's Leading Tech Watchdog', (May 2018) <https://www.nytimes.com/2018/05/24/technology/europe-gdpr-privacy.html> accessed on 15.10.2021

Thouvenin F, 'Informational Self-Determination: A Convincing Rationale for Data Protection Law?', 12 J. Intell. Prop. Info. Tech. & Elec. Com. L. 246 (2021)

Tomić A, 'Bosnia & Herzegovina – Data Protection Overview', OneTrust Data Guidance (August 2022) <https://www.dataguidance.com/notes/bosnia-herzegovina-data-protection-overview> accessed on 22.04.2023

Tomović D, 'Montenegro Adopts Controversial Surveillance Law', Balkan Insight (18.02.2015) <https://balkaninsight.com/2015/02/18/montenegoro-s-parliament-adopts-controversial-spying-law/> accessed on 08.03.2023

TRT Balkan, 'Dragoljub Reljić, Potrebno usvajanje novog zakona o zaštiti ličnih podataka' (27.02.2023), <https://bhsc.trtbalkan.com/region/bih-potrebno-usvajanje-novog-zakona-o-zastiti-licnih-podataka-11841199> accessed on 22.04.2023

Tverdova Y.V, Anderson C J, 'Choosing the West? Referendum choices on EU membership in east-central Europe', Electoral Studies, Volume 23, Issue 2 (2004)

Twinning project 'Support to the Implementation of the Modernised Data Protection Legal Framework in North Macedonia' (2021–2022)

Twinning Project, Albania – Italy – Austria, 'Institution-building for Alignment with the European Union Acquis on the Protection of Personal Data' (2020–2021)

Tzanou M, ‘Data protection as a fundamental right next to privacy? ‘Reconstructing’ a not so new right’ International Data Privacy Law, Volume 3, Issue 2, (May 2013)

Tzanou M, Addressing Big Data and AI Challenges: A Taxonomy and Why the GDPR Cannot Provide a One-size-fits-all Solution (17.07.2020)

UK Government, ‘Guidance International data transfers: building trust, delivering growth and firing up innovation’ (26.08.2021) <https://www.gov.uk/government/publications/uk-approach-to-international-data-transfers> accessed on 29.05.2023

UNCTAD, ‘Data protection regulations and international data flows: Implications for trade and development’, (2016) <http://unctad.org/en/PublicationsLibrary/dtlstict2016d1_en.pdf> accessed on 13.02.2022

United States Department of State, Bureau of Democracy, Human Rights and Labor, ‘2016 Country Report on Human Rights Practices Macedonia’, <https://www.state.gov/wp-content/uploads/2019/01/Macedonia-1.pdf> accessed on 20.05.2023

Uzelac A, ‘A Survival of the third legal tradition?’, Supreme Court Law Rev SCLR 49(2d) (2014)

Veil W, ‘The GDPR: The Emperor’s New Clothes – On the Structural Shortcomings of Both the Old and the New Data Protection Law’, Neue Zeitschrift für Verwaltungsrecht (07.01.2019)

Vesti.rs, ‘Brnabić: Poverenik zloupotrebio funkciju kada je kontrolisaio vinoteku u kojoj radi Danilo Vučić’ (13.11.2021) <https://www.vesti.rs/Novi-Sad/Brnabic-Poverenik-zloupotrebio-funkciju-kada-je-kontrolisao-vinoteku-u-kojoj-radi-Danilo-Vucic.html> accessed on 12.02.2023

Viel W, The GDPR: ‘The Emperor’s New Clothes – On the Structural Shortcomings of Both the Old and the New Data Protection Law’, Neue Zeitschrift für Verwaltungsrecht 10/2018 (December 21, 2018)

Vladisavljev S, ‘Policy Paper: China’s ’Digital Silk Road’ Enters the Western Balkans’, Association for International Affairs (AMO) (June 2021)

Von Cramon V, ‘Use of mass surveillance in Belgrade’, (29.09.2021) <https://violavoncramon.eu/en/news/content/use-of-mass-surveillance-in-belgrade/> accessed on 01.04.2023

Voss A, Position Paper on Fixing the GDPR: Towards Version 2.0 (25.05.2021)

Voss G, ‘Cross-Border Data Flows, the GDPR, and Data Governance’, 29 Wash Int’l L.J. 485 (2020)

Vrsaljko M, ‘Pracenje mobitela stavljeno na čekanje’ (10.04.2020) <http://balkans.aljazeera.net/vijesti/pracenje-mobitela-stavljeno-na-cekanje> accessed 29.03.2023

W Zweers V. Shopov, F. Van der Putten, M. Petkova, & M. Lemstra, ‘China and the EU in the Western Balkans’ Clingendael Report, 8. (2020)

Wagner J and Benecke A, ‘National Legislation within the Framework of the GDPR’, 2 Eur. Data Prot. L. Rev. 353 (2016)

Wagner J, ‘The transfer of personal data to third countries under the GDPR: when does a recipient country provide an adequate level of protection?’, International Data Privacy Law, Volume 8, Issue 4, (November 2018)

Wang F Y, ‘The Japanese Model of Data Privacy and the EU-Japan GDPR Adequacy Agreement’, McGill Guide 9th ed, 33:2 Harv J L & Tech, (2020)

Warren S and Brandeis DL, ‘The Right to Privacy’, Harvard Law Review, Vol. 4, No. 5. (Dec. 15,1890),

Watson A, ‘Legal Transplants: An Approach to Comparative Law’, University Press of Virginia (1974)

WBIF, 26th Call for Technical Assistance and Extension of 6th Call for Investment Grants, (14.06.2021) <https://www.wbif.eu/news-details/26th-call-technical-assistance-and-extension-6th-call-investment-grants> accessed on 18.12.2023

WESTERN BALKANS LEADERS DECLARATION ON COMMON REGIONAL MARKET: A catalyst for deeper regional economic integration and a stepping stone towards EU Single Market, CRM 2021–2024 AP(1) <https://www.rcc.int/docs/544/declaration-on-common-regional-market> accessed on 28.05.2023

Wittershagen L, 'The Transfer of Personal Data from the European Union to the United Kingdom post-Brexit', Volume 1 in the series Global and Comparative Data Law (2023)

Wong B, 'Delimiting the concept of personal data after the GDPR', Legal Studies, 39(3) (2019)

Wong R, 'The Data Protection Directive 95/46/EC: Idealisms and realisms', International Review of Law, Computers & Technology (2012)

Xinhua, 'Huawei aids Bosnia and Herzegovina in building smart city' (07.11.2018) <https://en.imsilkroad.com/p/118790.html> accessed on 03.04.2023

Xinhua, 'Sarajevo innovation conference explores China-CEEC cooperation opportunities', (17.11.2018) <http://www.xinhuanet.com/english/2018-11/07/c_137587059.htm> accessed on 01.04.2023

Zejnullahu Nj, 'Imposition of Monetary Sanctions as a Mechanism for Protection of Personal Data: Comparative Analysis of Kosovo and Slovenia', 2 Eur. Data Prot. L. Rev. 80 (2016)

Zejnullahu Nj, 'Personal Data Protection in Kosovo, Three Years of Failure', European Data Protection Law Review, Volume 6, Issue 2 (2020)

Zimmermann M, 'The GDPR two years on: Time for the EU to go after privacy violations by big tech', article published by European Digital SM Alliance (24.06.2020) <https://www.digitalsme.eu/the-gdpr-two-years-on-time-for-the-eu-to-go-after-privacy-violations-by-big-tech/> accessed on 01.12.2023

Zimmermann S, 'The Legal Framework of Data Protection in Israel: A European Perspective', 5 Eur. Data Prot. L. Rev. (2019)

Živić P, 'Problemi sa ličnim podacima na Balkanu: Od ličnih karata do video nadzora', BBC News (08.10.2019) <https://www.bbc.com/serbian/lat/balkan-49919849> accessed on 24.05.2022

Zotaj S, 'Protection of the Personal Data in Albania in Compliance with the General Data Protection Regulation', Central European University Private University (2021)

Zweigert K and Kötz H, 'An Introduction to Comparative Law', Clarendon Press, Oxford (1998)

Амповска М and Илиоски P, 'The Process of Civil Law Codification in Western Balkans', Macedonian Yearbook-Faculty of Law (2013)

FSC
www.fsc.org
MIX
Papier | Fördert gute Waldnutzung
FSC® C083411

Kolibri 360 GmbH
Ferdinand-Jühlke-Straße 7
99095 Erfurt, Deutschland
produktsicherheit@kolibri360.de